THE OXFORD HANDBOOK OF

INTERNATIONAL COMMERCIAL POLICY

THE OXFORD HANDBOOK OF

INTERNATIONAL COMMERCIAL POLICY

EDITED BY

MORDECHAI E. KREININ
AND
MICHAEL G. PLUMMER

OXFORD
UNIVERSITY PRESS

OXFORD
UNIVERSITY PRESS

Oxford University Press, Inc., publishes works that further
Oxford University's objective of excellence
in research, scholarship, and education.

Oxford   New York
Auckland   Cape Town   Dar es Salaam   Hong Kong   Karachi
Kuala Lumpur   Madrid   Melbourne   Mexico City   Nairobi
New Delhi   Shanghai   Taipei   Toronto

With offices in
Argentina   Austria   Brazil   Chile   Czech Republic   France   Greece
Guatemala   Hungary   Italy   Japan   Poland   Portugal   Singapore
South Korea   Switzerland   Thailand   Turkey   Ukraine   Vietnam

Published by Oxford University Press, Inc.
198 Madison Avenue, New York, New York 10016

www.oup.com

Oxford is a registered trademark of Oxford University Press

Library of Congress Cataloging-in-Publication Data

Oxford handbook of international commercial policy / edited by Mordechai Kreinin and Michael Plummer.
p.   cm.
Includes bibliographical references and index.

ISBN 978-0-19-537804-7
1. Commercial policy. 2. International economic relations.
I. Kreinin, Mordechai Elihau, 1930– II. Plummer, Michael G., 1959–
III. Title: Handbook of international commercial policy.
HF1411.O945   2012
382′.3—dc23   2011033275

1 3 5 7 9 8 6 4 2
Printed in the United States of America

on acid-free paper

Contents

....

CONTRIBUTORS

SVEN W. ARNDT (Ph.D., University of California, Berkeley) is the Charles M. Stone Professor of Money, Credit and Trade at Claremont McKenna College (CMC). He is adjunct professor at Claremont Graduate University. He was Director of the Lowe Institute of Political Economy at CMC. He has served on the faculties of the University of California in Los Angeles and in Santa Cruz. He has been visiting professor at Stanford University; the Johns Hopkins University School of Advanced International Studies campus in Bologna, Italy; the Institute for Advanced Studies in Vienna, Austria; the Universities of Konstanz and Mannheim in Germany; and the Chinese University of Hong Kong. He has served as Director, Office of International Monetary Research, U.S. Department of the Treasury; Visiting Scholar, Board of Governors of the Federal Reserve System; trade project director at the American Enterprise Institute; and research scholar with the U.S.-ASEAN Trade Initiative. He has served as President of the North American Economics and Finance Association and as Managing Editor of the *North American Journal of Economics and Finance*. He is currently the Senior Editor of that journal. He is a Distinguished Fellow of the International Banking, Economics and Finance Association and President-elect of the International Trade and Finance Association. He has authored and coedited several books, including *Fragmentation: New Production Patterns in the World Economy*. He has written articles in a variety of professional journals, including the *American Economic Review, Econometrica*, the *Economic Journal*, the *Journal of Political Economy*, the *Journal of Economic Asymmetries*, and the *North American Journal of Economics and Finance*. His current research interests include crossborder production networks and trade policy, exchange rate regimes, and global imbalances and financial instability.

ROBERT E. BALDWIN was Hilldale Professor of Economics, Emeritus, at the University of Wisconsin–Madison. He received his Ph.D. in Economics from Harvard in 1950 and taught at Harvard and the University of California at Los Angeles before moving to Wisconsin in 1964. He served as Chair of the Economics Department at UW-Madison in 1975–78 and Chair of the Social Systems Research Institute from 1986–1989. Baldwin published over a hundred theoretical, empirical, and policy-oriented articles in various professional journals and conference volumes in the fields of international trade and economic development. He was Chief Economist in the Office of the U.S. Trade Representative in Washington in 1963–64 and served as a consultant on trade matters in the U.S. Department of Labor (1975–1976), the United Nations Conference on Trade and Development (1975), the World Bank (1978–79), and the Organization for Economic Cooperation and Development

(1988, 1993, and 1997). He had also been a consultant to the Committee for Economic Development, the U.S. Chamber of Commerce, and the Atlantic Council. In 1991–1992, he served as Chair of the Panel on Foreign Trade Statistics for the National Academy of Science's Committee on National Trade Statistics, and was President of the Midwest Economics Association in 1995. He was a Research Associate at the National Bureau of Economic Research. In addition, he was a member of the Council on Foreign Relations and was on the Advisory Committee of the Institute for International Economics. He was a Fellow of the American Academy of Arts and Sciences. He served on an international panel of experts to advise the Director-General of the World Trade Organization, Mike Moore, in 2001–2003. He was a member of the Executive Committee of the Program for International Studies in Asia and served on the International Advisory Board for Ukraine for the Economics Education and Research Consortium. Sadly, Professor Baldwin passed away in April 2011. He will be greatly missed.

Torbjörn Becker is the Director of the Stockholm Institute of Transition Economics (SITE) at the Stockholm School of Economics (since August 2006). He is also Chairman of the board of the Kyiv Economic Institute in Ukraine and CenEA in Poland, as well as a board member of the Swedish International Development Cooperation Agency, and the International Faculty Committee at the International School of Economics in Tbilisi, Georgia. Prior to this, he worked at the International Monetary Fund in Washington, D.C., for nine years; his final position was as Senior Economist in the Research Department. In this capacity, his research and policy work focused on international financial architecture issues and particularly on how emerging markets can protect themselves against adverse shocks and what role international financial institutions could have in preventing and resolving crises. More generally, his work covers macroeconomics, international economics, financial markets, debt management, fiscal policy, and development issues. In previous positions at the IMF, he worked on emerging markets and developing countries in Eastern Europe and Russia, the Asia Pacific, and the Middle East. He holds a Ph.D. in economics from the Stockholm School of Economics, where he also did his undergraduate studies. He has also studied at U.C. Berkeley and the Manchester Business School.

Cristiane Carneiro is Assistant Professor at the International Relations Institute, University of Sao Paulo. She has taught at the University of Pennsylvania and at New York University. Her work focuses on dispute settlement at the World Trade Organization and on economic sanctions. She has published on economic sanctions and human rights (2009), as well as on the design of an arms trade treaty (2008). She holds a Ph.D. in Political Science from New York University.

Carl Davidson is Professor of Economics and current Chair of the Department of Economics at Michigan State University. He has published widely on many topics, most notably on the influence of labor market structure on issues related to international trade and the development of models of oligopolistic behavior designed to help us better understand how firms with significant market power interact. His work has appeared in such outlets as the *Journal of Political Economy, Review of Economic Studies, Economic Journal, Rand Journal of Economics, International Economic Review*, and *Journal of International Economics*. He is also the author of *Recent Developments in the Theory of Unemployment, Search Theory and Unemployment* (with Stephen Woodbury), *International Trade and Labor Markets: Theory, Evidence and Policy Implications* (with Steven Matusz), and *International Trade with Equilibrium Unemployment* (with Steven Matusz).

ALFRED E. ECKES, JR., is a former Chairman and Commissioner (1981–1990) of the U.S. International Trade Commission. He is Eminent Research Professor Emeritus of History at Ohio University in Athens, Ohio. His latest book, *The Contemporary Global Economy: A History since 1980*, was published by Wiley-Blackwell in 2011.

ANDERS FREDRIKSSON received his Ph.D. in Economics from the Institute for International Economic Studies at Stockholm University in 2009. After completing his thesis, he worked at the Stockholm Institute of Transition Economics and he is currently a postdoc at the University of Namur, Belgium. Currently his work includes projects related to bureaucracy, corruption, and the informal economy in developing countries.

HAL HILL is H. W. Arndt Professor of Southeast Asian Economies, Arndt-Corden Department of Economics, Crawford School, Australian National University (ANU). His professional research career of some 35 years has focused on the economies of Southeast Asia, especially Indonesia and the Philippines. In recent times, he has been engaged in book-writing projects on Cambodia and Malaysia. At the ANU, he has served as Head of the Indonesia Project and Head of Department. He is the author or editor of 16 books and about 130 book chapters and journal articles. He has consulted widely for several governments and international agencies, is on the editorial boards of 13 academic journals, and contributes to various newspapers and online sites.

GARY CLYDE HUFBAUER has been the Reginald Jones Senior Fellow at the Peterson Institute for International Economics since 1992. He was on leave as the Maurice R. Greenberg Chair and Director of Studies at the Council on Foreign Relations (1996–1998), and he formerly held positions as Marcus Wallenberg Professor of International Finance Diplomacy at Georgetown University (1985–1992), Senior Fellow at the Institute (1981–1985), Deputy Director of the International Law Institute at Georgetown University (1979–1981); Deputy Assistant Secretary for International Trade and Investment Policy of the U.S. Treasury (1977–1979); and Director of the International Tax staff at the U.S. Treasury (1974–1976). Dr. Hufbauer holds an A.B. from Harvard College, a Ph.D. in economics from King College, Cambridge University, and a J.D. from Georgetown University Law Center. He has written extensively on international trade, investment, and tax issues. His publications include *Global Warming and World Trading System (2009), Economic Sanctions Reconsidered*, 3rd ed. (2007), *US Taxation of Foreign Income* (2007), *US-China*

Trade Disputes: Rising Tide, Rising Stakes (2006), *NAFTA Revisited: Achievements and Challenges* (2005), and *Reforming the US Corporate Tax* (2005).

TIMOTHY JOSLING is Professor, Emeritus, at the (former) Food Research Institute at Stanford University; a Senior Fellow at the Freeman Spogli Institute for International Studies; and a faculty member at the Institute's Europe Center. His research focuses on agricultural policy and food policy in industrialized nations; international trade in agricultural and food products; the development of the multilateral trade regime; and the process of economic integration. He is currently studying the reform of the agricultural trading system in the World Trade Organization, including the current round of trade negotiations; the use of geographical indications in agricultural trade; the role of health and safety regulations in trade; the impact of climate change legislation on agricultural trade policies; and the treatment of biofuel subsidies in the WTO.

MASAHIRO KAWAI joined the Asian Development Bank Institute as Dean and CEO in January 2007 after serving as Special Advisor to the ADB President on regional economic integration and cooperation. Prior to this tour, he was Professor of Economics at the University of Tokyo. He began his career as Research Fellow at the Brookings Institution (1977–1978) and as Assistant and Associate Professor in Economics at the Johns Hopkins University (1978–86), and then served as Associate and Full Professor of Economics at the Institute of Social Science, University of Tokyo (1986–2008). During this period, he worked as Chief Economist for the World Bank's East Asia and the Pacific Region (1998–2001) and as Deputy Vice Minister of Finance for International Affairs of Japan's Ministry of Finance (2001–2003). He has published a number of books and more than 120 academic articles in English on international finance, the Asian financial crisis, the international currency system, and regional economic integration and cooperation in East Asia. Some of the books he has edited include *The New World Fiscal Order* (Urban Institute, 1996); *Exchange Rate Regimes in East Asia* (Routledge Curzon, 2004); *Policy Coherence towards East Asia: Development Challenges for OECD Countries* (OECD, 2005); *Managing Capital Flows: Search for a Framework* (Edward Elgar, 2010); and *Asian Regionalism in the World Economy: Engine for Dynamism and Stability* (Edward Elgar, 2010). He graduated with his B.A. and M.A. degrees in Economics from the University of Tokyo. He earned his M.S. in Statistics and Ph.D. in Economics from Stanford University.

MORDECHAI E. KREININ is University Distinguished Professor of Economics at Michigan State University and past President of the International Trade and Finance Association. He is the author of about 200 articles and 11 books in economics, including the widely used text *International Economics*. He has been a consultant to numerous international and national (U.S.) organizations in both the public and private sectors. He is listed in (Marquis) *Who Is Who in the World, Who Is Who in America, Distinguished Educators in America*, and many other bibliographies and is the recipient of numerous awards. He has been a visiting professor at 10 universities in the United States, Canada, Europe, and Australia, and has also lectured to both professional economists and lay audiences (business, government, and other groups) in the United States and many foreign countries, including 15 around-the-world or regional lecture tours. He works extensively in both print and electronic media. He has also been very active in university governance, and in the 1980s developed university-wide plans to deal with financial exigencies that were adopted at Michigan State and several other universities throughout the United States.

PETER LLOYD is Professor Emeritus of the University of Melbourne. His interests are international trade, both theory and policy, and microeconomic theory. He has published extensively in these areas. He has also served as a consultant to the Australian and New Zealand governments, to ASEAN, and to multilateral organizations including the World Trade Organisation, the World Bank, the IMF, and UNCTAD.

RACHEL MCCULLOCH is Rosen Family Professor of International Finance in the Department of Economics and the International Business School at Brandeis University. Prior to joining the Brandeis faculty in 1987, she taught at the University of Chicago, Harvard University, and the University of Wisconsin-Madison. In 2004–2005, she was the AGIP Professor of International Economics at the Bologna Center of the Johns Hopkins School of Advanced International Studies. She currently serves on the Academic Advisory Council of the Federal Reserve Bank of Boston and the Advisory Committee of the Peterson Institute for International Economics, Washington, D.C. She has also been a consultant to the Asian Development Bank and the World Bank and a member of the Technology Assessment Advisory Council of the U.S. Congressional Office of Technology Assessment (1979–1987), the President's Commission on Industrial Competitiveness (1984–1985), and the Committee on International Relations Studies with the People's Republic of China (1984–1992). She holds a Ph.D. in economics from the University of Chicago.

JAYANT MENON, a Malaysian national, is Principal Economist in the Office for Regional Economic Integration at the Asian Development Bank. Prior to this, he was at the ADB Institute, and he has worked on the India Desk, Regional Economic Monitoring Unit, and the Southeast Asia Department. Before joining ADB, he was Senior Research Fellow at the Centre of Policy Studies at Monash University in Melbourne, Australia. He has also worked at the University of Melbourne and Victoria University, and has held visiting appointments at the Australian National University, University of Malaya, Institute of Southeast Asian Studies in Singapore, and American University in Washington, D.C. He serves on the editorial board of several journals, and his academic publications relate mostly to trade and development issues, particularly as they relate to Asia. He received his Ph.D. from the University of Melbourne.

PATRICK A. MESSERLIN is Professor of Economics and Director of Groupe d'Economie Mondiale at Sciences Po, Paris. He was a special advisor to Mike Moore, WTO Director-General (2001–2002), and served with Ernesto Zedillo, former

President of Mexico and Director of the Yale Center for the Study of Globalization, as cochair of the United Nations Millennium Development Goals Task Force on Trade for Development (2003–2005) and of the World Bank Task Force on Global Finance and Trade Architecture (2008–2011). He is currently chairing the Global Trade Council 2010 of the World Economic Forum. He specializes in trade policy and regulatory reforms, more particularly WTO issues, EC commercial policy, services liberalization, and the "Better Regulations" initiatives. His work includes numerous articles and books, most recently *Measuring the Costs of Protection in Europe: European Commercial Policy in the 2000s* (Peterson Institute for International Economics, 2001) and *Europe after the No Votes* (Institute of Economic Affairs, 2006). He received a Ph.D. in economics from the University of Paris.

MICHAEL MICHAELY is Aron and Michael Chilewich Professor Emeritus of International Trade at the Hebrew University of Jerusalem. He specializes in commercial policy, trade structure, trade and growth, and open-economy macro-economics. He has published a dozen books and many articles on these and several other issues in economics, as well as on the economy of Israel. He was awarded several prizes for his publications. He has been Visiting Professor at universities and research organizations in the United States, Australia, and Sweden. After retiring from the University, he worked for a decade at the World Bank in Washington, codirecting a major multicountry study of trade liberalization and serving as Lead Economist for part of Latin America. At the Hebrew University, he was Chairman of the Department of Economics (1961–1965) and Dean of the Faculty of Social Sciences (1968–1971). He was President of the Israeli Economic Association (1982–1984). He served on various government committees in Israel on economic policy and chaired several committees on issues of higher education. He was a member of Israel's Higher-Education Council.

MICHAEL G. PLUMMER is Head of the Development Division in the Trade and Agriculture Directorate of the Organization for Economic Cooperation and Development and Eni Professor of International Economics at the Johns Hopkins University, SAIS-Bologna. He is Editor-in-Chief of the *Journal of Asian Economics;* Director, American Committee for Asian Economic Studies; and a nonresident Senior Fellow of the East-West Center. Previously, he held teaching, research, and management positions at Brandeis University and the East-West Center. He has also been a Fulbright Chair in Economics (Viterbo) and Pew Fellow in International Affairs (Harvard University). His main academic interests relate to international trade, international finance, and economic integration, especially in the Asian context. He has published extensively in these areas. He serves on the editorial boards of the *Asian Economic Journal, World Development*, and the *ASEAN Economic Bulletin*. His Ph.D. in economics is from Michigan State University.

NICHOLAS SLY is Assistant Professor of Economics at the University of Oregon. Before moving to Oregon, he received a Ph.D. in economics from Michigan State University. His research examines the relationship between international trade and structure of labor markets across countries. In particular, he has examined how labor mobility, differences in worker abilities, skill accumulation, and bargaining among workers influence firm behavior in open economies.

SHUJIRO URATA is Professor of Economics at the Graduate School of Asia-Pacific Studies, Waseda University, Faculty Fellow at the Research Institute of Economy, Trade and Industry, Research Fellow at the Japanese Center for Economic Research, and Senior Research Advisor, Economic Research Institute for ASEAN and East Asia. He was a Research Associate at the Brookings Institution and an Economist at the World Bank before joining Waseda University. His research specializes in international economics. He has held numerous research and advisory positions, including Senior Advisor to the Government of Indonesia, Consultant to the World Bank, the OECD, and the Government of Japan. He has published and edited a number of books on international economic issues and is an author and coauthor of numerous articles in professional journals. Some of the books he recently edited include *Bilateral Trade Agreements: Origins, Evolution, and Implications* (Routledge, 2005); *Multinationals and Economic Growth in East Asia* (Routledge, 2006); and *Free Trade Agreements in the Asia-Pacific* (World Scientific, 2010). He received his B.A. in Economics from Keio University and his M.A. and Ph.D. in Economics from Stanford University.

GANESHAN WIGNARAJA has been on the staff of the ADB since 2004 and is presently Principal Economist in the Office of Regional Economic Integration. He also represents the ADB on the WTO Director-General's Advisory Group on Aid for Trade and at the WTO Committee on Trade and Development. Formerly, he was Head of Competitiveness and SME Strategy at Maxwell Stamp PLC and Chief Programme Officer at the Commonwealth Secretariat. He has also held research positions at Oxford University, the OECD, the Overseas Development Institute, and the United Nations Institute for New Technologies. He has published 12 books on trade, competitiveness, regional integration, and industrial technology. He has a doctorate in economics from Oxford University and a BSc. in economics from the London School of Economics.

INTRODUCTION
AND OVERVIEW

....

MORDECHAI E. KREININ AND
MICHAEL G. PLUMMER

INTERNATIONAL trade has been growing at a fast pace in the postwar period, halted only temporarily by the 2008–9 global recession. World trade grew faster than the world GDP, while foreign investments grew even faster than trade. Indeed, globalization has become associated with a country's economic success, while failure to open up markets is often viewed as a cause of economic stagnation. This is predicted by economic theory and verified by empirical investigations. One reason for the growth of trade is the impressive reduction of trade barriers over the past 60 years; namely the pursuit of liberal commercial policy by many countries, led by the United States.

Commercial policy is the field that deals with a nation's policies that affect the flows of international trade and investment. Policies such as tariffs, import quotas, export subsidies, preferential trade agreements, and measures affecting foreign investment, fall under its rubric. It cuts through, and is part of, two general policy areas. On the one hand, it is an integral part of a country's foreign policy. Countries often use economic policy as an instrument in their overall foreign policy agenda. At the same time, commercial policy is a part of domestic economic policy because trade affects the domestic economy. Employment and income distribution are examples of such profound influences. Indeed, trade frictions and protectionism tend to rise during domestic recessions, as they did during the Great Depression and in the 2008–9 recession. These domestic effects go a long way toward explaining the widespread backlash against globalization, the criticisms of international trade among large groups of voters in all countries, the impasse at the Doha Development Agenda negotiations, and related phenomena. Arresting any protectionist trend has been a major objective of international institutions concerned with trade liberalization, from the WTO to the G-20, during the 2008–2009 recession.

Hence, there is a crying need for a volume that would explore the various aspects of commercial policy—theoretical, empirical, and institutional—beyond the standard texts in international economics. This is the topic to which this volume is devoted. What is *not* covered in the book is a related subject of international financial relations, which may warrant a separate companion book.

As the table of contents shows, this volume is divided into two parts: chapters 1–8 cover general approaches to commercial policy, while chapters 9–16 are devoted to country or regional studies. Each chapter is authored by one or two experts who have published extensively on the specific topic they tackle. Abstracts of all chapters, written by their respective authors, are given at the end of this introduction. In what follows, we give a brief summary of their contents.

The volume opens with a theoretical chapter by Professor Sven Arndt. The author demonstrates that although the traditional case for free trade is made under conditions that are at variance with today's reality, new conditions such as imperfect competition and economies of scale do not add up to an argument for protectionism. There follows a chapter by Professor Rachel McCulloch on the international trading system. It focuses on the tension between the principle of nondiscrimination of GATT/WTO (the MFN) and the proliferation of discriminatory trading practices, including regional agreements and preferred treatment of exports from low income countries.

Chapter 3, by Professor Alfred Eckes, deals with the administration of trade policy, focusing on the implementation of trade agreements and the governmental departments involved in the process in the United States, the EU, other countries, and the WTO. Chapter 4, by Professors Carl Davidson and Nicholas Sly, reviews recent literature on the importance of worker heterogeneity for a variety of trade issues.

Arguably, agriculture is the most distorted sector in the global economy and is certainly one of the most sensitive issues in trade negotiations. Chapter 6, by Professor Tim Josling, surveys the trade-distorting policies in the farm sector and shows how these policies are slowly changing into a more trade-neutral, nondistortionary form. Chapter 7, by Professors Kreinin and Plummer, reviews the theoretical literature on customs unions and free trade areas, as well as empirical models designed to measure their welfare effects. Chapter 8, by Professors Carneiro and Hufbauer, is devoted to a "rule-based trading system." The authors draw on political science concepts and historical episodes to explain the rise and design of a rule-based system.

Chapter 9 initiates the country-regional part of the volume. Authored by Professor Robert Baldwin, it reviews U.S. policies in light of the underlying economic and political conditions that shaped them. Chapter 10, by Professor Patrick Messerlin, among other things, reviews the current level and costs of EU protection, as well as the mechanism of decision-making on trade issues within the EU. Chapter 11, by Professors Kawai and Urata, on Japan's commercial policy during 1985–2010, covers both the multilateral approach through the GATT/WTO, the trade relation with the United States, and more recently, reliance on bilateral and plurilateral partnership agreements with Asian economics.

In Chapter 12, Ganeshan Wignaraja considers the commercial policy experience of the two giant countries, China and India. While China surged ahead of India in import and foreign direct investment liberalization, India acquired competitive capabilities in skill-intensive services. Both had favorable initial conditions of large domestic markets and low-cost labor. The author expects the gap of performance between the two to narrow over time.

While this volume does not deal with currency issues, we wish to note the divergence of the two countries' approaches to their exchange rates. While India permits the exchange level of the rupee to be determined generally by market forces, China keeps the yuan largely pegged to the U.S. dollar, thereby leading to criticisms that it is significantly undervaluing its currency, particularly given its massive buildup in foreign-exchange reserves. Faced as China is with a combination of large, external surpluses, high domestic inflation, and excessive exposure to external shocks, it is in China's interest to revalue or appreciate the yuan, which would also contribute considerably to reducing global imbalances and trade conflicts with its key trading partners. As of this writing, only minimal and inadequate changes have occurred in this policy. Emphatically, these are the humble views of the editors, and may not be shared by the chapter's author. They are expressed herein only because of the global significance of the issue. The IMF appears to share this view.

Chapter 13, authored by Professor Peter Lloyd, concerns Australian commercial policies. Both goods and services have been relatively open to imports since the mid-1980s. Recently, subsidies replaced tariffs as a main instrument of industry protection, and there is new emphasis on technology development. The number of bilateral and regional agreements increased from one to six. Chapter 14, by Professors Becker and Fredriksson, devoted to the "European Transition Economics," covers the commercial policy of 21 countries, including the transition from planned to market economies, with the EU being a strong external anchor for many reforms, as many of them aspired to membership. Chapter 15, by Professor Michael Michaely, traces the 50-year process of trade liberalization in a small open economy, Israel. By the year 2000, that process was completed, and the country is free of trade restrictions. A special section is devoted to policies regulating transactions with the Palestinian territories.

Finally, chapter 16, by Professors Hill and Menon, considers regional integration by the 10-member Association of Southeast Asian Nations economic bloc. The bloc achieved limited success in terms of regional economic cooperation prior to the 1990s, but since then has put in place the ASEAN Free Trade Area and is currently implementing the ASEAN Economic Community program, which is intended to create a single market and production base in ASEAN.

Abstracts

....

Chapter 1: Sven W. Arndt

....

Free trade as the widely preferred policy regime has enjoyed a very long and largely successful run. In recent years, however, political support for it has cooled substantially, especially in the arena of multilateral trade negotiations. Its wide acceptance was in part nurtured by memories of the devastating protectionism of the interwar years. Interestingly, the strongest and most unequivocal intellectual support for it comes from a model whose assumptions are more than a little at odds with modern reality. The case for free trade becomes more ambiguous under circumstances involving product differentiation and intraindustry trade, economies of scale, imperfect competition, and externalities.

Nevertheless, while introduction of greater realism weakens the universality of the case for free trade, it does not add up to an argument for protectionism. When markets are free, it can readily be shown that trade should also be free. In the years since World War II, trade barriers have been reduced significantly, while many markets have become less free, with greater concentration of economic power and rising volumes of transactions that do not take place in markets at all. This is particularly true in the financial services industries. Hence, the alternatives to free trade are not just simply a return to protection but strengthening competition in markets that are encumbered by public and private distortions.

Chapter 2: Rachel McCulloch

....

This chapter describes the evolution and structure of the international trading system, focusing on the tension between the fundamental GATT/WTO principle of most-favored-nation treatment and the proliferation of discriminatory trading arrangements, including regional agreements as well as new versions of special and differential treatment of low-income countries. It also discusses the increasing pressure to use the enforcement power of the GATT/WTO system to achieve member compliance with social norms in the areas of labor and environment. The chapter concludes by considering some significant challenges that currently face the international trading system and possible directions of the system's evolution in response to these challenges.

CHAPTER 3: ALFRED E. ECKES, JR.

This chapter focuses on the implementation of trade agreements, and examines the international and national authorities most involved. Much attention is devoted to trade administration in the WTO, the United States, Canada, the European Union, and other jurisdictions. The author finds that while international economists played major roles in designing the GATT/WTO system, and in negotiating key agreements, they have relatively little influence over the trade administration process. Instead, lawyers and judges appear to control these procedures, despite the costly and time-consuming nature of the judicial decision-making process.

CHAPTER 4: CARL DAVIDSON AND NICHOLAS SLY

A new literature has started to emerge that highlights the importance of worker heterogeneity for a variety of trade issues. New models that allow for nontrivial distributions of talent across the workforce have been developed, and they have raised a whole host of new and interesting questions. In this chapter we survey this literature, highlight a few of the more intriguing issues, and suggest some avenues that we believe are ripe for further investigation. In doing so, we concentrate on the relationship that trade has with how the talents of individual workers interact with each other, and with the technologies firms use. Key questions include: how does trade affect the labor market sorting of heterogeneous workers across sectors of the economy, across heterogeneous firms within a sector, and how does trade influence team formation within a firm?

CHAPTER 5: TIM JOSLING

Agricultural trade policy has always been among the most politically sensitive topics on the agenda of international trade institutions. Developed countries have protected and subsidized their farm sectors and contributed to the hardships of agriculture in the developing world. But these trade-distorting policies have been slowly changing into a more trade-neutral form, including the substitution of direct payments to farmers in place of price supports. The rapid globalization of the food industry has helped to propel this trend. Multilateral trade rules have followed this evolution, from the de facto exclusion of agricultural products from the GATT disciplines to the establishment of the Agreement on Agriculture under the WTO. The current Doha Round would, if completed, cut domestic support dramatically, eliminate export subsidies, and lower tariffs on agricultural imports by about 50%. Only a few of the markets for the most sensitive products (such as rice, cotton, sugar, and dairy products) would continue to be significantly distorted by domestic farm policies. But the continued improvement of the conditions for world trade in farm products depends essentially on the future of domestic farm policies in developing as well as developed countries. Developing countries will have the scope, if not the resources, for expanding trade-distorting policies. In addition, trade rules will have to deal with new issues ranging from the growth in the use of private standards in the food industry to the implications of policies designed to reduce the emission of greenhouse gases. Agricultural and food trade policy will continue to pose challenges for multilateral and regional trade agreements.

CHAPTER 6: MORDECHAI E. KREININ AND MICHAEL G. PLUMMER

Over the past decade, preferential trading agreements have become an increasingly important feature of the international trading system. Such accords are varied in terms of their composition, scope, and ambition: they include bilateral, plurilateral, subregional, and regional agreements; they occur between developed countries, developed and developing countries, and developing countries; they are comprehensive as well as "shallow." This chapter considers the economics of these preferential trading agreements from theoretical and empirical perspectives. In addition, given the increasing importance of preferential arrangements in the developing world and the rising importance of South–South trade, we evaluate the economic implications of such accords in the context of the "special case" of developing countries.

CHAPTER 7: CRISTIANE CARNEIRO AND GARY CLYDE HUFBAUER

Most contemporary observers regard rules-based systems as the "natural order" of international trade relations. Yet the rules-based trading system evolved long after early societies and nation-states engaged in commerce with one another. In this chapter, we summarize four theories drawn from the teachings of political science that explain the rise and design of rules-based systems: compliance theory, issue density, reputation, and regime type. We then draw on historical episodes to illustrate how the theories inform the evolution of the trading system. We start with the emergence of customary international law, centered on the most-favored-nation principle, in the seventeenth and eighteenth centuries, and then turn to the landmark Cobden-Chevalier Treaty (1860) between Britain and France. Our next illustration is drawn from the period between World War I and the Havana Conference, which created the General Agreement on Tariffs and Trade in 1947. Our final illustration covers the period between the founding of that agreement and the creation of the World Trade Organization in 1995. In each period, we find that themes from the four theories play a role in the formation of the dense system of rules that now regulates international trade.

CHAPTER 8: ROBERT E. BALDWIN

It is with profound sorrow that we inform our readers that the author of this chapter passed away in April 2011. For over half a century Professor Robert Baldwin was a leading light in the field of international economics. Active in both the academic and policymaking spheres, he was a tireless fighter for liberal trade policy and a promoter of the GATT/WTO approach to international economic relations. A brilliant researcher and conference organizer, he was an good friend and a devoted colleague. He will be sorely missed.
  The editors

This article presents a comprehensive but relatively brief historical survey of U.S. trade policy over the last 75 years. It is aimed at individuals who are not already familiar with the concepts and terminology used in discussions of trade policy or the domestic and international institutional framework within which U.S. trade policies are formulated and implemented. Particular attention is devoted to exploring the underlying economic and political conditions that have shaped U.S. trade policies since 1934.

CHAPTER 9: PATRICK A. MESSERLIN

First, the chapter describes the slow (trade in goods) and yet-to-be complete (trade in services) emergence of the "exclusive competence" of the EC (as distinct from the Member States) in trade matters. Consensus remains the rule on key trade issues; hence the occurrence of bursts of intra-EC conflicts at the end of trade negotiations. Second, we review the level of EC protection (still substantial in some sectors) in the early years of the decade 2000–2010 and provide estimates of the corresponding costs of protection. Third, we provide information on the changes in EC protection that would be generated by the Doha Round (on the basis of what has been achieved as of late 2008). Finally, we examine EC initiatives in concluding preferential trade agreements and explain why this policy has yet to be a confirmed success.

CHAPTER 10: MASAHIRO KAWAI AND SHUJIRO URATA

In this chapter we examine the changing nature of Japan's commercial policy over the last 25 years while reviewing Japan's changing structure of trade, foreign direct investment, and economy that underlay policy changes. We argue that until the late 1990s, Japan adopted a two-track approach of relying on multilateral liberalization under the GATT/WTO and open regionalism under Asia-Pacific Economic Cooperation on the one hand and on the bilateral trade relationship with the United States on the other. Although the Japan-U.S. bilateralism sometimes resulted in "managed trade" and encountered negative perceptions of the U.S. approach in Japan, overall, it had a positive impact on the Japanese economy in opening domestic markets through various reforms and deregulation measures. Japan's more recent commercial policy focuses on bilateral and plurilateral economic partnership agreements particularly with—but not limited to—East Asian economies. We argue that agricultural sector liberalization is key to the further integration of Japan with the Asian and global economies.

CHAPTER 11: GANESHAN WIGNARAJA

This chapter analyzes the link between commercial policies and exports through a comparative analysis of the giants China and India. China has surged ahead of India to dominate world manufactured exports, but India has acquired competitive capabilities in skill-intensive services. Favorable initial conditions (e.g., large domestic markets and low-cost productive labor) laid the foundations for the giants' export success. While the gradual switch to market-oriented commercial policies in the late 1970s drove trade-led growth in the giants, China was swifter and more coordinated. It introduced an open door policy toward foreign direct investment, actively facilitated technological upgrading of it, steadily liberalized a controlled import regime, ensured a competitive exchange rate, and concluded more comprehensive free trade agreements with Asian developing economies. India has attempted to develop more appropriate commercial policies since 1991, particularly to attract foreign direct investment and liberalize imports. Therefore, one might expect the gap in trade performance to between China and India to narrow over time. However,

both giants face an uncertain world economic environment after the global financial crisis, and future export success will depend on evolving commercial policies.
Critical areas are how the giants respond to the risk of protectionism, manage real
exchange rates, promote use of free trade agreements among businesses, and implement complementary policies.

CHAPTER 12: PETER LLOYD

This chapter reviews Commonwealth government border and nonborder policies
that affect the competitiveness of Australian industries. It covers goods and service
industries. Both have been opened up in Australia to more international competition since the mid-1980s. In recent years, there have been shifts in the pattern of
government intervention and regulation; subsidies replaced tariffs as the main instrument of industry assistance, there is a new emphasis on technology development, and the number of bilateral and regional agreements has increased from one
to six, with several more under negotiation. Australia is also a net recipient of both
capital and labor flows. Restrictions on annual inflows of both people and of foreign
direct investment have been relaxed in recent years. The chapter also reviews the
methods of policy review and implementation used by the Commonwealth
government.

CHAPTER 13: TORBJÖRN BECKER
AND ANDERS FREDRIKSSON

This chapter discusses trade policy in 21 European transition countries since 1989.
This period includes a fundamental transition from planned to market economies
for most of the countries covered, and trade and trade policy played an important
role in this process. The EU was a strong external anchor for many reforms and in
particular trade-related reforms. This was very much the case for countries that
entered the EU, but the EU also greatly influenced prospective members' reform
efforts and to some extent also countries with less clear ambitions to join the EU.
The trade reforms have led to relatively low tariff levels in the region compared with
other parts of the world. Not so surprisingly, trade with the old EU countries has
increased significantly for the new member states, but trade among the new member states has increased even faster. This is at least to some extent linked to the trade
agreements that were made for subsets of countries in Europe, such as CEFTA,
before EU accession, that fostered trade among the neighboring new member
states.

CHAPTER 14: MICHAEL MICHAELY

Israel started its existence, in 1948, as an economy highly dependent on capital imports but in other senses as a fairly closed, intensely controlled, and regulated economy. In early 1952, a process of liberalization and opening started; it persisted, though rather slowly, over 50 years, at the end of which the economy became highly free in its commercial policy and open in its performance. The process consisted of various phases. It started from a shift from a highly overvalued currency to a real exchange rate close to equilibrium, thus relaxing the need to control imports as a means of allocation of foreign exchange. It then moved through an ambivalent stage of freeing imports of intermediate goods while intensely using nontariff barriers as means of protecting the local production of final consumer goods. These quantitative barriers were then replaced by tariffs and other price measures, presumably intended to grant equivalent protection but in fact lowering it significantly. Following this, tariffs on imports from the United States and the E.U. were gradually lowered, and mostly eliminated. Finally, a similar liberalization policy was applied to imports from "the rest of the world"—mostly Asia. By the turn of the new millennium, the process of opening has thus been completed.

CHAPTER 15: HAL HILL AND JAYANT MENON

The 10-member Association of Southeast Asian Nations is arguably the most durable and successful regional grouping in the developing world. Established in 1967, it has contributed greatly to regional harmony and prosperity. The Association is characterized by great internal diversity, generally high economic growth, and a reluctance to establish a strong supranational organizational structure. Beginning in 1976, the member countries have initiated a range of economic cooperation and integration programs, initially for merchandise trade, in the 1990s focusing on services trade, investment, and labor and in the past decade extending to some broader macroeconomic and financial measures, the latter in cooperation with its Northeast Asian neighbors. Its members have adopted what appear to be formal preferential trade arrangements, but in practice these have usually been multilateralized. The Association has informally practiced what is sometimes termed "open regionalism." There is little likelihood in the foreseeable future of it adopting deep EU-style economic integration behind a common external trade regime.

PART I

GENERAL APPROACHES TO COMMERCIAL POLICY

CHAPTER 1

FREE TRADE AND ITS ALTERNATIVES

SVEN W. ARNDT

1. INTRODUCTION

The era of free or freer trade is now well over half a century old. Trade in goods, as well as services, is significantly less encumbered than at the end of World War II, and most of the world's economies are more open and more fully integrated into the global system than ever before. World trade has grown more rapidly than world production, and many traded goods and services have become internationalized as crossborder production networks have multiplied. Even nontradables are feeling the winds of foreign competition, as some of their parts and constituent activities and tasks have become tradable.

The belief that free trade is superior to its alternatives has enjoyed wide and robust support in many parts of the world and has served as the guiding principle for the series of multilateral trade negotiations that began shortly after the war, but are currently stalled in the Doha Round. Yet much of the theoretical case for free trade is based on a model that assumes an economic world in which markets are perfectly competitive and free of distortions and populated by firms that are small and not too-big-to-fail. There are no externalities or scale economies in this world; all goods and services are tradable, trade is always balanced, and economic growth just happens.

This view of the world is more than a little at odds with reality. While reduction of trade barriers and opening of national economies have brought fresh winds of competition, market structures in many parts of the world have evolved in the opposite direction, with fewer firms and more concentration of economic power, with capture of economic policy by private interests in a variety of instances, and with nontrivial information asymmetries and assorted externalities. There may be grounds for arguing that freeing markets from the trade restrictions that remain may be less urgent than freeing markets from the welter of other distortions and barriers to efficient utilization of the world's productive resources.

This chapter begins by reviewing the basic case for free trade in terms of the workhorse factor-proportions model. The conclusions of this "benchmark" model are then stress-tested by removing each of the key assumptions in turn. Not surprisingly, the case for free trade becomes less airtight, as a variety of specific market situations arises in which trade-based barriers such as tariffs or nontrade interventions such as production and other subsidies can produce superior welfare outcomes. But these theoretical findings of superiority do not necessarily translate into interventionist policy prescriptions, because in many cases the costs associated with practical implementation may exceed the expected benefits.

2. The Benchmark Model

This model assumes perfect competition in all markets, constant returns to scale, and no externalities or market distortions of any kind. It focuses on "comparative advantage" based on differences across countries in resource endowments and across industries in factor intensities. Countries are assumed to be differentially endowed with the main factors of production—land, labor (skilled and unskilled), and capital—and technologies are assumed to differ across products, ensuring that the factors will be combined in different proportions at given relative factor prices.

The essential conclusion of this model is that the economic welfare of each country is best served when it focuses on producing goods and services that make intensive use of the factor or factors of production with which it is relatively well endowed. Each will then produce more than it consumes of goods and services in which it has *comparative advantage*, while producing less than it consumes of goods in which it has comparative disadvantage. Each exports its excess production of the former, while importing the latter in order to bridge the shortfall of domestic production relative to consumption. It is within these conditions that the welfare results of free and restricted trade are compared.

The Small Country in Partial Equilibrium

There are two widely used approaches to the analysis of economic welfare in this context. One, the so-called partial-equilibrium approach, focuses on the market for a single good or service, while the other considers economy-wide effects. In both cases, the welfare results depend on whether a country is small or large vis-à-vis the rest of the world, where smallness means that the country has no influence on the world price of any product.

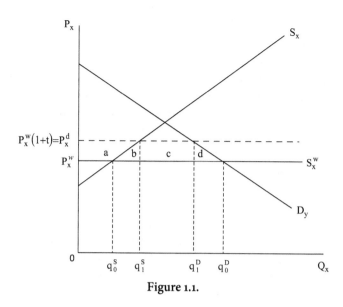

Figure 1.1.

On the import side, the partial-equilibrium version of the small country case is depicted in figure 1.1. The smallness assumption ensures that the country faces a horizontal world supply curve, S_x^w, and given world price P_x^w. At that price, domestic production is at q_0^S, domestic consumption is at q_0^D, and imports of $q_0^S q_0^D$ cover the gap between domestic demand and supply. Imposition of an import tariff works like a tax by raising the tariff-inclusive price to P_x^d, which is equal to $P_x^w + t$ if the tariff is a "specific" tariff or $P_x^w(1 + t)$ if the tariff is an ad valorem tariff. At this price, domestic production expands to q_1^S, while consumption shrinks to q_1^D. Imports fall to $q_1^S q_1^D$.

The concepts of consumer and producer surplus are used in this context to assess the welfare effects of the tariff. Consumer surplus shrinks by area a + b + c + d; producer surplus expands by area a and government collects tariff revenue equal to area c. It is clear that the bulk of the tariff's effect is to redistribute income or economic well-being from consumers (who are the losers in this case) to producers and the beneficiaries of government expenditures funded by tariff revenue.

In order to assess the overall welfare effect, the benchmark model makes an assumption that may not always be true in the real world: it assumes that winners and losers attach equal value or utility to the transferred amounts. Hence, the loss of area a is worth as much to consumers as its gain is to producers. The same calculation is applied to area c, which transfers income from consumers to government. Under this assumption, the winners' gains "cancel" the losers' losses, implying that this income redistribution has no net effect on "national" welfare.

That leaves the effects captured by triangles b and d, known as the efficiency or "deadweight" losses. The first is the result of "trade diversion" from lower-cost world producers to higher-cost domestic firms, and the second represents the loss of consumption brought about by the price increase. The net effect of the tariff is thus a welfare loss to the nation equal to area b + d. In the absence of the assumption of equal marginal utilities, the net result will be more or less negative, depending on whether consumers attach greater or lesser value to the transfer than the recipients.

The tariff creates welfare losses for the economy because it reduces the efficiency of resource utilization. It is an inefficient means of supporting home production, because it burdens consumers with higher prices. Any alternative policy that can achieve the same increase in domestic output without raising the price paid by consumers will be superior. As we shall see later, a per-unit production subsidy, equal to $P_x^w P_x^d$, the gap between the world price and the tariff-inclusive domestic price, achieves the same increase in production at lower welfare cost. The subsidy is a more efficient method of achieving the domestic policy objective, but it is also more transparent than the tariff and hence is politically less appealing.

Just because winners and losers value the transfer equally does not imply that the potential losers should not oppose the policy. Consider the following bargaining scenario. Could the losers compensate the winners in order to make them indifferent between the two trade regimes and still come away "better off" with free trade than with the tariff? Could the winners, on their part, compensate or "bribe" the losers to accept the tariff and still be better off with the tariff than with free trade?

In order to make producers and government outlay recipients indifferent between the two trade regimes, consumers would have to offer them compensation in the amount of areas a and c, respectively. Maintaining free trade would thus cost consumers area a + c, while the tariff regime costs consumers a + b + c + d. On the other side, producers and the government would have to pay consumers a + b + c + d in order to make them indifferent between the two trade regimes. Clearly, this would be an inferior solution by the amount b + d. This "double-bribe criterion" is another way of showing the superiority of free trade.

The Large Country in Partial Equilibrium

The large country is able to influence world prices by changes in its behavior. It is a price "maker" rather than a price "taker" in world markets. When such a country raises or lowers its demand for imports, it forces foreign suppliers to adjust their prices. When the large country imposes a tariff, thus reducing its demand for imports, the world price of those imports falls. This "terms-of-trade" effect has positive implications for the country's welfare. It is, however, harmful to the rest of the world and is known for that reason as a "beggar-thy-neighbor" policy.

In figure 1.2, two countries, A and B, both large enough in relation to each other to affect each other, trade good X. The left panel depicts the domestic situation in the importing country, A, while the right panel reflects conditions in the exporting country, B. The two curves in the middle panel represent A's net import demand and B's net export supply functions, respectively. Every point on each of these two curves is the difference between the respective domestic supply and demand at each respective price. Trade equilibrium occurs at the price at which the export supply forthcoming from country B just matches the import demand of country A. That price is P_x^W. At that price, distances $q_{0A}^{S}q_{0A}^{D}$ in the left panel, $q_{0B}^{D}q_{0B}^{S}$ in the right panel, and oq_0 in the middle panel are equal.

As in the small country case, imposition of an import tariff by country A may be depicted as a vertical addition to country B's export supply curve in the middle panel. If the tariff is a specific tariff, the tariff-inclusive supply curve will be parallel to the free-trade export supply curve. If the tariff is an ad valorem tariff, then the tariff-inclusive curve will have a steeper angle than the free-trade curve.

It is clear in the middle panel that consumers in country A will not want to maintain the free-trade level of imports, once the tariff is added to P_x^W. The quantity demanded falls to oq_1, forcing producers in country B to drop their price. In the new equilibrium, the price received by B's producers is P_x^B, the price paid by A's consumers is P_x^A, and the quantity traded, oq_1, in the middle panel is equal to $q_{1A}^{S}q_{1A}^{D}$ in the left and $q_{1B}^{D}q_{1B}^{S}$ in the right panel, respectively. While the difference between the two prices is once again equal to the tariff, in the large country case the tariff is added to a lower export supply price, implying that the domestic price in country A rises by less than the full amount of the tariff.

The welfare analysis proceeds along the lines discussed in the small country case. Consumer surplus falls in country A by the area a + b + c + d. Producer surplus rises by area a and government revenue increases by area c + e. Under the assumption of equal marginal utilities among the parties involved, the area that remains after taking account of the internal income redistribution is equal to e - b - d. Area e is positive in the sense that it represents government revenue not paid by consumers. Rather, it is extracted from foreign producers through the decrease in B's supply price and thus represents a welfare transfer from B to A. Triangles b and d are the negative deadweight losses. The net effect on national welfare in country A depends on the relative magnitudes of the positive and negative elements. Hence, welfare may decrease as it did in the small country, but it may also increase if the gains from the terms-of-trade improvement are larger than the deadweight losses.

Thus, while the "optimal" tariff, that is, the welfare-maximizing tariff, is clearly zero for the small country, it may be positive for a large country. The optimal tariff is the tariff that maximizes e - b - d. A stronger terms-of-trade effect makes for a larger decline in P_x^B relative to P_x^W and thus for a smaller rise of P_x^A relative to P_x^W. This, in turn, reduces the deadweight losses and increases the transfer from abroad.[1]

Unlike the small country's tariff, trade protection by the large country imposes welfare losses on its trading partner(s). In country B, consumer surplus rises by area f + g, while producer surplus falls by area f + g + h + s + v. The net effect on national welfare in country B is given by area h + s + v, which represents a loss to the nation at large. Area f + g is an internal transfer from producers to consumers, while area h is a transfer from B's producers to A's government, and areas s and v are deadweight losses. The effect of A's tariff on world welfare requires an additional assumption about the equivalence of marginal utilities between the two countries. Then areas e and h are offsetting from the point of view of world welfare, so that the effect on world welfare is given by area m + n in the middle panel, where m is the sum of areas b and d in the left panel and area n is the sum of areas s and v in the right panel. This is the deadweight loss to the world.

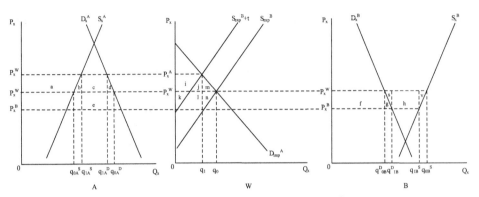

Figure 1.2. A large country levies a tariff.

Import Protection in General Equilibrium

The general equilibrium version of the benchmark model considers the effect on the rest of the economy of protecting the import-competing industry. In the two-commodity framework, the rest of the economy is the export sector, Y. There are no nontradable goods or services in the benchmark model. If the economy's productive resources are fully employed in the two sectors in figure 1.3, then free-trade production occurs at point Q_0 and consumption at point C_0, with the world price ratio given by P_w. This is a relative price measuring the amount of Y that must be given up in order to obtain a certain amount of X. If the money prices of the two goods are P_x and P_y, then P_w and P_d express the ratios P_x / P_y for free trade and the tariff situation, respectively. When a small country imposes a tariff on imports of X, the world price ratio is unaffected, while the domestic price ratio rises to P_d. The angle between the two price lines represents the size of the tariff.

In the new equilibrium, domestic producers and consumers adjust their behavior in light of the new tariff-inclusive home price ratio, but the country continues to trade at the world price ratio, P_w. Production moves to point Q_1, where output of the good X has risen in response to the rise in its price; at full employment, this increase comes at the expense of a decline in output of good Y. Consumption retreats to C_1 on a lower indifference curve (IC_1), with less of both goods being consumed. Community welfare clearly has been reduced by the policy.

In the case depicted in the diagram, the new "trade triangle" ($Q_1S_1C_1$) has shrunk along both dimensions, with exports and imports both smaller than before. This is a feature of import protection that is often overlooked in the policy debate: the tariff reduces not only imports but exports as well. It causes the country to "despecialize" along both dimensions.

In general equilibrium, community welfare is represented in terms of indifference curves.[2] Even without indifference curves, however, figure 1.3 provides useful information about the welfare changes that have taken place. In the movement from C_0 to C_1, the fact that less of both goods is consumed would suggest a loss of welfare even without recourse to the community indifference curve.

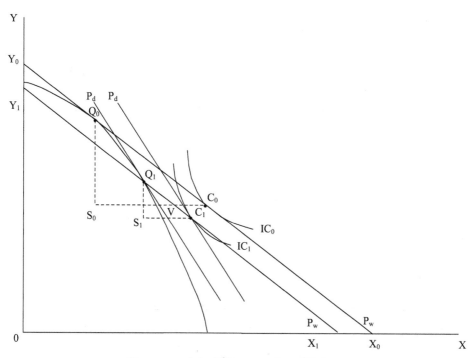

Figure 1.3. A tariff in general equilibrium.

It is possible under different sets of preferences, however, for the tariff to lower consumption of the import good while raising consumption of the exportable product. The increase in the price of X gives rise to a substitution effect, which shifts consumption from X to Y. It also introduces an income effect, which tends to reduce consumption of both goods. Together, the two effects reduce consumption of X, but they work in opposite directions on consumption of Y. If the substitution effect dominates the income effect, consumption of good Y will rise.

Aggregate output (and income) in this economy can be measured in terms of either of the two goods. In terms of good X, aggregate output in the initial situation is given at the intersection of the free trade price line, P_w, with the horizontal axis at point X_0. Measured in terms of good Y, it is given at the intersection of the same price line with the vertical axis at point Y_0. After the tariff has been imposed, the level of aggregate output has declined to X_1, when measured in terms of X, and to Y_1 when measured in terms of good Y. While consumers will attempt to mitigate the negative welfare effects by substituting away from the product that becomes more expensive, their overall spending is nevertheless bound by an inferior budget constraint.

The welfare losses sustained by the country's consumers, as opposed to the country overall, are implicit in the relative sizes of the trade triangles. Under free trade, the country exported Q_0S_0 units of good Y in exchange for imports of S_0C_0 units of good X. After the imposition of the tariff, exports have fallen to Q_1S_1 units and imports have declined to S_1C_1 units. However, in the new equilibrium, consumers receive only S_1V units of those X-imports, while the rest goes to the government in the form of tariff revenue. The government may decide to distribute this quantity to consumers, but it may also elect to spend the tariff proceeds in ways that do not benefit consumers directly, but may still be expected to affect them indirectly as citizens of the country.

It is worth noting for future reference that the benchmark model assumes trade to be fully balanced at all times. Exports pay for imports, so that the problem of lasting and unsustainable imbalances does not arise. Any incipient trade imbalance is immediately corrected by a change in the terms of trade.

A second important feature of the benchmark framework is that it is a single-period model, meaning that current output is completely absorbed or consumed in the current period. There is no saving and no recognition of depreciation, and economic growth is taken as exogenous.

Effects of Tariffs on Factor Prices

The Heckscher-Ohlin factor-proportions model provides additional insights into the adjustment process that follows imposition of a tariff. As the import-competing industry X expands production, it must offer higher wages and capital rentals in order to attract factors of production from the export sector. It can, of course, afford to pay higher wages and rentals, because the price of its product has risen from P_w to P_d. The Y-sector shrinks and releases labor and capital.

If the import-competing industry is relatively labor-intensive at the economy-wide factor-price ratio, then the proportion in which the export industry, Y, releases labor relative to capital at the initial factor-price ratio will be lower than the proportion required by the X industry at that same factor-price ratio. Consequently, wages will tend to rise relative to rentals in the move from point Q_0 to Q_1 in figure 1.3. It is important to note that when factors of production are perfectly mobile between the two sectors, then this realignment of factor returns will take place throughout the entire economy. If factors are immobile, as in the specific-factors version of this model, then the tariff raises returns in the X-industry relative to the Y-industry.

Under complete factor mobility, the factor of production used intensively in the import-competing industry is the beneficiary of the protectionist policy, while the other factor is worse off. In other words, the tariff has implications for the distribution of income in the economy: it tends to redistribute income among the country's own factors of production. In the case at hand, workers throughout the economy benefit at the expense of capital owners and investors.[3] The distributional aspects of the tariff, therefore, amount to redistribution first from consumers to producers and second in favor of factors of production used intensively in the protected industry.

In the small country, internal income redistribution and an increase in inefficiency are the main results of protection. In the large economy, an import tariff exerts downward pressure on the world price of the country's imports as the reduction in demand for those goods forces exporting countries to offer price concessions. This improvement in the tariff-imposing country's terms of trade brings about a crosscountry redistribution of income from the trading partner to domestic residents.

For the large country, price line P_w in figure 1.3 would thus rotate in a counterclockwise direction (not shown); it would become flatter, implying that the tariff reduces the world price of the import good. As a result, price line P_d in the figure would also become flatter than in the small country case. Consequently the post-tariff consumption point would lie on an indifference curve located somewhere between the two curves given in the figure. Indeed, if the terms-of-trade gain exceeds the inefficiency losses discussed above, then the new consumption point will lie on an indifference curve higher than curve IC_0. The tariff will have improved welfare.[4]

As noted, the optimum-tariff scenario is clearly an important argument in favor of protection. However, since country A's gains come at the expense of its trading partners, this policy is widely viewed as "beggar-thy-neighbor" in nature and is thus likely to invite retaliation from other countries.

Nontariff Trade Policies

The foregoing has focused on tariffs as the instrument of protectionist trade policy. In this section we briefly examine nontariff barriers such as import quotas and voluntary export restraints (VERs). While the basic welfare results continue largely unchanged, some of the many quantitative restrictions available to policy-makers may actually generate results that are more costly to national and/or world welfare than their tariff equivalents.

Import quotas are quantitative restrictions imposed by importing countries, while VERs are quantitative restrictions imposed on their own exports by exporting countries (very typically under pressure from importing countries). A binding quantitative restriction is one that limits imports to an amount less than that brought into the country under free trade (quantity $q_0{}^S q_0{}^D$ in figure 1.1). If the quota amount is set at $q_1{}^S q_1{}^D$, then there will be an excess demand at the free-trade price, forcing the domestic price to rise until the quantity imported just fills the gap between the demand and supply curves.

This quota is said to be "equivalent" to the tariff of figure 1.1 and vice versa. As before, consumer surplus declines by area a + b + c + d, while producer surplus rises by area a. Under the usual assumptions about comparable marginal utilities, area a is an internal transfer and areas b and d are deadweight losses. What happens to area c, which denoted revenue collected by the government in the case of a tariff, now depends on how the quota "rents" are distributed.

Quota licenses may be auctioned off, in which case the government will collect quota rents equal to area c. Licenses may also be given away, in which case the rents accrue to the holders of the licenses, who obtain the product at the world price and sell it at the domestic price, $P_x{}^d$. If the holders are domestic residents, such as importing companies, and the assumptions pertaining to marginal utility comparisons hold, then area c will be a domestic transfer from consumers to importers. If the holders are foreign entities, then area c is a transfer abroad, and the loss of national welfare expands to area b + c + d. From the national welfare point of view, therefore, this type of quota is clearly inferior to the tariff and to the auctioned quota. Voluntary export restraints have effects on welfare similar to those of quotas whose licenses are allocated to foreigners, except that under VERs the rents accrue automatically to foreigners, who produce the product at the world price and sell it at the importing country's domestic price.

Nontrade Policies

It is clear that, with the exception of the optimum tariff, the protectionist policies examined above are all inferior to free trade. Their main effects are income redistribution among domestic interest groups and inefficiencies in resource utilization. Domestic policy alternatives exist that are capable of achieving the objective of raising domestic production at lower welfare cost. One such policy is the domestic production subsidy.

A subsidy per unit of production equal to the difference between the domestic and world prices in figure 1.1 increases output to q_1^S. Producers sell that output at the world price—P_x^w—and receive a subsidy payment equal to the difference on every unit they produce, while consumers continue to pay the world price. Hence, there is no change in consumer surplus, while producer surplus again rises by area a. The cost of the subsidy to the government is area a + b. Under the stated assumptions about utility comparisons, area a is a transfer from taxpayers to producers, while area b represents the efficiency loss to society.

Although free trade with domestic production subsidies is still inferior to free trade, the welfare costs are smaller than under any of the trade-based policies discussed above. The main problem with subsidies is that they are more transparent for the income redistribution that is involved and thus tend to be less popular with industry and more difficult to implement politically. In recent years, moreover, a consensus has emerged among the member countries of GATT/WTO that subsidies of this type are beggar-thy-neighbor policies, because they create employment at home at the expense of unemployment among trading partners. A series of "subsidy codes" has been negotiated among WTO members, which sharply restricts the use of production subsidies as a viable policy option.[5]

Export Promotion

The preceding has dealt with trade policy intervention designed to protect import-competing industries from foreign competitors. In recent years, however, trade intervention designed to increase exports and to help domestic firms penetrate foreign markets has become an important preoccupation of governments. Export promotion policies include export subsidies, production subsidies to exportables industries, subsidized interest rates to finance exports, and undervaluation of the domestic currency.

Export Subsidies

An export subsidy offers domestic producers a payment for each unit of a commodity that is exported. It thus differs from a production subsidy, which is paid on each unit produced. Figure 1.4 provides a partial-equilibrium perspective on the effects of export subsidies. In the initial equilibrium at world price P_y^w, the country produces q_0^s units of commodity Y, consumes q_0^D units, and exports the difference. When the subsidy program is implemented, firms in a small country can sell all of their output in the world market at the world price and then collect the subsidy for every unit exported.

Together, these payments add up to a price-equivalent of P_y^d. Under these circumstances, there is no incentive to sell any part of their production domestically unless they can receive a price equal to the world price plus the subsidy. Hence, domestic consumers will be forced to pay P_y^d. It is important to note, however, that this outcome is possible only if consumers are prevented from importing the product at the world price.[6] This issue is examined in a later section.

In figure 1.4, consumer surplus falls by area a + b, producer surplus rises by area a + b + c, and the cost of the subsidy to government is b + c + d. Assuming equal marginal income utilities across interest groups, area a + b amounts to domestic income redistribution from consumers to producers with no effect on national welfare. Area c represents income redistribution from taxpayers to producers, while area b + d takes income from taxpayers that does not go to any other group in society. This is the increase in inefficiency, the "deadweight" loss, brought about by the subsidy policy.

If, on the other hand, consumers are able to access the world market for good Y, they will continue to purchase oq_0^D units, implying that the entire domestic output of the product will be exported and that the government will pay the export subsidy on the entire output. After accounting for internal transfers from taxpayers to producers, area d remains as the deadweight loss to society. Note that this is equivalent to a production subsidy in its effects and costs.[7]

Exchange Rate Protectionism

Exchange rate manipulation offers countries a way of simultaneously promoting exports and protecting imports. Undervalued currencies make exports cheaper abroad, but more expensive at home, while imports become more expensive at home. This result is equivalent to the combined effect of export subsidies and import tariffs. For a small country, whose export prices are determined in world markets, a rise in the exchange rate (defined as the price of foreign currency in terms of the home currency) raises receipts per unit exported in terms of domestic money. In a diagram like figure 1.4, currency undervaluation raises firms' export receipts to P_y^d, thereby encouraging greater production and a rise in exports. As under the export subsidy, home consumers end up paying the higher price.

On the import side, in a diagram similar to figure 1.1, undervaluation raises the home price of imports at given world prices, thereby allowing domestic firms to

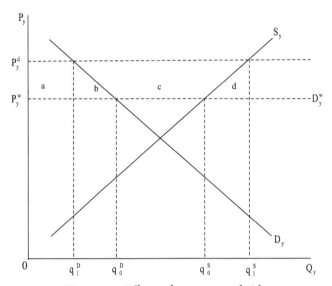

Figure 1.4. Effects of an export subsidy.

expand production and sales. Consumers pay a higher price for imports and import-competing goods and services. The welfare effects of undervaluation follow the line developed for import tariffs.

Of course, at full employment it is not possible in our two-good economy for production in both industries to rise, unless the economy is growing. Hence, domestic export and import prices rise proportionately, with no change in relative prices, no change in the output mix, and no change in the trade balance. In real-world economies, however, exports and imports, the so-called tradables sectors, make up only part of total domestic output. Many other industries produce nontradable goods and services, allowing production of both imports and exports to rise by drawing productive resources from these nontradables sectors.[8]

While a small country is a "price taker" in the world markets for its imports and exports, a large country will depress world market prices of both imports and exports, as the undervaluation of its currency reduces its import demand and raises its export supply. On the import side, figure 1.2 is a useful tool for assessing the effects. In the middle panel, effective foreign supply shifts left, not because the tariff imposes additional costs, but because the depreciation of the importing country's currency raises the price of imports in terms of the home currency. As we have seen, for the small country, that price will rise to fully reflect the extent of the depreciation. For the large country, the drop in imports lowers their foreign-currency price, implying that the rise in their home-currency price is less than the depreciation.

When the country is large, a rise in exports exerts downward pressure on the world price, implying that the resulting rise in the home-currency price of those exports will be less than the undervaluation. From the point of view of the exporting country, the policy leads to a loss of national welfare. From the point of view of the importing country, the positive terms-of-trade effect hurts local producers, but brings larger gains to consumers and thus raises national welfare. Producer surplus will decline by area f + g + s + h + v, while consumer surplus will rise by area f + g, leaving a net welfare loss of area of s + h + v. Area h represents the welfare transfer from trading partners to the currency manipulator, while area s + v reflects deadweight efficiency losses.

If there are countries in the world that are net importers of commodity Y, they will benefit from the repercussions of currency manipulation by a large country. Assume for simplicity that they import the commodity under free-trade conditions. Then a decline in the world price of good Y will raise consumer surplus by more than it reduces producer surplus and hence will raise national welfare.

3. INTRAINDUSTRY TRADE

The benchmark model was designed to explain *interindustry* trade, where countries' imports and exports belong to different industries and where domestic and foreign goods from the same industry are perfect substitutes. In the era following World War II, however, there has been an explosion of *intraindustry* trade, where countries' imports and exports contain goods belonging to the same industry but domestic and foreign goods from the same industry are no longer perfect substitutes. German car exports to France and German car imports from France may belong to the same industry, but they are subject to varietal differences that matter to consumers.

Intraindustry trade based on *product differentiation* may be horizontal or vertical. Horizontal intraindustry trade is the dominant pattern among advanced countries and is broadly characterized by two-way flows of end products of similar quality. Vertical intraindustry trade takes place between advanced and emerging economies involving trade in end products that differ in quality (Lancaster 1979; Linder 1961). In this instance, varieties exported by advanced countries tend to be of higher quality than the varieties exported by emerging economies.

In recent years, however, vertical intraindustry trade associated with crossborder production networks has grown particularly rapidly. Here, the constituent activities of production are dispersed across two or more countries, with each country taking responsibility for the stage or activity in which it has a comparative advantage. In this instance, finished end products may be exported by a country that imports some of the components contained in those end products. As the product goes through its various production phases, it may repeatedly cross borders. This modern version of vertical intraindustry trade is exemplified by the flow of automobile parts and components from the United States to Mexico and the movement of assembled automobiles from Mexico to the United States, or by the flow to China of electronic parts and components from a number of East Asian countries for assembly into finished products destined for shipment to the United States and other advanced-country markets.

The benchmark model's focus on factor endowments and factor intensities works very well in understanding interindustry trade and both types of *vertical* intraindustry trade, but it is limited in its ability to explain horizontal intraindustry trade. The model's focus on factor endowments and factor intensities, makes it a very useful tool for analyzing interindustry trade, where differences in factor proportions play a key role. As Lancaster (1979) has shown,[9] factor-proportions are also important in end-product trade between advanced and emerging economies. Here, a labor-abundant emerging economy has comparative advantage in the production of more labor-intensive varieties in a given industry, while its advanced trading partner can use its abundant supplies of skilled labor and capital to advantage by producing more technologically refined, high-quality varieties.[10]

The inability of the factor-proportions approach to explain *horizontal* intraindustry trade among advanced countries is due to the overwhelming similarities among those countries of factor endowments and factor intensities. The "new" trade theories, developed in the second half of the last century by Brander and Spencer (1981, 1984), Helpman (1984), Krugman (1979, 1981), and others were intended to overcome these difficulties in order to provide a better understanding of these trade patterns. In these trade models, economies of scale and imperfect competition, as well as product differentiation, play key roles.[11]

Scale Economies and Product Differentiation

On the demand side, the new theories explore the possibility that consumers may derive benefits from product variety, in which case *product differentiation* comes to play a key role. "Love of variety" is an important element in the contribution by Dixit and Stiglitz (1977), in which trade increases consumer welfare by increasing the varieties available within each product category. On the supply side, increasing returns to scale are introduced and with them the possible erosion of competition. In this world, each country's producers specialize in a subset of all varieties, thereby generating longer production runs in order to take advantage of cost-saving scale economies.[12]

When each country produces and exports a subset of varieties while importing the rest, overall demand for each country's domestic brands tends to rise as its market expands into other countries. Some domestic demand for domestic varieties falls as home consumers shift to foreign brands; indeed, some domestic varieties may disappear as they are replaced by foreign substitutes. Production runs for the surviving varieties tend to expand, thereby enabling producers to exploit the cost savings inherent in scale economies.[13]

With horizontal intraindustry specialization, equilibrium outcomes depend on such factors as the number of countries involved, the length of production runs needed to reach optimum scale in each industry, and the degree of product differentiation. A large number of participating countries makes for a larger integrated market. Each firm needs to decide on the number of varieties to bring to market and in which country to market them. Since each firm is large and thus a price maker and since it typically faces demand conditions that vary across countries, profit maximization typically involves price discrimination across national markets.

Firms compete for market share across borders. Each has an interest in protecting its own market against imports of foreign varieties, while seeking to promote exports of its brand. The short-run effects of import tariffs work very much like those discussed in connection with figures 1.2 and 1.3. Each firm faces an upward-sloping short-run supply curve, with capital fixed and labor mobile. A tariff on imports of the foreign variety raises its price, reducing consumer surplus, while raising government revenue. The net effect is a welfare loss. The rise in the home price of the foreign variety shifts domestic demand toward the domestic brand, raising price and increasing output. There are additional repercussions and spillover effects, but our main interest is in the long run when capacity changes and scale economies are won or lost.

In the long run, domestic firms respond to the rise in price of the domestic brand by expanding productive capacity. If the economies of scale are internal to the firm, this increase in size reduces each firm's cost, implying that the new short-run supply curve has shifted out and down, enabling firms to cut prices on domestic brands and thereby improve their overall competitiveness.

The experience of foreign firms is likely to run in the opposite direction. The tariff imposed by the home country reduces demand for the foreign variety and thus puts downward pressure on prices and production abroad (along the lines discussed in relation to figure 1.2). If foreign firms respond by eliminating capacity, then their long-run costs rise along the slope of the long-run cost curve. There is a leftward displacement of the new short-run supply curve, a rise in costs, and a rise in price. Each country's firms have an interest in fighting off encroachment on the size of their operations. The home country's tariff—sometimes referred to as a scale-snatching tariff—makes them less competitive and reduces their market share and is thus likely to meet with retaliatory countermoves.

As the foregoing suggests, the welfare effects of trade intervention are not easily generalized, given the importance of initial conditions on both the demand and supply sides.[14] We do, however, have some empirical evidence in the experience of the European Union (EU), where many countries have historically employed industrial and trade policies to support and protect "national champion" firms in key industries, including motor vehicles. Both tariffs and nontariff barriers have been employed to reserve national markets for home producers. Formation of the customs union (CU) was aimed at elimination of inefficiencies caused by trade barriers, while the Single Market project standardized competition policy across borders and removed many other distortions and impediments. Creating a large and uniform market was expected to reduce the overall number of firms, thereby allowing the survivors to expand production and reduce costs.[15]

When intraindustry specialization is vertical in the manner of Linder (1961) and Lancaster (1979), advanced countries produce and export varieties at the high-quality end of the spectrum and import varieties at the low-price, low-quality end from less advanced countries. For the majority of developing countries, local markets are too small to allow exploitation of scale economies. Hence, access to the markets of large countries and to the world market more generally is critical. Export-led growth has been a very important policy model, particularly in East Asia.

We saw earlier that vertical intraindustry specialization may be the result of endowment differences. In addition, differences in technological know-how also play a role. The Heckscher-Ohlin (1966) model, on the other hand, assumes away such differences in knowledge. As Vernon's (1966) view of the product cycle predicts and as postwar economic history shows, advanced countries find it very difficult to protect their knowledge-based edge. Over time, the advantage conferred by their endowment of "knowledge capital" is eroded as emerging economies catch up. Often, technology is appropriated by foreign rivals before the costs of research and development have been paid off. Protection of intellectual property rights is thus a very important part of trade relations. Important strides have been made in recent years at the level of the GATT/WTO to create a global framework for the protection of intellectual property.

Some critics see in the gradual erosion of advanced-country competitiveness in vertical intraindustry trade a key argument against free trade; it explains to them why free trade "doesn't work" (Fletcher 2010). They advocate tariffs just large enough to protect the advantages conferred by scale effects. Imposition of such tariffs, however, would not easily pass WTO muster. Concerns about WTO sanctions sometimes lead to VERs. The United States, for example, employed political pressure to move the Japanese government to impose limits on motor vehicle exports to the United States. This transferred large quota rents to Japanese producers, who promptly used them to upgrade the quality of their exports. Moreover, unlike the Heckscher-Ohlin model, in which there is no allowance made for foreign direct investment (FDI), Japanese firms responded to "Japan-bashing" by establishing production facilities in the U.S.

Protection through VERs may provoke tariff-jumping FDI, which replaces imports from abroad with local production of foreign brands for the home market. In an earlier age, American firms responded to discriminatory trade liberalization in Europe in the 1950s by moving production of their brands into Europe. From the point of view of firms in the importing country, this undermines the extent to which they are protected from foreign competition. From the point of view of jobs protection, the case is more complicated. The jobs "saved" by the tariff will be lost once foreign firms begin production, but new jobs will be created in the production of foreign varieties. The welfare effects again depend on the specifics, especially with respect to similarities and symmetries of cost structures.

The foreign affiliates' cost structures are likely to be affected by offsetting forces. Their cost conditions will be higher if they produce only for the local market, meaning a smaller scale of operations. Costs will be lower if they can acquire labor at better terms than domestic firms, along the experience of Japanese auto producers in Tennessee relative to Detroit or American firms in Ireland relative to German and French firms in their respective high-wage markets. If affiliate costs are higher than in the pretariff situation, then domestic firms receive a measure of protection. If they are lower, imposition of the tariff worsens their competitive situation.

Production Networks and Vertical Intraindustry Trade and Investment

Vertical intraindustry production sharing works particularly well among dissimilar economies, including economies with different factor endowments. But since the Heckscher-Ohlin model assumes that technologies are not only similar but identical across countries, its usefulness in explaining this type of trade may remain limited. However, the modern version of vertical intraindustry trade occurs largely within crosscountry production networks anchored by multinational companies. Those companies typically transfer essential technologies and capital to labor-abundant emerging economies, thus ensuring that technologies are "identical" where needed and that relative labor abundance is the key determinant of intra-product specialization.[16]

It clearly makes no sense for a member of a production network to impose trade restrictions of any kind on imports of parts and components that are brought in for further processing or assembly. Such restrictions would raise costs along the rest of the value chain. The argument against such imposts is provided by the theory of effective protection (Corden 1966). On the other hand, countries may compete for a place in a production network by offering concessions and incentives in order to attract multinationals.

Ireland's support of its electronics industry is an important example. Such support can play a key role even when scale economies are external to the firm. Government may aim its support at improving the competitiveness of the network and its constituents. This includes policies that lower transactions costs, costs related to infrastructural and administrative inefficiencies, and the like.

In key respects, vertical specialization has effects similar to technological change. Fragmentation and crossborder sourcing may be sector-specific or economy-wide. Like technical change, production possibility blocks like that pictured in figure 1.3 shift out along the axis or axes representing the sectors in which change occurs. Vertical specialization may also be factor-specific, with advanced countries tending to outsource low-skill-labor-intensive elements of production, while emerging economies outsource capital- and technology-intensive elements of production. The results for employment, factor prices, and changes in the output mix are sensitive to the specific features of a given episode.[17]

4. IMPERFECT COMPETITION

In the benchmark model, all markets are perfectly competitive. While some international trade, especially in some standardized components and commodities, may be reasonably treated as if it were perfectly competitive, much of modern trade in both goods and services involves markets with imperfectly competitive structures.

A significant share of trade in both goods and services is in reality dominated by large multinational companies. We have already noted that internal economies of scale tend to promote the formation of large firms and the concentration of market power. In this section, we explore the implications of trade intervention in the presence of imperfect competition.

In a world of imperfect competition, it is much more difficult to find easy generalizations regarding the welfare effects of alternative trade regimes. We have already encountered this problem in connection with scale economies, and it carries through to other departures from the assumptions of the benchmark model. When everybody is a price taker, "markets" resolve imbalances in ways that achieve socially optimal outcomes. Imperfect competition is a form of market distortion that undermines the ability of markets to achieve socially optimal allocations of an economy's resources. Monopolistic elements encourage firms to restrict output and raise price relative to the outcome under perfect competition. Hence, any trade policy that strengthens this power by reducing competition from abroad is likely to be welfare-reducing.

However, in an economy with multiple distortions, introduction of an additional distortion may raise or lower welfare, depending on whether it augments or offsets the effects of existing distortions. Removal of one among multiple distortions gives rise to similar ambiguities, which means that elimination of a trade barrier in an economy with multiple distortions may reduce rather than raise welfare. These considerations are aspects of the economics of the "second best" (Corden 1974); they create significant problems for policy-makers.

Although broad generalizations are not easily forthcoming in the presence of market distortions, economists have studied trade intervention in specific cases of imperfect competition.[18] In the next subsection, we focus on monopoly, not because it is the most typical of imperfectly competitive market structures in international trade but because the cases chosen illustrate several policy themes.[19] If monopoly power is the ability to influence prices, to be a "price maker," then we have already encountered one example of such price-making power, namely, the "optimum-tariff" argument for large countries. That argument continues to be relevant in the context of imperfect competition.

Domestic Monopoly

In figure 1.5, a country's domestic import-competing industry is assumed to be a monopolist, whose product is a perfect substitute for goods produced abroad. The country is assumed to be small in relation to the world market. In autarky, the firm faces downward-sloping domestic demand, D, with associated marginal revenue, MR. It produces an amount q_0^S, where marginal cost, MC, equals MR, and sells that amount at price P_0. Free trade and the resulting competition from abroad renders the firm's marginal and average revenue curves horizontal at the level of the world price, but the implications depend on the exact level of the world price.

If the world price is P_w^0, then the firm produces quantity q_0^S and sells it at that price, at which quantity demanded domestically is q_0^D. Hence, the country ends up

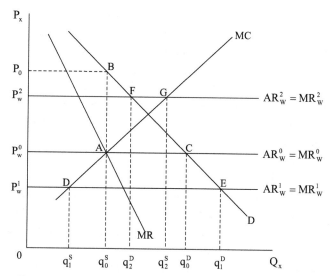

Figure 1.5. A domestic monopolist and the trade regime.

importing an amount AC of the product. In this case, the move to free trade reduces price but leaves domestic production unchanged, unlike the benchmark model, in which domestic production falls. If the world price is as low as P_w^1, however, domestic production does decline, and imports rise to DE. If the world price is as high as P_w^2, domestic production increases to q_2^S. At that price, the quantity demanded domestically is less than output, and the firm exports FG units.

In all three cases, free trade eliminates the monopolist's ability to restrict output and raise price by forcing it to behave like a perfect competitor. This is the well-known function of free trade as an antitrust instrument and may be the most powerful and compelling argument for free trade under imperfect competition. It is not surprising that domestic production may actually increase with free trade, given monopolists' tendency to restrict production in order to raise price.

Introduction of a tariff into this picture raises domestic price in all three cases. As the intersection of the tariff-inclusive horizontal price line (not drawn) rises along the MC curve between point D and its intersection with the downward-sloping demand curve, domestic production rises, domestic consumption falls, and imports decline. This outcome matches the results obtained with the benchmark model. It is important to note that the monopolist continues to be constrained to behave as a competitor for as long as domestic consumers are free to access the product at the world price and pay the tariff, that is, as long as arbitrage between the home and foreign markets is not restricted. As in the benchmark model, the effect of the tariff is to reduce net national welfare. It reduces consumer surplus, increases producer surplus, and provides government with tariff revenue, but after accounting for domestic income transfers, the typical deadweight losses remain.

If a tariff is introduced when the free-trade price is P_w^2, at which the firm is an exporter of the product, the firm can charge the tariff-inclusive price on units of the product sold domestically, but is constrained to sell all additional units in the world market at the world price. In that case, the firm effectively faces a kinked AR/MR curve. We return to this case after discussing figure 1.6 below.

It was important in the preceding discussion that consumers' ability to arbitrage between the home and foreign markets be preserved in order to force the monopolist to behave like a competitor. In figure 1.6, we suppose that the monopolist has the ability to prevent such price arbitrage. Governments prevent arbitrage by means of import tariffs and other regulatory restrictions.[20]

Under the stated conditions, the monopolist produces quantity q_0 and charges price P_0 in autarky. When the economy is opened to trade on the export side, with world price at P_w, the monopolist's marginal revenue curve follows the bold kinked line (ACDMR$_1$), descending initially from point A to C and then becoming horizontal at the world price. This curve intersects the marginal cost curve at point D, indicating a profit-maximizing output level of q_2. The firm sells Oq_1 units domestically at price P_1 and exports the rest at the world price. This profit-maximizing behavior may be viewed abroad as "dumping," selling a product at a lower price in the foreign market than at home. Such a policy might be pursued by countries seeking "export-led" growth. Domestically, this restrictive version of open trade reduces availability of the product and raises its price, to the obvious detriment of consumers.

Returning briefly to figure 1.5, if a tariff is imposed when the world price is at P_w^2, the firm would again face a kinked marginal revenue curve, descending initially along the downward-sloping MR curve, becoming horizontal at the tariff-inclusive price ($P_w^2 + t$), becoming vertical when it hits the demand curve, dropping down toward the world price line, and becoming horizontal at that price line. Production

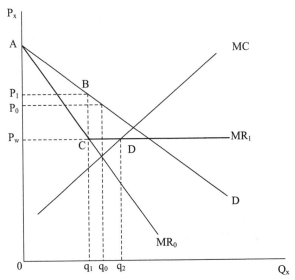

Figure 1.6. Domestic monopoly when arbitrage is restricted.

would occur at point G, where the kinked MR curve intersects MC. Domestic sales would occur at a price that would place home demand somewhere along the segment BF, and the rest of the firm's production would be exported.

It is important to note the new context within which the analysis of the previous paragraphs takes place. In the benchmark model, there are no distortions under free trade in either the domestic or the world economy. Markets function efficiently and well. They can be relied on to bring about the most productive utilization of national and world resources. In that model, the gains from trade arise simply from a more efficient allocation of productive resources. Trade intervention is thus welfare-reducing precisely because it interferes with market efficiency. In the benchmark model, trade intervention is the sole distortion in an otherwise undistorted world.

Monopoly, on the other hand, represents a distortion that interferes with the market's allocative functions and generates inefficiencies in resource utilization. In that distorted world, free trade introduces competition and thereby curbs or eliminates the distortion. As noted earlier, however, the theory of second best (Corden 1974) shows that in a world of multiple distortions it is not possible to say whether removal of one of those distortions improves or worsens welfare, just as it is not possible to say whether introduction of an additional distortion improves or worsens welfare.[21]

Foreign Monopoly

Consider the case of a foreign, rather than domestic, monopoly supplier of a country's imports of goods or services. The essence of the argument, illustrated in figure 1.7, is similar to the discussion of domestic monopoly. Under free trade conditions, the foreign monopolist, assumed to be the sole supplier of good X to the home market, produces output level q_0, where marginal cost and marginal revenue are equal, and sells it for price P_0. The foreign firm's monopoly profits are equal to area P_0ABC.

The country may have an interest in breaking or at least curbing the monopolist's market power by imposing constraints on its price-making power. Recall that in the example of the domestic monopolist, the price limit was provided by competition in the world market. In the present case, the country may decide to impose a specific tariff the effect of which is to shift the marginal cost curve to MC + t. This new curve intersects the marginal revenue curve at output q_1, for which the monopolist charges price P_1 in the domestic market. The tariff allows the monopolist to raise the price paid by consumers and thus reduces consumer surplus by area P_1DAP_0. The firm's monopoly profits decline to area P_1DEF, and the home country's government collects area FEGC in revenue, which it may recycle to consumers or use for other socially desirable purposes.

This type of tariff has come to be known as a "rent-snatching" tariff. Its effect is to raise national welfare, given that the government's rent receipts are larger than the loss in consumer surplus. Rents collected by the government will be larger than consumer surplus loss, provided that the MR curve is steeper than the D curve.

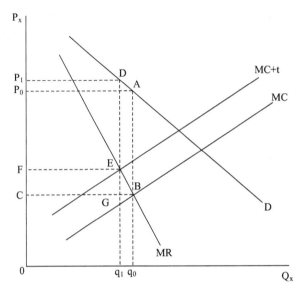

Figure 1.7. Foreign monopoly and the trade regime.

Then, the reduction in quantity from q_0 to q_1 generates a larger vertical change along the steeper MR curve than along the flatter D curve.

However, while the tariff has redistributed some of the monopolist's profits to the home country's government, the two distortions—monopoly and tariff—together have further reduced the efficiency of resource utilization.

5. OTHER MARKET DISTORTIONS

Externalities

The benchmark model assumes that private and social costs and benefits are equal throughout the economy. In reality, positive and negative externalities abound, implying that the "private" demand and supply curves in figures 1.1 and 1.2, on the basis of which producers and consumers make their respective decisions, do not correctly reflect costs and benefits to society. A well-known example is environmental pollution in agriculture and manufacturing, which raises social relative to private costs to the extent that private producers are not required to absorb the costs of environmental degradation. On the demand side, positive or negative externalities or spillovers may analogously separate private from and social benefits.

Economists agree that trade policy is generally not the best means of dealing with such externalities and that it is inferior to production and consumption taxes and subsidies, for reasons similar to those discussed in relation to production subsidies in section 2. A tariff may achieve a socially desirable increase in output, if social costs are below private costs, but it does so by introducing a distortion on the demand side embodied in the higher prices consumers must pay.

Environmental and Labor Standards

In recent years, two issues seemingly unrelated to trade have been introduced into the policy debate, in which opponents have argued that free trade can be "unfair" trade, especially between countries with very different environmental and worker protection standards. If countries like the United States have tough laws forcing firms to absorb the costs of environmental degradation and to protect workers from harsh and abusive conditions in the work place, then the resultant increase in private costs will place domestic producers at a competitive disadvantage relative to countries with more relaxed standards. This has led some to propose tariffs just large enough to offset such "unfair" advantages, much like an antidumping duty seeks to eliminate foreign price discrimination.

It is clear, however, that imposition of such a levy in the context of figure 1.1 would create the welfare losses analyzed before, without having any direct effect on the externalities in the exporting countries. While a production subsidy to the domestic industry would also "level the playing field" without introducing a distortion on the side of domestic consumption, it too would have no direct impact on foreign "unfair" practices.

When such a duty is imposed by a large country, its effect is to reduce price and production abroad (as in figure 1.2). If the objective is to penalize foreign firms for environmental degradation, then proponents may assert that the reduction in foreign producer surplus achieves that objective and, further, that the decline in output abroad serves to protect the global environment by shifting production from a high-polluting to a low-polluting country. It is even possible for the tariff to improve net welfare at home if the tariff is an optimum tariff.

If, on the other hand, the tariff is imposed in order to penalize the foreign country for abusive labor practices and inadequate worker protection, then the reduction in foreign production and rise in unemployment could worsen the plight of workers there. This has led some observers to propose that advanced countries like the United States might consider providing income transfers to poorer countries in order to help them pay for environmental and worker protection.

Preferential Free Trade Agreements (PTAs)

One of the most powerful conclusions of the benchmark model is that trade liberalization brings net welfare gains to a country regardless of whether its trading partners also adopt free trade. It makes the case for unilateral rather than negotiated free trade. In practice, however, the multilateral trade negotiations that have taken place since the end of World War II have from the beginning been based on reciprocity. Policy makers have found it easier to overcome domestic opposition to trade liberalization if they could show that opening their own markets was matched by more open foreign markets. Thus, in the public mind the perceived "cost" of lost import protection must be offset by the perceived gains from export promotion. Unfortunately, as the number of countries participating in multilateral trade negotiations has grown over the years, reaching a negotiated multilateral agreement has become more difficult and the negotiating process more protracted.

An important, but narrower and more limited, form of negotiated trade liberalization occurs in the context of PTAs, the two most popular examples of which are the free trade area (FTA) and the CU. In both instances, trade among members is liberated, but in the FTA each country retains its own tariffs on trade with non-members. In the CU, on the other hand, members adopt a common external tariff (CET) vis-à-vis non-members.

The main regional PTAs are the EU and Mercosur, both CUs; the North American Free Trade Agreement (NAFTA); and the ASEAN Free Trade Agreement. There are, in addition, numerous nonregional PTAs, such as those between the U.S. and Israel and between Singapore and the EU.

This form of selective and discriminatory trade liberalization may or may not increase national welfare, because it typically generates both positive and negative welfare effects. The positive effects are due to the shift from high-cost domestic production to lower-cost imports from member countries. This effect is known as "trade creation."

However, the lowest-cost member of the PTA may not be the lowest-cost producer in the world, in which case preferential elimination of the tariff in favor of PTA members diverts imports from lowest-cost nonmembers to higher-cost members. This cost-raising shift is known as "trade diversion." It follows that the net effect on the country's welfare depends on the relative magnitudes of trade creation and trade diversion.

In general, the larger the number of the world's low-cost producers included in the PTA, the greater the likelihood that the PTA will raise welfare. This insight provides an important explanation for the failure of the Latin American Free Trade Area, a discriminatory FTA that excluded too many of the world's low-cost producers of too many products (including the U.S. and the EU). In that event, negative effects of trade diversion overpowered the gains from trade creation.

As noted in earlier sections, large countries are price makers and thus their welfare also depends on movements in their terms of trade. If a country entering a PTA is "large" in relation to other member countries, then the shift from domestic production to imports will tend to raise prices, and this negative terms-of-trade effect introduces an additional welfare-reducing element.

On the other hand, to the extent that member countries are large relative to nonmembers, the diversion of imports will tend to reduce the price of imports from the rest of the world, providing members with potentially important terms-of-trade gains. Indeed, regional trade pacts may be beneficial from the point of view of small countries if, in addition to providing price-making power, they increase bargaining power in multilateral trade negotiations and multilateral institutions. The potential of membership in a regional trading group to confer market power upon small countries, including influence over the group's terms of trade with nonmember trading partners, is an important attribute of PTAs that has not been widely discussed in the literature (see Arndt 1968; 1969).

The lack of a common external tariff (CET) in an FTA allows importers in a high-tariff member country to by-pass the domestic tariff by bringing in goods, parts and components from outside the area through a low-tariff member country. This is an evasive maneuver that is not possible in a CU. In order to prevent such tactics, FTA members establish "rules of origin," also known as regional content requirements, which specify the percentage of an end product that must have been produced in member countries in order to take advantage of tariff-free passage across internal borders. Enforcement of these rules at road crossings, airports, and seaports within NAFTA, for example, is so costly that roughly half of the intra-NAFTA trade that is eligible for the zero tariff does not take advantage of that privilege, because the costs of compliance exceed the tariff advantage. This maneuver becomes increasingly cost-effective as the most-favored-nation tariff declines. At an average tariff of 4%, compliance costs can easily exceed that amount.

6. Concluding Comments

The case for free trade is at its strongest, but least relevant, when made in the context of a perfect economic environment. In such a world, protectionism introduces a distortion into an otherwise undistorted universe and thereby disturbs the "best" (most productive) utilization of productive resources. The inevitable and necessary consequence is a loss of welfare, as defined in that model. The benchmark model is useful not so much in providing a reasonable representation of reality as in spelling out the many conditions that must be satisfied in order to nail down the case for free trade. It is useful, especially, in making clear that when resources are fully utilized, import protection or export promotion policies make some people better off, but only at the expense of making others worse off. We see such policies for what they are, namely, opaque approaches to income redistribution, among domestic interest groups in small countries and partly away from foreigners in large countries. Moreover, in bringing about income redistribution, trade intervention creates welfare-reducing inefficiencies.

In the presence of imperfect competition, a principal benefit of free trade may be simply that it introduces competition into the home market and forces the monopolist or oligopolist to behave like a competitor. It is a great antitrust policy with which to tame and control domestic monopolistic elements. However, free trade may give foreign monopoly or oligopoly undesirably easy access to rents in the home market, in which case a tariff is useful in "snatching" back part of those rents. In the absence of workable antitrust policies for dealing with globally concen-trated industries, rent-snatching tariffs may some day become the last recourse for many an individual country.

Scale economies, especially when they are internal to the firm, nurture and promote imperfect competition. It is not always easy to say whether the cost savings inherent in larger firm size justify the adverse price changes introduced by atten-dant monopoly elements. Add various types of externalities into the brew, and the welfare implications of any policy action, whether toward or away from freer trade, become even murkier. This is a challenge that not only has stymied economic analysis but handicaps policy-making as well.

Meanwhile, the world has made significant progress toward global free trade since the end of World War II, driven in part by policy and in part by cost-reducing innovations in transportation and communication technologies. Indeed, the degree of success is so extensive as to suggest that for many goods and services, trade is now freer than the markets themselves. In many areas of economic endeavor, with the notable but not the only exception of agriculture, the trade barriers that remain are probably less detrimental to welfare than some of the other distortions, parti-cularly those involving imperfect competition. One example is suggested by the banking and financial industries. It would be difficult to show that opening world markets even more completely to the global banking and financial oligopolies would bring greater welfare benefits to society, however defined, than would increasing the degree of competition and facilitating entry and, most important, exit.

NOTES

I am indebted to Nik Miller, Nanako Yano, and Saumya Lohia for valuable research assistance and to Max Kreinin for helpful advice and guidance.

1. For detailed discussions of the optimum-tariff argument for protection, see Heffernan and Sinclair (1990) and Vousden (1990).

2. The assumptions underpinning the construction of community indifference curves are not uncontroversial. For additional discussion, see Markusen and Melvin (1984).

3. Some of the implications of factor mobility are explored in the "specific-factors" version of the benchmark model, which typically assumes that capital is immobile in the short run. Consequently, the rise in labor demand by the expanding industry boosts wages throughout the economy, while capital rentals rise in the expanding industry, but fall in the contracting industry. In the long run, when capital becomes fully mobile, the economy adjusts toward the results discussed in the previous paragraph.

4. See Markusen and Melvin (1984) for more on the general equilibrium framework.

5. Although the stated objective of the subsidy (as of the other policies) is to raise output and employment in the import-competing sector, the underlying imperative is to preserve incomes in the sector.

6. The EU's variable levy on food imports is a noteworthy example of a policy that limits consumers' access to low-cost imports from world markets.

7. Note that an income subsidy equal to area a + b + c paid directly to producers would raise producer surplus by the same amount, while leaving consumer surplus unchanged. The cost to taxpayers would be a + b + c. There would be no effect on national welfare. Output and exports of good Y would remain unchanged. In a recent study, Fletcher (2010) raises important concerns about the benchmark model's view of global competition, particularly with respect to its assumption that technological know-how is uniformly distributed across countries and that there are no economies of scale. We examine these issues in a subsequent section.

8. The existence of large pools of underemployed labor in many developing countries generates wage behavior that is quite different from that envisaged in the benchmark model. See Lewis (1954).

9. See also Vousden (1990).

10. To Linder (1961), this type of specialization may emerge from variations in local usage based on factor endowments. To Vernon (1966), such differences tend to disappear in the course of the "product cycle." Fletcher (2010) sees this catching up by emerging economies as a major threat to the long-run competitiveness of high-income countries. It is a key element in his critique of free trade.

11. For excellent selections from this literature, see Grossman (1992), Helpman and Krugman (1985), Kierzkowski (1984) and Krugman (1990).

12. Scale economies that are internal to the firm tend to create incentives for large firm size and thereby undermine the perfect competition assumption of the benchmark model. Scale economies that are external to the firm encourage firm clustering and agglomeration of productive activities, which is also incompatible with the benchmark model. On this, see Barba Navaretti and Venables (2004).

13. When the EU embarked on its "Single Market" project in the 1980s, achieving scale economies in passenger vehicles and other industries in order to compete more effectively with the U.S. and Japan was an important objective. The prevailing view in Brussels was that countries had protected their national markets for "national champion" firms, thereby limiting the size of the market and hence the ability of firms to fully exploit scale economies. See Jacquemin and Sapir (1989) and Emerson et al. (1988) for further discussion. See also Mertens and Ginsburgh (1985).

14. Vousden (1990) provides detailed analyses of a number of possible scenarios. See Mertens and Ginsburgh (1985) for a study of structural models with various combinations of market power and product differentiation.

15. In preparing the Single Market project, European leaders established regulations preventing member countries from seeking "first-mover" advantages for their industries by means of subsidies and other forms of support.

16. For a discussion of recent developments in "arms-length off-shoring," see Ando, Arndt, and Kimura (2005).

17. For specifics, see Arndt (1997), Arndt and Kierzkowski (2001), Deardorff (2001), and Feenstra (1998).

18. For a number of these studies, refer to the works listed in note 11.

19. For applications to other forms of imperfect competition, see Kjeldsen-Kragh (2001).

20. See Mertens and Ginsburgh (1985, p. 157), for a discussion of such policies in Europe.

21. Moreover, in the complex modern economy, many transactions do not take place in markets as defined in the benchmark model. This is especially true in financial markets, where many derivative products are traded over the counter. It is often difficult to say what the effect of such transactions is on economic efficiency and welfare.

REFERENCES

Ando, M., S. W. Arndt, and F. Kimura (2006). "Production Networks in East Asia: Strategic Behavior by U.S. and Japanese Firms." (Japanese version published 2007)

Arndt, S. W. (1968). "On Discriminatory vs. Non-preferential Tariff Policies." *Economic Journal* 78, 312, pp. 971–979.

Arndt, S. W. (1969). "Customs Union and the Theory of Tariffs." *American Economic Review* 59, 1, pp. 108–118.

(1997). "Globalization and the Open Economy." *North American Journal of Economics and Finance* 8, 1, pp. 71–79.

Arndt, S. W. (2004). "Global Production Networks and Regional Integration." In M. G. Plummer, ed., *Empirical Methods in International Trade*. Northampton, Mass.: Edward Elgar.

Arndt, S. W., and H. Kierzkowski, eds. (2001). *Fragmentation: New Production Patterns in the World Economy*. Oxford: Oxford University Press.

Barba Navaretti, G., and A. J. Venables (2004). *Multinational Firms in the World Economy*. Princeton: Princeton University Press.

Brander, J. (1984). "Tariff Protection and Imperfect Competition." In H. Kierzkowski, ed., *Monopolistic Competition and International Trade*. Oxford: Clarendon Press.

Brander, J., and B. Spencer (1981). "Tariffs and the Extraction of Foreign Monopoly Rents under Potential Entry." *Canadian Journal of Economics* 14 (August), pp. 371–389.

Caves, R. E. (1996). *Multinational Enterprise and Economic Analysis*. 2nd ed. Cambridge: Cambridge University Press.

Corden, W. M. (1966). "The Structure of a Tariff System and the Effective Protection Rate." *Journal of Political Economy* 74, 3, pp. 221–237.

Corden, W. M. (1974). *Trade Policy and Economic Welfare*. Oxford: Clarendon Press.

Deardorff, A. V. (2001). "Fragmentation in Simple Trade Models." *North American Journal of Economics and Finance* 12, 2, pp. 121–137.

Deardorff, A. V. (2006). *Terms of Trade: Glossary of International Economics*. London: World Scientific.

Dixit, A. K., and J. E. Stiglitz (1977). "Monopolistic Competition and Optimum Product Diversity." *American Economic Review* 67 (June), pp. 297–308.

Emerson, M., et al. (1988). "The Economics of Europe 1992: An Assessment of the Potential Economic Effects of Completing the Internal Market of the European Community." *European Economy* 35, 3,

Feenstra, R. C. (1998). "Integration of Trade and Disintegration of Production in the Global Economy." *Journal of Economic Perspectives* 12 (Fall), pp. 31–50.

Fletcher, I. (2010). *Free Trade Doesn't Work*. Washington, D.C.: U.S. Business and Industry Council.

Grossman, G. M., ed. (1992). *Imperfect Competition and International Trade*. Cambridge, Mass.: MIT Press, 1992.

Heffernan, S., and P. Sinclair (1990). *Modern International Economics* Oxford: Blackwell.

Helpman, E. (1984) "Increasing Returns, Imperfect Markets, and Trade Theory." In R. W. Jones and P. B. Kenen, eds., *Handbook of International Economics*, vol. 1. New York: North-Holland.

Helpman, E., and P. R. Krugman (1985). *Market Structure and Foreign Trade*. Cambridge, Mass.: MIT Press.

Jacquemin, A., and A. Sapir, eds. (1989). *The European Internal Market: Trade and Competition*. Oxford: Oxford University Press.

Kierzkowski, H., ed. (1984). *Monopolistic Competition and International Trade.* Oxford: Oxford University Press.

Kjeldsen-Kragh, S. (2001). *International Trade Policy.* Copenhagen: Copenhagen Business School Press.

Kreinin, M. E. (1987). "Comparative Advantage and Possible Trade Restrictions in High-Technology Products." In D. Salvatore, ed., *The New Protectionist Threat to World Welfare.* New York: North-Holland.

Krugman, P. R. (1979). "Increasing Returns, Monopolistic Competition, and International Trade." *Journal of International Economics* 9 (November), pp. 469–479.

Krugman, P. R. (1981). "Intra-industry Specialization and the Gains from Trade." *Journal of Political Economy* 89, pp.

Krugman, P. R., ed. (1986). *Strategic Trade Policy and the New International Economics.* Cambridge, Mass.: MIT Press.

Lancaster, K. (1979). *Variety, Equity and Efficiency.* New York: Columbia University Press.

Lewis, W. A. (1954). "Economic Development with Unlimited Supplies of Labour." *Manchester School of Economic and Social Studies* 22, 2, pp. 139–191.

Linder, S. B. (1961). *An Essay on Trade and Transformation.* New York: Wiley.

Markusen, J. R., and J. R. Melvin (1984). "The Gains-from-Trade Theorem with Increasing Returns to Scale." In H. Kierzkowski, ed., *Monopolistic Competition and International Trade.* Oxford: Oxford University Press.

Mertens, Y., and V. Ginsburgh (1985). "Product Differentiation and Price Discrimination in the European Community: The Case of Automobiles." *Journal of Industrial Economics* 34, 2 (December), pp. 151–166.

Pomfret, R. (1992). "International Trade Policy with Imperfect Competition." Special papers in international economics, no. 17. Princeton, N.J.: International Finance Section, Department of Economics, Princeton University.

Vernon, R. (1966). "International Investment and International Trade in the Product Cycle." *Quarterly Journal of Economics* 80 (May), pp. 190–207.

Vousden, N. (1990). *The Economics of Trade Protection.* New York: Cambridge University Press.

CHAPTER 2

THE INTERNATIONAL TRADING SYSTEM AND ITS FUTURE

RACHEL McCULLOCH

THE international trading "system" comprises many thousands of unilateral, bilateral, regional, and multilateral rules and agreements among more than 200 independent nations. Atop this complex and rapidly evolving mass of political and economic arrangements is the World Trade Organization (WTO), with 153 members that together account for nearly all of world trade.[1] Created in the Uruguay Round of multilateral negotiations as a successor to the General Agreement on Tariffs and Trade (GATT), the WTO provides a legal and institutional framework for national policies that directly or indirectly affect international trade among its members. Like the GATT, the primary goal of the WTO is to promote freer and more predictable conditions of trade. However, practice has gradually moved away from the principles that shaped the original GATT. In the WTO, nondiscrimination among trading partners remains a fundamental principle, as laid out in the original GATT (now known as GATT 1947) and also in the updated GATT 1994, produced in the Uruguay Round. Yet GATT rules also allow for preferential (i.e., discriminatory) policies, and these have become an increasingly important feature of the international trading system. Likewise, although reciprocity has always played a key role in GATT/WTO procedures for multilateral trade negotiations and dispute settlement, the scope of nonreciprocal arrangements intended to benefit poorer countries has steadily expanded.

The WTO is the latest embodiment of multilateral efforts to promote cooperation among trading nations that began even before the end of World War II. At the

1944 Bretton Woods Conference, which created the International Monetary Fund (IMF) and International Bank for Reconstruction and Development (World Bank), participating nations also recognized the need for a third institution, to be called the International Trade Organization (ITO). The ITO was designed to prevent a resurgence of the protectionism of the prewar period and continue the efforts toward reciprocal trade liberalization that were already in progress before the onset of the war. In addition to trade policies, the new organization's authority was to include national policies toward foreign investment and business practices. However, plans for the ITO were derailed when the U.S. Congress failed to ratify its ambitious draft charter. In its place, the more limited 1947 GATT treaty emerged as a "temporary" solution, one for which U.S. participation did not require congressional approval.[2]

Despite its limited scope and resources, the GATT endured for nearly 50 years, its membership (formally, contracting parties or signatories) growing from an initial 23 to 128 by 1994.[3] Prior to the Uruguay Round, which began in 1986, the GATT had already sponsored seven rounds of multilateral trade negotiations. These had achieved a significant cumulative reduction in tariff rates. By 1986, the trade-weighted average of tariffs on manufactured goods had been reduced to about 6.4%, from about 35% in 1947.[4] The GATT has thus been credited with a key role in facilitating the massive growth in the volume of world trade during the postwar era (Irwin 2002, 165–170).

Yet the GATT left some critical issues unresolved (Crowley 2003). Although average tariff rates had been reduced substantially, stubborn peaks for individual products remained. Some major industries, notably agriculture and textiles and apparel, had been excluded from normal GATT guidelines. Even in covered sectors, importing nations were making extensive use of "administered" protection—such as antidumping actions, countervailing measures, and voluntary export restraints—to limit competition from abroad. Moreover, GATT rules pertained mainly to trade in tangible goods, a significant limitation with international trade in services growing at a rapid rate. Other issues closely linked to trade but not covered by GATT rules included national policies toward foreign direct investment and intellectual property. And perhaps most central, the GATT provided no effective way to resolve disputes among the contracting parties.

Concerns about these shortcomings of the GATT provided much of the agenda for the ambitious Uruguay Round (1986–1994), which culminated in the establishment of the WTO. Yet despite the fanfare surrounding the WTO's birth in 1995, doubts regarding the new organization soon began to materialize. These doubts were heightened by lack of progress in the Doha Round begun in 2001, the first round of multilateral negotiations sponsored by the WTO. Some critics have called for a new Bretton Woods conference to reconfigure the three major international economic organizations and reallocate responsibilities among them. The goal would be to increase their overall effectiveness in addressing problems in global governance not anticipated in the 1940s, including huge bilateral trade imbalances and national efforts to limit climate change.

Section 1 of this chapter describes the evolution and structure of the GATT/ WTO system. Section 2 deals with the tension between the fundamental GATT/ WTO principle of most-favored-nation (MFN) treatment, that is, nondiscrimination among trading partners, and the trend toward discriminatory trading arrangements, including the proliferation of regional agreements, as well as new versions of special and differential treatment of low-income countries. Section 3 focuses on participation of developing countries in the system and the effort to use special treatment to promote development objectives. Section 4 discusses the pressure to use the enforcement power of the GATT/WTO system to achieve member compliance with social norms in the areas of environment and labor. Section 5 assesses some significant challenges that currently face the international trading system. Section 6 concludes by considering possible directions of the system's evolution in response to these challenges.

1. THE WTO

Notwithstanding repeated threats of its imminent collapse over nearly eight years of negotiations, the Uruguay Round made remarkable headway in addressing some of the most important shortcomings that had plagued GATT 1947. While negotiators continued the traditional GATT-era work of reducing tariff and nontariff barriers to manufactured goods trade (average tariff rates were reduced by 40%), they also broke new ground with agreements to bring trade in services, textiles and apparel, and agricultural products into greater conformity with GATT norms. The Round's significant achievements included negotiation of commitments to reduce agricultural subsidies, to phase out the Multifibre Arrangement (over a 10-year period) and thus apply the same rules to trade in textiles and apparel as to trade in other manufactured goods, and to strengthen protection of intellectual property rights (with phase-in periods based on members' level of economic development). Other agreements improved rules and procedures dealing with a variety of nontariff measures, including subsidies, technical barriers to trade, and sanitary and phytosanitary measures. The goal of these agreements was to balance member governments' acknowledged need to address domestic concerns against the potential for abuse of such policies as a disguised form of import protection or discrimination among trading partners.

The Uruguay Round also departed from precedent in a fundamental respect. With minor exceptions, all WTO members agreed to comply with the obligations spelled out in all the agreements, which were included in the "Single Undertaking." This requirement of consensus among all participants was in contrast to the approach used in the Tokyo Round, in which various "codes" governing use of nontariff barriers were endorsed by only some members, primarily the most advanced countries. Rules in the Tokyo Round codes then applied only to trade among signatories.

However, there has recently been discussion of reverting to a system that does not require all members to move toward WTO goals at the same rate.[5]

The most significant departure from the system created by GATT 1947 was a revamping of procedures for settling disputes among trading nations. The WTO Dispute Settlement Understanding (DSU) introduced a systematic rules-based approach to resolving disputes concerning a member's alleged failure to meet its WTO obligations. This system is usually described as self-enforcing, in that the WTO itself has no power to police national trade policies. Rather, an affected member must initiate each dispute. Under the current system, any dispute that cannot be resolved through direct negotiation among affected countries is referred to a panel of three experts, almost always specialists in international commercial relations, for example, diplomats and trade lawyers. The panel report is intended to provide a neutral judgment as to whether the challenged member has violated GATT/WTO rules.[6] If the panel affirms that the contested policy is inconsistent with the member's WTO obligations, the member can appeal the decision, amend its policies, or face authorized retaliation from trading partners that have lost market access as a result of the violation. Authorized retaliation (and often merely the threat of retaliatory action)—in the form of partners' increased barriers designed to reduce the member's market access by an amount commensurate with the effect of the contested policy—provides the enforcement mechanism that maintains adherence to WTO rules and thus protects members' export market access. The DSU is an important improvement over the GATT system, in which any country could in effect veto a panel decision that was contrary to its own political or economic interests.

Similar to the role played by the GATT until the end of the Uruguay Round, the WTO serves as a forum for multilateral trade liberalization negotiations among its members. The current Doha Round, initiated in 2001, is the first round of multilateral negotiations to be held under WTO sponsorship and is thus seen as a test of the new organization's ability to maintain forward momentum in trade liberalization. The stalled round therefore brings the WTO framework into question. But the WTO has important functions separate from its role as the facilitator of multilateral trade negotiations. Most important is its role discussed above as neutral arbitrator of trade disputes, that is, in helping to assure that members actually receive the anticipated trade benefits of reciprocal liberalization. The WTO also serves a monitoring and information-dissemination function, again building on its GATT roots. The WTO collects and publishes data on trade flows as well as changes in trade policy undertaken by members between negotiating rounds (members are required to notify the WTO of certain policy changes, such as antidumping actions). Under the Trade Policy Review Mechanism, the WTO carries out periodic reviews of each member's trade policy regime; scheduled frequency of review is highest for the largest trading economies.[7] The results of the reviews, including the responses of member country officials, are made available on the WTO website. Finally, as discussed in section 3, the WTO has also continued to expand the role gradually taken on by the GATT in promoting the trade interests of developing countries.[8]

2. GATT/WTO Principles and Discriminatory Trading

At the start, the primary goal of the GATT was to promote nondiscriminatory trade liberalization. The fundamental guidelines were nondiscrimination (MFN treatment among signatories), reciprocity, and transparency. MFN treatment was deemed important enough to be the subject of Article I of the GATT 1947. The principle of reciprocity was reflected in the agreement's preamble, which called for members to enter into "reciprocal and mutually advantageous arrangements directed to the substantial reduction of tariffs and other barriers to trade," and in Article XXVIII, requiring "compensatory adjustment" when previously agreed concessions are modified. The need for increased transparency was expressed in several GATT articles, especially Article X, requiring prompt publication by signatories of new laws and regulations affecting trade, and Article XI, calling for general elimination of quantitative restrictions on trade. The underlying goal was to ensure that foreign suppliers would face known and constant barriers, ones that could be overcome by sufficiently competitive producers. The strong preference specifically for the use of tariffs over quantitative restrictions or other types of trade policies also stemmed from the view that reliance on tariffs would simplify the future process of reciprocal liberalization.

The early GATT priorities reflected the negotiating nations' desire to undo the harm to the international trading system that had occurred during the 1930s. The Smoot-Hawley tariffs enacted by the U.S. Congress in 1930 had soon been followed by similar "beggar-thy-neighbor" actions of other countries, as well as discriminatory arrangements such as the United Kingdom's imperial preferences, which entailed lower tariffs on imports from its colonies and dominions. With the United States and England taking the leading roles, negotiators resumed efforts begun before World War II to lower barriers to trade through reciprocal reductions in bound tariff rates (reciprocity),[9] to replace quantitative restrictions and other nontariff barriers by tariff protection (transparency), and to eliminate discriminatory arrangements (MFN treatment).

The initial success of the GATT in achieving these goals reflected mutual gains to the participating nations, but, given the overwhelming dominance of the United States in the world economy, the key factor was U.S. willingness to abide by GATT principles. Cuts in the first GATT round (1947) reduced U.S. average bound tariff rates by 26% (Martin and Messerlin 2007). However, changing conditions gradually diluted U.S. commitment, pushing the contracting parties toward a multitier system of responsibilities. The first change was the surge in exports of manufactured goods from Japan and then from four even newer suppliers (Hong Kong, Singapore, Taiwan, and South Korea) collectively termed the Newly Industrializing Economies (NIEs) or Four Tigers. To manage the increase in competing imports, the United States and the European Union used discriminatory policies involving extra-GATT bilateral agreements with individual exporters rather than the GATT's own safeguard procedures (Article XIX), which are meant to be applied on an MFN basis. The result was the spread of negotiated quantitative restrictions, first from Japan[10] to the NIEs and then, especially for textiles and apparel, to many additional exporters. By 1974, worldwide trade in textiles and apparel was controlled by the Multifibre Arrangement (MFA), a system of bilateral quotas limiting trade between most of the world's rich importers and most of the world's poor exporters of these products.

At the same time, the list of contracting parties gradually expanded to include more of the world's poor countries. The new signatories were often former colonies of the original participants. Perhaps inevitably in an organization operating on the basis of unanimity, provision for "special and differential treatment" of nations at an earlier stage of economic development expanded far beyond the initial vague commitment in GATT Part IV, which had been added in 1964. Attention to the trade concerns of less developed nations increased further during the "New International Economic Order" crusade of the 1970s. The issues raised by the increasing majority of poor countries among participants in the GATT/WTO system are discussed in section 3.

A final important change in the GATT/WTO system has been the surge in negotiation of preferential trade agreements (PTAs)[11] among subsets of participating nations. From the start, the GATT made provision for PTAs in Article XXIV, even though such arrangements represented an explicit departure from the GATT/WTO guiding principle of nondiscriminatory trade among signatories, that is, MFN treatment. In the WTO, Article XXIV of GATT 1994, together with the Uruguay Round "Understanding on the Interpretation of Article XXIV of the General Agreement on Tariffs and Trade," set rules governing PTAs for goods; Article V of the General Agreement on Trade in Services (GATS) contains corresponding rules for services.

The GATT/WTO position on PTAs recognizes the desirability of increasing trade through voluntary agreements between two or more members. However, there is also the concern that such agreements should facilitate trade among the partner countries without raising barriers to trade with nonpartner countries.[12] Article XXIV therefore places some significant restrictions on the common external tariffs applied by members of a customs union as well as the required product coverage, which is supposed to include "substantially all trade." In practice, however, the GATT/WTO system has taken a laissez-faire attitude, with virtually no effort to ensure that agreements are consistent with the guidelines. Moreover, almost all the new PTAs—the notable exception is the European Union—have been free trade agreements rather than customs unions with common external tariffs. The result has been what Jagdish Bhagwati termed a "spaghetti bowl" of PTAs, with selective product coverage, lengthy phase-in periods, and complex rules of origin.[13]

Beyond an expectation that new PTAs will be notified to the WTO, the rules on preferential trading appear to exercise little if any discipline over such arrangements. In practice, no preferential agreements among GATT or WTO members, whether developed or developing, have ever been challenged by other members. This laissez-faire posture has given rise to increasing concern about the effects of proliferating free trade agreements on progress toward multilateral trade liberalization.

This deleterious effect could arise for either of two reasons (Krueger 2007). First, the limited capacity of many countries to conduct international trade negotiations may be taxed by efforts to form PTAs. Second, WTO members' incentives to engage in multilateral liberalization may be lessened, to the extent that the benefits derived from current PTA membership would thereby be eroded. However, these concerns do not seem to be discouraging members from pursuing new PTAs.[14] Moreover, some theoretical and empirical research suggests that formation of free trade areas may actually stimulate rather than retard multilateral liberalization—PTAs may act as building blocks rather than stumbling blocks (Estevadeordal, Freund, and Ornelas 2008; McCulloch and Petri 2007).

3. Developing Countries in the International Trading System

Although the 23 nations participating in the negotiations that produced the original GATT in 1947 included 12 developing countries, in its early days the GATT was disparaged as a "rich man's club."[15] The GATT initially focused almost entirely on trade in manufactured goods, that is, goods that were then exported mainly by the developed countries, and GATT rules for poor countries were mostly the same as those for rich countries. However, developing countries were accorded special treatment through exemptions from some rules, for example, permission under Article XVIII to use tariffs and quotas to promote an infant industry or to deal with balance of payments problems (Dam 1970, ch. 14). Developing countries also benefited via MFN treatment from the liberalization commitments of the advanced nations without being required to engage in reciprocal opening of their own markets.

The principle of special treatment for developing countries was formalized by the addition in 1966 of Part IV, "Trade and Development," to the GATT. The Tokyo Round went even further with adoption of the Enabling Clause (officially, "Differential and More Favorable Treatment of Developing Countries") in 1979. The Enabling Clause allows advanced countries to discriminate in favor of poorer countries, and especially the least developed countries—as had already been done through the enactment of the Generalized System of Preferences. The Enabling Clause also allows developing countries to negotiate preferential trade agreements that do not satisfy the usual GATT criteria as spelled out in Article XXIV.[16]

Notwithstanding their special status, most of the poor countries remained poor, and those that prospered—mainly the NIEs and other East Asian countries—did so through export-oriented growth strategies. Yet these new exporters were soon subjected to discriminatory trade restrictions, and the GATT did little to shield them from policies that violated at least the spirit of its rules. Moreover, even after successive rounds of GATT-sponsored multilateral trade negotiations, labor-intensive manufactured products like shoes and especially textiles and apparel remained highly protected, while world prices of many agricultural products were depressed by generous subsidies in the United States and European Union.

The GATT's special treatment of developing countries turned out to be at best ineffective and perhaps even counterproductive.[17] To begin with, it was predicated on the assumption, now largely discredited, that trade liberalization is less desirable for developing countries than for developed countries. Facing less external pressure to open their markets to trade, the developing countries obtained less of the potential benefits to be derived from integration into world markets. Moreover, relieving the developing countries of the requirement for reciprocity meant that these countries remained on the sidelines in shaping multilateral negotiations. The developing countries thus lost the opportunity to exchange access to their own domestic markets (whether as a group or, for some larger countries, individually) for desired liberalization commitments from developed countries. By remaining nonparticipants in the successive rounds of GATT tariff reductions, they also lost the opportunity to contest disadvantageous exceptions to basic GATT rules for specific sectors, especially textiles and apparel and agriculture. Finally, because MFN liberalization reduces the benefits enjoyed by countries with preferential access to important markets, the existence of one-way preferences may retard progress toward global free trade.[18]

By September 1986, when the Uruguay Round negotiations began, the total number of GATT contracting parties had grown to 91, and the majority of the additions were developing countries, including newly independent nations in Africa and elsewhere. More developing nations joined the GATT during the negotiations that eventually produced the WTO, which commenced operation on January 1, 1995, with 128 members.

But despite ongoing efforts to provide benefits for poor countries, the operation of the GATT system was still dominated by the concerns of the developed nations, and those concerns continued to play an important role in the Uruguay Round. By 2008, an overwhelming majority of the 153 WTO members were developing countries, with 32 of the poorest classified as least developed countries (LDCs). Yet even with the rapid increase in their numbers, many observers, and especially those representing the interests of poor countries, judge that participation in the Uruguay Round and in the WTO has so far yielded few benefits for these countries.

Of the accomplishments from the Uruguay Round, the eagerly sought dismantling of the MFA proved to be a major disappointment to most developing countries, as China's share of export markets for textiles and apparel exploded and competition among suppliers dissipated quota rents. The Agreement on Trade-Related Aspects of Intellectual Property Rights (TRIPS) has been criticized as causing, at least potentially, an adverse movement in the terms of trade of poorer countries, which are overwhelmingly importers of proprietary technologies created mainly in a few rich countries.[19] Promised elimination of U.S. and European Union agricultural subsidies has stalled, disappointing middle-income developing countries with comparative advantage in sugar, rice, cotton, soybeans, and other agricultural products. And the Doha Development Round, aimed specifically at addressing post–Uruguay Round concerns of poor countries, has been declared dead on numerous occasions.

But laments regarding lack of progress in the Doha Round have tended to over-shadow the increasing benefits already being derived by many developing countries from another achievement of the Uruguay Round: creation via the DSU of an enhanced process that allows members to self-enforce the market access to which their trading partners have agreed. Data on disputes brought to the WTO show a steady stream of WTO self-enforcement actions undertaken by developing countries throughout the WTO era, in contrast to the declining trend of self-enforcement actions undertaken by the developed countries over the same period (Bown and McCulloch 2010). These actions have allowed at least some developing countries to maintain the market access to which they are entitled in situations when trading partners have failed to uphold their WTO commitments.

Yet the ability of developing countries to engage in successful self-enforcement actions remains limited by two important factors. First, most developing countries have small markets for imports. This is due partly to small total demand but also to significant import barriers, which on average are still much higher than those of the developed countries. Since the self-enforcement process relies on the threat of WTO-authorized retaliation, its potency is limited by import market size. Thus, only larger developing countries are in a position to take full advantage of the self-enforcement process. In addition, information about foreign actions that reduce market access may be difficult to obtain, especially when the actions in question are less easily observed than new trade barriers. Developing countries have therefore focused their self-enforcement actions on types of WTO violations that are directly observable by exporting firms and governments, especially unjustified application of antidumping measures, rather than on subtler domestic measures that also limit imports.[20] Although WTO litigation costs of developing countries' self-enforcement actions are already heavily subsidized by the Advisory Center on WTO Law, the significant informational costs of determining when such an action is justified remain a significant deterrent (Bown 2009).

4. TRADE SANCTIONS AS A MEANS OF ENFORCING SOCIOECONOMIC NORMS

The WTO is unique among international organizations in possessing an effective system by which its rules can be enforced. As a result, there has been continuing pressure going back to the GATT era to use the WTO to enforce socioeconomic norms shared by a significant number of participating countries. The justification for involving the GATT/WTO is that failure to honor social norms usually confers a cost advantage. A country's failure to meet such norms may therefore be regarded as "social dumping" and treated in an analogous way. The main areas of domestic policy potentially affected are those concerned with environmental protection and labor standards, although as discussed in section 5.2, there has been recent discussion of using trade sanctions as a way to force macroeconomic "rebalancing."

Underlying the controversy regarding use of WTO-authorized trade sanctions to enforce socioeconomic norms is that national attitudes regarding environmental protection and labor standards are strongly affected by per capita income—these norms tend to be "luxury goods" whose demand rises along with citizens' incomes. Expecting poor countries to meet the same standards as rich ones may place poor countries at an important competitive disadvantage and may also be economically inefficient. For example, to the extent that labor productivity is higher in rich countries, mutually beneficial two-way trade between rich and poor countries may *require* similar differences in wages.[21]

Poor countries argue that norms should be adjusted to take into account differences in stage of development, pointing out that present labor and environmental conditions in their economies are no worse, and in some cases far better, than those that prevailed in the now-industrialized nations during an earlier era. Although actual GATT/WTO links between market access and social norms have so far been minor,[22] the issue is poised for greater significance as many developed countries begin to impose broad restrictions on carbon emissions and pressure developing countries, especially large ones like China and India, to make corresponding commitments.

5. EMERGING ISSUES

It is easy to point to shortcomings in the world trading system that bode ill for the future. The Doha Round had stalled repeatedly even before the onset of the global financial crisis of 2008–9. Despite a trimmed-down agenda, many observers have grown pessimistic about completion of the round. But on the positive side, even the extreme economic disruptions accompanying the global crisis did not give rise to the feared surge in protectionism and defection from WTO disciplines. Although many countries implemented some new protection, this was done almost entirely in ways that did not violate their WTO commitments, that is, through antidumping and safeguard actions, or by raising applied tariffs that were initially below the corresponding bound rates (Bown and Kee, 2010).

Meanwhile, the development of an unprecedented bilateral imbalance between the United States and China has placed an increasing strain on a system based on reciprocity, and a continuing surge of new preferential, that is, discriminatory, trading arrangements has increased the tension between the GATT/

WTO's key MFN principle and trade realities. The designation MFN has now come to mean *least*-favored-nation treatment, that is, paying the "list price" at the border. Beneficiaries of one-way preferences argue that fairness requires compensation for erosion of benefits when successful MFN liberalization cuts the preferential margin they now enjoy. And finally, the perceived need to reverse the growth of carbon emissions will pose an important new challenge for the WTO, as participating countries seek trade policy measures to deal with "carbon leakage" from countries not willing to join in these efforts. How are these situations likely to play out in terms of evolution of the world trading system?

5.1 The Doha Round

As of late 2011, the stalled Doha Round, which was initiated in November 2001 as the Doha Development Round, had already exceeded the length of any of its predecessors, and with no end in sight. In contrast, even the ambitious and protracted Uruguay Round had required "only" seven years and seven months from inception to signing. Economists and public officials are divided on both the feasibility of completing the round and the importance of doing so.[23] An increasing number see the lack of progress as a reflection of the problems inherent in achieving consensus among such a large and diverse group of nations and even question whether there is any future for multilateral trade liberalization along the lines of the GATT rounds of the past. This view gains some credence from the heightened pace at which new preferential agreements have been initiated and concluded over the same period. Moreover, the recent economic woes of the advanced countries have further reduced domestic political support for any new concessions to developing countries.

Even those who argue for completing the round are divided on what is to be gained by doing so. Some see the fate of the Doha Round as significant mostly for what it implies about global support for the WTO as an institution. In this view, a failed round could undermine the WTO's authority in setting and enforcing guidelines for national policies toward trade (Hoekman, Martin, and Mattoo 2009). However, others see a Doha failure mainly as a missed opportunity to continue the GATT/WTO's progress in promoting a more open and transparent trading system. In direct contrast to proposals to further limit the scope of the negotiations as a way to facilitate agreement, Hufbauer, Schott, and Wong (2010) argue for a more ambitious package that would increase anticipated gains for major parties and thus justify the political effort required to bring the round to a successful conclusion. Whether this approach is feasible remains to be seen, but it is certainly true that progress can only be made if each participant perceives a net benefit from going forward; raising the stakes could energize the moribund process. However, with world leaders already challenged by more urgent priorities, it is not obvious where the necessary leadership for a step in this direction can be found.

5.2 Reducing Bilateral Imbalances

As the world emerges from the global financial crisis, the need for "rebalancing" supply and demand across countries and continents has become evident. But where does the responsibility for rebalancing lie, and how should it be achieved? Accomplishing this goal during a still-fragile recovery beset with other important international dilemmas, such as the fate of the Euro, poses a formidable challenge.

Many believe that a major appreciation of China's currency is a necessary condition for sustained shrinkage of its bilateral surplus with the United States. If so, is it appropriate for the WTO to become the enforcer of this prescription? Mattoo and Subramanian (2009) argue for joint action by the IMF and the WTO—the WTO's participation required because the IMF has no ability to enforce its policy prescriptions on a member such as China that is not requesting IMF loans. However, use of trade restrictions to force an exchange rate appreciation would represent a major shift in the mission of the GATT/WTO, which normally focuses on measures that affect the composition of trade flows rather than aggregate imbalances (Bown and McCulloch, 2009). Moving in this direction would open the door to further actions whenever a country's exports seemed "too large" or imports "too small"—according to criteria still to be determined.

Some argue that by maintaining a low international price for the yuan, China is in effect subsidizing its exports, and that a countervailing duty equal to the extent of yuan undervaluation would be appropriate under WTO rules. However, there is no consensus among economic experts on the extent of yuan undervaluation. Moreover, an analysis by Staiger and Sykes (2010) raises analytical doubts concerning this approach. Staiger and Sykes conclude that the difficulty of determining the trade effects of China's currency practices "calls into question the wisdom and legitimacy of countermeasures that have been proposed." In any case, even a large revaluation of the yuan in terms of the dollar would not be enough to restore bilateral balance between China and the United States unless accompanied by a substantial, sustained increase in national saving in the United States and a corresponding reduction in China and other surplus countries.

5.3 The Trend toward Preferential Trading

Sharply contrasting with the absence of progress in multilateral trade negotiations is continued momentum in the negotiation of new preferential agreements. The attraction of moving in this direction is obvious—with a small number of participants it is much easier to craft terms that are mutually beneficial. While excluded countries as a group may be harmed, this effect is usually sufficiently dispersed to avoid any major fallout. Yet even the most ardent supporters of the preferential approach see it as a complement to multilateral liberalization rather than a substitute. The real challenge is to avoid creating a thicket of inconsistent policies that further complicate the task of achieving liberalization multilaterally (Baldwin 2006). Plummer (2007) advocates a multilayered liberalization process in which regional agreements are based on "best practices" (the lasagna bowl). These might include a requirement that PTAs accept new members, perhaps after an initial waiting period.

Kawai, Petri, and Sisli Ciammara (2009) and Lawrence (2008) envision the evolution of the WTO into a host organization for regional "clubs" formed by subsets of its members. In contrast to the current laissez-faire approach toward PTAs, the WTO could develop and enforce guidelines for club actions and also serve as a neutral arbiter of disputes arising among club members.

The tension between preferential trading and multilateral liberalization is greatest in the case of poor countries that are the beneficiaries of one-way preferences. While it may be laudable to bend WTO rules in a way that ensures gains for even the poorest participants, there may be other ways to achieve this goal without creating built-in opposition to multilateral liberalization (which reduces the value of trade preferences). One approach that has received increasing attention in recent years is aid for trade—provision of resources that help poor countries achieve gains from trade, through measures ranging from expert assistance in identifying areas of comparative advantage to improvements in port facilities and customs procedures. Measures of this kind facilitate mutually beneficial trade by accelerating the integration of poor countries into world markets, rather than creating an artificial advantage for a particular group of exporters. Another approach is to maintain the model of a single undertaking, but, as in the Uruguay Round, allow developing countries a longer period in which to achieve compliance. A third option is to focus MFN tariff-cutting efforts on the goods of greatest interest to developing country exporters.

5.4 Trade and Climate Change

Reconciling WTO rules with national policies to limit greenhouse gas emissions is sure to pose a major challenge for the world trading system. Countries contemplating across-the-board action to reduce emissions face strong domestic political opposition, especially from industries whose costs will rise significantly as a consequence. Unless all countries adopt comparable measures, national policies raise obvious concerns about lost international competitiveness in the short run and migration of high-emissions industries to other countries in the longer run—in either case severely undermining the effectiveness of national actions in reducing global emissions. Policy proposals have therefore typically included border measures (taxes and subsidies intended to neutralize the impact on trade competitiveness) as well as government subsidies intended to reduce the private cost of complying with new standards or to spur innovation.

Hufbauer, Charnovitz, and Kim (2009) identify the areas in which national climate change policies currently under review are most likely to conflict with WTO principles and thus result in a surge of new WTO disputes. These authors argue for negotiating a Code of Good WTO Practice on Greenhouse Gas Emissions Controls that would create a "green policy space" within which WTO members could take appropriate measures to limit emissions. In principle, the green space would allow countries some leeway within WTO rules to maintain the competitiveness of their own industries while raising environmental standards. At the same time, the Code would prevent the misuse of environmental policies to discriminate against goods and services produced abroad or to favor imports from preferred source countries.

A related and more immediate issue concerns trade policies toward green goods and services—the inputs used to reduce greenhouse gas emissions. Negotiations on trade in green goods and services are on the Doha Round agenda, and Pascal Lamy, director-general of the WTO, argues that WTO members have a strong interest in opening their markets to such goods as a way to improve the efficiency of their economies.[24] But Lamy's argument applies equally to liberalizing imports of almost any type of industrial input, and it thus ignores the need to overcome opposition from competing domestic producers.[25] In practice, such a negotiation is likely to be complex and protracted, beginning with the determination of exactly which goods and services should be included.

Compared to other environment-related policies that have generated past WTO disputes (e.g., protection of dolphins and turtles), both costs and benefits associated with efforts to limit climate change are likely to be very large, and their effects experienced over many economic sectors. For these reasons, such a negotiation is urgent. However, finding the necessary common ground for agreement in a large and diverse group of nations is sure to be difficult—perhaps the largest challenge yet for the international trading system.

6. Looking Ahead

This chapter has reviewed the evolution and structure of the GATT/WTO system, as well as several emerging issues likely to affect its performance in achieving its various goals. However, the current state of the international trading system provides good reasons for optimism. Most important, the system has survived more or less unscathed the worst global economic conditions since the Great Depression and the inevitable resurgence of protectionist sentiment worldwide. The WTO disciplines, backed by the dispute settlement mechanism, remain a potent safeguard against unchecked unilateral measures to limit foreign competition. Despite some increase in (GATT-legal) temporary protection, trade flows have rebounded vigorously as world economic growth has revived. But as discussed in the previous section, the system has yet to deal with some pressing issues. Thus, the status quo, while representing an important achievement in terms of multilateral cooperation, will not be enough to maintain the open and predictable market access that WTO members have come to expect.

Can the necessary progress be made? In the past, U.S. hegemony played a key role in shaping international institutions, but the United States does not appear ready to assume anything beyond shared responsibility for the provision of global public goods.

New problems have also been raised by the emergence of large and economically powerful developing countries, such as China, India, and Brazil. Still poor relative to the
United States and other industrialized countries, these countries are reluctant to participate in international agreements on the same terms as their much richer counterparts, yet their impact on the global economy and on global emissions is too large to
be exempted without undermining the overall effectiveness of the system. The solution may lie in a two-part strategy that builds on the success of the WTO via completion of the Doha Round while also dealing flexibly with some complex issues by
building from the bottom up, that is, by channeling PTA formation and expansion
along lines that provide a clearer path toward multilateral liberalization.

NOTES

Thanks are due to Chad Bown, Peter Petri, and Max Kreinin for helpful suggestions.

1. An overwhelming majority of the 153 members are developing countries, with 32
of the poorest classified as least developed countries (LDCs); 29 as of 2011, additional
"observer" nations were working toward WTO membership. www.wto.org/english/
thewto_e/whatis_e/whatis_e.htm (accessed 3/8/2010). Significant nonmembers included
the Russian Federation and several other major oil exporters. The Russian Federation was
expected to receive membership in 2012

2. The GATT was an agreement rather than a full-fledged international organization
and had "contracting parties" rather than members. It came into effect *during* the ITO
negotiations, with the goal of achieving immediate tariff reductions among the 23 participating countries (Hudec 1998).

3. www.wto.org/english/thewto_e/gattmem_e.htm (accessed 3/8/2010).

4. Crowley (2003) quoting Hoekman and Kostecki (1995).

5. Hoekman and Kostecki (2009, 529–530). An approach in which common policies
are implemented at different rates is often called "variable geometry," a phrase due to
Jacques Delors. However, because it refers to differences in speed of convergence to
common policies, it leaves aside the more difficult situations in which there is no
agreement on what the common policy should be.

6. More precisely, the panel report indicates whether the challenged policy is
WTO-inconsistent. This broader category also includes "nonviolation complaints." In
contrast to the more common disputes involving an allegation that a member has violated
a WTO rule, these refer to situations in which the complainant has not received the
anticipated benefit even though no rule has been violated. Such complaints aim at preserving the balance of benefits intrinsic to reciprocal bargaining.

7. This timing scheme is the opposite of what might be recommended, given that it
dedicates most resources to the major countries, for which other agencies and organizations already provide ample and often more timely information. Moreover, the review
process is influenced by political as well as economic considerations. To avoid controversy,
reviewers may fail to emphasize the kinds of information that would be most helpful in
ensuring members' adherence to their WTO commitments (Bown 2009, 219–220).

8. In the early decades, poor countries were called "less developed" countries
(LDCs). Since adoption of the more optimistic but often inaccurate current terminology,

LDC has become the acronym used to designate the *least* developed countries, i.e., the poorest of the poor.

9. In the United States, the 1934 Reciprocal Trade Agreements Act authorized the president to conduct bilateral negotiations with major trading partners to reverse the protectionist Smoot-Hawley tariffs on a reciprocal basis. The U.S. tariff cuts achieved through these negotiations were then extended to other trading partners through MFN treatment. Negotiated reductions required no enabling legislation by Congress.

10. The United States had already negotiated bilateral trade restraints with Japan for textiles prior to World War II.

11. The WTO documents refer to these as Regional Trade Agreements, even when partner countries are on separate continents.

12. Even in the absence of higher MFN tariffs, the preferential margin created by a PTA in effect raises barriers to trade with nonpartner countries, resulting in *trade diversion*, i.e., the substitution of partner imports for lower-cost imports from nonpartners. Some economists have suggested that countries forming free-trade areas should be required to *reduce* MFN tariff rates to offset this tendency.

13. More lenient rules on preferential trading between developing countries are contained in the Tokyo Round agreements signed in 1979.

14. Pomfret (2007) argues that the extent of PTA formation has been exaggerated by use of faulty measures. He also notes that the most important PTAs in terms of trade volume affected, notably the European Union, coordinate policies in many areas in addition to trade, thereby achieving "deep integration" among their members. Such agreements have complex implications for the health of the multilateral trading system going far beyond the usual trade creation/trade diversion analysis.

15. Beginning in 1964, the United Nations Conference on Trade and Development (UNCTAD) provided a forum where concerns of poor countries could be aired. The UNCTAD agenda included issues such as one-way trade preferences for manufactured exports of poor countries, stabilization of commodity export prices—primary commodities had accounted for about 80% of export earnings of these countries, and a nonfuel commodity was the leading export for many—and unconditional grant aid. However, much of the agenda required the cooperation of rich countries for funding or market access. Some parts of the agenda became reality, including the Generalized System of Preferences enacted by most industrialized countries and export-earnings stabilization schemes implemented by the International Monetary Fund and the European Economic Community.

16. For example, such agreements may cover only a limited range of products rather than "substantially all trade" as specified in Article XXIV.

17. Jones (2010, 24–27). Some analysts foresaw the problematic outcome of the Tokyo Round's emphasis on "special treatment" of developing countries. See McCulloch (1983).

18. In the Doha Round, some beneficiary countries have requested compensation for the erosion of benefits from preferential market access as MFN protection is negotiated downward.

19. In practice, implementation delays and favorable pricing practices, especially for pharmaceuticals, have so far minimized the feared effects.

20. The preponderance of cases involving antidumping may also reflect the global proliferation in this particular form of import protection.

21. Consider a simple Ricardian model in which labor productivity in the richer country is four times as high in the export industry and twice as high in the import-competing industry as in the poorer country. Two-way trade is then possible only if the

richer country's wage rate is at least twice but no more than four times as high as that of the poor country, when both are measured in the same currency.

22. Their role is greater in preferential agreements. Beginning with the North American Free Trade Agreement, many preferential agreements, and particularly those involving the United States, have explicitly linked market access to enforcement of environmental and/or labor policies, though these have so far had minimal impact on the policies themselves.

23. Martin and Messerlin (2007) review the history of previous rounds of multilateral negotiations in order to evaluate alternative explanations for the Doha Round's lack of progress. In the end, they remain cautiously optimistic about the round's eventual success. Baldwin (2009b) likewise draws parallels with past rounds, pointing out that the history of past negotiations is also "littered with lengthy stalemates."

24. Reuters, "WTO's Lamy Sees Trade Pact Boosting Green Goods," May 20, 2010, www.reuters.com/article/idUSLDE64J13F20100520 (accessed 5/26/2010).

25. An early indication of the potential problem is the October 2011 trade complaint brought by U.S. producers of solar panels, accusing Chinese rivals of benefiting from unfair government subsidies and dumping their products in the U.S. market.

REFERENCES

Baldwin, Richard E. (2006). "Multilateralizing Regionalism: Spaghetti Bowls as Building Blocs on the Path to Global Free Trade." *World Economy* 29(11), 1451–1518.

Baldwin, Robert E. (2009, December 15). "Standstills in GATT/WTO Trade Negotiations Are Not All That Unusual." VoxEU.org.

Bown, Chad P. (2009). *Self-Enforcing Trade: Developing Countries and WTO Dispute Settlement*. Washington, D.C.: Brookings Institution.

Bown, Chad P., and Hiau Looi Kee (2010, May). "Trade Barriers, Developing Countries, and the Global Economic Crisis." World Bank working paper. Washington, D.C.: World Bank.

Bown, Chad P., and Rachel McCulloch (2009). "U.S.-Japan and U.S.-China Trade Conflict: Export Growth, Reciprocity, and the International Trading System." *Journal of Asian Economics* 20(6), 669–687.

Bown, Chad P., and Rachel McCulloch (2010). "Developing Countries, Dispute Settlement, and the Advisory Centre on WTO Law." *Journal of International Trade & Economic Development* 19(1), 33–63.

Crowley, Meredith A. (2003). "An Introduction to the WTO and GATT." *Economic Perspectives* 7(4), 42–57.

Dam, Kenneth W. (1970). *The GATT: Law and International Economic Organization*. Chicago: University of Chicago Press.

Estevadeordal, Antoni, Caroline Freund, and Emanuel Ornelas (2008). "Does Regionalism Affect Trade Liberalization toward Nonmembers?" *Quarterly Journal of Economics* 123(4), 1531–1575.

Hoekman, Bernard, and Michel Kostecki (1995). *The Political Economy of the World Trading System*. Oxford: Oxford University Press.

Hoekman, Bernard, and Michel Kostecki (2009). *The Political Economy of the World Trading System*. 3rd ed. Oxford: Oxford University Press.

Hoekman, Bernard, Will Martin, and Aaditya Mattoo (2009, November). "Conclude Doha: It Matters!" World Bank Policy Research Working Paper 5135. Washington, D.C.: World Bank.

Hudec, Robert E. (1998). "The Role of the GATT Secretariat in the Evolution of the WTO Dispute Settlement Procedure." In Jagdish Bhagwati and Mathias Hirsch, eds., *The Uruguay Round and Beyond: Essays in Honour of Arthur Dunkel*. Berlin: Springer-Verlag, 101–120.

Hufbauer, Gary Clyde, Steve Charnovitz, and Jisun Kim (2009). *Global Warming and the World Trading System*. Washington, D.C.: Peterson Institute for International Economics.

Hufbauer, Gary Clyde, Jeffrey J. Schott, and Woan Foong Wong (2010, February 22). "Figuring Out the Doha Round." VoxEU.org.

Irwin, Douglas A. (2002). *Free Trade under Fire*. Princeton, N.J.: Princeton University Press.

Jones, Kent (2010). *The Doha Blues: Institutional Crisis and Reform in the WTO*. New York: Oxford University Press.

Kawai, Masahiro, Peter A. Petri, and Elif Sisli Ciamarra (2009, October). "Asia in Global Governance: A Case for Decentralized Institutions." ADBI Working Paper no. 157. Tokyo: Asian Development Bank Institute.

Krueger, Anne O. (2007). "An Enduring Need: Multilateralism in the Twenty-First Century." *Oxford Review of Economic Policy* 23(3), 335–346.

Lawrence, Robert Z. (2008). "International Organisations: The Challenge of Aligning Mission, Means and Legitimacy." *World Economy* 31(11), 1455–1470.

Martin, Will, and Patrick Messerlin (2007). "Why Is It So Difficult? Trade Liberalization under the Doha Agenda." *Oxford Review of Economic Policy* 23(3), 347–366.

Mattoo, Aaditya, and Arvind Subramanian (2009). "From Doha to the Next Bretton Woods: A New Multilateral Trade Agenda." *Foreign Affairs* 88(1), 15–26.

McCulloch, Rachel (1983). "The Tokyo Round and the Future of the GATT." *Portfolio* 8(2), 1–17.

McCulloch, Rachel, and Peter A. Petri (1997). "Alternative Paths toward Open Global Markets." In Keith E. Maskus, Peter M. Hooper, Edward E. Leamer, and J. David Richardson, eds., *Quiet Pioneering: Robert M. Stern and His International Economic Legacy*. Ann Arbor: University of Michigan Press, 149–169.

Plummer, Michael (2007). "'Best Practices' in Regional Trading Agreements: An Application to Asia." *World Economy* 30(12), 1771–1796.

Pomfret, Richard (2007). "Is Regionalism an Increasing Feature of the World Economy?" *World Economy* 30(6), 923–947.

Staiger, Robert W., and Alan O. Sykes (2010). "'Currency Manipulation' and World Trade." *World Trade Review* 9(4), 583–627.

CHAPTER 3

ADMINISTRATION OF TRADE POLICY

ALFRED E. ECKES, JR.

"War is too serious a matter to be left to military men," Georges Clemenceau commented after he became prime minister of France during World War I. Years later Margaret Thatcher, the prime minister of the United Kingdom, jibed, "Economics is too important just to be left to the economists."[1]

In this chapter, focusing on the implementation and enforcement of trade agreements, readers may discover a contemporary corollary. Without a doubt, the thinking of international economists, working in the classical tradition of Adam Smith and David Ricardo, provides the intellectual infrastructure for six decades of trade liberalization following World War II. But to implement that economic model, governments turned increasingly to lawyers and judges after the Uruguay Round (1986–1994) negotiations resulted in a complex set of rules, laws, and procedures. The structure of the contemporary world trading system is perhaps best described as a legal regime, negotiated by trade lawyers and diplomats, and administered by lawyers and judges. In effect, litigation has replaced negotiation. As this chapter shows, economists, who played such a significant role in designing the GATT system, have experienced only modest success in establishing a role for themselves and their analytical models in the WTO's trade administration process. The same appears to apply in the trade regulatory institutions of leading commercial nations.

Focusing on the arcane world of trade administration, this chapter examines the individuals, ideas, and institutions that shape the trade regulation process. Much of this section concerns the rules-based global trading system (the World Trade Organization [WTO]) and how the United States and other leading nations implement their obligations. The chapter also provides readers with extensive bibliographical information, so that they can learn more about technical aspects of this broad subject.

BACKGROUND

As other contributors to this book make clear, international economists have over more than two centuries developed a logical, and persuasive, rationale for removing barriers to trade and for integrating national markets. On matters relating to trade theory, economists working in the classical tradition of Adam Smith and David Ricardo spoke with a persuasive voice. Their argument that free trade enhances efficiency and welfare, making people around the world better off, proved compelling to policy-makers.[2] Indeed, economists were prominent in wartime negotiations about the post–World War II international economic order. It is worth remembering that Nobel laureate James E. Meade (UK) fashioned an early draft of the International Trade Organization (forerunner of the GATT). Later, Harold Wilson, Lionel Robbins (both UK), and Clair Wilcox (U.S.) were among the economists heavily involved in the 1947 GATT negotiations.[3]

From influential positions in the academy, the media, think tanks, and international institutions, international economists continue to shape public debate and influence the trade liberalization process. Jagdish Bhagwati, Jeffrey Sachs, and Joseph Stiglitz of Columbia University have maintained a visible presence in the national media, as has Paul Krugman of Princeton University, through his column in the *New York Times*. The Peterson Institute for International Economics in Washington, D.C., founded by C. Fred Bergsten, is another influential voice on trade and financial matters. Gary Hufbauer, an international economist with a law degree, frequently comments and testifies on trade-related issues. Many other prominent economists—including Anne Krueger, the former deputy managing director of the IMF who is now at Johns Hopkins University, and Patrick Low, the director of economic research and statistics at the WTO, have trumpeted the case for trade liberalization from their positions in international institutions. As defenders of the free-trade faith, economists exert considerable influence over the broad contours of public policy.

But within the WTO and the institutions of major trading powers, economists acting as economists do not typically have major operational responsibilities for regulating and enforcing trade agreements. In trade administration, economists appear to have a supportive role, analyzing data and preparing reports for decision-makers. The few Ph.D.-level economists who occupy key administrative or regulatory positions usually have acquired considerable experience in government positions where inductive fact finding, and political and bureaucratic skills, are more important than deductive analysis. An example is former Thai deputy prime minister Supachai Panitchpakdi, who early in his career earned a Ph.D. in economics in the Netherlands working with Nobel laureate Jan Tinbergen and later served as director-general of the WTO for three years.[4] In that role he presided over the launching of the Doha Development Round of multilateral negotiations. At the close of his term, Supachai moved from the WTO to become secretary-general of the UN Conference on Trade and Development (UNCTAD), an organization focused on policy discussion, research, and integration of developing economies into the world economy. Although UNCTAD has no responsibilities for administering trade laws and agreements, its research and analysis make important contributions to the discussion of policy issues.

GLOBAL TRADE ADMINISTRATION

The WTO

At the apex of the world system of trade administration is the WTO, an organization with 153 national members and a mission to liberalize trade in goods and services. It is a forum for negotiations, as well as a tribunal where governments bring disputes for resolution in accordance with internationally negotiated rules. For 2011, the WTO had a budget of 196 million Swiss francs and 640 employees of some 70 nationalities.

Until the Uruguay Round established the WTO in 1994 and accelerated the judicialization of world trade, the multilateral trading regime had been the preserve of an insider network of low-profile diplomats and civil servants who operated in a consensual way to sustain and extend the free-trade-inspired system.[5] Diplomats and career public servants provided the GATT's early leadership, and a wider network of economists, lawyers, and retired government officials supported their endeavors. Indeed, of the nine individuals who have led the international trade organization (since the founding of the GATT in 1947), each has had extensive service in diplomacy and government service. Four also had law degrees.[6] Only Supachai held a doctorate in economics; his dissertation related to human-resource planning and economic development. Pascal Lamy, the current director-general, previously served as the EU commissioner for external trade and as a civil servant in France.

Senior-level managers and professionals at the WTO have similar career patterns and professional credentials. Director-general Lamy has four deputies. All of them have extensive diplomatic and political experience working in various national bureaucracies. They mirror the regional diversity of the WTO's membership, coming from Chile, India, Rwanda, and the United States. Two of the deputies hold law degrees and one a doctorate in industrial economics. Interestingly, the Chilean deputy responsible for the economic research unit is a diplomat and lawyer, whereas the Indian deputy, who has a doctorate in economics from Oxford University, oversees divisions concerned with agriculture and commodities, services, and the environment.[7]

On its website, the WTO says that its "professional staff is composed mostly of economists, lawyers, and others with a specialization in international trade policy."[8]

This may overstate the involvement of economists. One study of staffing patterns at the WTO found only eight Ph.D.-level economists in the economic research unit and a few others sprinkled in other units of the WTO. According to economist Chad Bown, WTO staffing of legal affairs, rules, and economic research did not change in the 2001–2007 period, despite a surge in additional personnel to support Doha Round negotiations. The growth in WTO employment occurred in Informatics and Language Services.[9]

One of the most important, new responsibilities of the WTO is its binding dispute settlement mechanism, a product of the Uruguay Round negotiations.[10] This is a self-enforcing mechanism, relying on members to file complaints. When a member government complains that another government is in violation of its WTO obligations, the WTO's Dispute Settlement Body undertakes consultations and may appoint a three-member panel to hear the complaint. Panelists tend to be current or retired trade officials with a legal background. Many are diplomats based in Geneva.[11] The panel makes an initial ruling, and it is either endorsed or rejected by the WTO's full membership. Appeals go to three members of a seven-member Dispute Settlement Body. These judges hold four-year terms, and all are international lawyers or career civil servants, many with extensive experience in trade diplomacy. None of the current members hold doctoral degrees in economics. The WTO's website makes clear the primacy of law and the role of lawyers. "The WTO's procedure underscores the rule of law, and it makes the trading system more secure and predictable."[12]

Other evidence that lawyers drive the dispute resolution system can be found in the special waiver that is provided to lawyers in the dispute management system. While only governments have standing to bring complaints to the WTO, private lawyers may represent those government parties. Because many developing countries did not have the lawyers familiar with WTO procedures, the WTO permitted members to retain private counsel for both panel and appellate proceedings. Thus, the U.S. law firm White and Case represented Costa Rica in the battle over Europe's tariffs on bananas.[13] Even cases brought by large countries on behalf of private firms, such as the banana case the U.S. trade representative (USTR) filed for Chiquita, typically involve substantial involvement of private attorneys behind the scenes. They assist government trade officials in preparation of cases.[14] Often the private lawyers retain consulting economists to provide economic analysis and models for the proceedings, so economic arguments are frequently advanced.

However, some economists believe that the WTO judicial process should be more accessible to economic analysis and economists. Bown suggests that the WTO dispute settlement process should give greater weight to technical analysis in its decisions, and provide better economic staffing to support the panels. Bown examined the professional credentials of 23 arbitrators involved in 10 dispute settlement panel decisions and concluded that only one was "an individual who another economist would likely classify as an analytical research economist at the level necessary either to interpret technical economic evidence or to construct the economic counterfactuals that are of utmost importance to arbitration proceedings in particular." In his view, each dispute settlement panel should have from inception at least one econ-omist assigned to it for staff support.[15] He thinks it desirable for each case to have two Ph.D.-level economists so they may collaborate, as economists are trained to do.[16]

Within the WTO, there is apparently some resistance in dispute settlement cases to more extensive use of economic models and analysis. The WTO economist Alexander Keck has responded to calls for change with the observation that while there may be room for better economic analysis, it cannot determine outcomes in dispute settlement cases. Dispute settlement, he observes, is about fairness, not about optimal outcomes. He notes that panelists in a Korean beverage case stated: "Quantitative analyses, while helpful, should not be considered necessary."[17]

To assist developing countries in the dispute settlement process, the WTO, other international organizations, national governments, and even private associa-tions have established training programs for officials of developing countries.[18] Much of this effort has gone to training lawyers. One intergovernmental organiza-tion, the Advisory Centre on WTO Law (ACWL), trains young trade lawyers from developing countries and provides support to developing countries in dispute set-tlement proceedings.[19] In 2009, the ACWL with a staff of eight lawyers, provided 194 legal opinions and support to developing countries in six disputes, and awarded 34 certificates of training to those participating in training courses.[20] The ACWL apparently does not provide technical economic analysis to help developing coun-tries assess that side of their arguments in dispute settlement proceedings.[21]

However, another new group, which is based in Toronto and supported by the World Bank and various national aid programs, does provide economic and legal assistance to developing countries in trade negotiations. It is the International Lawyers and Economists Against Poverty (ILEAP). It provides analytical assistance and capacity building but does not apparently assist in dispute resolution cases.[22]

The World Customs Organization (WCO)

One of the less visible international organizations important to global trade adminis-tration is the small WCO, located in Brussels. It is an intergovernmental body repre-senting 177 customs administrations and has about 100 employees, including technical specialists and support staff, and a budget in 2007–2008 of 14 million euros.[23]

Traditionally, the mission of customs officials has been to control the move-ment of goods and safeguard revenue collection. They also combat smuggling, col-lect data, and enforce a variety of laws applicable to international trade, such as rules of origin, antidumping and countervailing duty laws, and orders excluding goods that infringe intellectual property rights. They face the difficulty of applying import laws in a world of complex and overlapping bilateral, regional, and multilat-eral agreements. A major function of the WCO is promoting the harmonization of tariff classification and valuation practices, and training customs officials from de-veloping countries. The WCO administers the Harmonized System, a multipurpose product nomenclature for classifying and coding goods. The EU and 135 countries apply this uniform system to classifying their imported goods.

The WCO does not have a binding dispute settlement mechanism. When questions occur over the Harmonized Code, a committee of the WCO is expected to offer an advisory option. Several disputes involving customs issues have gone to the WTO Dispute Settlement Body for consultations and binding dispute settlement. In one involving the EU's classification of frozen chicken cuts from Brazil and Thailand, the WTO ruled against the EU and ordered it to bring its customs classification into conformity with its WTO obligations.[24]

The WCO's secretary-general is Kunio Mikuriya, a Japanese customs official. Customs officials are on the front line of administering tariffs, trade laws, and rulings. While the organization emphasizes its efforts to make globalization work, from an economist's point of view, customs officials may often exhibit a law enforcement— and sometimes a protectionist—regulatory mindset.[25]

The World Intellectual Property Organization (WIPO)

In recent years issues involving intellectual property have become an integral part of the WTO-based international trading system. The WIPO, a specialized agency of the United Nations, has a mandate to promote intellectual property protection throughout the world, through cooperation with member states and other international organizations.[26] The WIPO administers several international treaties, including the Paris Convention for the Protection of Industrial Property (1883), the Madrid system for registration of trademarks (1891, 1989), and the Strasbourg Agreement Concerning the International Patent Classification (1971). The WIPO has an agreement with the WTO over implementation of the Trade-Related Intellectual Property agreement (TRIPS). With these treaty obligations, WIPO has an evolving enforcement responsibility against counterfeiting and pirated goods. It also has an educational role in helping developing nations prepare to implement intellectual property systems and obligations. Much of WIPO's educational activity involves teaching the elements of patent and intellectual property law to officials of developing countries so that they can implement their TRIPS obligations.[27]

Member states (185 altogether) determine the organization's strategic direction and activities. It has a budget of 618.6 million Swiss francs and 1044 regular staff. The director-general of WIPO is usually a lawyer. Australian lawyer Francis Gurry replaced Kamil Idris of Sudan in 2008.[28]

TRADE ADMINISTRATION IN THE UNITED STATES

At the national level, the legal approach to trade administration continues to gain ground, reflecting the need of nations to know and employ WTO-based trade law. In the United States, the legalization trend is far advanced. Government economists appear to have important supporting roles in most agencies, but lawyers and civil servants retain operational responsibilities for trade policy, negotiations, and administration of trade laws and agreements. One proxy for the increased involvement of lawyers is the length of trade agreements. In 1947, when economists and diplomats handled the negotiations, the GATT agreement with appendices, and modifications, came to 65 pages. By the Uruguay Round (1994) lawyers had control of the negotiating process, and 60 agreements totaled 550 pages. The same pattern applied to bilateral agreements: NAFTA has 824 pages, the U.S. FTA with Singapore 1,586 pages, and the CAFTA-Dominican Agreement 3,725 pages.

Office of the U.S. Trade Representative (USTR)

This office, with some 229 employees and a budget of $48 million in 2010, is the most important agency on the trade front. It has broad responsibility for coordinating trade policy, negotiations, and administration. It is part of the Executive Office of the President, but the U.S. trade representative reports to both the president and Congress, reflecting the bifurcated nature of trade policy. In the United States, only the president can negotiate, but only Congress can pass tariff legislation and approve treaties and international agreements. Not only does USTR coordinate U.S. trade policy and negotiate agreements, it has oversight responsibility for the generalized system of preferences, unilateral Section 301 complaints against foreign unfair trade practices, safeguards, and certain intellectual property infringement cases.[29]

In recent years, Congress has directed USTR to monitor the implementation of agreements and report annually to Congress. As a result, USTR now has an assistant USTR who focuses exclusively on monitoring and enforcement issues. This official is a lawyer. On enforcement issues, USTR prepares and issues reports such as the *National Trade Estimate Report on Foreign Trade Barriers*. The president's annual report on the trade agreements program is also useful.[30]

At USTR, the workload involves negotiations with other governments and consultation with other branches of the U.S. government over politically sensitive technical and legal issues. Not surprisingly, presidents usually nominate an individual with legal qualifications to handle the USTR's portfolio. Since 1960, 16 persons have served as trade representative. Of these, 12 were lawyers and two had doctorates, one of these in public administration and the other in agricultural economics. The agricultural economist (Clayton Yeutter) was also a lawyer. Only President George W. Bush's last trade representative, Susan Schwab, a university of Maryland administrator, came to USTR from the academy. She previously spent a decade on Capitol Hill working on trade issues. Most USTRs have held elective office or have worked as staffers for elected officials in Congress. Many have also have had extensive business experience.[31]

Among the senior staff at USTR, lawyers enjoyed a strong presence in 2010. Along with the USTR, Ron Kirk, and his three principal deputies, there were nine other lawyers among 25 key professional staff. Many other lawyers worked at middle-level staff positions. In early 2003, one scholar found over two dozen lawyers working on trade matters, and that figure did not include lawyers working as diplomatic negotiators. Nor did it include USTR's practice of relying on lawyers from other agencies on specialized matters before the WTO.[32] By contrast, in the early years of USTR such economists as W. Michael Blumenthal and Harald Malmgren, both with doctorates in economics, held key top-tier posts. Before the Tokyo Round, one had to reach down to the lower levels of USTR to find a lawyer.[33]

Outside lawyers, including many former USTR officials, play an important role in the U.S. trade administration process. Alan W. Wolfe, a former deputy USTR during the Carter administration, has been especially active representing U.S. steel companies and in building support in Congress for USTR's trade agreements. Before USTR files a complaint with the WTO or pursues unilateral action, it consults extensively with the complaining industry and reviews documents prepared by its lawyers. Often these materials include analysis by private economists retained by law firms representing domestic industries with a trade complaint.[34]

Appreciating that many foreign countries lack resources to defend their trade-agreement interests, the USTR and other agencies of the U.S. government make large contributions to the trade-capacity-building process. In 2008, the USTR and other agencies spent nearly $2.3 billion on this subject, including $1 billion for Sub-Saharan Africa. The goal is to expedite the integration of developing countries into the WTO system and enable them to benefit from global trade.[35]

U.S. Department of Commerce

The U.S. Department of Commerce, a cabinet-level agency with over 38,000 employees and a budget of $6.5 billion, has broad responsibilities for enforcing trade laws. Commerce is a vast government conglomerate whose activities range from weather forecasting to census collection and economic development. The divisions most important for the administration of trade laws are the Bureau of Industry and Security (BIS) and the International Trade Administration (ITA).

On the export-control side, BIS administers laws and regulations designed to prevent certain advanced technology items from being exported to China, Cuba, North Korea, Iran, and certain other governments. Its mission is to "advance U.S. national security, foreign policy, and economic objectives by ensuring an effective export control and treaty compliance system and promoting continued U.S. strategic technology leadership." A remnant of the Cold War export control program, BIS requires export licenses. In 2009, the bureau says, it processed 20,351 export license applications for goods valued at $62.4 billion. In 2010, BIS had a budget of some $108 million, and it had 362 employees in 2008.[36]

One of the most important units of Commerce is the ITA. It has broad responsibility for promoting exports, maintaining foreign trade zones, administering import laws, and ensuring compliance with existing trade agreements.

The ITA is headed by an undersecretary, and it had a budget of some $465 million and 1,881 employees in 2010. President Obama nominated Frank Sanchez, a Tampa lawyer and businessman, as undersecretary. This position usually goes to a lawyer with strong political connections. The Import Administration (IA), headed by an assistant secretary, is one of the ITA's principal units concerned with trade administration and regulation. The assistant secretary who holds this key position is usually a talented lawyer. Among the former occupants of this position are top-flight international trade lawyers, like Gary Horlick, Alan Holmer, and Judy Bello, and others who have moved on to more senior positions in trade policy and administration. The IA had a budget of $68 million in 2010 and 351 employees.

The ITA shares responsibilities with the U.S. International Trade Commission (ITC) for administering U.S. unfair trade laws dealing with subsidies and dumping. The ITA also administers textile and steel monitoring programs, as well as foreign trade zones.[37] There has been much discussion in the legal and economic literature of Commerce's controversial zeroing methodology for calculating duty rates for foreign producers and exports under investigation. Simply stated, it was alleged that U.S. officials counted only positive dumping margins and set aside negative dumping margins, that is, where the exported good sold at a higher price than in the domestic market. This practice led to a formal complaint by the European Union, and in 2008 a WTO dispute panel ruled against the United States. That finding was upheld by the WTO's Appellate Body.[38]

The Department of Commerce, an executive-branch agency, has also experienced difficulties with domestic court review from the Court of International Trade and the Court of Appeals for the Federal Circuit. One academic study concludes that Commerce has had more problems than the independent ITC.[39] Political scientists concluded that ITA makes "protectionist decisions based on national interest and foreign policy concerns as well as domestic political concerns."[40]

Another important area for ITA in trade administration involves market access and compliance. The ITA has an assistant secretary for Market Access and Compliance (MAC), with a budget of $43 million in 2010 and 207 employees. This office seeks to identify and help businesses overcome trade barriers, resolve trade disputes, and ensure that trading partners fully meet obligations under trade agreements.[41] Commerce's Trade Compliance Center advertises itself as a one-stop shop for businesses, and the website contains the text of U.S. international agreements together with a search tool.[42]

Another little-known but important division of Commerce is the Patent and Trademark Office. It had a budget of about $2 billion and employed 9,614 individuals in 2010. It reviews applications for patents and trademarks, and assists USTR with efforts to promote global respect for U.S. intellectual property.[43]

At Commerce, like other trade agencies, more and more lawyers hold top positions. In key regulatory positions, senior officials tend to have law degrees and experience working on Capitol Hill or in the executive branch. Economists, however, are more visible in research divisions, such as the Bureau of Economic Analysis and the Census Bureau. While their studies and reports impact trade policy, these units do not administer trade laws.[44]

Customs and Border Protection

One other front-line agency for U.S. trade administration warrants attention: Customs and Border Protection in the Department of Homeland Security. In 2010 it had a budget of about $10.1 billion and in 2008 a workforce of 57,519.[45] On its website, Customs and Border Protection offers detailed information about its trade-related activities. The most important are enforcing countervailing and antidumping orders, intellectual property, textile regulation, and agriculture and safety laws. In 2007, before the global recession depressed trade, Customs and Border Protection says, it collected $32 billion for the federal government.[46]

In the contemporary era, customs inspectors are career civil servants, who are supported by lawyers and commodity specialists. Their decisions are often reviewable in federal court, where the U.S. Court of International Trade has a traditional role overseeing customs decisions. The judicial approach to customs administration is quite different from eighteenth-century century practice. Then Adam Smith, author of the *Wealth of Nations*, spent over 12 years as a Scottish commissioner of customs. In that role, the famous economist-turned-administrator had to enforce many of the very laws he disagreed with on philosophical grounds against the real free traders of that era, smugglers. According to a biographer, Smith, though he served as only one member of the customs board, was something of an innovator and used his position to "promote changes he viewed as both useful and just."[47]

Other Executive-Branch Agencies

Several other executive agencies have important trade-related administrative functions. The U.S. Department of Agriculture (USDA) has overall responsibility for agricultural trade. Its Foreign Agricultural Service helps U.S. exporters to access foreign markets and overcome foreign trade barriers.[48] The USDA's Food Safety and Inspection Service is charged with inspecting and monitoring the safety of meat, poultry, and egg products. The Food and Drug Administration, in the U.S. Department of Health and Human Services, is responsible for protecting public health by assuring the safety of the nation's food supply. With a budget of some $3.5 billion and nearly 9,500 employees, it has broad regulatory responsibilities for imported food.[49]

The U.S. Department of Labor oversees trade adjustment programs, offering benefits to workers dislocated as a consequence of imports or of shifts in production out of the United States. The Employment and Training Administration supervises these programs. In 2010 the U.S. spent $1.82 billion on these programs, up from $934 million in 2008. The Trade and Globalization Assistance Act of 2009 substantially expanded benefits to workers impacted by imports.[50]

The Department of State, which controlled trade policy before the establishment of the Special Trade Negotiator's Office, forerunner of the USTR, in 1962, continues to have a role in interagency trade policy-making and negotiations. The Bureau of Economic, Energy and Business Affairs has a voice in a great variety of issues from transportation to energy, trade, and investments. It helps to administer economic sanctions and intellectual property enforcement. During the Carter and Reagan presidencies, the undersecretary for economic affairs was usually a prominent academic economist, such as Richard N. Cooper and W. Allen Wallis, who both held the position. Perhaps as evidence of the new emphasis on legal and financial dimensions of economic diplomacy, President George W. Bush appointed to this position a lawyer and former head of the Commodity Futures Trading Commission.[51] The Obama administration has appointed Robert Hormats, until recently an investment banker with Goldman Sachs. Earlier in his career Hormats, who holds a Ph.D. from the Fletcher School of Law and Diplomacy, held international economic positions in the Nixon, Ford, Carter, and Reagan administrations.

The International Trade Commission

This commission, an independent quasi-judicial agency, is responsible for administering various trade remedy statutes. In 2010, the ITC had a budget of $82 million and 394 employees.[52] In quasi-judicial antidumping and countervailing duty proceedings, as well as safeguard investigation, the ITC is asked to make injury determinations. In antidumping and countervailing duty cases, the standard is material injury, or threat thereof. It is defined in the statute as injury "which is not inconsequential, immaterial, or unimportant." The Commission is directed to evaluate the volume of imports, the effect of imports on prices for like products, and the impact of imports on domestic producers.[53]

Reviewing courts have said the Commission may use economic analysis, including modeling, to help it reach statutory determinations, but the ITC does not have discretion to rely on economic models at the exclusion of other factors. Indeed in *Altx v. United States* (June 2004), the Court of Appeals for the Federal Circuit held "it is within the Commission's discretion to refuse to abide by a theoretical economic model that proves inconsistent with empirical data." The appeals court agreed with the first reviewing court, the Court of International Trade, that an economic "model alone cannot substitute for consideration of the statutory factors and the record data. The court has repeatedly recognized that the ITC may reasonably base a decision on facts in the record that vary from a theoretical economic model."[54] Unlike some other areas of legal practice, such as competition law, the specific statutory language appears to leave trade administrators with little discretion. As a result of the Commission's judicial-type decision-making, its detailed evidentiary records, and its independence from political influence, the ITC has performed "remarkably better in court than the Department of Commerce," says one scholar.[55]

By contrast, in antitrust investigations the role of economists is well established. Lawrence White, a former FTC economist, notes that antitrust statutes are terse, and a long history of court interpretation has led to increase roles for economists especially in merger analysis and vertical relationships and restraints. A prominent economist, with the title deputy assistant attorney general, usually heads the Department of Justice's staff of 60 Ph.D.-level economists. At the Federal Trade Commission, a bureau director is a leading economist and supervises 70 Ph.D.-level economists.[56]

Along with judicial review, the ITC experiences close congressional oversight. It is not unusual for members of Congress to testify at agency's proceedings or to raise pointed questions at oversight hearings. After the Commission turned down the domestic steel industry's antidumping petition involving cold-rolled steel from Argentina, and seemingly relied on the respondents' econometric model, the steel industry counterattacked politically.[57] In 2000, for example, the House Appropriations Committee voiced concern in budget hearings that the ITC was "expending resources to analyze theoretical constructs of the conditions of competition, rather than focusing on the market realities faced by domestic industries injured by foreign unfair trade practices in accordance with the statutorily mandated factors to be analyzed in Sec. 771(7) of the Tariff Act of 1930 (as amended) such as import volume and process, and their impact on domestic shipments, capacity utilization, employment, prices, profitability, investment, etc." Members of the Committee threatened to cut appropriations and demanded a list of the agency's economists and their specific functions.[58]

Does congressional pressure influence ITC decisions on cases? An econometric study of ITC decision-making in antidumping and countervailing duty cases between March 1985 and June 1992 found "no support for the hypothesis that ITC decisions are influenced by congressional pressure." The results also "strongly supported" the thesis that "economic criteria are used appropriately by the ITC commissioners."[59]

Given the rules-based WTO regime, the specific language in U.S. trade law, and extensive oversight and review, the ITC has become increasingly more judicial in its approach and its composition over the last 30 years. Until the mid-1960s, there was normally at least one Ph.D.-level economist on the six-member commission. In appointing the first Tariff Commission, President Woodrow Wilson selected three Ph.D.-level economists—Professor Frank Taussig from Harvard University, perhaps the nation's most renowned international economist, as well as Thomas Walker Page from the University of Virginia and William O. Culbertson, who was also a lawyer. Secretary of State Cordell Hull, author of the reciprocal trade program, placed two of his aides with economics doctorates (Lynn Ramsey Edminster and Henry F. Grady) on the Commission. However, since 1980, when the Tokyo Round agreements were implemented, the vast majority of appointees have been lawyers. During this period the ITC has had 28 commissioners (independent decision-makers), 16 of them lawyers. Three others had doctorates—two in international relations and one in history. Like top decision-makers at USTR and Commerce, most of these appointees had worked for members of Congress or held elective office.[60] None came to their decision-making posts directly from universities.

The absence of presidential appointees with advanced degrees in economics is conspicuous and a departure from the Commission's historical tradition. One explanation may be that senators, who must confirm presidential appointees, are wary of economists. Some perceive that economists are inclined to apply trade laws as they think they should be written rather than as Congress has enacted them.[61] During Carter administration, the White House did nominate two prominent international economists, Gardner Patterson of Princeton (a former deputy director general of the GATT) and Robert Baldwin of the University of Wisconsin. Neither was confirmed, reportedly because of opposition from Senate Finance Committee Chairman Russell Long (a Democrat from Louisiana) and organized labor. During the Reagan administration several other names of economists were circulated informally, but none attracted favor on Capitol Hill.

JUDICIAL REVIEW

The Court of International Trade and the Court of Appeals for the Federal Circuit review actions of the Customs and Border Protection, and for that reason must be considered in any discussion of U.S. trade administration.

The Court of International Trade

This court, in New York City, is a trial-level court with nine members, serving life terms.[62] It has exclusive authority to hear civil cases against U.S. officials or agencies, growing out of administration of international trade laws. Many of the cases involve appeals of antidumping and countervailing duty courses before the Department of Commerce and the U.S. ITC. Since the 1890s, earlier versions of this court have addressed disputes about the valuation and classification of goods for tariff purposes. That traditional function now occupies less than 20% of the court's published opinions.

As a result of changes to its mandate in 1980, Congress provided a comprehensive system for judicial review of civil actions in trade transactions. The new Court of International Trade became actively involved in antidumping and countervailing duties. Approximately half of the court's opinions in 2005 involved these so-called unfair trade cases. The chief judge has estimated that because cases are consolidated, this type of case consumes three-quarters of the court's resources. The court is also actively involved in customs litigation over administration of unfair trade laws, as well as a significant number of cases pertaining to trade adjustment assistance.[63] Typically, the court will sustain an antidumping or countervailing duty decision of the U.S. ITC or the Department of Commerce unless it is "unsupported by substantial evidence on the record, or otherwise not in accordance with law."[64]

The court has taken a cautious approach to the use of economic analysis in the ITC's causation analysis. On the one hand, it has upheld the use of valid economic models; on the other, it has rejected elasticity analysis when the underlying elasticities were not part of the trial record.[65]

Political scientists say the court tends to reverse decisions from Commerce more frequently than from the independent ITC. The court, they say, "does not" appear to push U.S. trade policy "significantly in either a protectionist or nonprotectionist direction."[66]

The Court of Appeals for the Federal Circuit

This court, a specialized appellate court, is one of 13 appellate courts in the federal judicial system. It has 12 judges and has jurisdiction over cases involving international trade, government contracts, patents, trademarks, certain money claims against the U.S. government, federal personnel, and veterans' benefits. Appeals come from all federal district courts, as well as the Court of International Trade. The Court of Appeals for the Federal Circuit also reviews decisions of the U.S. ITC in patent cases. According to the court, some 55% of its cases involve administrative law issues and 31% intellectual property cases. Another 11% involve money damages against the United States[67] As noted elsewhere, the court has upheld use of economic analysis but, like the Court of International Trade, has insisted that the ITC address each of the factors listed in the statute.[68] Some scholars claim the Court of Appeals for the Federal Circuit has a protectionist bias, settling a majority of cases to the benefit of U.S. companies.[69]

TRADE ADMINISTRATION IN OTHER COUNTRIES

The advent of the WTO with its system of trade rules and mandatory dispute settlement has accelerated the trend toward legalization and judicialization of trade policy in many countries. Here are some examples.

Canada

Since 1982, the Department of Foreign Affairs and International Trade Canada has overall responsibility for trade policy, and some facets of trade administration.[70] That division of the department is headed by the minister for international trade, who in the hierarchy ranks second to the minister of foreign affairs. Beneath the deputy minister, a career civil servant, are assistant deputy ministers responsible for air negotiations, communications, business development and investment, resources, trade law, and trade policy and negotiations. The trade law bureau lists 45 individuals with the title of counsel, or lawyer, and has expanded rapidly as Canada has implemented its WTO obligations and sought to use the dispute settlement regime to improve export opportunities. As of October 2011, it had filed 33 cases (more than any members but the EU and the U.S.) and served as respondent in 17 others.[71]

As in the United States, Canada has a bifurcated process for investigation of antidumping and countervailing duty complaints. A five-member, quasi-judicial panel, the Canadian International Trade Tribunal (CITT) has duties similar to those of the U.S. ITC to make injury determinations to domestic industries. The panel is assisted by 87 permanent staff members. It is responsible for safeguards, anti-dumping, and countervailing duty investigations. Of the five members of the CITT, four are lawyers or jurists, and the other is a career civil servant.[72] Some academics complain that the CITT seldom accepts a public interest argument to set aside anti-dumping duties. They fault the CITT for an injured producers bias and insensitivity to consumer welfare considerations.[73]

When an antidumping complaint is filed, CITT reviews it, and if the application reveals a reasonable indication of injury to the domestic industry, the complaint is referred to the Canada Border Services Agency (CBSA) for examination. The CBSA, like the U.S. Department of Commerce, attempts to determine margins of dumping.[74] As in the United States, there is a chain of judicial review, with some appeals of CBSA determinations going to the CITT, then to the Federal Court of Appeal, and if needed to the Supreme Court of Canada. As a result of trade agreements such as NAFTA and the WTO, the courts of Canada have an expanded role in trade administration.[75]

The EU

As the EU expanded from 6 to 27 members, and engaged the WTO, the importance of law and lawyers grew. Brussels, which once preferred the diplomatic approach to resolving trade disputes, has increasingly adopted the legal approach to enhance market opportunities for its exporters. Next to the United States, the EU has filed more complaints with the WTO than any other member. As of October 2011, the EU had filed 85 cases and responded to 70 others. The U.S. had initiated 98 complaints (and been designated as respondent in 113 others).[76]

The EU has been successful in some major cases, including its successful challenge of export tax subsidies for U.S. foreign sales corporations. The EU has also successfully challenged numerous U.S. countervailing and antidumping decisions, use of the 1916 Antidumping Act, and the Byrd amendment providing awards to petitioners from collected antidumping and countervailing duties. In addition, the EU has challenged U.S. unilateral sanctions under Section 301 and the Bush administration's steel restraints.[77]

Nonetheless, EU practice differs from that of the United States. In Europe the bureaucracy is stronger, and government is less reliant on private counsel in formulating cases. However, once the decision to file a case has been made, the EU legal staff may retain outside counsel. On occasion, it has even employed U.S. law firms in bringing, or defending, cases involving the United States.[78]

The classic example of an EU public-private partnership is the Boeing-Airbus subsidy dispute. While the EU assigned a dozen lawyers to the case, they were supported by the U.S. private law firm Sidley Austin, which Airbus hired. Boeing retained former U.S. trade representative Charlene Barshefsky, and soon both sides were estimated to be spending about $1 million per month on the high-profile case.[79]

In the EU bureaucracy responsible for trade, professional civil servants tend to occupy senior positions, but lawyers are increasingly visible. The Legal Services division has 17 lawyers working on subsidies and dumping, and another 13 assigned to trade policy and the WTO.[80] Within the trade directorate, the office responsible for legal aspects of trade policy has 13 professionals, including one economist. The trade directorate even has an office of the chief economist, with several Ph.D.-level economists. There are others sprinkled through the bureaucracy, including some who function as diplomats.[81]

Japan

The same legalization trend is manifest in Japan, a country with a strong government bureaucracy and a relatively weak judiciary. Until recently, Japan had only 16,000 lawyers, or 126.5 per million people, compared to 900,000 in the United States, or 2,873 per million people. When trade disputes required solutions, Japan relied on extralegal, diplomatic approaches such as export restraint agreements. But at the outset of the WTO in 1995, Japan devised a new strategy for managing trade disputes. Hereafter, it would rely on international trade law as a sword and shield to advance its interests within the multilateral framework. Political scientist Saadia Pekkanen says that "Japan's aggressive legalism is here to stay."[82] But Keisuke Iida, a Japanese political scientist, argues that the radical change is largely tactical, inasmuch as Japan hires foreign counsel to prepare its legal briefs. Unlike other governments that have developed in-house counsel to protect their interests under the WTO, Japan has relied heavily on American lawyers for legal expertise. One reason for utilizing foreign law firms, he says, is that "few Japanese are competent enough to write such complex technical documents in English."[83]

Nor are Japanese government agencies apparently building high-powered, in-house economic analysis units to support their legal initiatives. In its 2009 report on foreign trade barriers, the USTR recommends that the Japanese Fair Trade Commission "improve its economic analysis" with employees who have "postgraduate economics training."[84] This commission has primary responsibility for enforcing antimonopoly law, and its responsibilities touch on patent, antidumping, and competition issues, all subjects of WTO negotiations.

According to WTO records, Japan had filed 14 dispute settlement complaints by October 2011 and been named as a respondent in 15. Two of its officials, Mitsuo Matsushita, a former Tokyo University law professor, and Shotaro Oshima, a former deputy foreign minister, have served on the seven-member WTO Appellate Body for disputes.[85]

Trade Administration in Developing Countries

Developing countries have been slower than Canada, the EU, and the United States to use the WTO dispute settlement mechanism to advance their interests. Brazil, India, and Mexico have been among the more active. Brazil has filed 25 complaints (respondent in 14), India 19 (respondent in 20), and Mexico 21 (respondent in 14). But smaller and poorer countries have largely been invisible. No Sub-Saharan Africa country has filed a complaint. By October 2011, for example, only 42 of 153 WTO members had filed complaints.[86] Shaffer notes that developing countries typically have fewer trading interests, and less resources to invest in litigation. Developing countries typically have few lawyers and must rely on outside counsel. Representation may cost $500–600 per hour, and bringing a major cast to the WTO could cost complainants and respondents upward of $10 million. There are exceptions, as when the Venezuelan oil company hired U.S. private lawyers to help the government of Venezuela to file a gasoline case against the United States.[87]

Brazil

Brazil is a classic example of how emerging powers can adapt to a rules-based international system and become major players. According to legal scholars, Brazil adapted to the requirements of WTO's judicial approach to administration and has become a successful model for other developing countries.[88] To do this, the Brazilian government transformed its bureaucracy to give greater emphasis to legal approaches. Its businesses hired top-flight international legal talent to help the government present its WTO cases. Petrobras, for example, retained a Washington, D.C., law firm to prepare its first dispute settlement complaint against the United States on reformulated gasoline in 1995. In an aircraft case involving Embraer, the hired U.S. lawyers even attended the WTO panel hearings as part of Brazil's delegation.[89]

In the successful case brought against U.S. cotton subsidies, Brazil again retained U.S. lawyers (Sidley Austin) and economists to assist with the case. In that instance, economic analysis had a major bearing on the outcome. Economist Daniel Sumner, a faculty member at the University of California at Davis and a former U.S. assistant secretary of agriculture, prepared an analysis showing how U.S. cotton subsidies impacted the international cotton trade. His report worked against the interests of California cotton growers. The growers cried foul and accused the state university professor of unethical conduct.[90]

Other developing nations also have retained foreign firms to train local lawyers in WTO dispute procedures. China and India are among them. When China hires foreign law firms, it requires them to work with local law firms so as to facilitate the transfer of knowledge about trade litigation to local talent.[91] Vietnam is another developing country that has relied on foreign legal talent, including one former USTR lawyer, to gear up for the new world of trade litigation. Incidentally, that lawyer— Daniel Price—easily crossed traditional professional boundaries and served as deputy national security adviser for international economic affairs in the administration of

President George W. Bush. In that role he was the senior White House official on matters dealing with the international economy.[92]

International law firms boast of their involvement in the WTO process. Sidley Austin, a U.S.-based international law firm with 70 international trade lawyers, says its attorneys have participated in more than 230 of some 400 complaints brought to the WTO. This firm's professionals have been counsel to Brazil, the EU, Japan, Norway, and the United States in various high-profile cases such as the Boeing-Airbus dispute and Brazil's challenge of agricultural subsidies. The firm claims: "Our extensive experience means that we have shaped—and continue to shape—the development of WTO law."[93]

Another leading firm, Steptoe and Johnson, boasts that it was one of only two law firms in the world to receive a top-tier ranking from Chambers & Partners for its WTO practice. Steptoe represented China in a WTO dispute and South Korea in free-trade negotiations, both with the United States on the other side.[94] In a brochure, written in English and Chinese, Troutman and Sanders boasts of representing clients from Brazil, Canada, and South Korea in WTO and NAFTA dispute settlement proceedings involving the United States.[95] Miller and Chevalier asserts: "Our representations extend beyond advising from 'outside of the room'—we frequently have attended negotiations as experts accredited as part of a negotiating team."[96]

Gary Horlick, the former head of Import Administration in the Department of Commerce, notes on his website that he "is the highest-ranked international trade lawyer in the world." He has served as counsel to other governments (including the United Kingdom, Canada, Mexico, Chile, and South Africa), and chaired WTO and MERCOSUR panals.[97]

Many of the law firms have economists on the professional staff to advise clients on the economic dimensions of cases. Frequently, these in-house economists hold graduate degrees, but not doctorates, in economics. However, Sidley's WTO practice group lists one Ph.D.-level economist in its Geneva office who can advise clients on the economic dimensions of cases.

EVALUATING THE JUDICIALIZATION OF TRADE ADMINISTRATION

Why the Preponderance of Lawyers?

So why have lawyers taken over the regulation and administration of trade from the economists and diplomats who conceived the global economy and shaped its evolution in the first decades after World War II? Several factors stand out. First, until the Tokyo Round, trade administration largely involved tariffs and quota issues. In dealing with these border barriers, economists had centuries of relevant expertise, a comparative advantage based on a logical, and relatively simple, model. But as trade negotiations and trade administration moved to liberalize, and harmonize, the impact of internal regulatory systems on international flows of goods and services, the subject became infinitely more complex. The focus turned to issues involving services, procurement, investments, intellectual property, and dispute settlement. Trade administration intersected complex issues of international law, domestic regulatory processes, sovereignty, and equity. These are areas where lawyers have established expertise and can claim a comparative advantage.

To resolve the conflicting claims, and reduce the appeals for congressional intervention to aid import-impacted industries, legislators accepted a more judicial decision-making process. They empowered ad hoc panels of specialists or nonpartisan institutions such as the U.S. ITC to hear cases. And to keep the administrators focused on statutory criteria, legislators empowered courts to review decisions.[98] With increased court review of administrative determinations, agency proceedings necessarily became more formal and transparent. Decision-makers faced strict timetables and needed to develop substantial evidence to support their decisions. In effect, parties to trade disputes became litigants, and trade administrators became judges.[99] It is thus not surprising that the judicial nature of proceedings became a powerful argument for the appointment of decision-makers with legal experience and a sensitivity to legal patterns of thought.

There may be other reasons why economists appear to have a limited role in trade administration. Legal scholar Andreas F. Lowenfeld says that economic theory does not "provide clear guidelines for international economic law."[100] John H. Jackson, himself a former general counsel of the USTR's office, has suggested that "much of the economic literature is too theoretical and technical" for decision-makers.[101]

Economists offer different insights about their lack of influence on public policy generally. One recent study shows there are more economists [of all specialties] in "policymaking positions" [sic] than in earlier generations, but that economists have had relatively less success in promoting their ideas. The study concludes that to succeed in government, economists are "forced to become lawyers," trading off economic analysis for "quick and clever arguments." While lawyers develop political skills, "building political relationships is not in the skill set of most economists."[102]

Nonetheless, as this chapter has shown, national and international courts do take notice of economic analysis. But at the WTO and in various national courts, such as the U.S. Court of International Trade, there has been a noticeable reluctance to substitute conclusions based on economic models for reliance on explicit statutory factors. While that may change over time as judges and lawmakers become more familiar with economic analysis, the present reality is that contemporary trade administration is heavily based on legal covenants, written by and applied by lawyers and judges.

Costs of Judicialization

The judicialization of trade policy may produce fair decisions, though not necessarily decisions that will survive close scrutiny in the economics classroom. The judicial approach is also costly and time-consuming for all concerned. Those aspects warrant brief discussion. The WTO dispute settlement litigation process can drag out for three years, if parties appeal the panel decision and subsequently contest implementation of the decision. The costs of litigation, exclusive of public relations and political lobbying, probably exceed $500,000 for a complainant in a market access case. Parties in the Japan–Photographic Film cases reportedly had legal bills exceeding $20 million. In the U.S.–EU dispute over aircraft subsidies, billings reportedly topped $1 million each per month in mid-2005 for both Boeing and Airbus.[103]

The U.S. trade remedy process is also time-consuming and costly. It can take as much as three years to navigate the process, from time of original filing through appellate reviews. Washington, D.C., attorneys John Greenwald and Peggy Clarke have estimated that a modest antidumping case in the United States could cost $1 million, including appeals, and from $150,000 to $1 million for each respondent. This, of course, does not include opportunity costs and executive time consumed with litigation. The cost of corporate resources is perhaps twice the cost of outside counsel, they say.[104]

Over the last 20 years, international trade law, and litigation, has been a growth industry. According to Martindale Hubbell, there are 509 international trade lawyers in the District of Columbia engaged in private practice.[105] This does not include hundreds in government and corporate practice, and many others not listed in the Martindale Hubbell directory.[106] Estimates of total billings in national and international proceedings vary, but they probably exceed $1 billion annually.[107] While lawyers defend their fee structure as the cost of maintaining a transparent and fair system of resolving trade disputes, it is not surprising that some scholars are beginning to ask whether trade administration has become too expensive and time-consuming to be left only to lawyers.[108]

In *Henry VI*, one of William Shakespeare's characters, Dick, a butcher and a conspirator in a rebellion against government authority, wisecracks: "The first thing we do, let's kill all the lawyers."[109] The barb may, or may not, have reflected Shakespeare's personal sentiments. But the populist remarks apparently won applause from those in Elizabethan England who considered the legal system burdensome. Four centuries later, Dick the butcher's words may still resonate among economists and others who would prefer a less costly and time-consuming approach to trade administration. But so far, as this article shows, their alternative approaches have encountered skepticism among legislators, and have made only limited contributions to decision-making in the trade judiciary and the WTO.

NOTES

1. A. B. Wilson. "Thatcher Wouldn't Have Gone Wobbly on Detroit," *Wall Street Journal* (December 20, 2008).

2. K. Bagwell and R. W. Staiger, *The Economics of the World Trading System* (Cambridge, Mass.: MIT Press, 2002), 111–121.

3. It is worth remembering that economists played a similar role in the parallel financial negotiations to establish the International Monetary Fund and World Bank. At Bretton Woods, economists Harry Dexter White (U.S.) and John Maynard Keynes (UK) dominated negotiations.

4. Jan Tinbergen of the Netherlands shared the first Nobel Prize in economics (1969) for his work in dynamic modeling of economic processes. Supachai was one of his graduate students at the time.

5. R. Howse, "From Politics to Technocracy—and Back Again: The Fate of the Multilateral Trading Regime," *American Journal of International Law* 96 (2002), 94.

6. Author's review of biographical information for Eric Wyndham White, Olivier Long, Arthur Dunkel, Peter Sutherland, Renato Ruggiero, Mike Moore, Supachai Panitchpakdi, and Pascal Lamy.

7. Information obtained from WTO website, www.wto.org, regarding Alejandro Jara (Chile), Valentine Sendanyoye Rugwabiza (Rwanda), Harsha Vardhana Singh (India), and Rufus Yerxa (U.S.).

8. WTO, *Annual Report 2008*, 109.

9. C.P. Bown, "The WTO Secretariat and the Role of Economics in DSU Panels and Arbitrations," August 2008 version, 20, accessed April 2009 at http://graduateinstitute.ch/ webdav/site/ctei/shared/CTEI/events/workshop%20sanction/Bown-Secretariat-August-2008.pdf.

10. For further information on the WTO and its dispute settlement activities, see www.wto.gov/.

11. P. Van Den Bossche, *The Law and Policy of the World Trade Organization: Text, Cases and Materials*, 2nd ed. (New York: Cambridge University Press, 2008), 245.

12. www.wto.org/english/thewto_e/whatis_e/tif_e/disp1_e.htm#appeals.

13. P. D. Ehrenhaft, "The Role of Lawyers in the World Trade Organization," *Vanderbilt Journal of Transnational Law* 34(4) (2001), 963; M. D. Goldhaber, "Trade Warriors: In the Contest for World Supremacy at the WTO, It's Europe vs. America, Airbus vs. Boeing—and Wilmer vs. Sidley," *American Lawyer* (January 2006), accessed May 2009 at Factiva, Inc., http://factiva.com/index_i7_w.asp.

14. G. C. Shaffer, *Defending Interests: Public-Private Partnerships in WTO Litigation* (Washington, D.C.: Brookings, 2003), 48–50.

15. There is also an argument that WTO panels would benefit from the inclusion of scientists and technicians. See M. Iynedjian, "The Case for Incorporating Scientists and Technicians into WTO Panels," *Journal of World Trade* 42:2 (2008), 279–297.

16. Bown, "WTO Secretariat," 15, 18, 34.

17. A. Keck, "WTO Dispute Settlement: What Role for Economic Analysis? A Commentary of Fritz Breuss," *Journal of Industry, Competition and Trade* (2004), 365–371.

18. C. P. Bown and B. M. Hoekman. "WTO Dispute Settlement and the Missing Developing Country Cases: Engaging the Private Sector," *Journal of International Economic Law* 8:4 (2005), 861–890.

19. Advisory Centre on WTO Law, *The ACWL after Four Years: A Progress Report by the Management Board* (October 5, 2005), accessed April 2009 at www.acwl.ch/e/tools/doc_e.aspx.

20. Advisory Centre on WTO Law, *Report on Operations 2008*, accessed April 2009 at www.acwl.ch/pdf/Oper_2008.pdf.

21. Bown and Hoekman, "WTO Dispute Settlement," 876.

22. www.ileap-jeicp.org/publications/index.html.

23. For further information on the WCO, see www.wcoomd.org/.

24. "European Communities—Customs Classification of Frozen Boneless Chicken Cuts—Complaint by Thailand," WTO dispute panel, report adopted September 27, 2005, WT/DS269, available at www.wto.org/english/tratop_e/dispu_e/cases_e/ds286_e.htm.

25. For additional information on customs administration, see World Bank, *Customs Modernization Handbook* (Washington, D.C.: World Bank, 2004), and M. Keen, ed., *Changing Customs* (Washington, D.C.: IMF, 2003), see www.imf.org/external/pubs/nft/2003/customs/index.htm.

26. For additional information, see www.wipo.int/.

27. P. Salmon, "Globalization's Impact on International Trade and Intellectual Property Law: Cooperation between WIPO and the WTO," *St. John's Journal of Legal Commentary* 17 (2003), 429.

28. WIPO, *An Overview* (2010). Accessed October 2010 at www.wipo.int/.

29. USTR budget and personnel data from www.whitehouse.gov/omb/budget/fy2010/assets/eop.pdf.

30. For discussion of USTR's enforcement activities, see *President's Annual Report on the Trade Agreements Program.* Accessed April 2009 at www.ustr.gov/Document_Library/Reports_Publications/2009/2009_Trade_Policy_Agenda/Section_Index.html.

31. Author's review of USTR biographical information from *Washington Post, New York Times*, and other news sources.

32. Shaffer, *Defending Interests*, 120–121.

33. S. Dryden, *Trade Warriors: USTR and the American Crusade for Free Trade* (New York: Oxford University Press, 1995), 69–70, 106–107, 191.

34. Shaffer, *Defending Interests*, 25.

35. USTR, *2009 President's Trade Policy Agenda and 2008 Annual Report*, 231–233. See www.ustr.gov/assets/Document_Library/Reports_Publications/2009/2009_Trade_Policy_Agenda/asset_upload_file86_15410.pdf. For further information on USTR, see www.ustr.gov/.

36. For detailed information on the export control program, see www.bis.doc.gov/. For links to other agencies and departments with export control responsibilities, see www.bis.doc.gov/about/reslinks.htm. Commerce Department budget and personnel data from www.whitehouse.gov/omb/budget/fy2010/assets/com.pdf.

37. For more information on ITA's Import Administration, see http://trade.gov/ia/index.asp.

38. Valerie A. Slater and Jarrod M. Goldfeder. "'Show Me the Money': A Practitioner's Guide to the Intersection of Customs and AD/CVD Law," *University of Pennsylvania Journal of International Economic Law* 28:1 (2007), 51. See also WTO, "United States—Continued Existence and Application of Zeroing Methodology." WTO dispute panel, report adopted June 2, 2009, DS350, available at www.wto.org/english/tratop_e/dispu_e/cases_e/ds350_e.htm.

39. Wendy L. Hansen, Renee J. Johnson, and Isaac Unah, "Specialized Courts, Bureaucratic Agencies, and the Politics of U.S. Trade Policy," *American Journal of Political Science* 39:3 (August 1995), 529–557, and Isaac Unah, "Specialized Courts of Appeals' Review of Bureaucratic Actions and the Politics of Protectionism," *Political Research Quarterly* 50:4 (December 1997), 851–878.

40. Wendy L. Hansen and Kee Ok Park, "Nation-State and Pluralistic Decision Making in Trade Policy: The Case of the International Trade Administration," *International Studies Quarterly* 39 (1995), 207.

41. For more information on Commerce's market access and compliance, see http://trade.gov/mac/index.asp.

42. See http://tcc.export.gov/Trade_Agreements/index.asp.

43. For more information on the Patent and Trademark Office, see www.uspto.gov/main/policy.htm.

44. For further information on the U.S. Department of Commerce and its activities, see www.commerce.gov/.

45. www.whitehouse.gov/omb/budget/fy2010/assets/dhs.pdf.

46. See www.cbp.gov/xp/cgov/trade/priority_trade/.

47. See I. Simpson, *The Life of Adam Smith* (Oxford: Clarendon Press, 1995), 320–333, quotation 333.

48. For further information, see www.fas.usda.gov/ustrade.asp/.

49. See www.fda.gov/.

50. See www.doleta.gov/tradeact/.

51. Several others with academic credentials have held the post—including Joan E. Spero, Richard McCormack, and Alan Philip Larson. For further information, see www.state.gov/e/eeb/index.htm#.

52. U.S. International Trade Commission budget and personnel data from www.whitehouse.gov/omb/budget/fy2010/assets/oia.pdf.

53. *19 USC 1677.*

54. *Altx, Inc., v. United States*, 370 F.3d 1108, *Altx, Inc., v. United States*, 26 C.I.T. 1425.

55. Unah, "Specialized Courts," 851, 871.

56. L. J. White, "Economics, Economists, and Antitrust: A Tale of Growing Influence," www.aeaweb.org/annual_mtg_papers/2008/2008_180.pdf. White's article traces the rising influence of Ph.D. level economists in the Federal Trade Commission and the Justice Department's Antitrust Division. Also, in the 1980s the FTC had its first commissioners who were Ph.D. economists.

57. J. P. Durling and M. P. McCullough, "Teaching Old Laws New Tricks: The Legal Obligation of Non-attribution and the Need for Economic Rigor in Injury Analyses under U.S. Trade Law," in *Handbook of International Trade*, edited by E. K. Choi and J. C. Hartigan (Oxford: Blackwell, 2005), 95–96.

58. U.S. House of Representatives, Committee on Appropriations, *Departments of Commerce, Justice, and State, the Judiciary, and Related Agencies Appropriations Bill, Fiscal Year 2001*, 106th Cong., 2nd sess., House Report 106–680.

59. J. M. Devault, "Economics and the International Trade Commission," *Southern Economic Journal* 60:2 (1993), 476–477.

60. Author's research using *U.S. Government Manual*, various issues.

61. Robert H. Nelson, an Interior Department economist, has observed that economists in government must "tailor their advocacy" to the "political environment in which they work." See R. H. Nelson, "The Economics Profession and the Making of Public Policy," *Journal of Economic Literature* 25:1 (1987), 41–91, especially 50.

62. For information about the court, see www.cit.uscourts.gov/.

63. J. A. Restani, "A Special Year in the Life of the United States Court of International Trade," *Georgetown Journal of International Law* 38 (2006–7), 1.

64. S.M. Rosen and G. Husisian, "Judicial Review by the U.S. Court of International Trade and the U.S. Court of Appeals for the Federal Circuit under 19 U.S.C 1581(c) of Antidumping and Countervailing Duty Determinations Issued by the Department of Commerce," *Georgetown Journal of International Law* 38 (2006–7), 11.

65. See *Maverick Tube v. United States* 12 C.I.T. 444 (May 1988).

66. Hansen, Johnson, and Unah, "Specialized Courts, Bureaucratic Agencies," 529–557.

67. For information about this court, see www.cafc.uscourts.gov/.

68. *Altx, Inc., v. United States*, 370 F.3d 1108.

69. Unah, "Specialized Courts," 872.

70. For additional information see www.international.gc.ca/commerce/index.aspx.

71. www.wto.org/english/tratop_e/dispu_e/dispu_by_country_e.htm. Accessed May 2009.

72. www.citt.gc.ca/biographies/index_e.asp.

73. V. Stevens, "The Political Economy of Anti-dumping in Canada: Section 45 of the Special Import Measures Act," *University of Toronto Faculty of Law Review* 64:1 (2006), 1–44.

74. For more information on the Canada Border Services Agency, see www.cbsa. gc.ca/.

75. S. McBride, "Quiet Constitutionalism in Canada: The International Policy Economy of Domestic Institutional Change," *Canadian Journal of Political Science* 36:2 (2003), 251–273.

76. World Trade Organization. See www.wto.org/english/tratop_e/dispu_e/dispu_by_country_e.htm.

77. G. Shaffer, "What's New in EU Trade Dispute Settlement? Judicialization, Public-Private Networks and the WTO Legal Order," *Journal of European Public Policy* 13:6 (2006) 836–837.

78. Shaffer, *Defending Interests*, 116–118.

79. Shaffer, "What's New in EU Trade Dispute Settlement?," 844. See also Goldhaber, "Trade Warriors."

80. My data taken from *EU Staff Directory*. Accessed May 2009 at http://ec.europa. eu/staffdir/plsql/gsys_page.display_index?pLang=EN. In a 2003 study Shaffer reported sixteen lawyers in two EU directorates primarily focused on WTO matters. In addition, lawyers in other directorates monitored WTO activities impacting their responsibilities, *Defending Interests*, 121.

81. http://ec.europa.eu/.

82. S. M. Pekkanen, "Aggressive Legalism: The Rules of the WTO and Japan's Emerging Trade Strategy," *World Economy* 24 (2001), 732; also S. M. Pekkanen, *Japan's Aggressive Legalism: Law and Foreign Trade Politics beyond the WTO* (Stanford, Calif.: Stanford University Press, 2008).

83. K. Iida, *Legalization and Japan: The Politics of WTO Dispute Settlement* (London: Cameron May, 2006), 9–12, 41–42.

84. USTR, *2009 National Trade Estimate Report on Foreign Trade Barriers* (Washington, D.C.: USTR, 2009), 270, accessed August 2009 at www.ustr.gov/.

85. www.wto.org/english/tratop_e/dispu_e/appellate_body_e.htm.

86. www.wto.org/english/tratop_e/dispu_by_country_e.htm.

87. G. Shaffer, "How to Make the WTO Dispute System Work for Developing Countries," in *Toward a Development-Supportive Dispute Settlement System in the WTO* (Geneva: International Centre for Trade and Sustainable Development, March 2003), 14–16. See also "United States—Standards for Reformulated and Conventional Gasoline," DS2, WTO, www.wto.org/english/tratop_e/dispu_e/cases_e/ds2_e.htm.

88. G. Shaffer, M. R. Sanchez, and B. Rosenberg, "Winning at the WTO: What Lies behind Brazil's Success?" *Cornell International Law Journal* 41:2 (2008), 383.

89. Ibid., 457–558.

90. Ibid., 460; on the claims of unethical conduct, see P. Blustein, "In U.S., Cotton Cries Betrayal," *Washington Post* (May 12, 2004). Accessed May 2009, Lexis Nexis Academic.

91. Shaffer, Sanchez, and Rosenberg, "Winning at the WTO," 461.

92. D. A. Gantz, "Doi Moi, the VBTA and WTO Accessions: The Role of Lawyers in Vietnam's No Longer Cautious Embrace of Globalization," *International Lawyer* 41:3 (2007), 873. See also Sidley Austin, LLP, press release, www.sidley.com/64/s1148/newsre-sources/newsandpress/Detail.aspx?news=3922.

93. wwwsidley.com/internationaltrade/, accessed May 2009.

94. Chambers and Partners, "International Trade/WTO: Global," accessed May 2009 at www.chambersandpartners.com/Editorial.aspx?ssid=30626.

95. Troutman Sanders, "International Practice Group 2008," 15–17, accessed May 2009 at www.troutmansanders.com/.

96. www.millerchevalier.com/tradepolicywtoandmarketaccess/.

97. Accessed May 2009 at www.ghorlick.com/ghorlick/.

98. A. E. Eckes, Jr., *Opening America's Market* (Chapel Hill: University of North Carolina Press, 1995), 257–277; E. L. Stewart, "Existing Remedies and the Trade Deficit: The Promise of Reform through Judicial Review," *New York University Journal of International Law and Policy* (1985–86), 1166–1188.

99. P. Ehrenhaft, "The 'Judicialization' of Trade Law," *Notre Dame Law Review* 56 (1980–81), 595–613.

100. A. F. Lowenfeld, *International Economic Law* (New York: Oxford University Press, 2002), 8.

101. J. H. Jackson and W. J. Davey, *Legal Problems of International Economic Relations*, 2nd ed. (St. Paul, MN: West, 1986), 10.

102. S. Beaulier, W. J. Boyes, and W. S. Mounts, "The Influence of Economists on Public Attitudes toward Government," *American Economist* 52:2 (2008), 68, 70. See also Nelson, "Economics Profession," 41–91.

103. H. K. Nordstrom and G. Shaffer, "Access to Justice in the World Trade Organization: A Case for a Small Claims Procedure?," *World Trade Review* 7:4 (2008), 588; Bown and Hoekman, "WTO Dispute Settlement," 870; Shaffer, "What's New in EU Trade Dispute Settlement," 844.

104. J. Greenwald and P. A. Clarke, "An Overview of Trade Remedy Law," in T. C. Brightbill, L. S. Chang, and P. A. Clarke, eds., *Trade Remedies for Global Companies* (Chicago: Section of International Law, ABA, 2006), 21; Shaffer, *Defending Interests*, 120.

105. Accessed May 2009 at www.martindale.com/.

106. Shaffer reported 2,100 individuals registered as trade lawyers in Washington, D.C., *Defending Interests*, 120.

107. In 2007 the *American Lawyer* reported that the 100 largest U.S. law firms had revenues of $64.5 billion. See Aric Press and John O'Connor, "Lessons of the Am Law 100," *American Lawyer* 30:50 (May 1, 2008), 131. The Commerce Department reported that exports of all legal services, not simply trade-related work, amounted to $6.4 billion in 2007, or about 10% of the largest firms' revenue. See U.S. Bureau of Economic Analysis, *Survey of Current Business* (October 2008), 38–39. This sum may well understate the overall significance of international trade in legal services. It does not take into account the sales of legal services by foreign affiliates of U.S. law firms.

108. For one imaginative suggestion, see Nordstrom and Shaffer, "Access to Justice in the World Trade Organization." They suggest that a small claims procedure might enable countries with small trading stakes to pursue claims at less expense, perhaps without the need for legal counsel.

109. Accessed at www.william-shakespeare.info/act4-script-text-henry-vi-part2.htm.

CHAPTER 4

TRADE AND THE LABOR MARKET: RECENT DEVELOPMENTS AND NEW FRONTIERS

CARL DAVIDSON AND NICHOLAS SLY

THE pure theory of international economics emphasizes that differences create opportunities for trade and that such trade has distributional consequences. Traditional trade theory, as embodied by the Ricaro-Viner (Specific Factors) and Heckscher-Ohlin-Samuelson (HOS) models, focuses on differences across countries (e.g., in technologies, factor endowments, and factor mobility) and across sectors (e.g., in the factor intensities of production) as the sources of trading opportunities. "New trade theory" emphasizes that there are important differences within an industry as well. The assumption of perfect competition in the product market has been abandoned in favor of more sophisticated models of monopolistic competition in which firms produce differentiated products and the variety of goods offered for sale directly effects consumer satisfaction. While these new models were primarily developed to explain intraindustry trade, they have also resulted in a rich body of predictions linking globalization to price-cost markups, firm sizes, export behavior, and productivity (both at the firm and industry levels). Moreover, availability of new firm-level and plant-level data has allowed for tests of these predictions as well as the establishment of a wide variety of new "stylized facts" concerning the evolution of industrial structures in dynamic open economies. Attempts to explain these stylized facts have forced trade theorists to extend their models even further with the introduction of firm-side heterogeneity (in terms of costs or productivity), now viewed as an essential component.

Perhaps inspired by the work on firm heterogeneity, a new literature has started to emerge that underscores the role that worker heterogeneity plays for a variety of trade issues. New models that allow for nontrivial distributions of talent (or skills) across the workforce have been developed, and they have raised a whole host of new and interesting questions. Our goal in this chapter is to survey this emerging literature, highlight a few of the more intriguing issues that have been addressed, and suggest some avenues that we believe are ripe for further investigation.

The idea that the distribution of talent has important consequences both at the micro and macro level is certainly not new—see, for example, the seminal contributions of Rosen (1981) and Murphy, Schleifer, and Visnhy (1991). There is also substantial evidence that the distribution varies considerably across countries, suggesting that this might have important implications for international trade. If we assume that worker skills are tied to educational attainment, we can look to Barro and Lee (1993, 1996, 2001) and the OECD (1998) for rough estimates of the distribution of skills across countries. Both of these studies break workers over the age of 25 into groups based on the highest level of education attained. Barro and Lee use four categories: no school or primary, partial secondary, full secondary, and tertiary; whereas the OECD uses three: below upper secondary, upper secondary, and tertiary.[1] Table 4.1 provides the estimates for seven countries,[2] grouped together based on their aggregate endowments (as measured by the average years of schooling over the population).

As the table clearly indicates, the distribution of schooling varies considerably across these populations. To be more precise, focus on the Barro and Lee estimates, use the heading "unskilled labor" to refer to the workers in the first category, and then use low-skilled, medium-skilled, and high-skilled for the remaining groups. Turn first to the first three countries listed in the table: Canada, New Zealand, and Sweden. All three have populations with roughly 11.2 years of schooling per worker, but the three clearly have different distributions of educational attainment. Canada has a large stock of highly skilled workers, with the remaining workers distributed

Table 4.1. Barro-Lee and OECD estimates of educational attainment in 1995

	Barro-Lee estimates				OECD estimates			
	No school or primary	Second-ary partial	Second-ary full	Tertiary	Average years of school	Below upper secondary	Upper second-ary	Tertiary
Canada	22	16	13	49	11.2	25	28	47
New Zealand	34	18	9	39	11.3	41	34	25
Sweden	20	15	44	21	11.2	25	46	28
Australia	27	28	21	24	10.3	47	29	24
Switzerland	31	24	31	15	10.2	18	61	21
Denmark	34	8	39	19	9.9	38	42	20
Finland	31	14	35	19	9.8	35	45	21

almost uniformly over the remaining categories. New Zealand has large stocks of unskilled and highly skilled workers but very few workers with low or moderate skills. Finally, Sweden has a large stock of workers with moderate skills, with the remainder of its workforce split roughly evenly over the remaining categories. A similar picture emerges if one focuses on the OECD estimates for these countries or if one looks at the second group of countries listed in the table. Note that Australia and Switzerland have distributions that are almost uniform across all categories, while Denmark and Finland have workforces that are dominated by unskilled and moderately skilled workers.[3]

Variation in the distribution of skills across countries raises new issues about international trade and forces us to reconsider traditional insights. For the purposes of this review, we will concentrate on the relationship that trade has with how the talents of individual workers interact with each other, and with the technologies that firms use. We begin in section 2 by considering a set of articles similar to traditional trade theory, in that product markets are assumed to be perfectly competitive, all firms within an industry are assumed to be identical, and industries differ in the manner in which workers' skills are used in the production process. The key questions that must be addressed are how the market sorts heterogeneous workers across the sectors of the economy and how trade alters that sorting. In section 3 we turn to models that allow for heterogeneous firms within an industry. The sorting problem then changes, with workers and firms within the same industry seeking appropriate matches.

For the most part, the articles surveyed in sections 2 and 3 tend to focus on the manner in which the talents of a worker mesh with the skill requirements of the technologies that firms use. However, some of these articles also allow for team production, where the ability to combine the talents of several workers become important. In section 4, we focus our attention on models that explicitly highlight the role of team production in the presence of a heterogeneous workforce. The central issues that must then be addressed are how teams are formed and how globalization and the labor market integration that comes with it affect the composition of teams.

When workers produce in teams, the organization of production becomes vitally important. There is a large and growing literature on organization and trade, both theoretical and empirical, and we will make no attempt to survey that literature here.[4] Instead, we will point to a few of the more interesting empirical results that are relevant for our discussion of the relatively small number of articles on trade and organization that explicitly allow for a diversity of talent.

At an aggregate level, the last two decades have seen polarization of the workforce in both the United States (Autor, Katz, and Karney 2006) and in Europe (Goos, Manning, and Salomons 2009). High-skill and low-skill tasks account for larger employment shares than observed 20 years previously, while middle-skill jobs have been disappearing. These changes in labor demand are linked strongly with the dynamics in wage distributions. Given the definition of tasks according to skill content, examining the role of trade in this trend (if any) requires theories that incorporate labor heterogeneity.

Looking at skill compositions of specific firms, Bernard and Jensen (1999) find that exporting firms in the United States use a larger share of nonproduction workers (a crude measure of skill). Cunat and Guadalupe (2009) observe that intensified trade competition increases the demand for talent among U.S. firms. Similar patterns arise in developing countries. Fernandes (2007) finds higher demands for skill among Colombian exporters. Furthermore, reallocation of skilled workers appears to be a key source of productivity gains following Colombian trade reform. As for the specific role of skill in exporting firms, Verhoogen (2008) shows that a higher-skilled workforce produces and exports products with relatively higher quality. Guadalupe and Wulf (2009) examine the structure of teams within firms and show that trade competition tends to "flatten" firms by reducing the number of levels between the upper and lower echelons of management. In short, the composition of the skilled workforce across exporting and nonexporting firms is a dynamic and crucial feature of trade.

The link between skill composition and production in open economies is well established. Less clear is the link between skill composition and labor market outcomes in open economies. Burstein and Vogel (2010) compare the within- and across-industry relationship between trade, skills, and wages. In particular they demonstrate that the *within*-industry effect of trade in raising wage inequality across all countries dominates the *between*-industry effect of trade on wages that reduces (increases) wage inequality in skill-scarce (-abundant) countries. Focusing squarely on firms, Frias, Kaplan, and Verhoogen (2009) explore changes in wage structures in Mexican firms during the peso crisis in the mid-1990s. Looking at average wages paid by firms in *levels*, they find that skill composition explains approximately one-third of the higher wages paid by large exporters. However, looking at *changes* in average wages as firms alter their export behavior, they find no relationship to changes in skill composition. Regardless, they reject the possibility of competitive wages. Workers earn rents based on the firm and other workers they are matched with. This suggests that modeling imperfections in the labor market may be a key step to gaining an understanding of how labor markets with heterogeneous workers adjust to globalization. We take up this issue below, when we summarize two contributions that add search frictions to models with heterogeneous workers.

1. SORTING ACROSS INDUSTRIES

The first article to emphasize the importance of talent diversity across populations for trade is Grossman and Maggi (2000).[5] Working with a traditional competitive framework, they consider an economy in which workers differ in human capital and countries differ in the distribution of human capital across their populations. They also assume that the technologies used to produce different goods vary in the manner in which workers with different talents interact—thus, there is team production. For some goods, workers with different skill levels are complementary—they each perform different tasks, and since each task is vital for the production of the good, the production process "is only as strong as its weakest link." In this case, production is said to be *supermodular*, so that the marginal return to talent of an individual worker is increasing in the skill of her partner. Grossman and Maggi point to any complicated manufacturing process, such as O-ring production, as a prime example of supermodularity, because failure at any stage of the production process destroys the value of the good (see also Kremer 1993).

In contrast, other goods are produced using a technology in which the talents of workers are substitutable for each other. This implies that production will be roughly tied to the productivity of the most talented worker engaged in the production process. In this case, production is said to be *submodular*. The authors' motivating example of submodularity is software programming, since it only takes a breakthrough by one of the engineers working on a project to achieve success.

When both types of goods are produced, efficiency dictates that similar workers form teams in the supermodular sector (so that high-productivity workers do no suffer from inept partners) whereas workers should be crossmatched in the submodular sector (so that no high-productivity worker's talent will be wasted). Although they generate several interesting results, the one we will highlight is that in a two-good world, the country with the *more diverse* talent base will have a comparative advantage in the good that is characterized by crossmatching. The logic is based on the fact that the country with the more diverse talent base has more workers with extreme productivity measures, and their low-productivity workers can be swept under the rug by pairing them in the submodular sector with those workers with extremely high-productivity measures. Moreover, since trade expands that sector, it is the workers with extreme productivity measures, those at the top and bottom of the wage distribution, who gain from trade, while those with moderate productivity are harmed. These wage effects are unlike anything that arises in traditional trade models and are generated by the interaction of heterogeneity in worker ability and differences in the substitutability of worker talents across industries.

Grossman and Maggi close their article by considering what happens if talent is imperfectly observable and show that even though this leads to imperfect matching, their results with respect to comparative advantage are strengthened. Grossman (2004) picks up on this theme by considering a model in which worker ability is private information that can be observed to varying degrees based on the type of production process the worker is engaged in. Production processes such as large-scale manufacturing require work in teams, which makes it difficult to ascertain the skill level of each particular team member. In such sectors, compensation will be tied to team production, which makes that type of employment unattractive to highly skilled workers. In contrast, there are other production processes in which individual contributions play a key role. Examples of this can be found in the service sector, where attorneys, financial advisors, and doctors often work independently, and in high-tech industries, where the productivities of individual engineers and managers are often easy to observe. Sectors that value individual contributions will be attractive to highly skilled workers, since they will not only be compensated for their talents but also will be able to signal their productivity to outsiders and thereby increase their bargaining power. Grossman shows that when countries differ in their distributions of talents across workers, the country with the more heterogeneous workforce will have a comparative advantage in the sector in which individual productivity is easier to discern. Moreover, since trade expands that sector, trade will tend to exacerbate inequality by pushing up the incomes of the country's most talented workers.

In a related article, Bougheas and Riezman (2007) use a two-good, two-country model to focus on the impact of trade on inequality in the presence of labor-market heterogeneity. In their article, the two goods are produced in a primary sector, where all workers are equally productive, and a high-tech sector, where productivity is positively related to the worker's endowment of human capital. Workers differ in human capital, and the *only* difference between the countries (A and B) is between their distributions of human capital. There is no team production, and human capital is observable, which differs from the setup of Grossman and Maggi (2000) and Grossman (2000). They show that *any* difference in the distribution of human capital is sufficient to generate trade.

With respect to specific trade patterns, Bougheas and Riezman produce two results. First, if country B has a distribution that dominates country A's in the sense of first order stochastic dominance, then trade patterns will be consistent with Heckscher-Ohlin, in that country B will export the human-capital-intensive good. Second, if country A's distribution is more diverse than country B's (in the usual Rothschild-Stiglitz sense) and the demand for one good is sufficiently strong, then country B will export that good. This second result is an artifact of the assumption that human capital plays no role in the primary sector.

To see this, note that if we fix primary-sector output, country A will have greater production in the high-tech sector than country B. This is because country A has more workers with high measures of human capital, which increases the production of the high-tech good. The fact that they also have more workers with low measures of human capital is not costly, since those workers are employed in the primary sector where human capital plays no role. Thus, with no other differences between countries, the PPF in country A is a radial expansion of country B's PPF, implying that preferences help determine the pattern of trade. With respect to inequality, Bougheas and Riezman show that trade increases inequality in the country that exports the human-capital-intensive product and reduces inequality in the other country and that trade can lower aggregate welfare in a country in which inequality rises and marginal utility is decreasing in income. Thus, the basic message of Bougheas and Riezman is similar to that of Grossman and Maggi (2000) and Grossman (2004): the distribution of talent matters for trade issues, particularly in North-North trading relationships in which the aggregate endowments are similar.

In the articles we have discussed so far, workers differ in one attribute and, while countries have identical aggregate endowments of labor, workers differ in their distribution of talent. Ohnsorge and Trefler (2007) develop a framework that is similar, in that workers are heterogeneous in the talents that they offer, but these authors make an attempt to place the analysis firmly in a traditional trade setting by adopting many of the features of the HOS model. In particular, they assume that countries face identical technologies but differ in factor endowments and that all factors are perfectly mobile across sectors.

With respect to workers, it is now assumed that each one has two attributes that are important for production (e.g., problem solving and communication skills). Industries differ in their skills requirements, and workers sort across industries based on their comparative advantage—that is, they take the job that pays them the most for their particular bundle of skills.[6] Ohnsorge and Trefler show that this model is much more powerful than either the HOS or Ricardo-Viner model, providing sharper predictions about trade patterns, the demand for protection, and the link between trade and the distribution of income. One key result is that the correlation between the workers' two attributes plays a critical role in shaping a country's comparative advantage and determining how trade affects income inequality within a country. Thus, just as in Grossman and Maggi (2000) and Grossman (2004), higher moments of the distribution of worker skills are critical for understanding the effects of trade.

The manner in which workers are matched to industries based on relative bundles of skill is, in many senses, much more satisfying than what takes places in traditional models such as HOS or Ricardo-Viner. Workers are free to sort into any industry; that is, as in a HOS framework, there is perfect factor mobility. However, workers choose to sort into specific industries based on the comparative advantage granted by their bundle of skills. This makes workers specific to sectors, as in Ricardo-Viner, but the ties to sectors arise endogenously; they are not assumed.

We can be more precise about Ohnsorge and Trefler's results by describing their framework in greater detail. Following their conventions, let H and L denote each of a worker's two skill levels, use T (H,L) to denote the worker's marginal product, and assume that T($\bullet$) is subject to constant returns to scale. Then we can think of each worker's attributes as H/L (a measure of relative skills) and L (a measure of absolute skills). A worker with a high value for H/L will have a comparative advantage in H-intensive industries, while L will determine the worker's absolute advantage. One key parameter in the model is ρ, which measures the degree of correlation between relative ability (H/L) and total ability (L) across the population. While an increase in ρ does not affect the sorting behavior of workers, it does increase the measure of workers endowed with high level of both attributes.

Ohnsorge and Trefler derive "correlates" of the Rybczynski and Heckscher-Ohlin theorems, which predict that an increase in ρ leads to an increase in production and exports in industries that are H/L-intensive. These correlates indicate how the traditional intuition of the HOS model carries over to a world with multidimensional worker heterogeneity. However, their framework allows us to go beyond this and builds on the insights of Grossman and Maggi (2000) and Grossman (2004) by offering "variants" of Rybczynski and Heckscher-Ohlin that link inequality in endowments to the pattern of trade. To do so, they must first define "endowment inequality," which is a nontrivial issue when workers differ in more than one attribute. Based on their definition, an increase in endowment inequality occurs when the variances of H/L and L increase without altering their means or conditional means. If we order industries based on their H/L-intensity, then the Rybczynski and Heckscher-Ohlin "variants" predict that an increase in endowment inequality causes countries to export goods at the two extremes of the ordering. In other words, a country with greater endowment inequality will specialize in the goods produced in industries that have either high H/L-intensity or high L-intensity but produce less in industries ranked in the middle of the ordering.

Working with multidimensional heterogeneity creates technical difficulties that force Ohnsorge and Trefler to make a number of assumptions to keep the analysis tractable. One key assumption is that there is no teamwork between workers. As a result, dispersion in the individual attributes of a worker play no role in the Ohnsorge and Trefler's framework, while dispersion of talent alone was a source of comparative advantage in Grossman and Maggi. In this sense, the analyses should be viewed as complementary as opposed to competing.

Another simplifying assumption made by Ohnsorge and Trefler is that the joint distribution of worker attributes is multivariate normal. Together, individual production and multivariate normal distributions of ability provide descriptions of both the demand for attributes and the supply of attributes that allow for a tractable examination of trade with labor heterogeneity. Yet these are not necessary conditions for labor heterogeneity to influence trade patterns. A recent contribution by Costinot (2009) explores the general conditions under which trade patterns are determinant in a world with heterogeneous factors of production.

Costinot explains that the key to comparative advantage is a form of complementarity called "log-supermodularity." Considering production functions across industries, log-supermodularity implies that the marginal returns to worker ability are *relatively* increasing in the skill intensity of production methods.[7] This is stronger form of complementarity than supermodularity, in that it relates the marginal returns to ability across all skill levels. Considering factor supplies, log-supermodularity in the distribution of workers across countries implies that a skill-abundant country has *relatively* more high-ability workers. This definition corresponds to the well-known feature of monotone likelihood ratio dominance.[8]

When factor usages across sectors and factor supplies across countries satisfy log-supermodularity, and factors are perfectly substitutable within all sectors, then Costinot demonstrates that factor abundance generates a unique pattern of comparative advantage so that trade patterns are determinant in a world with labor heterogeneity. Furthermore, log-supermodularity of factor usages and factor supplies are minimally sufficient conditions for trade. As the literature moves forward, Costinot (2009) provides theoretical guidance on how economies must be structured for labor heterogeneity to play a systematic role in international markets.

Using the power of log-supermodularity to generate comparative advantage, Costinot and Vogel (2010) examine trade patterns and the distributional consequences of trade as a continuum of workers in each economy are assigned to a continuum of production tasks. Considering North-South trade, where the North is defined as being relatively skill abundant, international exchange leads to rising wage inequality and skill downgrading in the North, with falling wage inequality and skill upgrading in the South. These implications reflect traditional Stopler-Samuelson effects with continua of worker types and factor intensities. If the North is defined as a country using relatively more skill-intensive methods of production (i.e. skill-biased technology) then trade magnifies the skill bias in the North, via skill upgrading of tasks, and leads to skill downgrading in the South. One interesting feature of their analysis is that North-South trade based on the skill intensity in production reduces inequality in the North and raises inequality in the South. The intuition is that trade allows more individuals in the North to gain employment in tasks that rewards skill highly, with trade having the opposite implication for the South.

Even though countries appear similar in their aggregate endowments, Grossman and Maggi, Bougheas and Riezman, Ohnsorge and Trefler, and Cositnot and Vogel have demonstrated that higher moments alone can generate trade. In other words, differences in levels of diversity can lead to North-North trade. For example, Costinot and Vogel extend the implications of Grossman and Maggi to the case of a continuum of workers and show that North-North trade leads to skill upgrading of low-skill tasks, and skill downgrading of high-skill tasks within the relatively more diverse trading partner.

As the theoretical implications of labor diversity are beginning to be understood, a nascent empirical literature has emerged that evaluates the influence of higher moments of the labor distribution on trade. Sly (2011) builds a simple model where laborers perform intermediate tasks that are complementary in production. The model predicts that dispersion in labor endowments and the median skill level across countries jointly influence factor productivity as heterogeneous workers sort across tasks and industries. He the examines factor trade between OECD countries (i.e. North-North) empirically to assess the role of labor heterogeneity. Consistent with the predictions of the model, in countries with high median ability, dispersion erodes the comparative advantage implied by factor abundance, while in countries with low median ability, dispersion amplifies comparative advantage implied by factor endowments and thus influences trade patterns between developed countries. In addition, Bombardini, Gallipoli, and Pupato (2011) show that trade patterns reflect the level of diversity in labor endowments in a multisector version of Grossman and Maggi.[9]

The articles discussed in this section have incorporated labor heterogeneity into traditional theories of interindustry trade. As has long been recognized, much of world trade occurs within sectors. The next section discusses the allocation of heterogeneous workers within sectors and its interaction with international market opportunities.

2. SORTING WITHIN AN INDUSTRY

While the papers surveyed in section 2 highlight the importance of labor market heterogeneity for understanding trade issues, they all assume that firms within an industry are identical. The empirical work of the late 1990s, primarily motivated by studies such as Bernard and Jensen (1995, 1997, 1999) and Roberts and Tybout (1997), made it clear that this assumption is counterfactual with respect to firm participation in international markets. Moreover, these studies emphasized the importance of taking firm heterogeneity into account in order to explain how product markets adjust to globalization. The theoretical work that stemmed from Melitz (2003) gave us a better understanding of these adjustment processes and demonstrated that firm heterogeneity could be included in models without sacrificing tractability. However, the vast majority of the work on trade with heterogeneous firms assumes that labor markets are perfectly competitive and that they are populated by identical workers.

Matters get far more complicated and interesting when heterogeneous firms within the same industry face a workforce with diversity in skills and/or ability. When there is heterogeneity on both sides of the labor market, one must be concerned about the types of matches that are generated—should the most productive workers be matched with the most efficient firms? Or would it be more efficient to pair together low-productivity workers and high-productivity firms? This is an issue that has been studied in labor economics (where it is known as an assignment problem; see Sattinger 1975, 1993), the literature on the economics of marriage (Becker 1973), and search theory (Legros and Newman 2002 and Shimer and Smith 2000). If production is supermodular, then positive assortative matching, in which good workers are paired with good firms, is optimal. If wages are determined in a competitive market, then a supermodular production function is sufficient for equilibrium matches to be positively assorted. However, in the case where wages are bargained at the individual level and there are no side payments (i.e. nontransferable utility), then Legros and Newman (2007) demonstrate that the individual payoffs to both parties, as opposed to simply the joint surplus, must exhibit complementarities in order for positive assortative matching to occur in equilibrium.[10]

Yeaple (2005) provides a simple examination of trade and worker heterogeneity. Firms in the same monopolistically competitive industry must choose which type of technology to implement. Firms are ex ante identical but can choose between two technologies to produce their differentiated products. The better (or more sophisticated) technology is more costly to adopt but allows for the potential to achieve positive exporting profits. Thus, equilibria exist in which firms choose to adopt

different technologies, with a firm-indifference condition determining the proportion of firms that adopt the more sophisticated technology. Yeaple assumes that
worker ability and technologies exhibit complementarities and that labor markets
are perfectly competitive. As a result, the best workers are employed by exporting
firms using low-marginal-cost technologies.[11]

It is worth noting that Yeaple's approach to firm heterogeneity differs from that
of Melitz (2003). In Melitz, workers are identical, and firm heterogeneity is driven
by exogenous random draws on firm productivity. In Yeaple, a diversity of talent in
the workforce provides a rationale for ex ante identical firms to make different
decisions with respect to technology. Some firms choose to pay the high cost of in-
stalling a sophisticated technology, while others adopt a cheaper basic technology.
The high-tech firms recruit more productive workers and pay higher wages, but
because their workforce is more highly skilled, they produce more and have an
easier time covering the fixed cost of exporting. The extra profits they earn from
exporting are just enough to cover their higher production costs. Thus, firm heterogeneity arises endogenously, and this allows Yeaple to examine how the degree of
heterogeneity varies with transport costs.

One of Yeaple's main goals is to show that his model can explain many of the
stylized facts that motivated the new literature of firm-level adjustment to globalization. For example, he shows that a reduction in trade costs increases the incentives
for firms to adopt the more sophisticated technology. This causes market share reallocation with the more productive firms expanding as the weaker firms contract.
Since the better firms employ more highly skilled workers, this increases the demand
for the most talented workers and pushes up their wages. In addition, since more
firms are now using the sophisticated technology, the reduction in transport costs
causes the average productivity of labor employed in the industry to rise.

In Yeaple's framework, gains from trade arise because of traditional selection,
variety, and scale effects. However, with competitive wages, frictionless labor markets, and individual production (i.e., there are no teams), trade liberalization has no
effect on the matching pattern between workers and firms at the intensive margin.
As transport costs fall, the best workers remain matched with firms offering complementary production modes. All the action takes place at the extensive margin, with
more firms adopting the best technology available. Thus, the only new avenue for
gains from trade is that a greater share of the workforce has an opportunity to use
complementary production modes. However, one can easily imagine that with heterogeneity in both production modes and labor ability, there are potential gains
along the intensive margin if trade can improve any mismatches that arise when
labor markets have frictions, are segmented, or if wages are not set competitively.
This is a particularly intriguing question in light of the recent evidence that wages
paid in international markets are not competitive (see the discussion of Frias, Kaplan,
and Verhoogen, 2009, at the end of the first section) and that matching in labor markets is not perfect (see, for example, the articles discussed in Lopes de Melo 2009).[12]

One article that deviates from frictionless labor markets and includes both
worker and firm heterogeneity is Davidson, Matusz, and Shevchenko (2008). As in

Yeaple, workers differ in skill and are hired to manage production processes with different productivities. Firms produce homogeneous goods but differ in the technologies they choose to adopt. Labor markets are imperfect in that it takes time and effort for unemployed workers and firms with vacancies to find each other. Firms can elect to use a modern production process, but this requires them to recruit a high-skilled manager and pay a high wage. Alternatively, they can use a basic production process, which can be managed by any worker and pay a lower managerial wage. In equilibrium, firms of both types coexist and earn the same profits. The firms that use the modern technology have a harder time filling their managerial vacancy and must pay a higher wage rate, but once the vacancy is filled, they produce more output.

Given the assumptions made about the production process, positive assortative matching would be efficient—that is, highly skilled managers *should* be paired with those firms that adopt the modern technology. However, with search required to find a job, some high-skilled workers may wind up employed by low-tech firms. This occurs if the gap in the revenues earned by the two types of firms is not too large. If this is the case, then the compensation that the two types of firms can offer high-skilled workers will be sufficiently close, and it will be optimal for high-skilled workers to accept the first job they are offered. Thus, some high-skilled workers will be underemployed in equilibrium.

Davidson, Matusz, and Shevchenko focus on how international trade affects the degree of underemployment. As in any model of trade with heterogeneous firms, it is the firms that adopt the modern technology (the most productive firms) that have the greatest access to international markets. If these firms compete in an export-oriented market, then as trade costs fall, the most productive firms will benefit relatively more with even greater access to foreign markets. This will widen the gap between the revenues earned by the two types of firms and make it *more difficult* for low-tech firms to attract high-skilled workers. As a result, globalization increases the degree of positive assortative matching in an export-oriented market. This can be viewed as another source of gains from trade.

In contrast, if the good is sold in an import-competing industry, globalization decreases the degree of positive assortative matching. In this case, as trade costs fall, import penetration rises, pushing down the (common) domestic price for the good. Since this price is applied to a larger stock of output for high-tech firms, they are harmed more by this change than their low-tech counterparts. As a result, the gap in revenues earned by the two types of firms shrinks, making it *easier* for low-tech firms to attract high-skilled workers. The increase in underemployment that follows can be viewed as another cost of globalization.

This section has reviewed a short but potentially rich literature that examines worker heterogeneity and trade when the allocation problem each economy must solve is to match workers with technologies. Within the boundaries of firms, workers often cooperate through team production. The next section discusses how globalization influences team formation between heterogeneous workers, both within and across borders.

3. Team Formation and Trade

A traditional view of trade is that countries produce domestically and exchange final goods on international markets. However, two recent contributions from Kremer and Maskin (2006) and Antràs, Garicano, and Rossi-Hansberg (2006) consider the possibility of production in teams within and across borders. They each take a view of globalization as integrating labor markets through offshoring, facilitating trade in intermediate goods/services. With this perspective, they consider improvements in team formation across countries with different distributions of ability that arise due to globalization.

Kremer and Maskin (2006) take a simple approach in an attempt to address failures of traditional trade theories to predict observed changes in wage inequality and trade volumes between countries. In particular, they begin their article by pointing out that traditional models predict that bilateral trade will be highest among countries that are vastly different, with little or no trade between similar countries, and that such models also tend to predict that if trade increases inequality in one country (usually the rich country) it is likely to lower inequality in the economy of its trading partner (a poor country). They then survey a large amount of empirical evidence that runs counter to these predictions. Their goal is to provide a model in which changes in the organization of production can provide explanations for the stylized facts.

Kremer and Maskin assume that there are two tasks in the production process: a managerial task and an assistant's task, with the managerial task being relatively skill intensive. A firm's output is then determined by the skill of the two workers assigned to these tasks. In particular, production is given by H^2L, where H is the skill of the manager and L is the skill of the assistant. There are two countries (rich and poor), one consumption good, and four types of labor differentiated by skill (skill levels are A–D with A > B > C > D). The rich country has workers of type A and B, while the poor country has workers of type C and D. With this production function, it is straightforward to check that it is always optimal to assign your most skilled worker to the managerial task and that it may be more efficient to have workers crossmatched (forming teams of workers with different skill levels) rather than self-matched (forming teams of workers with the same skill levels). This will be the case if the skill levels of the workers are not too different. For example, if a country has two workers each with skill levels H and L, self-matching results in output of $H^3 + L^3$, whereas crossmatching results in output of $2H^2L$. Crossmatching is optimal as long as $H < 1.6L$.

If we assume that A and B are not too different and that C and D are sufficiently close, then autarky in both country entails crossmatching in production. Now, suppose that globalization results in the two labor markets becoming integrated so that all crossmatches are possible. Then, if C is well below B, as would be the case if the rich and poor country are significantly different (Kremer and Maskin use the U.S. and Chad as examples), then there will be no change in the teams formed since it would be inefficient for any worker in the rich country to match with any worker in the poor country. Thus, there would be no trade between countries that are significantly different (since there is only one consumption good, all trade must be due to team formation across borders).

Now, suppose instead that C is close to B and that D is far below C. In autarky, there would be crossmatching in the rich country and self-matching in the poor country. When countries become more integrated in the global economy, type A managers in the rich country are willing to hire type C assistants from the poor country. They are willing to do so since they can pay their new assistants lower wages than they were paying in autarky. The type A and C workers clearly benefit from such a match, while type B workers lose, since they are forced to self-match. As a result, trade increases inequality in both countries. When labor markets become integrated and global production is possible, the reformation of teams leads to wage effects that are consistent with observed rising wage inequality in developing countries.

The simple framework in Kremer and Maskin provides a first look at how international team formation can be important, but lacks the ability to provide a detailed analysis of the welfare effects of globalization, the role of firms in global production, and the types of workers that are likely to form international production teams. Moreover, there is no attempt to explain how labor market integration occurs at all. To these ends, Antràs, Garicano, and Rossi-Hansberg (2006) examine international team formation by examining the manner in which firms organize worker knowledge effectively.

Production within each firm occurs as individual workers attempt to solve tasks with random difficulties. Hierarchical organization of workers according to skill is the most efficient means of production. Low-skill workers draw tasks from a known distribution of difficulties. If they have the requisite knowledge, they complete the task and production ensues. However, if they cannot solve a particular problem, they pass the task along to their supervising manager, albeit with communication costs. The hierarchal structure of firms shields managers from menial tasks that workers could easily solve, and managerial skill ensures that worker efforts in communicating tasks are not wasted. In other words, the knowledge-hierarchy production process generates endogenous complementarities between worker abilities.

The competitive equilibrium derived by Antràs, Garicano, and Rossi-Hansberg exhibits several appealing characteristics. First, because of complementarities, there is positive assortative matching between workers and managers. Second, the assignment to roles as "workers" or "managers" occurs endogenously. The workers with the most skill pursue jobs as managers; in the hierarchal organization of the firm, a managerial position rewards skill more intensively, since they can focus only on difficult tasks beyond the skills of workers to solve. Third, the model is unique in that it generates one-to-many matching outcomes; that is, one manager is matched with many workers.

Globalization reduces communication costs between workers and managers, so that workers in the South have the potential to form cost-effective teams with

managers in the skill-abundant North. Two key parameters dictate the consequences of globalization: the cost of communication and the level of overlap in the
distribution of labor ability. If the distributions of skill between the North and
South overlap to a significant degree, and communication costs are low, then the
authors show that crossborder matches exist in a low quality equilibrium. Specifically, all labor in the South are employed as workers under the supervision of managers in the North. The reason that such an allocation is called "low quality" is that
relatively unskilled workers in the South are paired with the best workers in the
North, failing to exploit complementarities in skill. However, if communication
costs are relatively high, and there is little overlap in the distributions of abilities
across countries, then globalization leads to a high quality equilibrium. Managers
appear in the South and, because of positive sorting, match with low quality workers
in the South. On the other hand, managers in the North form better teams with
workers in the North and South.

The wage effects of globalization depend on both the skill of individual workers
and the type of equilibrium obtained. Regardless of the type of equilibrium that
emerges, the ability to form crossborder teams leads to destruction of jobs as managers (i.e., firms) and the creation of jobs as workers. Moreover, the formation of
crossborder teams always leads to more efficient production through better matching. In short, globalization improves team formation.

Segmented labor markets can inhibit the global economy from creating optimal
matches between workers. But focusing solely on domestic labor markets, positive
matching between worker skills may not arise if wages are not set in competitive
markets, as found by Frias, Kaplan, and Verhoogen (2009), or if the return to skill
differs across both job types and firms. Sly (2008) considers the (mis)matching
behavior of domestic workers in a global economy when firm recruit workers only
from the domestic labor market. Because only some firms can access foreign markets, trade liberalization has the potential to alter the distribution of rents across
firms, and this difference impacts worker matching behavior.

In Sly's framework, monopolistically competitive firms recruit a team of
managers to supervise production of a unique variety. The two managers are each
assigned to a single task. Within each firm, the managers' skills are complementary,
but because of differences in the skill intensity of tasks, their skills are not perfectly
substitutable. Firm heterogeneity arises endogenously, as workers form teams
voluntarily.

Sly allows the two managers to negotiate over any surplus retained from
domestic and foreign sales. The manager who performed the skill-intensive task
contributed relatively more to the production process, and thus is able to negotiate a relatively larger share of the firm's operating profits. Recognizing the premium paid to skill-intensive tasks, workers have distinct preferences for good
task assignments. In fact, when forming teams, all workers are willing to sacrifice
match quality at the margin in order to secure jobs that pay for their skills more
intensely. The only way to secure a skill-intensive job is to match with a worker of
lesser skill.

The best-managed firms are productive enough to overcome trade costs and earn positive profits from exporting. Thus, managers face a potential trade-off: on the one hand, they desire high-ability partners to gain access to surpluses from foreign revenues; on the other hand, they desire low ability-partners to secure a larger share of the firm's total surplus during negotiations. Trade liberalization tips this balance in favor of better team formation.

At the margin, some managers begin to reject task assignments in favor of matches that will lead to profits from foreign markets as trade barriers are reduced. Yet the adjustment in the matching between workers is not limited to firms on the margin of exporting[13]. The shift in matching behavior away from good task assignments generates slack in the labor market. As a result, all managers rethink their preliberalization match so that trade initiates inframarginal changes in the skill composition of all firms.

The adjustments in matching between heterogeneous workers in open economies lead to more segregated team formation; high-skill workers match with relatively higher-skilled partners as trade barriers fall. Because of complementarities in production, the greater degree of segregation improves productivity within all surviving firms. Trade rationalizes the matching behavior of skilled workers in that the benefits to firm-level productivities are a source of gains from trade, distinct from the gains that occur through exit of low-productivity firms and reallocations of production across firms.

Sly also considers the impact of worker matching behavior on the distribution of income. Intuitively, greater openness increase the wages of skilled workers employed at exporting firms relative to those employed at nonexporters. However, the likelihood that a worker benefits from trade is not necessarily increasing in skill. When skilled workers are rent-seekers and negotiate wages with their employer, better skill does not always benefit their bargaining position as trade barriers fall. Finally, the reformation of matches in an open economy influences wage dispersion within firms. More segregated matching outcomes reduce wage dispersion among skilled workers employed at the same firm.

A change in the matching pattern between domestic workers provides a new source of gains within all surviving firms. Sly (2008) also emphasizes how the dynamics of trade adjustment through worker matches differs from previous analyses that include sunk investment costs. Trade liberalization brings market access immediately, and so workers act immediately to obtain jobs at exporting firms. Reallocation in the labor force arises as workers actively pursue better jobs, rather than waiting for their initial job to be destroyed, as in Melitz (2003), Yeaple (2005), and Davidson et al. (2008). Furthermore, adjustments in worker matching behavior occur even when firm production techniques remain fixed.

Labor market distortions such as frictions or differences in the return to skill across firms can each alter the incentives of workers to form optimal matches. These we explored in a trade context separately in Davidson et al. (2008) and Sly (2008). A recent article by Helpman, Itskhoki, and Redding (2010) merges these two labor market structures and then analyzes the effects of trade liberalization. In their framework, workers must search for jobs offered by heterogeneous firms à la Melitz (2003). Firms hire many workers but screen their abilities, at a cost, to ensure that they have the requisite talents to join the firm's production team. Firm productivity and worker "quality" are complementary during production. So in equilibrium, the best firms screen and accept only the best workers. This generates differences in the returns to skill across firms. And since labor markets are characterized by frictions, matched workers and firms do not have the same outside option as those that are unmatched. Wages are thus set through multilateral bargaining.

Before discussing their model and results further, we should point out that worker heterogeneity arises ex post. All workers are ex ante identical, and worker quality, which is determined by a random draw once the worker and firm meet, is match-specific. All unmatched workers have the exact same opportunities in the labor market for any level of trade costs. Therefore, the consequences of trade on the wage distribution discussed by Helpman, Itskhoki, and Redding (2010) should be interpreted as consequences for residual wages, or the *within-group* wage distribution. Recall that Frias, Kaplan, and Verhoogen (2009) found that this was indeed the most important channel by which trade influenced average firm wages.

Opening the economy to trade increases the revenues for those firms that export. In turn, exporting firms begin to screen workers more intensely in order to recruit a stronger workforce to better access foreign markets. On the other hand, domestic firms begin to screen less intensively. This follows from the fact that increased competition from foreign firms reduces domestic revenues, making screening relatively more costly. Firm productivity adjustments following trade reflect changes in worker match quality.

Through multilateral bargaining, firm-level wages depend partially on average match quality. At the aggregate level, the response of the wage distribution to trade liberalization depends on how exclusive international participation is among firms. As a result, the relationship between trade and the wage distribution is nonmonotonic. When few firms export initially, then the benefits of trade liberalization through export wage premia are confined to only the best-matched workers in the economy. However, when many or all firms are able to access foreign markets, the reverse is true. Increases in trade costs raise wage inequality because they act to limit export opportunities to only a portion of the labor force. The nonmonotonic relationship between trade and inequality is a key feature of the Helpman, Itskhoki, and Redding approach.

Labor market frictions induce equilibrium unemployment, and the authors examine the relationship between market openness and employment. More intense screening by exporting firms decreases the hiring rate, since a smaller range of match qualities are accepted. Furthermore, reallocation of production across firms induces more matches to arise between workers and efficient firms with high standards in the screening process. These effects tend to increase unemployment. However, trade can also raise the level of tightness in the labor market as firms increase total hiring. The net effect of trade on unemployment is determined by the opposing impacts on the hiring rate and labor market tightness. Generally speaking trade has an ambiguous impact on unemployment.

Team production benefits from efficient team formation. This section has reviewed recent work on how globalization can improve team formation both across and within borders. One question yet to be explored is how relative levels of diversity affect the decisions of multinational firms to enter foreign markets when they must recruit entire teams of foreign workers (note: this is different than forming crossborder teams). Inexpensive foreign labor may not equate to inexpensive foreign teams. Differences in labor heterogeneity across borders may prove to be informative about the incentives to conduct vertical foreign direct investment.

4. CONCLUSION

The Davidson et al. and Helpman et al. models yield sharp predictions about how openness should affect the types of worker–firm matches that we observe. Likewise Sly (2008) and Antràs, Garicano, and Rossi-Hansberg (2006) make predictions about the relationship between openness and team formation within firms. Each analysis also yields interesting predictions about the impact of openness on the wage distribution within an industry and on productivity at the firm and industry levels. Fortunately, over the past decade a number of worker–firm matched data sets have become available, and this opens up exciting new possibilities in terms of empirical research on labor market adjustment to globalization. First, the fundamental predictions about trade and the skill compositions of firms and teams need to be vetted against these data. Going forward, the implications of trade for worker–firm and worker–worker matching need to be related to now common features of trade behavior. For example, if trade were shown to improve the organization of a heterogeneous workforce across firms, what does this imply about price markups, firm product variety, number of export destinations, or product quality? Skill composition may interact with these firm behaviors in many different ways.

In a similar vein, the Grossman and Maggi (2000), Grossman (2000) and Ohnsorge and Trefler (2007) articles surveyed in section 2 all yield predictions about the implications of worker heterogeneity for trade patterns and inequality by looking at sorting behavior across industries. Although some empirical work is already under way testing these predictions (e.g., Bombardini, Gallipoli, and Pupato (2011) and Sly [2011]), there is still important work to be done considering the role of teams and diversity across industries. Data regarding the degree of teamwork and complementarities of skill across industries are available from the O*NET occupational survey. These data rank industries according to their skill substitutability along three dimensions: teamwork, impact on coworker productivity, and level of communication/interaction. Combined with information from Barro and Lee (2001) about educational attainment across countries, these models which predict trade based on diversity of endowments can be tested.

All of these models of trade with heterogeneous labor predict specific flows of workers across firms and occupation types. The dynamic aspects of the labor market suggested by these models veer from traditional thought, and thus warrant empirical analysis. We should be able to obtain new insights about the incidence of worker dislocation, the manner in which openness affects the job search process, and the manner in which the gains and losses from freer trade are distributed across firms and their workers within industries. In other words, it should be possible to do for the labor market what has already been done for the product market.

It is difficult to predict which lines of future research will be most fruitful. However, we can point to areas that are conspicuously missing from the current body of literature concerning trade and labor heterogeneity. A political economy of trade, where heterogeneous workers sort across industries, firms, occupations, and teams, is needed. Incorporating the role of labor differences may provide new insights about how regional trade agreements form, the impact of trade sanctions such as antidumping legislation, or the determinants of protectionism. In addition, recent work regarding trade and technologies has emphasized skill bias, primarily in response to the stylized facts regarding average skill content within firms discussed in the introduction (see, e.g., Bernard and Jensen 1999). Recognizing the importance of overall skill heterogeneity, new models relating trade to the composition of jobs offered by firms are required.

NOTES

1. Barro and Lee actually separate out "no school" and "primary," but we combine these two since the numbers for "no school" are close to zero for all of the countries in table 4.1.

2. These seven countries were chosen for illustrative purposes. Both studies include data on a broad spectrum of additional countries.

3. For additional evidence, see the introduction of Grossman and Maggi (2000), where data on the distribution of literacy scores across countries are reported and discussed.

4. See Antràs and Rossi-Hansberg (2009) for a review of recent contributions emphasizing organizations and trade.

5. An earlier article by Bond (1986) generates firm heterogeneity by assuming that managers at firms vary in their entrepreneurial abilities. Although there is a diversity of talent present, Bond's primary focus is on how firm heterogeneity and the entry and exit of marginal firms alter impact of endowment changes and changes in world prices. Bond also holds the distribution of entrepreneurial ability fixed throughout his analysis.

6. Ohnsorge and Trefler's model is an extension of Heckman and Sedlacek (1985), which allows for a continuum of industries.

7. The implications of log-supermodularity applies generally to any attribute of workers and industries. Per the emphasis here, we discuss the results in Costinot (2009) in terms of labor skill and skill intensity in production.

8. Considering the framework of Ohnsorge and Trefler, it is worthwhile to note that the normal distribution satisfies monotone likelihood ratio dominance.

9. We should note that the framework in Bombardini et al. follows Helpman and Itskhoki (2010) and Helpman et al. (2010), where labor markets are characterized by search frictions and heterogeneity refers to residual differences among workers. Thus, observed labor heterogeneity is revealed ex post and plays no allocative role in the economy. We return to this issue below.

10. In fact, a primary contribution of Legros and Newman (2002, 2007) is to show that positive assortative matching arises when a condition called general increasing differences are satisfied. This is a weaker condition than supermodularity. Thus, supermodularity in production functions in the transferable utility case—and in the payoff functions in the nontransferable utility case—should be viewed as a sufficient but not necessary condition.

11. The structure Yeaple's model allows firms in the traded sector to adopt one of two technologies and hire a single worker. Yet the previously discussed frameworks in Costinot (2009) and Costinot and Vogel (2009), with a continuum of both worker types and production tasks, are general enough to apply to firms matching one-to-one with workers of differing ability in competitive labor markets.

12. This is actually not quite right. The literature we are referring to fails to find evidence of positive assortative matching—that is, the "best" workers matching with the "best" firms. This could be due to imperfections in the matching process (i.e., search frictions), or due to a lack of complementarities in production, or due to shortcomings in the econometric techniques that are being employed. The third of these is the main focus of Lopes de Melo's article.

13. Recall that in Yeaple (2005), the better matching between workers and technologies occurred only at this margin.

REFERENCES

Antràs, Pol, Luis Garicano, and Esteban Rossi-Hansberg, 2006. Offshoring in a knowledge economy. *Quarterly Journal of Economics* 121(1): 31–77.

Antràs, Pol, and Esteban Rossi-Hansberg, 2009. Organizations and trade. *Annual Review of Economics* 1: 43–64.

Autor, David, Lawrence Katz, and Melissa Kearney, 2006. The polarization of the U.S. labor market. *American Economic Review Papers and Proceedings* 96(2): 189–194.

Barro, Robert, and Jong-Wha Lee, 1993. International comparisons of educational attainment. *Journal of Monetary Economics*, 32: 363–394.

Barro, Robert, and Jong-Wha Lee, 1996. International measures of schooling years and schooling quality. *American Economic Review* 86: 218–223.

Barro, Robert, and Jong-Wha Lee, 2001. International data on educational attainment: Updates and implications. *Oxford Economic Papers* 53: 541–563.

Becker, Gary, 1973. A theory of marriage: Part I. *Journal of Political Economy* 81(4): 813–846.

Bernard, Andrew, and J. Bradford Jensen, 1995. Exporters, jobs and wages in U.S. manufacturing, 1976–87. *Brookings Papers on Economic Activity: Microeconomics*, 1995: 67–112.

Bernard, Andrew, and J. Bradford Jensen, 1997. Exporters, skill upgrading, and the wage gap. *Journal of International Economics* 42(1/2): 3–31.

Bernard, Andrew, and J. Bradford Jensen, 1999. Exceptional exporter performance: Cause, effect or both? *Journal of International Economics* 47: 1–25.

Bombardini, Matilde, Giovanni Gallipoli, and German Pupato, 2011. Skill dispersion and trade flows. *American Economic Review*, forthcoming

Bond, Eric, 1986. Entrepreneurial ability, income distribution, and international trade. *Journal of International Economics* 20(3/4): 343–356.

Bougheas, Sprios, and Raymond Riezman, 2007. Trade and the distribution of human capital. *Journal of International Economics* 73: 421–433.

Burstein, Ariel, and Jonathan Vogel, 2010. Globalization, technology and the skill premium: A quantitative analysis. NBER Working Paper 16459, October.

Costinot, Arnaud, 2009. An elementary theory of comparative advantage. *Econometrica* 77(4): 1165–1192.

Costinot, Arnaud, and Jonathan Vogel, 2010. Matching and inequality in the world economy. *Journal of Political Economy* 118(4): 747–786.

Cunat, Vicente, and Maria Guadalupe, 2009. Globalization and the provision of incentives inside the firm: The effect of foreign competition. *Journal of Labor Economics* 27(2): 179–212. *Papers and Proceedings* 99(2): 58–63.

Davidson, Carl, Steven Matusz, and Andrei Shevchenko, 2008. Globalization and firm level adjustment with imperfect labor markets. *Journal of International Economics* 75(2): 295–309.

Fernandes, Ana, 2007. Trade policy, trade volumes and plant-level productivity in Columbian manufacturing industries. *Journal of International Economics* 71(1): 52–71.

Frias, Judith, David Kaplan, and Eric Verhoogen, 2009. Exports and wage premia: Evidence from Mexican employer-employee data. Mimeograph.

Goos, Maarten, Alan Manning, and Anna Salomons, 2009. *American Economic Review*.

Grossman, Gene, 2004. The distribution of talent and the pattern and consequences of international trade. *Journal of Political Economy* 112: 209–239.

Grossman, Gene, and Giovanni Maggi, 2000. Diversity and trade. *American Economic Review* 90: 1255–1275.

Guadalupe, Maria, and Julie Wulf, 2010. The flattening firm and product market competition: The effect of trade liberalization on corporate hierarchies. *American Economic Journal: Applied Economics* 2(4): 105–127.

Heckman, James, and Guilherme Sedlacek, 1985. Heterogeneity, aggregation and market wage function: An empirical model of self-selection in the labor market. *Journal of Political Economy* 93: 1077–1125.

Helpman, Elhanan, and Oleg Itskhoki, 2010. Labor market rigidities, trade and unemployment. *Review of Economics Studies* 77(3): 1100–1137.

Helpman, Elhanan, Oleg Itskhoki, and Stephen Redding, 2009. Inequality and unemployment in a global economy. *Econometrica* 78(4):1239–1283.

Kremer, Michael, 1993. The O-Ring theory of economic development. *Quarterly Journal of Economics* 108(3): 551–575.

Kremer, Michael, and Eric Maskin, 2006. Globalization and inequality. Working Paper 2008-0087. Weatherhead Center for International Affairs, Harvard University.

Legros, Patrick, and Andrew Newman, 2002. Monotone matching in perfect and imperfect worlds. *Review of Economic Studies* 69: 925–942.

Legros, Patrick, and Andrew Newman, 2007. Beauty is a beast, frog is a prince: Assortative matching with nontransferabilities. *Econometrica* 75(4): 1073–1102.

Lopes de Melo, Rapael, 2009. Sorting in the labor market: Theory and measurement. Mimeograph, available at http://isites.harvard.edu/fs/docs/icb.topic818278.files/sorting_paper.pdf.

Melitz, Marc, 2003. The impact of trade on intra-industry reallocations and aggregate industry productivity. *Econometrica* 71: 1695–1725.

Murphy, Kevin, Andrei Shleifer, and Robert Vishny, 1991. The allocation of talent: Implications for growth. *Quarterly Journal of Economics* 106(2): 503–530.

OECD, 1998. *Human Capital Investment: An International Comparison.* Paris: Centre for Educational Research and Innovation, OECD.

Ohnsorge, Franziska, and Daniel Trefler, 2007. Sorting it out: International trade with heterogeneous workers. *Journal of Political Economy* 115(5): 868–892.

Roberts, Mark, and James Tybout, 1997. The decision to export in Columbia: An empirical model of entry with sunk costs. *American Economic Review* 87(4): 545–564.

Rosen, Sherwin, 1981. The economics of superstars. *American Economic Review* 71(5): 845–858.

Sattinger, Michael, 1975. Comparative advantage and the distribution of earnings and abilities. *Econometrica* 43: 455–468.

Sattinger, Michael, 1993. Assignment models of the distribution of earning. *Journal of Economic Literature* 31(2): 831–880.

Shimer, Robert, and Lones Smith, 2000. Assortative matching and search. *Econometrica* 68(2): 343–369.

Sly, Nicholas, 2008. Labor matching behavior in open economies and trade adjustment. MPRA Working Paper 25693. University Library of Munich, Germany.

Sly, Nicholas, 2011. International productivity differences, trade, and the distributions of factor endowments. *Review of International Economics*, forthcoming

Verhoogen, Eric, 2008. Trade, quality upgrading, and wage inequality in the Mexican manufacturing sector. *Quarterly Journal of Economics* 123(2): 489–530.

Yeaple, Stephen, 2005. A simple model of firm heterogeneity, international trade, and wages. *Journal of International Economics* 65: 1–20.

CHAPTER 5

AGRICULTURE

TIM JOSLING

"I don't want to hear about agriculture from anyone but you, Ken," President John F. Kennedy is reported to have said to his advisor John Kenneth Galbraith, "and I don't want to hear about it from you, either." For many interested in public policy, agricultural issues are at best a distraction and at worst a maze into which one enters with no assurance of being able to find the exit. Similarly, trade policy students often find the "exceptional" treatment of agriculture an anomaly reflecting political sensitivities with little economic rationale. This chapter attempts to provide in a succinct way a road map for those wandering into the territory of agricultural policy and trade. I hope it will encourage some to explore the subject further.

The starting point of any discussion of agricultural trade policy has to be the network of agricultural policies that have grown up in the period since the 1930s. All developed countries adopted such policies, and several developing countries have tried similar interventions though constrained by other budget priorities and by the regressive effect of higher food prices on urban consumers. Developed-country farm policies have focused in the main on supporting domestic price levels and incomes but in the process have used instruments at the border to allow those policies to be effective. Import tariffs have been needed to prevent foreign supplies from undercutting the domestic prices set by policy. Quantitative import restrictions have been even more effective: issuing licenses for imports only when needed to supplement home supplies has been a favorite way of controlling the market. Export subsidies have been necessary to dispose of surpluses onto world markets to avoid price collapse at home. Export taxes have been employed when domestic supplies threaten to flow abroad and increase domestic prices to consumers. State trading has been a common way for exporting countries to dispose of surpluses without the need for explicit subsidies: food aid has continued for 50 years largely because it has the support of producer groups looking to increase exports with the help of public funds.

The chapter begins with a brief discussion of the linkages between domestic farm policies and trade policies and the implications of those linkages for world markets. The second section deals explicitly with the treatment of agriculture within the GATT and later the WTO, and considers the significance of the current Doha Round for improving trade rules and lowering protection. A third section considers the situation with respect to regional and bilateral trade agreements, where agriculture has been a reluctant player but has over time been influenced significantly by this trend toward regional solutions to trade problems. A final section gives some indication of where the trade policies and trade rules in agriculture may be heading.[1]

AGRICULTURAL POLICY AND TRADE POLICY

The links between domestic farm and food policies and trade policies are forged in the basic expressions of statehood. Most governments profess a concern for the security of their country's food supply and the level and stability of the income of their rural sector. This concern has translated itself, in importing countries, into caution about relying on imports for basic foodstuffs and a conviction that protection from overseas competition is necessary for the health of the rural economy. Those countries with export potential have long decried such sentiments, arguing that they can provide a regular supply of foodstuffs at lower prices and that supporting inefficient domestic production is not a sound basis for development. But even the most enthusiastic of exporting countries maintain import controls to shelter their less competitive agricultural sectors. Hence, opening up markets for agricultural products has proved a stumbling block for trade negotiations, at both the regional and multilateral level.

The domestic policies that are aimed at supporting agricultural production and maintaining farm incomes have taken a number of forms, often reflecting the market situation as well as the political philosophy of the government and the pressures from farm lobbies. At one extreme, governments have taken a major role in the planning of agricultural production and been involved in the marketing of farm products. In such cases, state trading has been common, as it would be difficult to control supplies if private firms could import farm products. And quantitative trade barriers have been used even when private firms are allowed to import. At the other extreme, some countries have left markets comparatively open while giving their farmers income supports and other financial assistance to enable them to maintain production. Trade policies under these circumstances are generally in the form of tariffs, and the level of such tariffs helps to control government financial obligation. In between these two extremes are a range of instruments to either control domestic supply (in which case import restrictions are necessary), reduce farm costs (by input subsidies), or boost demand (by purchasing surpluses off the domestic market). Intervention to buy up surplus involves their disposal, often abroad with the aid of export subsidies.

Given the existence of strong and effective lobbies devoted to keeping these farm policies, and a tendency for rural areas to be overrepresented in legislatures, the possibility of negotiating effective multilateral rules for agricultural trade was minimal. Reform of farm policies was a prerequisite for trade reform. Twenty years ago, the edifice of agricultural protection couched in the need to maintain domestic production began to show cracks. Reform started in such countries as New Zealand and Chile with the notion that the government could not artificially provide the demand for farm products in small exporting countries in the light of macroeconomic distortions and locational disadvantages. It spread to those countries that were stifling their farm sectors with marketing arrangements that provided little incentive for quality. Together with the paradigm change in the management of the economy, toward deregulation and the provision of more appropriate incentives, the change in agricultural policies away from market intervention and toward direct payments has now transformed the policies and provided a new environment for agricultural trade.

The changes in the agricultural policy in the EU have been particularly dramatic. Once the poster child for agricultural protectionism, the EU began in 1992 to shift the emphasis from maintaining high internal prices to supporting farmers through direct payments not tied to their current volume of production. This reform accelerated over the 1990s as farm policy shifted to include environmental and quality aspects of food production, culminating in the reforms of 2003 that virtually eliminated for arable agriculture any link between farmer support payments and commodity market conditions. Progress in the United States has been less linear, with a move in 1996 to delink payments from production but then some recidivism in 1998 with the "emergency payments" that were incorporated in the 2002 and 2008 Farm Bills. Commodity-based price support programs proved to have strong support in the farm lobby and in Congress.

This shift in policy instruments for domestic support has made it possible to change trade policies as well. The introduction of direct payments has made possible the reduction of support prices toward the world price level. This helps both to allow tariff reductions (and the removal of quotas and levies that vary with world prices) and to remove the need to subsidize exports to keep up domestic price levels. As discussed below, it was this change that allowed the Uruguay Round to finally come to grips with the need for rules on agricultural trade that could be enforced and that would provide a discipline on domestic farm policies that had been lacking in the GATT.

It is possible that some of these changes would have occurred as a result of the process of "globalization" in world trade. Agriculture was always likely to be a laggard in this process, but the food sector (both processors and retail firms) began to develop longer supply chains, and farm input suppliers (seed and chemical companies) consolidated and became global in scope (Coleman et al., 2004). This has fundamentally changed the nature of trade in farm products. Twenty years ago, much of the trade in primary agricultural products passed through the hands of parastatal bodies acting as sales or purchasing agents for producers and wholesalers, or of companies whose function was to distribute temperate and tropical products through established channels. The role of state trading has shrunk markedly, with the adoption of policies to allow more private activity in marketing. Large companies now have a considerable role in the processing and marketing of farm products, as they have had for some time in the trading function. Most of these private actors operate in several countries, and so food trade has become much more of a global business. The share of such trade that is categorized as "high value added" has correspondingly increased, leaving the trading of commodities and raw materials a significantly smaller part of agricultural trade. Such trends explain the growing interest by large food and retail firms in removing trade barriers that act to inhibit worldwide marketing.

As a result of these changes, both in political perception and structural reality, agricultural trade negotiations have been somewhat more successful in recent years in opening markets, and have even made some progress in the past decade in reducing trade-distorting subsidies. One probable reason for this is the fact that most countries now have interests as both importers and exporters of farm products and foodstuffs. This has blurred the easy categorization of a country's trade policy by its trade balance. Developing country importers often join with developing country exporters in voicing concerns about trade issues, particularly about the subsidies given to domestic producers in rich countries. Developed country exporters have "sensitive" sectors that apparently need to be sheltered even while espousing more open markets for other products. Developed country importers with high protection are often major importers of farm products needed for processing or for animal feed, and press for restraints on export taxes and embargoes. Perhaps only in the market for tropical agricultural products is it still possible to identify typical "importer" and "exporter" views, but even in this case there are clear distinctions between those that have preferential access into industrial country markets and those that don't benefit from such preferences, and between those that sell the raw material and those that successfully add value in the domestic economy.

AGRICULTURE IN THE GATT

The treatment of agriculture in the GATT and subsequently in the WTO reflects this gradual tendency to incorporate agriculture more fully into the trade rules that have governed manufactured trade for 60 years. For most of that period, agricultural trade lagged far behind in the process of multilateral economic integration under agreed rules. The GATT, as it emerged in 1947, applied to agricultural trade but also included two articles that specifically modified the impact of the general provisions relating to trade in goods. Article XI, which established the principle that nontariff trade barriers could be only be used under specific circumstances, made room for some types of agricultural programs. The article recognized the case where an agricultural product is subject to quantitative restrictions on domestic production (Article XI:2[c]): under such circumstances quantitative import restrictions were allowed (Josling, Tangermann, and Warley, 1996).[2] Many countries relied on this clause to restrict imports by quantitative trade barriers when domestic markets were being managed. The other agricultural "exception" was to specify different rules for export subsidies of manufactures and primary products. Though the original GATT subjected both primary and manufactured product export subsides to the same notification and consultation procedures, in 1955 it was agreed to add an explicit prohibition on export subsidies on manufactured goods (Article XVI). Agricultural export subsidies were constrained only by the obligation not to use such subsidies to capture "more than an equitable share" of world markets. Successive GATT panels failed to come up with a satisfactory definition of this concept, and agricultural export subsidies in effect escaped any disciplines (Josling and Tangermann, 2003).

The Kennedy Round tried but failed to introduce rules for agricultural trade that would constrain the domestic subsidies of the EU and the United States. Instead, the discussion on agriculture focused on the setting-up of commodity agreements that would coordinate the reaction of governments to high and low prices. The EU wished at one stage to go further, projecting its new market management regime onto the international stage, a convenient mixture of pragmatism and ideology. One such commodity agreement, for grains, did emerge from the Kennedy Round, but it failed to stop the slide in the international prices of agricultural commodities caused in large part by the generous domestic price support policies of the United States and the EU.

The Tokyo Round, initiated in 1974 and concluded in 1979, did not do much better for agricultural trade. Coming at a time when world prices were high, the emphasis was on coordinating stockpiles of basic foodstuffs rather than in reducing support levels and trade barriers.[3] A further international commodity agreement on wheat was negotiated but barely survived the end of the Round. A plurilateral subsidies code (applicable only to the signatories) was agreed on, as was one on standards, both aimed in part at constraining agricultural protection. A dairy agreement and a bovine meat accord attempted to address some of the problems in these sectors but had little impact on the behavior of the developed country governments and the direction of their domestic policies. So the first 30 years of the GATT had produced almost nothing that constrained developed country farm policies.

The fundamental weakness in the treatment of agriculture in trade rules was recognized and discussed in two committees at the beginning of the 1980s: the Trade and Agriculture Committee of the GATT (1982) and the combined Agricultural and Trade Committees of the OECD (1984), acting under a mandate from the ministers. The GATT Committee discussed ways the agricultural rules could be brought more into line with those for trade in manufactured goods. This included the notion that nontariff barriers be converted into tariffs. Though no agreement was reached at that time, many of the ideas of the Committee found their way into the Uruguay Round discussions. The OECD Committee took a different approach, requesting from the Secretariat credible information on the extent to which domestic policies gave incentives to production (and reduced consumption) and hence had an effect on trade. The Secretariat calculated an indicator, the Producer Subsidy Equivalent, that provided the basis for a more intensive and focused debate in the Uruguay Round on the disciplines that could be applied to domestic support.

AGRICULTURE IN THE WTO

The Uruguay Round of trade negotiations under the GATT marked a transition of the multilateral trade system from a limited intergovernmental agreement on rules of conduct for trade in goods to a more comprehensive treaty covering trade in services and trade-related aspects of intellectual property protection as well as goods trade. In addition to the broadening of the multilateral trade rules, further deepening took place. Two issues were addressed: the consolidation of the Tokyo Round Codes (which had been set up as plurilateral agreements that countries could sign if they chose) and the absorption of agricultural and textiles into the mainstream of the trade system. The issues of agriculture and textiles were considered to be an important part of the agenda for developing countries, balancing negotiations over services and intellectual property that favored developed countries.

The Uruguay Round Agreement on Agriculture (URAA) marked a turning point in the treatment of agricultural goods in the multilateral trade system. It devised agriculture-specific rules that obliged the conversion of nontariff border measures to tariffs. The restrictions on border policies included restraints on export subsidies. In particular, the URAA addressed the question of the impact of domestic farm policies on trade flows. It imposed restraints on the level of support provided by domestic programs and introduced incentives to shift to less trade-distorting measures. Moreover, it introduced institutional monitoring of compliance with the rules and schedules, sheltered some types of agricultural subsidy from challenge under the new subsidy agreement, and committed member governments to further talks on agricultural policy reform. It represented a move toward the more complete integration of agriculture in the trade system, though paradoxically it made agriculture more "different" in certain respects. As the URAA is still in operation (unless or until it is modified by the outcome of the Doha Round) its provisions constitute the multilateral framework for agricultural trade and domestic policies for all WTO members.

A brief overview of the main provisions of the URAA is necessary, along with a discussion of how it has been implemented, to put current issues into context. The URAA defines rules related to what have become known as the three "pillars" of market access, export competition and domestic support.[4] But in addition, important parts of the agreement defined special treatment for developing countries, limitations on the possibility for challenge to subsidies, the establishment of a monitoring institution, and the commitment to the continuation of reform.[5]

MARKET ACCESS

Restrictions on market access for agricultural goods ranged from high tariffs to quantitative import controls and variable levies. The Uruguay Round introduced significant changes to the conditions for market access for agricultural products. The most significant changes included the following:

- Nontariff barriers had to be converted into tariffs (tariffication)
- Tariff-rate quotas (TRQs) were introduced for these "tariffied" products: current access and minimum access provisions ensured that markets would remain open even with high tariffs.[6]
- A Special Safeguard (SSG) was allowed for tariffied products (if specified in country schedules): temporary additional duties could be assessed if prices fell or quantities of imports increased.
- Tariffs were to be bound and reduced by 36% on average (15% minimum for each line item): lower reductions were required of developing countries, and no cuts were required of Least Developed Countries (LDCs).[7]
- Schedules of tariffs offered, verified, and agreed became part of treaty provisions
- Developing countries were allowed to bind tariff "ceilings" rather than calculate tariff equivalents.[8]

Conversion of nontariff barriers took place with very few problems. The delay agreed for rice was used by Japan and Korea, but Japan instituted a tariff for rice in 2000. Some tariffs were set at rather higher levels than price gap warranted ("dirty tariffication") by the choice of an unrealistic world price. As a result of the conversion of nontariff measures to tariffs, agriculture emerged with a higher proportion of bound tariffs than nonagricultural sectors. The SSG has been used by some importers (Japan and the EU particularly) to restrict imports without the need for evidence of domestic injury.

Though the new rules offered the possibility of more open markets, market access for agricultural products did not greatly improve as a result of the tariff reduction schedules. Many of the tariff cuts merely reduced the "water" in the tariff schedules (the superfluous protection given by a tariff that is higher than that which would close off any imports). Ceiling bindings were often set at high levels even though applied tariffs were much lower. The introduction of TRQs, though arguably an improvement on the quantitative restrictions that they replaced, still restricted trade in the more sensitive products. So the task of reducing tariffs to a level more in keeping with nonfarm tariffs was left to subsequent rounds of negotiations.

EXPORT COMPETITION

The new provisions included in the URAA in the area of export competition included the following:

- No new export subsidies were allowed to be introduced.
- Existing export subsidies were defined in country schedules and had to be reduced in expenditure (by 36%) and in quantity of product subsidized (by 20%).
- Disciplines on export credits were to be discussed elsewhere.
- Food aid was not to be used to avoid restrictions on export subsidies.[9]
- Developing countries were allowed to keep transportation and marketing subsidies on exports (Article 9.4).

Restraints on export subsidies have generally been effective. No new export subsidies of an explicit kind have been introduced, though WTO panels have found that some less direct export subsidies were introduced or maintained in violation of the scheduled amounts. Countries did not use all export subsidy "entitlements," as prices initially were high in the 1996 and 1997 crop years. In fact, the majority of export subsidies have for the past few years been paid by the EU, particularly in dairy products. The export credit talks (in the OECD) were not successful in defining when such credits could be used.

Countries have continued to complain about use of food aid as an export subsidy and about implicit subsidies involved in state-trading exporters. In particular the EU, as it became the predominant user of export subsidies, expressed increasing concern that these other practices were going on unchecked.

DOMESTIC SUPPORT

The rules on domestic support broke new ground by both classifying subsidies provided by measures inside the border and by defining the levels of such subsidies in country schedules. The following elements were particularly significant:

- Domestic support was classified by extent of trade distortion: Amber Box policies were those tied to production or price; Blue Box policies those constrained by supply control; and Green Box those that were "decoupled" from price and production.[10]
- Blue Box policies were capped (at 1992 levels) but not included in reduction commitments.
- Green Box policies were unrestricted, thus encouraging countries to move to instruments of support compatible with the definition in Annex 2.

- De minimis exclusions of 10% of the value of production—5% product specific and 5% non–product specific—were allowed.
- Total Aggregate Measure of Support (AMS), calculated as total domestic support less Green Box, Blue Box, and de minimis payments, was to be reduced (by 20%).
- Developing countries were allowed some additional scope for domestic policies related to development, as well as larger de minimis allowances.

Many developed countries have reformed farm policies since the base period (1986–88) chosen for reduction commitments, and generally have not used all their domestic support "entitlements."[11] The general move to targeted and decoupled payments has been consistent with the constraints imposed by the URAA.

However, not all countries have been content with the operation of the rules on domestic support. Developing countries and competitive exporters have accused developed countries (the U.S. and EU, primarily) of "box-shifting" to avoid restraints. As this was indeed one of the objectives of the URAA (to shift policy instruments toward less trade-distorting alternatives) this may seem somewhat inconsistent. But the problem has emerged as to whether significant payments given directly to farmers really do reduce the incentive to produce. So the question for policy-makers is whether to subdivide the Green Box and hence impose some constraints on direct payments even if not tied to current output levels.

So the outcome of the Uruguay Round has had a major impact on the conduct of trade policy, and domestic farm policy, in particular in developed countries. The URAA introduced effective disciplines on agricultural trade by establishing special rules.[12] A tariffs-only regime was instituted (hence Article 11.2[c] is no longer needed), though the SSG and the creation of TRQs make provision for those cases where tariffs replaced quantitative restrictions. The URAA banned new export subsidies and limited existing export subsidies but did not eliminate them. Thus, special agricultural rules still apply in this area, though the number of countries that use such subsidies is small. The URAA disciplined domestic subsidies but classified them differently from the SCM and therefore set up an apparently parallel set of criteria for judging the trade impact of such measures. Institutional innovations, such as the establishment of the Agriculture Committee, have had some limited success in providing greater transparency.

Several other agreements that were concluded at the Uruguay Round have had an effect on trade in the agricultural and food sectors. These include the Agreement on Sanitary and Phytosanitary Measures (SPS Agreement), the Agreement on Technical Barriers to Trade (TBT Agreement) and the agreement on Trade-Related Aspects of Intellectual Property Rights (TRIPS agreement). The significance of these agreements for agriculture has increased in recent years, as a result of the increased trade in processed and high-value products. The SPS Agreement was negotiated largely to limit the extent to which countries could use health and safety measures to restrict imports when no agreed threat to health (of humans, plants, or animals) was involved. Exporting countries such as the United States, Canada, and

Australia were concerned that importers such as the EU, Japan, and Korea would introduce "economic" considerations when enacting health and safety regulations.[13] The solution was to require all countries when making such regulations to frame them in the context of a risk assessment, to use international standards when possible, and to be prepared to justify with scientific evidence any restrictions more exacting than those standards. In addition, a system of notification of new standards was established and a committee to consider complaints about restrictions considered to be out of compliance. The transparency of the system has been greatly improved, and the majority of complaints have been resolved without resort to dispute settlement (Josling, Roberts, and Orden, 2004).

The TBT Agreement covers all regulations not related to health and safety. In such regulations relating to food and agricultural products (e.g., labeling and container size restrictions) scientific evidence is not likely to be in question. But the agreement also suggests adherence to multilateral standards and requires countries to achieve legitimate objectives with the least disruption to trade. Though the TBT Agreement has not had the visibility of the SPS Agreement, it, too, has forestalled several conflicts through the discussions in the TBT committee. Not all conflicts have proved easy to resolve: issues such as the labeling of foods containing genetically modified organisms (GMOs) have bounced between the SPS and TBT committees with little progress apparent.

One aspect of global expansion of food markets is that of avoiding the misuse of geographical names that might mislead consumers. This question has been handled in limited agreements between countries (mostly European) for the past hundred years. The inclusion of an agreement on trade-related intellectual property in the Uruguay Round provided an opportunity for those countries that made extensive use of such "Geographical Indications" (GIs) to have them incorporated into the TRIPS agreement.[14] Moreover, for wines and spirits, an additional level of protection was provided in that the GIs could not be usurped even if no confusion of consumers was claimed. Thus the effect of the TRIPS Article 23 was to go beyond consumer protection and give a valuable right to producers in a particular region to use a geographical name. It is not surprising that conflicts have continued between countries intent on facilitating the development of local and regional foods and those that are interested more in securing brand recognition and willing to use "generic" geographical terms when helpful to establish such brands.[15]

Another significant development at the Uruguay Round that has influenced trade in the area of agriculture is the strengthening of the rules relating to trade disputes. Agricultural trade has generated more than its share of disputes in the past fifty years (Josling, 2009a). Lack of a clear structure of rules to constrain government activity in these markets, coupled with the particularly sensitive nature of trade in basic foodstuffs, has been the main cause of this disproportion. With the introduction of the URAA, much of the ambiguity was removed, but this did not stem the flow of disputes. Indeed, the strengthened legal provisions of the Dispute Settlement Understanding (DSU) gave encouragement to complainants to attempt to settle long-standing disputes that had eluded the weaker GATT dispute settlement process.

The rush to make use of the enhanced dispute settlement procedures was not immediate. A temporary exemption was given (for nine years) to certain subsidies from challenge in the WTO (URAA Article 13, known as the Peace Clause): in effect, it allowed agricultural subsidies to avoid challenge under the SCM that was also a part of the Uruguay Round package. However, the expiry of the Peace Clause in 2003 and a growing willingness on the part of exporters to challenge domestic farm programs in other countries through action under the DSU has once again stirred the agricultural pot. Now trade disputes are more frequently leading to litigation, encouraged by the slow progress in the Doha Round of trade negotiations. New types of disputes also emerged, reflecting changing trade patterns and structures. Many of these new disputes related to health and safety issues, taking advantage of the more structured rules included in the SPS Agreement. Others dealt with market access issues, in part over the interpretation of the new obligations. More recently, agricultural disputes have challenged the scope for domestic and export subsidies, under the Agreement on Agriculture and the Agreement on SCM (also part of the Uruguay Round outcome). In the absence of an agreement in the Doha Round, one might expect these conflicts to intensify, as countries attempt to use litigation to achieve what might otherwise be gained through negotiation. And if the Agreement on Agriculture does become revised in a successful Doha conclusion, there will no doubt be several more issues that will need to be resolved through the DSU.

AGRICULTURE IN THE DOHA ROUND

The current discussions in the WTO Doha Round about further reform of the agricultural trade system can be thought of as a follow-up from the Uruguay Round. The Doha Round is intended to bring the liberalization in agricultural markets that was promised but not delivered in the Uruguay Round. The main aims of the negotiators are to reduce agricultural tariffs substantially (albeit with some flexibility for "sensitive" and "special" products, as defined in the text). The Round also includes talks on services, and non-agricultural market access (NAMA) as well as on trade facilitation. Progress in all areas is needed for a successful conclusion, and the slow pace of the agricultural component has prevented agreement in the other areas. The agenda shift was in response to the demands by developing countries that the Doha Development Agenda would encourage and facilitate development and if possible remove some of the impacts of asymmetry in the operation of the trade system.

Trade negotiations of this complexity and importance are commonly a long-drawn-out process of exploring possible approaches. Member governments agree to deadlines to give structure and urgency to the process but often find agreement difficult when the deadline arrives. The early phase of the talks was marked by a large number of submissions on the way the agricultural talks might be focused, as well as specific comments on particular items of interest. The incorporation of the agricultural talks in the Doha Round increased the scope for trade-off and for an ambitious outcome.

The Doha Round has limped from one missed deadline to another. Agricultural difficulties have been a major reason for the slow progress. However, in early 2008 talks began coalescing about draft documents circulated by the chairman of the agricultural negotiating committee, and a miniministerial in July 2008 pushed resolutely toward an agreed modalities document. This agreement has proved elusive, though a compromise had emerged on most of the issues, and these are included in a revised modalities draft dated December 6, 2008 (WTO, 2008).[16] The process is currently (October 2011) on hold and may yet be declared to have failed. In any case, as a result of the U.S. election cycle, no final agreement would be possible before 2013.

The importance of the Doha Round to agricultural trade policy is hard to overstate. The final elimination of export subsidies would be a major step, and the pegging of trade-distorting support at a relatively low level would prevent a shift backward in policy reform. Cutting bound tariffs by over one-half would begin to bring border protection levels in agriculture more into line with non-agricultural tariffs. However, the main sticking point is now the degree of flexibility that countries will have to protect particular sectors against import surges.[17] It is proving a striking demonstration of the diverging interests of the major negotiating parties in the Doha Round. It is tempting to interpret the meaning of these positions as indicating the future evolution of agricultural trade policies. If the reluctance of major developing countries to further liberalize the imports of special and sensitive products proves to be the cause for the collapse of the Doha Round, then that bodes ill for future trade liberalization.

AGRICULTURE IN REGIONAL TRADE AGREEMENTS (RTAs)

Over the same period that the multilateral trade rules were being established and refined, countries were negotiating regional and bilateral trade agreements that dealt with many of the same issues. Agricultural trade has always been a contentious issue for these agreements, as it has been for multilateral negotiations. Agricultural trade is regarded as a subcategory of trade in goods for the purposes of bilateral, regional, and multilateral trade agreements and hence notionally subject to trade liberalization. But in virtually all such agreements, agricultural trade is subject to special treatment.

How have sensitive sectors of agriculture been protected from competition from regional and bilateral partners? A review of the various ways agriculture has been treated shows that this is most often done by quantitative restrictions on imports (Josling, 2009b). On some occasions. the sensitive sector is excluded altogether. More frequently, the tariff on imports from partners is reduced more slowly than that for other goods. But even with this special treatment, regional and bilateral trade agreements are slowly constraining the ability of governments to maintain a high level of protection for agricultural producers.

The exclusion of agriculture from RTAs in any case poses the issue of their consistency with WTO rules (specifically with Article XXIV of GATT 1994). Article XXIV requires "substantially all trade" to be covered, and the level of preference to be 100%. Though there has as yet been no agreement on the interpretation of "substantially all trade," agriculture is often the sector where the question arises. On the other hand, the prospect of competing exporters challenging the exclusion of agriculture in an RTA is remote: they benefit from the exclusion. And exporters within the RTA have implicitly agreed to the exclusion, and would be reluctant to make a challenge against a partner in respect to mutually agreed decisions.

The European Union led the way in the incorporation of agriculture into regional trade pacts, and in some respects still is in the vanguard. The agreement on the shape of the Common Agricultural Policy (CAP) in 1962 represented an attempt to develop at a regional level the market regulations for farm products that had existed in almost all members. By 1967, the six countries of the EEC had moved to common prices for the major products under a common regime of import levies and export subsidies at the border and intervention to take surpluses off the domestic market. In 1973 the UK, the largest import market for foodstuffs in Europe, joined the EEC along with Denmark and Ireland. Enlargement to include the Southern European countries took place in the 1980s, so that by the time of the Uruguay Round the EU had twelve members and the CAP was the most significant (and controversial) agricultural trade system in the global economy.[18]

In 1960 the countries of South America attempted to borrow from the European experience and set up the Latin America Free Trade Area (LAFTA), which encompassed most of the countries of the region.[19] The European model of open trade was constrained, however, by the economic paradigm prevalent in Latin America of import substitution industrialization that involved high protection for domestic sectors that could reduce dependence on imports from the industrial countries. Agriculture was seen as low on the list of priorities for such treatment and was generally omitted from sectors that were "offered" as candidates for regional investment. The Andean Pact, which emerged as a spinoff from LAFTA, also made little progress in rationalizing regional agriculture. The Caribbean countries that had gained their independence over this period formed a Caribbean Free Trade Area (CARIFTA) that has developed over time to become the Caribbean Community (CARICOM).

The nature of the trade agreements in the Latin American and Caribbean region shifted sharply in the mid-1980s, as country after country abandoned the import substitution model in favor of an opening of the economy to competition through low tariff barriers and less government intervention in markets. By the time of the

Uruguay Round, the prevailing economic paradigm was moving decisively in the direction of lower trade barriers, whether negotiated in multilateral or regional agreements or decided unilaterally. Moreover, the incorporation of agricultural trade in these agreements had begun, though with exceptions for particularly sensitive products (Almeida et al., 2009). It is unlikely that the region will ever be satisfied with markets close to home: Latin American countries played, and continue to play, a major role in pushing for more open trade in farm products in the WTO.

In Africa a number of postcolonial free-trade areas were formed, though they did not address issues with respect to the main trade flows of agricultural products and raw materials between these countries and the European market. These agricultural trade relations developed under the auspices of the EU, as a series of nonreciprocal preferential trade pacts, consolidated in the Lomé agreements. As part of a major revamping of its trade policy with its former colonies (known as the African, Caribbean and Pacific countries, the ACP) the EU has been converting the nonreciprocal preference agreements to fully reciprocal free-trade agreements with groups of the ACP.[20] The dominance of trade with the EU has led to stagnation in the development of regional markets. Internal African food trade has been hampered by all manner of problems, from political conflicts to inadequate roads. The goal of an African Economic Union has been espoused over the years. The reality, at least for agriculture, is that intraregional trade has not expanded along with the growth of RTAs in Africa.

Asia was left far behind in the development of regional trade agreements until recently: the one major regional initiative in the period up to 1995, the Association of South East Asian Nations (ASEAN), was set up mainly for political and security reasons and economic integration (through the ASEAN Free Trade Agreement) emerged as an afterthought. But like that of a recent convert, the enthusiasm for free-trade agreements in the area has been striking. The trickle of such agreements a few years ago, when Singapore began to court trade partners, has become a flood. Moreover, agricultural trade is not excluded from such agreements, though sensitive products such as rice and palm oil are usually treated with delicacy. Internal ASEAN trade in agricultural and food products has grown recently, and the diverse nature of the region and its outreach to Australia and New Zealand, as well as to Latin America, promises to maintain this trend. The participation of Japan in such agreements and the recent interest of China and India in forging free-trade agreements make this a dynamic region for agricultural trade.

The parallel development of regional and multilateral trade systems was exemplified by the discussions among the United States, Canada, and Mexico leading up to the North American Free Trade Agreement (NAFTA) in 1992.[21] The United States had already negotiated a free trade agreement with Canada (the Canada-US Free Trade Area, or C-USFTA) in 1986 (at the start of the Uruguay Round), and much of the content and language of the C-USFTA found its way into the GATT drafts. The treatment of agriculture in NAFTA was a mix of boldness and caution. U.S.-Mexican trade was opened up (with a long transition period for some key commodities) but the U.S.-Canada bilateral respected the sensitivity of Canadian farmers and excluded products where "supply control" was a part of Canadian policy (basically dairy and poultry). So the North American agricultural market remains hampered by national policies, and particularly the impact of U.S. domestic farm policies, but is broadly integrated in terms of investment and distribution.

The 15 years since NAFTA has seen a remarkable change in the U.S. approach to bilateral trade agreements. The U.S. began to negotiate several bilateral free-trade agreements as an expression of a policy of "competitive liberalization" as articulated by the U.S. special trade representative. This policy consisted of offering swift negotiations to any country that was willing to conform to the terms consistent with the mandate of the U.S. administration, as specified in the Trade Promotion Authority. The list of willing trade partners included Singapore, Chile, and Australia, to be joined by Morocco, Bahrain, and Oman. Talks with South Korea, Colombia, Panama, Ecuador, and Peru have been completed, though the agreements with Korea, Colombia, and Panama have yet to be approved by the U.S. Congress.

The United States and five Central American countries—Costa Rica, El Salvador, Guatemala, Honduras, and Nicaragua—began negotiations for a Central American Free Trade Agreement (CAFTA) on January 27, 2003. President Bush notified Congress of his intent to enter into the CAFTA on February 13, 2004. Negotiations with the Dominican Republic (DR) were concluded on March 15, 2004, that would fully integrate that country into the CAFTA. The CAFTA/DR agreements will conclude the establishment of free-trade agreements between the United States and almost all of the countries in Central America.

What agricultural provisions do these free-trade agreements contain? All of them have provisions for tariff reductions that affect many food and agricultural goods. However, with few exceptions, the agreements control trade in a range of products considered politically sensitive in one or both partners. For the United States, these sensitivities include sugar, citrus fruits, peanuts, and dairy products, and for the partners the list includes corn and beans along with rice. Mediterranean products do not generally reach the level of sensitivity to be granted exceptions. With the partial exception of wine (where the bilateral with Chile gave a major wine exporter free access to the U.S. market) and tomatoes and citrus (where Mexico had the capacity to expand exports in competition with Florida), the partner countries have not posed any significant threat to U.S. producers of Mediterranean products. Similarly, these products have not been particularly sensitive in the partner country.

The EU negotiated a free-trade agreement with Mexico in 1995, just after the entry into force of NAFTA. The EU-Mexico free-trade agreement does not reach the ambition of NAFTA, with the creation of a tariff- and quota-free zone for agricultural products covering Mexico and the United States. However, some agricultural trade is included. Current levels of trade in Mediterranean products between Mexico and the EU are small, in part because of the proximity of the U.S. Mediterranean production areas to Mexico.

A more significant bilateral is that negotiated between the EU and the Republic of South Africa (RSA). The EU-RSA agreement had a strong political imperative, as

Europe's contribution to the support of the political changes in South Africa. However, granting the RSA easy access to the EU market was not without its controversy. In particular, the wine and spirit sector posed significant challenges, as the RSA had developed a number of products often aimed at the UK market that capitalized on name recognition of similar products from Southern Europe (notably port and sherry).[22] The trade agreement was held up by this controversy. The RSA finally agreed to discontinue the use of European names even when other countries had been able to use these as generic terms.

The EU negotiated a bilateral free trade agreement with Chile that came into effect in 2003. The EU is the primary trading partner of Chile. Commentators have noted that the style of this agreement is considerably different from those with the Mediterranean countries. While those agreements list products and their corresponding tariff reductions, the Chile agreement contains lists of different products grouped by the number of years until total liberalization. This indicates not just a simple reduction of tariff rates from most-favored-nation (MFN) levels, but a firm commitment to completely eliminate tariffs on certain products over a scheduled timeframe. In other words, the EU-Chile agreement includes a timetable and a commitment that is missing in many of the more sensitive EU agreements.[23]

Among those that are most significant for developing countries are those negotiated under the European Partnership framework. Traditionally, the EU has used the policy of trade preferences as a strategy of cooperation for development. Trade concessions have been granted by the EU on unilateral basis to other countries. Now, Europe-Mediterranean agreements take further steps for trade liberalization on a bilateral and reciprocal basis. Since the first Euro-Mediterranean Conference in November 1995, the EU and 12 Mediterranean countries have been engaged in negotiating Association Agreements (the Barcelona Process). The overall objective is to form one Euro-Mediterranean free-trade area from the separate agreements in place. To date, bilateral Association Agreements have been concluded with seven trade partners: Tunisia (1995), Israel (1995), Morocco (1996), Jordan (1997), the Palestinian Authority (1997), Algeria (2001), and Lebanon (2002).

Agriculture is a key sector in the debate between trade partners, as it is seen as necessary to establish a balance of commercial opportunities through the increase in both industrial and agricultural exports from the region. However, trade in agriculture is subjected to weak liberalization, within the present framework of the Association Agreements. No specific liberalization road map has been defined for the agricultural sector as a whole. Only for certain products have specific concessions for liberalization been determined.

The EU offers enhanced preferences beyond those of other developing countries to Sub-Saharan African, Caribbean, and Pacific countries (the ACP countries) under the Cotonou Agreement. There are individual protocols for bananas, beef, veal, and sugar. These products accounted for three-quarters of the value of ACP preferences in the late 1990s, including industrial products, which are all eligible for duty-free access. The regime of tariff preferences was maintained through 2007 to allow the EU time to negotiate with subregional

ACP country groupings. Such negotiations were broadly concluded by the end of 2007, but not all ACP members have yet agreed to their terms.

The EU also discriminates in favor of LDCs. Market access barriers were removed under the Everything But Arms (EBA) initiative introduced in 2001, which grants duty-free access, without any quantitative restrictions, to all imports from LDCs (except arms and munitions). Liberalization was immediate except for three products (fresh bananas, rice, and sugar), for which the tariff was gradually reduced to zero (in 2006 for bananas and 2009 for rice and sugar). The effect of the EBA initiative, however, is likely to be limited in the short and medium run, since the LDCs were not exporting the products that were immediately liberalized under EBA.

LOOKING FORWARD

Though there has been considerable progress through the parallel processes of domestic reform and multilateral trade agreements toward a more open system for agricultural trade, the sector remains among the most protected. Moreover, the process of trade and domestic policy reform has been uneven among sectors. The so-called white goods—rice, cotton, sugar, and milk—have among the highest tariff barriers and the most pervasive domestic subsidies. The sensitivity of these goods extends to exporting countries. The United States, normally a supporter of low tariffs, has come under pressure from trading partners to reduce subsidies on each of these products. This has complicated the position of the United States in trade talks, arguing for others to open up markets but being more cautious in offering to cut support or lower tariffs where domestic interests are vocal. The EU also has its sensitive products, including dairy and beef, though it has recently modified its domestic policies for rice, sugar, and cotton. The Uruguay Round did relatively little to improve the situation in the "white goods" markets, and their inclusion in regional trade agreements has often been politically sensitive. Sugar, for instance, was left out of the U.S.-Australia Free Trade Agreement and was given a "temporary" exclusion from the MERCOSUR trade arrangements.

In addition to the reduction of protection for these sensitive products, other issues remain before agricultural trade can fulfill its role as the basis for a secure global food system. One such issue is the future of farm programs in developed and emerging economies. So a key issue for the next decade or so is whether the domestic reform process will continue, so that all developed countries will in essence have rural policies that emphasize land stewardship and rural development, nutrition policies that focus on quality and food safety, and agricultural policies that are aimed specifically at issues of productivity enhancement and risk management. Such a world would be consistent with a more open trade system and the removal of the many impediments that developing countries face in supplying food to the industrial country markets. But reform could become unhinged if attitudes changed, perhaps as a result of food shortages or a collapse of world trade. It would not be difficult for those who would prefer the old policies of protection of producers by governmental management of markets to make the case that the "free market" had not worked. And the benefit of keeping the major developed countries moving along the same path, albeit at different speeds, is clear. It would be difficult to imagine the EU following a reform agenda that removed government from involvement in commodity markets if the United States were moving in the other direction by increasing that involvement. So this is one area where the backstopping of the multilateral trade system is particularly useful. The Doha Round will play a major role in ensuring that the market-oriented reforms of the past 20 years in developed country farm policies are not reversed.

The more difficult question is whether developing countries will follow the same pattern with respect to the protection of domestic markets and producers. Much of the impetus for public intervention in developed country markets came as a reaction to different rates of growth in the agricultural and the non-agricultural sectors. Strong growth in manufactures and services can put pressure on the government to intervene to help agriculture. But how that assistance is given, and under what conditions, is important. The Agreement on Agriculture will continue to be a significant international constraint on this choice.

There are two typical strategies from which developing countries choose when considering their agricultural trade policy. The first is that common in Latin America, which entered the 1980s with considerable protection for its agriculture and highly regulated domestic markets. These countries, often with the support of the World Bank, the Inter-American Development Bank, and the International Monetary Fund, began a process of "structural adjustment" that emphasized opening up the agricultural sector along with other parts of the economy. As a result, applied tariffs even on agricultural products are now relatively low, though the bound rates are often higher. This type of agricultural policy has been conducive to growth of trade and to stronger regional markets. However, the process could always go in reverse: serious income problems in rural areas of Latin America could spur a resurgence of protectionism. A disruption of exports to the United States and Europe might be enough to bring two decades of relatively open trade policies to a close.

The second strategy that may be followed is more typical of Asia, where agricultural trade policy owes more to debates about self-sufficiency and poverty alleviation than about access into the lucrative U.S. market. This has led to an increase in agricultural protection as countries experience rapid economic growth. The pattern has been repeated in several countries since the 1960s, first in Japan, then in Korea, and now in China and India. How the emerging countries manage the stresses of relative agricultural decline will determine the extent to which they will agree to further liberalization in agricultural trade. The holdup in the Doha Round in July 2008 illustrated the problem. Negotiators failed to agree on modalities that included a special safeguard mechanism for developing countries that would have allowed them to raise tariffs to protect their agriculture when world prices fell.

The choices made by the larger developing countries will help to set the agenda for the next set of trade negotiations in agriculture. The Doha Round, if successful, will have eliminated export subsidies and some policies such as export credit guarantees, aid to parastatal exporters, and export enhancement through food aid. Domestic support will have been reduced to a fraction of existing limits, and will no longer allow countries to maintain expensive trade-distorting price support systems. Tariffs will have been sharply cut, and will be weakened even further by the multiple concessions granted through regionals and bilaterals. What will remain is relatively high protection for a small group of products, including rice, cotton, dairy, and sugar (the white goods). The reduction of these tariffs will have to wait until the next set of negotiations.

What will be left of the domestic support programs is direct payments (not linked to output or to price) and infrastructure support for the sector. It is likely that some clarification of the way domestic support is notified may be needed within a year or two. Market price support (in the Aggregate Measure of Support) is now virtually without meaning for most developed countries: the administered prices, the eligible quantities, and the reference prices are increasingly irrelevant to the question of policy reform. And the Green Box, which was intended to capture trade-neutral subsidies, now includes a raft of payments tied to environmental aims.

It would be misleading to suggest that the processes of globalization in farm and food trade and of reform of domestic policies have removed all the obstacles to open trade in agricultural goods. The process of reform has taken place at different speeds in different countries. So the pace of trade negotiations is still controlled to a large extent by the slowest reformers. Among the developed countries this includes Japan, Norway, and Switzerland. Not only is protection high in these countries but the types of policies used still rely heavily on protection at the border. Hence, they have been prominent members of the Group of Ten, in the context of the WTO Doha Round, arguing for generous exclusions for "sensitive products," more modest tariff cuts, and no cap on the height of tariffs. Among the developing countries, the reluctant importers have formed the Group of 33, and emphasized the need for adequate provision for "special products" and the inclusion of a "special safeguard mechanism" to allow them to reimpose tariffs if domestic markets are disrupted. These two groups, though negotiating separately, have effectively limited the "level of ambition" of the market-access talks on agriculture.

The global food system has seen dramatic changes over the past 20 years, and the trade rules are in the process of catching up with these developments. The main manifestation of globalization of the food sector has been the establishment of global supply chains, with the driving force behind such chains being supermarkets and food processors. The increasingly aware consumer has played a willing role in this development. In developed countries, the successful attempt by retailers to package attributes of health and environmental responsibility with foodstuffs, along with animal welfare and in some cases labor conditions, has transformed the economics of food trade. In developing countries, consumers have increasingly embraced the availability of nonlocal foods and the better reliability and quality control that can come with firm size and management expertise.

A further trend is noticeable in developed country markets toward local foods and more diverse distribution systems—such as farmers' markets. Though still a small part of total food consumption, this trend poses some interesting questions for food trade. The balance between increased globalization of the food system and the "localization" of food supplies has implications for developing-country food suppliers. Longer food chains have integrated many developing countries into the global marketplace, though also leading to a bifurcation of the suppliers into those that have the capacity to meet strict standards and those that don't. But the push for local food in several developed countries has made it somewhat harder for overseas suppliers to compete. The organic foods movement has exacerbated this problem by introducing a series of private standards that are both market-specific and costly to adopt. Once again, foreign suppliers often struggle to meet the conditions for entry into lucrative markets.

This has set up some potential conflicts in the area of food trade. Governments negotiated at length to establish the rules for national health and safety regulations contained in the SPS Agreement. This circumscribed the ability of governments to set import standards that were not justified by risk assessment and based on scientific evidence. But tconsumers in many cases decided that governments and their scientific advisors were underplaying certain subjective risks to health and to the environment. Headline issues such as biotech crops became grist for the mill in the competition for market shares among retailers. But this was merely the tip of the iceberg, as private standards tied to particular marketable attributes began to proliferate. The SPS Agreement has been very successful in increasing transparency, particularly in the area of animal and plant diseases and curbing the egregious use of SPS barriers for the protection of domestic producers, but has not been so effective in cases where public sentiment has dominated scientific consensus. And the role of private standards, unconstrained by the need to exhibit scientific justification, further complicates an already difficult corner of the trade system.

The question that countries will have to face in the next few years is whether to try to amend the SPS Agreement to allow government regulations to respond to consumer concerns that have not been found to have scientific merit. Exporting countries clearly see this as a possible end to the SPS Agreement as a constraint on governments: who is going to arbitrate on whether subjective fears pass some test of credibility and legitimacy? But in the absence of some sort of solution to this problem, the SPS Agreement will increasingly become irrelevant for most food trade. This could be compounded by the adoption of standards related to such longer-term health topics such as obesity. The SPS Agreement relates to regulations governing the safety of foods, but eating too much of a "safe" food can cause health problems. So it is not inconceivable that an agency such as the World Health Organization could find itself advocating policies that are in contradiction to the SPS Agreement.

Potentially overwhelming all these issues is that of climate change, or at least the actions taken by governments to slow down global warming. Most actions will increase the price of oil-based inputs, and some will allow for another valuable output from agriculture—the sequestration of carbon.[24] The impact of these policies on the competitive position of agriculture and hence on agricultural production and trade is complex, particularly if combinations of policies are used (Blandford and Josling, 2009). The effects depend on such factors as whether agriculture is the target of the policies or is affected by policies applied to other sectors, whether the policies generate private incentives to change production methods or the volume of output or whether this is solely generated by a publicly funded incentive, and whether the net effect is to create an incentive to increase agricultural output in the aggregate or to change its composition. In general, policies that restrict current activities (e.g., take land out of production) will have a depressing effect on production. Policies that subsidize particular practices will tend to encourage output.

The main constraint from the viewpoint of trade rules is that in order to qualify for the environmental component of the Green Box under the WTO Agreement on Agriculture, subsidies should be limited to the extra costs incurred by farmers. Tying current direct payments to sequestration or other beneficial aspects of farming activity may be subject to challenge, as they would almost certainly exceed the additional costs involved. Moreover, such a link would weaken the claim that the payments are unrelated to current production activity and hence trade-neutral. In other words, care has to be taken to assure that climate change subsidies respect the criteria of the Green Box. Alternatively, the Green Box criteria may need to be clarified to reflect desirable policy.

Domestic climate change legislation is constrained by international trade obligations, but a carefully crafted program should not raise insuperable problems (see Hufbauer et al., 2009, for a full treatment of this issue). It should be possible to devise domestic schemes that contribute to effective international action. However, an international consensus on what measures are likely to be effective is crucial for avoiding trade disputes. The move toward "decoupled" payments unrelated to price and current output has provided an opportunity for such a consensus. Recoupling these payments in such a way that climate change mitigation is encouraged, without jeopardizing food security, may be a constructive first step.

GLOSSARY

Aggregate measure of support (AMS)	The AMS aggregates all domestic support payments that are considered to distort trade. Current Total AMS is notified and compared with the allowable AMS (the Final Bound AMS) as in the schedule.
Domestic support	Assistance to farmers given by subsidies and support prices other than those administered at the border (tariffs, etc.).
Export competition	Conditions of export competition as distorted by export subsidies and other assistance to export sectors, including surplus disposal through food aid, subsidies to state trading enterprises and the granting of export credit at other than commercial rates.

Market access	The terms of entry into import markets, particularly tariffs, quotas, licenses, along with safeguard actions.
Amber Box	Elements of domestic support that are deemed trade-distorting and hence included in the Aggregate Measure of Support (AMS).
Blue Box	Elements of domestic support that are linked with supply controls (payments conditional on crop or livestock limitations, as defined in Article 6.5(a) of the Agreement on Agriculture). These payments are deemed to be less trade-distorting than Amber Box policies but more so than Green Box policies.
Green Box	Elements of domestic support that are considered non- or minimally trade-distorting, and satisfy the conditions in Annex 2 of the WTO Agreement on Agriculture. They should not be tied to current price and output levels.
Export credits	Schemes that guarantee payments to exporters in the event of default by importing firms.
Special products	Products that are of particular significance in developing countries as a result of being essential for food security and livelihood security.
Sensitive products	Products that are deemed sensitive by importers and for which they can choose to use alternatives to tariff cuts (i.e. quota increases) to improve market access.
Tariff rate quota (TRQ)	A two-tier tariff whereby a low (or zero) tariff is charged on the first tranche of imports. (Also referred to as a tariff-quota.)
Special Safeguards	The Special Safeguard for Agriculture (SSG) allows countries to impose import restrictions if import prices are lower than trigger prices or quantities surge by more than particular amounts. It is only available for products that have undergone "tariffication."
MFN	Most-favored-nation principle, whereby each WTO member must grant to all as favorable access as it grants to the "most favored" nation. In other words, discrimination among members is not allowed.
Preferences	The granting of access to particular trading partners. This inconsistency with MFN is allowed under certain conditions, such as Customs Unions and Free Trade Areas, and in favor of developing countries.
Geographical indications	Terms relating to the geographical region or place where goods are produced that are protected by countries as the intellectual property of producers in that region.

State trading enterprises	Parastatal and state owned firms or agencies that import or export products, usually with exclusive responsibilities for such trade.
Multifunctionality	A term relating to the varied functions of agriculture including the stewardship of the countryside and the employment of rural people in addition to the production of farm goods.
Nontrade concerns	Concerns that enter into the decision on trade liberalization not strictly related to commercial benefits
Tariff reduction formula	Methods of reducing tariffs in negotiations. Main types include "across-the-board" cuts of a particular percentage and "harmonizing" formulae that cut higher tariffs by a greater percentage. Tiered and banded approaches use different percentage cuts within defined bands.
Peace Clause	This refers to Article 13 of the Agreement on Agriculture that sheltered Green Box policies for a period of nine years from actionability under the Subsidies and Countervailing Measures Agreement (SCM) and Amber and Blue Box policies from actionability if payments did not increase relative to the 1992 levels. Export subsidies were also nonactionable for the period of the Peace Clause.
Tariffication	The conversion of nontariff import barriers into tariffs, using the tariff-equivalent (the tariff that would have the same impact on imports).
Ad Valorem equivalents	The equivalent in percentage terms of a tariff expressed in "per ton" or other specific or conditional form.
De Minimis provisions	Nominal amounts of domestic support that are not included in the Current Total AMS when comparing with scheduled levels. Product-specific and non-product-specific de minimis levels were set at 5% for developed countries and 10% for developing countries.
Tariff escalation	Tariffs that increase with the degree of processing. Lower-priced raw materials give additional protection to the processors and increase their "value added."
Bound tariffs	Tariffs that are bound cannot be increased without negotiations with principle suppliers usually leading to compensation through reductions in other tariffs.
Applied tariffs	Tariffs actually applied can be well below the "bound" tariffs notified to the WTO.
Ceiling bindings	Binding many tariffs at a nominal (usually high) level was allowed to developing countries as an alternative to line-by-line calculation of tariff equivalents (tariffication).

NOTES

1. Agricultural trade policy has its own jargon. While an attempt has been made to explain terms in the text, a glossary is appended to help the reader over linguistic hurdles.

2. Even this provision did not constrain the use of quotas to defend farm policy in developed countries. A prominent example of this was the imposition of quotas by the United States under Section 22 of the Agricultural Adjustment Act (as amended) that mandated quantitative restrictions on imports of a number of goods whenever domestic programs were "materially interfered with" by imports. This required a waiver of the U.S. obligations under Article 11, a waiver that was renewed annually until made irrelevant by the Uruguay Round outcome (see below). The EU also avoided restraints on its Common Agricultural Policy (CAP), which used "variable levies" to stabilize the duty-paid price of imports. Such an instrument was not easily classified as either a customs duty or a quantitative restriction. The Uruguay Round Agreement on Agriculture specifically bans such variable levies.

3. An exception to this was the successful removal of many of Japan's quantitative restrictions on imports.

4. There are of course linkages between the pillars. For instance the subsidization of exports requires some restraints on imports. Domestic programs often work in conjunction with border measures to keep domestic prices high. Indeed, at the beginning of the Uruguay Round there was discussion of the notion of using an overall measure of support (including that from border measures) as the vehicle for liberalization. This was however rejected in favor of disciplines on the three pillars individually.

5. See the glossary for clarification of the sometimes arcane vocabulary of the agricultural agreement.

6. Tariff-rate quotas are more commonly called tariff quotas in other branches of commercial policy.

7. A bound tariff cannot be increased without consultation and negotiation with affected suppliers. See the glossary.

8. Many of these ceilings were set at high and arbitrary levels, such as 100 or 200%, and applied across a wide range of products.

9. Competing exporters have long considered that food aid programs cross the line between meeting the needs of countries that would not otherwise be able to purchase food on world markets and disposing of surpluses by selling food at low prices to developing countries on the pretext of meeting these needs.

10. The term "amber box" is not defined in the URAA, but has become used in place of the more formal Total Aggregate Measure of Support (AMS). For a more complete explanation of the terms used in describing domestic support see Orden et al. (2011), chapter 2.

11. A recent study has explored in more detail the link between domestic support notifications by the major developed countries and the policy changes that took place coincidentally (Orden et al. 2011). In some cases, there is a clear causal link between the URAA and domestic reform, but the degree of flexibility given by the high base period support levels (world price levels were low in the late 1980s) and the modest reduction requirements (20%) has meant that the WTO constraints have not been the main cause of domestic policy reform.

12. This is in contrast to the treatment of trade in textiles and clothing, where a temporary regime, the Agreement on Textiles and Clothing, was set up. The Agreement on Textiles and Clothing expired in 2005, and no special rules now exist for this sector. Protection levels remain high, however, and constraints on trade negotiated as part of China's entry into the WTO are still in place (see WTO 1995).

13. One issue that had concerned exporters was the possibility, reportedly under discussion in the EU, to take into account market needs when considering health regulations in the area of livestock trade. The EU ban on imports of beef treated with hormones (i.e. from the U.S. and Canada, where this was a normal practice) was taken as a prelude of things to come.

14. Geographical Indications are a type of intellectual property right that enables groups of producers exclusive use of a geographical name that may have market value through its reputation with consumers. Many of these GIs are for European wines, cheeses, meats, and other "quality" foods that might otherwise face competition from non-European producers using the same of similar names.

15. Among the issues that have been the cause of trade tensions are trademarks for Parma ham and Roquefort cheese used (legitimately) by firms that are not selling products from those particular European regions. In the case of wine, the issues have revolved around a list of generic names often used by wine makers outside Europe to identify wine types rather than their provenance.

16. Previous revisions to the original July 2007 Draft were issued on 8 February, 19 May, and 10 July 2008.

17. The Mini-Ministerial held in Geneva at the end of July 2008 broke up when the negotiation over the Special Safeguard Mechanism (SSM) reached stalemate. Most other agricultural issues were within reach of an agreement. However, the negotiations did not address the difficult issue of deeper cuts in cotton subsidies.

18. Countries that had stayed outside the EEC formed a less comprehensive free trade area (the European Free Trade Association) that excluded agriculture and fisheries from its operations.

19. The countries of Central America had established a Central American Common Market in 1958, though political tensions among the members limited its effectiveness.

20. The move to reciprocal preferences was also driven by the desire to avoid having to renew the WTO waiver for the Lomé agreement, which was considered discriminatory.

21. In 1990, Mexico decided that access to the United States was essential to its own development, and sought a free trade area with the United States. The eventual NAFTA was a trilateral agreement with three bilateral market access agreements.

22. Similar problems arose with purveyors of alcoholic drinks on sale in the RSA market that used Greek and Italian names.

23. Turkey negotiated a Customs Union with the EU in 1995. Notable about this agreement is that it excluded agricultural products. Thus the trade in Mediterranean products between Turkey and the EU is in limbo, awaiting progress in the accession negotiations.

24. Some types of land use, particularly forestry, absorb (sequester) carbon dioxide and thus lessen the emission of greenhouse gases. Under some climate change mitigation schemes, agriculture would be able to be paid for this positive contribution to climate change mitigation.

REFERENCES

Almeida, Juliana Salles, Carlos M. Gutierrez, Jr., and Matthew Shearer (2009). *The Treatment of Agriculture in Regional Trade Agreements in the Americas, Integration and Trade Sector (INT)*. Washington, D.C.: Inter-American Development Bank.

Blandford, David, and Tim Josling (2009, September). *Greenhouse Gas Reduction Policies and Agriculture: Implications for Production Incentives and International Trade Disciplines*. ICTSD/IPC Policy Issues no. 1. Geneva: International Centre for Trade and Sustainable Development

Coleman, William, Wyn Grant, and Tim Josling (2004). *Agriculture in the New Global Economy*. Cheltenham, England: Edward Elgar

Hufbauer, G. C., S. Charnovitz, and J. Kim (2009). *Global Warming and the World Trade System*. Washington, D.C.: Peterson Institute for International Economics.

Josling, Tim (2009a). "Agricultural Trade Disputes in the WTO." Chapter 10 of James C. Hartigan, ed., *Frontiers of Economics and Globalization*, vol. 6. Bingley, England: Emerald Group.

Josling, Tim (2009b). "Agriculture." In Simon Lester and Bryan Mercurio, eds., *Bilateral and Regional Trade Agreements: Commentary and Analysis*. Cambridge: Cambridge University Press.

Josling, Tim, Donna Roberts, and David Orden (2004). *Food Regulation and Trade: Toward a Safe and Open Global System*. Washington, D.C.: Peterson Institute for International Economics.

Josling, Tim, and Stefan Tangermann (2003). "Production and Export Subsidies in Agriculture: Lessons from GATT and WTO Disputes Involving the US and the EC." In Ernst-Ulrich Petersmann and Mark Pollack, eds., *Transatlantic Economic Disputes*. Oxford: Oxford University Press.

Josling, Tim, Stefan Tangermann, and Thorald K. Warley (1996). *Agriculture in the GATT: Past, Present and Future*. Basingstoke, England: Macmillan.

Orden, David, David Blandford, and Tim Josling, eds. (2011). *Disciplining Domestic Agricultural Support through the WTO*. Cambridge: Cambridge University Press.

World Trade Organisation (1995). *Results of the Uruguay Round of Multilateral Trade Negotiations: The Legal Texts*. Geneva.

World Trade Organisation (2008, December 6). *Revised Draft Modalities for Agriculture*. TN/AG/W/4/Rev4. Geneva.

CHAPTER 6

THEORY AND ECONOMIC MODELING OF PREFERENTIAL TRADING ARRANGEMENTS

MORDECHAI E. KREININ AND MICHAEL G. PLUMMER

PARTICULARLY since the current Doha Development Agenda of the WTO has reached an impasse, countries interested in further trade liberalization have been pursuing bilateral and regional trading agreements with partner countries. According to the WTO Secretariat, the total number of such agreements notified to the WTO and are currently in force is 272, about a half of which came into effect after 2000. Moreover, 159 of these bilateral and regional trading agreements (or 58%) are free-trade agreements (FTAs). There appears to be a strong tendency toward entering into new bilateral and plurilateral accords as the multilateral process has stalled. It also appears that as globalization proceeds apace, the private sector is demanding that commercial policy keeps up: doing so is much easier at the bilateral and regional levels than at the multilateral level.

The European Union (EU) is the most famous and offers the most successful model of progressive regional cooperation. It began as a customs union with the Treaty of Rome in 1957 and advanced to a common market in 1986, completed a decade later. It has expanded to 27 member-states, of which 16 have adopted monetary union under the euro. The North American Free Trade Agreement (NAFTA) between Canada, Mexico, and the United States began in 1994 and is (economically) the largest FTA in the world. Arguably, it also marked the beginning of the modern wave of FTAs that has been sweeping international commercial relations. But the lion's share of emerging preferential trading arrangements involve developing countries, either paired with developed ("Northern") countries or among each other ("South-South" cooperation). The two most prominent South-South accords in this light would be, first, the Association of Southeast Asian Nations (ASEAN), which was initiated in 1967 and is currently comprised of 10 Southeast Asian countries.[1] It negotiated the ASEAN Free-Trade Area (AFTA) in 1992 and pledged in 2007 to create a stylized common market known as the ASEAN Economic Community by the end of 2015. Second, Mercosur (in English, the "Southern Common Market") was established in 1991 and is a loose customs union made up of four South American countries, that is, Argentina, Brazil, Paraguay, and Uruguay.

But apart from filling in a void left by the impasse at Doha, there are many economics-related arguments in favor of forming a regional agreement. First, there are potentially strong efficiency effects that can be derived from a well-constructed FTA. This chapter will discuss what these effects are; suffice it to note that the more an FTA can promote efficiency while minimizing discrimination against third countries, the greater the potential salutary effects. Second, negotiating economic liberalization with a select group of trade partners is more likely to lead to an agreement than bargaining at the multilateral level. It is easier, for example, to agree on sensitive commitments regarding market access between the like-minded ASEAN countries than in the highly diverse WTO with its 157 members. Third, a country may join a regional agreement because it needs a commitment device to underpin domestic policy reform. By signing an agreement, the government raises the cost of backsliding, thereby reducing vulnerability to special interest lobbies. For example, many North American economists supported NAFTA not for the direct effects of the agreement but rather to lock in the salutary reforms hitherto undertaken by Mexico in anticipation of joining NAFTA. Fourth, countries may also form a regional bloc to negotiate as a group with nonmember countries and therefore increase bargaining power. This has been done very effectively in the case of the EU.

This chapter provides a concise guide for policy-makers to the economic theory of FTAs and the modeling methods used to assess their effects. The focus is on FTAs because this appears to be the preferred regional trading agreement, perhaps because it is the shallowest form of integration compared to customs unions, common markets or economic unions. The main body of this chapter is comprised of three sections. The first section discusses the underlying economic theory of FTAs, focusing on the static net welfare effects. This will begin with analysis of the basic conceptual model developed by Viner (1950), which details the fundamental concepts of trade creation and trade diversion, and the modern analysis of FTAs. Next, it discusses the "dynamic effects" of an FTA and covers other issues that are relevant to anticipating the economic effects of an FTA (that is, "ex-ante assessment").

The second section explains the theoretical features of a computable general equilibrium (CGE) model that simulates the potential impact of an FTA. These

CGE models have become the most popular tool for evaluating the economic implications of an FTA. We also analyze the practical strengths and limitations of CGE analysis in evaluating a FTA. This type of ex ante model is followed in section II by analysis of ex-post approaches, in particular import-growth models and the gravity model. Section III considers extensions of our analysis to the special case of developing countries. Finally, Section V offers brief concluding remarks.

I. The Potential Economic Effects of an FTA: Theory

This section provides the theoretical foundation for the economic analysis of FTAs.[2] We employ a simple model that should help elucidate the basic economic consequences of modern FTAs.

We begin with definitions. An FTA is a commitment by the signatory members to remove tariffs between member states while continuing to maintain independent tariff regimes on imports from third countries. A customs union goes one step further by employing a common tariff regime against outsiders. Beyond a customs union, a commitment to free flows of goods, services, and factors of production (i.e., labor and capital) is called a "common market." An economic union is generally referred to as a common market with monetary union.

These are textbook definitions. In reality, the border-lines across definitions are blurred. For example, some FTAs exclude agriculture and/or services but may well include investment. Some customs unions have many exclusions to the "common external tariff" (CET), to the extent that they look like FTAs that just happen to have equal tariffs in some sectors. And the European Economic Community (EEC) was often called a "common market" when it was little more than a customs union for the first 30 years of its existence. Keeping in mind that these definitions may be slippery, we focus mostly on FTAs defined in the traditional way, given their predominance among bilateral and regional cooperative groupings in the international trading system. Besides, the basic principles inherent in an FTA apply generally to deeper forms of integration as well.[3]

What economists are primarily concerned with when analyzing the trade and welfare effects of an FTA is their preferential or discriminatory nature. Nondiscriminatory trade liberalization allows countries to export their products if they are the most efficient producers and to source their imports from the lowest-cost suppliers. In contrast, an FTA creates preferences in favor of partner-country producers, who may not be the most efficient, so a member won't necessarily source from the lowest-cost producer. A member country may be able to export its products to another member country simply because it enjoys tariff preferences under the FTA. This suggests that the importing partner will be paying more for its imports; in other words, its terms of trade (the price of exports in terms of imports) deteriorate.

The typical economic analysis of the trade and welfare effects of regional integration is based on the seminal customs union model by Jacob Viner (1950). This model illustrates the well-known effects of trade creation and trade diversion, which are explained later in this section.

In an FTA, the fact that each member country maintains its own tariff regime vis-à-vis nonmembers (unlike a customs union) raises two important issues. First, an FTA must be based on rules of origin. If there were no such rules, then transshipment can exist, where by nonmembers export a good to the member of an FTA with the lowest tariff and then reexport it to other FTA members, bypassing higher tariff barriers. The FTA would effectively become an unofficial customs union in which each tariff line would have the lowest tariff among the members' tariffs. Rules of origin are, therefore, a necessity for a true FTA, and there may be costs associated with implementing, administering, and complying with these rules (they may also be used as a form of "hidden protection" and distort investment decisions). Second, although each member of an FTA retains autonomy over its tariff regime against nonmembers, the autonomy may make each government more susceptible to special interest groups at the national level. By contrast, in a customs union these groups would have to lobby at the regional level to air their interests.

A. Static Effects of FTAs

To expound the basic economic theory of preferential trading arrangements, we begin with Viner's conceptual framework of trade creation and trade diversion. In short, trade creation is the displacement of less efficient national production in favor of more efficient partner-country production. It is measured as the diminution of output in the importing member. This leads to a gain in economic efficiency, as the country's resources are allocated more efficiently. This is the same positive effect obtained from nondiscriminatory trade liberalization (say, in the context of the WTO). But unlike nondiscriminatory liberalization, the preferential treatment extended to partners in the FTA can lead to the displacement of more efficient nonpartner imports in favor of less efficient partner-country sourced imports: the "trade diversion" effect. This effect is costly to the importing partner.

Figure 6.1 illustrates demand and supply of a certain good in the domestic market of a country that plans to join an FTA.[4] We will refer to this country as the "home" country, other FTA-member countries as "partner" countries, and nonmembers as "outsiders." We assume at present that the home country is "small" in an economic sense, meaning that it is unable to influence international prices, and therefore can always buy its imports at a constant price from abroad. Prior to the FTA, the home country imposes a tariff on all imports of the good regardless of the source. The tariff in this model can be expressed as either a specific tariff (i.e., a certain amount of money per unit imported), or ad valorem (percentage of price), which are the same when price doesn't change. Tariff revenue is simply the tariff multiplied by the quantity of imports.[5] We also assume that the outsider is the lowest-cost producer of the good.

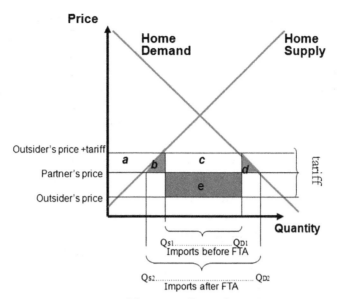

Figure 6.1. The static effects of an FTA.

Prior to the FTA, domestic producers supply Qs1 units of the good, and domestic consumers purchase QD1 units, which is the sum of Qs1 domestically produced units plus imported units from the outsider, who is able to supply the product at a lower price than the partner country. However, after joining the FTA, the removal of the tariff on imports from the FTA partner makes these imports cheaper than those from the outsider to the *consumer*. Domestic production contracts due to the greater competition from the partner country, and it now supplies only Qs2 units of the good. As consumers now face lower prices, they purchase more (QD2). The country now sources all its imports from an FTA partner rather than an outsider.

Gross trade creation is the amount of total imports after the FTA, (QD2-Qs2), minus total imports before the FTA, (QD1-Qs1). The actual trade creation effect is the reduction in domestic production that is now met by more efficient imports (Qs1-Qs2), but to this we add the rise in consumption (QD2-QD1), or the "consumption effect." In sum, the trade creation effect is positive because cheaper imports from the partner country encourage consumption and discourage higher-cost domestic production.

The FTA also causes trade diversion because the imports previously sourced from the outsider, (Qd1-Qs1), are displaced by imports from the partner country. The country loses tariff revenue on this quantity of imports. The shifting of the source of imports from the outsider to the FTA partner occurs because the FTA makes imports from member countries cheaper relative to those from non-members for the consumer. However, the country itself now imports from a higher-cost source.

Intuitively, the trade diversion concept is simple. Suppose that before the FTA, prices of imports from the partner and outsider countries came to $12 and $10, respectively. If there is a tariff of 30%, then to consumers in the home country, the price of partner-country sourced imports would be \$16, and the price of outsider imports would be \$13. Home would buy from the outsider. Note that while the *consumers* pay \$13, the home *country* still pays only \$10, the difference being the tariff (which ends up as government revenue). Now, if there is an FTA and, hence, no tariffs on partner-country imports, then the price of partner-country imports (\$12) is cheaper than the price of outsider-sourced imports with a tariff (\$13). The home-country consumers buy from the partner country. But note that at the *country* level, home now spends \$12 per unit for goods that used to cost only \$10. Since it no longer receives tariff revenue, that revenue is lost. This is why we calculate trade diversion as a terms-of-trade effect: there is no change in the price of our exports, but the price of our imports rises.

Viner was the first to show what has been come to be known as the "second-best" nature of FTAs and customs unions. Before Viner, the "oral tradition" suggested that if a grouping lowered its tariff to zero and didn't raise tariffs on outsiders, it must be efficient. Viner noted the fallacy in this argument: the discrimination against outsiders could actually lead the world, and even the home country, to be worse off than without the FTA. The efficiency effects of the FTA would be the net of the positive (trade creation) and negative effects (trade diversion). If the former exceeded the latter, the FTA would be efficient. Otherwise, it would be inefficient. This is unlike multilateral liberalization, which has only positive effects, for it is nondiscriminatory. Disagreements among economists regarding the economic desirability of preferential trading arrangements centers on this difference.

So far, the analysis has centered exclusively on changes in quantities. We next consider the welfare implications for consumers, producers, and the government.

Producer surplus captures how much domestic producers benefit from selling their output in the market. It is the difference between the market price of the good and the marginal cost of each unit of output, and is represented as the area above the supply curve but below the market price. Consumer surplus is a measure of the consumers' net benefit from the market, which is the difference between the amount consumers are willing to pay for each unit and what they actually have to pay. It is represented in figure 6.1 as the area below the demand curve but above the market price.

The net welfare effect of the FTA in the home country is the combined effect of the changes in domestic producer surplus, consumer surplus, and tariff revenue. In figure 6.1, the loss in producer surplus corresponds to the trapezoid *a*, while the gain in consumer surplus is the sum of the areas *a*, *b*, *c*, and *d*. The loss in tariff revenue is the total area of rectangles *c* and *e*. So the net welfare effect of the FTA is $(b + d - e)$.

Areas *b* and *d* show the net gains from trade creation.[6] Area *b* represents the gain from switching from higher-cost domestic output to lower-cost imports (also known as a *production effect*). Area *d* represents a gain from being able to consume more of the good given the lower price of imports (also known as a *consumption effect*). Area *e* shows the net loss from trade diversion; it depends on the original quantity of imports and the difference between the partner's and outsider's prices exclusive of tariffs. It is an efficiency loss because the discriminatory tariff regime

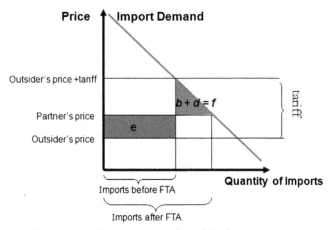

Figure 6.2. The import market of the home country.

under the FTA causes the country to lose tariff revenue while forgoing the lowest-cost imports.

The net welfare effect of the FTA on the home country can also be illustrated with reference to the home country's import market. Figure 6.2 contains the home country's import demand, which is the difference between the quantity demanded and quantity supplied in the home country's market at each price below the autarkic equilibrium price level (i.e., the price that would prevail if the home country did not import the good). The net welfare effect on the home country boils down to the relative size of the two efficiency gains from trade creation versus the efficiency loss from trade diversion. The two efficiency gains are shown in figure 6.2 as the area $f = b + d$. If the sum of the efficiency gains, as represented by the area f, is larger than the efficiency loss shown by area e then the FTA is beneficial to the home country. Otherwise, the net welfare effect is negative. Thus, the net welfare effect of an FTA on an importing country is ambiguous.

For the policy-maker, the Viner model provides some guidelines to evaluate the net welfare effect of an FTA in a particular sector. Each of the following guidelines characterizes the size of the FTA's efficiency gains ($f = b + d$) or the efficiency loss (e):

1. The closer are the partner country's and outsider's prices, the larger the efficiency gains ($f=b+d$), and the smaller the efficiency loss (e), thus increasing the likelihood of positive net welfare effect.
2. The higher the home country's initial tariff, the larger the efficiency gains ($f = b + d$), the smaller the efficiency loss (e), thus increasing the likelihood of a positive net welfare effect.
3. The more responsive import demand is to price changes (i.e., more elastic home supply and demand), the larger the efficiency gains ($f = b + d$), thus increasing the likelihood of a positive net and positive welfare effect.
4. The more countries participate in the FTA, the more likely a partner country's price is to be closer to the outsider's price as in the first guideline

above, thus increasing the likelihood of a net positive welfare effect. (For more, see Kreinin 1959, 1960).

B. Extensions to the Viner Model

The above analysis contained several assumptions, which we now relax in order to extend the model. First, there was the assumption that the lowest-cost source of imports was an outsider. If this was changed to make the partner country the cheapest import source, then the FTA would have only a trade creation effect, because imports would come from that partner country even before and after the FTA, that is, there would be no trade diversion. So the FTA would be unambiguously beneficial to the home country; it would have the same effect as nondiscriminatory liberalization.

Second, we assumed that foreign exporters produced at constant marginal cost so that their export supply curves were horizontal.[7] This assumption focused the analysis on the home country as an importer because changes in its imports would have no welfare effects (i.e., no changes in producer surplus) on the outsider or the partner country.[8] In other words, this assumption abstracted from any welfare effects beyond the home country. The assumption that foreign producers have constant marginal costs also implies that a country always imports a good from only one foreign country and never from multiple countries. This implication is definitely not realistic in the case of a good with multiple varieties, but even in the case of a homogenous good, a country may import from many sources, both FTA members and nonmembers, because any one source is unable to fulfill the country's demand, or perhaps due to an explicit diversification strategy.

A more realistic assumption would be that the partner country produced with an increasing-cost technology while the outsider produced at constant cost. This assumption would fit most FTAs because of their small size, that is, FTA members are small countries in terms of their share of world trade of a certain good. In terms of exports, "smallness" would imply that exporting FTA members have a limited capacity to produce and additional output would be at a higher cost. In terms of imports, "smallness" would imply that the import demand of FTA members would be negligible to outside suppliers and, therefore, not have an impact on the outsiders' marginal cost, that is, the outsiders' cost per unit remains constant.[9]

C. Modern Analysis of FTAs

Many authors have contributed to the theory of FTAs since Viner's pioneering work. The Vinerian analysis now fits into a more general theory called the General Theory of Second Best of Lipsey and Lancaster (1956/57). This theory holds that, given a distorted economic system, eliminating one set of distortions does not guarantee an improvement in overall economic welfare so long as other economic distortions remain unchanged. In the context of an FTA, this theory implies that reducing

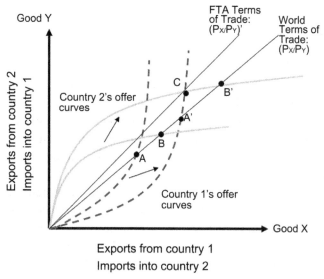

Figure 6.3. International markets for goods X and Y.

tariffs on a discriminatory basis may not improve welfare for individual countries or the world economy because other tariffs are maintained.

Modern authors examined FTAs in the context of many traded goods, whereas the Viner model is only a single-good partial-equilibrium analysis. The previous section focused on the markets of one good and ignored any interaction with other goods' markets and changes in the terms of trade (i.e., the relative price of exports to imports). We next consider trade in multiple goods in a general equilibrium framework, following work by Meade (1955) and Lipsey (1970). This FTA model incorporates a long-term equilibrium condition of balanced trade (i.e., each country has a zero trade deficit) and produces terms of trade effects.

Reciprocal (trade) offer curves are used to represent the international interaction of markets. A trade offer curve records the quantity of one good that a country is willing to export to the world in exchange for an imported quantity of another good at any given the terms of trade (i.e., relative prices of exports to imports). Figure 6.3 illustrates trade offer curves for two countries and two traded goods. Country 1 exports good X and imports good Y and has dashed offer curves. Country 2 exports good Y and imports good X and has solid offer curves. The offer curve for each country has the typical shape of sloping upward and bending back toward the axis of the imported good.[10] The terms of trade are represented in figure 6.3 by the slopes of rays from the origin (i.e., P_x/P_y for Country 1 and the inverse ratio for Country 2). To simplify the analysis, we assume that (1) countries 1 and 2 are small and, therefore, their trading volumes have no influence on world prices, and (2) the post-FTA external tariffs are high enough to eliminate all trade with outsiders. The pre-FTA traded quantities are shown as point A for Country 1 and point B for Country 2. The difference between the two points represents trade with the rest of the world.

Now introduce an FTA between the two countries. The FTA shifts both countries' offer curves to the northeast because intrabloc trade liberalization increases the desired quantities of imports and exports at any given terms of trade.[11] As external tariffs are prohibitive, both countries do not trade with outsiders after the FTA and trade only with each other. The intrabloc (FTA) terms of trade are then determined by the intersection of the new trade offer curves at point C. We can see that the terms of trade move in favor of Country 1 and against Country 2.

From the perspective of Country 1, the FTA represents an improvement as it moves from point A to C, improving its terms of trade and increasing its volume of trade.[12] Moreover, point C is better than Country 1 can do by eliminating its tariff unilaterally and thus moving to A'. The FTA is the best alternative for Country 1. However, as the FTA has changed the terms of trade adversely for Country 2, the FTA is not the best alternative for Country 2. It is uncertain how Country 2's welfare at C (i.e., after the FTA) compares with its original position. But if Country 2 eliminates its tariffs unilaterally and moves to point B', it will be better off compared to points B and C. Therefore, it would be in Country 2's interest to simply remove its tariffs instead of joining the FTA.

From the perspective of the FTA as a whole, it can be shown mathematically that Country 2's loss from joining the FTA instead of removing its tariffs unilaterally is larger than Country 1's gain from the FTA compared to unilaterally removing its tariffs. So, although Country 1 would like Country 2 to join the FTA, Country 1's gain would not be sufficient to compensate for Country 2's loss. This illustrates a fundamental problem in the creation of trade agreements: when the interests of members are different, their policies may not be compatible. In this situation, Country 1 might have to transfer all its static welfare gains and offer a side-payment to Country 2 in order to form an FTA.

However, as Wonnacott and Wonnacott (1981) show, if the World (i.e., outsiders) has import tariffs or there are transportation costs on trade with the World, then an FTA may actually be the dominant strategy for both countries. To see this, consider Figure 6.4, which shows three rays from the origin depicting the World terms of trade. The steepest ray shows the World terms of trade when the World either imposes tariffs on imports of good Y or Country 2 has to pay transportation costs for exporting good Y to the World. The tariff or transportation cost, in effect, depresses the price on good Y that exporters from Country 2 receive. The flattest ray shows the World terms of trade when the World either imposes tariffs on imports of good X or Country 1 has to pay transportation costs in order to export good X to the World. Its slope can be understood using a similar logic as that for the steepest ray. Trade barriers to the World, thus, create a wedge between the World terms of trade as seen by Countries 1 and 2.

Prior to the FTA, Countries 1 and 2 have the option of trading with the World or each other. To simplify the analysis, we assume that these countries choose to trade only with each other before the FTA.[13] Figure 6.4 shows this because the intersection of the countries' initial offer curves at C represents a higher level of welfare than point A for Country 1 and point B for Country 2, both representing

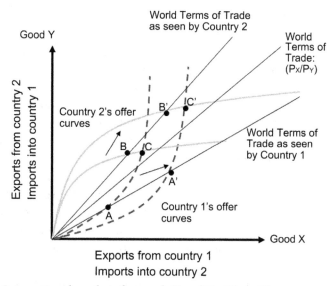

Figure 6.4. International markets for goods X and Y with tariffs or transportation costs on exports to the world.

trade with the World. After the FTA, both countries continue trade with each other instead of with the World because point C' represents a higher level of welfare than points A' and B', which both represent unilateral rather than preferential trade liberalization by each country. Therefore, both countries will choose to join the FTA. We obtain this result because the intersection point of the post-FTA offer curves lies in the wedge formed between the rays illustrating the World terms of trade as seen by each country. In practical terms, this says that if the World's trade barriers are high enough to make the two countries trade exclusively with one another after the FTA, then an FTA is welfare-improving for both countries.

The main policy implication from this analysis is that a group of small countries may gain from an FTA rather than unilateral trade liberalization if outsiders have high trade barriers against them or the group faces high transportation costs in exporting to outsiders. This is one explanation for the formation of FTAs among countries that are geographically close but distant as a group from outsiders.

Note that we have assumed that the countries are small, which by definition does not allow the World's terms of trade to change. If trade between these countries, as a group, and the World were substantial enough to influence the World's terms of trade, then an FTA would be one means for the group to achieve more favorable terms of trade vis-à-vis the World. By using external tariffs, these countries would reduce their demand for imports from the World, which—by the assumption of balanced trade—would reduce these countries' supply of exports to the World. The price of their exports would rise while the price of their imports would fall. The large size of the FTA allows for improved collective terms of trade and greater bargaining power in trade negotiations. Such improvement in the terms of trade does not, however, imply that all countries in the FTA benefit. A member would stand a better chance of benefiting from terms-of-trade improvement after the FTA, if the FTA as a whole was a net exporter and importer to the World of the member's export and import goods, respectively.

An important outgrowth of this literature was discussion of the economic rationale of FTAs and customs unions. That is, is there a trade liberalization policy that could always lead to a more economically advantageous outcome? The economic thesis put forward by Cooper and Massell (1965?) and expounded more generally by Berglas (1979) suggested that there is: unilateral liberalization would be a "dominant" strategy in that it always generates a better outcome than a preferential trading arrangement. The proposition is simple: if the home country were to reduce the nondiscriminatory tariff to the price of the partner country, then the country would get all the positive effects of trade creation, but no trade diversion effect, as the country would continue to import from the cheapest-cost source (the outsider). In figure 6.1, this would be equivalent to reducing the nondiscriminatory tariff such that (outsider's price + tariff) = partner's price. All changes in imports would, therefore, be trade creation.

This would seem to put to rest the debate regarding FTAs: it is always better to liberalize unilaterally than engage in preferential trading arrangements. Wonnecott and Wonnecott (1981) point out a problem inherent in this analysis. They note that countries don't engage in FTAs simply to reduce their own tariffs: they do it to open up access to other markets. This key motivation for an FTA is left out of the Vinerian model. A simple illustration underscores their point. Suppose there are three economies in the world: the United States, the EU, and Nepal. Assume that the United States and the EU each accounts for 49% of the global market, whereas Nepal accounts for 2%. According to the protagonists of "unilateral liberalization dominance," it would make no sense for the United States to form an FTA with the EU, as by unilaterally liberalizing it could also gain from imports from Nepal. But if the United States had an FTA with the EU, the EU would be forced to lower its barriers to imports from the United States, thereby leading to an increase in demand for U.S. exports. Clearly, the marginal effects of trade diversion due to the exclusion of Nepal in the FTA would be far less than the positive economic effects of greater access to the EU market.

Note that Wonnecott and Wonnecott do not suggest that an FTA dominates unilateral liberalization: they just note that the opposite is not true. We always need to consider market access to partner-country markets.

Lastly, the Kemp-Wan Existence Theory considers the possibilities that an economic arrangement such as a customs union can always be efficient if constructed correctly. Their proposition requires three elements. First, countries in the customs union need to create a CET such that the imports from outside countries do not change. That is, if there is potential trade diversion from one outside market, then the CET would have to be lowered in order to ensure that the discrimination inherent in the customs union does not change trade with that market. Second, the customs union would have to embrace total internal free trade, thereby leading to greater efficiency through trade creation. Third, since it is theoretically possible that some countries in the customs union would be worse off with this arrangement (e.g., depending on the effects of the CET), there would have to be a compensation mechanism, such that any losing country would be completely compensated. As the customs union would guarantee greater overall efficiency, it is certain that this is possible. Hence, Kemp and Wan show that a theoretical possibility exists that this customs union would lead to no one being worse off and at least some countries being better off (i.e., a customs union that would be "Pareto optimal").

For many years, this was thought to be merely a theoretical possibility without much policy relevance. But the embrace of the idea of "open regionalism" in the context of the Asia-Pacific Economic Cooperation (APEC)[14] organization led to an increase in its popularity. Open regionalism is a nondiscriminatory approach to regionalism, that is, liberalization of trade barriers within the grouping would be extended to outsiders. This approach has no trade diversion, as it is nondiscriminatory, yet it has trade creation and, hence, is unambiguously efficient.

Although economically attractive, there are at least two problems with this approach in the real world. First, it is politically untenable. For example, while the United States may gain economically from completely free trade with APEC, it is unlikely that the U.S. Congress would look favorably on reducing U.S. tariffs to zero on EU imports in exchange for nothing from the Europeans! Second, within APEC there is currently no compensation mechanism, which would be necessary in order to ensure the type of Pareto optimality sought by Kemp and Wan. It is no surprise that APEC's major achievements have been in the area of trade facilitation; the "Bogor Vision" of 1994, in which the APEC leaders committed to create an "open region of trade and investment" by 2010 for developed-country members and 2020 for developing countries, has fallen well short of its goals. Instead, at the APEC Summit in Yokohama, Japan, in November 2010, the group agreed to work toward a "Free Trade Area of the Asia Pacific" by 2020 (the "Yokohama Vision").

D. Dynamic Effects of FTAs

The previous section focused on the theoretical effects of changes in tariffs within the context of an FTA. We compared economic outcomes before and after the introduction of an FTA, analyzing the welfare effects of one-time price changes, or "static" changes. We ignored any dynamic effects, that is, medium- and long-term implications of FTAs. Because dynamic effects may be more substantial and pervasive, we now consider the following dynamic effects in the context of FTAs: economies of scale and variety, technology transfer and foreign direct investment (FDI), and structural policy change and reform, as well as competitiveness and long-run growth.

1. *Economies of Scale and Variety*

The definition of economies of scale is a reduction in average costs as output expands. Economies of scale may occur because of improved technical efficiency in large-scale production, increased ability to spread administrative costs and overhead over a bigger operation, bulk discounts from suppliers, or improved logistics because of bigger volumes. Economies of scale exist in the production of agricultural, natural-resource-intensive, and manufacturing and services sectors, as well as ser-vices. By creating a larger market for firms operating in partner countries, an FTA allows producers to take advantage of a larger customer base and, hence, produce at a lower average cost on all sales. Firms are even able to lower prices for existing cus-tomers—the "cost-reduction effect" (Corden 1972). As a result, these firms become more competitive not only at home but also in foreign markets. Customers in each member country also enjoy more varieties the goods they can purchase, because the larger market created by the FTA allows firms to sell in more markets and, given economies of scale, introduce new varieties that were too costly and unprofitable before the FTA.

2. *Technology Transfer and Foreign Direct Investment (FDI)*

Foreign direct investment is an important means of transferring technology and know-how from developed to developing countries. It is one of the primary reasons why many developing countries seek to attract FDI inflows through unilateral trade liberalization and other means. Bilateral and regional FTA formation attracts such long-term, risk-sharing investment flows by creating a more integrated marketplace within which multinational corporations can enjoy a regional division of labor with low transaction costs, and exploit economies of scale (Kreinin 1959b, 1964). Foreign direct investment patterns following an FTA may be similar to the effects of trade creation and trade diversion. A multinational corporation that believes that an FTA will lead to greater economic dynamism may be compelled to invest more in one of the members, thus resulting in "investment creation." However, if the multinational decides to invest in the member because it now has preferential access to the FTA market, the result is "investment diversion." In other words, although investing in an outsider might have been more cost-effective, the multinational diverts investment to the FTA because of this regional accord. The motivation would be the same as in "tariff-hopping" FDI.

There is a similar effect of "investment diversion" associated with rules of origin discussed in section I. If rules of origin are restrictive, it may create an incentive for a multinational corporation to increase the proportion of value-added of produc-tion of a good within the confines of an FTA than would otherwise have been the case. For example, the rule of origin on automobiles in NAFTA is 62.5% of value-added. Thus, if, say, a Korean car manufacture moves intermediate production from Indonesia to Mexico, it may be able to meet the value-added requirements of NAFTA and thereby gain free access to the U.S. market. While this may make sense from the point of view of the Korean manufacturer, and Mexico may be happy for the additional FDI, investment is diverted from the most efficient country (Indone-sia), thereby hurting Indonesia as well as global efficiency.

3. *Structural Policy Change and Reform*

Free-Trade Agreements have traditionally focused on commercial policy at the border, but they are increasingly affecting deeper integration by addressing behind-the-border measures. Examples of these behind-the-border areas are quality standards; complex measures specific to the service sectors; laws related to corporate and public governance; customs procedures; the national treatment of partner-country investors; competition policy, including the reform of state-owned enterprises; and other "sensitive sectors" with important links to the rest of the economy. The inclusion of these areas in FTAs shows how instrumental these agreements have become in shaping and harmonizing the national economic policies of members. Free-Trade Agreements allow like-minded countries to address these nontraditional areas that improve the business environment by reducing costs, leveling the playing field for foreign investors, and pushing policy reforms toward best practices (Plummer 2007). Doing so at the multilateral level would be extremely difficult if not impossible because of diverse interests. In ASEAN, for example, this is being done within the context of the ASEAN Economic Community (AEC).

4. *Competitiveness and Long-Run Growth Effects*

Although trade liberalization in an FTA is preferential, the reduction in trade barriers still allows members to benefit from healthy increased intrabloc competition. Increased exposure to competition from partner countries weeds out less productive firms and favors more productive ones. It also gives firms an incentive to invest in more efficient productive processes and technology. For each member economy and the FTA as a whole, these competitive forces may improve structural efficiency and resource allocation as different members specialize in the production of different final and intermediate commodities. All the effects of increased competition on productivity and efficiency combine to raise the FTA members' long-run growth prospects. The FTA is placed on a higher growth trajectory.

5. *Other FTA Issues: Preconditions for Success*

Lastly, we consider some of the preconditions that are critical if an FTA—or any trade-policy innovation—is to be successful. First, the success of an FTA depends on the soundness of its member countries' domestic economic policies. Few firms can benefit from preferential trading if there is macroeconomic instability, weak property rights, corruption, or opaque tax laws and business regulations. While an FTA may affect some reform in domestic economic policy, the initial economic policy configuration has to be sufficiently conducive to growth if the FTA is to succeed in the first place. Second, the success of an FTA also depends on the efficiency of the transportation infrastructure. To realize benefits from the FTA, the transportation and logistics networks between member countries should have enough capacity to handle increased trade volumes. Realization that transportation and other forms of "hard" and "soft" infrastructure are necessary conditions is a driving force behind the "aid for trade" initiative that is being embraced by the WTO, the Asian Development Bank, the OECD, and others. Third, the distribution of economic gains among countries in an FTA may be very unequal. Some members may face net losses even if an FTA as a whole is welfare-enhancing.[15] Members of an FTA have to decide on whether and how to redistribute the FTA's gains from those countries that gain to those that lose.

Finally, a country needs to compare the costs and benefits of trade liberalization within an FTA versus that in a multilateral, nondiscriminatory trade liberalization context. Preferential trade liberalization has ambiguous net welfare effects, whereas nondiscriminatory trade liberalization is certain to result in a net welfare gain. Some authors have even raised the issue of regionalism blocking multilateralism.[16] An example might be the problem of scarce human resources in Least Developed Countries (LDCs) that are devoted to bilateral and regional agreements at the cost of working on the Doha Development Agenda. But conversely it may be that experience gained through FTA negotiations can train trade policy-makers and deepen their understanding of multilateral issues, allowing them to become more effective at all levels.

Bilateral/regional and multilateral processes may differ in terms of the coverage of goods and services and the potential to undertake liberalization. Free Trade Agreements have tended to be more comprehensive in coverage, whereas the GATT/WTO agreements have been piecemeal, leaving protection on some agricultural and labor-intensive products practically untouched after successive multilateral rounds. Regionalism may also be more advantageous over multilateralism, in that it allows like-minded countries to address far more issues and in a shorter period of time. By choosing one or several partners with similar policy goals, countries are able to make more progress in deep integration than they could in the extremely diverse WTO context.

II. Economic Modeling of the Potential Impact of FTAs

The second-best nature of FTAs suggests that empirical analysis is necessary in order to anticipate the economic consequences of any given FTA, as well as analyze the effects of an FTA already in place. The former is called "ex ante" analysis and the later "ex post" analysis. The literature is replete with such studies, in terms of both partial and general equilibrium analysis. The ex ante models are the most common due to both supply and demand reasons. First, they are easier to simulate—since ex post models have to come up with a counterfactual example that tends to be tricky to form. Second, policy-makers are more interested in being informed of the potential economic effects of an accord they are considering making rather than the economic implications of an accord they made in the past.

This section reviews both ex ante and ex post models. The former focuses on a general equilibrium approach to estimating the economic effects of an FTA, which has become the most common in the ex-ante literature. For the ex post models, we review two modeling approaches that have been used frequently: the "import-growth" approach and gravity models.

A. Ex Ante Approaches to FTAs: The CGE Model

For analytical tractability, theoretical models of FTAs have usually restricted the number of countries and goods in the analysis.[17] They have also ignored character-istics like economies of scale or imperfectly competitive markets. To overcome these limitations and to provide more relevant policy advice, researchers have turned to computer-based modeling. This type of modeling can include any number of commodities and partner countries or economic features, provided there are no data or memory restrictions. These computer-based models fre-quently perform general equilibrium analysis with many dimensions. It takes account of all the important interactions between markets and can give more com-plete and precise answers to policy questions, *albeit* formulated in a basic way. When computer based, this type of analysis is known as computable general equi-librium (CGE) modeling.

There are several reasons to use CGE models for the analysis of FTAs. First, CGE modeling is based on explicit assumptions in a framework consistent with microeconomic theory. Second, as CGE models produce quantitative results that are clear and exact, policy-makers can assess who gains and loses from an FTA. Third, as an FTA involves changes in trade policy in multiple markets, the analysis may be too complex using algebraic or geometric methods. Lastly, CGE analysis may generate fresh insights about the role of certain economic assumptions in determining the results of an FTA.

Section Ic reviewed a type of general equilibrium analysis that focused only on the price and trade linkages between two international markets. There are several other ways one market is linked to other markets. A change in the price of a good in a particular market affects the demand for related consumption goods (substitutes or complements) and the demand for production inputs such as raw materials, labor, machinery, and factory premises. In turn, this may change the incomes of different households and their demand for other goods and services, some of which may be imported. This may also change the government's budget, particularly in terms of tax revenue and government subsidies. For an open economy, equilibrium in the balance of payments must also hold.

The crux of general equilibrium analysis is that no market remains with excess demand or supply, that is to say that the circular flows of income and expenditure must all be balanced. To achieve market equilibrium, prices are assumed to adjust until demand for factors of production equals available endowments, consumers have chosen the desired basket of goods given their incomes, and firms have chosen production levels that maximize their profits. Because an FTA introduces a set of policy changes in an economy, CGE models simulate an economy where markets have adjusted and a new general equilibrium has been reached. The effect of an FTA can be estimated by comparing welfare under the old equilibrium with that under the new equilibrium.

A CGE analysis is a study of these market linkages using mathematical modeling and real-world data from a benchmark year. The mathematical modeling is based on a set of neoclassical economic assumptions about the motivation of agents in the economy, market structure, consumer preferences, production technology, and market equilibrium conditions. These assumptions are coded in mathematical functions and equations, which contain parameters that capture important behavioral relationships. In a CGE model, most of these parameters are elasticities (i.e., they measure the responsiveness of one variable to changes in another) or share parameters such as the share of consumption demand in aggregate demand. Some of these parameters will have known values, while others will have to be calibrated in the mathematical model with real-world data. Calibration is a step in CGE analysis when values are selected to make the CGE model's output agree with real-world data from the benchmark year.

A CGE model essentially captures demand and supply in each sector and the linkages among sectors. The model has exogenous variables (i.e., variables that have given values determined outside the model) and endogenous variables (i.e., variables that are solved within the model). In the analysis of an FTA, the exogenous variables typically correspond to the trade policy variables, elasticities, and share parameters. The rest of the variables in a CGE model of an FTA are endogenous, including prices, import and export volumes, household income, tariff revenue, consumer surplus, producer surplus, and so on.

1. *Characteristics of Agents in a Typical CGE Model*

A typical CGE model has three agents: (1) firms, (2) consumers, and (3) government. Firms produce output, which is purchased by both consumers and the government. Firms are profit-maximizers and use market prices in deciding how much output to produce and with which inputs. In the typical CGE model, each sector has only one firm that produces a single good. The sector's production is represented by a production function, which shows the relationship between inputs and output. Various functional forms such as the Cobb-Douglas, the Leontief, or the constant elasticity of substitution (CES) functions may be used to model production in a CGE model.[18] These production functions are usually assumed to exhibit constant returns to scale and be weakly separable between primary factors and intermediate inputs.[19] Further, these production functions include parameters called elasticities of substitution, which define the substitutability of one input for another. The elasticities of substitution are therefore an important determinant of demand for various inputs.[20] In addition, production in a CGE model typically involves a multilevel or nested production process. The use of a nested structure allows for differing elasticities for each pair of factors and makes it easier to incorporate intermediate inputs into the analysis.

Consumers are often modeled by a representative household. Market prices factor into the decisions of the representative household (i.e., consumers' decisions) on how much of each good to purchase. Consumers are utility-maximizers, and their preferences are captured by utility functions, which include parameters that capture the elasticities of substitution between final goods. Consumers also act as factor owners in a CGE model. They are endowed with capital, land, labor, and other factors of production. Based on market prices, they supply their factors and receive income in return. This income is used to purchase goods and pay direct taxes (e.g., income tax) and indirect taxes (e.g., import tariffs, sales tax, etc.), and in dynamic CGE models, some of this income may be saved.

Government, in a CGE model, administers only market-related policies such as taxes, subsidies, trade tariffs, quotas, and so on. The government is often assumed not to have an objective function. For this reason and the fact that the effects of government policies are of primary interest, policy variables often enter exogenously in CGE models.

2. CGE Models of International Trade and FTAs

Computable general equilibrium models are commonly used to evaluate the effects of trade policy, because policy-makers require quantitative assessments of the impacts of any policy in order to make decisions. As we have seen, economic theory only provides qualitative conclusions, which are sometimes ambiguous. For example, in the case of FTAs, trade creation and trade diversion have opposing effects on welfare, so the net effect may be positive or negative. Computable general equilibrium models provide an empirical foundation for policy analysis that can quantify the magnitudes of the effects identified by theory, and suggest the likely net welfare effect.

In CGE models of international trade, the set of goods available to firms, consumers, and government includes imported goods. For a particular good, the imported and domestically produced varieties are typically modeled as substitutable but not perfect substitutes. Besides relative prices, the choice between the domestic versus the foreign variety of a good depends on a parameter known as the Armington elasticity. This parameter distinguishes goods by their national origin and captures the substitutability between goods from different countries. Armington elasticities are key in determining the impact of trade policy in CGE models. They also produce more realistic trade responses than models without national differentiation. Further, the use of these elasticities results in intraindustry trade (i.e., a country imports and exports different varieties of the same good). Another advantage of the Armington assumption is that complete specialization does not occur.

To simulate an FTA, the CGE modeler must first make sure that the model is producing outcomes that match the actual observed values of endogenous variables such as prices or trade volumes to recreate the baseline situation. Once this is achieved, simulating an FTA is a simply a matter of setting trade barriers to zero between FTA partners in the model and running the model to produce new estimates. The simulation represents what the economy would look like if the FTA had occurred. By comparing post-FTA outcomes with the baseline situation, the modeler can study changes in welfare (changes in consumer and producer surplus or other welfare indicators such as equivalent variation),[21] changes in the terms of trade of each partner and the FTA as a whole, changes in production by sector, changes in the returns to the factors of production (i.e., labor by skill, capital, landowners), and changes in imports and exports by sector and by partner. The modeler may also wish to compare the potential effects of different possible FTAs with different partners, different scenarios that may include or exclude different sectors, or combinations of trade agreements. By comparing the welfare outcomes of all scenarios, a policy-maker would be able to determine the scenario that benefits a country the most.

3. *Limitations of CGE Analysis of FTAs*

Computable general equilibrium analysis is not without problems. First, the data requirements to analyze FTAs are extensive, and frequently certain data items are arbitrarily picked by the modeler. Second, the model's results may be very sensitive to the assumptions and data used. To address these first two concerns, almost all CGE exercises include a sensitivity analysis to get a range of results based on different assumptions or data. In this way, the modeler can check the robustness of the results. Third, a CGE analysis lacks a time dimension. These models are essentially simulations that allow economists to trace the impact of trade-policy innovations, but the approach is essentially static in nature, allowing us to compare the nature of the economy postinnovation to preinnovation. So analysis of an FTA will not provide results on how long it does take for economies to adjust and reach the new equilibrium. Recent work in CGE modeling has attempted to include some dynamic effects via financial markets, but this work is far from capturing the dynamic features that are most relevant to FTAs. Fourth, it is difficult to model certain nontariff barriers if these are included in an FTA. Moreover, incorporating the level of production on services trade is challenging, as very little data exist. Fifth, while some modelers have tried to endogenize productivity spillovers in CGE models, which we believe to be extremely important, this is an extremely complicated operation. Finally, CGE models are sometimes unable to answer key questions that interest policy makers. Typical CGE models include, for example, macroeconomic "closures," such as full employment of labor and constant current account balances, which prevent analysis of the effects of an FTA on employment or the trade balance.

B. Ex Post Approaches: Import Growth and Gravity Models

2. *Import Growth Approaches*

The AFTA has mainly been in place for the original ASEAN countries for the past several years. What have been its effects on trade flows? Answering this question requires a very different approach from a CGE model: we already know what happened, but what would have happened in the absence of AFTA? Import growth approaches answer this question by attempting to estimate what would have happened to trade flows if there had been no AFTA. Thus, it creates a "counterfactual" to which the actual flows can be compared. This is a way of estimating how much the changes in trade flows can be attributed to AFTA, as well as trade creation and trade diversion. The literature reveals that there are at least two ways to arrive at the counterfactual import growth rate: the standard normalized approach and the import-share-in-apparent-consumption approach.

The standard normalized approach estimates the counterfactural import growth rate by using a control country as a normalizer. Pioneered by Kreinin (1972, 1973), this approach posits a modified control country's (or countries') import growth rates as a proxy for the growth rate of the importing country (or countries) in the counterfactual. The principal argument for using a control country approach is that simple projection of trends in pre-FTA growth rates can lead to substantial biases, due mainly to the differing historical economic environments in the pre-FTA relative to post-AFTA years. For example, assume that a modeler wishes to measure changes in import growth rates due to AFTA for Indonesia. The AFTA agreement was signed in 1992; therefore, we would need to use import growth rates for Indonesia prior to 1992 in order to estimate a counterfactual for the years 2007–2009, when most of Indonesia's AFTA commitments were put in place (we would obviously not use the 1992–2006 period, as that period's import growth would have been partially affected by AFTA itself). But Indonesia's economy prior to 1992 was very different from the one in 2008; part of this may be due to AFTA, but much of it would have also been due to rapid (non-AFTA-related) policy change. Moreover, the devastating effects of the Asian financial crisis, which lasted from 1997 until 2004 for Indonesia, and the most recent global economic crisis of 2008–2009 would lead to a considerable bias in the results. The counterfactual would estimate much higher growth rates prior to 1992 than could have been expected in light of all these (non-AFTA) shocks. We would have a tendency to extrapolate higher trend growth rates than what would have been possible, and the results would have us believe that AFTA had a more negative effect on trade flows than would have been the case if the counterfactual were measured accurately.

Thus, pre-FTA growth rates are biased if the subjective economic environment in the pre-FTA phase is different from that in the post integration phases. In fact, given the extensive economic gyrations in the past two decades for most economies, a country's past is a poor normalizer for itself in the present.

In order to produce a more efficient proxy, Kreinin (1972) suggests that a country (or countries) with similar characteristics to those being considered be used as a normalizer. The more similar the country, the better the predictor. Ideally, this country should be at the same level of economic development, have comparable import patterns, not be a part of an integration process, and undergo similar exogenous economic changes in the domestic and international realms. Such a country is difficult to find, but a ranking of countries can be compiled and the best control(s) chosen according to their degree of appropriateness. There is no perfect control country. This explains in part why ex post modeling is less common in the literature.

Following is the functional form of a standard normalized approach. Trade creation in Country i and Commodity Group k is estimated by adjusting imports in period 1 by the import growth rate of the control variable to derive counterfactual total imports (M_{ik2}^{T*}). This value is subtracted from actual imports in period 2:

$$TC = [MT_{ik2}^{T} - MT_{ik2}^{*}] \tag{1}$$

where: $M_{ik2}^{T*} = [M_{ik1}^{T}(1 + M_{nk}^{T})]$; and M_{nk} = growth rate of imports in Control Country n from t_1 to t_2.

This figure is summed over all k categories in Country i to derive total trade creation for that country. The sum of trade creation over all integrating countries yields the total trade creation effect of integration.

Trade diversion is estimated in Country i and Commodity Group k by subtracting from counterfactual external imports M_{ik2}^{X*} the actual external imports in t_2, M_{ik2}^{X*}:

$$TD = [M_{ik2}^{X*} - M_{ik2}^{X}] \tag{2}$$

where: M_{ik2}^{X*} $[M_{ik2}^{X}(1 + M_{nk}^{X})]$ and $M^{X}nk$ = growth rate of external imports in n from t_1 to t_2.

This value is summed over all k categories in Country i to compute total trade diversion for that country, and summing over all i yields the total trade diversion.

Instead of focusing on the growth rate of total imports in the counterfactual, the normalized import-share-in-apparent-consumption approach focuses on changes in imports relative to apparent consumption. A control country or group of countries is chosen analogously to the standard approach, but changes in the ratios of imports to *apparent consumption* are used to construct the counterfactual. Thus, trade creation is measured as follows:

$$TC = [(M_{ik}^{T} / C_{ik})_2 - (M_{nk}^{T} / C_{ik})^*]^* C_{ik2} \tag{3}$$

where: C_{ikT} = apparent consumption (domestic production plus imports minus exports) in period t, t = 1, 2; $(M_{nk}^{T} / C_{ik})^* = [(M_{ik}^{T} / C_{ik})_1 (1 + (M_{nk}^{T} / C_{nk})]$; and $(M_{nk}^{T} / C_{ik})]$ = rate of growth in imports to apparent consumption from period 1 to period 2 in Control Country n.

Hence, trade creation is derived in the same way as above, except that the changes are expressed in ratios. But it is necessary also to multiply the change in the ratios—which are expressed in percentage terms—by total apparent consumption in period 2, the post-FTA year.

Trade diversion is estimated analogously to the standard normalized approach:

$$TD = [(M_{ik}^{*} / C_{ik})^* - (M_{ik}^{X} / C_{ik})_2)]^* C_{ik2} \tag{4}$$

where: $(M_{ik}^{X} / C_{ik})^* = [(M_{ik}^{X} / C_{ik})_1 (1 + (M_{mk}^{X} / C_{nk}))]$.

The growth rate in the control country's external imports share in apparent consumption is used in the trade diversion equation to estimate what that ratio would have been in the absence of integration. The percentage change in actual values of import shares in apparent consumption are subtracted from the percentage change in counterfactual external import shares in apparent consumption to calculate trade diversion.

Another variant is formulated under the assumption that the ratio of external imports relative to total imports does not change. In that case, the appropriate estimator of trade diversion is:

$$TD=M^T_{ik_2}[(M^X/M^T)_{ik_1} - (M^X/M^T)_{ik_2})] \tag{5}$$

This technique is unbiased as long as exogenous economic disturbances that influence import growth throughout the period under consideration affect external and total import growth equally.

There are several advantages to the control group techniques. First, it is possible to avoid the time-trend problem of different historical conditions. Second, even though no ideal control groups exist, it is possible to exclude those commodities for which the importing country and the control country are unacceptably different, or one could use another control country as a surrogate. Indeed, several control countries can be used. Third, divergent income growth rates in the importing and control countries can be scaled upward or downward, as is appropriate, to correct for biases. This is necessary even in the import-share-in-apparent-consumption approach, because if the control country's income growth rate were faster than the importing country's income growth rate, trade creation would be understated and trade diversion overstated. This is because the income elasticity of *import* demand with respect to real income is significantly greater than the income elasticity of demand for domestically produced goods. Hence, the change in imports relative to apparent consumption in the counterfactual would be biased upward. Last, it is possible to correct for divergent changes in price competitiveness in the control and importing countries, resulting from differential inflation rates or real exchange rate variations. If changes in price competitiveness do occur, potential biases could result. For example, if the control country's inflation rate were higher than the importing country's, one would expect, ceteris paribus, a relative decline in the former country's competitiveness. Thus, the counterfactual trade creation and trade diversion would be biased downward and upward, respectively, if one does not adjust for inflation differentials.

2. *Gravity Models*

Like CGE models, gravity models have been extremely popular in the literature. In fact, over the past two decades, they have been the most frequently used econometric model to estimate the determinants of trade flows, in much the same way that CGE models have dominated trade-policy modeling. Gravity models have been less frequently used to estimate a counterfactual in order to gauge trade creation and trade diversion effects. Rather, they have been employed to see if a given trade grouping has had a statistically significant effect on trade flows or not.

In short, gravity models are econometric models that attempt to explain bilateral import demand (X_{ij}) with a variety of explanatory variables, for example, income of the importing country (Y_i), income of the exporting country (Y_i), per capita income of the importing and exporting countries (N_i and N_j, respectively), a variable that accounts for the distance between the importing and exporting countries (D_{ij}), and vector of additional variables that may be employed if thought to be relevant (V_i).[22] Expressed in logarithmic form, a characteristic gravity model of bilateral trade takes on the form

$$\ln X_{ij} = A + \delta_1 \ln (Y_i * Y_j) + \delta_2 \ln (Ni * Nj) + \delta_3 \ln D_{ij} + \delta_z \ln V_z + \ln e_{ij} \qquad (6)$$

where i = importing country; j = exporting country; A= intercept; δ_i = coefficients of the explanatory variables; and log e_{ij} = lognormal error term.[23]

A common way to use gravity models is to include an FTA binary variable(s) to estimate whether or not formal economic cooperation has had a statistically significant effect (Frankel 1997). If it is significant and positive, we can deduce that the FTA had a positive effect on trade flows, with the magnitude relating the size of the coefficient (we have to be careful to remember that this is a semilog function and, hence, need to interpret the estimated coefficient on binary variables, which are not in log form).

However, this approach does not reveal whether the statistically significant effect is due to trade creation, trade diversion, or both. To this end, we need to use the parameters estimated from the gravity model to create a counterfactural. These estimates can then be compared these to actual trade flows with partner and outsider countries in order to estimate trade creation, trade diversion, and the net effect.

C. Final Comments on Empirical Modeling

The above discussion summarized the most popular models used to estimate the economic effects of trade agreements in general and FTAs in particular. All models have shortcomings. Nevertheless, these models provide an understanding of what the possible effects of bilateral and regional FTAs might be (ex ante) or what the actual effects of an already established FTA has been (ex post).

It would, perhaps, be useful to give some examples of the empirical results derived using these approaches. To give a comprehensive summary of such studies would be well beyond the scope of our objectives; in fact, given the popularity of regional economic cooperation agreements and myriad studies devoted to estimating their potential effects, such a comprehensive approach would take several volumes. Hence, we offer just a few examples to give some idea of the magnitude of the estimates.

First, the EU's Single Market Programme, which was devoted to extending the existing customs union to create a full-blown common market, has been extensively researched, as the process of creating the single market was politically difficult. In order to push through the program, politicians needed to know what the potential gains would be. The famous "Cecchini Report" (Cecchini 1988) estimated that the ultimate effect of the Single Market Programme would be to increase EC GDP by up to 6.5%. This is on top of any integration measures already in place after 30 years of regional cooperation. Economies of scale, which is one of the main advantages of creating the EC single market and production base, alone accounted for a 2% increase in EC GDP.

Second, one prominent study on the East Asian region was undertaken by Brooks, Roland-Holst, and Zhai (2005). In order to show the important differences between "traditional estimates"—induced by liberalization of tariff and tariff-equivalent non-tariff barriers—of gains due to trade liberalization in Asia (Scenario 1) and more general trade-cost reduction effects such as improving customs clearance, lower transaction costs, and facilitation of international market access (Scenario 2), they run simulations to compare the aggregate impact on real income, exports, and terms of trade in the context of various East Asian FTA configurations.[24] By comparing Scenario 1 and Scenario 2, they are able to show the value-added of "modern" or "deep" integration initiatives, compared to traditional approaches. They assume that non-policy-related trade costs are around 120% and are cut by half over a 20-year period for East Asia, Southeast Asia, and South Asia.[25] The results are illuminating. Under Scenario 1, real income rises in the range of 0.9–2.9% for East Asia, 1.9–6.6% for Southeast Asia, and 0.3–0.6% for South Asia. Such magnitudes are fairly standard in the literature. Under Scenario 2, the gains are many times as large, that is, 8.1–53.8%, 35.5–116.6%, and 10.4–22.4%, respectively.

Also in light of the need to evaluate modern FTAs, Hertel, Walmsley, and Itakura (2001) analyze the potential gains from the Japan-Singapore FTA, which it calls a "new age" (modern) agreement. Moreover, since Japan's average tariff is less than 2% in manufactures and Singapore essentially has a zero average tariff, the traditional effects of an FTA would essentially be insignificant. They essentially develop a dynamic CGE/GTAP-based model using an ex ante simulation but with some ex post features in estimating some "dynamic" and policy-related changes that one would expect from a deep-integration accord such as the Japan-Singapore FTA. Thus, they add to traditional trade barrier effects of the harmonization of e-commerce standards, liberalizing rules in trade in services, automating customs services in Japan (to be consistent with Singapore), and investment flows. Interestingly, given the nature of this "new age" agreement, *all* regions of the world gain, including, of course, Japan and Singapore. Fully 70% of the gains accrue to Japan (a good share of which is due to improved customs services). This study shows that features of modern FTAs could actually be "building blocks" in favor of the multilateral system and the welfare of the global economy takes us well beyond traditional Vinerian approaches.

Third, Plummer and Chia (2009) use a CGE model to estimate the potential benefits of the ASEAN Economic Community above AFTA itself by removing all nontariff barriers, allowing for increases in foreign direct investment, and reducing trade costs due to induced efficiency by a conservative 5%. They find that ASEAN economic welfare should rise by 5.3%, or $69 billion, that is, above what was estimated (on average) in the Cecchini Report for the European Single Market. It is also six times what the estimated effect of completing AFTA alone would be.

In short, economic modeling of the types used in this section can be extremely useful in capturing the potential economic effects of regional cooperation, which in turn may be a necessary condition to solicit political interest. But gauging the economic implications of "modern" agreements is often more of an art than a science; we know, for example, that harmonization of customs facilities, improved treatment of foreign investors, and better intellectual property regimes will have significant economic implications, but modeling these changes is extremely difficult and requires many simplifying assumptions. This is especially true in the area of services, which tend to be much more restricted than the goods sector, but their complex nature makes creating effective proxies of protection extremely difficult (to the point that no good proxies current exist). Thus, interpreting the actual economic implications of the results of these models must be done carefully.

III. Developing Countries: Additional Issues

Much of the theoretical and empirical modeling reviewed above was developed in the context of developed countries.[26] In particular, the evolution of economic integration in the context of the EEC and, later, the EU has greatly influenced this literature. However, developing countries require special consideration in the context of formal regional cooperation agreements. Least developed countries do not respond to changes in tariffs and nontariff barriers in the same way developed countries do. A complementary policy framework and infrastructure need to be in place in order to increase the probability of success. This section considers briefly some of the more salient preconditions for success.[27]

A. Macroeconomic Stability

There is general consensus that macroeconomic stability is critical to the continued success of any development strategy. Even short-term bouts of instability can haunt an economy for many years to come; Latin America's long struggle with inflation is only now beginning to be won, and this has been accomplished at considerable economic cost (through unemployment and foregone output) and social tension.

Promoting macroeconomic stability is difficult in developing countries, and external means to support this process are often necessary.

In particular, exchange-rate stability is vital for the smooth functioning of the economy, particularly in the tradable sector. Developing countries tend to rely on variations of fixed exchange rate regimes for a number of reasons, including vulnerability to inflation. What became clear during the Asian crisis is that the internationalization of these economies, though having many benefits, also expose them more to "external shocks" originating abroad (particularly for countries with fixed exchange rates), and intraregional interdependence, as well as the perception that Asia is increasingly performing as a group,[28] suggest that strong policy externalities exist in the region. That is, macroeconomic instability created by, say, an asset bubble in one market could have an important effect on the other markets. Hence, closer integration at the real and policy levels imply the need for greater cooperation at the macroeconomic level as well.

Preferential trading arrangements can help encourage macroeconomic stability in a number of ways. Real-financial links endemic to preferential trading agreements require stable macroeconomic policies if the agreement is to function smoothly. In order to ensure a stable partnership, countries must share information, cooperate in advocating stable fiscal and monetary policies, and engage in strong "peer pressure" against unstable policies. In advanced ("modern") regional agreements, countries find that they must focus on nontraditional areas affecting trade and investment if they are to advance economic integration, including competition policy and government procurement. These "nonborder" measures force a stronger market orientation, inject greater microeconomic competition by reducing the power of domestic monopolies and "rent seeking," and put constraints on government spending through, say, the abolition of export subsidies and restrictions on industrial policies. Thus, such "forced macroeconomic stability" could be highly beneficial to the economic development strategies of participating countries.

B. Technology Transfer and FDI

The link between FDI and technology transfer has been firmly established (Plummer 2007). It is one of the primary reasons why Asian countries have consistently sought means to lure FDI inflows. Regional integration is one means to attract such long-term investments by creating a more integrated marketplace within which multinationals can enjoy a regional division of labor with low transactions costs and exploit economies of scale. It is often said that AFTA itself is more of an investment agreement than a trade agreement, in that it is designed to enhance inward FDI more than intraregional trade flows.

The relationship between trade and technology transfer is less well known than that of FDI and technology transfer, or at least less well appreciated. Through trade liberalization, countries are also able to stimulate technological development. Trade leads to the adaptations of new technologies from abroad by increasing the potential for success in using these technologies to crack foreign markets. In addition, increased competition forces domestic firms to place a higher priority on creating their own or importing new technologies (Pissarides 1997). This implies a strong incentive for developing countries emphasizing technology transfer to liberalize even unilaterally.

Moreover, to best take advantage of these new technologies, countries find that they must establish strong intellectual property protection laws and means of enforcement. Without a protective environment in which multinationals can operate and in which domestic firms can invest in new innovations, the process of technology transfer is significantly inhibited. Formal free-trade areas can help create a strong underlying framework for the protection of intellectual property.

When developing countries team up with developed countries in an FTA, they are also able to encourage technology transfer specifically, either through internal promotional means (e.g., in terms of training facilities, regional research and academic institutes, research consortia) or in jointly devising means to bring in appropriate technologies from abroad. The U.S.-Singapore FTA, for example, tries to bring down barriers to greater cooperation in higher education and the establishment of foreign universities.

C. Structural Policy Change and Reform

Related to points A and B are various reforms in developing countries that are not directly pertinent to trade or even investment/financial flows per se but are essential to the modernization and competitiveness of an economic system. While often pushed by economists and technocrats, these reforms may not find special interest groups within the body politic that are able to push them. And since they tend to be controversial (with clear losers), they are difficult to promote, even if the economic gains in terms of increasing competitiveness are clear. Examples include the need for better laws related to corporate (and public) governance; competitions policy, including reform of state-owned enterprises, financial, and other services; and other "sensitive sectors" with important links to the rest of the economy.

Regional integration can help push reforms in these areas by providing the rigor of a formal accord. Since developing countries require such reforms more than most developed countries, regional integration can generate greater gains. For example, the creation of the EEC and the U.S.-Canada Free Trade Area arguably made relatively little progress in promoting structural reforms, as these were agreements between developed countries. However, when the EEC took in Greece, Spain, and Portugal in the 1980s, these countries, which were really "newly industrialized" rather than developed, made significant gains in terms of structural reforms, leading to greater competitiveness and productivity. The same can be said of Mexico in NAFTA; while it has a long way to go before becoming a truly "developed" economy, Mexico has made great progress in providing a more stable economic framework, modernizing and liberalizing previously undeveloped sectors (such as financial services, which now has significant foreign penetration), and increasing productivity.

D. Harmonization Issues

An important effect of the Single Market Programme in the EU can be classified under the rubric of "harmonization issues," such as product testing, professional certification, standards conformance, customs and transit, and so forth. Gains in all of these areas would be maximized by adopting global harmonization standards. But doing so at the global level is much more difficult, particularly for developing countries, who often feel threatened by such programs. By conforming as a group to some global standards, the agreement clearly reinforces the global system.

E. Political-Economy and Policy Issues

Most existing preferential trading arrangements were either created as economic arrangements in support of political goals or at least were consistent with the diplomatic strategy of the founding countries. Economic cooperation is seen as an important vehicle through which political goals can be pursued. The EU has been effective in using preferential trading arrangements as diplomatic tools over the past 40 years, in part out of necessity: commercial policy was the only unified policy at the regional level.

To the extent that these regional accords add to the political stability of the region, they do service to economic development in general and the goal of policy reform in particular, even if the arrangements have weak substance to them. This is an important part of the early success story of ASEAN. Although most ASEAN countries had only recently achieved independence and were struggling to create nation-states, the arrangement established an important dialogue that prevented overt hostilities between these countries. To say that the weak economic cooperation initiatives in ASEAN had nothing to do with the subsequent dynamic growth in the region is to seriously understate its role.

In sum, while regionalism is a second-best policy, there is reason to believe that bilateral and plurilateral accords could potentially generate far greater gains than standard models would suggest, given the critical importance of dynamic and non-border/policy changes that are inherent in such accords. Moreover, developing countries in Asia stand to gain relatively more from these "deep" policies than developed countries, provided that the region's FTAs are open—that is, trade-creating rather than trade-diverting—and other regulatory and nonborder conditions are met.

IV. Concluding Remarks

Preferential trading accords such as FTAs have both positive and negative effects. This is why they are known as "second-best" initiatives. However, when the "first-best" (i.e., multilateral liberalization) is unobtainable, they provide an alterative vehicle for trade policy. This chapter has considered the theoretical effects of such arrangements, as well as models that can be employed to estimate their potential economic effects. While some of the most important effects of FTAs, such as the "dynamic" effects and the salutary influence on macroeconomic and microeconomic policy, are excluded from formal modeling, they could prove to be the most important to developing countries on the path to outward-oriented economic development.

NOTES

The authors would like to thank David Cheong for his substantive input and contributions.

1. Namely, Brunei Darussalam, Cambodia, Indonesia, Laos, Malaysia, Myanmar, the Philippines, Singapore, Thailand, and Vietnam.

2. This section borrows from Plummer, Cheong, and Hamanaka (2010).

3. The analysis of regional integration in a customs union has been extended to the case of an FTA (Krueger 1995; Panagariya and Findlay 1996; and Krishna and Panagariya 2002). These authors show that some of the qualitative results from Viner's customs union model are similar to those from FTA models, but important differences remain.

4. The exposition here follows the partial equilibrium analysis in Johnson (1960).

5. For an ad valorem tariff, the analysis needs to be only slightly modified for the same qualitative results.

6. These triangular areas are also known as "Harberger triangles" after Arnold Harberger. In his article (1971) on the measurement of consumer and producer surplus, he discusses the geometric measurement of welfare.

7. Constant marginal-cost production is defined as incurring the same extra costs for each additional unit produced.

8. An equivalent assumption to constant marginal costs would be that the home country had a small share of these foreign countries' exports, so changes in the home country's imports would be marginal to the foreign exporters.

9. For a FTA analysis with rising supply curves see Kreinin (2010, pp. 116–118).

10. The upward slope of the offer curve says that as the relative price of imports falls, the country is willing to export more for additional quantities of imports. This implies that the demand for imports is price elastic. If demand for imports becomes price inelastic at low import prices, then the offer curve bends back.

11. The size of the shift will depend on the size of the initial tariff, preferences, production technology, and factor endowments.

12. In this model, for any shift of the offer curve away from the origin, a higher volume of tradables at the same terms of trade is associated with higher welfare. Further, any point that is higher on the same offer curve is also associated with higher welfare.

13. The main analytical results do not change if we allow the countries to trade with the World before the FTA.

14. APEC currently is comprised of 21 economies in the Asia-Pacific region. It is comprised of the NAFTA countries, ASEAN countries (save Cambodia, Laos, and Myanmar), Japan, Russia, South Korea, China, Hong Kong, Chinese Taipei, Australia, New Zealand, Papua New Guinea, Chile, and Perù.

15. We discussed this some in the context of Kemp and Wan (1976), but see also Panagariya and Krishna (2002) for a discussion of these conditions.

16. See Bhagwati (2008) for a survey of the arguments against regionalism.

17. This subsection on CGE models borrows from Plummer, Cheong, and Hamanaka (2010).

18. A general Cobb-Douglas production function is $y = A \prod\limits_{i=1,n} x_i^{a_i}$, where y is the quantity of output, xi is the quantity of input i, A is a scalar for productivity, and α_i is a parameter for each factor used. A general CES production function is

$$y = A\left[\sum_i \left(a_i x_i\right)^r\right]^{\frac{1}{r}},$$ where y is the quantity of output, x_i is the quantity of input i, A is a scalar for productivity, α_i is a parameter for each factor used, and ρ is a parameter related to the elasticity of substitution. A general Leontief production function is

$$y = \min\left(\frac{x_1}{\alpha_1}, \cdots, \frac{x_n}{\alpha_n}\right),$$ where y is the quantity of output, xi is the quantity of input i, and α_i is a parameter.

19. Separability is a mathematical property of a function. When it is assumed that production functions are weakly separable between primary and intermediate inputs, this implies that the marginal rate of substitution between any pair of primary factors is independent of the amount of intermediate inputs used. In other words, the demand for any two primary factors depends only on the price ratio of primary factors, and is independent of prices of intermediate inputs.

20. If a Leontief function is used to represent production, then there is no substitutability between inputs. If the Cobb-Douglas function is used to represent production, then the elasticity of substitution between inputs is equal to 1, i.e., a 1% reduction in the use of one input needs to be offset by a 1% increase in the use of another input to maintain a given level of output. For more flexibility, modelers often use the CES function, which allows them to choose any value for the elasticity of substitution.

21. Equivalent variation is a technique used to estimate changes in consumer welfare with a change in price.

22. These could be to delineate a common border through a binary variable, whether countries have a fixed exchange rate or monetary union, even cultural variables. As discussed in the text, we could also include a binary variable for an FTA or customs union.

23. Standard trade theory would suggest that the coefficients of the explanatory variables would have the following signs: $\delta_1 > 0$, $\delta_2 > 0$, $\delta_3 < 0$, and the rest would depend on the vector of additional explanatory variables. For example, we would expect that binary variable for a FTA partner would be positive.

24. Brooks, Roland-Holst, and Zhai (2005) model the Scenario 2 liberalization as an "iceberg effect," in which a fraction of goods and services "melt away in transit due to the trade costs" (p. 4 n. 4).

25. It is important to note that this value is a guesstimate and is not derived systematically or empirically.

26. For additional analysis of preferential trading arrangements in the context of developing countries, see Kreinin and Plummer (2000, 2002).

27. Parts of this section borrow from Plummer (2007).

28. What we mean here is that as ASEAN cooperation deepens, markets begin to view it as one entity. Besides, business cycles in the ASEAN countries have become more correlated (see, for example, Bayoumi, Eichengreen, and Mauro (1999) and Kim, Kose, and Plummer 2003).

REFERENCES

....

Bayoumi, Tamim, Barry Eichengreen, and Paolo Mauro. 1999."On Regional Monetary Arrangements for ASEAN." Paper prepared for the ADB/CEPII/KIEP Conference on Exchange Rate Regimes in Emerging Market Economies, Tokyo, December 17–18.

Berglas, Eitan. 1979. "Preferential Trading Theory: The n commodity case." *Journal of Political Economy* 87 (April): 315–331.

Bhagwati, Jagdish. 2008. *Termites in the Trading System: How Preferential Agreements Undermine Free Trade*. Oxford: Oxford University Press.

Brooks, Douglas H., David Roland-Holst, and Fan Zhai. 2005, September. Asia's Long-Term Growth and Integration: Reaching beyond Trade Policy Barriers. ADB ERD Policy Brief no. 38.Manila: Asian Development Bank.

Cecchini, Paolo. 1988. *The Cost of Non-Europe*. Brussels: EC Commission.

Cooper, C. A., and B. F. Massell. 1965. "A New Look at Customs Union Theory." *Economic Journal* 75 (December): 742–747.

Corden, W. M. 1972. "Economies of Scale and Customs Union Theory." *Journal of Political Economy* 80(3): 465–475.

Frankel, Jeffrey A. 1997, October. *Regional Trading Blocs in the World Economic System*. Washington, D.C.: Peterson Institute for International Economics.

Harberger, Arnold C. 1971. "Three Basic Postulates for Applied Welfare Economics." *Journal of Economic Literature* 9(3): 785–797.

Hertel, T. W., T. Walmsley, and K. Itakura. 2001. "Dynamic Effects of the 'New Age' Free Trade Agreement between Japan and Singapore." *Journal of Economic Integration* 16(4) (December): 446–484.

Innwon Park and Soonchan Park. 2009. "Free Trade Agreements versus Customs Unions: An Examination of East Asia." *Asian Economic Papers, MIT Press* 8(2) (June): 119–139.

Johnson, Harry. 1960. "The Economic Theory of Customs Union." *Pakistan Economic Journal* (10 March): 14–32. Reprinted in Richard Pomfret, ed., *Economic Analysis Of Regional Trading Arrangements*. London: Edward Elgar, 2003.

Kawai, Masahiro, and Ganeshan Wignaraja. 2008. "Regionalism as an Engine of Multilateralism: A Case for a Single East Asian FTA." Working Papers on Regional Economic Integration 14, Manila Asian Development Bank.

Kemp, Murray A., and Henry Wan. 1976. An Elementary Proposition Concerning the Formation of Customs Unions. *Journal of International Economics* 6(1) (February): 95–97.

Kim, Sunghyun Henry, M. Ayhan Kose, and Michael G. Plummer. 2003. "Dynamics of Business Cycles in Asia: Differences and Similarities." *Review of Development Economics* 7(3) (August): 462–477.

Kreinin, Mordechai E. 1959a. "European Integration and American Trade." *American Economic Review* 49(4) (September): 615–627.

Kreinin, Mordechai E. 1959b. "On the Trade Diversion Effect of Trade Preference Areas." *Journal of Political Economy* 67(4) (August): 398–401.

Kreinin, Mordechai E. 1960. "The Outer-Seven and European Integration." *American Economic Review* 50 (June): 370–386.

Kreinin, Mordechai E. 1964. "On the Dynamic Effects of a Customs Union. *Journal of Political Economy* 72 (April): 193–195.

Kreinin, Mordechai E. 1972. "Effect of the EEC on Import of Manufactures." *Economic Journal* 82(327) (September):, 897–920.

Kreinin, Mordechai E. 1973. "The Static Effects of EEC Enlargement on Trade Flows." *Southern Economic Journal* 39(4), vol (April): 559–568.

Kreinin, Mordechai E. 2010. *International Economics: A Policy Approach*. New York: Pearson.

Kreinin, Mordechai E., and Michael G. Plummer. 2000. *Economic Integration and Asia*. London: Edward Elgar.

Kreinin, Mordechai E., and Michael G. Plummer. 2002. *Economic Integration and Development*. London: Edward Elgar.

Krueger, Anne O. 1995. "Free Trade Agreements versus Customs Unions." NBER Working Papers 5084. Cambridge, Mass.: National Bureau of Economic Research.

Lipsey, Richard. 1957. "The Theory of Customs Unions. Trade Diversion and Welfare." *Economica* 24(93): 40–46.

Lipsey, Richard. 1970. *The Theory of Customs Unions: A General Equilibrium Analysis*. London.

Lipsey, Richard, and K. J. Lancaster. 1956/57. "The General Theory of Second Best." *Review of Economic Studies* 24 (October): 11–32.

McMillan, John, and Ewen McCann. 1981. "Welfare Effects in Customs Unions." *Economic Journal* 91(363): 697–703.

Meade, James E. 1955. *The Theory of Customs Unions*. Amsterdam: North-Holland.

Panagariya, Arvind. 2000. "Preferential Trade Liberalization: The Traditional Theory and New Developments." *Journal of Economic Literature* 38: 287–331.

Panagariya, Arvind, and Ronald Findlay. 1996. "A Political Economy Analysis of Free Trade Areas and Customs Unions." In Robert Feenstra, Douglas Irwin, and Gene Grossman, eds., *The Political Economy of Trade Reform: Essays in Honor of Jagdish Bhagwati*. Cambridge, Mass.: MIT Press.

Panagariya, Arvind, and Pravin Krishna. 2002. "On Necessarily Welfare-Enhancing Free Trade Areas." *Journal of International Economics* 57(2): 353–367.

Pissarides, Christopher A. 1997. "Learning by Trading and the Returns to Human Capital in Developing Countries." *World Bank Economic Review* 11(1) (January): 17–32.

Plummer, Michael G. 2007. "Best Practices in Regional Trading Agreements: An Application to Asia." *World Economy* 30 (December): 1771–1796.

Plummer, Michael G., David Cheong, and Shintaro Hamanaka. 2010. *Methodology for Impact Assessment of Free Trade Agreements*. Manila: Asian Development Bank.

Plummer, Michael G., and Ganesh Wignaraja. 2006. "The Post-crisis Sequencing of Economic Integration in Asia: Trade as a Complement to a Monetary Future." *Economie Internationale* 107: 59–85.

Plummer, Michael G., and Chia Siow Yue, eds. 2009. *Realizing the ASEAN Economic Community: A Comprehensive Assessment*. Singapore: ISEAS.

Shoven, J., and J. Whalley. 1992. *Applying General Equilibrium*, Cambridge: Cambridge University Press.

Viner, Jacob. 1950. *The Customs Union Issue*. New York: Carnegie Endowment for International Peace.
Wonnacott, P., and R. J. Wonnacott. 1981. "Is Unilateral Tariff Reduction Preferable to a Customs Union? The Curious Case of the Missing Foreign Tariffs." *American Economic Review* 71(4): 704–714.

CHAPTER 7

THE RULES-BASED TRADING SYSTEM

CRISTIANE CARNEIRO AND GARY CLYDE HUFBAUER

TEACHINGS FROM INTERNATIONAL RELATIONS

"A people . . . who are possessed of the spirit of commerce, who see and who will pursue their advantages may achieve almost anything."

—George Washington (letter to Benjamin Harrison, October 10, 1784)

Since times immemorial, international commerce has been celebrated as a fountain of prosperity.[1] Trade flourished long before trade regulations ever came into being. The subsequent creation of trade regulations did not preclude trade in unregulated goods, services, and property, nor has it eliminated smuggling and contraband. Evidently trade and regulations often exist independent from each other. But over the course of history, trade has become increasingly regulated. In this chapter, we focus on the evolution of trade regulations and the development of a rules-based system.

Why Rules between Sovereign Countries?

If exchange among trade partners is such an attractive proposition, why have intense levels of international commerce not emerged spontaneously, that is, without the framework of state-sponsored regulation? In other words, why did states feel compelled to regulate international trade in the first place? Related to that question, how can we account for the trading system's uneven regulatory developments since the late eighteenth century? This chapter is concerned with puzzles presented by the rules-based trading system that we inherited from the past and now take for granted.

Our inquiry does not start with a blank slate. Scholars have analyzed factors that contributed to the emergence of a rules-based trading system, and the impact of the system on the economic structure. We survey these varied approaches and argue that they are not mutually exclusive. Rather, we believe that an understanding of the rules-based trading system that we have today requires an appreciation of several theoretical approaches, regardless of the direction of causation. To that end, we examine the role of compliance theory, issue density, reputation, and regime type as they play out in the development of an international trade regime.

Compliance Theory

In an anarchic world system, where no authority has the power to enforce commitments, the emergence and sustainability of cooperation among self-interested actors can be facilitated by international agreements. Agreements clarify the content of obligations and signal a willingness to comply. Whether compliance follows formalized commitments or the other way around, and related to that, whether formal commitments improve the levels of compliance, are central research questions of compliance theory.

Chayes and Chayes (1993, p. 176) argue that it is "plausible and useful" to assume: (1) that states have a propensity to comply with international agreements; (2) that instances of noncompliance are often unintentional; and (3) that international agreements should be deemed successful if they reach "acceptable levels of compliance," as opposed to full compliance.[2] Along these lines, the regulation of international trade can be seen as a compliance-enhancing mechanism. Trade partners welcome the regulatory initiative as a means to tie their own hands, and the hands of their partners, thereby taming the temptation to defect that is inherent in all prisoner dilemma scenarios.

In a prisoner's dilemma, each player in a single game does better when she defects and the other player continues to cooperate. For an example in the realm of international trade, consider a most-favored-nation bilateral agreement. In the absence of a formal agreement, the trading partner who violates the most-favored-nation status unilaterally will most likely improve her terms of trade—she will buy goods more cheaply from the partner that is still required to pay the tariff, since that partner has to compete with another partner who enjoys duty-free access to her market. In this situation, compliance theory proposes that the presence of formal commitments will improve observance of the most-favored-nation rule.

Based on the main tenets of compliance theory, we expect systems of trade regulation to emerge whenever the "temptation to defect" from informal commitments is high. By the same token, existing regulatory arrangements will become more legalized, with tighter rules, in face of greater incentives to defect.[3] These propositions will guide our overview of the historical evolution of the rules-based trading system, as we know it today.

But before we proceed to the other theoretical frameworks that shed light on the evolutionary process, we point to a selection bias identified by Downs, Rocke, and Barsoom (1996) with respect to mainstream compliance theory—theory that the three authors label the "managerial school." The selection bias arises because the managerial school focuses on international agreements that required relatively little behavior modification from states. For Downs, Rocke, and Barsoom (1996), these agreements are easy to negotiate and to carry out because the required level of cooperation is shallow—in comparison to agreements that call on states to substantially change their behavior. The latter agreements offer a better test of the challenges that compliance entails, except that such agreements are infrequent precisely because the compliance hurdles are high. However, for Downs, Rocke, and Barsoom (1996), international agreements that involve a certain "depth of cooperation," measured by the required level of behavior modification, should be the focus of analysis (p. 93).

In the realm of international trade regulation, the agreement by all members of the World Trade Organization (WTO) to protect intellectual property—the so-called TRIPs agreement (Trade Related Intellectual Property Rights)—called for substantial modification in countries where patent infringement and copyright piracy were normal business practice. In the decade since the Uruguay Round was concluded at Marrakech in 1994, which included the TRIPs agreement, many of these "scofflaws" have enacted and even enforced their own intellectual property laws.

Deep agreements often contain enforcement mechanisms to help counter the disincentives that states face, when it comes to negotiating agreements, maintaining them in force, and complying with their terms. The question of when and how enforcement mechanisms emerged over the history of the rules-based trading system is a matter of considerable interest. Given the challenges of reaching deep cooperation on the one hand and the incentives to defect on the other, how can we account for the emergence of enforcement mechanisms to mitigate these problems? This question is addressed in Keohane (1982), who focuses on the role of issue density.

Issue Density

For Keohane (1982), a marketplace exists for international regulations, which bears similarities to markets in everyday commerce. But contrary to market mechanisms as we know them in microeconomics, in international relations both the demand for regulations and their supply are functions of a single state or a small group of states. The single state is usually the hegemon, such as the Great Britain in the nineteenth century or the United States today; the small group of like-minded states is illustrated by the Hanseatic League, an informal association of about 200 north

German towns (Schulz 2005, p. 1) or the European Common Market of the 1960s (six members).

Regime *demandeurs* sponsor the creation of international regulations in response to three—at times compounding—defects in the existing state of affairs (Keohane 1982):

(1) Absence of a clear framework establishing liability for actions
(2) Information imperfections—information is costly to acquire
(3) High transactions costs in carrying out business

Regimes are more likely to emerge when these three defective conditions exist at the same time. Information imperfections and transaction costs are in fact two sides of the same coin, as Keohane notes, and their combined pressure for regime development is directly proportional to the density of the issues under consideration (Keohane 1982). In other words, when several issues are at the same time afflicted by the defects on Keohane's list, the pressure is greater to develop a regulatory framework. Issue density also aggravates the liability problem, because with more issues at stake, the absence of a legal umbrella implies greater uncertainty: if country A ignores the informal rules on issue X, country B may in turn ignore the rules on issue Y. Issue density thus constitutes a major force behind the emergence of international regimes.

Issue density makes regulation more urgent because of the potential for spillover from issue to issue—and the greater the number of issues, the larger the risk of harmful spillovers. For our purposes—to explain the emergence of a rules-based trading system—it is sufficient to match peaks of issue density to regulatory efforts on the part of states. Conversely, when the issue space becomes more rarefied, a feeble regulatory effort should be observed.

So far, our discussion has overlooked the characteristics of states that participate in the regulatory effort—either as suppliers, as *demandeurs*, or as subjects. Do we have information about how these states acted in the past? Are they reliable partners? Answers to these questions can be summarized in a theory of reputation, which among its predictions suggests how information on the reliability of individual states (their reputation) has shaped the outcome of regulatory enterprises. We rely on the recent work of Tomz (2007) to discuss the role of reputation, either as a known or unknown quality, on the evolution of a rules-based trading system.

Reputation

For Tomz (2007), reputation is a function of observable behavior in the context of particular events. He analyzed the role of reputation in the realm of international foreign debt over three centuries. During this time, first-time borrowers acquired a reputation, which was subsequently put to the test when a changing context imposed harsh repayment conditions on them. Lenders, at their next turn, priced loans according to the risk associated with each borrower, based on reputation. The usefulness of Tomz's theory resides in the fact that reputations evolve as a function of the borrower's behavior over time, given a specific economic context. Following this logic, there are three types of borrowers: lemons, fair-weathers, and stalwarts. The first type fails to meet its responsibilities even in good times, the second only fails during economic downturns, and stalwarts pay up in good as well as bad times. Related to that, a first-time borrower will often pay a premium for not having a track record that speaks for its creditworthiness. Subsequently, the borrower's behavior in context will perhaps establish a good reputation, and earn cheaper loans.

This framework is tested against competing theories, ultimately revealing its wide explanatory power. Because the international financial system developed almost simultaneously with the rules-based trading system, we believe the reputation story so elegantly formulated in Tomz (2007) illuminates the history we tell in this chapter. Our theoretical expectations converge toward four conjectures:

- At early stages of development of the rules-based trading system, regulations were harsh, because a risk premium was built in to cover the lack of knowledge that states had about each other's reliability (reputation).
- As regulatory initiatives developed, new entrants were penalized with more demanding terms, as compared to seasoned trade partners, again because of the lack of information.
- As new entrants had an opportunity to establish good reputations, terms extended to them improved.
- Economic downturns presented states with an opportunity to revise their regulatory systems—often to less demanding thresholds—and with these revisions, a chance to reestablish reputations presented itself.

Finally, before we embark on the historical illustrations in this chapter, we would like to emphasize that the emergence and development of modern democracy has impacted the trading system. Most prominently, as argued in Bueno de Mesquita et al. (2003), democratic leaders need to meet the demands of a larger group of constituents in order to further their political survival. Thus, the waves of democratization that the world has witnessed since the eighteenth century have brought significant, though unintended, consequences to the rules-based trading system.

Regime Type

Leadership survival is the centerpiece of contemporary research on regime type. Incumbents are primarily concerned with holding on to power; as a consequence, most policy decisions—from the provision of public roads to taxation and foreign policy—are guided by the goal of political survival. To that end, the "selectorate" model proposes that any polity can be understood in terms of four features (Bueno de Mesquita et al. 2003): (1) a winning coalition, or the group of individuals whose support is essential to keep a leader in power; (2) a selectorate, the group that possesses the means to join the winning coalition; (3) the disenfranchised; and (4) the leader.

Autocratic regimes typically rely on small winning coalitions. It follows that an autocratic leader needs only to please a select few to remain in power. The most effective way to accomplish this task is to reward this group with private goods. Among other advantages, private rewards bring more loyalty.

Typically, as states undergo the process of democratization, leaders will increasingly embrace the provision of public goods. This is so because incumbents in a democratic regime must meet the needs of a larger winning coalition, and public goods are an effective way of doing so, given their characteristic of nonrival consumption (many people can drive on a public highway at the same time without interfering with each other). The regulation of international trade is neither a pure public good nor a pure private good. We argue instead that trade regulation can extend across a spectrum. Regulation with the characteristics of a pure public good should accompany waves of democratization; regulations with characteristics more akin to a pure private good should be the flavor of autocracy.

We draw on the selectorate model to account for the impact that several waves of democratization have exerted on the development of a rules-based international trading system. We are particularly interested in highlighting the moments in history when trade regulations ceased to benefit a select few and became a policy instrument to bolster the population as a whole—in other words, episodes when the trading system distanced itself from the characteristics of a private good and shifted toward the features of a public good.

Historical Illustrations

The Role of Customary International Law

The efforts of sovereign states to regulate trade beyond their borders is a response to the demands of their own merchants, initially for guaranteed access to foreign markets, and later for better terms of access. Brown (2003, p. 50) credits these early initiatives for the emergence of the most-favored-nation (MFN) clause, which would play such an important role in subsequent regulatory efforts. Initially, the negotiation of MFN status sought to harmonize regulations on access to ports, as well as the payment of port dues and taxes, for foreign ships carrying foreign cargo. In particular, Great Britain acted with a fierce persistence to secure the most viable maritime routes for its trading companies that possessed a monopoly on lucrative international markets: the West Indies Company and the East Indies Company. The Dutch followed suit.

Initially these regulatory efforts were not formalized into multilateral treaties but rather were shaped through the norms of customary law. International law scholars agree that the law of the sea and the ensuing practices followed by international traders are among the early examples of international law in modern history (Dunoff, Ratner, and Wippman 2006). The creation of binding obligations in that manner was made easier by the small number of sovereign states during the colonial era: the emergence of a norm of customary international law only required the following of a practice with a sense of legal obligation. Unless a state objected to the custom in the beginning of the process of norm formation, the state would automatically become bound by the norm. As new states came into being, they were likewise expected to adopt the norm.

Thus, MFN regulation did not require the execution of treaties. Some legal scholars argue that the nature of the incentives associated with this norm led to self-enforcing agreements, and the negotiation of international treaties would have been superfluous (Goldsmith and Posner 2005). More specifically, because the demand for harmonization of access and equal treatment was ubiquitous, states had a powerful self-interest in complying with the established custom—otherwise withdrawal of MFN privileges would harm the state's own merchants who traded abroad. Reciprocity ruled! Much later, the need to go beyond MFN, in order to guarantee treatment similar to that reserved for domestic merchants, engendered a race toward the negotiation of bilateral treaties.

Bilateral Treaties

The proliferation of bilateral treaties during the second half of the eighteenth century sought to extend national treatment to foreign merchants, as said before, but it can also be seen as an attempt to strengthen commitments at a time of great political instability in Europe. Goldsmith and Posner (2005, p. 84) argue that explicit agreements—as opposed to customary international law—are useful to enhance cooperation in situations that involve problems of coordination or prisoner dilemma scenarios. Extension of national treatment often entails one or the other. For example, if foreign and domestic merchants are to be taxed in the same manner by two states, the specific package and its conditions must be well understood by both parties. A bilateral treaty helps accomplish this goal.[4]

It can also be argued that with the shift of power toward legislative branches of government, the negotiation and ratification of bilateral treaties enhanced the standing of national treatment commitments in the eyes of future officeholders. This is certainly the case in Britain and in America. While in Britain Parliament became the center of the political process in the eighteenth century, in America the Constitution explicitly granted the Congress plenary powers relating to domestic and foreign commerce.

International custom and bilateral treaties represent the first steps toward a regulatory system that would only come into existence much later, as a response to international economic and security concerns. The road that culminated with the General Agreement on Tariffs and Trade in 1947 traversed a series of failed revolutions in Europe in 1848, two great depressions, and two world wars. No less important, the collapse of the trade monopoly of the British and Dutch companies, as well as shifting fortunes within major European powers and across the Atlantic, generated unparalleled pressure in favor of protectionist policies toward the final decades of the nineteenth century and after World War I, pressure that could not be dealt with on a bilateral basis.

An Infant Multilateral Regime

During the nineteenth century, a web of bilateral MFN treaties was negotiated, pioneered by Great Britain's unilateral trade liberalization efforts. In 1823, the Reciprocity of Duties Act led to MFN treaties between Britain and France, Prussia, Austria, Sweden, the Hanseatic League, Denmark, the United States, and most Latin American states (Conybeare 2002, p. 44). In the aftermath of the Opium Wars with China (1839–1842)[5] and following the reintroduction of the income tax (1841), all export duties on British goods were lifted. Great Britain was well positioned for the vast expansion in world trade that would take place between 1843 and 1873.

Partly because Great Britain was spared the "great troubles" of 1848, its production capacity was unaffected by the many revolutionary movements that seized European capitals during that year (and then failed). Historians credit Britain's timely passage of legislation to improve welfare and work conditions with taming the political unrest that engulfed the Continent (Conybeare 2002, p. 40). The British entered the 1850s reassured of their industrial dominance and ready to pursue MFN negotiations more aggressively and on a more formalized manner, which ultimately led to the landmark Cobden-Chevalier Treaty of 1860 between Great Britain and France.

This treaty became a benchmark of the multilateral regime, precisely because it spawned several bilateral treaties, mostly between France and other European nations. The treaty is also seen as a response to the "ordinary business cycle downturn" that started in 1857, affecting France most directly (Gourevitch 1977, p. 281). In 1873, when France denounced the Cobden-Chevalier Treaty, the seeds of a great depression were already in place, and the trade liberalization chapter of the mid-nineteenth century was about to close. During the prolonged depression, which continued in fits and starts until 1896, countries resorted to higher tariffs and protectionist measures of various sorts. The feeble rules-based multilateral trade experiment was short lived.

The Nineteenth Century: Compliance, Issue Density, Reputation, and Regime Type

We argued earlier that various explanations can be combined to account for the emergence of a multilateral international trade regime in the mid-nineteenth century. We turn to each now, as they relate to the first period under analysis. Great Britain's unilateral move toward liberalization can be understood as a direct consequence of advances in technology and production methods. Unilateral liberalization at that juncture demanded little "behavior modification" on Britain's part, as expounded by Downs, Rocke, and Barsoom (1996)—which had not been the case at the beginning of the Industrial Revolution. At a later stage, again according to their argument, states would negotiate treaties that entailed little or no behavior modification; these treaties would subsequently enjoy good levels of compliance and evolve into international regimes. This is precisely what happened in Britain and continental Europe, through a cascade of bilateral treaties.

Coupled with the compliance literature argument, issue density and state reputation also played a role. The most notable concentration of issues resulted from the combination of security and trade questions. Added to that, the trade explosion that followed the Industrial Revolution demanded the expansion of several distinct markets, in Europe, in the Americas, in Asia, and in Africa. This could be accomplished most efficiently through an international trade regime. The liberalization that started with Britain's unilateralist policies in the 1820s offered states an ideal stage to establish their international reputation. The regime provided the background against which states would become known as stalwarts, fair-weathers, and lemons and able to negotiate correspondingly favorable trade deals (Tomz 2007). As a trade partner improved its reputation, it would be granted more benefits, often negotiated in the context of an MFN treaty. The record of the British unilateral liberalization policies, as well as the Cobden-Chevalier Treaty and its aftermath, confirm this pattern.

Finally, we argue that the deepening of democracy in Great Britain throughout the nineteenth century had important redistributive consequences, because it entailed an expansion of the winning coalition. With this expansion, leaders engaged in an effort to enhance the provision of public goods, as opposed to private goods, which work best at ensuring the loyalty of a small winning coalition. The first pieces of welfare and labor legislation were passed at that time; it was expected that trade liberalization policies would lead to cheaper food and more jobs, thus favoring the new elements in the winning coalition.

The Twentieth Century: From World War I to the Havana Conference

The new century followed the path toward multilateralism that states had initiated a few decades earlier. This time, not only international trade but also international warfare became global with the most perverse consequences for peoples and markets. Setting aside the devastating legacy of the two world wars, we comment on their impact for the development of a rules-based trading system.

It goes without saying that during the war years international trade flow was acutely disrupted and the infant system that supported it, already weakened by the depression of the late nineteenth century, suffered a major blow to its raison d'être. In this context, two phenomena had an important impact on the development of a rules-based trading system: (1) the suppression of gold convertibility in 1918, and (2) the emergence of strong nationalist sentiments within states. In the next paragraphs we discuss the role of both during the interwar years.

The regime of floating exchange rates that replaced the gold standard during the first half of the 1920s presented states with the tempting opportunity to use exchange rate policy as a tool to address balance-of-payments problems. Adverse systemic consequences from this new usage of floating exchange rates were addressed by raising tariffs—to the extent that Brown speaks of "tariffs as a weapon against exchange rate dumping" (2003, p. 68). The race toward protectionism could not be reversed when most countries returned to the gold standard between 1925 and 1927. In 1927 states got together for the International Economic Conference and proclaimed a "tariff truce" (p. 71). During this time, the adoption of unconditional MFN treatment by the United States, following the 1922 Fordney-McCumber Tariff Act, is said to have been inconsequential. The apex of escalating tariffs, in the United States, was the infamous Smoot-Hawley Tariff Act of 1930.[6] The trend toward protectionism was only partially reversed in 1934, with the passage by the U.S. Congress of the Reciprocal Trade Agreements Act. Unlike Britain in the 1820s, the United States refused to liberalize unilaterally. In both countries, the introduction of the income tax as an alternative revenue source to customs duties seems to have assisted trade liberalization forces; nevertheless, in the United States that process demanded reciprocal tariff reductions (Irwin 2002, p. 61).

The protectionist policies embedded in high tariffs nicely suited domestic constituents who saw trade barriers as a justified expression of nationalist sentiment. In fact, the memory of World War I remained fresh in the minds of soldiers and civilians, who suffered so much loss and deprivation during the war years. They were not ready to grant nondiscriminatory tariff treatment to former enemies. Thus, the preference for protectionist policies took root in the minds of leaders and constituents, even though it was based on noneconomic premises. The alignment of protectionist preferences within states reinforced the prisoner's dilemma nature of the international trade liberalization game, increasing the incentives for defection. By defecting, each country could taste the elixir of temporary employment gains in protected industries, no matter the adverse effect on trading partners. Thus was coined the phrase "beggar thy neighbor" policy.

Intimately linked to this unhappy juxtaposition of forces was the Great Depression, which began with the stock market crash of 1929 and lasted through most of the 1930s, only to be followed by World War II. It was only after experiencing the downward spiral of depression and the horrors of the war that states representing 60% of world trade—23 countries altogether—met in Havana to discuss the creation of an international trade liberalization regime, premised this time both on the centuries-old MFN clause *and* on the more recent principle of national treatment. The General Agreement on Tariffs and Trade (GATT) was born.

The Twentieth Century: Compliance, Issue Density, Reputation, and Regime Type

Our same network of theoretical explanations can account for the failings of the trade regime during the first half of the twentieth century. According to the behavior modification story proposed by Downs, Rocke, and Barsoom (1996), when trade liberalization commitments demanded behavior modification that became too costly, states simply abandoned their obligations. This pattern is best illustrated by the rise in tariffs that preceded World War I and continued with renewed force after the bloodbath.

The reputation argument sees the high tariffs of the 1920s and 1930s as punishment for defection from prior trade liberalization commitments, not to mention various nonaggression promises. When states fail to uphold treaty obligations— such as the ones contained in the several MFN agreements negotiated during the nineteenth century—they lose their good standing in the marketplace; their reputations, much like those of borrowers that do not repay on time, are downgraded, and they are charged a corresponding premium in the form of higher tariffs.

According to the regime type explanation, the new wave of authoritarianism favored the provision of private goods over public goods. During the first half of the twentieth century this trend is noticeable in at least two areas: protectionism, as said before, and human rights. In fact, because the new authoritarian leaders needed the support of a select few to remain in power, they could please this minority quite efficiently by enacting made-to-order protection. Meanwhile the suppression of civil liberties and political rights furnished a quick solution for reconciling competing interests. As history has shown, this policy combination eventually leads to lower incomes and indiscriminate repression, but in the short run it certainly helps authoritarian leaders stay in power.

With respect to issue density, the regulatory environment was so complex at the time that information sharing and the search for equilibrium took a lot longer than would be normal. The war years and the world depression can be understood as a long period of realignment that would culminate with the new order, marked by U.S. hegemony, by the Cold War, and by the creation of the Bretton Woods institutions in which the GATT figured prominently.

The Twentieth Century: From the GATT to the WTO

The GATT was created in 1947 to meet the regulatory preferences of a few powerful countries, principally the United States, Canada, and their European allies. The communist bloc was not part of the original GATT, nor were most developing countries. Moreover, important sectors soon escaped the liberalization commitments embedded in the GATT, most prominently agriculture and textiles. Services were not covered. With respect to sectors that were subject to core GATT principles— MFN and national treatment—member countries (known as "contracting parties") enjoyed ample flexibility in the form of escape clauses and the ability to veto adverse dispute settlement findings.

Throughout the decades, GATT's evolution into what we know today can be seen as a response to both internal and external forces. Internally, as states had an opportunity to establish their reputations within the regime's parameters, the level of commitment deepened. This can be observed in the progressive reduction of trade barriers, and the willingness of states to give greater respect to the determinations of dispute settlement panels. The custom developed to appoint a panel of three experts to hear the arguments in a dispute between member states and make recommendations. Despite the absence of enforcement mechanisms, these recommendations were followed far more often than not (Hudec 1993).

Only modest levels of behavior modification were institutionalized in the GATT, corroborating the proposition from compliance literature of the "lowest common denominator." In the event that agreed levels of behavior modification could not be met by a single member, an adverse dispute settlement ruling would usually suffice to bring about compliance, given the concern of member states about their reputations. However, in blockbuster disputes, involving agricultural protection or tax practices, behavior modification was too painful domestically, and member states tarnished their reputations by ignoring the rulings.

Among the many external factors that influenced the evolution of the GATT, we chose to highlight:

- The European Economic Communities (EEC)
- The admission of developing countries
- The end of the Cold War
- The pressure to cover new issues

Each one of these developments ignited a wheel of institutional revision within the GATT, almost always within the framework of one of the eight negotiating "rounds." Issue density, according to Keohane's framework (Keohane 1982), explains how the GATT responded to the new challenges. The slow trend toward democratization called for more liberalization, while the preoccupation of the United States and European powers with consolidating the nascent world trading system fostered the role of reputation in international politics.

Brown refers to the formation of the EEC in 1957 as "by far the most important event in international trade relations in the 1950s" (2003, p. 99). After their experience using cooperative mechanisms to overcome the "dollar shortage" that followed the World War II, the six western European countries saw that greater economic integration might enable Europe to reassert itself as a competitive force in the international marketplace. The chosen instrument was the creation of a customs union with free trade among the members and a common tariff against outsiders. The implications for American trade supremacy and for the non-EEC members of GATT were immense. The Kennedy Round (1964–1967) was the institutional response to the European enterprise (p. 97). The big idea of GATT negotiations in the 1960s was to lower the common EEC external tariff so as to reduce discrimination against the "outsiders"—Europe's trading partners. As a direct outcome of the Kennedy Round, tariff reductions in the order of 36 to 39% of pre-Round levels were agreed by GATT members.[7]

Between 1964, the start of the Kennedy Round, and 1979, the end of the Tokyo Round, 24 countries acceded to the GATT. Among these countries, only Switzerland could be singled out as a developed nation. The United States and Europe wanted to bring these 23 developing countries into the trading system, as one of several bulwarks against the communist bloc (then led by the Soviet Union and China). But neither the existing GATT members nor the new recruits wanted to pay a high price in terms of behavior modification. One part of the deal was the Multi-Fiber Arrangement (MFA) and continued high tariffs on other labor-intensive products like footwear and toys. Moreover the "quad" countries—the United States, the EEC, Canada, and Japan—would continue to run the GATT negotiations through the Tokyo Round. According to the deal, new GATT members were granted the General System of Preferences and other forms of "special and differential treatment." Very little was asked of new members in that era—as part of the accession process, they did not have to cut or even bind their tariff barriers very much, or end their quota regimes—but still they did get a reputational boost.

We spoke earlier of sectors that were not included in the trade liberalization umbrella created by the GATT. Sectors like agricultural products and transportation services were left out because the level of behavior modification that regulation and liberalization in these matters entailed was above and beyond the acceptable thresholds for most GATT members. The Kennedy Round witnessed another compliance theory adjustment, this time related to the textile and apparel industries. At issue was competition between East Asian, European, and American producers; and producers in the industrial countries were well represented in legislative bodies. The quagmire led to the MFA, an agreement that institutionalized a complex system of import quotas, in direct contradiction with GATT's tenet of nondiscrimination and its strictures against quantitative barriers.

The MFA festered in the minds of developing countries as evidence of the power game that took place within the GATT. These countries were joining the GATT in greater numbers with the decolonization process.[8] Often membership in the GATT was handed down from former colonial powers. The newcomers, along with developing countries that were original signatories, quickly identified common interests and proceeded to congregate in an informal gathering that became known as the Group of Seventy Seven. Among the common interests was resistance to the idea of reciprocity. Developing countries felt that they needed "special and differential treatment" in order to prosper. That agenda led to two outcomes: a widely accepted understanding that developing countries would not be asked to reduce their barriers much if at all during the course of GATT negotiating rounds, and the General System of Preferences, which allowed developed countries to give preferential access to imports from developing countries (Brown 2003, p. 103).

The end of the Cold War and, equally important, China's conversion to a market economy, were landmark events in the midst of the Uruguay Round (1986–1994). With these dramatic changes, the United States and Europe felt less need to humor developing countries to keep them from slipping into a communist camp that was rapidly shrinking in size and importance. The United States and the European Union wanted to surround China with the disciplines of GATT; on their part, the Chinese leaders wanted to use these disciplines as a means of pushing market reforms. Meanwhile, the Group of Seventy Seven were getting more frustrated with the MFA—and they failed to foresee the rise of China as a dominant exporter of textiles and apparel. The result of these forces was lots of behavior modification— acceptance by developing countries of the nominal inclusion of services in the system, through the General Agreement on Trade in Services, but without major liberalization, and also the acceptance of intellectual property protection via TRIPs. The developed countries on their side agreed to phase out the MFA. For its part, China embarked on a 13-year accession process, as much to accelerate market reforms within China as to burnish its reputation as a world trader.

The coverage of new issues in a big way, beyond tariffs and quotas, got started in the Tokyo Round (1973–1979) with the discussion of various codes. These put teeth in GATT provisions that could not be effectively enforced solely through dispute panels. Most important, the codes of conduct addressed various nontariff trade barriers. The Code on Government Procurement (1979) and the Code on Subsidies and Countervailing Duties (1979) are exemplary. These and other codes sought to raise the punishment for defection. They clarified the obligations of signatory countries within the GATT and aimed at increasing the reputational costs of free riding; however, the codes were only binding on those GATT members that elected to join.

The same process resumed during the Uruguay Round (1986–1994), this time with greater ambition, particularly since the agreements generally applied to all GATT members. This was the concept of a "single undertaking," which meant that members could not excuse themselves from the new codes (with very few exceptions), but rather had to embrace the revisions as part of a deeper GATT. Thus, the new General Agreement on Trade in Services, the new TRIPs, as well as the Agreement on Subsidies and Countervailing Measures, the Agreement on Trade Related Investment Measures, and a few others came under the umbrella of the new WTO. Despite the provisions contained in the "single undertaking," flexibility existed through a scheduling process that accommodated countries' temporary needs. The outcome mirrored the discussion in Gilligan (1997): higher levels of cooperation were attained by relaxing the commitment to the same terms for all members.

The WTO was charged with overseeing implementation of these new codes and the associated deepening of member-state obligations. The "crown jewel" of the WTO was its dispute settlement mechanism (DSM), which strengthened the system that existed under the GATT by reversing the consensus rule. Now, only a unanimous vote of the members can overturn a final decision rendered by the Appellate Body. This institutional reform represented a major step in the direction of legalization and sharply increased the stakes for member-states with respect to their reputation for abiding by WTO agreements. In fact, the DSM created by far the strongest international tribunal in today's global system of state-to-state relations.

However, the WTO witnessed a stalemate in its role as a negotiating forum. The twin institutional obstacles are the rule of consensus decision-making in a 153-member body and the concept of a "single undertaking," which means that nothing is agreed until everything is agreed. At this writing, the result is that the Doha Development Round is entering its tenth year of talks, with the conclusion still over the horizon. Institutional paralysis in the WTO has contributed to the proliferation of regional and bilateral trade agreements; through these agreements, some states have accomplished highly ambitious liberalization nested in strong legal commitments.

CONCLUDING REMARKS

We started this chapter by emphasizing the role of four theoretical frameworks as useful explanatory tools in the evolution of the rules-based trading system that we know today. From the scholarship on compliance, we derived an association between the levels of behavior modification demanded and the emergence of new rules. The argument on issue density helped us point to the role of "new developments" in the evolution of regulations, whereas the recent literature on reputation and regime type illuminated the response of states to pressures both from the international community and domestic constituents.

The rules-based trading system has attained unparalleled accomplishments over the last two centuries. Income, wealth, and innovation have all multiplied through liberalization. The trading system has conveyed important and positive consequences for other areas of international politics, such as international security, human rights, and democratization. This process is far from complete and in all likelihood will continue to unfold over future generations. The analysis of the historical developments offered here, as well as their framing in terms of international relations theory, can perhaps help policymakers better understand the terrain that they labor to shape.

NOTES

1. Views expressed are the opinions of the authors.
2. The authors entertain three circumstances that can lead to unintentional noncompliance: "(1) ambiguity and indeterminacy of treaty language, (2) limitations on the capacity of parties to carry out their undertakings, and (3) the temporal dimension of the

social and economic changes contemplated by regulatory treaties" (Chayes and Chayes 1995, p. 10).

3. Legalization can be viewed as a continuum, in which ever greater levels of formalization are negotiated over already legalized agreements—an idea proposed by Abbott and Snidal (2000) and Goldstein et al. (2000). For these authors, legalization encompasses three aspects: obligation, or the degree to which commitments are legally binding; precision, or the degree to which the content of commitments clearly identifies the conduct that is required, authorized, or proscribed; and delegation, or the degree to which the interpretation, the monitoring, and the implementation of commitments is transferred to a third party (Goldstein et al. 2000, p. 387).

4. In a game of coordination, it is in both players' self interest to implement the treaty, whereas in a prisoner's dilemma, both players have an incentive to cheat, even when the other player cooperates.

5. The Opium Wars with China offer one of the few good examples of successful gunboat diplomacy in pursuit of trade objectives. On the whole, however, the use of limited military intervention to secure foreign policy goals, commonly referred to as gunboat diplomacy, has a spotty record. Tomz identifies four leading motivations that historically prompted gunboat diplomacy: civil wars, territorial conflicts, tort claims, and foreign debt collection. Trade disputes are not on the list of leading motivations (the Opium Wars were the exception, not the rule). Moreover, Tomz argues that even bondholders held few expectations that gunboat diplomacy would deliver satisfactory results (2007, p. 232).

6. Some scholars downplay the impact of the Smoot-Hawley Tariff, since it did little to raise applied tariffs, simply because trade barriers were already so high (Irwin 2002). However, as a symbol of protectionist spirits, Smoot-Hawley was unrivaled in its own time and still is to this day.

7. To be more specific, for the EEC and the United States the average tariff reduction was 36%, while Britain and Japan reached an average cut of 39% (Brown 2003, p. 103).

8. Between 1947 and 1965, 35 more developing countries joined the GATT (Brown 2003, p. 107).

REFERENCES

Abbott, Kenneth W., and Duncan Snidal. 2000. "Hard and Soft Law in International Governance." *International Organization* 54(3), pp. 421–56.

Acemoglu, Daron, Simon Johnson, and James Robinson. 2001. "The Colonial Origins of Comparative Development." *American Economic Review* 91(4), pp. 1369–1401.

Acemoglu, Daron, Simon Johnson, and James Robinson. 2003. "The Rise of Europe: Atlantic Trade, Institutional Change and Economic Growth." *American Economic Review* 95(3), pp. 546–79.

Brown, Andrew G. 2003. *Reluctant Partners: A History of Multilateral Trade Cooperation 1850–2000.* Ann Arbor: University of Michigan Press.

Bueno de Mesquita, Bruce, Alastair Smith, Randolph Siverson, and James Morrow. 2003. *The Logic of Political Survival.* Cambridge, Mass.: MIT Press.

Chayes, Abram, and Antonia Chayes. 1995. *The New Sovereignty: Compliance with International Regulatory Agreements.* Cambridge, Mass.: Harvard University Press.

Chayes, Abram, and Antonia Handler Chayes. 1993. "On Compliance." *International Organization* 47(2), pp. 175–205.

Conybeare, John A. C. 2002. "Leadership by Example? Britain and the Free Trade Movement of the Nineteenth Century." In Jagdish Bhagwati, ed., *Going Alone: The Case for Relaxed Reciprocity in Freeing Trade*. Cambridge: Cambridge University Press.

Downs, George. 1998. "Enforcement and the Evolution of Cooperation." *Michigan Journal of International Law* 19(2), pp. 319–44.

Downs, George, and Michael Jones. 2002. "Reputation, Compliance, and International Law." *Journal of Legal Studies* 31 (January), pp. 95.

Downs, George, David Rocke, and Peter Barsoom. 1996. "Is the Good News about Compliance Good News about Cooperation?" *International Organization* 50(3), pp. 379–406.

Dunoff, Jeffrey, Steven Ratner, and David Wippman. 2006. *International Law: A Process-Oriented Approach*. New York: Kluwer Law.

Gilligan, Michael J. 1997. *Empowering Exporters*. Cambridge, Mass.: Cambridge University Press.

Goldsmith, Jack, and Eric Posner. 2005. *The Limits of International Law*. New York: Oxford University Press.

Goldstein, Judith, Miles Kahler, Robert O. Keohane, and Anne-Marie Slaughter. 2000. "Introduction: Legalization and World Politics." *International Organization* 54(3), pp. 385–99.

Gourevitch, Peter. 1977. "International Trade, Domestic Coalitions, and Liberty: Comparative Responses to the Crisis of 1873–1896." *Journal of Interdisciplinary History* 8(2), pp. 281–313.

Hiscox, Michael. 2001. "Class versus Industry Cleavages: Inter-industry Factor Mobility and the Politics of Trade." *International Organization* 55(1), pp. 1–46.

Hudec, Robert. 1993. *Enforcing International Trade Law: The Evolution of the Modern GATT Legal System*. Salem, Mass.: Butterworth Legal.

Irwin, Douglas A. 2002. *Free Trade under Fire*. Princeton, N.J.: Princeton University Press.

Keohane, Robert. 1982. "The Demand for International Regimes." *International Organization* 36(2), pp. 325–55.

Keohane, Robert, ed. 2005. *After Hegemony: Cooperation and Discord in the World Political Economy*. Princeton, N.J.: Princeton Classic Editions.

Keohane, Robert, and Lisa Martin. 1995. "The Promise of Institutionalist Theory." *International Security* 20(1), pp. 39–51.

Krasner, Stephen. 1982. "Structural Causes and Regimes Consequences: Regimes as Intervening Variables." *International Organization* 36(2), pp. 185–205.

Milgrom, Paul R., Douglas C. North, and Barry Weingast. 1990. "The Role of Institutions in the Revival of Trade: The Law Merchant, Private Judges, and the Champagne Fairs." *Economics and Politics* 2(1), pp. 1–23.

Milner, Helen. 1998. "International Political Economy: Beyond Hegemonic Stability." *Foreign Policy* 110 (spring), pp. 112–23.

Moravcsik, Andrew. 1997. "Taking Preferences Seriously: A Liberal Theory of International Politics." *International Organization* 51(4), pp. 513–53.

Rogowski, Ronald. 1987. "Political Cleavages and Changing Exposure to Trade." *American Political Science Review* 81(4), pp. 1121–37.

Schattschneider, E. E. 1935. *Politics, Pressures and the Tariff*. New York: Prentice-Hall.

Schulz, Heiner. 2005. "The Institutional Structure of the Hanseatic League." Unpublished manuscript.

Snidal, Duncan. 1985. "The Limits of Hegemonic Stability Theory." *International Organization* 39(4), pp. 579–614.

Srinivasan, T. N. 1999. *Developing Countries in the World Trading System: From GATT, 1947, to the Third Ministerial Meeting of WTO, 1999.* Keynote speech at the High-level Symposium on Trade and Development, WTO, Geneva, March 17, 1999. Cambridge: Blackwell.

Tomz, Michael. 2007. *Reputation and International Cooperation: Sovereign Debt across Three Centuries.* Princeton, N.J.: Princeton University Press.

Yarbrough, Beth V., and Robert M. Yarbrough. 1987. "Cooperation in the Liberalization of International Trade: After Hegemony, What?" *International Organization* 41(1), pp. 1–26.

Wendt, Alexander. 1992. "Anarchy Is What States Make of It: The Social Construction of Power Politics." *International Organization* 46(2), pp. 391–425.

Williamson, Jeffrey. 2004. "The Tariff Response to World Market Integration in the Periphery before the Modern Era." Paper presented at World Market Integration Workshop, Florence, July 1–4.

PART II

COUNTRY (REGIONAL) STUDIES

CHAPTER 8

U.S. TRADE POLICY SINCE 1934: AN UNEVEN PATH TOWARD GREATER TRADE LIBERALIZATION

ROBERT E. BALDWIN

Since 1934, when the Congress transferred much of its tariff-setting powers to the president, there has been a remarkable decline in the average level of U.S. tariffs on dutiable imports. This average duty was 51.2% in 1931 just after the Smoot-Hawley Tariff Act of 1930, 26.3% in 1946 just prior to the first General Agreement on Tariffs and Trade (GATT) round of multilateral trade negotiations, 12.2% in 1960 just before the Kennedy Round of trade negotiations, and 4.8% in 2004 during the Doha Round.[1] What is not fully appreciated, however, is the extent to which this decline has been due not to tariff-reducing negotiations among nations but simply to the tariff-reducing effects of rising import prices in conjunction with specific or compound duties, namely, import duties that are fixed in terms of their dollar amounts per unit of imports or that are a mix of specific and ad valorem duties. For example, Irwin (1996) estimates that 70% of the 99% decline in the average tariff rate on dutiable imports between 1932 and 1954 was due to a rise in import prices (tariff acts constant) and only 29% was attributable to tariff acts alone (import price constant). The tariff reduction over the entire period that is not attributable to changes in import prices is still very impressive, however. Moreover, there has been a significant decline in protection from nontariff measures such as quantitative import restrictions.

This chapter describes various U.S. legislative and executive branch actions over the last 75 years that have produced the reduction in protectionism and explores the underlying economic and political conditions that have influenced these events.

1. TRADE LIBERALIZATION UNDER THE RECIPROCAL TRADE AGREEMENTS PROGRAM, 1934–1962

A. The Early Years, 1934–1945

With Cordell Hull, the secretary of state in the administration of Franklin D. Roosevelt, taking the leadership role in advocating tariff reductions and the Democrats gaining control of the House and Senate, Congress passed the Trade Agreements Act of 1934. This legislation gave the president the power to reduce tariffs by 50% over a three-year period through reciprocal negotiations with other countries. A major argument used in seeking passage of this measure was that it would provide an outlet for the disposition of American surplus products, especially agricultural ones. The votes in favor of the measure were 274 to 111 in the House and 57 to 33 in the Senate. Sixteen trade agreements with 17 countries (Belgium and Luxembourg representing one agreement) were concluded between 1934 and 1937.

The Trade Agreements Program was extended in 1937, in 1940, and again in 1943 without any new tariff-reducing authority. The arguments favoring extension gradually shifted from being based mainly on domestic policy objectives to being based on foreign policy goals. In 1937 Secretary Hull argued that the program was needed not only to alleviate depression conditions but also to contribute to world peace in a period of increasing tensions in international relations. By 1940, President Roosevelt argued in his State of the Union message that the Trade Agreements Act was "an indispensable part of the foundations for any stable and durable world peace" (Roosevelt 1940). In 1943, administration officials linked the extension of the program to both wartime and postwar planning. However, concern on the part of Republicans that Congress would have the opportunity to terminate the program at the end of the war resulted in its renewal for two rather than the usual three years.

In March 1945, Roosevelt delivered a message to Congress urging that the Trade Agreements Program be extended for another three years and that further tariff-cutting authority be included in the legislation. He argued that the continuation of the program was needed "if the economic foundations of the peace are to be as secure as the political foundations."[2] He also pointed out that much of the tariff-cutting authority granted in the 1934 act had been used up and another 50% was needed to carry out the program effectively. The renewal bill passed in the House by a vote of 258 to 153 and in the Senate by 53 to 21.

B. The Ill-Fated International Trade Organization

In July 1944, delegates from 44 of the Allied Nations met at Bretton Woods, New Hampshire, and established the International Monetary Fund to maintain a stable international monetary system and the International Bank for Reconstruction and Development to promote economic growth in both the war-torn developed countries and the developing countries. It was always envisioned that these institutions would be supplemented by an international trade organization aimed at promoting a more open trading system, but this objective proved more difficult to achieve. In 1945, the United States invited its World War II allies to enter into negotiations to establish such an organization, and by 1948 the Havana Charter for an international trade organization was completed. However, it was never implemented, mainly because of the opposition of the American business community. This group alleged that the elaborate and detailed rules on such matters as commercial policy, restrictive business practices, international commodity agreements, international investment, and dispute settlement procedures contained so many exceptions that most countries could comply with the Charter's rules without actually freeing trade from existing restrictions.[3]

C. The 1947 Round of Multilateral Trade Negotiations in Geneva

The U.S. trade negotiators did not wait for an approval or disapproval decision by Congress on the International Trade Organization before launching new tariff-reducing negotiations. Instead, using their new tariff-reducing powers under the 1945 extension of the Reciprocal Trade Agreements Program, they invited the world's major trading nations to participate in a multilateral round of tariff reductions held in Geneva, Switzerland, in 1947. During these negotiations, the United States agreed to a 21.1% cut in its average tariff level.[4]

The tariff-reducing procedure followed in the 1947 negotiations—as well as in the four rounds that took place between 1949 and 1962—began with an exchange of offer and request lists. Offers of a tariff concession on a particular product were made to the trading partner that was the principal or important supplier of the product to the country. The request list covered those items for which the country sought tariff reductions from a trading partner where the partner was the principal supplier of the item to the country. The bilateral negotiations that followed the exchange of offer and request lists aimed at utilizing each country's tariff-cutting authority to the maximum extent, subject to the limits imposed by their respective national governments and the constraint that each country was to regards the set of final concessions as being balanced.

D. The General Agreement on Tariffs and Trade

A unique feature of the results of the 1947 Geneva Round was that it consisted not only of schedules of tariff reductions but a set of international rules covering government behavior in international trade, namely, the GATT. The rules are essentially those set forth in the commercial policy section of the Havana Charter. The two key ones are the most-favored-nation and national treatment rules. The most-favored-nation principle specifies that the lowest tariff rate imposed by a GATT member on imports of a product from another member must be the rate that the latter country charges on similar imports from any other GATT member.[5] An important exception to this principle is made, however, with respect to free-trade areas and customs unions. National treatment means that a country's internal taxes, rules, and regulations shall not be applied in a manner that affords protection to domestic producers. The initial membership of the GATT was 23 countries, with the Secretariat based in Geneva.

Two other GATT rules that have played important roles in U.S. trade history relate to antidumping and countervailing duties. "Dumping" refers to foreign exporters either charging less on the products they sell abroad than they do at home or selling their products abroad for less than their cost of production. If these actions[6] cause or threaten to cause material injury to an established domestic industry, the importing country can levy an antidumping duty equal to the margin of dumping. "Countervailing duties" are duties permitted to offset subsidies by foreign countries on the production or export of their goods.[7] Other notable provisions of the GATT are the general elimination of quantitative restrictions and the escape or safeguard clause, which permits temporary increases in protection on any product being imported in such increased quantities as to cause or threaten to cause serious injury to domestic producers.

E. Shifts in the Views of Republicans and Democrats toward Trade Liberalization

When the Republicans took control of both Houses of Congress in the election of 1946, longtime Republican opponents of the Trade Agreements Program hoped to bring an end to it. However, in the early post–World War II period there were important changes in the views of both Republicans and Democrats toward trade policy. The Republican business community realized that the postwar economic dominance of the United States in most international markets meant it was in their interest to support a policy of trade liberalization. Moreover, a greater number of Republicans supported the view that trade liberalization played an important role in promoting world peace. Thus, the administration of Harry S. Truman was able to deflect efforts to prevent trade liberalizing negotiations in Geneva by issuing an executive order in 1947 that required the insertion of an escape clause in all trade agreements permitting the United States to modify trade concessions that caused or threatened to cause serious injury to domestic producers. Whether serious injury or the threat thereof exists is determined by the U.S. International Trade Commission (called the U.S. Tariff Commission before 1974), a six-person government agency whose members are nominated by the president and approved the Senate. The president need not implement an affirmative decision of the Commission if he or she believes this would not be in the national interest.

The Truman administration was also able to prevent the Trade Agreements Program from expiring in 1948 by agreeing to a one-year extension that included a so-called peril point provision. Under this provision, the U.S. International Trade Commission held hearings aimed at determining the extent to which tariff rates proposed for possible reduction in trade negotiations could be lowered without threatening injury to domestic producers. The House version of the bill also included a provision stipulating that Congress would have the right to adopt a concurrent resolution of disapproval of any trade agreement with duty concessions outside the limits set by the Commission. However, this provision was dropped from the final version of the bill.

In 1949, the Democrats again obtained majorities in both the House and Senate and promptly passed the Trade Agreements Extension Act of 1949, which repealed the act of 1948 with its peril point provision and extended the program for three years from its 1948 expiration date. In 1949, the administration used this authority to undertake a second round of tariff-reducing multilateral negotiations within the GATT framework. The extent of liberalization was modest. The average level of U.S. duties declined by only 1.9 percentage points. A third round of multilateral negotiations followed shortly thereafter. These negotiations, which were held in Torquay, England, beginning in September 1950, also produced only a modest reduction in duties. Average U.S. duties declined only 3.0 percentage points.

By 1951, the views of Democrats on both the peril point and escape clauses had changed significantly. Enough Democrats supported these protectionist provisions that they were included in the bill that passed and extended the program for another two years. The fact that most of the Democrats voting in favor of these provisions came from the South or from border states indicates that increased international competition in labor-intensive products such as textiles and apparel was a factor in this policy shift. The U.S. trade negotiators had also learned that the existence of these provisions had not had the dire consequences many had feared.

F. The Eisenhower Years

With the election in 1952 of a Republican president and Republican majorities in both the House and Senate, one might have expected a rapid and extensive shift in U.S. trade policy toward protectionism. Such was not the case, however. President Dwight D. Eisenhower proposed a one-year extension of the Trade Agreements Act pending a thorough review of U.S. foreign economic policy by a commission composed of members of both houses of Congress and private citizens. This action seemed to undercut the attempt by some Republicans to pass a highly protectionist bill, and the program was extended for another year with only modest new protectionist features.

A majority of the members of the U.S. President's Commission on Foreign Economic Policy, also known as the "Randall commission," established under the 1953 Extension Act to advise the president on trade-related aspects of foreign policy and national security, favored a lowering of existing trade barriers through multilateral trade negotiations. However, the key congressional members of the commission supported tariff changes that would equalize the price differences in goods produced in the United States and in other countries. Consequently, a deadlock quickly developed in Congress when in 1954 Eisenhower requested a three-year extension of the Reciprocal Trade Agreements Act with new tariff-reducing authority. It was resolved by again passing a one-year extension without any new tariff-reducing authority.

As in 1949, a shift in 1954 in the control of Congress from Republicans to Democrats was critical for achieving further trade liberalization. In 1955, Eisenhower was able to obtain a three-year extension with an additional 15% duty-cutting authority. However, the need to satisfy the increasing proportion of Democrats in both the House and Senate who supported protectionist policies meant that the final bill contained provisions making it easier to gain import protection under the escape clause provision and permitting the imposition of import quotas in industries where imports were threatening an industry deemed essential to national security. Import quotas on oil were introduced in 1959 under this provision. The Eisenhower administration also pressured the Japanese into accepting voluntary restraints on their exports of cotton textiles.

In 1955, the United States obtained a GATT waiver covering agricultural products that effectively removed all trade in these goods from GATT discipline. Article 12:2 of the original document already permitted countries to introduce import restrictions on agricultural and fishery products necessary for the enforcement of governmental measures that operate to restrict the production or marketing of the like domestic product. The 1955 waiver allows the United States to apply import restrictions without regard to whether measures are in place restricting the production or marketing of such products. Other countries followed the United States in utilizing this waiver.

Eisenhower was again successful in 1958 in extending the Trade Agreements Program, this time for four years with an additional 20% tariff-reducing authority. The main concession to protectionist groups was a provision permitting Congress to override presidential decisions on Tariff Commission escape clause decisions by a two-thirds majority vote in both the House and Senate.

The Eisenhower administration used the tariff-reducing authority it obtained in the 1955 and 1958 extensions of the Reciprocal Trade Agreements Program to enter into the fourth (1955–1956) and fifth (1961–1962) GATT rounds of multilateral trade negotiations. Both took place in Geneva and, like the second and third negotiating rounds, produced only modest average duty reduction. The average level of U.S. duties declined by only 3.5 percentage points in the fourth round of negotiations and by 2.4 percentage points in the fifth.

2. 1962–1994: Significant Multilateral Reductions in Tariffs and Nontariff Trade Barriers but with Selective Protectionism

A. The Trade Expansion Act of 1962 and the Kennedy Round of Trade Negotiations, 1963–1967

The Trade Expansion Act of 1962 and subsequent Kennedy Round of trade negotiations begins a new period of stand-alone trade-liberalizing multilateral negotiations that continues to the present time. Under the Trade Expansion Act, the president was given the power to enter into trade agreements with other countries before July 1, 1967, that reduced U.S. duties by up to 50% of their 1962 levels. In addition, tariff levels of 5% or less could be cut by up to 100%.

The administration of John F. Kennedy pressed Congress for this significant new tariff-cutting authority for both economic and foreign policy reasons. Economic relations with the European Economic Community (EC),[8] which had been formed in 1957, played an important role in the decision to seek this extensive tariffcutting authority. Leaders in both U.S. political parties favored the formation of the EC because it would greatly reduce the possibility of future military conflicts among its members. Trade officials recognized, however, that the elimination of duties among its members meant that some U.S. exports to EC members would be displaced by similar products produced by other EC members, since these products would no longer be subject to import duties. Negotiating a general decrease in levels of protection would, they argued, reduce the margin of preference for these members. The benefits of tariff-liberalizing negotiations in strengthening political ties within the Atlantic Community and in preventing communist economic penetration were also stressed.

Some concessions to protectionist interests were made to help gain the new negotiating authority, however. In 1962, for example, the United States became a signatory to the Long-Term Agreement regarding Trade in Cotton Textiles, which established import quotas for this product. President Kennedy also approved affirmative safeguard decisions by the International Trade Commission on glass and carpets. The 1962 act eliminated the peril point clause, but the Tariff Commission was charged with advising the president as to the probable economics effects of tariff reductions. In addition to including a safeguard clause, the act for the first time also included adjustment assistance to domestic firms and workers injured by increased imports. Qualifying firms could receive technical and financial assistance, while workers who qualified could receive extended unemployment payments, retraining allowances, and relocation allowances. Shifting the administration of trade negotiation away from the State Department to a special trade representative located in the executive offices of the president was also regarded as a concession to protectionist interests.

The act easily passed in both the House and Senate. The House vote was 299 in favor of passage and 128 against; the Senate vote was 78 yeas and 8 nays.

At the outset of the Kennedy Round negotiations in 1962, there was general agreement among the major participants to replace the item-by-item approach of earlier negotiating rounds with a formula approach to cutting tariffs. As the number of countries participating in GATT-sponsored trade negotiations increased,[9] item by item negotiations had become increasingly cumbersome and time-consuming. The fact that the volume of imports for which one country served as the principal supplier to another country need not match the volume of trade for which the latter country was the principal supplier to the first country, coupled with countries' objective of achieving an overall balance of concessions from other countries, also limited the extent of the overall tariff reduction possible. The United States proposed that all tariffs be reduced by 50% with a bare minimum of exceptions. The developing countries were not expected to provide reciprocity, however. The EC proposed a formula that would reduce high tariff rates by a greater percentage than low rates. In particular, the EC proposed that duties on manufactured goods be reduced by 50% of the difference between their existing levels and 10%. Duties on semimanufactures and raw materials were to be cut by 50% of the difference between the existing rate and 5% and zero, respectively. Agricultural products were not covered by this proposal. The United States strongly opposed the EC tariff-cutting rule, on the grounds that it would only yield an average reduction for the main trading nations of about 15% and would also require a substantially greater average cut for the United States than the EC.

After intense negotiations, the EC finally accepted the U.S. position that the cuts be linear and uniform, but with the proviso that special rules would apply where there are significant disparities in tariff levels. However, such special rules were never agreed on by the major trading nations, and the EC ended up by simply excluding from linear cuts a number of items where it believed significant disparities in tariff rates existed. Fortunately, the number was not sufficiently large to unravel the entire tariff-cutting exercise. The average reduction in dutiable imports of nonagricultural products for the United States, the EC, the United Kingdom, and Japan was in the range of 36 to 39%

Trade negotiations covering agricultural products proved even more difficult in the Kennedy Round than those relating to manufactured goods. The main concern of the United States was that the implementation of a common agricultural policy by the EC would result in a significant reduction of U.S. agricultural exports to Europe. The initial offers of the EC confirmed this conclusion, and a stalemate on agricultural negotiations ensued that lasted until the end of the Kennedy Round. Bilateral negotiations between the U.S. and EC finally broke the deadlock, with each side backing off their initial positions. The average tariff reduction on dutiable agricultural imports of the major industrial countries was 20%, or considerably less than in nonagricultural sectors.

B. Tariff Preferences for Developing Countries

A key proposal of the first United Nations Conference on Trade and Development, held in 1964 during the Kennedy Round, was that the developed countries should grant preferential tariff treatment to imports of manufactured and semi-manufactured goods originating in developing countries. The United States was somewhat reluctant to accept such a recommendation, due to its long-standing opposition to discriminatory trading arrangements, but soon followed other industrial countries in providing zero-duty treatment on imports of most manufactured goods from developing countries. Authority for doing so has since been regularly included in U.S. trade legislation. Initially, it was necessary to obtain a GATT waiver to grant such preferences, but during the Tokyo Round the so-called enabling clause was included in the GATT permitting members to grant such preferences routinely.

C. Particular Protectionism of the 1970 and 1980s

Beginning in the late 1960s, there was a rapid rise in import penetration ratios in many U.S. manufacturing sectors.[10] The result was a wave of protectionism that restricted imports from various countries on steel, textiles and apparel, footwear, color television sets, and automobiles at various times during the 1970s and 1980s. In 1970 a bill sponsored by Wilbur Mills, the chairman of the Ways and Means Committee, that would have imposed import quotas on a wide range of manufactured goods passed in the House. The protectionism of this period was driven in part by a shift in the policy position of organized labor from supporting trade liberalization to advocating import restrictions.

D. The Trade Act of 1974 and the Tokyo Round of Trade Negotiations, 1973–1979

A widely held view among business and labor groups in the early 1970s was that the increased competitiveness of foreign producers was due in no small measure to the use of unfair nontariff trade measures on their part. It was this view that helped the administration of Richard M. Nixon to secure passage of the Trade Act of 1974, which directs the president to undertake multilateral negotiations aimed at harmonizing, reducing, or eliminating nontariff barriers to international trade as well as at reducing tariffs by up to 60%. However, the 1974 act for the first time required that any agreement reached with other countries must be approved by a majority vote in both the House and Senate. Under this so-called fast-track procedure or, as it is now called, trade promotion authority, no amendments to the agreement submitted by the president are permitted by Congress. Without this provision, other countries are reluctant to agree on a negotiating package for fear that Congress will withdraw some of the U.S. trade concessions involved in the agreement.

Another important provision of the 1974 Trade Act, namely, Section 301, permits the president to take retaliatory actions against a foreign country that "maintains unjustifiable, or unreasonable" tariffs or import restrictions, engages in "discriminatory or other acts which are unjustifiable or unreasonable," or provides "subsidies . . . which have the effect of substantially reducing the sales of the competitive United States product."

The Trade Act of 1974 passed in the House by a vote of 272 to 140 and in the Senate by a vote of 72 to 4.

In the Tokyo Round of trade negotiations that followed passage of the 1974 Trade Act, the United States negotiated a series of detailed codes covering nontariff measures that set forth permissible and nonpermissible GATT-consistent behavior. The main subjects covered were subsidies and countervailing duties, antidumping practices, government procurement policies, valuation and licensing practices, and technical barriers to trade (standards). Signing the codes was made voluntary on the part of the participants in the negotiations.

The tariff-cutting formula for industrial products accepted by all participants in the Tokyo Round negotiations was proposed by the Swiss, namely,

$$Z = AX/(A + X), \tag{1}$$

where Z is the new tariff rate, A is a constant, and X is the current tariff rate. The constant was set at 14 for the United States and 16 for the EC. Thus, a U.S. duty of 20% was reduced to 14 x 20 / (14 + 20) = 8.23%. The United States was somewhat constrained by this formula in that it could not cut duties more than 60%, but it was able to raise its average rate of reduction to the levels achieved by other industrial countries by utilizing its statutory power to reduce duties 5% and below by up to 100%. Taking into account the various exceptions to applying the Swiss formula, the average reduction in tariffs on industrial product in the Tokyo Round was about 35% for both the United States and EC.[11]

As in the Kennedy Round, reaching an agreement with the EC covering agricultural products proved to be the most difficult part of the negotiations. An impasse between the U.S. and the EC over agriculture was not broken until mid-1977, when the two trading powers agreed to separate agricultural negotiations from other matters and to engage in bilateral negotiations. The main concession by the United States was to increase the import quota on cheese, while the main concession by the EC was to increase the import quota for high-quality beef.

The various codes as well as the tariff concessions were implemented by the United States in the Trade Act of 1979. This Act also extended "fast-track" authority for another eight years.

E. The Uruguay Round of Trade Negotiations, 1986–1993

The most successful post–World War II multilateral trade negotiation as measured by the depth and scope of liberalization was the Uruguay Round (1986–1993).[12] Three new subjects not covered in previous negotiating rounds were introduced: trade in services, trade-related intellectual property rights, and trade-related aspects of investment measures. In addition, a special effort was made that brought agriculture and textiles/apparel under GATT discipline. The negotiations also covered such traditional topics as tariff liberalization, subsidies, dumping, government procurement policy, technical barriers to trade, dispute settlement, and institutional reform.[13]

An important feature of the framework agreement negotiated for services is that it covers not only crossborder trade in services but services supplied by foreign firms within a country to consumers in that country and services supplied by domestic firms to nationals of other countries who are visiting the country. The General Agreement on Trade in Services commits WTO signatories to a set of general principles that includes most-favored-nation treatment, transparency with regard to domestic laws affecting trade in services, and the progressive liberalization of traded services.

In fashioning policies covering intellectual property, namely, creations of the mind such as inventions, literary and artistic works, and symbols, names, images, and designs used in commerce, society must balance two output-creating forces. One is the output gains that that come about from distributing an existing body of knowledge as widely as possible. The other is the output gains that arise because inventors and other creators of intellectual property are granted temporary monopolies that prevent others from copying their intellectual creations before they have had a chance to reap the monetary gains that make their creative efforts worthwhile. The Uruguay Round agreement on the trade-related aspects of intellectual property attempted to overcome some of the drawbacks of the existing system. For example, all countries are now required to provide copyright, trademark, and patent protection on goods and services for a specified number of years. However, developing countries and the least developed countries were given extra time to implement this requirement. In addition, countries are required to establish civil judicial procedures whereby individuals and firms can seek to enforce their intellectual property rights. Criminal procedures must also be put in place to deal with willful trademark counterfeiting or copyright piracy on a commercial scale. In a notable ruling in 2009, a WTO dispute-settlement panel ruled that China violated WTO rules by barring copyright protection for movies, music, and books that have not been approved for publication or distribution in China.

The GATT dispute settlement procedures were notoriously weak prior to the Uruguay Round. For example, the losing party in the report of a GATT dispute-settlement panel could block the adoption of the panel's report. However, as a result of the Uruguay Round negotiations, formation of panels and adoption of their reports are now all automatic.

One of the biggest disappointments with the codes approach utilized in the Tokyo Round was the failure of many countries to sign some of the key agreements. In an effort to curtail the resultant free riding and to bring together existing and new trading rules, the Final Act of the Uruguay Round established a new international organization, the WTO, encompassing the General Agreement on Tariffs and Trade, the results of past liberalization efforts, and all the results of the Uruguay Round. Members are required to accept all its provisions, with the exception of the so-called Plurilateral Trade Agreements—consisting of the agreement on government procurement, the agreement on civil aviation, the international dairy arrangement, and the arrangement regarding bovine meat.

As in previous negotiating rounds, differences between the United States and EC[14] made reaching agreement covering agricultural products especially difficult. However, bilateral negotiations held in Washington in the waning days of the Bush administration formed the basis of the final agreement in agriculture. In restoring GATT discipline to this sector, nontariff barriers such as quotas, variable levies, and voluntary export restraints were converted to tariffs and these tariffs then reduced. Internal support measures and export subsidies were also reduced.

The negotiations on tariff reductions in the industrial sector went surprisingly smoothly. A request-offer format between principal supplying countries for individual products was followed with the objective of achieving a one-third reduction target. In addition, there were zero-for-zero duty reductions in some sectors by the major developed countries (Canada, the EU, Japan, and the U.S.). The end result was that industrial tariffs were reduced by more than one-third.

F. Omnibus Trade and Competitiveness Act of 1988

This act set forth not only the principal negotiating objectives of the United States with respect to such traditional subjects as unfair trade practices, safeguards, agriculture, and developing countries but also new negotiating topics such as trade in services, intellectual property rights, worker rights, foreign direct investment, and dispute settlement. In doing so, it granted the president an additional 50% duty-reduction authority and extended fast-track authority another five years. This authority expired in 1994 after Congress had extended it for one year in order to approve the Uruguay Round agreements. An effort in 1998 to pass fast-track authority was defeated in the House by a vote of 180 to 243, with only 29 Democrats voting in the affirmative.

The 1988 Trade and Competitiveness Act also increased the authority of the U.S. trade representative to take action under Section 301 against unfair trade practices of foreign countries, in addition to spelling out in more detail the nature of these practices.

3. THE POST–URUGUAY ROUND PERIOD: WANING SUPPORT FOR MULTILATERAL TRADE LIBERALIZATION

A. The Trade Act of 2002

In addition to renewing and expanding the trade adjustment program, this legislation again provided the president with trade promotion authority. The vote in the House was 215 in favor of passage and 212 against. Twenty-five Democrats voted in the affirmative, 183 in the negative.[15] House Republicans favored passage 190 to 27. In the Senate, the bill passed 64 to 24, with 20 Democrats voting in the affirmative and 19 in the negative. Senate Republicans favored passage by 42 to 5.

This new fast-track authority expired in June 2007. However, during this second period of fast-track authority, Congress enacted implementing legislation for the United States–Chile Free Trade Agreement, the United States–Singapore Free Trade Agreement, the United States–Australian Free Trade Agreement, the United States–Morocco Free Trade Agreement, the Dominican Republic–Central America–United States Free Trade Agreement, the United States–Bahrain Free Trade Agreement, the United States–Oman Free Trade Agreement, and the United States–Peru Free Trade Agreement. The United States has signed free trade agreements with Colombia, South Korea, and Panama, but Congress has yet to implement these agreements at the time of this writing.

The United States had long opposed regional trade agreements, both on the grounds that the resulting discrimination among countries had an unfavorable effect on international political stability and because of the uncertain economic welfare effects of such agreements. However, this policy changed during the Uruguay Round when the decision was made to pursue U.S. trade policy objective not only through multilateral negotiations and unilateral Section 301–type policies but also through regional and bilateral trade agreements.

B. The Doha Round

The ninth round of multilateral trade negotiations under GATT/WTO sponsorship was scheduled to begin in 1999 in Seattle and to be known as the Millennium Round. However, objections by the developing countries over how the agricultural negotiations were being handled as well as over the efforts of the developed countries to include such issues as competition and investment policies as part of the negotiations led to a breakdown of the Ministerial Meeting and a postponement of the effort to start a new round. It was not until 2001 that a new round was successfully launched in Doha, Qatar.

An important concession made by the European Union (EU)[16] that facilitated the start of these negotiations was a pledge to discontinue all export subsidies by 2013. The so-called Singapore issues (trade-related investment, competition policy, government procurement policy, and trade facilitation or procedures and controls governing the movement of goods across national borders) were included in the work program outlined in the Ministerial Declaration, but negotiations on these topics were scheduled to begin only after "explicit consensus" by the participants. Discussion of these four issues first arose in the WTO at the 1996 Ministerial Meeting in Singapore in 1996. Most developed countries favored negotiations that would introduce antitrust policies into WTO rules, limit government controls on foreign direct investment, open up government purchasing to greater competition from private firms, and simplify customs procedures. Developing countries, on the other hand, generally wanted to retain government controls over these matters as a means of implementing the type of economic development they desired.

Among the long list of other topics included in the Doha Round work program were agriculture, services, market access for nonagricultural goods, intellectual property rights, antidumping and subsidy rules, regional trading rules, implementation-related issues, trade and the environment, and dispute settlement. Each topic included a statement that developing countries would receive special and differential treatment in the negotiations on the subject.

Progress in agreeing on the framework for negotiating on the issues covered by the Doha Ministerial Statement proved difficult right from the outset.[17] For example, at the Cancun Ministerial Meeting in 2003, which was called mainly to check on the progress made to date, it became apparent that the views of developed and developing countries were far apart on most issues. In particular, they could not agree on whether to include negotiations on competition policy, trade-related investment issues, government procurement policy, and trade facilitation. As a result, the meeting ended without a declaration setting forth a future agenda. It was not until July 2004 that WTO members agreed on a new work program for the Doha Round. Of the Singapore issues, only trade facilitation was included as an agenda item.

C. The July 2008 Collapse of the Doha Round Negotiations

By July 2008, sufficient progress appeared to have been made in both the agricultural and non-agricultural negotiations to warrant another Ministerial Meeting that would resolve the remaining issues in these negotiations. Unfortunately, this meeting resulted in yet another failure. The key issue was a disagreement between the United States and India over the extent to which developing countries would be allowed to raise agricultural duties in response to import surges. India wished to have the unencumbered right to raise duties to the level it deemed necessary to protect the livelihood conditions of its farmers. The United States was concerned that this freedom of action would lead to tariffs being raised to levels above those agreed on in the Uruguay Round negotiations and thus would represent a step backward from the hard-won liberalization gains of that Round in agriculture.[18]

In an effort to break the resulting deadlock that arose at the July 2008 Ministerial Meeting over this issue, WTO director-general Pascal Lamy proposed as a compromise that pre-Doha tariff rates could be exceeded only if the increase in imports in the current year was at least 40% greater than the average for the preceding three years. Susan Schwab, the U.S. trade representative, accepted this figure as a compromise point, but Kamal Nath, the Indian commerce and industry minister, summarily rejected it with the remark "I reject everything. I cannot put the livelihoods of hundreds of millions of people at risk."[19]

The prospects for a successful conclusion of the Doha Round are uncertain, but world political leaders are urging the resumption of negotiations. For example, at their meeting in July 2009, the G-8 industrial countries together with the major developing countries included in their final declaration the statement that they "are committed to an ambitious and balanced conclusion of the Doha Development Round in 2010." They also directed their respective trade ministers to explore all possible avenues for direct engagement in the WTO and to meet prior to the G-20 Summit in Pittsburgh in September 2009.

There has clearly been a shift in negotiating power within the WTO away from the developed countries and toward the developing countries as the developing countries' share of world exports has increased. This share rose from 17% in 1990 to 27% in 1999 and then to 38% by 2008.[20] The rapid growth in the trade and gross domestic product levels of India and China coupled with the accession of China to the WTO in November 2001 has been crucial in this power shift. These countries, as well as most other developing countries, do not have a long tradition for the type of trade-liberalizing policies that the developed countries have implemented within the WTO/GATT framework. They are wary of both the domestic economic adjustments these policies involve and the nature of the economic development they encourage. Consequently, the developing countries are using their increased influence in WTO trade negotiations not only to block market-opening negotiations on such matters as government procurement policy, foreign direct investment, and competition policy but also to slow down the pace of traditional liberalization for agricultural goods and in the services sector. This shift in the power structure involved in trade negotiations coupled with the increased resistance to trade liberalization within the developed countries in recent years means that the prospects for significant trade liberalization in future years are not very favorable.

4. SOME CONCLUSIONS ABOUT THE VARYING FORCES SHAPING U.S. TRADE POLICY

Since the Trade Agreements Act of 1934, there have been two main direct decision-making centers with respect of U.S. trade policy, namely, the president or executive branch and the U.S. Congress. These decision-making entities have, in turn, been influenced by the policy positions and relative political power of the Democrat and Republican parties and individuals within them, the policy stances and relative political power of various other nongovernmental organizations such as labor unions, business organizations, professional organizations and individuals within these groups, the policies of other governments, and perceptions about the views of the general public.

In making trade-policy decisions, the president and Congress are motivated by both U.S. domestic and foreign policy goals. Their decisions include such diverse actions as providing domestic producers with expanded export opportunities by reducing foreign trade barriers and preventing income declines for particular domestic groups by raising levels of protection on imports that compete with domestic production. Their decisions also affect the manner in which the country interacts with other countries politically, socially, and militarily. Reducing U.S. trade barriers may, for example, strengthen the ability of foreign governments to resist regime changes that lead to governments hostile to the United States. Frequent exogenous changes in underlying economic and political conditions change the mix of trade policies appropriate for implementing the domestic and foreign policy goals of policy-makers.

A. The Trade Agreements Program: Protecting Members of Congress while Making the President Responsive to Congressional Protectionist Wishes

The stage for a significant shift in U.S. trade policy in the early 1930s was set by the passage of the Smoot-Hawley Tariff Act of 1930, which raised import duties to unprecedented heights; by the worldwide collapse of economic activity; by the subsequent sharp increase in trade barriers against U.S. goods; and by the capture by the Democrats of both houses of Congress as well as the presidency. Democrats traditionally preferred lower tariffs than the Republicans but, as Irwin argues,[21] the U.S. depression precluded a unilateral reduction in trade barriers. By tying reductions in U.S. tariffs to reciprocal cuts in the import duties of other countries, Cordell Hull, the architect of U.S. trade policy in the Roosevelt administration, was able to argue that the United States could dispose of its surpluses of goods without changing overall employment conditions significantly and without increasing import prices relative to export prices.[22] As Destler argues,[23] by granting the president the power to reduce tariffs by up to a certain percentage for a given time period, members of Congress were able to protect themselves from the direct, one-sided pressures from protectionist interests but still have considerable power over the nature and extent of import protection.

B. The Importance of Foreign Policy Goals and of the Role of the President

Trade policy decisions have frequently been motivated by foreign policy objectives. This was particularly true during the early years of the Cold War. Presidents Truman, Eisenhower, and Kennedy all argued that a liberal U.S. trade policy by expanding the markets for foreign goods increases the ability of other countries to resist the spread of communism. One of the stated purposes of the Trade Act of 1962 is, for example, "to prevent Communist economic penetration."

A historical survey of trade policy also reveals the importance of the president's role in shaping the nature of trade policy. For example, at the outset of his Administration, President Eisenhower appeared to be only mildly supportive of the Reciprocal Trade Agreements Program and played a rather passive role in the one year extensions in 1953 and 1954. However, in 1955 the expression of strong support for the program by his secretary of state, John Foster Dulles, and other cabinet officers played a significant role in obtaining a three-year extension. The vigorous efforts by President Kennedy and key members of his administration to build support for the Trade Expansion Act both within Congress and among the general public stand out as another example where the role of the president was important in shaping trade policy. A more recent illustration where the president played a crucial lobbying role in obtaining trade liberalizing legislation was the passage of the Trade Act of 2002 during the administration of President George Bush.

C. The Importance of the Political Division of Congress between Democrats and Republicans

For much of the period covered by this study, the most important determinant of trade policy has been the percentage division of members of Congress between the Republican and Democratic parties. In the 1930s, most Republicans still believed that U.S. manufacturing needed to be protected against foreign competitors who often engaged in unfair trade practices such as dumping and government subsidization. They opposed tariff reductions, therefore, even on a reciprocal basis. However, by the early post–World War years, Republican opposition to any trade liberalization had eased as the international demand for U.S. goods increased sharply. But they still were fearful that reductions in U.S. manufacturing tariffs would not infrequently result in import increases that seriously injured particular industries. Therefore, they sought escape clause and peril point provisions in U.S. trade legislation.

Democrats in the 1930s maintained that high tariffs raised the prices of goods to factory workers and farmers and reduced their living standards. But by the 1950s they, too, were concerned about the possible injurious effects of tariff reductions and supported the inclusion of the escape clause in U.S. trade legislation. The import surges of the late 1960s further increased these concerns, and by the 1970s a major force in the Democratic Party, namely, U.S. labor unions, began to oppose trade liberalization. Nonunion supporters of the Democratic Party also became more concerned about the effects of trade liberalization in reducing the real wages of unskilled workers. Indeed, by the late 1990s votes in the House reveal that a majority of Democrats opposed such trade-liberalizing legislation as the North American Free Trade Agreement (1998), the fast-track extension (1998), and the Trade Act of 2002. The failure by Congress to implement the free-trade agreements negotiated by the Bush administration with Columbia, Korea, and Panama indicates that support for trade liberalization is weak among members of both political parties.

The various restraining actions taken by Congress over the years, such as imposing time limits on the trade-liberalizing powers of the president, introducing safeguard rules and the peril point clause into U.S. trade law, shifting the main trade policy powers from the States Department to the Office of the U.S. Trade Representative, providing for unilateral actions against other countries under Section 301, and requiring trade agreements to be approved by Congress before taking effect can all be viewed as successive efforts by Congress to make the president more responsive to the wishes of Congress. None of these measures seem to have completely satisfied the Congress, however, and now members seem reluctant even to grant trade promotion authority to the president. Although President Obama has indicated his support for concluding the Doha Round in 2010, it is not clear that he has the political power to ensure congressional approval of an agreement acceptable to the developing countries.

NOTES

1. Irwin, 2007, table 2.
2. Quoted from Woolley and Peters, n.d.
3. See Diebold, 1952, for a detailed analysis of why the ITO failed.
4. Lavergue, 1981.
5. The United States adopted the most-favored-nation principle in 1923.
6. Antidumping legislation was first introduced into U.S. law in 1916.
7. U.S. countervailing law can be traced back to the Tariff Act of 1897.
8. The six members were Belgium, France, Germany, Holland, Italy, and Luxembourg.
9. Sixty-six countries took part in the Kennedy Round negotiations.
10. See U.S. Congress, House Committee on Ways and Means, 1973.
12. Winham, 1986, p. 267. The EC consisted of nine countries by the end of the Tokyo Round, with Denmark, Ireland, and the United Kingdom becoming members in 1972.
12. See Preeg, 1995, for a comprehensive analysis of the Uruguay Round.
13. See Baldwin, 1995, for an economic evaluation of the Uruguay Round Agreements.
14. The European Community consisted of 12 countries at the outset of the Uruguay Round, with Greece joining in 1981 and Spain and Portugal joining in 1986.
15. Two Independents also voted against passage of the bill.
16. The European Union was formed in 1993 out of the institutions of the European Economic Community. Its founding members were Belgium, Germany, Italy, France, Luxembourg, and the Netherlands. As of 2009, its size had increased to 27 members.
17. See Baldwin, 2009a, for an analysis of key issues facing negotiators in the Doha Round.
18. See Baldwin, 2009a, for a more detailed analysis of the cause of the 2008 collapse in the negotiations.
19. See Blustein, 2008, 9. This is an especially valuable account of the December 2008 breakdown because Blustein interviewed key participants in the negotiations and had access to their notes on the meetings.
20. Based on trade data collected by the WTO.
21. Irwin, 1998.
22. For a theoretical analysis of reciprocal trade agreements driven by terms-of-trade effects, see Bagwell and Staiger, 1999.
23. Destler, 2005, ch. 2.

REFERENCES

Bagwell, Kyle, and Robert Staiger. 1999. "An Economic Theory of GATT." *American Economic Review* 80: 2155–2248.

Baldwin, Robert E. 1965. "Tariff-Cutting Techniques in the Kennedy Round." In R. E. Baldwin et al., *Trade, Growth, and the Balance of Payments: Essays in Honor of Gottfried Haberler*. Chicago: Rand McNally.

Baldwin, Robert E. 1979. *The Multilateral Trade Negotiations: Toward Greater Liberalization?* Special analysis, no. 79-2. Washington, D.C.: American Enterprise Institute.

Baldwin, Robert E. 1995. "An Economic Evaluation of the Uruguay Round Agreements." In S. Arndt and C. Milner, eds., *The World Economy: Global Trade Policy 1995*. Oxford: Blackwell, 155–172.

Baldwin, Robert E. 2009a, March 11. *The Botched Doha Round Negotiations on a Special Safeguards Mechanism*. http://VoxEU.org.

Baldwin, Robert E. 2009b, December 15. "Standstills in WTO Trade Negotiations Are Not That Unusual." *Vox*. Available at www.voxeu.org/index.php?q=node/4380.

Blustein, Paul. 2008. *The Nine-Day Misadventure of the Most Favored Nations: How the WTO's Doha Round Negotiations Went Awry in July 2008*. Brookings Global Economy and Development. Washington, D.C.: Brookings Institution.

Destler, I. M. 2005. *American Trade Politics*. 4th ed. Washington, D.C.: Institute for International Economics.

Diebold, William, Jr. 1952. *The End of the I.T.O.* Essays in International Finance, no. 16. International Finance Section. Princeton, N.J.: Princeton University Press.

Irwin, Douglas. 1996. "Changes in U.S. Tariffs: Prices or Policies?" NBER Working Papers 5665. Cambridge, Mass.: National Bureau of Economic Research.

Irwin, Douglas. 1998. "Changes in U.S. Tariffs: The Role of Import Prices and Commercial Policies." *American Economic Review* 88: 1015–1026.

Lavergne, Real P. 1981. "The Political Economy of U.S. Tariffs." Ph.D. diss., University of Toronto.

Preeg, Ernest H. 1970. *Traders and Diplomats: An Analysis of the Kennedy Round of Negotiations under the General Agreement on Tariffs and Trade*. Washington, D.C.: Brookings Institution.

Preeg, Ernest H. 1995. *Traders in a Brave New World: The Uruguay Round and the Future of the International Trading System*. Chicago: University of Chicago Press.

Roosevelt, Franklin D. 1940. State of the Union Address, January 3, 1940. Available at www.infoplease.com/t/hist/state-of-the-union/151.html.

U.S. Congress. House Committee on Ways and Means, prepared by the staff of the U.S. Tariff Commission. 1973. *Comparisons of Ratios of Imports to Apparent Consumption, 1968–72*. Washington, D.C.: GPO.

Winham, Gilbert R. 1986. *International Trade and the Tokyo Round Negotiation*. Princeton: Princeton University Press.

Woolley, John T., and Gerhard Peters. N.d. The American Presidency Project. University of California, Santa Barbara. Available at www.presidency.ucsb.edu/ws/?pid=1659.

CHAPTER 9

THE EUROPEAN COMMUNITY COMMERCIAL POLICY

PATRICK A. MESSERLIN

THE European Community (the correct legal term in trade matters, hereafter EC) is still a recent and ongoing process. Fifty years is a short time span for such an endeavor (the appendix to this chapter lists the 17 treaties that have formed its legal basis).[1] It is strictly an economic process because a straightforward political unification of Europe was out of reach, then, now, and for the decades to come. This ambiguous relation between economics and politics explains why the EC commercial policy often was given the status of a foreign policy instrument. This was the case in the EC relation with former colonies (during the 1960s), developing countries (the 1970s), the central European countries formerly in the Soviet sphere (the 1990s), and neighbors or emerging economies (the 2000s).

Yet economic analysis shows that the trade policy of a country reflects domestic conflicts between consumers, import-competing producers, and exporters of the country more than its international relation. Hence, this chapter begins (section 1) by examining the EC domestic scene—the balance between "the EC and its Member States," the sacrosanct expression used in the trade treaties signed by the EC. The development of the EC commercial policy can be seen through the tensions between the Treaty, the European Court of Justice, the Commission, and the EC Member States (ECMSs).

Subsequent sections describe briefly the level of protection of the EC in the early 2000s, before examining the EC approach to the Doha Round of the WTO during the last decade, and the possible return to trade preferences most recently. A final section concludes.

1. THE TREATY, THE COURT, AND THE PRACTICES

The Treaty of Rome confers on the Community as such (not the Commission) power to conduct commercial policy. This so-called principle of the Community's "exclusive competence" makes the ECMSs' Council the decision-maker giving to the Commission a mandate to act on its behalf, with the final decision remaining in the Council's hands.[2] This choice reversed the choice made in the 1951 Treaty of Paris, which created the European Coal and Steel Community (the EC precursor), which had kept most trade policy instruments under the control of the individual ECMS. The main exception to that rule was a then little-known and used instrument: antidumping.

In the early decades of the EC, commercial policy was by far the most important of the four policies under exclusive competence.[3] The EC competition policy seemed odd in the 1960s, when no other ECMS than Germany had a true competition policy. In fact, some ECMSs were looking at planning rather than markets as the ideal way to manage economies. The two other policies under exclusive competence (taxation issues related to the functioning of the customs union, and conservation of marine biological resources) were of more limited scope. The Common Agricultural Policy was shaped later (in the mid-1960s) and placed under the "mixed competence" of the EC and the ECMSs.[4]

Extending the Coverage of "Exclusive Competence" in Trade in Goods

But the Treaty did not define precisely the instruments covered by commercial policy. It mentioned clearly only tariffs. Indeed, as early as the Kennedy Round (1964–1967) the Commission started to negotiate on tariffs on behalf of the ECMSs (at that time the EC was nicknamed the "Geneva ghost") despite the fact that only the ECMSs were GATT members (the Treaty of Rome was notified to GATT but not substantially reviewed by it).[5]

The progressive extension of exclusive competence to the other instruments of trade policy in goods—quotas of all types and other nontariff barriers—was completed only at the end of the Uruguay Round (1995). This was the result of several converging evolutions. First, the European Court of Justice released several rulings (most notably, the 1976 *Donckerwolcke* ruling) that included nontariff barriers in the EC commercial policy. Second, a Treaty provision (Article R115)[6] allowed ECMSs to impose barriers to imports of specified products into their own territory (these goods being imported freely in the rest of the EC) as an alternative to EC-wide barriers. Its use was conditioned on a Commission's authorization that had to be renewed on a yearly basis, a condition that gradually made Article R115 obsolete.[7] Third, in the late 1970s, the ECMSs began to use a "European" facade for getting tailor-made trade barriers by using antidumping procedures (antidumping cases can be easily tailor made to the interests of individual ECMS).

Last but not least, today, ECMSs still have a last recourse to limit exclusive competence in goods. They can oppose changes in the EC commercial policy that they find contrary to their interests by vetoing, or threatening to veto, decisions in other EC policies that require unanimity or qualified majority of the ECMSs. The "vetoing" ECMS would drop its opposition to the other policies if EC commercial policy was made favorable to its interests. That practice reduces de facto the scope of commercial policy within the competence of the EC.

As a result, the current situation remains somewhat fluid. For a vast majority of trade issues in goods, ECMSs abide by exclusive competence, and tend to devolve trade policy to the Commission, to the point of giving the impression that the Commission is fully in charge. However, when an ECMS has a critical trade interest at stake, it can act precipitously and vigorously confront the Commission. This makes the EC trade policy more unpredictable than it used to be when ECMSs were closely monitoring the Commission's actions, with the last months of important trade negotiations witnessing fierce intra-EC disputes on deals tabled by the Commission. Solving such conflicts could require giving satisfaction to the ECMS, at the risk of blocking negotiations. It could also involve "compensation" to the "losing" ECMS. For instance, at the end of the Uruguay Round, France dropped its opposition to the agreement in exchange for an additional package of farm subsidies from the other ECMSs.

Services and Other Commercial Issues

If the Uruguay Round closed the debate on the Community's exclusive competence in trade in goods, it opened the debate on its exclusive competence in the other commercial issues that were included in the world trade regime by the Uruguay Round (1995), in particular trade in services. Things continue to be complex in these matters.

Services are by far the most important issue in commercial policy: they constitute 70% of GDP in most ECMSs and the core of future liberalization. Although written in 1955–1956 (few people thought about services at that time) Treaty Article R60 (F57) covers services, defined as economic activities "provided for remuneration, in so far as they are not governed by the provisions relating to freedom of movement of goods, capital and persons."[8] As no country was interested in trade in services before the Uruguay Round negotiations, the Treaty provisions remained largely inert until the mid-1980s and early 1990s.

At the end of the Uruguay negotiations, the European Court of Justice released its 1/94 opinion (November 1994), which launched an official process of extending the Community's exclusive competence to commercial policy in services. The Lisbon Treaty solidifies such a competence in its Articles R131 (F206) and R133 (F207) by stating: "The Commission shall make recommendations to the Council, which shall authorise it to open the necessary negotiations. The Council and the Commission shall be responsible for ensuring that the agreements negotiated are compatible with internal Union policies and rules."

Yet exclusive competence is much more difficult to implement in services where liberalization consists largely of regulatory reforms. In the 1970s, the hope that service regulations could be fully harmonized in the EC (a necessary condition for a meaningful concept of exclusive competence) collapsed. The following decades witnessed a constant retreat from this approach—from harmonization to mutual recognition and to mutual evaluation. As the ECMSs are expected to stay in charge of regulatory reforms in services for a long time to come, mixed competence will de facto prevail. The apparent Community's exclusive competence combined with the reality of ECMS-based regulatory reforms in services generate an unsatisfactory situation for EC trading partners. They have to negotiate a trade agreement in services with the Commission, but most details of the negotiations and, even more crucially, the effective enforcement of the agreement need to be delivered by the ECMSs.

The most important other commercial issues are public procurement, trade-related intellectual property rights, and foreign direct investment (FDI) treaties. The first item leaves, by definition, a high degree of freedom to the ECMSs, and even to the subnational entities such as regions, provinces, and towns. As a result, the EC disciplines in this domain are mostly of procedural nature (transparency, nondiscrimination, etc.).

The Lisbon Treaty includes FDI and trade-related aspects of intellectual property rights (TRIPs) in the same Articles—R131 (F206) and R133 (F207)—that cover services. However, it is unclear to what extent these new provisions will be operational soon, particularly in FDI matters. During past decades, a few ECMSs (notably Britain and Germany) have been able to develop a wide set of bilateral investment treaties that they may not be ready to make easily available to the other ECMSs.

2. THE LEVEL AND COSTS OF EC PROTECTION AT THE DAWN OF THE DOHA ROUND (2001)

In the late 1990s, Lord Brittan, then Sir Leon Brittan, the EC trade commissioner, floated the idea of the new round of trade negotiations at the WTO that ultimately became the Doha Development Agenda (Doha Round). This proposal marked a deep change in the EC approach to GATT Rounds. Until then, the EC initial position in new Rounds varied from cautious to reluctant, because many EC quarters perceived these Rounds as an attempt to dissolve the EC in a wider free-trade area, hence as an obstacle to the long-term political goal of European unification.

From a more economic perspective, Lord Brittan's proposal also surprised many Europeans who perceived the EC as a very open economy, compared to the other large economies. This belief was, and still is, best illustrated by the repeated assertions that the EC is the largest world importer, without recognizing that its sheer size and some features (such as the absence of EC territories capable of producing tropical crops) necessarily make it so. Yet at the dawn of the twenty-first century, the EC still has much protection.

Protection of Agriculture and Manufacturing

Tariff protection has two main dimensions: the average tariff level and the tariff dispersion allowing tariff "peaks" (defined in what follows as tariffs higher than 15%). From an economic perspective, tariff peaks cause most economic distortions, hence deliver the largest welfare gains to consumers when eliminated. They are also key from a political perspective because they are a sure sign of powerful lobbies, capable of protecting very inefficient sectors, even after more than five decades of liberalization.

The EC protection uses other instruments than ad valorem tariffs (tariffs expressed in percent of world prices). It includes:

- Specific tariffs, mainly tariffs expressed in euros per physical unit, which cover a third of the agricultural products
- Quantitative import and export restrictions
- Quotas enforced by the EC or "voluntary" restraints imposed by the EC but enforced by its trading partners
- Antidumping measures, which can take the forms of ad valorem or specific tariffs, de facto voluntary quantitative export restraints, or minimum price schemes
- Safeguard measures, which can also take all of the above forms
- Antisubsidy measures, which can take the forms of ad valorem or specific tariffs
- Production and export subsidies, massive in agriculture
- Norms and standards stringent enough to make difficult or impossible the import (or export) of foreign (EC) goods, as best illustrated by the ban of selling some genetically modified food

It would be ideal to have estimates on the EC "global" protection that would aggregate all the above measures in one tariff equivalent, expressed in percent of world prices for each product. But since this is not possible, the following estimates are limited to three instruments: ad valorem tariffs, the ad valorem equivalent of antidumping measures, and ad valorem estimates of key quantitative import restrictions.

In table 9.1, column 1 shows the average level of the EC global protection covering the above three instruments at the dawn of the Doha Round, and column 6 shows peak protection. Table 9.1 also compares these estimates with the ad valorem tariffs alone (columns 2 and 3 for the averages, columns 7 and 8 for the peaks) for the same year (1999) and for the most recent year. Finally, table 9.1 provides the available data for China, in order to get a sense of the relative speed of trade liberalization in the EC and in China (data on China are only on tariffs).

Table 9.1 provides four main results. First, the level of EC global protection in 1999 is 11.7%—five percentage points above the ad valorem average tariff. This means that a substantial share of EC protection is delivered by opaque instruments (antidumping and quantitative restrictions) with well-known perverse distortionary effects.

Second, the Uruguay Round has only moderately reduced EC protection. Its impact has been notable in manufacturing, with a decline of average global protection from 9.5% in 1990 to 7.7% in 1999. But it has been negligible in agriculture, in sharp contrast to a wide belief in Europe. The EC farmers and politicians who attribute their problems to alleged farm liberalization of the Uruguay Round are wrong.

Third, columns 6 and 8 show that severe tariff peaks in the EC remain (moreover, some of these peaks are based on specific tariffs that vary with world prices). Such high tariffs still protect a substantial share of the EC economies. In 1999, the level of global protection was higher than 10% in sectors representing more than one-fourth of the EC value-added, and higher than 20% in sectors representing more than one-sixth of the EC value-added. The highly protected sectors are agribusiness (which is much more protected than farmers per se), chemicals, textiles and clothing, and, to a lesser extent, steel and cars.

Last but not least, table 9.1 compares the EC to China in order to better understand the emerging world trade landscape (??environment). The average Chinese protection is becoming close to EC level—it is lower in agriculture, despite the fact that this sector represents a huge share of China's workforce compared to 4% in Europe. This situation is all the more remarkable because China begun to liberalize

Table 9.1. Global border protection in the EC (2000 and 2008) and China (2001–2008)

	Average border protection (%)					Maximum tariffs (%)				
	EC			China [c]		EC			China [c]	
	1999 [a]	1999 [b]	2008	2001	2007	1999 [a]	1999 [b]	2008	2001	2005
	1	2	3	4	5	6	7	8	9	10
Agricultural products	24.1	17.3	17.2	23.1	15.3	n.a.	236.4	604.3	121.6	65.0
Manufacturing products	7.7	4.5	3.7	14.4	8.8	41.7	26.0	89.8	90.0	50.0
All products	11.7	6.9	6.7	15.6	9.7	N.A.	236.4	604.3	121.6	65.0

N.A.: not available. All averages are unweighted.
Sources: [a] Messerlin (2001). [b] WTO Secretariat, Trade Policy Review (2001 and 2009). [c] WTO Secretariat, Trade Policy Review (2001, 2006, 2008).

only in the very late 1970s–early 1980s, 30 years after Europe started. Similar observations can be made about India or Brazil—though to a lesser extent, and with the key caveat that these countries apply tariffs much lower than the tariffs they bound at the WTO (hence they could increase their applied tariffs with no legal consequence in the WTO forum) while for China and the EC the bound and actual tariffs are the same. Chinese tariff dispersion tends to be smaller than the EC. The dramatic shifts in level and dispersion of protection of the major trading partners, with the emerging economies becoming rapidly as open as the EC and the United States, explain the tectonic changes observed in the world economic relations during the last decade.

Protection of Services

Services represent about 70% of the European economy, but not all of them have been the main target of European integration since the mid-1980s. Treaty Article R63 (F59) provides that *"priority* [for liberalization] *shall as a general rule be given to those services which directly affect production costs or the liberalisation of which helps to promote trade in goods."* As a result, the *acquis communautaire* (the set of EC-wide regulations, hereafter the *acquis*) in this sector is concentrated in a limited number of services, as illustrated by table 9.2. In particular, the *acquis* in the middle of the decade 2000–2010 does not include key services supplied by public entities in most of the ECMSs such as health and education, as well as private services of huge economic importance, including retail distribution and tourism, which were included only very recently in the *acquis*, with the 2006 Services Directive (Breuss et al. 2008).

The key question is: has this regulatory effort improved access to ECMSs services by service providers from the rest of the world? Until the late 1990s, there was a naive feeling in the EC that adopting the *acquis* in services—the so-called 1992 Programme, then the Internal Market programme—would be sufficient to create an effective "Internal Market" in services, despite the robust evidence that it was not the case (Messerlin 2001). It was only in the middle of the decade 2000–2010 that the Commission recognized that creating an Internal Market was much less simple than expected.

That said, protection is much more difficult to document in services than in goods. What follows relies on three sources: data on trade in services, direct information on regulatory barriers in services, and direct information on barriers to FDIs, a key instrument for acceding to foreign markets in services.

Data on trade in services are notoriously incomplete, and a notable share is included in the data on trade in goods. Comparing intra-EC and extra-EC trade flows in services shows two main results. Between 1995 and 2005, the share of intra-EC and extra-EC trade in services in world trade has not changed much. During the same period, the GDP shares of intra-EC and extra-EC trade in services have increased, but roughly at the same rate as the GDP shares of intra-EC and extra-EC trade in goods (Gros 2007; Ilzkovitz et al. 2007).

Table 9.2. The *acquis communautaire* in services, mid-2000s

	Number of texts						All (shares) (%)
	1958–1985	1986–1990	1991–1995	1996–2000	2001–2005	All	
Freedom of workers	4			1	8	13	2.2
Right of establishment, freedom to provide services	5	1		3	1	10	1.7
Free movement of capital	1	2	1	5	4	13	2.2
Financial services							
Banking and financial conglomerates		1	2	5	2	10	1.7
Insurance and occupational pensions	10	5	7	4	11	37	6.3
Securities markets and investment services	1		1	2	9	13	2.2
Others				1	10	11	1.9
Information society and media							
Audiovisual policy		2		3	3	8	1.4
Electronic communications		2	2	7	39	50	8.6
Information society directive				4	2	6	1.0
Transport policy							
Land transport: road	6	5	16	25	27	79	13.6
Land transport: rail	1		3	6	25	35	6.0
Inland waterways	5	4	10	9	4	32	5.5
Maritime transport	5	6	8	20	50	89	15.3
Air transport		1	17	21	49	88	15.1
State aid	3	2	10	4	4	23	3.9
Energy							
Electricity					3	3	0.5
Gas					3	3	0.5
Hydrocarbons	4		2	1		7	1.2
Coal					2	2	0.3
New and renewable sources of energy	1		2	2	10	15	2.6
Nuclear energy	2	4	4	6	5	21	3.6
Trans-European networks							
Transport			1	2	5	8	1.4
Energy			1	3	3	7	1.2
Acquis communautaire in services in % of total	48 8.2	356.0	87 14.9	134 23.0	27 47.9	583 100.0	100.0

Source: EC legislation in force. Author's calculations.

A first direct information on market opening in services is provided by the OECD indicators on the product-market regulations.[9] Table 9.3 presents the evolution of these indicators for 1998, 2003, and 2008 for 26 OECD members, for various groups of ECMSs, and for a group of OECD "reference countries." Table 9.3 suggests three main results. First, the "founding" ECMSs have slightly improved their average relative performance compared to the OECD reference countries between 1998 and 2003, but not since 2003. Second, other long-standing ECMSs (Western ECMSs #2) have made no progress. Last but not least, the most recent ECMSs (the Central European ECMSs) have substantially reduced their regulatory backwardness, to the point of having caught up some long-standing ECMSs (Western ECMSs #2).

In short, none of these results presents the *acquis* as an autonomous and vigorous source of services liberalization. Founding ECMSs are not at the forefront of market openness and some long-standing-time ECMSs are losing ground while recently acceded ECMSs are quickly catching up. These results are confirmed by other available databases on regulatory reforms (Messerlin 2007, 2008).

Finally, the international provision of services relies heavily on FDI. Table 9.4 presents the available direct evidence of restrictions in specific barriers to FDI flows as estimated by the OECD FDI restrictiveness indexes (FDIRIs).[10] Table 9.4 shows a wide range of situations among ECMSs. Only a few ECMSs are very open to the rest of the world, and only those ECMSs are likely to be also open vis-à-vis the other ECMSs. By contrast, the ECMSs with high FDIRIs with respect to the rest of the world are likely to be also close vis-à-vis the other ECMSs for the services in question.

Table 9.4 also shows substantial differences in the openness level of the three large economies (EC, Japan, U.S.), with the EC27 being the least open, except in air and maritime transport (compared to both Japan and the U.S.), banking and insurance (compared to the U.S.), and fixed telecom and accounting (compared to Japan).

The Costs of EC Protection: Estimates

There are two alternative methods to estimate the costs of EC protection. The first concentrates on the peaks of protection. This requires the use of a partial equilibrium approach, since available data do not allow the use of a general equilibrium approach when focusing on the precise goods subjected to peaks. Such an approach (Messerlin 2001) can cover a relatively wide set of trade barriers, take into account some consequences of imperfect competition, and cover some services. It suggests two main results: protection costs are close to 5% of the value-added of the sectors under scrutiny, if markets are assumed competitive; these costs increase to 7% of the EC GDP if imperfect competition, widely spread in services, is taken into account.

The second alternative is to adopt a general equilibrium approach that allows for key interactions between sectors and operators. But it relies on trade-weighted measures of protection to aggregate the information into a manageable set of

Table 9.3. Product market regulations (PMR) indicators

Group	Countries	1998	2003	2008
RC	United States	1.28	1.01	0.84
EW1	Britain	1.07	0.82	0.84
EW1	Ireland	1.65	1.35	0.92
RC	Canada	1.29	1.14	0.95
EF	Netherlands	1.66	1.36	0.97
EW2	Spain	2.55	1.68	1.03
EW1	Denmark	1.59	1.18	1.06
RC	Japan	2.19	1.41	1.11
RC	Switzerland	2.48	1.72	1.18
EW3	Finland	2.08	1.30	1.19
RC	Australia	1.52	1.16	1.23
RC	New Zealand	1.36	1.14	1.26
ECC	Hungary	2.30	1.91	1.30
EW3	Sweden	1.93	1.49	1.30
EF	Germany	2.06	1.60	1.33
EF	Italy	2.59	1.81	1.38
EF	Belgium	2.17	1.59	1.43
EW2	Portugal	2.25	1.64	1.43
EW3	Austria	2.33	1.76	1.45
EF	France	2.52	1.75	1.45
RC	Korea	2.35	1.78	1.47
EF	Luxembourg	–	1.48	1.56
ECC	Czech Republic	2.99	1.98	1.62
ECC	Slovakia	–	1.84	1.63
ECC	Poland	3.97	2.95	2.26
EW2	Greece	2.99	2.58	2.37
EF	Founding ECMSs	2.20	1.60	1.35
EW1	Western ECMSs #1	1.44	1.12	0.94
EW2	Western ECMSs #2	2.60	1.97	1.61
EW3	Western ECMSs #3	2.11	1.52	1.31
ECC	Central ECMSs	3.09	2.17	1.70
RC	Reference countries	1.78	1.34	1.15

Source: OECD, Product Market Regulation Database (website). The indicators range from 0 (most promarket regulations) to 6 (least promarket regulations).

Table 9.4. Foreign direct investment restrictiveness indexes, 2006

		1. Legal services	2. Accounting	3. Architecture	4. Engineering	5. Fixed telecoms	6. Mobile telecoms	7. Construction	8. Distribution	9. Insurance	10. Banking	11. Hotels/resto	12. Air transport	13. Maritime transport	14. Road transport	15. Electricity
EF	Belgium	22	22	22	22	72	72	22	22	44	44	22	122	248	72	22
EF	France	233	33	33	33	72	72	22	22	138	94	22	198	198	72	322
EF	Germany	22	22	22	22	122	122	22	22	116	72	22	248	198	22	122
EF	Italy	22	22	22	22	72	72	22	22	88	144	22	494	66	22	122
EF	Netherlands	11	11	11	11	11	11	11	11	55	33	11	411	355	11	611
EW1	Britain	17	17	17	17	17	17	17	17	83	67	17	267	361	17	17
EW1	Denmark	1000	562	22	22	72	72	22	22	44	22	22	422	22	122	122
EW1	Ireland	22	22	22	22	122	122	22	22	88	44	22	466	66	22	1000
EW2	Greece	462	506	462	462	122	122	22	22	88	88	22	522	254	22	1000
EW2	Portugal	22	66	22	22	122	122	22	22	116	172	22	1000	122	22	122
EW2	Spain	512	66	22	22	322	322	22	22	226	182	22	304	316	22	22
EW3	Austria	348	348	348	348	172	172	172	172	272	172	172	322	472	222	172
EW3	Finland	550	550	110	110	110	110	110	110	110	160	110	310	210	154	210
EW3	Sweden	556	292	66	66	166	166	66	66	116	116	66	316	266	166	166
ECC	Czech Rep.	125	375	50	50	50	50	100	50	150	150	50	450	100	100	450
ECC	Estonia	1000	22	22	22	22	22	22	22	122	22	22	322	366	22	622
ECC	Hungary	100	100	100	100	100	100	100	100	150	100	100	500	400	150	200
ECC	Latvia	0	0	0	0	0	0	0	0	0	0	0	132	0	100	1000
ECC	Lithuania	50	50	50	50	50	50	50	50	50	100	50	350	94	50	650
ECC	Poland	225	175	75	75	375	375	75	75	75	325	75	375	75	125	175
ECC	Romania	250	50	50	50	150	150	50	50	50	175	50	750	150	50	450

ECC	Slovakia	75	375	75	75	72	72	72	72	172	172	72	372	122	72	322
ECC	Slovenia	125	125	100	100	200	100	100	100	100	100	100	740	244	100	700
EC27	All ECMSs	250	166	75	75	117	108	50	48	107	111	48	408	205	76	374
RC	Japan	100	100	25	25	286	25	25	25	25	75	25	675	275	25	25
RC	United States	75	25	25	25	25	25	25	25	175	275	25	650	275	25	125
EF	Founding ECMSs	62	22	22	22	70	70	20	20	88	77	20	295	213	40	240
EW1	Western ECMSs #1	346	200	20	20	70	70	20	20	72	44	20	385	150	54	380
EW2	Western ECMSs #2	332	213	169	169	189	189	22	22	143	147	22	609	231	22	381
EW3	Western ECMSs #3	485	397	175	175	149	149	116	116	166	149	116	316	316	181	183
ECC	Central ECMSs	217	141	58	58	124	102	63	58	97	127	58	443	172	85	508

Source: OECD (2007). The indexes measure deviations from "national treatment" on a 0 to 1,000 scale, with 0 representing full openness and 1,000 a prohibition of FDI. GDP-weighted averages for the groups of ECMSs.

sectors, an approach that systematically underestimates tariff peaks, hence the costs of protection. As a result, these models suggest a much lower welfare cost of EC protection (generally less than 1%).

These results call for two additional remarks. First, the EC protection is inefficient: it saves a limited number of jobs at a much higher costs than the average wage in the sectors in question. This conclusion is reinforced by the following fact. As most ECMSs have relatively inefficient labor markets, the number of jobs truly saved by trade barriers per se is probably even lower, since these jobs would have been protected anyway by existing labor regulations. As shown by economic analysis, saving jobs requires much better targeted and monitored policies than trade policy.

Second, the EC protection tends to generate high rents to the protected sectors. Such rents are estimated to represent a third of the global cost of protection (compared to a fifth or a fourth for tariff revenues) (Messerlin 2001). Such a high share is due to the fact that the EC markets where protection is high (steel, chemicals, food products, etc.) are also characterized by a relatively low level of competitive pressures, which results from a mix of a tight net of regulations and of a widespread tendency to collusive behavior (Amatori 1999). The large share of rents runs against the general perception of protection in the European opinion, which often sees protection as protecting "public interest" and opening the economy as favoring narrow private interests. The reality is quite the opposite. Protection favors the "happy few," to the detriment of a much wider crowd of consumers and producers.

Last but not least, the costs of EC protection may be larger than those in comparably large industrial countries because the Internal Market in goods and services remains so imperfect. In 2005, price dispersion among the 15 oldest ECMSs is still substantial, with a coefficient of variation of 13% for goods (down from 20% in 1991) and 36.2% in services (Ilzkovitz et al. 2007). During the 1997–2006 period, 8 manufacturing sectors and 7 services sectors (out of 11 manufacturing sectors and 12 services sectors) showed notable to substantial signs of "integration problems" (Ilzkovitz et al. 2008).

3. THE EC COMMERCIAL POLICY IN THE DECADE 2000–2010

In the late 1990s, the EC Commission became a champion of new WTO trade negotiations. However, it was very slow to realize the profound changes in the world situation that occurred in the decade 2000–2010—particularly the increasingly cooler U.S. attitude toward trade liberalization and the rising influence of the emerging economies, and their insistence on opening the U.S. and EC markets for products of interest to them—precisely those that had been most protected during the previous decades.

The Doha Round negotiations are moving at a slow pace, if at all, since December 2008. This has induced the EC commercial policy to pay more attention to preferential trade agreements (PTAs) under the form of bilateral agreements (hereafter bilaterals). The EC renewed interest in bilaterals is driven by two very different motives from those that were behind its staunch support to PTAs until the late 1980s. First is a foreign policy motive. The EC fell behind the U.S. initiatives in terms of bilaterals, negotiated or signed with countries in the Middle East, in Latin America or in Asia Pacific, which were largely driven by political reasons. The second motive was a desire to change radically the logic of the PTAs with the African, Caribbean, and Pacific countries (ACPs), which are the oldest PTAs in the history of the EC commercial policy.

The Doha Round

The EC, as has the United States, has entered the Doha negotiations with a mentality of "business as usual." It considered itself the dominant player along with the United States, so that it could trade small opening of its agricultural markets for concessions in topics it was not able to settle during the Uruguay Round (1995) although it priced them highly: geographical indications in agriculture,[11] competition policy, rules in investment and public procurement, and trade facilitation, to mention the most important ones.

The 2003 Cancun Ministerial eliminated these topics from the Doha list of topics to be negotiated, with the exception of trade facilitation and, more problematically, geographical indications. It was only then that the EC fully realized that opening its agricultural markets was the key condition to get more open industrial markets in the developing and emerging countries.

The Doha negotiations took shape only at the 2005 Hong Kong Ministerial. They have led to the Doha "modalities" released in December 2008 by the Chairs of the WTO negotiating groups for agriculture and "nonagricultural market access" (NAMA). What follows refers to these "2008 Doha texts" because they are seen as the "best approximation" of what could be the final results of the Doha Round.

NAMA

In the negotiations on industrial products ("nonagricultural market access" in the Doha Round jargon) the EC is mostly a demandeur since its own level of protection is generally low, with the exception of peak tariffs. The 2008 Doha texts would imply that the EC average tariff would be reduced from 3.7% to just above 3%, while EC peak tariffs would be sharply cut, from 50% to less than 8%.

Turning to the tariffs of the EC trading partners, the European manufacturing sector was looking for a simple outcome of the Doha Round: "*no single [industrial] tariff above 15 percent at the end of the implementation period, except for LDC)*" (Businesseurop 2001). The 2005 Hong Kong Ministerial adopted a "Swiss" formula as the formula for cutting tariffs.[12] The Businesseurop request would require the adoption of a Swiss coefficient of 18–20 by the EC major trading partners. The current Swiss coefficients mentioned in the 2008 Doha texts, ranging from 20 to 25, are close to satisfying this request, except for a small number of tariff lines (Messerlin 2011).

But this result still depends on the exceptions to the Swiss formula that the 2008 Doha texts will offer to the developing countries. Some exceptions (in particular, the possibility to keep unbound tariffs or to impose no cuts on 5–7.5% of the tariff lines) could seriously reduce the very positive impact of the aforementioned Swiss coefficients.

Second, Swiss coefficients ranging from 20 to 25 mean that developing countries would mostly bind their tariffs at their current levels—that is, would eliminate the existing "water in tariffs" (the difference between bound and applied tariffs). Henceforth, developing countries would no longer have the option of raising their applied tariffs to their bound tariffs. Such a reversal was very much feared at the peak of the 2008–2009 crisis, and it would have cost $450–900 billion to the world GDP (Bouët and Laborde 2009; Productivity Commission 2009).

Such cuts of bound tariffs would not change drastically the existing level of openness of the emerging markets, which are de facto relatively open. So it does not create great enthusiasm among European businesses. But although the offensive interests of European business have largely been achieved (assuming only few exceptions to the Swiss formula) the EC negotiators are continuing to insist on getting more concessions in NAMA from the emerging economies. They have two opposite reasons for such a tactic. By doing so, they may try to open more the NAMA markets of the emerging economies. But they may also try to limit the opening of the EC agricultural markets, because demanding more concessions in NAMA may be a way to induce the emerging countries to demand less concessions in agriculture.

Negotiations in "Agriculture"

The term "agriculture" in the Doha Round is a misnomer. The current negotiations deal with three times as many agroindustrial or "food" products as farm products. This little-recognized feature is crucial because trade liberalization in food products is likely to be similar to trade liberalization in industrial products, and could therefore benefit from the long experience in the latter.

Negotiations on tariffs. Largely under the EC influence, the Doha negotiators on farm and food products have adopted a liberalization formula, known as a "tier-based" formula, that is much more opaque than the Swiss formula.[13] A tier-based formula has also the key shortcoming of cutting the initially high tariffs by less than a Swiss formula. Yet, from an economic perspective, the tariffs that should be cut most are the high tariffs, which generate the highest welfare costs.

Table 9.5 provides the tariff cuts to be expected from the 2008 Doha text for the whole agricultural sector and for its farm and food components.[14] It shows the strong "tariff escalation" in the current EC schedule: the more processed the goods are, the higher their level of protection. The average tariff of bulk farm products

(19.7%) is substantially lower than the average tariff of the processed food products (32.6%), and, even more strikingly, the highest tariff for farm products (93.6%) is much smaller than the highest tariff on processed food (407.8%).

Second, as the Doha tier-based formulas are softer on the highest tariffs than the Swiss formulas, the tariff cuts in the current EC proposal protect *food producers* much more often than *farmers*. Table 9.5 shows that the post-Doha tariffs would be 7.8% for the bulk farm commodities, compared to 12.3% for processed food products, while the post-Doha maximum tariff would be 28.1% for the farm products, compared to 122.3% for processed food. Moreover, the food products that would remain the EC's most protected items after the Doha Round are a strange hodge-podge of waste products (dog and cat food, offal, whey, etc.), goods with a tiny potential in international trade (yoghurts), and products of questionable importance (cucumbers, gherkins, etc.).

As in NAMA, the 2008 Doha texts on agriculture raise serious problems because they provide too generous exceptions to tariff cuts, hence risking unravelling the impact of the tier-based formula. In the same vein, the EC has been pushing hard for an intensive use of "tariff-rate quotas" as the preferred instrument for exceptions. Tariff-rate quotas are well known for their opacity and their perverse effects. The quota rents they generate are likely to go not to European farmers but rather to EC-based importing firms or even to foreign exporting firms.

Table 9.5. Expected cuts of the EC tariffs in farm and food products

	Current ad val. Equivalent tariffs %	Post-Doha tariffs (%)		
		EC initial offer	Doha text 2008	Swiss formula*
All "agricultural" products (2,011 tariff lines)				
Average tariffs	24.4	12.9	9.4	9.4
Bulk farm commodities (117 tariff lines)				
Average tariffs	19.7	11.0	7.8	7.8
Maximum tariff	93.6	46.8	28.1	21.8
Other/horticulture farm products (273 tariff lines)				
Average tariffs	13.6	8.1	6.0	7.3
Maximum tariff	118.9	59.5	35.7	23.0
Semiprocessed food products (488 tariff lines)				
Average tariffs	12.6	7.1	4.9	5.3
Maximum tariff	174.9	70.0	52.5	24.5
Processed food products (1,120 tariff lines)				
Average tariffs	32.6	17.6	12.3	11.9
Maximum tariff	407.8	163.1	122.3	26.6

* The Swiss coefficient of 28.5 would ensure that the average tariff on all the farm and food products is the same as the tariff generated by the tier-based formula suggested by the 2008 Doha texts (9.4%).
Source: EC tariff schedule, including the ad valorem equivalents of the specific tariffs.

Negotiations on farm subsidies. If tariffs cover farm and food products, subsidies are concentrated on farm products. In the EC system, some agrifood firms may receive subsidies, particularly export subsidies. But these subsidies are mostly compensation for high prices of the farm products that these agrifood firms have to pay European farmers. In short, EC agribusiness firms are "quasi-public" agencies for distributing subsidies to the farmers.

The EC has been in a better negotiating position in the Doha negotiations on farm subsidies than the United States because since 2004, it has shifted roughly 25 billion euros out of the perimeter of the prohibited subsidies ("overall trade distorting support" in the Doha jargon).[15] Indeed, table 9.6 shows that the 2008 Doha texts would essentially bind the EC and U.S. future subsidies at the current or shortly expected within a few years level. In short, the huge "water in domestic support" would be largely eliminated—echoing the aforementioned elimination of the huge "tariff water" in NAMA for the emerging economies.

Yet serious problems remain. First, subsidies outside the coverage of the "overall trade distorting support" may be less perverse than production-based subsidies, but they still have an indirect impact on trade flows. Hence, they should be revisited. This perspective fits well the growing recognition in Europe that decoupled farm subsidies go mostly to large farmers, which are facing an increasing legitimacy problem because few Europeans want to fight for them. With time, it will become increasingly unsustainable politically to grant subsidies to farmers on the basis of outputs produced in an increasingly distant past.

Second, recent years have witnessed worrisome developments in certain EC subsidy schemes: the huge subsidies granted to biofuels leading to effective rates of protection of almost 10,000%, despite the fact that such biofuels of the first generation have a strong negative impact on the environment; the emergence of antidumping measures in agriculture (on biofuels imported from the U.S.); and the reactivation of export subsidies for dairy since the 2008–2009 economic crisis.

A concluding remark on agriculture. Whether the Doha negotiations fail or succeed, they have achieved an important objective in the EC farm sector. They have made European farmers and policy-makers increasingly aware of the fact that the impact of the Common Agricultural Policy varies with each member state's production structure. An ECMS producing mostly farm goods protected by high EC tariffs and/or subsidies is, on average, "more" protected than an ECMS producing mostly farm goods protected by low or moderate EC tariffs or subsidies.

Table 9.7 illustrates this point by weighting each ECMS' farm production by the EC-wide level of protection, be it measured by tariffs or by the combined protection granted by tariffs and subsidies, as measured by the OECD "producer support equivalents." It shows that producer surplus equivalents vary from 1 to 2.6 and tariffs from 1 to 1.4.

Contrary to common belief, French farmers are not among the most protected in the EC: farmers from ECMSs favoring freer trade (Britain or Sweden for instance) are on average more protected. This situation should induce French farmers to be among the most supportive of market opening in agriculture, since a large share of

Table 9.6. The liberalization formulas in the "overall trade distorting support" (OTDS)

	Support in billion U.S. dollars [a]		Support in % of agricultural output [b]	
	U.S.	EC15 [c]	U.S.	EC15
The Uruguay bound commitments	55.0	149.0	47.4	70.6
Effective OTDS (2004)	23.0	78.0	19.8	37.0
Estimated OTDS (2013) [d]	12.4	30.0	10.7	14.2
The Doha draft text (December 2008)				
Base levels	48.2	149.0	41.6	70.6
Formula cuts (in %)	70	80	-	–
Commitments	14.5	29.8	12.5	14.1

Notes: The overall trade distorting support includes all the farm subsidies deemed to be highly trade-distortive. [a] Figures for the EC are expressed in euros in the Chair text, and are translated in U.S. dollars on the basis of an exchange rate of 1.35 U.S. dollar per euro prevailing in December 2008. [b] Average value added in agriculture for the years 1995–2000. [c] Past figures for the OTDS for the EC 27 are roughly 106% higher than those for the EC15. OTDS for 2013 is estimated for the whole EC27. [d] Support for 2013 are estimated by Kutas (2010) for the EC and by Orden, Josling, and Blandford (2010) for the U.S.
Source: WTO Agriculture Chair text, TN/AG/W/$/Rev.4, 6 December 2008. Author's computations.

French agriculture is not protected by the Common Agricultural Policy and since, for those protected farm products, French farmers are often considered among the most efficient in Europe.

The Other Topics Included in the Doha Round

The Doha Round negotiations cover potentially many other important topics: services; selected industrial sectors (such as environmental products and equipment goods), which are candidates for full liberalization, including nontariff barriers; geographical indications; rules for antidumping and antisubsidy; and trade facilitation. But so far, all these topics, except trade facilitation, have not been subjected to intensive negotiations because the Doha negotiators have agreed to a sequential approach—first negotiate on industrial and agricultural goods, then on the other topics. As a result, the EC and all the other developed countries have no visibility on what are the opportunities and gains to be expected in services, when these activities represent 70% of EC GDP and may be the source of substantial comparative advantages. This sequential approach has been detrimental to a rapid and successful conclusion of the Doha Round.

Table 9.7. Level of protection by EC Member States, 2004

EC Member States	Global protection [a]	Tariffs (%) [b]
Ireland	91	26.2
Luxemburg	69	25.6
Britain	66	25.5
Finland	65	26.5
Sweden	65	25.5
Lithuania	58	26.6
Germany	56	24.5
Latvia	56	25.3
Austria	55	22.9
France	55	21.6
Czech Republic	54	26.6
Belgium	53	22.7
Slovenia	52	21.2
Estonia	51	27.2
Slovakia	51	25.2
Netherlands	50	19.1
Denmark	49	26.1
Poland	45	24.5
Hungary	41	23.5
Italy	41	19.1
Spain	41	19.1
Portugal	40	18.3
Greece	37	18.7
Malta	35	18.6
EC (16 Member States)	51	21.9
EC (24 Member States)	57	23.3

Sources: OECD, WTO. Notes: [a] PSE: producer surplus equivalent, as calculated by the OECD. [b] Ad valorem tariffs in 2004 (specific tariffs excluded). It is impossible to update these results because the European agricultural policy has been increasingly modulated by the ECMSs since 2004.

Back to Preferential Trade Agreements

In November 2006, Lord Mandelson, then trade commissioner, released a working document on "Global Europe" reaffirming the EC support to the Doha negotiations but also developing a massive European strategy of future bilaterals (no less than 24), hence giving a strong impression of a deep change in the EC commercial policy (European Commission 2006). It seemed that the EC was going back to the "addiction" to discrimination that marked its trade policy from the 1960s to the 1990s, a policy that has left deep scars in the world trade system: a third of the current PTAs notified to the

WTO are intra-European bilaterals, mainly deals between countries located on the European continent. This large number mirrors the way Europeans are building their Single Market: any new bilateral negotiated by the EC mechanically generates "clone" negotiations by the European countries linked to the EC by trade agreements—the European Free Trade Association countries, Turkey, and so on.

However, the "Global Europe" document suggests that the new bilaterals have a new raison d'être: a substantial foreign policy component. This aspect explains the Commission's repeated statement that the EC is lagging behind in terms of bilaterals. This perception was largely created by the fact that most recent U.S. bilaterals were politically loaded.[16]

The fact that the motive behind the "Global Europe" agenda is largely "political" raises a key question. Would the bilaterals envisaged by the EC be dominated by "market opening" forces or by "market preference" forces? The former case occurs when negotiating countries apply low tariffs on goods imported from countries other than the signatories of the deal and enforce domestic procompetitive regulations on services and investment. Such bilaterals are likely to have a net positive economic effect on the signatories, and no significant negative impact on the rest of the world. They may be stepping stones to world trade liberalization and, by the same token, enhance EC political influence without costing the EC or its PTA partners much.

By contrast, market-preferences-dominated bilaterals, namely high tariffs on goods imported from the rest of the world and anticompetitive domestic regulations on services and investment, are likely to be economically harmful. The higher the preferences, the more distorted the bilateral trade flows that result, and the higher the costs of the bilateral deal to the consumers of the products and services imported from the trading partner. Hence, the higher the likelihood of the collapse of the bilateral agreement, and the more painful the "erosion" of these preferences for the signatories. If such bilaterals are likely to be stumbling blocks to world trade opening, then they are politically costly to the EC, and perhaps to its partners as well.

Table 9.8 compares the EC bilateral policy, when launched in 2006, with the equivalent policies of six other countries. It gives—in an admittedly crude way—a sense of the "market opening" versus "market preference" nature of the 91 bilaterals signed by these countries in 2006, and of the 100 bilaterals under negotiation or under consideration by these seven countries.

Columns 2 and 3 give the GDP shares of the seven countries' trading partners in the world GDP calculated both at current and purchasing power parityexchange rates. Thus they offer a sense of the *coverage* of the market preferences that could be created by the size of the partners in the existing and future bilaterals of the seven countries in question. Multiplying the coverage indicator by indicators of the *level* of preferences yields the *magnitude* of the expected preferences. Columns 2 and 3 show the diversity of the situations. The current bilaterals cover a very low share of world GDP, except for the two smallest economies. But the inclusion of the bilaterals under negotiation or consideration dramatically changes the picture. The

Table 9.8. Comparing Global Europe to the strategies of other selected countries, 2006

	Number of partners	Market size [a]		Average industrial tariff [b]		Regulatory ranking [c]				
		At current USD	At PPP USD	Applied	Bound	Trading across borders	Dealing with licenses	Ease of doing business	Registering property	Protecting investors
	1	2	3	4	5	6	7	8	9	10
A. Bilaterals signed										
Singapore	10	48.5	39.3	4.8	9.2	35.8	41.7	28.0	35.3	16.7
Chile	20	79.0	70.4	5.5	8.0	34.1	70.8	41.5	39.6	46.3
Korea	14	4.1	5.8	7.1	21.5	58.8	70.3	69.0	59.2	68.7
USA	15	7.6	6.5	7.5	19.6	42.9	41.9	29.2	50.1	34.0
China	14	2.9	5.9	8.0	25.4	63.1	77.3	72.8	66.7	55.4
EC	14 [d]	6.4	8.2	9.2	18.3	76.8	91.9	67.1	80.4	53.4 1
Japan	4	2.7	3.3	10.0	27.4	69.4	62.4	55.6	76.6	52.4
B. Bilaterals under negotiations or consideration										
Singapore	12	90.6	81.2	5.7	9.0	40.0	68.9	43.5	42.3	41.0
Chile	9 [e]	81.6	77.7	6.4	10.3	43.2	77.8	49.4	45.5	45.1 1
Korea	11	49.1	57.4	7.3	13.3	43.3	85.3	57.6	39.8	40.4
Japan	18	13.4	16.4	7.5	20.0	53.5	58.3	54.8	60.6	56.6
USA	14	14.9	16.5	8.8	21.3	54.1	69.7	52.2	64.7	44.2
China	12	10.4	17.0	10.1	25.5	83.1	96.4	83.5	76.1	47.2
EC	24	23.4	44.2	10.3	17.8	71.1	125.6	91.2	61.8	64.8

Notes: [a] GDP (in U.S. dollar, 2004) as a share of world GDP. [b] WTO Trade profiles. [c] Doing Business indicators (2007). [d] Counting as one the 10 countries having acceded to the EC in 2004. [e] Counting as one the EC.
Sources: WTO Secretariat, Trade profiles [website]. World Bank, Doing Business [website].

Commission's proposal generates such a change of scale in bilateralism that it could trigger a race to bilaterals among the large countries, if China and/or the United States feel compelled to follow a strategy as aggressive as the one designed in the EC proposal.

    Columns 4 and 5 of table 9.8 focus on tariffs, the first key instrument that could determine the level of preferences in trade in goods.[17] A low average of applied tariffs suggest bilaterals more focused on market opening than on market preferences. By contrast, bilaterals behind a high average of applied tariffs are prone to market preferences. The same could be said in case of high average bound tariffs. Column 4 shows that the EC partners have the highest average applied tariffs of the bilaterals under negotiation or consideration by the Commission's proposal. Column 5 suggests, again, based on bound tariffs, possible substantial market preferences for the bilaterals under negotiation or consideration by the four largest countries. In sum, the bilaterals involving the smaller economies tend to focus on market access, in sharp contrast to the EC bilaterals that are dominated by market preferences.

Columns 6 and 7 focus on nontariff barriers, the other key instrument that could determine the level of preferences in trade in goods. As there is no direct measure of such barriers, table 9.8 relies on the ranking of the partners of the seven countries in two respects: the ease of trading across borders and the ease of dealing with licenses, two indicators estimated by the Doing Business database. Ranks are crude indicators. But the average ranks in columns 6 and 7 exhibit differences among of the seven countries' partners so large that they are likely to be meaningful. Once again, the bilaterals under negotiation or consideration by the EC appear the more prone to market preferences.

Columns 8–10 look at services and investments, also with the help of indicators provided by the Doing Business database. The services dimension is captured by the global indicator of the ease of doing business with the various trading partners of the seven countries examined, whereas the investment dimension is indicated by the ranks in property registering and in investors protection among trading partners. These indicators show the EC and China on the one hand and on the opposite side the five other countries. Once again, the bilaterals under negotiation or consideration by the EC appear to be more dominated by market preferences.

To conclude, bilaterals under negotiation or consideration by the Commission's Global Europe agenda seem to be seriously biased toward substantial market preferences. Their short-term political benefits for the EC may be quickly eliminated by their long-term economic costs, generated by market preferences and their erosion following new bilaterals or multilateral trade negotiations. They may also create serious systemic risks in the world trade regime. In particular, they magnify the risk that the aggressive approach of the Commission might trigger a race to bilaterals, by inducing the United States, China, and Japan to "catch up" in terms of bilaterals.

The Economic Partnership Agreements between the EC and the ACPs

A series of bilaterals currently under negotiations by the EC deserves a special attention: the Economic Partnership Agreements (EPAs) with 75 ACPs.

To some extent, negotiating these EPAs was required by WTO rules. The Yaoundé (1963, 1971), then Lomé (1975, 1981, 1985, 1990), then Cotonou (2000) Conventions did not require reciprocity: the EC eliminated its tariffs on ACP products while the ACPs were allowed to keep their own tariffs on EC products.[18] As a result, these Conventions were not fully consistent with the WTO nonreciprocity, rule which is possible for least developed countries but not for developing countries where reciprocity is the rule (roughly half of the ACPs are developing countries). This partial inconsistency was protected by a waiver that was due to expire by

December 31, 2007. Despite the fact that the EC and the ACPs started their discussions on the postwaiver regime as early as 2000, nothing happened before October 2007.

Then, suddenly, the Commission decided to launch negotiations on the new EPAs, and it pledged to conclude them by December 2007. The Commission argued that the waiver deadline had to be strictly enforced, an interpretation that was contested by many WTO experts.[19]

Of their tariff lines for products imported from Europe, EPAs require ACPs to eliminate tariffs on 80%, so that the trade between the EC and each ACP would be tariff-free on 90% of the tariff lines (the average of 100% on the EC side and 80% on the ACP side).[20] It was the EC that defined this threshold of 90%, assuming that it would be high enough to meet a key provision of GATT Article 24 (*"substantially all the trade between the constituent territories"* should be covered by a PTA). The ACPs unwilling to sign EPAs have only one alternative. Least-developed ACPs (39 countries) could adopt the EC "Everything but Arms" initiative, if not yet done. Developing ACPs could turn to the Generalized System of Preferences, an alternative representing a serious reduction in the access of ACPs' producers to EC markets.

Will EPAs be costly to the ACPs (Delpeuch and Harb 2007) The main reasons for a positive answer are captured by the following example. Nigeria's average bound tariffs are 150% in agriculture and 66% in NAMA. If the EC products enter the Nigerian markets duty free, the EC firms could price their products at up to 1.5 and 0.6 times higher than the world price, respectively. The resulting distortions in ACP economies are huge. Behind such high tariffs, inefficient EC firms could charge high prices, and still be preferred to efficient exporters from the rest of the world which have to pay the high ACP tariffs. In such a case, the preferences granted by the ACPs in the EPAs are equivalent to ACP subsidies paid by the (very) poor ACP consumers to these inefficient EC firms. Meanwhile, behind such high tariffs, efficient EC firms could also charge high prices in order to grab the rents generated in the ACP markets by the high tariffs imposed by the ACPs on imports from non-EC sources. In sum, Nigerian consumers, including Nigerian firms, which are often large consumers, will hardly benefit from liberalization. At the same time, the Nigerian government will lose tariff revenues, and Nigerian firms will have a hard time entering their own markets—once fully open to EC firms—losing opportunities to diversify the Nigerian economy.

It could be said that this example provides too dark a picture of the situation because the effectively applied tariffs may be lower than bound tariffs. Table 9.9 suggests that this caveat should be treated with great caution. First, half of the ACPs have average applied tariffs higher than 15% in agriculture, and one-fourth have average tariffs higher than 15% in manufacturing.

Second, table 9.9 shows that the "peak" tariffs applied by the ACPs are very high: almost 50% on average for all the ACPs in agriculture, and 40% in manufacturing. These peak tariffs are concentrated in domestically produced products (a feature meaning that, politically, these are the tariffs the most likely to be kept unchanged

Table 9.9. ACPs current bound and applied tariffs: An overview

	Agriculture (farm and food)				Manufacturing (NAMA)				Overall
	Bound tariffs		Applied tariffs		Bound tariffs		Applied tariffs		binding coverage
	Average	Maximum	Average	Maximum	Average	Maximum	Average	Maximum	
	1	2	3	4	5	6	7	8	9
Number of countries with available data	55	11	62	11	55	11	62	11	53
Average tariff or binding coverage	78.1	85.9	17.1	48.4	46.2	75.9	12.0	40.0	64.3
Number of countries with:									
Bound tariff higher than 30%	48	9	–	–	37	8	–	–	37
Bound tariff higher than 50%	37	9	–	–	23	8	–	–	30
Bound tariff higher than 70%	33	7	–	–	12	6	–	–	28
Applied tariff higher than 15%	–	–	33	11	–	–	15	11	–
Applied tariff higher than 20%	–	–	18	8	–	–	3	9	–
Applied tariff higher than 30%	–	–	2	4	–	–	1	4	–

Sources: WTO Member Information (WTO website) and Tariff Profiles when data are not available in Member Information files. Applied tariffs are for 2001. Author's calculations.

under the EPAs by the ACPs since they are backed by large lobbies) and because they are the source of the largest welfare costs for the imposing country.

Last, many ACPs tariffs are still not bound. As a result, they can be increased without restraint, thus representing huge risks for foreign traders. For instance, half of the African ACPs have bound less than a third of their tariff lines. Indeed, the increase of imports from the EC following the implementation of the EPAs is likely to induce ACPs governments to raise their unbound tariffs on non-EC imports. This is economically unsound, yet a politically likely reaction from the ACPs.

As of May 2010, less than two third of the ACPs have initialled (19 ACPs) or signed (26 ACPs) EPAs. No EPA has been ratified. Moreover, a key initial goal of the EPAs, to favour regional integration among ACPs, had to be abandoned. All concluded EPAs are de facto or de jure bilateral, with the exception of the EPA which involve the 15 Caribbean ACPs.

Why such a slow, limited and uneven process? First is the fact that the aggressiveness with which the Commission undertook the negotiations under Commissioner Mandelson generated deep oppositions in the ACPs and serious concerns in many ECMSs, such as Britain or France. Lady Ashton (the Trade Commissioner succeeding Lord Mandelson) did not fully remove these concerns despite her efforts to introduce some flexibility in the rigid format of the EPAs. The second reason is that the ACPs did not try to come up with better alternatives for themselves because most of their governments are still convinced that any additional trade liberalization would be detrimental to their growth and development. So, they ended up by trying to increase the number of products which could remain protected, making the EPAs even more costly to themselves.

Lastly, if the EPA's are costly for the ACPs, they may become a political trap for the EC. In the long run, they will be perceived by the ACPs as a way to provide a preferred access to EC firms to the detriment of the efficient firms from emerging economies, such as Brazil in agriculture or China in manufacturing. The political cost of what could be branded as neo-imperialism could be enormous for the EC in the long run.

CONCLUSION

In 2010 the EC is facing a severe crisis, with several eurozone members in great difficulties or even on the verge of bankruptcy. As this crisis will not disappear quickly, it raises several important questions.

First is the EC capable of assuming again initiatives on the trade front in the coming months or years (from mid-2009 to mid-2010, the EC has been already relatively inert on the WTO front) An important way for the EC to show its dynamism would be to launch exploratory talks in services. This sector is not only large, but it is still plagued by huge transaction costs—two to three times those in goods (Miroudot, Sauvage, and Shepherd 2010). As the Doha Round is stuck with its self-inflicted constraint of the sequencing of the negotiations ("*let us settle goods first*") such exploratory talks on opening services should find another forum. There are several options, the most logical being the Transatlantic forum. If satisfactory, such talks would be very likely to trigger interests among the 10 or so largest trading partners of the United States and the EC. If successful in this wider context (the U.S., the EC, and these 10 large countries would represent more than 80% of the world value added in services), these talks could then be repatriated into the WTO forum and contribute to unlocking the Doha negotiations.

Second, the EC should seriously review its use of trade policy as a foreign policy instrument. As suggested, the short-term benefits of such an approach should be balanced against the long-term costs, which are almost unavoidable for the following reason: the logic of foreign policy is to sign as many bilaterals as possible. In trade terms, this logic implies that future bilaterals will erode the preferences created by today's bilaterals—a sure way to make businesses disoriented and dillusioned.

Appendix: The Treaties Establishing the European Community and Union

Dates	City of signature	Name of the Treaty
1951	Paris	European Community of Steel and Coal (ECSC)
1957	Rome	European Economic Community (EEC)
1957	Rome	European Community of the Atomic Energy (Euratom)
1965	Brussels	The Merger Treaty
1970	Brussels	The Budgetary Treaty
1972	Brussels	Acts of Accession (Denmark, Ireland and the United Kingdom)
1975	Brussels	The Budgetary Treaty
1979	Athens	Act of Accession (Greece)
1985	Lisbon, Madrid	Acts of Accession (Portugal and Spain)
1986	Luxembourg, The Hague	The Single European Act
1992	Maastricht	The Treaty on European Union (TEU)
1994	Corfu	Acts of Accession (Austria, Finland and Sweden)
1997	Amsterdam	The Treaty of Amsterdam
2001	Nice	The Treaty of Nice
2003	Athens	Acts of Accession [a]
2004	Rome	The Treaty establishing a Constitution for Europe
2005	Neumunster Abbey	Acts of Accession [b]
2009	Lisbon	Consolidated Version of the Treaty on the Functioning of the European Union

Notes: [a] Cyprus, Czech Republic, Estonia, Hungary, Latvia, Lithuania, Malta, Poland, Slovakia, Slovenia. [b] Bulgaria, Romania.
Sources: Official Journal.

Last, commercial policy is only one of the many policy instruments available to a government. "Overusing" such an instrument is a strong tendency in the EC because of the way the Treaty is designed, and because it allows the Commission to maximize its role. But such an overuse may be a source of problems. A good illustration is the so-called EC "energy dependency" with respect to Russia. What seems to be a trade problem (EC imports gas from Russia and Central Asian countries) is fundamentally an EC domestic problem: the absence of a competitive EC energy market. Improving competition in the EC energy markets would be one of the best ways to reduce the EC "dependency."

NOTES

I would like to thank Mordechai Kreinin, Alan Matthews and Michael Plummer for their extremely useful help.

1. For simplicity's sake, this chapter uses the generic term "Treaty" as often as possible to refer to the series of treaties that have established the EC over time.

2. A parallel could be made with the United States, with the Council having the role of the U.S. Congress and the Commission the role of the U.S. administration.

3. Since the creation of the euro, the monetary policy is covered by exclusive competence for the ECMs members of the eurozone.

4. Hence, "renationalizing" the CAP by the ECMs is a possibility that is not inconsistent with the Treaty.

5. The Kennedy Round was instrumental to EC progress. It helped the ECMSs with initially high tariffs to enforce the cuts imposed by the Common External tariff by obtaining more open markets in the U.S. and other GATT Members.

6. As the numbering of the articles has been changed in each successive treaty, every article number provided in this chapter begins with a letter that refers to its treaty: e.g., Article $R115$ is contained in the Treaty of *Rome*. Article numbers beginning with F refer to the most recent treaty, known as the "Functioning" or "Lisbon" Treaty.

7. Article $R115$ became a mere paragraph in the Nice Treaty (Article $N134$) and is not included in the Functioning Treaty.

8. The four freedoms (free movement of goods, services, people, and capital) are the building blocks of the Treaty.

9. These indicators constructed by the OECD (which focus on the network sectors targeted by the Directives) range from 0 (most promarket regulations) to 6 (least promarket regulations) (Conway et al. 2005, Nicoletti 2000).

10. These indicators constructed by the OECD range from 0 (most promarket regulations) to 6 (least promarket regulations).

11. Geographical indications are place names (or words associated with a place) used to identify the origin and quality, reputation, or other characteristics of products.

12. The basic Swiss formula is $T = [rt / (r + t)]$, where t is the initial tariffs, T the postnegotiation tariffs, and r the reduction coefficient (the "Swiss coefficient"). The Swiss coefficient is thus the only element to be negotiated.

13. A tier-based formula splits the whole range of the existing tariffs into several tiers (four to five in the Doha Round). Tariffs pertaining to a tier are cut by a constant

percentage. For instance, in the case of developed countries, tariffs ranging from 0 to 20% would be cut by 50%, while those ranging from 20% to 50% would be cut by 57%, etc.

14. The concordance table used has been established by the U.S. Department of Agriculture. It splits the whole universe of the "agricultural" products into four subsets: the bulk farm commodities, the produce/horticulture products, the semiprocessed products, and the processed products.

15. For simplicity's sake, this comment refers only to the "overall trade distorting support," but the 2008 Doha texts include other disciplines on subsets of different types of subsidies (see Kutas 2010; Orden, Josling, and Blandford 2010; or WTO website).

16. The U.S. administration has taken few initiatives in terms of bilaterals (Australia, Korea, Latin America), and these were fundamentally driven by foreign policy motives (from the Iraq war to the drug wars). At this juncture, the United States has no pending "grand vision" of bilaterals. The Free Trade Area for the Americas looks like a sleeping beauty; the U.S. calls for an Asian Pacific initiative are incantatory but inconsequential. Finally, the ordeals to get the recent bilaterals approved by the U.S. Congress and the mood of the newly elected Congress (revealed by the request for a review of the bilaterals demanded by the new Democratic majority) do not suggest that strategic changes are high on the agenda.

17. This is why the seven countries are ranked by the increasing level of the average tariffs applied by their partners in bilaterals.

18. It is worth noting that the nonreciprocity feature was to be a favor to the ACPs. In fact, it was quite costly for them, as underlined by Kreinin (1973).

19. Last but not least, the EPA issue was intertwined with a very controversial issue: the EC regime of banana imports. Since 1958, the EC regime was imposing all kinds of nontariff barriers in an effort to discriminate in favor of ACPs' bananas and against bananas from Latin America. It was only in December 2009 that a solution was finally accepted by all the parties: the ACPs, the Latin American producers, the United States, and the EC.

20. As underscored by A. Matthews, the EU requirement is also to liberalize 80% of trade value. The "smallness" of the ACP economies makes the impact of this requirement similar to the one based on tariff lines.

REFERENCES

Amatori, F. 1999. European business: New strategies, old structures. *Foreign Policy* (summer), pp. 78–89.

Australian Productivity Commission. 2009. Reform beyond the Crisis. Annual Report 2008–2009. Australian Government, www.pc.gov.au Canberra.

Bouët and Laborde. 2009. The potential costs of a failed Doha Round. Discussion paper 886. IFPRI, Washington, D.C.

Breuss, F., G. Fink, and S. Griller. 2008. Services Liberalization in the Internal Market. Vienna: Springer.

Conway, P., V. Janod, and G. Nicoletti. 2005. Product Market Regulations in OECD Countries: 1998 to 2003. Economic Department Working Papers. Paris: OECD.

Businesseurope. 2001. www.businesseurop.eu.

Delpeuch, C., and G. Harb. 2007. EPAs: Thinking outside the European Box. GEM working paper. Available at http://gem.sciences-po.fr.

European Commission. 2006. Global Europe: Competing in the World.

Gros, D. 2007, 19 February. EU Services Trade: Where Is the Single Market in Services? CEPS. Available at www.ceps.eu.

Ilzkovitz F., A. Dierx, V. Kovacs, and N. Sousa. 2007, January. Steps towards a Deeper Economic Integration: The Internal Market in the 21st Century. A Contribution to the Single Market Review. European Economy, no 271.

Ilzkovitz F., A. Dierx, and N. Sousa. 2008, August. An Analysis of the Possible Causes of Product Market Malfunctioning in the EU: First Results for Manufacturing and Services Sectors. Economic Papers 336. European Economy.

Kutas, G. 2010. Impact of the Doha Round on the European Agricultural Sector. Ph.D. diss., Sciences Po, Paris.

Kreinin, M. E. 1973, September. Some Economic consequences of reverse preferences. *Journal of Common Market Studies* Volume 11, Issue 3, pages 161–172.

Messerlin, P. 2001. Measuring the Costs of Protection in Europe. European Commercial Policy in the 2000s. Peterson Institute for International Economics.

Messerlin, P. 2007. Economic and Regulatory Reforms in Europe: Past Experiences and Future Challenges. Sixth Snape Lecture. Productivity Commission, Australia. www.pc.gov.au.

Messerlin, P. 2008. The EC neighbourhood policy: an economic review. *Journal of International Trade and Diplomacy* 2(2), pp. 25–54.

Messerlin, P. Forthcoming. The Doha Round. In A. Lukauskas, R. M. Stern, and G. Zanini, eds., Handbook of Trade Policy for Development. Oxford University Press.

Miroudot, S., J. Sauvage, and B. Shepherd. 2010, May. Measuring the Costs of International Trade in Services. GEM Working Paper. http://gem.sciences-po.fr.

Nicoletti, Giuseppe. 2000, 16 October. Regulation in Services: OECD Patterns and Economic Implications. OECD Economics Department Working Paper. Paris: OECD.

OECD. 2006. OECD's FDI regulatory Restrictiveness Index: Revision and Extension to More Economies. Working Papers on International investment, no. 2006/4.

Orden, D., T. Josling, and D. Blandford. 2010. WTO Disciplines on Agricultural Support: Seeking a Fair Basis for Trade.

World Bank, 2010. Doing Business. World Bank, Washington, DC.

World Trade Organization, 2001. Trade Policy Review: the European Communities. WTO, Geneva.

World Trade Organization, 2009. Trade Policy Review: the European Communities. WTO, Geneva.

World Trade Organization, 2001. Trade Policy Review: China. WTO, Geneva.

World Trade Organization, 2006. Trade Policy Review: China. WTO, Geneva.

World Trade Organization, 2009. Trade Policy Review: WTO, Geneva.

CHAPTER 10

CHANGING COMMERCIAL POLICY IN JAPAN, 1985–2010

MASAHIRO KAWAI AND SHUJIRO URATA

1. FROM MANAGING TRADE FRICTIONS WITH THE UNITED STATES TO FORGING ECONOMIC PARTNERSHIP AGREEMENTS

Japan is the first country in post–World War II East Asia that significantly benefited from the open multilateral trading regime and achieved rapid industrialization and economic growth through trade expansion. Since its accession to the General Agreement on Tariffs and Trade (GATT) in 1955, Japan began to liberalize crossborder trade restrictions through reductions of quantitative restrictions, tariffs, and other nontariff barriers mainly in manufactured goods trade. But its economic success created a series of trade frictions with other industrialized economies, particularly the United States, between the 1960s and the 1990s, due to Japan's explosive export growth and large trade surpluses.

Starting in the 1980s and continuing through most of the 1990s, Japan's trade policy was centered on how to handle the U.S. demands to curb Japan's explosive growth in exports of manufactured products, such as color televisions, industrial machinery, automobiles, and other machinery products, and to open its "closed" markets to U.S. imports such as semiconductors, automobiles, beef, agricultural products, and financial services. The United States often applied pressure on Japan by using the threat of protectionist measures such as Section 301 of the Trade Act of 1974 (Super 301), and Japan had to respond through "voluntary export restraints" and/or "voluntary import expansions."[1]

Japan's economic structure began to change significantly after the sharp, rapid yen appreciation following the Plaza Accord of 1985.[2] Japanese firms, through foreign direct investment (FDI), began to locate their production sites to more cost-effective Asian emerging economies, initially in the newly industrialized economies (NIEs)—that is, Hong Kong, Korea, Singapore, and Taipei,China—then to middle-income Association of Southeast Asian Nations (ASEAN) countries and, more recently, to China. This contributed to the formation of production networks and supply chains throughout East Asia. Japan began to trade more with these East Asian economies than with the United States, by using these economies as a production platform to manufacture goods for Japan's and other advanced countries' markets.

Such a fundamental change in Japan's trade and associated economic structures, together with the establishment of the World Trade Organization (WTO) in 1995, significantly reduced trade frictions with the United States. Japan's trade surplus, both overall and with the United States, persisted, but the U.S. trade deficit began to balloon to high levels, making Japan no longer the most important surplus country for the United States. The WTO's enhanced dispute settlement mechanism allowed Japan to bring the bilateral trade issues with the United States to the dispute settlement panel. Japan's commercial policy began to pay increasing attention to forging institutional ties with East Asian economies, which became the most important trade partner for Japan.

At the turn of the century, Japan started to shift the focus of commercial policy towards pursuing trade and investment liberalization and deepening economic relationships with its trade partners, particularly its East Asian neighbors, through economic partnership agreements (EPAs), which are more comprehensive than free trade agreements (FTAs). The Japan-Singapore Economic Partnership Agreement in 2002 was the first EPA ever implemented by Japan. The *White Paper on International Trade 2003*, published by Japan's Ministry of International Trade and Industry (presently Ministry of Economy, Trade, and Industry), argued the need for pursuing a multitrack approach to trade policy, centered on the WTO and bilateral and plurilateral EPAs. As it recognized the useful role of EPAs as an option for achieving trade liberalization, the Japanese government expected EPAs to play a positive role for promoting Japan's economic growth—through providing business opportunities for Japanese firms in EPA partner countries, strengthening economic ties and cooperation with EPA partners, and facilitating domestic policy reforms such as agricultural and labor market reforms in Japan.

This chapter examines the changing nature of Japan's commercial policy over the last 25 years. Section 2 reviews the changing structures of trade, FDI, and the economy in Japan that underlay policy changes. Section 3 focuses on Japan's commercial policy between 1985 and 1999, when policy-makers adopted a two-track approach of relying on multilateral liberalization under the GATT/WTO and open regionalism under Asia-Pacific Economic Cooperation (APEC) on the one hand and on the bilateral trade relationship with the United States on the other. Section 4 examines Japan's more recent commercial policy since the turn of the century as the country increasingly began to rely on bilateral and plurilateral EPAs, particularly with—but not limited to—East Asian economies. We argue that agricultural sector liberalization is key to the further integration of Japan with the Asian and global economies. Section 5 concludes.

2. Japan's Changing Trade and Economic Structure

It is well known that Japan's post–World War II economic reconstruction and industrialization was aided by the liberal international trading regime. With its accession to GATT in 1955, Japan began to liberalize international trade by reducing quantitative restrictions, tariffs, and other nontariff barriers on manufactured imports. In 1964, Japan became an International Monetary Fund (IMF) Article 8 member and eliminated exchange controls on current account transactions. In the same year, it joined the Organisation for Economic Co-operation and Development (OECD) and began to liberalize the policies and rules on international capital flows, particularly for FDI. Japan's trade started to expand in the 1960s, and its outward FDI became active in the 1970s.

Over time, the structure of Japan's exports shifted sequentially from labor-intensive products such as clothing and textiles to capital-intensive products such as electrical appliances, iron and steel, and automobiles, and then to technology-intensive products such as machine tools and semiconductors. The shift in the structure of exports reflected the changing patterns of Japan's comparative advantages. But it was in the mid-1980s when Japan's trade and FDI structures underwent a significant transformation.

Trade and Investment Expansion

Until the mid-1980s, Japan's major trading partners were the United States, Europe, East Asia, and oil-producing countries. Although the share of trade with East Asia was comparable to the share of trade with the United States in 1980, the United States was a prime, expanding market for Japan's producers. The share of exports to the United States rose in the 1980s, fueling Japan's trade frictions with the United States, as will be discussed in the next subsection. The importance of East Asia as a trading partner for Japan began to rise in the second half of the 1980s (see fig. 10.1).

The substantial rise in the yen's value following the Plaza Accord of 1985 (see fig. 10.2) provided a strong impetus for the change in patterns of Japan's trade and FDI. Facing the rising cost of domestic production, Japanese manufacturing firms decided to move to cost-effective emerging East Asia, in order to cope with the declining international price competitiveness of the products manufactured domestically.[3] In the 1980s, several emerging East Asian economies—starting with the NIEs

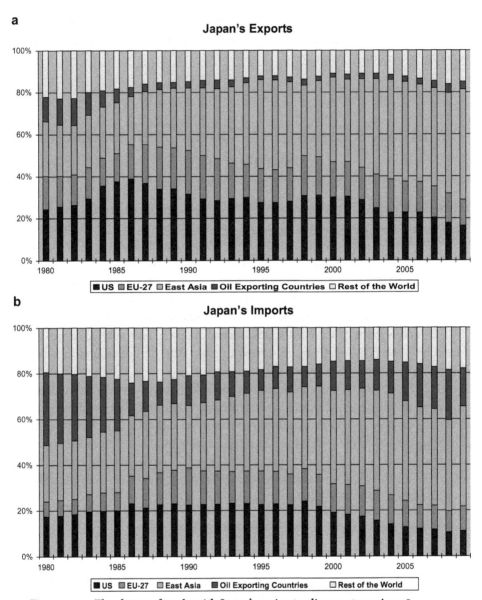

Figure 10.1. The shares of trade with Japan's major trading partners in 1980–2009.
Source: IMF, Direction of Trade Statistics, CD-ROM.

and middle-income ASEAN countries such as Malaysia, Thailand, Indonesia, and the Philippines—adopted outward-oriented policies of liberalizing trade and FDI regimes and deregulating domestic economic activities. Such policy changes were designed to alter the incentives in the economy from import substitution to export promotion and raise the attractiveness of these economies to foreign investors, thereby promoting economic growth. A combination of higher costs of production in Japan due to the sharp yen appreciation and outward-oriented economic reforms in emerging Asia motivated Japanese firms to invest in these economies.

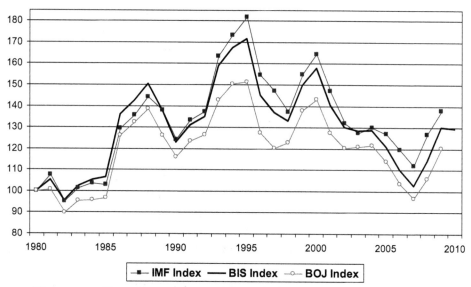

Figure 10.2. Alternative measures of the real effective exchange rate of the yen
(1980 = 100).

Source: IMF, International Financial Statistics, CD-ROM; Bank for International Settlements (BIS) and Bank of Japan (BOJ) websites.

In the second half of the 1980s and throughout the 1990s, Japanese manufacturing FDI expanded in emerging East Asia, initially to the NIEs, then to middle-income ASEAN countries, and more recently to China. Japanese multinational corporations (MNCs) began to form supply chains and production networks in East Asia, in industries such as electronics, automobiles, and other machinery products. Essentially, they fragmented the entire production process into several subprocesses, located these subprocesses throughout East Asia by taking into account each economy's comparative advantage—represented by its factor proportions and technological capabilities—and linked these subprocesses through trade across East Asia as if each economy were a factory.[4] In this way, Japanese MNCs developed vertical, inter-subprocess division of labor and intraindustry trade in East Asia, between their home country parents and foreign affiliates, or between the foreign affiliates. Such activities were supported by industrial infrastructure development such as power, telecommunications, and transport; a rapid reduction of information and communications costs due to the recent information and communication technology (ICT) revolution; and a reduction of the logistics cost, due to greater liberalization of business services that enabled different production subprocesses to be linked more easily. Intrafirm trade began to account for a substantial share of trade for these MNCs, particularly their Asian affiliates in their total trade with Japan.

Initially led by the Japanese MNCs and later joined by U.S. and European MNCs and, more recently, by emerging Asian firms, East Asia has been transformed into a large manufacturing base that serves the global market. This "factory Asia" has seen a persistent rise of intraregional trade in industrial materials, parts, and components, and capital goods for the production of finished manufacturing goods. Factory Asia has been built on the strong nexus between trade and investment. For example, Kawai and Urata (1998) presented some evidence that Japan's trade and FDI were largely complementary, that is, FDI created trade, and trade induced further FDI.

The Asian financial crisis of 1997–1998 had a significant economic and financial impact on many East Asian economies but had only a temporary negative impact on the region's trade and FDI. In fact, the recovery of the East Asian economies from the crisis was supported by a mutually reinforcing process of intraregional trade expansion as the global economy began to grow in 1999 and created demand for East Asian exports. The post–Asian financial crisis period saw a rapid rise of the role of China in "factory Asia." China emerged as one of the most active assemblers of Asian manufacturing products, importing technology-intensive parts and components from such neighboring economies as Japan, Korea, and Taipei,China. China began to expand its trade volume rapidly and became the most important trading partner for many East Asian economies, including Japan.

The global economy, trade, and investment grew briskly during the period 2002–2007, until the global financial crisis erupted in 2008. The crisis had significant contractionary effects on international trade and investment globally; international trade shrank by 23% in 2009 from 2008. Japan's exports and output were severely affected by the crisis. Its exports collapsed in late 2008 and early 2009, and real GDP fell sharply.

Japan's exports declined significantly for two reasons (Kawai and Takagi 2009). First, Japan's exports of consumer durables to the United States and Europe collapsed because of the sharp demand contraction there. Second, its exports of industrial supplies and capital goods to emerging Asia also collapsed because emerging Asia saw a decline in exports of manufactured products to the United States and Europe and, thus, reduced its import of the industrial supplies and capital goods necessary to produce its exports. By the second half of the 2000s, over 90% of Japanese exports consisted of highly income-elastic industrial supplies, capital goods, and consumer durables. Hence, once the U.S. and European economies collapsed rapidly, this exerted a severe negative influence on Japanese exports directly and indirectly through emerging East Asia.[5]

Changing Industrial Structure in Japan

The industrial structure of Japan has undergone significant transformations over time in the post–World War II period. In particular, the composition of the manufacturing sector has changed. In the 1950s and 1960s, high levels of investment in plant and equipment and imports of advanced technologies helped establish heavy industries, such as iron and steel, shipbuilding, machinery, and chemicals. The oil price shock of 1973 forced the Japanese industries to adopt energy-efficient technologies and develop higher value added products, such as automobiles, electronics, electric machinery, communication equipment and apparatus, and machinery with electronic controls. The industrial structure has changed since 1985, when the real effective exchange rate of the yen began to appreciate significantly (see fig. 10.2). The yen's real effective appreciation continued for 10 years as a trend; it peaked in 1995, when the level was some 80% higher than in 1980, and then began to decline as a trend until 2007, except for the brief 1999–2001 period when the value rose temporarily.

From a theoretical perspective, a high real value of the yen raises the price of nontradable goods relative to the price of tradable goods and, thus, encourages the production of nontradable goods relative to tradable goods; resources therefore should shift away from the tradable goods sector and toward the nontradable goods sector. As this relative price change reduces the international price competitiveness of manufacturing firms that produce tradable goods, it encourages them to shift their production activities abroad through FDI. Indeed, this is what we observed.

Figure 10.3 depicts the production of nontradable goods relative to tradable goods between 1980 and 2007 in terms of both nominal and real outputs. The two solid lines represent the respective trend lines.[6] The figure clearly indicates that the relative size of nontradable goods output rose steadily over this period in terms of nominal value, although the relative size of nontradable goods output was virtually flat when measured in terms of real values, reflecting the relatively more rapid growth of nontradable goods prices than tradable goods prices. An important point is that during the period of trend yen appreciation, that is, 1986–1995, the relative size of the nontradable goods sector rose. Even though the yen rate began trend depreciation in 1996, the size of nontradable goods output remained above the trend line—regardless of whether it is measured in nominal or real values—until 2002, because the real effective exchange rate, though declining, was still high.

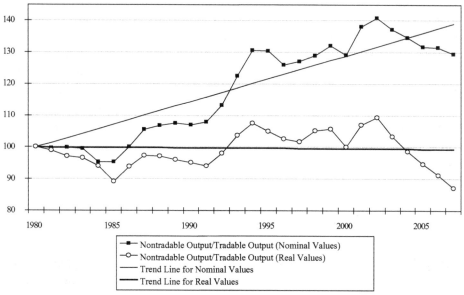

Figure 10.3. Production of nontradable goods relative to tradable goods (1980 = 100).
Source: Update of Kawai and Takagi (2011). Compiled from National Income Account, Cabinet Office.

It is interesting to note that when the real effective yen showed a clear sign of weakening, the size of nontradable goods output relative to tradable goods output began to decline from a peak achieved in 2002. This was matched by Japan's recovery from the "lost decade." When Japan began slowly to emerge out of the prolonged stagnation, it relied on the export sector as an engine of growth as the yen fell in real effective terms. As a result, not only did the GDP share of exports increase but also Japan's overall openness rose throughout the 2000s, until the country was hit by the global financial crisis. For instance, Japan's exports to GDP ratio, which was only 11% in 2000, rose to over 17% in 2008. Over the same period, trade openness, measured by the sum of exports and imports as a percentage of GDP, increased from about 20% of GDP to almost 35%.

3. JAPAN'S COMMERCIAL POLICY IN THE 1980S AND 1990S

Japan–U.S. Trade Frictions

Japan experienced various types of trade frictions with advanced economies, particularly the United States, due to its explosive export growth. Trade frictions between Japan and the United States go back to the 1950s and spread from Japanese exports of clothing and textiles, electrical appliances, and iron and steel to the exports and imports of automobiles and high-technology products—such as machine tools and semiconductors—and the imports of agricultural products in the 1980s.[7] Facing a surge of imports of certain products from Japan, the U.S. government occasionally requested that the Japanese government voluntarily restrain exports of these products. Textiles and steel were primary examples. Some Japanese industries that encountered trade threats in the United States, such as the textile, color television, and iron and steel industries, were persuaded to adopt "voluntary export restraints." Other firms started to invest in assembly or production plants in the United States, for example, in the electrical appliance and automotive industries, to avoid protectionist trade measures. Some Japanese firms shifted their production plants to East Asia to avoid discriminatory trade measures imposed by the U.S. authorities on Japanese products.

Bilateral Trade Frictions

In the early 1980s, when the Reagan administration adopted a mix of tight monetary policy and lax fiscal policy, U.S. imports surged and Japan's exports to the United States expanded, reflecting the rising demand in the United States and the real appreciation of the U.S. dollar. As a result, not only did both Japan's trade surpluses and the U.S. trade deficits rise (see fig. 10.4) but also the Japan–U.S.

bilateral trade imbalance expanded, which led to a new stage of Japan–U.S. trade frictions focusing on economy-wide structural issues, going beyond sectoral trade frictions.

The U.S. government took the view that Japan's distorted market structure, closed to foreign products and conducive to creating trade surpluses,[8] was the fundamental cause of both Japan's trade surplus and the U.S. deficits. The Japanese market was closed because of high import barriers to foreign products, due not only to border restrictions—such as tariffs and quantitative restrictions—but also to "behind-the-border" regulations and market practices. So the U.S. government argued that if the Japanese market had been opened by reducing such import barriers, U.S. exports to Japan would have risen and the U.S.–Japan bilateral trade imbalance and the overall U.S. deficit would have declined. Therefore, Japan should open up its economy to foreign competition by eliminating import-unfriendly restrictions and practices.

In contrast, the Japanese side took the view that the large trade imbalance reflected the large savings and investment imbalances in the United States and Japan (Komiya and Itoh 1988). Unless these domestic imbalances were corrected, the trade imbalance would persist. To reduce the trade deficit, the United States was advised to reduce the budget deficit and increase household savings. To reduce the trade surplus, Japan would stimulate domestic demand through structural reforms and deregulation of various restrictions. The so-called Maekawa Report (Kokusai Kyocho no tameno Keizai Kozo Chosei Kenkyukai 1986), produced in the mid-1980s, urged the Japanese government to implement such a policy.

In the "Structural Impediments Initiative" (1989–1990), the United States addressed squarely the need to deregulate Japan's "closed" markets for automobiles, color film, retail distribution services, and insurance services and demanded that

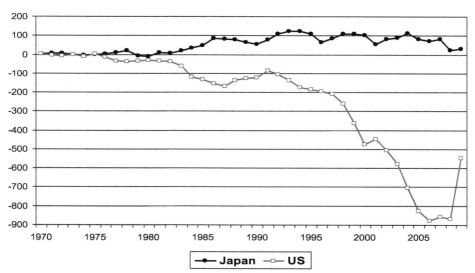

Figure 10.4. Trade imbalances of Japan and the U.S., 1970–2009 (billion US$).
Source: IMF, International Financial Statistics, CD-ROM.

the Japanese government dismantle undue restrictions and cease interventions that would limit imports from abroad. The U.S. side pointed out that exclusive transactions practices among Japanese firms, the Large-Scale Retail Store Law, and other measures restricted imports of foreign products. Exclusive transactions practices, based on the "*keiretsu* system" (a risk- and profit-sharing system among a group of companies with interlocking business relationships and shareholdings) were considered to put foreign competitors at a disadvantage because they were outsiders of the group.[9,10] The Large-Scale Retail Store Law, which limited the operations of large-scale stores, was considered to inhibit the import of goods to Japan through American-style large-scale retail stores. The United States argued that such unjust public interventions should be lifted so as not to impede imports of foreign products.

The Case of the Semiconductor Disputes

This case was an interesting one, as it resulted in "voluntary import expansion" on the part of Japanese firms. Japanese semiconductor producers had been expanding their market share for semiconductors globally, including in the United States and Japan. The Semiconductor Industry Association of the United States argued that U.S. producers were disadvantaged because of (1) the Japanese government's public support for Japanese firms and (2) the exclusive *keiretsu* relationships among Japanese firms in Japan, despite the fact that Japanese firms could freely compete against U.S. firms in the U.S. market.[11] The United States took the position that as the import barriers in Japan distorted the country's resource allocation, it would be desirable for the government to intervene in order to correct such distortions by raising the share of foreign products in the market. The United States pressured Japan to accept such market opening measures with the threat of using Section 301 of the Trade Act of 1974 (Super 301).[12] Given that the activation of Super 301 would severely restrict Japan's exports to U.S. markets, the Japanese government yielded to the U.S. demand. The two sides reached the semiconductor trade agreement (SCTA) in 1986 to increase the share of foreign-produced semiconductors to 20% in the Japanese semiconductor market, on the assumption that the Japanese government could manage market shares of the private semiconductor industry.[13]

Itoh and Shimoi (2009) argued that the Japan–U.S. bilateral semiconductor agreement was trade distorting. First, there was no convincing evidence of the presence of import barriers. Even if such barriers had existed, an appropriate policy would have been to directly address such barriers themselves rather than agreeing on a certain numerical target. Second, the U.S. intention was to increase the share of U.S.-produced, rather than foreign-produced, semiconductors in Japan's market. That is, the "voluntary import expansion" was not designed to increase overall imports of foreign semiconductors from abroad but to secure a certain market share of foreign (largely U.S.) products. To the extent that this type of "managed trade" did not expand overall import value or did not reduce semiconductor prices, it likely distorted the market and did not necessarily serve the interest of consumers.

In contrast, Tyson (1993) argued that the major impediments to the Japanese semi-conductor market were rooted in the unique character of Japanese business organiza-tions and their distinctive relationships with one another and with the Japanese government. She contended that voluntary import expansions were inferior to the first-best approach of unimpeded market competition, but that they could sometimes prove more useful than doing nothing when such competition was constrained by structural impediments and foreign trading practices. Hence, the SCTA was useful in stimulating competition in the Japanese market where competition was effectively hampered.

Essentially, the U.S. government used the threat of severely restricting imports of major products from Japan, and this aggressive U.S. policy toward Japan gener-ated resentment in Japan. Nonetheless, to the extent that the Japanese government addressed many "behind-the-border" regulations, there is no doubt that the policy had a positive impact on Japanese market openness, efficiency, and transparency and improved the economic welfare of Japanese consumers.

Japan–Europe Trade Frictions

Japan also had some trade frictions with Europe, although they did not become as contentious as the Japan–U.S. trade frictions. As was the case for Japan–U.S. trade frictions, expansion of Japan's trade surplus with Europe precipitated Japan–Europe trade frictions. Japan–Europe trade frictions in the post–World War II period began in the late 1960s, when the European Community (EC) imposed import restrictions on rapidly increasing Japanese exports of color televisions. Trade frictions contin-ued into the 1970s and 1980s as products that caused problems expanded to include electronic machinery, automobiles, and machine tools. During the 1970s, Japanese producers of automobiles, videocassette recorders, machine tools, microwave ovens, semiconductors, and other products responded to trade frictions mainly through voluntary export restraints. However, the EC began to use antidumping litigation and duties to limit Japanese exports of ball bearings, copying machines, printers, microwave ovens, and semiconductors. The European governments attempted to protect and promote European producers, particularly those in electronics indus-tries, by limiting imports of Japanese products. Responding to these measures, Japanese firms actively set up production bases in the EC by undertaking FDI.

One noted case of Europe's import restrictions against Japanese products took place in Poitiers, an inland city in France, between October 1982 and April 1983. In the so-called Battle of Poitiers, the French government limited the customs process-ing of all Japanese videocassette recorders to a small customs house in Poitiers.[14] As a result of this import-restricting measure, as many as 60,000 Japanese videocas-sette recorders were piled up in the warehouse one month after the implementation of the measure.[15] At that time, no French electronic producers were manufacturing videocassette recorders, so the French government's accusation claiming that the imports of Japanese videocassette recorders brought injury to French electronic producers was unfounded.

During the 1980s Japan's trade surplus against Europe expanded, and its magnitude was even larger than Europe's total exports to Japan. Irritated by this huge trade imbalance, European governments and the EC criticized Japan for having a closed market. Furthermore, emotional reactions, such as accusing Japanese people of being workaholics living in rabbit hutches, erupted in Europe.[16] Nonetheless, the Japan–Europe trade frictions did not go as deep as the Japan–U.S. trade conflicts in the sense of urging Japan to address the structurally "closed" nature of the economy and market. Japan–EC trade frictions dissipated in the 1990s mainly because of the yen appreciation, rise of Japanese FDI in Europe and the resulting expansion of local production, and less aggressive export behavior of Japanese firms.

The Role of the WTO and APEC

The Uruguay Round under GATT

The Uruguay Round of multilateral trade negotiations under the auspices of the GATT started in 1986 and was concluded in 1994. Although the negotiations lasted eight long years, the Uruguay Round made substantial progress toward liberalizing trade and FDI. The achievements included a reduction in tariff rates; framework agreements on trade in services, on intellectual property rights, and on trade-related investment measures; a timetable for phasing out all quantitative restrictions on trade; first steps toward bringing agricultural trade more firmly under a multilateral discipline; a stronger dispute settlement mechanism; and the establishment of the WTO.

Japan did not play a critical role in the Uruguay Round because it could not offer sufficient concessions on agricultural liberalization. In the negotiations, Japan argued that agricultural goods trade should be treated differently from manufactured goods trade because of the multifunctional role of agriculture—such as protecting the environment and preserving nature. But due to the lack of international support, Japan could neither lead nor exercise influence over the negotiations. Domestically, agricultural interests strongly advocated the continuation of protection, while nonagricultural interests did not present a sufficiently compelling case for opening the agricultural goods market.

Nonetheless the Uruguay Round agreement had significant impacts on Japan's commercial policy. First, partial liberalization of agricultural trade, including rice imports, was achieved. Japanese trade negotiators were persuaded that the country could no longer maintain the policy of protecting the agricultural sector while enjoying the benefit of liberalization of manufacturing trade. Although their original position stated that "no grain of rice would be allowed to come to the Japanese market," in the end they had to accept the "minimum access" approach to rice imports. Essentially, Japan abandoned its policy of prohibiting the import of rice and began to allow a certain amount of rice imports, equivalent of 4–8% of domestic consumption. Soon after this, Japan shifted to tariffication of rice imports by setting a prohibitively high tariff rate of 778% on rice imports.

To deal with the trade adjustment in agriculture, necessitated by the partial liberalization of rice imports, the Japanese government provided to the domestic agricultural industry as much as 6 trillion yen. Although the intention could be justified, the program was not successful in facilitating meaningful adjustment, because a large part of the funds were not spent for upgrading skills of impacted workers, enhancing labor productivity, or concentrating farmland in the hands of large-scale productive farmers but for different purposes, such as drilling for hot springs or paving country roads.

Second, the way Japan handled the bilateral trade frictions with the United States changed in a fundamental way. Before the establishment of the WTO, Japan tended to respond to the U.S. pressure to reduce its exports to the United States and open its market to U.S. products by agreeing to "voluntary export restraints" and "voluntary import expansion," respectively. With the establishment of the WTO, Japan began to use its enhanced dispute settlement mechanism.[17]

The Japanese government essentially found three reasons for bringing the bilateral issues to the multilateral mechanism of WTO dispute settlement. First, the multilateral forum would deliver decisions based on objective trading rules and norms rather than on the asymmetric bargaining power between disputing parties. Second, even if Japan lost the case, it would be easier for the government to convince the domestic stakeholders to accept the WTO decisions and to make the appropriate national policy responses, such as adjustment policies. Third, such policy responses would take the form of addressing the fundamental problem, such as changing domestic regulations, rules, and procedures, rather than putting in place "managed trade" measures such as numerical targets.

Japan indeed took the case of the color film dispute to the WTO panel. Eastman Kodak argued that Japan's film market was unduly controlled by Fuji Film and, as a result, closed to foreign products, such as Kodak film, and in 1995 presented the case for sanctioning Japan to the U.S. trade representative. The Japanese government argued against Eastman Kodak and brought the case to the WTO. The WTO panel delivered its decision in support of Japan in 1998.

Since this incident, there has been no major Japan–U.S. bilateral trade dispute. Six factors could explain this. First, the availability of the WTO's dispute settlement mechanism may well have deterred the U.S. authorities from resorting to bilateral negotiations with trade sanction threats. Second, Japan undertook a number of policy reforms such as those in the financial system and corporate governance, the areas that were the main focus of U.S. concerns over the structure of the Japanese economy. Third, Japanese firms began to expand production in the United States through FDI and, thus, created a local constituency that sometimes opposed U.S. government policy-making that could have limited imports from Japan. Fourth, Japan's trade surplus was no longer the most important source of the U.S. trade deficit, as the U.S. deficit began to balloon in the second half of the 1990s. The trade and economic structure of Japan had changed in such a way as to not run a large bilateral trade imbalance with the United States. Fifth, the stagnation of the Japanese economy after the bursting of the asset market bubble may have reduced the U.S. perception of the Japan threat. Finally, rising competition from, and expanding trade deficits with, emerging East Asian economies began to divert U.S. attention away from Japan toward these economies, such as China.

APEC

A voluntary and unilateral approach under APEC has also contributed to the liberalization and facilitation of trade and FDI for Japan as well as emerging East Asian economies. Established in 1989, APEC began with 12 members and has grown into a transregional cooperation organization with 21 members.[18] This forum's membership includes some countries with great influence in the world economy, such as the United States, Japan, China, and Russia. APEC has been the only international economic forum in which the U.S. and East Asian economies hold policy dialogue on a wide range of economic issues and pursue trade and investment liberalization outside the GATT/WTO.

The aim of APEC has been to promote free and open regional trade and investment and contribute to economic growth in the Asia-Pacific region and the world. The means employed to attain this end have been to liberalize and facilitate trade and investment and to engage in economic and technical cooperation. Decisions to act are left to the discretion of each member without including legally binding negotiations, treaties, and conventions, such as those imposed by the WTO. In addition, APEC liberalization measures are also applied to nonmembers, thereby enforcing most-favored-nation (MFN) treatment without discrimination. Thus, APEC's approach has been termed "open regionalism."

Japan has played an important role in APEC. On the occasion of the organization's birth, it joined with Australia in performing the role of midwife and subsequently has made major contributions in many areas, including organization-building and cooperative activities. In Bogor, Indonesia, APEC in 1994 agreed on what was considered to be its primary goal: the achievement of free and open trade and investment by no later than 2010 in the case of developed economies and no later than 2020 in the case of developing economies. But it was in Osaka, Japan, that APEC in 1995 adopted an action plan for achieving this goal, the Osaka Action Agenda. This agenda specified principles, frameworks, and actions in the three areas of trade and investment liberalization, trade and investment facilitation, and economic and technical cooperation. Among the general principles for liberalization and facilitation were comprehensiveness, WTO consistency, comparability, and nondiscrimination. The economic and technical cooperation was to be implemented by the APEC members as soon as they were ready, making use of action, forums, and other means. For Japan—and other developed economies in the APEC region—2010 was both the deadline to meet the Bogor Goals and the year in which it hosted the annual APEC summit.

The APEC leaders assessed the achievement of the Bogor Goals for 13 economies and reported that while more work remains to be done, these 13 economies made significant progress toward achieving the Bogor Goals (APEC 2010).[19] They highlighted the areas where barriers to trade and investment remain and, accordingly, where more concerted progress can be made by APEC.

One of APEC's most significant achievements was to help both China and Taipei,China to join the WTO in December 2001 and January 2002, respectively. However, the effectiveness of APEC has been challenged recently, due to the limited role it played at the time of the 1997–1998 Asian financial crisis and the slow progress of unilateral, voluntary liberalization since the early 2000s.

Japan's Slow Tariff Reduction

Since its accession to the GATT, Japan has been liberalizing trade by cutting tariff rates, reducing quantitative restrictions, and addressing other nontariff barriers. Figure 10.5 demonstrates how Japan has been reducing the average tariff rates over the past 20 years. Japan saw a significant tariff reduction in 1995 as a result of the conclusion of the Uruguay Round, but the tariff reduction since then has been very slow. This is in sharp contrast with other high-income OECD countries and the world as a whole. Although Japan's average tariff rates are much lower than the world average and marginally lower than the high-income OECD country average, the rest of the world has been reducing tariffs since 1996, while Japan has not. This implies that if the Doha Development Round negotiations

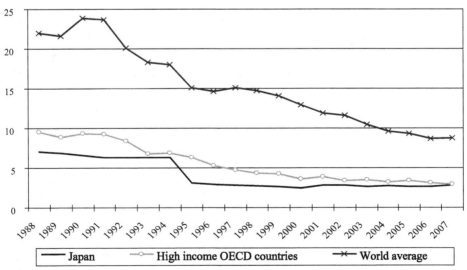

Figure 10.5. Trends in Japan's average applied tariff rates, 1988–2007 (unweighted in percent).

Source: Various sources from UNCTAD TRAINS database, WTO IDB database, World Bank, OECD, and IMF.

should become stalled, Japan needs to find another way to further reduce the tariff rates.

4. JAPAN'S COMMERCIAL POLICY SINCE 2000

Adoption of EPA Initiatives

At the turn of the century, Japan began to adopt the policy of promoting trade and investment liberalization through bilateral and plurilateral trade arrangements. Notably, since November 2002, Japan has implemented 10 bilateral EPAs with seven ASEAN members, Mexico, Chile, and Switzerland and one plurilateral EPA with ASEAN, while pursuing official negotiations with five trading partners (see table 10.1 for a summary of Japan's EPA initiatives). Japan's move to use EPAs as a commercial policy tool has spawned FTA moves by other East Asian economies, particularly China, Korea, and ASEAN countries. In response to the Japan–Singapore EPA negotiations that began in January 2001, China and ASEAN began official negotiations on closer economic partnership that were concluded in November 2002. Then Japan completed a series of bilateral EPAs with Malaysia, Thailand, Indonesia, Brunei Darussalam, the Philippines, and Viet Nam, while implementing an EPA with ASEAN as a group. Japan, China, and ASEAN have been joined by Korea, India, Australia, and New Zealand in active FTA moves. In this sense, there have been domino and bandwagon effects among these and other economies in their drive for FTAs/EPAs.

Mexico was the first country that approached Japan for a possible EPA. Following the Mexican president's proposal to establish a possible Japan–Mexico EPA in November 1998, think tanks in both countries conducted a study on a possible bilateral EPA, and an official study group was set up in September 2001 to examine the details of a possible EPA. Official negotiations began in November 2002, followed by an agreement in September 2004. The Japan–Mexico EPA was enacted in April 2005. The most serious obstacle in the negotiations was Japan's strong resistance to liberalization of trade in agricultural products, specifically pork, beef, and chicken products, oranges, and orange juice. In the end, Japan agreed to open up these markets by increasing import quotas—not by removing tariffs, as it should under FTAs that are consistent with the WTO rules—in exchange for Mexico's agreement to liberalize steel and automobile markets within 10 and 7 years, respectively. Mexico opened its market to all imports from Japan, while Japan opened its market to only 84% of its imports from Mexico. The Japan–Mexico EPA was strongly supported by the Japanese business sector, which felt that their business was suffering from the loss of market access and business opportunities, including government procurement, in the absence of an EPA with Mexico.

Table 10.1. Japan's EPAs implemented or under official negotiations

	Partner country/ region	Date negotiation begun	Date signed	Date implemented
Implemented	Singapore	January 2001	January 2002	November 2002
	Mexico	November 2002	September 2004	April 2005
	Malaysia	January 2004	December 2005	July 2006
	Chile	February 2006	March 2007	September 2007
	Thailand	February 2004	April 2007	November 2007
	Indonesia	July 2005	August 2007	July 2008
	Brunei Darussalam	June 2006	June 2007	July 2008
	Philippines	February 2004	September 2006	December 2008
	ASEAN	April 2005	April 2008	December 2008
	Switzerland	May 2007	February 2009	September 2009
	Viet Nam	January 2007	December 2008	October 2009
	India	January 2007	February 2011	August 2011
Under official negotiation	Korea[1]	December 2003		
	GCC[2]	September 2006		
	Australia	April 2007		
	Peru	May 2009		

[1] Japan's EPA negotiations with Korea began in December 2003 but were suspended in November 2004.
[2] Cooperation Council for Arab States of the Gulf.
Source: Ministry of Foreign Affairs.

Japan's approach has been to establish an EPA, rather than simply an FTA, by covering wider issues of WTO-plus elements. Such elements include the four Singapore issues (trade facilitation, investment, government procurement, and competition policy) and other provisions such as intellectual property rights, labor standards and mobility, and cooperation on the environmental, information technology, and small- and medium-sized enterprises. The four Singapore issues were conditionally included in the work program for the Doha Round in November 2001 but were subsequently dropped at the WTO Ministerial Conference in Cancun in 2004. Japan's EPAs with Indonesia and the Philippines include provisions on the movement of natural persons in the area of nursing and old-age care. Intellectual property rights are included in all the EPAs Japan has concluded.

Motives behind Japan's EPA Strategy

Japan came to recognize EPAs as one of its trade policy options, in addition to the multilateral framework under the WTO.[20] Several factors contributed to this shift in Japan's trade policy.

First, greater access to foreign markets was one of the important motives that aroused Japan's interest in EPAs. Japan was one of the few countries in the world that did not have any bilateral, plurilateral, or regional trade arrangement such as FTAs until the early twenty-first century, despite the fact that an increasing number of FTAs had become established globally. Facing the world market, which had many discriminatory trading arrangements, in particular those in Europe and North America, Japan felt an urgent need to secure market access for Japanese firms by setting up EPAs. As an EPA eliminates trade barriers in EPA partners, Japanese firms are able to enjoy more business opportunities, especially when multilateral trade negotiations under the Doha Development Agenda were making little progress.

For internationally competitive Japanese firms, it is very important to have more business opportunities when competing with foreign companies. For example, EPAs with East Asian countries would increase Japan's exports to these countries, which are presently protected with high tariff and nontariff barriers.[21] In addition, Japanese firms could expand their business operations in EPA partners via FDI, as an EPA includes FDI liberalization and other measures contributing to creating a business-friendly environment.[22] Japan's EPA strategy focuses on East Asia, as establishing EPAs with East Asian countries would contribute to economic prosperity and, hence, political and social stability in the region, which in turn would benefit Japan.

The market access motive clearly played an important role for Japan in pursuing an EPA with Mexico. Thanks to the North American Free Trade Agreement (NAFTA) and the European Union (EU)–Mexico FTA, EU and U.S. firms could export their products to Mexico without tariffs. In order to export their products to Mexico, Japanese firms had to pay high tariffs, an average of 16.2% for all imports in 2001, which protected the Mexican market. Among Japanese manufacturing sectors, the automobile and steel industries were eager for the government to sign an EPA with Mexico. Japan's automobile industry was interested in expanding exports of finished cars to Mexico, while its steel industry was interested in exporting steel products, which were used for the production of electronics, household electrical appliances, general machinery, and automobiles by Japanese assembly firms operating in Mexico. In addition, the Mexican government allowed only FTA members to participate in the government procurement market. Mexico could impose such restrictions on government procurement because it was not a signatory to the WTO's government procurement code. Faced with these market access problems in Mexico, the Japanese business community vigorously pushed its government to obtain an EPA with Mexico. Essentially, the Japanese government used EPAs to combat discrimination in foreign markets, like Mexico, which favored those of Japan's competitors that were engaged in FTA networks.[23]

Second, stimulating structural reforms, which are required by EPAs, was considered essential to revitalize the Japanese economy. After the collapse of the asset price bubble in the early 1990s, the Japanese economy entered a long period of stagnation. Indeed, the 1990s was characterized as the "lost decade" for Japan. Although

Japan's post–World War II system contributed to high economic growth until the bubble arose, it became ineffective after it burst. To put Japan back on a sustainable growth path, a series of structural reforms are needed, including those addressing the rapid demographic change associated with a population that is aging and declining in number. From this perspective, EPAs can trigger a series of structural reforms in Japan, such as labor market and agricultural reforms.

Third, Japan expects to contribute to the strengthening of the world trade system under the WTO, as FTAs/EPAs could have harmful impacts on the world trade system because of their discriminatory nature. While acknowledging the possibility of such a harmful effect, it would be possible to maximize the favorable effects from EPAs to more than offset it. For example, Japan could contribute to the WTO system by successfully forming EPAs that include many "WTO-plus" elements.

Japan's Approach to Regional Economic Integration

Forming a Region-Wide EPA

There is increasing recognition in Japan of the merits in forming a region-wide EPA as a means to consolidate the "noodle bowl," a plethora of bilateral and plurilateral agreements in East Asia. Such a large EPA would confer various economic benefits: (1) increase market access to goods, services, skills, and technology; (2) increase market size to permit specialization and realization of economies of scale; (3) facilitate the FDI activities and technology transfer of MNCs; and (4) permit simplification of tariff schedules, rules, and standards.

With key ASEAN+1 agreements—such as the ASEAN–Japan EPA, ASEAN–China FTA, ASEAN–Korea FTA, ASEAN–India FTA, and ASEAN–Australia and New Zealand FTA—implemented, the policy discussion in Asia is focusing on competing region-wide agreement proposals. They are an East Asia Free Trade Area (EAFTA) among ASEAN+3 countries (10 ASEAN member countries, China, Japan, and Korea) and a Comprehensive Economic Partnership for East Asia (CEPEA) among ASEAN+6 countries (ASEAN+3, India, Australia, and New Zealand). Japan takes the view that the region should create a CEPEA while China advocates the EAFTA. An important challenge is to identify which of the two, an EAFTA or a CEPEA, is more beneficial in terms of economic welfare for the regional and global economy.

Figure 10.6 presents the results of a computable general equilibrium (CGE) analysis for economies in Asia reported in Kawai and Wignaraja (2011). Three overall results can be highlighted from the CGE exercise in terms of change from 2017 baseline income projections: (1) a region-wide FTA, whether an EAFTA or CEPEA, offers larger gains to world income than the current wave of bilateral and plurilateral FTAs; (2) the CEPEA scenario, which is broader in terms of country coverage, offers larger gains to the world as a whole in terms of income than the EAFTA scenario; and (3) third parties outside either an EAFTA or CEPEA lose little from being

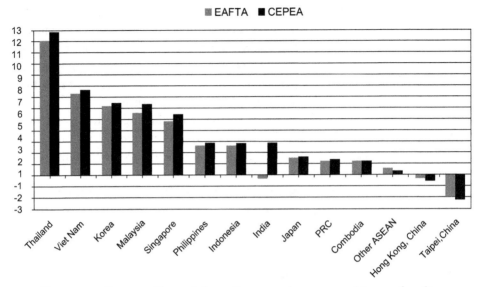

Figure 10.6. Income effects of alternative scenarios compared to 2017 baseline
(% change in GDP by economy).

Source: Kawai and Wignaraja (2011).

excluded from a region-wide agreement. The benefit to Japan as a result of an EAFTA or a CEPEA is around 1.5% of baseline GDP, which is smaller than the benefits to many other economies, but sizable for a large economy like Japan.

Thus, the CGE analysis demonstrates that a region-wide agreement in East Asia—particularly a CEPEA—would provide welfare gains over the present wave of ASEAN+1 FTAs. The gains to members of such an agreement are notable, while losses to nonmembers are relatively small. Accordingly, arguments for, and moves toward, a CEPEA are supported by economic modeling.

Political Economy Considerations of an East Asia–Wide EPA

Even though the consolidation of FTAs/EPAs into a region-wide agreement would yield large economic gains to Japan and Asia, the future path seems unclear. An important reason to establish an EAFTA is that production networks have been developed most significantly among the ASEAN+3 countries, and harmonizing rules of origin among these countries can produce a tangible benefit. The logic for a CEPEA is that the production network is beginning to embrace Australia and India. In addition, it would take more time to produce a region-wide EPA including India if that country were slow to liberalize, whereas it would be easier to form a CEPEA if India were to make tangible progress.

To form an East Asia–wide FPA, whether it would be an EAFTA or a CEPEA, it is important to create preconditions—or building blocks—for this. The missing link is an FTA/EPA among the "plus-three countries"—China, Japan, and Korea—which would need to coordinate their trade and FDI regimes.

On a possible Japan–China EPA, the Japanese government is concerned about the competitiveness of China's manufacturing sector and agricultural products. Japan wishes to treat China as a nonmarket economy so that it can safeguard against a surge of Chinese imports into Japanese markets, but the Chinese government insists on market economy status for itself. Japan also argues that China has yet to clearly demonstrate progress toward implementation of WTO entry commitments, with significant issues including clarity of regulations and rules over firms and protection of intellectual property rights. Japan would like to see improvements in government procurement practices and the elimination of policy bias favoring indigenous innovation by Chinese firms. Food safety issues are also a concern for Japan. The Japanese government has taken the position that an investment treaty should be a first condition before starting an EPA negotiation.[24]

Japan's primary concern over a Japan–Korea EPA is the competitiveness of Korea's agriculture and fishery sectors. In contrast, Korea is concerned about Japan's competitiveness in manufactured products (intermediate inputs), Korea's large tariff concessions required due to high MFN tariffs, and the risk of greater bilateral trade deficits with Japan.

Despite these problems, if Japan is able to craft a trilateral EPA with China and Korea or separate EPAs with each of them, a strong foundation for a possible EAFTA and a CEPEA could be built. This will require political commitment from the governments of all three countries. Forming a Free Trade Area of the Asia-Pacific (FTAAP) involving APEC members would be more complex than forming a CEPEA. An FTAAP could possibly be established, if a significant number of APEC economies (particularly including the United States) join the Trans-Pacific Partnership (TPP) agreement, the East Asian economies (particularly including China) conclude an EAFTA or CEPEA, and the two processes are merged. From this perspective, Japan may wish to join the TPP so that it could influence the future trade rule-making in the Asia-Pacific region.

Obstacles to Further Liberalization for Japan

Whether pursuing liberalization through the WTO or EPAs, Japan faces various obstacles. This section examines them.

Although trade and investment liberalization brings economic benefits to Japan as a whole, the benefits do not accrue to all sectors and individuals equally. Some sectors or groups are likely to suffer from negative consequences. Specifically, competitive sectors are likely to gain large benefits as firms in these sectors can find business opportunities in overseas markets, while uncompetitive sectors are likely to lose because competitive foreign firms would be able to compete successfully with them. These mixed impacts are expected from any type of trade liberalization, whether under the WTO or from a bilateral EPA.

For Japan, agriculture is the most sensitive sector in trade liberalization, regardless of its form, that is, whether a bilateral or regional framework under an EPA or a multilateral framework under the WTO. Japan has relatively low tariff protection on agricultural products in general, compared to other agricultural-product-importing countries. What is notable about agricultural protection in Japan is the very high protection given to several products through complicated protection systems, which combine import quotas and high tariffs. For example, the ad valorem tariff equivalent for some selected items, such as rice, wheat, sugar, butter, and *konnyaku* potato, are very high. In addition, as a part of the Uruguay Round agreement, Japan introduced a special safeguard system to deal with the damages caused by import surges.

Policies to protect the agricultural sector have been an obstacle in EPA negotiations for Japan. Japan excluded agricultural products from trade liberalization in the Japan–Singapore EPA, even though agricultural production in Singapore was very small. Pork products became a contentious issue in the Japan–Mexico EPA negotiations. Despite a strong demand from Mexico to reduce the level of protection on pork imports, Japan did not give in and instead increased import quotas on beef, chicken, oranges, and orange juice, which were not included in the initial request. Japan's EPA negotiations with other countries have also encountered the problem of import liberalization of agricultural products. The EPA negotiations where the import of various agricultural products faced Japan's strong opposition include the Japan–Philippines EPA (bananas, rice, wheat, starch, dairy products, beef, pork, sugar, canned pineapples), the Japan–Thailand EPA (rice, sugar, boneless chicken, processed chicken), and the Japan–Chile EPA (fish products, pork). In addition to the products listed above, various agricultural products could be identified as possibly sensitive in the TPP or FTAAP negotiations, for example, rice (Australia, U.S., China), beef and pork (Australia, U.S.), sugar (Australia), and dairy products (Australia, U.S.).

Among these highly protected items, rice is by far the most difficult item for Japan to liberalize, for several reasons. First is its importance in agricultural production, with its share amounting to approximately 25% of agricultural production.[25] Second is the geography of its production, with rice grown throughout Japan. Finally, farmers have a relatively strong voice in agricultural policy issues, due to the disproportionately high electoral powers allocated to rural areas. These factors result in strong political dynamics. In order to make agricultural production more efficient, productive, and competitive, it is essential to accelerate reform of the agricultural sector. The government should encourage the concentration of farmland in the hands of large-scale productive farmers, while at the same time assisting the farmers and farmworkers who are forced to leave the agricultural sector in upgrading their skills and knowledge so that they can be employed in other sectors of the economy.

5. Conclusion: The Way Forward

In the post–World War II period, Japan made use of global institutions (e.g., GATT, IMF, and OECD) and bilateral external pressures (especially, those from the U.S.) to reform its domestic economy through trade liberalization. Structural reforms contributed significantly to improve the competitiveness and productivity of the Japanese manufacturing sector. Indeed, until the 1990s, Japan pursued trade liberalization within the multilateral framework of GATT/WTO and open regionalism of APEC, while undertaking domestic "behind-the-border" liberalization under a series of bilateral negotiations with the United States. Although the Japan–U.S. bilateralism sometimes resulted in "managed trade" and encountered resistance to the U.S. approach in Japan, overall it had a positive impact on the Japanese economy in opening domestic markets through various reforms and deregulation measures.

The U.S. pressure on Japan concerning trade-related issues weakened after the establishment of the WTO in 1995 for various reasons. First, the United States, Japan, and other WTO member countries began to use the strengthened dispute settlement mechanism of the WTO for settling trade disputes. Second, Japan undertook a number of policy reforms, such as those in the financial system and corporate governance, the areas that were the main focus of U.S. concerns over the structure of the Japanese economy. Third, Japan's trade surplus was no longer the most important source of the U.S. trade deficit, which began to balloon in the second half of the 1990s. The trade and economic structure of Japan had changed, which limited the bilateral trade imbalances against the United States. Fourth, the stagnation of the Japanese economy since the bursting of the asset market bubble may have mitigated the U.S. perception of Japan's threat, in the face of rising competition from, and expanding trade deficits with, emerging East Asian economies, particularly China.

At the turn of the century, Japan's trade policy shifted from a dual-track approach centered on the GATT/WTO and APEC and on U.S. bilateralism to a multitrack approach that would also focus on bilateral and plurilateral EPAs and on regional economic integration in East Asia. Japan made this shift in response to the changing global and regional trading environment. First, trade liberalization under the WTO was stalled due to emerging differences in the views among the WTO members toward trade liberalization, which in turn was attributable to the increasing number of WTO members and to the increasing influence of emerging economies, such as China, India, and Brazil, with a more reserved view toward trade liberalization. Second, a rapid expansion of FTAs globally and the successes of European market integration and NAFTA prompted Japanese policy-makers to consider EPAs as an important commercial policy tool and to create a series of EPAs with economies inside and outside Asia. Third, Japan's trade and FDI activities have shifted away from the United States toward East Asia, and this has generated growing interest in regional cooperation with East Asian economies. Furthermore, the integration of the Japanese economy with dynamic emerging economies in East Asia is now considered as an important component of Japan's growth strategy.

At its onset, Japan's EPA policy was, however, both passive and defensive in nature, aiming to avoid being discriminated against in foreign markets, which were rapidly captured by FTA networks. Japan's EPA policy became proactive as Japan found that it could use EPAs to achieve various objectives, including not only increasing market access in EPA partner countries for Japanese firms but also improving the business environment of partners, strengthening economic cooperation, and increasing economic integration with emerging East Asia. Japan has so far enacted 12 EPAs, mainly with East Asian countries, which account for approximately 18% of Japan's overall trade. Although the Japanese government has made economic cooperation and integration with emerging East Asia through EPAs a high-priority policy, the prospect of achieving this goal could be limited, due to strong opposition from domestic agricultural interests. If Japan is to effectively pursue EPA policies, it must make agricultural product liberalization a high priority and undertake needed structural reforms in agriculture. Reform of the agricultural sector is also needed to revitalize Japan's economy and to help the WTO resume its practically stalled Doha Development Agenda trade negotiation.

NOTES

The authors are grateful to Mordechai Kreinin and Michael Plummer for their comments on an earlier version of this chapter and to Barnard Helman for his competent editorial assistance. The findings, interpretations, and conclusions expressed in this chapter are entirely those of the authors alone and do not necessarily represent the views of the Asian Development Bank, its Institute, its executive directors, or the countries they represent.

1. Voluntary export restraints (VERs) and voluntary import expansions (VIEs) are forms of "managed" trade. Typically, VERs establish a quantitative limit on a country's exports to its trading partner(s) and, thus, implicitly set up a quantitative limit on the imports from a trading partner. Often, VIEs establish a minimum target for the share of a country's market to be supplied by imports or foreign producers. Tyson (1993) claimed that VERs restrict trade and competition, while VIEs can promote trade and competition in economies where policies or structural factors limit access for foreign suppliers.

2. The yen had started to appreciate in the spring of 1985, but it was after September that the yen began to appreciate significantly due to policy support.

3. As part of the policy of recycling Japan's current account surplus, Japanese firms were generally encouraged to invest abroad, but without explicit policy support such as subsidies and/or favorable tax treatments.

4. See, for example, Kawai and Urata (1996, 1998), Athukorala (2005), Kimura and Ando (2005), and Asian Development Bank (2008).

5. Asia's production networks created a significant amount of intraregional trade in parts and components and, thus, involved double counting in the trade data in terms of value added. This may have exaggerated the volume of trade prior to the global financial crisis and the drop of trade during the crisis.

6. Here, the nontradable goods sectors include construction, electricity, gas, water, wholesale and retail trade, banking and insurance, real estate, transportation, telecommunication, and services. The tradable goods sector includes manufacturing.

7. See Komiya and Itoh (1988) for a review of Japan's commercial policy between 1955 and 1984.

8. Lawrence (1987) attempted to demonstrate that the Japanese economy was different and relatively closed in comparison to other advanced economies by using a gravity model. However, Saxonhouse (1993) showed that Japan's market was not necessarily "closed" once its factor endowments and resource availabilities were taken into account.

9. Based on surveys on the purchasing behavior of Japanese, U.S., and European subsidiaries in Australia, Kreinin (1988) found that Japanese firms abroad had an unusually strong preference to buy from Japanese rather than other foreign suppliers. Specifically, according to his results, Japanese subsidiaries were more tightly controlled by the respective parent company, procured more of their equipment from the home country, and owned and operated more machinery produced in the home country than their U.S. and European counterparts. He concluded that Japan's industrial structure and buyers' preferences played an important role. Using econometric models, Lawrence (1991) demonstrated that *keiretsu* links were barriers to foreign sales in Japanese markets. That is, he showed that the larger the share of industrial output produced by firms that were *keiretsu* members, the smaller the import penetration in that industry.

10. See articles in Krugman (1991) for a comprehensive treatment of the economic, industrial, and financial structures of Japan that were perceived as a source of the "closed" nature of the Japanese economy.

11. See Wolf, Gadbaw, Howell, and Richards (1985).

12. "Super 301" is an enhanced version, introduced in 1988, of Section 301 of the 1974 U.S. Trade Act. This allowed the U.S. government to impose sanctions against countries it deemed were engaging in unfair trade practices and erecting trade barriers against U.S. products and services.

13. Tyson (1993) documented that in a confidential side letter to the SCTA, the Japanese government "would make efforts to assist foreign companies in reaching their goal of a 20% market share within five years." When the SCTA was renewed in 1991, an explicit target of the 20% market share was mentioned, to be realized by the end of 1992.

14. See Kimura (2005) for more detailed discussions.

15. Iwaki (2007) provides a concise overview of the Japan–EU Economic relationship with a focus on trade issues.

16. See Kimura (2005) for more detailed discussions.

17. One innovation under the WTO was the introduction of the negative consensus approach to dispute settlement. That is, a case could now be heard unless there was the unanimous objection of the panel members.

18. Starting with 12 members (Australia, Canada, Japan, New Zealand, South Korea, the United States, and the six members of ASEAN: Brunei Darussalam, Indonesia, Malaysia, the Philippines, Singapore, and Thailand), 9 additional economies have subsequently joined APEC, including Chile, China, Hong Kong, Mexico, Papua New Guinea, Peru, Taipei,China, Viet Nam, and Russia.

19. Besides five developed economies, eight developing economies, Chile, Hong Kong, Korea, Malaysia, Mexico, Peru, Singapore, and Taipei,China, volunteered to be assessed. The assessment was conducted for these economies individually, but the results of the

assessment were reported for these economies as a group, probably to avoid possible disputes.

20. Pempel and Urata (2006) discussed Japan's EPA policy in conjunction with its bilateral trade agreements with the United States in semiconductors and others in the 1970s and 1980s.

21. In sectors other than electronics whose MFN tariffs are already low.

22. See Solis and Urata (2007) for the discussion of Japan's activist foreign economic policy.

23. See Urata (2009) for this observation.

24. China, Japan, and Korea embarked on negotiations for a trilateral investment agreement in March 2007.

25. Ministry of Agriculture, Forestry, and Fisheries home page, www.maff.go.jp/hitokuti/top.htm#mokuji1.

REFERENCES

Asian Development Bank. 2008. *Emerging Asian Regionalism: A Partnership for Shared Prosperity*. Manila: Asian Development Bank.

Athukorala, Prema-chandra. 2005. "Product Fragmentation and Trade Patterns in East Asia." *Asian Economic Papers* 4(3), pp. 1–27.

Itoh, Motoshige, and Naoki Shimoi. 2009. "Baburuki Defureki no Nihon no Tsusho Seisaku [Japanese commercial policy during the bubble and deflationary period]." In Motoshige Itoh, ed., Kokusai Kankyo no Henka to Nihon Keizai [Changes in international environment and the Japanese economy]. Tokyo: Keio University Press, pp. 88–123.

Iwaki, Shigeyuki. 2007, October. "Nihon-EU Kankei no Shinten to Kadai: Keizai Tsushoo Chuushinni [Developments and issues on Japan-EU relations: Focus on economic and international trade]." *Reference* (Research Department, National Diet Library), pp. 9–29.

Kawai, Masahiro, and Shinji Takagi. 2011. "Why Was Japan Hit So Hard by the Global Financial Crisis?" In Daigee Shaw and Bih Jane Liu, eds., *The Impact of the Economic Crisis on East Asia: Policy Responses from Four Economies*. Cheltenham, England: Edward Elgar, pp. 131–148.

Kawai, Masahiro, and Shujiro Urata. 1996, October. "Trade Imbalances and Japanese Foreign Direct Investment: Bilateral and Trilateral Issues." In Ku-Hyun Jung and Jang-Hee Yoo, eds., *Asia-Pacific Economic Cooperation: Current Issues and Agenda for the Future*, East and West Studies Series, 39. Institute of East and West Studies, Yonsei University, pp. 61–87.

Kawai, Masahiro, and Shujiro Urata. 1998. "Are Trade and Direct Investment Substitutes or Complements? An Empirical Analysis of Japanese Manufacturing Industries." In Hiro Lee and David W. Roland-Holst, eds., *Economic Development and Cooperation in the Pacific Basin: Trade, Investment, and Environmental Issues*. Cambridge: Cambridge University Press. pp. 251–293.

Kawai, Masahiro, and Ganeshan Wignaraja. 2011, February. "Asian FTAs: Trends, Prospects and Challenges." *Journal of Asian Economics* 22:1, pp. 1–22.

Keizai Kozo Chosei Kenkyukai [Advisory Group on Economic Structural Adjustment]. 1986, April. "Kokusai Kyocho no tameno Keizai Kozo Chosei Kenkyukai Hokokusho [Report of the Advisory Group on Economic Structural Adjustment for International Harmony]." Government of Japan.

Kimura, Fukunari, and Mitsuyo Ando. 2005. "Two-Dimensional Fragmentation in East Asia: Conceptual Framework and Empirics." *International Review of Economics and Finance* 14:3, pp. 317–348.

Kimura, Takayuki. 2005. "The EU Enlargement and the EU-Japan Economic Relationship." In Takako Ueta and Eric Remacle, eds., *Japan and Enlarged Europe: Partners in Global Governance*. Brussels: P.I.E.-Peter Lang, pp. 175–188.

Komiya, Ryutaro, and Motoshige Itoh. 1988. "Japan's International Trade and Trade Policy, 1955–1984." In Takeshi Inoguchi and Daniel I. Okimoto, eds., *The Political Economy of Japan*, vol. 2, *The International Context* Stanford: Stanford University Press, pp. 173–224.

Kreinin, Mordechai E. 1988. "How Closed Is Japan's Market? Additional Evidence." *World Economy* 11 (December), pp. 529–542.

Krugman, Paul R., ed. 1991. *Trade with Japan: Has the Door Opened Wider?* Chicago: University of Chicago Press for the National Bureau of Economic Research.

Lawrence, Robert Z. 1987. "Imports in Japan: Closed Markets or Minds?" *Brookings Papers on Economic Activity* 2, pp. 517–554.

Lawrence, Robert Z. 1991. "Efficient or Exclusionist? The Import Behavior of Japanese Corporate Groups." *Brookings Papers on Economic Activity* 1, pp. 311–330.

Pempel, T. J., and Shujiro Urata. 2006. "Japan: A New Move toward Bilateral Trade Agreements." In Vinod K. Aggarwal and Shujiro Urata, eds., *Bilateral Trade Agreements in the Asia-Pacific: Origins, Evolution, and Implications*. New York: Routledge.

Saxonhouse, Gary R. 1993. "What Does Japanese Trade Structure Tell Us about Japanese Trade Policy?" *Journal of Economic Perspectives* 7:3, pp. 21–43.

Solis, Mireya, and Shujiro Urata. 2007. "Japan's New Foreign Economic Policy: A Shift toward a Strategic and Activist Model?" *Asian Economic Policy Review* 2:2, pp. 227–245.

Tyson, Laura D'Andrea. 1993. *Who's Bashing Whom? Trade Conflict in High-Technology Industries*. Washington, DC: Institute for International Economics.

Urata, Shujiro. 2009. "Exclusion Fears and Competitive Regionalism in East Asia." In Mireya Solis, Barbara Stallings, and Saori N. Katada, eds., *Competitive Regionalism: FTA Diffusion in the Pacific Rim*. London: Palgrave Macmillan, pp. 27–53.

Wolf, A., R. M. Gadbaw, T. Howell, and T. Richards. 1985. *Japanese Market Barriers in Microelectronics: Memorandum in Support of a Petition to Section 301 of the Trade Act of 1974*. Washington, D.C.: Semiconductor Industry Association.

CHAPTER 11

COMMERCIAL POLICY AND EXPERIENCE IN THE GIANTS: CHINA AND INDIA

GANESHAN WIGNARAJA

THE rise of the two Asian giant economies—the People's Republic of China (hereafter China) and India—will have profound implications for the world economy for decades to come.[1] Until the late 1970s, China and India were poor economies with inward-oriented trade and investment regimes, central planning, and lackluster export sectors. A shift in commercial policies thereafter saw their rise as huge global exporters. Already, they make up over one-third of the world's population and about one-tenth of its exports. The giants' exports increasingly comprise sophisticated manufactures and services, rather than simple labor-intensive exports. Rapid trade-led growth has lifted hundreds of millions out of poverty in both economies. And the giants' exports and growth have rebounded faster than many others following the 2008 global financial crisis. This success is remarkable among Asian newly industrializing economies and even large developed countries (Amsden 2001; Gerhaeusser et al. 2010; Madison 2007).

A growing body of literature has focused on the giants' rise in world trade and the influence of commercial policies. Four major lines of research can be distinguished. The first suggests that China's remarkable structural transformation enabling the production of manufactures for export beginning in the late 1970s was largely unforeseen. Informed analysts note that China's performance "already has been the largest growth surprise ever experienced by the world economy" (Winters and Yusuf, 2007, p. 1) and project the two giants to be among the world's largest trading economies within a couple of decades (Madison, 2007; Winters and Yusuf, 2007). The second line of research differentiates between the giants and credits India with turning the corner beginning in the 1990s but argues that its export performance is still in a different league from that of China (Panagariya, 2007). It is further argued that both countries started economic liberalization in the late 1970s but China was swifter, with the launch of an open-door policy toward foreign direct investment (FDI) in 1978, while India did not adopt a major reform package until 1991 (Lardy, 2003; Kowalski, 2010; Panagariya, 2006, 2007). The third notes that freer trade and markets were pivotal to the giants' export success, but that active industrial policies in China played a complementary role in nurturing domestic capabilities in consumer electronics and other advanced areas that might not have developed in their absence (Amsden, 2001; Rodrick, 2006). Implicit in this third line of thinking is that the absence of any new reform policies since 1991 may in part explain why India lags behind China in advanced manufactured exports. Fourth, concerns have been expressed that the giants' recent pursuit of free-trade agreements (FTAs) may be detrimental to exporting, due to the shallow coverage of agreements and an Asian "noodle bowl" of overlapping FTAs (Baldwin, 2008; Suominen, 2009).

This chapter explores the link between commercial policies and export performance through a comparative analysis of China and India. Existing research underlines the complexity of the giants' commercial policy mix and suggests further exploration of four interesting questions: (1) Have China's exports outpaced India's? (2) What role has liberalization of trade and investment regimes played in the giants' export records? (3) Is the recent emphasis on FTAs detrimental to exports? And (4) what are the emerging commercial policy challenges in the post-2008 global financial crisis era?

Building on existing research, the remainder of the chapter tackles these questions. Section I looks at initial conditions influencing trade and trade performance. It examines the giants' export record by describing the evolution of trade flows at the aggregate and sectoral levels (focusing on growth and structural change in manufactured and services exports). Section II explores the link between shifts in key commercial policies (e.g., import liberalization, export promotion, and FDI policies) and trade flows. Section III examines the impact of FTAs on exporting. It evaluates FTA quality in terms of some simple criteria and provides evidence on the use of FTAs at the firm level. Section IV explores emerging commercial policy challenges in the post–global financial crisis era. Section V concludes.

Commercial policies are defined somewhat broadly here to include the spectrum of trade and investment policies affecting imports, exports, and FDI. In the context of economic reforms, commercial policies encompass import liberalization, export promotion measures, real exchange rates, FDI policies, and FTAs.

I. Initial Conditions and Trade Performance

Initial Conditions

Initial conditions often shape trade outcomes following economic liberalization. Three key initial conditions laid the foundations for the trade pattern and performance of the giants after economic liberalization in the late 1970s.

One condition is geographical proximity to a major developed economy, resulting in spillovers for neighbors. China's strategic location in East Asia and shared history with the region meant it was well placed to attract export-oriented manufacturing FDI from Japan, the Republic of Korea (Korea), and the economies of the members of the Association of Southeast Asian Nations (ASEAN). Geographical proximity, along with low-cost labor and large market size, may have also influenced the relocation of production networks and supply chains from ASEAN economies to China. India is less well placed geographically to attract FDI from East Asia but is closer to Europe than China and shares greater ties due to its legacy of British rule.

The second condition is large and growing domestic markets, which create a competitive advantage for any product that has substantial economies of scale (e.g., automobile or electronics assembly) and lower barriers to entry. So how large are the Chinese and Indian markets? It is estimated that industrial producers in China face a potential market of about $1 trillion, while India's industrial producers face a potential market that is one-quarter to one-third the size of China's (Yusuf, Nabeshima, and Perkins, 2007).

Third is ample supplies of low-cost, productive manpower to provide the basis for a comparative advantage in low-technology, labor-intensive exports and in attracting FDI. It is often suggested by various competitiveness studies that China's labor productivity is higher than India's and that this advantage underlies China's entry into labor-intensive manufactures (World Economic Forum, 2010). Meanwhile, the roots of India's relative success in information technology (IT) and business process outsourcing lie in other factors, including its exposure to English, linked to a long period of British colonial rule; the establishment of Indian institutes of technology, which provided a base of world-class IT professionals and engineers; close links with a diaspora of professionals and business people who provided relevant contacts, information, and capital; and falling telecommunications costs, which made it profitable to outsource services (Kowalski, 2010; Yusuf, Nabeshima, and Perkins, 2007).

Overall Trade Performance

To trace the link between economic liberalization and trade performance in the giants, table 11.1 shows the expansion of aggregate exports and imports of goods and services between 1978 and 2010. The data are from the World Bank's World

Table 11.1. Exports and imports of goods and services, 1978–2009

	China							India						
	1978	1985	1991	1998	2008	2009/ᵃ	2010	1978	1985	1991	1998	2008	2009ᵃ	2010
As % of GDP														
Exports of goods and services	6.6	9.9	20.8	20.3	36.6	28.4	31.8	6.4	5.3	8.6	11.1	22.7	19.7	22.9
Goods exports	...	8.2	15.5	18.0	33.2	25.6	25.4	4.8	4.1	6.8	8.2	16.2	12.7	15.2
Service exports	...	1.0	1.8	2.3	3.4	2.7	3.1	1.2	1.5	1.8	2.8	8.9	7.0	7.7
Imports of goods and services	7.1	14.1	17.2	16.0	28.5	24.8	28.9	6.6	7.7	8.6	12.8	28.0	26.0	30.9
Goods imports	...	12.5	13.2	13.4	24.8	21.4	25.4	5.5	6.6	7.9	10.8	27.2	20.0	22.7
Service imports	...	0.8	1.1	2.6	3.7	3.4	3.5	1.2	1.7	2.2	3.5	4.9	6.1	8.2
As% of the World														
Exports of goods and services	0.6	1.3	1.7	3.0	8.0	8.6	11.0	0.6	0.5	0.5	0.7	1.3	1.6	2.0
Goods exports	...	1.3	1.7	3.3	9.1	7.8	12.8	0.5	0.5	0.5	0.6	1.2	1.0	1.7
Service exports	...	0.7	0.8	1.7	3.8	0.8	4.9	0.6	0.8	0.5	0.8	2.7	0.6	3.2
Imports of goods and services	0.7	1.8	1.4	2.4	6.4	7.5	10.3	0.6	0.7	0.5	0.8	1.7	2.1	2.8
Goods imports	...	2.0	1.4	2.5	6.9	6.5	11.6	0.6	0.8	0.6	0.8	2.0	1.6	2.7
Service imports	...	0.6	0.4	1.9	4.5	1.0	5.9	0.5	0.9	0.6	1.0	1.6	0.5	3.6
Exports of goods and services (current US$, billion)	9.8	30.5	78.9	207.4	1581.7	1331.0	1748.0	8.6	12.2	23.0	46.4	262.8	241.0	326.0
Imports of goods and services (current US$, billion)	10.5	43.1	65.3	163.6	1232.8	1164.0	1587.0	9.0	17.8	23.0	53.4	324.8	318.0	440.0

Notes: . . . = data not available.
ᵃ Author's estimates based on WTO trade data.
Source: World Bank, World Development Indicators Online (accessed June 2010).

Development Indicators Database, and the indicators are presented as a share of GDP or world trade. The ratios of exports and imports to GDP are often used as proxies for openness, although also reflects the availability of foreign exchange. Four points are noteworthy.

First, China's earlier and swifter overall trade liberalization path since 1978 compared with India is highlighted by the ratio of exports of goods and services, and the similar ratio for imports. In 1978, China and India were at similar low levels of openness—exports- and imports-to-GDP ratios of 6–7% each—reflecting a history of restrictive trade regimes and state control. With increasing trade liberalization in China, its exports- and imports-to-GDP ratios more than doubled between

1978 and 1991, while India's ratios showed little change. In the aftermath of India's 1991 liberalization, a modest increase in its openness occurred between 1991 and 1998, and a significant one between 1998 and 2010. China maintained its openness through the 1990s and also saw a rise in exports- and imports-to-GDP ratios between 1998 and 2010. By 2010, in terms of exports (whether of goods or goods and services), China was considerably more open than India, but there was little difference in terms of imports-to-GDP ratios. China's ratio of exports of goods and services to GDP was 31.8% in 2010, compared with 22.9% for India. Meanwhile, the ratios for imports in 2010 were similar to each other, with 28.9% for China and 30.9% for India. Thus, China was relatively more open than India over several decades, but India has made considerable progress, particularly since the late 1990s.

Second, as China's GDP has grown faster than India's since the 1970s, the trade-to-GDP ratios understate the spectacular growth of China's trade. The respective dollar values of exports and shares of world exports give a better picture of the difference in export performance between the two giants. In 1978, the two giants had about the same level of exports of goods and services, as well as similar world shares of exports: China exported $9.8 billion worth of goods and services, compared with $8.6 billion for India. These figures were equivalent to about 0.6% of world exports of goods and services each. By 2010, China's exports of goods and services reached a staggering $1.8 trillion, or 11.0% of world exports. The comparable figures for India were $326 billion and 2%.

Third, the global financial crisis did not significantly disrupt the giants' trade. In the aftermath of the crisis, exports of goods and services in China fell to $1.3 trillion while India's increased slightly to $270 billion. In 2010, there were sharp rebounds in exports and imports in China and India. This underscores the relative resilience of the giants' trade performance and the growing importance of South–South trade cooperation (Wignaraja and Lazaro, 2010).

Fourth, as developed countries experienced a greater fall in exports than the giants and a muted response thereafter, the world export shares of China and India in 2010 rose to 11% and 2%, respectively. According to the World Trade Organization (WTO), China's 2010 world share of exports places it among the leading exporters on the planet. The United States is the world's largest exporter (12.1%). China is next followed by Germany (10.1%) and Japan (6.1%).[2] China is also the leading exporter among the so-called club of large BRIC nations, which also includes Russia (3%), Brazil (1.6%), and India, which is placed comfortably within the club.

Growth of Manufactures and Services

China's exceptional export performance since 1978 has been driven primarily by the production of manufactures for export. As table 11.2 shows, China's manufactured export growth in current US dollars (26.7%) was nearly twice as fast as India's (15.4%) during 1985–2008. Even more strikingly, perhaps, China increased its share of the world's manufactured exports from 0.5% to 10.8% between 1985 and 2008, while India's share rose from 0.5% to 1.3% over the same period.

Further differences are visible between the two giants in the composition of manufactured exports. Table 11.2 presents UN Commodity Trade data on manufactured exports for the two giants according to a technology-based classification developed by Lall (2001). This method distinguishes among resource-based, low-technology, medium-technology, and high-technology manufactures. The technology categories can be briefly described as follows. Resource-based products tend to be simple and labor-intensive (e.g., simple food or leather processing), but there are segments using capital-, scale-, and skill-intensive technologies (e.g., petroleum refining or modern processed food). Low-technology products tend to have stable, well-diffused technologies, primarily embodied in capital equipment (e.g., textiles, garments, and footwear). Medium-technology products, which consist of the majority of skill- and scale-intensive technologies in capital goods and intermediate products, lie at the core of industrial activity in developed countries. High-technology products have advanced and fast-changing technologies, with large R & D investments and a focus on product design (e.g., electronic and electrical products, aircraft, precision instruments, and pharmaceuticals). Annual average growth rates for these technological categories in current U.S. dollars during 1985–2008, shares in manufactured exports, and shares of world exports are provided.

The following can be noted:

- Within China's manufactures, high-technology exports grew the fastest and resource-based the slowest. Meanwhile, India's medium-technology exports grew the fastest and low-technology the slowest.
- Both giants have witnessed increasing technological upgrading of their manufactured exports since 1985, but China's speed of technological sophistication has been quite striking. Between 1985 and 2008, China's share of high-technology exports in its total manufactures increased more than five times to reach 27.7% in 2008. China's medium-technology exports also rose three times to 37.0% in 2008. During the same period, India's shares of high-technology exports and medium-technology exports doubled to 8.3% and 24.9%, respectively. Nonetheless, India's manufactured exports are typically concentrated in the lower end of the technology spectrum, with resource-based products accounting for one-third of manufactures and low-technology products accounting for another third.
- China has dominated world markets in low-technology products for well over a decade, and in 2008 it accounted for 18.1% of the world's low-technology exports. It also accounts for 10.3% of the world's medium-technology exports and 14.3% of high-technology exports. This is why China is viewed by many developing countries as the main competitive threat across the technological spectrum (Lall, 2001). It is also seen as an outlier in terms of the sophistication of its exports: "its export bundle is that of a country with an income per capita level three times higher than China's" (Rodrick, 2006, p. 4). Meanwhile, India accounts for less than 1% of total world medium-technology and high-technology exports, and is perceived as less of a

Table 11.2. Manufactured exports

Growth rate, 1985–2008 (%)		
China		
Manufactures	26.7	
Resource-based	18.6	
Low tech	24.2	
Medium tech	33.3	
High tech	36.2	
India		
Manufactures	15.4	
Resource-based	14.6	
Low tech	13.7	
Medium tech	20.2	
High tech	18.3	
Share of national manufactured exports, %	1985	2008
China		
Resource-based	38.9	8.5
Low tech	43.7	26.8
Medium tech	12.2	37.0
High tech	5.2	27.7
India		
Resource-based	40.6	35.0
Low tech	45.3	31.8
Medium tech	10.0	24.9
High tech	4.1	8.3
Share of world manufactured exports, %	1985	2008
China		
Manufactures	0.5	10.8
Resource-based	0.8	3.5
Low tech	1.2	18.1
Medium tech	0.1	10.6
High tech	0.1	14.3
India		
Manufactures	0.5	1.3
Resource-based	0.9	1.7
Low tech	1.2	2.5
Medium tech	0.1	0.8
High tech	0.1	0.5

Source: UN Comtrade (accessed December 2009).

competitive threat in the developing world. Even more revealing about India's manufacturing capability is that it has a limited global presence in low-technology exports (2.5% in 2008) and resource-based exports (1.7% in 2008).

India's recent expansion in exports has been led by services rather than manufacturing. India has also kept pace with China in services export growth. A profile of India and China's service exports during 1985–2008 is shown in table 11.3, including growth in service exports in current U.S. dollars, the composition of service exports by broad categories, and world market shares. India's service export grew at 16.1% per year, compared with 18.6% in China, during 1985–2008. In 1985, both giants were relatively small players in global service exports, with less than 1% of world service exports. By 2008, these shares had risen to 2.7% in India and 3.8% in China. These figures may mask the area where India has typically excelled: more sophisticated, skill-intensive services exports. India has done better in IT and business process outsourcing, as well as insurance and financial services. In 2008, India accounted for 4.7% of world IT and business processing outsourcing exports, compared with 4.1% for China. Similarly, India accounted for 1.9% of world insurance and financial services exports, while China's share was 0.6%.

Thus, the giants differ considerably in their trade performances. China has surged ahead of India in world export markets, with China's exports of goods and services over five times bigger. China's success is linked to the rise of manufactured exports, which have rapidly upgraded over time, and the expansion of some services. Meanwhile, India has done better in skill-intensive services than manufactures. Compared with developed countries, the giants' export performances have been relatively resilient in the aftermath of the global financial crisis. While initial conditions were influential, they cannot account for the whole story of exports in China and India. Commercial policies have also played a major role in facilitating specialization and trade. We turn to this topic next.

II. Shifting Commercial Policies and Exports

A central question concerns the role that the liberalization of trade and investment regimes has played in the giants' export records. This section focuses on key commercial policies—import liberalization, export promotion measures, and FDI policies—at the heart of China and India's reforms. The giants are considered separately below, followed by some comparisons of their commercial policies and export outcomes.

Table 11.3. Commercial Services Exports

Growth rate (1985–2008), %		
China		
Commercial services	18.6	
Computer, communications, and other services	24.2	
Insurance and financial services	10.0	
Transport services	15.9	
Travel services	17.7	
India		
Commercial services	16.1	
Computer, communications, and other services	17.4	
Insurance and financial services	23.6	
Transport services	14.3	
Travel services	11.8	
Share of national commercial service exports, %	1985	2008
China		
Computer, communications, and other services	15.3	44.7
Insurance and financial services	6.7	1.2
Transport services	44.5	26.2
Travel services	33.5	27.9
India		
Computer, communications, and other services	55.6	72
Insurance and financial services	1.3	5.5
Transport services	15.7	11
Travel services	27.4	11.5
Share of world commercial service exports, %	1985	2008
China		
Commercial services	0.7	3.8
Computer, communications, and other services	0.4	4.1
Insurance and financial services	1.2	0.6
Transport services	1.0	4.2
Travel services	0.8	4.1
India		
Commercial services	0.8	2.7
Computer, communications, and other services	1.5	4.7
Insurance and financial services	0.3	1.9
Transport services	0.4	1.2

Source: World Bank, World Development Indicators Online (accessed June 2010)

China's Commercial Policies

Inward-Oriented Strategy

China initiated reforms in 1978 to shift to a more open-market-oriented economy. The previous inward-oriented, centrally planned strategy had caused multiple economic distortions that hampered exports and private sector activity. The inward-oriented strategy—introduced in the 1950s—fostered import-substituting industrialization using stringent protection and state control of resource allocation. During the Maoist period, private sector firms, including foreign-owned firms, were gradually taken over, and private sector ownership was completely eliminated in 1958 during the Great Leap Forward. Instead, state-owned enterprises emerged at the forefront of the country's industrialization effort. A formal state-owned enterprise sector made up of large firms and a proletarian elite of workers with job security and generous welfare benefits coexisted with less-capitalized, small-scale industrial enterprises based mainly in rural areas where workers enjoyed less security and benefits (Maddison, 2007).

Some of the economic distortions that arose from China's inward-oriented strategy were as follows:

1. Stringent quantitative restrictions and other import controls led to a bias toward inefficient capital-intensive production by large, state-owned enterprises.
2. The exchange rate was fixed at an overvalued level to implicitly subsidize the import of high-priority capital goods that could not be produced domestically. A rigid system of exchange control also existed whereby exporters surrendered all their foreign exchange to the state.
3. Tight controls on the entry of foreign enterprises shut out FDI and technology transfer, resulting in technological obsolesce relative to global best practices.
4. Virtually all commodity trade was determined by central planning, primarily to ensure that state-owned enterprises could obtain cheap imports of capital goods and intermediates. A handful of foreign trade cooperatives owned and controlled by the ministry of foreign trade was responsible for carrying out the trade plan. Each of the foreign trade cooperatives dealt with a limited range of commodities for which it was the sole trading company.

Not surprisingly, owing to these inefficiencies and distortions, China witnessed lackluster export performance during much of the inward-oriented, centrally planned era. By 1978, its exports of goods and services had stagnated at less than $10 billion (or 0.6% of world exports of goods and services). The composition of exports was dominated by primary products, resource-based manufactures, and some low-technology manufactures. The time was ripe for a change in commercial policies toward export promotion and the private sector.

Open-Door FDI Policy and Other Reforms

The post-1978 reforms marked the start of a gradual and highly coordinated transition process in China over the next three decades. The initial focus of reforms was to promote exports by attracting FDI. In 1979, an export processing law was passed that provided incentives for the processing and assembly of imported inputs. These incentives were expanded in 1987 to provide for the duty-free import of all raw materials, parts, and components used in export production. Monopoly state trading was liberalized starting in the late-1970s and replaced with a complex and highly restrictive set of tariffs, nontariff barriers, and licenses. Reform of the complex import control regime was more cautious during the early transition years, but was strengthened from 1992 onward by extensive reforms China agreed to implement as a part of the WTO accession process. Accordingly, a dualistic trade regime existed from the mid-1980s onward that promoted exports via FDI alongside controlled liberalization of a protected domestic sector (Kowalski, 2010).

To attract export-oriented FDI, China implemented five main measures beginning in the late-1970s (Zhang, 2009). These included the following:

1. The easing of regulations governing the entry and operation of foreign enterprises through a series of laws, notably the Sino-Foreign Equity Joint Venture Law of 1979, the Sino-Foreign Cooperative Joint Venture Law of 1986, and the Wholly Foreign-Owned Enterprise Law of 1988. Such measures encouraged the formation of joint ventures between foreign and local investors, technology transfer to local partners, and domestic sourcing of inputs.
2. Providing efficient, cost-competitive infrastructure for export processing commencing with four special economic zones (SEZs) along China's southern coast. These zones enabled foreign producers to operate with good infrastructure and a minimum of undue interference.
3. Introduction of a complex system of tax incentives (including a 15% corporation tax rate, exemptions, and refunds) and facilitation of financing to channel FDI toward the SEZs.
4. Formalizing of a duty drawback system from 1987 onward to ensure duty-free access to all imported raw materials, parts, and components for export processing.
5. Relatively liberal labor regulations in SEZs were applied (with a minimum of legislative intervention and administrative "red tape") that ensured relatively low wages for ample supplies of skilled workers.

Two other policies were vital to export growth, especially among domestic enterprises (Lardy, 2003). First, there was the liberalization of the system of export licensing and quotas. Only 8% of exports were subject to export licensing and quotas by 1999, compared with a peak in 1991, when some two-thirds of all exports were so burdened.

Second, reforms of the foreign exchange system were initiated, starting with unification of dual exchange rates in 1994 (Hu, 2010). As a significant incentive for exporting, exporters were allowed to retain a share of their foreign exchange earnings, which enabled them to finance imports without needing to seek official permission. Over time, the state also devalued the domestic currency and, in 1997, moved to currency convertibility on current account transactions, making it even easier for exporters to obtain foreign currency. In mid-2005, China moved more systematically toward a managed floating exchange rate regime based on market supply and demand with reference to a basket of currencies.

Despite the various measures to attract FDI and promote exports, FDI inflows were modest in the first decade or so of reforms. As table 11.4 shows, annual average FDI inflows amounted to $1.6 billion a year during 1978–1990 and were largely destined for the four SEZs. From the early 1990s onward, however, China attracted

Table 11.4. Foreign Direct Investment (FDI) (current US\$, billion)

	CHINA	INDIA
Total FDI inflows (current US\$, billion)		
1978–2010	1098.7	191.3
Annual average FDI inflows (current US\$, billion)		
1978–1991	1.6	0.1
1991–2008	48.8	7.5
1991–2002	35.6	2.5
2003–2008	75.2	17.5
2008	108.3	40.4
2009	95.0	34.6
2010[a]	105.7	21.0
FDI (% of GDP)		
1991–1995	3.8	0.2
2004–2008	2.8	2.0
2009	2.0	2.8
Share of multinational companies in exports (%), most recent estimate[/b]	54	<10
Total outward FDI (current US\$, billion)		
1995–2009	182.0	73.1
Annual average outward FDI (current US\$, billion)		
1995–2005	3.8	1.0
2006–2008	31.9	16.0
2008	52.2	18.5
2009	48.0	14.9

[a] Authors estimate. [b] India from Kumar and Sharma (2009) and China from www.fdi.gov.cn.
Sources: Author's calculations based on data from the World Investment Report 2009 and 2010.

record levels of FDI, with inflows amounting to $54 billion per year during 1991–2010. Annual FDI inflows in 2003–2010 ($81.5 billion) were more than double that of the 1991–2002 period. Cumulative FDI inflows into China reached an impressive $1,098.7 billion in 1978–2010. As a result, China became the world's second largest FDI recipient after the United States. Interestingly, the global financial crisis did not significantly disrupt FDI inflows, which dropped modestly from $108.3 billion in 2008 to $95.0 billion in 2009. FDI inflows rebounded to precrisis levels in 2010 ($105.7 billion).

A strong regional element is visible in the host-country origins of China's FDI inflows. Much of the surge in FDI inflows into China after the 1990s came from overseas Chinese investors—primarily based in Hong Kong, Taipei, and Macao—who collectively accounted for 42.0% of accumulated FDI inflows during 1997–2006 (Zhang, 2009). Another 21% was from other East Asian countries—primarily Japan, Korea, and ASEAN members. Meanwhile, among nonregionals, the United States made up 7.8% and the EU 8.6%. Interestingly, the share of overseas Chinese investors rose significantly to 56.9% in 2008. Meanwhile, the shares of other East Asian countries (17.3%), the EU (6.7%) and the United States (6.4%) declined somewhat (Ministry of Commerce, PRC, 2011)

Foreign direct investment had a dramatic impact on China's exports. The share of foreign enterprises in total Chinese exports increased from 32% to 58% between 1995 and 2005;[3] it declined slightly to 54% in 2010 (January to August).[4] FDI inflows have been fundamental to China's success in manufactured exports by linking the country into production networks in key industries. Foreign direct investment brought not only capital but, more important, access to marketing channels, world-class technologies, and organizational methods. In the early years of reforms, FDI was central to the rise of low-technology, labor-intensive exports like textiles, garments, and footwear. Subsequently, the surge in FDI in the 1990s drove the rapid technological upgrading of manufactures into more complex activities like electronics and automotives.[5] China used active policies to facilitate technology upgrading and domestic technological development. Entry and operational regulations for foreign firms required them to form joint ventures with domestic firms, promote technology transfer to partners, and increase local content by sourcing inputs locally (Rodrick, 2006). Furthermore, China also invested heavily in R & D and in scientists and engineers to absorb imported technologies. Its ratio of R & D expenditure to GDP more than doubled from 0.6% to 1.5% between 1996 and 2007 (see table 11.7). Researchers in R & D per million people also doubled from 448 to 1,071 during this period.

More recently, China has become a major outward investor in the world economy. During 1995–2005, annual outward FDI from China was relatively small, at $3.8 billion per year. Such flows increased over fivefold to about $22 billion in 2006–2007 and peaked at $52.2 billion in 2008 on the eve of the global financial crisis. Following the crisis, there was a modest drop in China's outward investment to about $48 billion in 2009. The bulk of outward FDI has been into the primary and tertiary sectors, with relatively little so far going into manufacturing (Davies, 2010).

Most has gone to Asia, but Chinese FDI is now spreading throughout the world. In part, the growth of outward FDI from China reflects a combination of large export surpluses, rising wages, a global search for commodities to fuel industrialization, and the emergence of large, home-grown multinational corporations looking for overseas investment opportunities.

The liberalization of import controls began slowly and cautiously in China from the early 1980s onward.[6] Two parallel stages in import liberalization can be identified that led to significant cuts in overall import protection over time. First, to move away from the direct planning of all trade, a simplified system of import quotas and licensing was adopted in the early 1980s, and the number of products under import controls was reduced. The share of imports under quotas and licensing fell from 46% to 18% between the late 1980s and 1992, and still further to about 9% in 1997 (Lardy, 2002, p. 39). Second, more transparent price-based instruments—import tariffs—were introduced in the early 1980s to replace quotas and licenses, and tariff reduction subsequently commenced. In 1985, a new customs regulation was passed that rationalized the tariff schedule. More notable tariff cuts occurred following the adoption of a socialist market economy in 1992. The process of tariff reduction was also facilitated by the significant reforms the country agreed to implement as a part of its accession to the WTO in 2001.

The available tariff data indicate a move toward a more open and transparent import regime. Simple average import tariffs on all imports fell modestly from 55.6% to 43.2% between 1982 and 1992 (Lardy, 2002, p. 34). Thereafter, the pace of tariff reform accelerated. Table 11.5 provides data from the WTO Integrated Database and the WTO Tariff Profiles on simple average applied most-favored-nation (MFN) tariffs for agricultural products, nonagricultural products, and the total between 1996 and 2008. Average import tariffs fell to 23.7% in 1996 and still further to 15.9% on the eve of WTO accession in 2001. The continuing process of tariff reduction resulted in average import tariffs of 9.6% by 2008. Accordingly, China became one of the more open economies in the developing world. Nonagricultural products typically enjoyed less tariff protection than agricultural products and have experienced a swifter speed of tariff reduction. In 1996, average import tariffs for

Table 11.5. Simple Average Applied MFN Tariffs by Broad Sectors, 1996, 2001, and 2008

	China			India		
	1996	2001	2008	1996	2001	2008
All	23.7	15.9	9.6	38.7	31.9	13.0
Agricultural products	34.1	20.3	15.6	23.1	36.3	32.2
Nonagricultural products	22.8	15.5	8.7	40.1	31.4	10.1

Source: World Trade Organization Integrated Database (accessed February 2010); WTO, ITC, and UN, World Tariff Profiles 2009.

nonagricultural products (22.8%) were significantly lower than those for agricultural products (34.1%). By 2008, import tariffs for nonagricultural products reached 8.7% and those for agricultural products were 15.6%.

Table 11.6 provides the latest data on MFN applied tariffs and imports by product groups for 2008. There is relatively little dispersion in import tariffs for nonagricultural products, which range from 4.4% for wood and paper to 16.0% for clothing. Within this general picture, major high-technology products have lower tariffs than less dynamic low-technology products. Thus, import tariffs for electrical machinery, for nonelectrical machinery, and transport equipment are, respectively, 8.0%, 7.8%, and 11.5%. This compares with import tariffs of 16% for clothing and 13.4% for leather and footwear. In contrast, a larger dispersion in import tariffs is visible for agricultural products from 10.6% for oilseeds, fats, and oils to 27.4% for sugars and confectionary.

Exchange rate management has assumed more significance for exporting from China since the turn of the millennium. In essence, the Peoples Bank of China has pursued a managed floating exchange regime whereby the renminbi exchange rate is based on the supply and demand of the market, and adjusted with reference to a basket of currencies (Hu, 2010). A key policy objective is to maintain a relatively stable and predictable nominal exchange rate of the renminbi. A standard measure of international competitiveness is the real effective exchange rate (REER)—the weighted average of a country's currency relative to an index or basket of other major currencies adjusted for the effects of inflation. Figure 11.1 charts monthly Bank of International Settlements (BIS) data on the REER for China from January 2000 to June 2010. The base year for the REER series is 2005. The REER exhibits a U-shaped pattern during this period. After a short initial appreciation between January 2000 and April 2002, the REER remained depreciated between May 2002 and December 2007. Thereafter, the REER behave somewhat erratically, with an appreciating tendency. Thus, for much of the last decade, China's inflation was below that of its trading partners, and the rate of nominal exchange depreciation was sufficient to offset this inflation differential.

India's Commercial Policies

Inward-Oriented Strategy

The start of import substitution in the late 1950s in India introduced policy interventions on trade, and India developed into one of the most highly protected and inward-oriented regimes in the developing world. The regime continued, with some minor changes, into the 1980s. Popular discourse often equates India's commercial policy reforms with the post-1991 period. Partial reforms, however, were attempted in the previous decade. Accordingly, three phases can be identified in the history of India's commercial policies: (1) inward-oriented, state controlled policies (1950–1975); (2) partial liberalization (1976–1991), particularly since the mid-1980s; and (3) major reforms from 1991 onward (Panagariya, 2004).

Table 11.6. MFN Applied Tariffs and Share of Imports by Product, 2008

Product groups	China			India		
	MFN applied duties		Imports	MFN applied duties		Imports
	AVG	Max	Share, %	AVG	Max	Share, %
Animal products	14.7	25	0.2	31.6	100	0.0
Dairy products	12.0	20	0.1	33.8	60	0.0
Fruit, vegetables, plants	14.8	30	0.2	29.7	100	1.1
Coffee, tea	14.7	32	0.0	56.1	100	0.0
Cereals & preparations	23.9	65	0.2	30.8	150	0.7
Oilseeds, fats, & oils	10.6	30	2.1	26.2	100	1.3
Sugars and confectionery	27.4	50	0.1	34.4	60	0.0
Beverages & tobacco	22.9	65	0.2	70.8	150	0.1
Cotton	22.0	40	0.4	17.0	30	0.1
Other agricultural products	11.5	38	0.5	21.9	70	0.4
Fish & fish products	10.7	23	0.5	29.6	30	0.0
Minerals & metals	7.5	50	16.5	7.4	10	29.5
Petroleum	4.5	9	10.1	9.0	10	29.2
Chemicals	6.6	47	11.4	7.9	100	8.0
Wood, paper, etc.	4.4	20	2.5	9.1	10	2.0
Textiles	9.6	38	2.1	14.1	122	1.3
Clothing	16.0	25	0.2	19.9	97	0.0
Leather, footwear, etc.	13.4	25	1.6	10.1	70	0.8
Nonelectrical machinery	7.8	35	13.2	7.1	10	10.1
Electrical machinery	8.0	35	26.0	6.9	10	7.2
Transport equipment	11.5	45	3.6	14.8	100	5.1
Manufactures, n.e.s.	11.9	35	8.6	8.8	10	2.8

Source: World Trade Organisation Integrated Database (accessed August 2010).

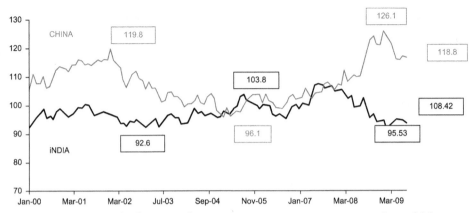

Figure 11.1. Real effective exchange rates, January 1994–June 2010 (monthly).
Source: Bank for International Settlements (data accessed August 2010, at www.bis.org/statistics/eer/index.htm).

During phases (1) and (2), balance-of-payments pressures in the 1950s led to comprehensive import controls to conserve foreign exchange. Such controls rapidly evolved into an explicit strategy to promote import-substituting industrialization behind high and variable import protection backed by central planning to allocate resources. A self-interested bureaucracy, famously dubbed the "license raj" by Bhagwati and Desai (1970), implemented a plethora of controls and restrictions on private sector expansion and exporting. A strict and cumbersome system of licensing and quotas was applied to imports of capital goods, consumer goods, and other inputs. To this formidable battery of trade and investment controls were added policies to foster indigenous technology. Controls were applied at various stages to access foreign technology in the form of foreign direct investments and licensing agreements. For instance, under the Foreign Exchange Regulations Act of 1973, foreign ownership beyond 40% equity was usually not permitted. For licensing, the government imposed strict controls on the payments permitted and the life of the contract. Shielded from competition, a handful of large private firms and state-owned enterprises occupied monopoly positions in major industrial and service sectors.

There were attempts at partial liberalization of imports and exports in phase (2). For instance, in 1979 India introduced an Open General Licensing list, which permitted limited imports of machinery and raw materials not produced domestically. In the mid-1980s, a few measures to promote exports were undertaken, including a passbook scheme for duty-free imports for exporters and the setting of the exchange rate at a more realistic level. Partial liberalization contributed to India's export development in the second half of the 1980s. Albeit from a low base, India's exports of goods and services rose modestly from $8.6 billion to $12.2 billion between 1978 and 1985. India's share of world exports of goods and services, however, fell from 0.6% to 0.5% during the same period. The hallmark of the trade and investment regime during phases (1) and (2) was an antiexport bias, which held back export growth and diversification. Tight controls on technology imports meant that there was only a trickle of FDI inflows and few technology licenses were granted. Overprotection resulted in technological obsolescence, and Indian industry rapidly fell behind world technology frontiers (Lall, 1987).[7] Largely shut out from external markets and technology transfer, India's economy grew unremarkably at the so-called Hindu rate of 3.5% per year during the period 1950–1980.

Economic Reforms

In phase (3), reforms of India's import-substituting industrializing strategy were undertaken from the 1990s onwards. A package of trade and investment reforms were introduced in 1991 and followed by deeper reforms over time, leading to four key changes as follows.

First, in a sweeping liberalization on the trade front, import licensing on machinery and raw materials was abolished in 1991. Licensing on consumer goods was abolished in 2001. This meant that import tariffs became the main protective instrument after 1991.

Second, a gradual reduction in the dispersion of high and variable import tariffs, which had risen significantly in the 1980s, also began in 1991. Tariff reform focused on a gradual compression of the top tariff rates, with simultaneous rationalization of the tariff structure via a reduction in the number of tariff bands.

Third, a depreciated exchange rate was maintained to boost export competitiveness, and better access to foreign exchange for exporting was introduced. The dual exchange rate was unified, and current account convertibility commenced in 1994 in line with International Monetary Fund (IMF) Article 7 obligations.

Fourth, restrictions on foreign ownership were gradually liberalized. A system of automatic clearance for FDI proposals fulfilling various conditions (e.g., ownership levels of 50%, 51%, 74%, and 100%) was established, and new sectors were opened up to foreign ownership (e.g., mining, banking, telecommunications, and various services). Subsequently, 100% foreign ownership was permitted in manufacturing, with some exceptions such as defense-related sectors. In 2005, a Special Economic Zones Act was passed to promote exports from both foreign and local enterprises more systematically.

The post-1991 reforms had a significant impact on India's profile as an international investment destination. Between 1978–1990 and 1991–2010, average annual FDI inflows increased from a tiny $100 million to an unprecedented $9 billion (see table 11.5). The annual averages mask the fact that most of the increase in FDI inflows took place in the second decade after the 1991 reforms, indicating a notable lag between the enactment of policy reforms and major FDI inflows. Annual average FDI inflows rose multifold from $2.5 billion to $20 billion between 1991–2002 and 2003–2010. Inflows of FDI peaked at $41.6 billion in 2008. But the global financial crisis exerted a negative effect on inward investment into India, and FDI inflows fell from this peak level to $34.6 billion in 2009 and remained depressed at $21 billion in 2010. Cumulative FDI inflows amounted to $191.3 billion in 1978–2010, with $155.3 billion occurring in the 1991–2010 period.

The attraction of significant FDI inflows into India is a major achievement of the 1991 reforms. The post-2003 surge in FDI flows is particularly encouraging, and the figures for 2008 and 2010 are starting to match FDI inflows into China in the 1990s. Nonetheless, cumulative FDI inflows are below the levels experienced by China and other high-performing East Asian economies. For instance, cumulative FDI inflows into India during 1978–2009 are only one-sixth of China's in the same period. The entry of FDI into India brought new technologies, skills, and marketing connections and began the process of making Indian manufacturing more internationally competitive. Thus far, India has yet to emulate East Asia's example in fully exploiting the potential for export-oriented FDI inflows into manufacturing. Foreign direct investment into Indian manufacturing has largely focused on serving the large domestic market rather than exports. It is estimated that the share of multinational enterprises in India's exports is small, at less than 10%, compared with 54% in China (Kumar and Sharma, 2009, p. 37; Ministry of Commerce, PRC, 2011). Following a focus on domestic manufacturing, FDI flows have increasingly shifted toward services—particularly IT and financial services. The United States is the single largest source of FDI into India after Mauritius, making up about 16% of total FDI inflows during 1991–2006 (Kumar and Sharma, 2009, p. 39). East Asian economies account for another 14%, and EU countries comprise 24%.

Another aspect of India's post-1991 reform FDI story is the emergence of outward investment. India had limited outward investment in the first decade and a half of reform, but has seen a marked increase thereafter. India's annual average outward FDI increased from a relatively small base of $1 billion to $16.7 billion between 1995–2005 and 2006–2008. There was a fall in outward investment to $14.9 billion in 2009, however, as a result of the global financial crisis. India's cumulative outward investment amounted to $73.1 billion in 1995–2009, which is equivalent to about 40% of China's during the same period.

Import tariffs, which became the main protective instrument following the abolition of licensing, steadily fell during the post-1991 period. On the eve of the 1991 reforms, India was reputed to have the highest import tariffs in the developing world, along with significant dispersion of import tariffs. In 1991, the simple average of all tariffs was 113%, with the highest tariff rate at 355% (Panagariya, 2004, p. 7). A reduction occurred thereafter, with simple average tariffs falling from this peak to 38.7% in 1996 and still further to 13.0% in 2008 (see table 11.5). The main thrust of tariff reduction since 1991 has been on nonagricultural rather than agricultural products. Tariffs on nonagricultural products fell somewhat modestly from 40.1% to 31.4% between 1996 and 2001, but the pace of tariff reduction accelerated in recent years with such tariffs falling to historic lows of 10.1% in 2008. In contrast, tariffs on primary products actually rose from 23.1% to 36.3% between 1996 and 2001, and subsequently reduced somewhat to 32.2% in 2008. In spite of progress in tariff reduction, India's average import tariffs remain higher than China's. While a narrow gap exists on the average tariffs for nonagricultural tariffs, India's average import tariffs on agricultural products are double those of China.

The growing gap between agricultural and non-agricultural tariffs in India also raised dispersion in tariffs. As table 11.6 shows, there is significant dispersion in the tariffs for nonagricultural products, which range from 6.9% for electrical machinery to 29.6% for fish and fish products. The dispersion of tariffs is considerably higher, however, for agricultural products, ranging from 17% for cotton to 70.8% for beverages and tobacco. Accordingly, tariff dispersion seems higher in India than in China.

Unification of the dual exchange rate along with current account convertibility increased the potency of the exchange rate as a trade policy instrument and improved foreign exchange availability for exporters. As figure 11.1 shows, India maintained a stable and predictable REER between January 2000 and May 2005. Since mid-2005, however, the REER has tended to behave more erratically with short periods of sharp depreciation, followed by sharp appreciation. More volatile REER behavior since 2005 reflects differences in inflation between India and its major trading partners. Particularly worrying is the emergence of an appreciating trend after March 2009 linked to rising inflation in India. Accordingly, the REER supported exporting activity between 2000 and mid-2005 but has provided more mixed signals in recent years.

Comparing Commercial Policies and Export Outcomes

China and India have each pursued a distinctive style of commercial policy to shift to an outward-oriented, market-based economy after a long period of inward-oriented, centrally planned policies. Contrary to the prevailing orthodoxy, which emphasized the merits of "big bang" comprehensive reforms pursued by Russia, starting in the late 1970s the giants initiated gradual and incremental reforms over several decades. The giants' interest in a gradualist approach reflects concerns about the strength of the supply response of the private sector to reforms, long process of creating market institutions, and social consequences of economic adjustment. China and India differ, however, in the process of implementing a gradual approach to reforms, including timing, speed, stages, and specific measures adopted. Accordingly, differences in commercial policies have influenced China's rise as a massive global exporter of manufactures and India's expansion into high-skill service exports alongside manufactures.

China was swifter, more coordinated, and more credible in its overall reform process than India. It introduced an open door to FDI in 1978, while India's major reforms came as late as 1991. Attracting export-oriented FDI into the manufacturing sector became the cornerstone of China's commercial policies in the early years of reform and underlies its success in manufactured exports. China evolved a comprehensive FDI policy that enabled it to attract record inflows of export-oriented FDI into manufacturing and to technologically upgrade it over time (via joint ventures and promoting technology transfer). Another FDI spillover is growing Chinese outward investment to Asia and the rest of the world.

India was slower in adopting a comprehensive policy framework for export-oriented FDI. It initially focused on liberalizing restrictions on foreign ownership, which is perhaps insufficient in a highly competitive international environment for attracting export-oriented FDI. For instance, other measures like SEZ legislation only date to 2005. Moreover, the somewhat cumbersome process of reforming FDI rules led to criticisms by foreign investors that the country's FDI regime was complicated and nontransparent. Inflows of FDI increased but remained below expected levels in the first decade of reforms, indicating caution about foreign investment in the Indian economy. Nonetheless, an improvement in India's investment climate in the second reform decade was accompanied by a surge in FDI inflows, particularly into services. If the FDI surge continues, India has the potential to become a significant global services hub with a respectable manufacturing export base.

Export promotion via FDI took place in China alongside controlled liberalization of a protected domestic sector. China was cautious in reforming its import control regime during the early transition years, but the process was strengthened from 1992 onward by reforms to accede to the WTO. Steady progress in tariff reform occurred, so that China has presently emerged as one of the more open economies in the developing world. Increased import competition induced increased efficiency, industrial restructuring, and exporting in a formerly protected domestic enterprise sector. India dramatically abolished import licensing on machinery and raw materials in 1991, and tariff reform has resulted in a far more open import regime than ever before. Nonetheless, India's average tariffs and their dispersion still remain higher than China's.

In an environment of gradual tariff reform, exchange rate management became a critical tool to encourage exporting activity in the giants. China introduced currency convertibility on current account transactions, while India unified the dual exchange rate and commenced current account convertibility. Following improved access to foreign exchange, the giants both pursued managed floating exchange rate policies to maintain relatively stable and predictable nominal exchange rates. Both also had some success in maintaining a favorable REER for exporting activity during the 2000s, but China seems to have done somewhat better than India in this regard.

III. PURSUIT OF FTA-LED REGIONALISM

In another marked shift in commercial policy since the early 2000s, the giants have each pursued a variety of bilateral and regional trade agreements alongside multilateralism. These moves have promoted some concerns about the possible detrimental impact of FTAs on exporting for two reasons. One is the shallow coverage of FTAs, which are said to be quite liberalizing when it comes to the goods trade, with the exception of agriculture, but quite thin and vague in scope compared with most agreements formed in the Americas or across the Pacific (Suominen, 2009). Second, there is the problem of the so-called Asian "noodle bowl" of FTAs. Informed by Jagdish Bhagwati's famous insight of a spaghetti bowl of FTAs and applied to

Asia, the noodle bowl description suggests that different tariffs and rules of origin in multiple FTAs have resulted in the problem of crisscrossing agreements that are characterized by excessive exclusions and special treatment (Baldwin, 2008). Quite apart from a potential distortion of trade toward bilateral channels, it is suggested that firms face large administrative burdens, such as the need to deal with multiple rules of origin, which results in little use of the FTAs. Are these concerns valid?

Motivations for FTAs

By October 2010, the giants were among the region's leaders in FTA activity, with 11 FTAs in effect each (see table 11.7). Looking at FTAs under negotiation and proposed FTAs suggests that such activity will rise in the future, as China has another

Table 11.7. Classification of FTAs in effect (as of October 2010)

	Country/FTAs	Goods liberalization[a]	Coverage of services sectors[b]	Coverage of Singapore issues[c]
China				
1	Asia–Pacific Trade Agreement (1976)	Partial	No provision	No provision
2	PRC–Thailand FTA (2003)	Partial	No provision	No provision
3	PRC–Hong Kong CEPA (2004)	WTO-compliant	Partial	No provision
4	PRC–Macao CEPA (2004)	WTO-compliant	Partial	No provision
5	ASEAN–China FTA (2005)	WTO-compliant	Partial	Partial (investment)
6	PRC–Chile FTA (2006)	WTO-compliant	Partial	Partial (trade facilitation)
7	New Zealand-PRC FTA (2008)	WTO-compliant	Partial	Partial (investment, trade facilitation)
8	PR–Pakistan FTA (2007)	Partial	Partial	Partial (investment)
9	PR–Singapore FTA (2008)	WTO-compliant	Comprehensive	Partial (trade facilitation)
10	PR–Peru FTA (2009)	WTO-compliant	Partial	Partial (investment, trade facilitation)
11	Economic Cooperation Framework Agreement[/d] (2010)	Partial	Partial	Partial (investment)
India				
1	Asia–Pacific Trade Agreement (1976)	Partial	No provision	No provision

Table 11.7. (*continued*)

	Country/FTAs	Goods liberalization[a]	Coverage of services sectors[b]	Coverage of Singapore issues[c]
2	India–Sri Lanka FTA (2001)	WTO-compliant	No provision	No provision
3	India–Nepal Treaty of Trade (2002)	Partial	No provision	Partial (trade facilitation)
4	India–Afghanistan PTA (2003)	Partial	No provision	No provision
5	India–Singapore CECA (2005)	WTO-compliant	Comprehensive	Partial (investment, trade facilitation)
6	South Asian FTA (2006)	Partial	Partial (SATIS signed)*	Partial (trade facilitation)
7	India–Bhutan Trade Agreement (2006)	Partial	No provision	Partial (trade facilitation)
8	India–Chile PTA (2007)	Partial	No provision	No provision
9	Indi–MERCOSUR PTA (2009)	Partial	No provision	No provision
10	Indi–Korea CEPA (2009)	WTO-compliant	Comprehensive	Comprehensive (government procurement cooperation only)
11	ASEA–India FTA (2009)	Partial	No provision	Partial (customs procedure cooperation only)

Notes: [a] An FTA is "WTO-compliant" following GATT Article 24, where tariffs are eliminated on at least 85% of either or both FTA members' tariff lines (or goods traded) within 10 years. Otherwise, it has partial coverage.
[b] Comprehensive coverage if an FTA covers the 5 key sectors of the GATS: business and professional services, communications services, financial services, transport services, and labor mobility/entry of business persons. "No provision" means there is no liberalization provision on services sector. "Partial" are those not otherwise classified as comprehensive or no provision.
[c] Comprehensive are those that covers all the Singapore issues of investment, competition policy, government procurement, and trade facilitation. Partial if only 1 to 3 Singapore issues are in the FTAs. No provision means those without any provision on Singapore issues.
[d] This refers to the FTA between China and Taipei that came into effect on 12 September 2010.
Source: Author's estimates based on ADB, Asian Regional Integration Center Database. (http://aric.adb.org)

14 agreements in the pipeline and India another 22. Meanwhile, the relatively limited (goods only) Asia-Pacific Trade Agreement (APTA) signed in 2001 is the only FTA between China and India.

The giants' interest in FTAs may seem somewhat surprising, as India is a founding WTO member and China only joined the WTO in 2001. This interest can be attributed to three main causes:[8] (1) the expansion of European and North American FTA-led regionalism, which highlights large economic gains (e.g., economies of scale, specialization, and inward investment) available from integrating fragmented regional markets; (2) the lack of progress in the multilateral WTO Doha Round trade negotiations, which has encouraged FTAs to be considered as an alternative means of securing market access in goods and services as well as venturing into new trade issues not covered by the Doha Round; and (3) increasing recognition that FTAs are a part of a supporting policy framework for deepening production networks and supply chains formed by global multinational corporations and emerging Asian firms.

Reflecting China's relatively recent FTA experience, it has FTAs with trading partners in the developing world—ASEAN members, Hong Kong, Taipei, Macao, Pakistan, Chile, and Peru—but only one agreement with a developed economy—New Zealand. China's FTA strategy appears to be driven by economic motivations related to China's emergence as the global factory though a pivotal role in Asian production networks. It views FTAs as supporting the functioning of Asian production networks in electronics and automotives, and as means of gaining preferential market access for manufactured exports. To this end, the ASEAN–China FTA, which is an important building block for an Asia-wide FTA, has effectively created the world's largest free trade zone facilitating the parts and components trade in ASEAN economies and final assembly in China. The agreements with Hong Kong, Taipei, and Macao are natural extensions of the free trade zone into the region. The impetus for such agreements to reduce trade barriers and costs has come from overseas Chinese investors, who account for the bulk of inward investment into China. The FTA with Pakistan provides initial access to the large and growing South Asian market. The FTA with New Zealand provided China with an opportunity to learn about negotiating comprehensive new-age FTAs with developed countries, as well as to attract FDI and technology transfer in the dairy industry. The FTAs with Chile and Peru are beachheads in the Latin American market and a means of fostering closer transpacific cooperation.

China's future FTAs consist of a mix of subregional and bilateral agreements. Prominent among the subregional FTAs is a China-Japan-Korea agreement, which is critical to the formation of an Asia-wide FTA and the deepening of production networks. The FTAs with the South African Customs Union and Gulf Cooperation Council facilitate access to commodity imports to fuel China's rapid industrialization and to regional markets for its manufactured exports. Unlike in the case of India, there is little sign of FTA discussions with China's major trading partners in the developed world—notably the EU and United States—which may reflect trading partners' concerns about the impact of China's highly competitive manufactured exports on domestic employment. For the same reason, there has been little movement in official FTA discussions with India.

China seems to be experimenting with alternative formats for FTAs in an attempt to eventually evolve a template akin to what the United States uses for FTA negotiations. In earlier FTAs with ASEAN and Chile, China has followed a gradual approach, whereby goods were liberalized first, then services and investment. A single undertaking, however, characterizes more recent bilateral FTAs with New Zealand and Singapore.

With a smaller manufacturing base and the relatively late adoption of trade liberalization, India's initial motivation for concluding FTAs appears to have been different from China's. Motivated by a political commitment to the Non-Aligned Movement, India has long supported the expansion of South-South trade though agreements focused on market access for good trade. In this vein, it was party to the region's first agreement (APTA) as early as 1976. Following a long period of detailed negotiation, a spate of bilateral FTAs followed with smaller South Asian neighbors, including Afghanistan, Bhutan, Nepal, and Sri Lanka; a subregional South Asian Free Trade Area in an attempt to access markets in Bangladesh and Pakistan; and bilateral agreements with Chile and MERCOSUR. The South-South thrust of India's FTA strategy continues, with agreements under negotiation with several Latin American and African countries. India's FTA strategy evolved to encompass major trading partners as economic motivations and market access became more prominent after the 1991 economic reforms. Recent extensions reflect India's Look East Policy of fostering economic ties with economically important East Asia and the needs of its growing services sector to access developed countries. India has put into effect FTAs with ASEAN, Singapore, and Korea as stepping stones toward an ASEAN+6 FTA. India is also engaged in active FTA negotiations with several developed countries, including Japan, the EU, Australia, and New Zealand. Developed country interest in negotiating FTAs with India reflects complementarities in factor endowments and trade patterns, as well as a recent surge in multinational investment focused on the large domestic Indian market.

Evaluating FTA Quality

What is the quality of China's and India's existing FTAs in relation to best practices? Evaluating FTA quality against best practices is difficult for two reasons. First, it requires detailed and often painstaking examination of the legal texts of FTAs. Second, an internationally accepted methodology for assessing the quality of FTA provisions against best practices is absent. One way forward is to attempt to evaluate the compatibility of China's and India's FTAs against existing (or future) global rules. Building on recent research, some simple legal and economic evaluation criteria were developed to gauge the giants' FTAs according to tariff elimination on the goods trade, coverage of services sectors, and coverage of trade issues beyond goods and services (Plummer, 2007; Wignaraja and Lazaro, 2010). The tariff elimination criteria reflected article 24 of the General Agreement on Tariffs and Trade (GATT). The FTAs that eliminated tariffs on at least 85% of tariff lines (of either or all FTA partners) within 10 years were classed as WTO-compliant. The criteria for services liberalization relied on the coverage of sectors included in the General Agreement on Trade in Services (GATS). The FTAs that covered five key sectors of the GATS were taken as "comprehensive," those with less than five sectors as "partial," and those without any coverage as "no provision." The four so-called Singapore issues[9] in the context of WTO negotiations—investment, competition policy, government procurement, and trade facilitation—are convenient for examining trade issues beyond goods and services. The FTAs that covered all four Singapore issues were classed as comprehensive and the remainder as partial or no provision.

Table 11.7 presents the details of the classification system and the results for individual FTAs in China and India. Legal texts from the FTA database of the Asian Development Bank (ADB) were used for the empirical application of these criteria. The results are quite revealing about the quality of China and India's FTAs in terms of existing or future global rules. The key findings are given below.

The overall quality of China and India's trade agreements varies. Of the giants' 22 FTAs, in effect, 10 are WTO-compliant on goods liberalization, three are comprehensive in services coverage, and one is comprehensive in coverage of Singapore issues. The best FTAs are probably the PRC-Singapore FTA, which is WTO-compliant on goods and comprehensive in services coverage, and the India-Korea Comprehensive Economic Partnership Agreement (CEPA), which is comprehensive in both services coverage and Singapore issues, in addition to being WTO-compliant on goods.

In terms of goods liberalization, China's FTAs seem better than India's. Seven of China's FTAs are WTO-compliant, compared with three for India. Some examples of WTO-compliant agreements are useful to highlight differences in the giants' approaches with their trading partners. Under the PRC-Singapore FTA, 95% of China's tariff lines are eliminated within one year. Singapore, of course, has virtually zero tariffs for most items, and tariff elimination is not considered a major trade policy issue. The New Zealand-China FTA allows for immediate elimination of 35% of China's tariff lines on entry into force and 96% within eight years. The ASEAN-China FTA allows for longer adjustment periods for Least Developed Countries and accordingly eliminates 90% of the tariff lines of China and the more advanced ASEAN economies within five years, while the economies of Cambodia, Myanmar, Lao People's Democratic Republic, and Viet Nam (CLMV) have 10 years. Meanwhile, the India-Korea FTA liberalizes 75% of India's tariff lines within eight years and 93% of Korea's. The India-Singapore FTA immediately eliminates tariffs on 80% of the value of India's imports from Singapore.

The coverage of services also seems better in China's FTAs than India's. The PRC-Singapore FTA allows for comprehensive coverage of services, while another seven of China's FTAs cover partial liberalization in services. The PRC-Singapore agreement significantly builds on the ASEAN-China FTA by allowing for the movement of natural persons. By comparison, and with the notable exceptions of the India-Korea CEPA and the India-Singapore CECA, India's FTAs seem more limited in services coverage. In a move to extend services coverage to the regional level, a South Asian Trade in Services Agreement was signed in April 2010.

The four Singapore issues are selectively covered in the giants' FTAs. Seven of China's FTAs cover one or two Singapore issues. For instance, investment and trade facilitation[10] are both covered in the PRC-New Zealand FTA and the PRC-Peru FTA, while the PRC-Pakistan FTA and the Economic Cooperation Framework Agreement covers only investment. More sensitive issues of government procurement and competition policy are absent from China's FTAs. Meanwhile, the India-Korea FTA comprehensively covers three Singapore issues. While there is no separate chapter on government procurement, there is a cooperation provision on government procurement that opens the door for liberalization in this difficult area. Another four of India's FTAs, including the South Asia Free Trade Area, only cover trade facilitation, while the India-Singapore FTA covers both trade facilitation and investment. China and India's remaining FTAs exclude the Singapore issues altogether.

Are FTAs Used?

Most unfortunately, neither China nor India publishes official data on FTA use from certificates of origin or information on impediments to using FTAs. This is a major gap that needs to be addressed in the future. Nonetheless, it is possible to explore this issue by looking at trade with FTA partners, which is indicative of potential use, and evidence from firm surveys.

The giants' increasing FTA numbers have been accompanied by trade with FTA partners gaining in importance over the first decade of the twenty-first century. While the majority of international trade is still with non-FTA partners, we estimate that about 27% of China's total trade and 23% of India's was potentially covered by FTAs in 2008.[11] Encouragingly, these figures are up considerably from less than 5% in 2003.

Relatively high FTA use among firms in China compared with other Asian countries is indicated by a recent multicountry, multienterprise ADB survey.[12] About 45% of the firms in the country-wide Chinese survey said that they had used FTAs, and more said they planned to do so in the future.[13] The use of FTAs in China is higher than previously thought for Asian countries (Baldwin, 2008). The ADB survey also highlights impediments to using FTAs at the firm level in China. Interestingly, few firms seemed concerned by the Asian noodle bowl effect, with only 6% of the Chinese sample expressing concerns about significant transactions costs arising from multiple rules of origin in overlapping agreements. As more FTAs come into effect, however, the noodle bowl remains a future risk for the region. Instead, the key impediments to FTA use in China turned out to be a lack of information on FTA provisions and business impacts, nontariff measures in overseas markets, small margins of preference, and the availability of alternative export incentives (e.g., export processing zone schemes and the Information Technology Agreement).

Unfortunately, information on use of FTAs is not yet available for Indian firms from the ADB survey or other sources. But our discussions with the Federation of Indian Industry and Commerce (FICCI) suggested that its members were increasingly aware of the benefits of FTAs, such as the Indo-Lanka FTA and the ASEAN-India FTA, and had begun to use them to facilitate the goods and services trade with FTA partners.[14] They also said that India's FTAs with Sri Lanka and ASEAN had facilitated an increase in intraregional investment in manufacturing and IT services.

Thus, there seems little evidence of detrimental effects on exports of China and India's FTAs. The giants' FTA strategies still appear to be in the formative stages. China's FTAs with regional developing economies are geared toward supporting its role as the global factory and the deepening of production networks. From an initial focus on South-South trade, India has recently moved toward seeking market access to East Asia and major developed countries. China's FTAs seem to have better coverage in terms of goods and services. Use of the FTA, at least in China, also seems higher than expected. Nonetheless, both countries can improve the coverage of Singapore issues in future FTAs and adopt best practices in designing rules of origin and origin administration.

IV. EMERGING CHALLENGES SINCE THE GLOBAL FINANCIAL CRISIS

Growth in China and India has rebounded from the 2008 global financial crisis, while the world economy remains sluggish (ADB, 2011). The global financial crisis marked the end of a period of respectable world growth and expanding employment in major industrial economies. Unprecedented fiscal stimulus efforts coupled with low interest rates averted a 1930s-style economic depression. Nonetheless, slow economic growth with high unemployment in much of the developed world appears to characterize the likely scenario in the medium term. This somewhat pessimistic scenario is linked to unusually high levels of public debt, the crisis in the eurozone economies, lackluster private investment, and fragile consumer confidence. Some developed countries are in the process of making large cuts in public expenditures, which may accentuate the slowdown at least in the short run. A lack of progress on the WTO Doha Round on the magnitude of reductions in agricultural subsidies and industrial tariffs continues to deprive the world economy of a major source of trade-led growth. Added to this are growing concerns about a double-dip recession in the United States and a slowdown in China's fast economic growth. While the magnitude of world economic growth in the medium term is difficult to forecast, the consensus forecast is for a downward direction.

The new world macroeconomic era will pose several important commercial policy challenges for China and India, including (1) the risk of protectionism, (2) exchange rate management, (3) increased FTA use by businesses, (4) removing impediments to China-India trade, and (5) complementary policies.[15] How well the giants tackle these challenges will partly determine the continued pace of their trade-led growth.

Risk of protectionism. High unemployment in the wake of the global financial crisis has prompted influential industrial lobby groups in G-20 economies to call for the protection of domestic industries. Mass public sector redundancies induced by public sector expenditure cuts are likely to accentuate such calls in the future. The

available evidence suggests a modest rise in protectionist measures in G-20 economies since 2008 with emphasis on less transparent nontariff measures (particularly SPS and TBT measures),[16] public procurement, and local buy-back schemes,
rather than industrial tariffs per se.[17] There has also been a rise in anti-dumping and
safeguard measures with some targeting of highly-competitive, labor-intensive
exports from China and India. Concluding the WTO Doha Round offers the best
insurance against rising protectionism and a modest deal is better than no deal at
all. The giants are well placed to steer WTO members towards a less ambitious Doha
deal involving some reductions in agricultural subsidies and industrial tariffs as
well as trade facilitation. Such a deal may be supported by increased aid for trade
and enhanced special and differential treatment to mitigate negative effects on
lesser-developed and small vulnerable economies. In addition, China and India
need to improve surveillance on non-tariff measures in overseas markets, improve
business support to cope with Sanitary and Phytosanitary (SPS) and the Agreement
on Technical Barriers to Trade (TBT) measures affecting specific exports, and
upgrade legal capacity to deal with antidumping cases at the WTO.

Exchange rate management. China is now under international pressure to revalue its currency. Section II discussed China's exchange rate policy and export
development. Recent policy attention, particularly in the United States, has been
devoted to the links between the management of the renminbi, China's trade surplus, and the U.S. trade deficit. It has been suggested that China's exchange rate does
matter for global rebalancing.[18] These findings have led to influential voices calling
in early 2010 for stepped-up multilateral initiatives in the IMF and WTO to promote appreciation of the exchange rate of the renminbi (Bergsten, 2010). On 19 June
2010, during the leadup to the G-20 meeting in Toronto, the Peoples Bank of China
announced that it would further reform the renminbi's exchange rate, thereby shifting to a more flexible exchange rate policy (Hu, 2010). In particular, the announce-
ment indicated continued emphasis on reflecting market supply and demand with
reference to a currency basket, and maintaining wider exchange rate floating bands.
Discussions in international fora and concerns about domestic inflation may lie
behind the latest reforms. On 29 September 2010, the U.S. House of Representatives
passed legislation that would allow the United States to use estimates of currency
undervaluation to calculate countervailing duties on imports from China and other
countries. This move has sparked fears of a looming currency and trade war. A prolonged dispute over the currency issue could damage China-U.S. trade and exert a
negative impact on the two economies and the world economy. Accordingly,
stepped-up international diplomacy may be necessary to resolve the issue. As India
becomes more prominent in world export markets, it is possible that its exchange
rate management may also emerge as an international policy issue.

Increased use of FTAs by businesses. Section III suggested that the giants have
pursued a variety of FTAs to liberalize the goods and services trade in the region,
and that FTA use among Chinese firms was reasonable. Awareness of FTA provisions, however, varies among business in China and other Asian countries. Small-
and medium-sized enterprises (SMEs) seem less well informed than large firms and

tend to use FTAs less. Some firms also complain about cumbersome bureaucratic procedures associated with exporting through FTAs, such as stringent rules of origin and poor origin administration. Accordingly, both giants (particularly India) need to adopt more proactive outreach measures to involve business associations in FTA negotiations and inform them of the benefits of FTAs through simple business guides and websites. They also need to adopt best practices in rules of origin in FTAs—coequality of rules, regional cumulation, and origin administration by business associations—and enhance technical and other business support services to assist firms to make use of FTAs. In the medium term, a move toward a broad and deep Asia-wide FTA would significantly enhance business use of FTAs. It could provide a common and predictable policy framework for business, enable the realization of economies of scale, and be attractive to inward investment (Chia, 2010). Model-based studies suggest that an ASEAN+6 FTA—including China, India, Japan, Korea, Australia, and New Zealand, along with the ASEAN economies, and covering goods, services, and trade facilitation—would bring higher welfare gains than alternative FTA scenarios. The formation of an ASEAN+6 FTA is expected to realize world income gains of around $260 billion (Kawai and Wignaraja, 2011). Interestingly, China is projected to see income gains of $43.6 billion under an ASEAN+6 FTA, while the figure for India is $19.2 billion.

Removing impediments to China-India trade. China-India trade has boomed in recent years as a sign of a rapidly deepening China-India economic relationship (Whalley and Shekhar, 2010). Each is deeply integrating into the world economy through trade and FDI flows. Global integration has fostered bilateral trade amid slow trade growth in traditional developed country markets. Two-way trade between China and India was estimated at $60 billion in 2010 (up significantly from a small base of only $2.3 billion in 2000). Some have raised concerns that such trade is unbalanced in the sense that China has a large trade surplus with India—and that India exports raw materials and semifinished products in return for manufactures from China. Nonetheless, trade with China has provided the spur of competition for Indian industry to upgrade technological capabilities and stimulated skill-intensive service exports to China (including information technologies). Acceleration of reforms in India in the 2000s also provides an opportunity to unleash the private sector and narrow the trade performance gap with China. On balance, therefore, growing China-India trade will bring gains to both parties in the long run.

To facilitate more two-way trade, China and India should continue lowering trade and nontariff barriers, invest in trade-related infrastructure, and streamline crossborder procedures to reduce trade costs, reduce barriers to services trade, and encourage more business-to-business contact. Improving bilateral trade policy cooperation would be an additional useful future step. An eventual China-India FTA can provide a means to cement gains from bilateral trade between the giants by providing a rules-based framework for trade and investment as well as expand market access and crossborder investment A China-India FTA needs to be consistent with WTO rules and comprehensive in its coverage of goods, services and investment.

Implementing complementary policies. Maintaining export competitiveness and shifting to new areas of comparative advantage in China and India in the new macroeconomic era will require complementary supply-side support in addition to continuing with gradual commercial policy liberalization. The liberalization of trade and investment regimes provides incentives for firms to invest in competitive technological capabilities and link up to production networks, while supply-side support provides requisite inputs for the process.

Enhancing crossborder infrastructure investment is a key area. A huge need for infrastructure investment in Asia, estimated at about $750 billion annually during 2010–2020, was identified by ADB/ADBI (2009). The study also identified about 20 priority infrastructure projects, including several involving the giants. With large financial reserves emanating from export surpluses, the giants can play an enhanced role in financing large multimodal, crossborder infrastructure projects involving neighboring economies and linking each other's markets. As table 11.8 shows, China spends more of its GDP on infrastructure than India. China also fairs better than India on indicators of overall infrastructure quality as well as the quality of roads and electricity supply according to opinion surveys of business people collected by the World Economic Forum.

Table 11.8. Infrastructure, business regulation, and technology

Indicators	Year	China	India
Infrastructure spending (% of GDP)[a]	2007–2008	11	6
Quality of overall infrastructure (where 1 = top quality)[b]	2008–2009	66	89
Quality of roads[b]	2008–2009	50	89
Quality of electricity supply[b]	2008–2009	61	106
Ease of doing business index (1 = most business-friendly regulations)[c]	2009	89	133
Starting a business[c]	2009	151	169
Registering property[c]	2009	32	93
Enforcing contracts[c]	2009	18	182
Closing a business[c]	2009	65	138
Research and development expenditure (% of GDP)[d]	1996	0.6	0.7
	2007	1.5	0.8
Researchers in R & D (per million people)[d]	1996	448	154
	2007/2005	1071	137

Sources: [a]India Economic Survey 2010. [b]World Economic Forum, Global Competitiveness Report (2006, 2010). [c]World Bank, Doing Business Report 2010. [d]World Bank, World Development Indicators Online (accessed August 2010).

Increasing industrial R & D efforts is another key area. For maintaining competitiveness in medium- and high-technology industries, and ensuring technology spillovers from FDI to local firms, R & D is a pre-requisite. Table 11.8 shows two measures of R & D efforts in China and India since 1996, R & D expenditures as a percent of GDP and researchers in R & D per million people. The data indicate India lags significantly behind China in both measures. Strikingly, India's R & D expenditures are just under half of China's, while its ratio of R & D researchers is about one-tenth of China's.

Reducing bureaucratic impediments to conducting business is a final area of complementary policies. Both giants score relatively high on the World Bank's overall ease of doing business index in 2009, meaning that they do less well compared with the world's top performers but China seems better placed than India. China does better, in particular, in registering property, enforcing contracts, and closing a business.

V. Conclusions

This chapter has analyzed the role of commercial policies in the rise of China and India in world trade over the last three decades. In a radical break with past economic policies, China and India adopted market-oriented commercial policies in the late 1970s to boost exports and the private sector. More recently, the giants have pursued FTA-led regionalism alongside multilateralism. Few foresaw the future impact the giants would collectively have on world trade patterns or the magnitude of adjustment required in the rest of the world.

The trade performance of China and India has been impressive by the standards of either developing countries or developed countries. Within a relatively short time span of about a generation, the giants have emerged both as major players in world trade and as notable outward investors. Following early entry into low-technology products, the giants have steadily upgraded into medium- and high-technology products, as well as skill-intensive services. While the two are often compared, China seems to have roared ahead in world trade in manufactures and is on the verge of challenging the United States as the world's largest exporter. India's export expansion has been primarily driven by services, and it is attempting to play catchup in a range of manufactured exports.

The foundations for the giants' success lie in initial conditions. These include China's proximity to Japan, which facilitated inward investment and a large, dynamic domestic market. Both India and China had access to ample supplies of low-cost, productive manpower.

The switch in commercial policies has played a significant role in the trade performance of China and India. China, of course, was swifter and introduced an open door policy toward export-oriented FDI in the late 1970s, alongside controlled liberalization of imports. India introduced some reforms in the late 1970s, but the major reforms came after 1991. The difference in trade performance between China and India, however, is not simply a matter of the timing of changes in commercial policies. Closer examination suggests that China had a more comprehensive approach to attracting export-oriented FDI, actively facilitated technological upgrading of FDI and exports, reduced import tariffs and the dispersion of tariffs in a more systematic manner, typically managed a more predictable and transparent REER, and provided for more comprehensive liberalization in goods and services provisions in its FTAs with Asian developing economies. In recent years, India has attempted to put in place appropriate commercial policies, particularly on attracting export-oriented FDI, and liberalizing tariffs. India is also attempting ambitious FTA negotiations with developed countries that could provide market access and FDI inflows, among other benefits. Therefore, one might reasonably expect the gap in trade and investment performance between the giants to narrow over time but China's dominance in manufactures to continue for at least the next decade.[19]

Both China and India face a new and more uncertain world economic environment in the post–global financial crisis era. The effect of this new economic era on trade performance in the giants will depend crucially on how each copes with the risk of protectionism, manages exchange rate issues, increases business use of FTAs, reduces impediments to bilateral trade, and implements complementary policies. The giants seem set to increase their dominance of world trade in the next decade, and adapting commercial policies, along with other measures, will play a notable role in success.

I am most grateful to Max Kreinin and Michael Plummer for comments, and to Anna-Mae Tuazon for efficient research assistance.

NOTES

1. The views expressed here are solely the author's and should not be attributed to the Asian Development Bank.

2. See WTO (2011).

3. 1995 and 2005 figures from Anantaram and Saquib (2010, p. 141).

4. 2010 (January to August) data from Ministry of Commerce, PRC, 2011.

5. For recent micro-level level studies of the relationship between imported technology (via FDI and foreign buyers) and innovation and learning in Chinese manufacturing (e.g. electronics, automotives, and textiles) see Wignaraja (2008, 2011). The evidence indicates that impressive levels of technological capabilities to use imported technologies efficiently underlie China's export success.

6. Zhang et al. (1998) evaluated the structure of trade protection in China and present estimates of static costs. They suggest that trade liberalization would lead to short-term costs in terms of lost domestic output and employment but estimate long-run benefits to be in the range of about $35 billion.

7. Lall's pioneering study of the acquisition of technological capabilities in Indian industry during the early 1980s concludes: "even the leading enterprises find themselves unable to undertake the development of major new products and process technologies. More interestingly, they find it difficult to copy many new advances in product technology (for sophisticated new equipment, for instance) on their own" (Lall 1987, p. 238).

8. See Kawai and Wignaraja (2011).

9. The Singapore issues refer to four working groups set up during the WTO Ministerial Conference of 1996 in Singapore. These groups are tasked with these issues: (1) transparency in government procurement, (2) trade facilitation (customs issues), (3) trade and investment, and (4) trade and competition. The four Singapore issues were conditionally included in the work program for the Doha Development Round global trade talks, but were dropped at the WTO Ministerial Conference in Cancun in 2004.

10. Trade facilitation refers to the simplification and harmonization of the customs procedures that regulate international trade to reduce cost burdens while safeguarding legitimate regulatory objectives.

11. The number of FTAs is relatively easy to track over time, but by themselves the numbers do not indicate the importance of FTAs to economic activity or trade at the national level. It is informative to get an idea of how much of a country's world trade is covered by FTA provisions. This is difficult to measure because of exceptions and exclusions contained in many agreements. Furthermore, official statistics on utilization rates of FTA preferences in Asia are hard to come by, and published data on the direction of services trade do not exist. Nevertheless, by making the bold assumption that all goods trade is covered by concluded FTAs, indicative estimates can be obtained.

12. The ADB surveys provided data on the incidence of firms that use FTAs in six Asian countries (Kawai and Wignaraja eds. 2011). Use of FTAs is as follows: China (45%), Japan (29%), Thailand (25%), Korea (21%), Singapore (20%), and the Philippines (20%).

13. Use of FTAs is closely linked to innovation and learning processes at the firm level in China, thereby underlining the importance of technology-based approaches to trade. Econometric analysis of the decision to export among a sample of Chinese firms reveals that FTA use, export experience, foreign ownership, and R & D expenditures all influence the probability of exporting (Wignaraja 2010).

14. Meetings with FICCI officials, including Manab Majumdar (assistant secretary-general, FICCI) and Manish Mohan (senior director, FICCI), in New Delhi, 12 April 2010.

15. Winters and Yusuf (2007) and Gerhaeusser et al. (2010) comprehensively deal with other future economic policy challenges facing the giants, including demographics, financial integration, the environment, and governance.

16. During the Uruguay Round of multilateral trade negotiations, member nations established the Agreement on the Application of Sanitary and Phytosanitary (SPS) Measures and the Agreement on Technical Barriers to Trade (TBT) to address the emerging debate over the use of standards in international trade. Generally speaking, the SPS Agreement is a compromise that permits countries to take measures to protect public health within their borders as long as they do so in a manner that restricts trade as little as possible. Similarly, the TBT Agreement strikes a delicate balance between the policy goals of trade facilitation and national autonomy in technical regulations.

17. OECD, WTO, and UNCTAD (2010) suggests that new import restricting measures introduced on 1 September 2009 covered 0.7% of G-20 imports and 0.4% of total world imports through mid-February 2010. Similar figures for October 2008—October 2009 were 1.3% and 0.8%, respectively. The joint report concludes that there is no indication of a significant increase of trade or investment restriction during the period under

review, but notes that some G-20 members have continued to put in place measures that potentially restrict trade, directly or indirectly. New trade restrictions tend to be concentrated in sectors that are relatively protected and also relatively labor intensive, including minerals, textiles, and metal products.

18. A recent econometric study by Cline (2010), for instance, based on certain assumptions, estimates that at a 2010 scale, a 10% real effective appreciation would reduce China's current account surplus by $170–$250 billion. The corresponding gain in the U.S. current account balance would range from $22–$63 billion.

19. Some popular accounts (e.g. see *Economist*, 2 October 2010) predict that India's growth may overtake China by 2013. Several factors are said to be in India's favor, including a relatively young and growing workforce, a base of world-class companies led by English-speaking bosses, and democratic institutions. Weighed against this is a much larger export base in China; much higher levels of investment in R & D, skills, and infrastructure; and better policy coordination and implementation. I am grateful to Alan Winters for clarifying this point about the giants' future prospects.

BIBLIOGRAPHY

ADB (2011). *Asian Development Outlook 2010 Update*. Manila: Asian Development Bank.

ADB/ADBI (2009). *Infrastructure for a Seamless Asia*. Manila: Asian Development Bank and Tokyo: Asian Development Bank Institute.

Anantaram, R., and M. Saqib (2010). "The People's Republic of China's Manufacturing Sector since 1978." In K. Gerhaeusser, I. Iwasaki, and V. B. Tulasidhar, eds., *Resurging Asian Giants: Lessons from the Peoples Republic of China and India*. Manila: Asian Development Bank.

Amsden, A. (2001). *The Rise of the Rest: Challenges to the West from Late-Industrializing Economies*. Oxford: Oxford University Press.

Baldwin, R. E. (2008). "Managing the Noodle Bowl: The Fragility of East Asian Regionalism." *Singapore Economic Review* 53(3), pp. 449–478.

Bergsten, F. C. (2010). "Correcting the Chinese Exchange Rate: An Action Plan." Testimony before the Committee on Ways and Means, U.S. House of Representatives, March 24, 2010. Washington, D.C.: Petersen Institute for International Economics, available at www.piie.com.

Bhagwati, J. N., and P. Desai (1970). *India: Planning for Industrialization*. Oxford: Oxford University Press.

Chia, S. Y. (2010). *Regional Trade Policy Cooperation and Architecture in East Asia*. ADBI Working Paper Series, no. 191 (February). Tokyo: Asian Development Bank Institute.

Cline, W. (2010). *Renminbi Undervaluation, China's Surplus, and the US Trade Deficit*. Peterson Institute for International Economics Policy Brief, no. PB10–20 (August). Washington, D.C.: Peterson Institute for International Economics.

Davies, K. (2010). *Outward FDI from China and Its Policy Content*. Columbia FDI Profiles. New York: Vale Columbia Center on Sustainable Development (18 October).

Gerhaeusser, K., I. Iwasaki, and V.B Tulasidhar, eds. (2010). *Resurging Asian Giants: Lessons from the Peoples Republic of China and India*. Manila: Asian Development Bank.

Hu, X. (2010). "A Managed Floating Exchange Rate Regime Is an Established Policy." Speech (15 July). Beijing: Peoples Bank of China. Available at www.pbc.gov.cn.

Kawai, M., and G. Wignaraja (2011). "Asian FTAs: Trends, Challenges and Prospects." *Journal of Asian Economics* 22, pp. 1–22.

Kawai, M., and G. Wignaraja, eds. (2011). *Asia's Free Trade Agreements: How Is Business Responding?* Cheltenham, England: Edward Elgar.

Kowalski, P. (2010). "China and India: A Tale of Two Trade Integration Approaches." In B. Eichengreen, P. Gupta, and R. Kumar, eds., *Emerging Giants: China and India in the World Economy.* Oxford: Oxford University Press.

Kumar, N., and P. Sharma (2009). "India." In J. Francois, P. Rana, and G. Wignaraja, eds., *National Strategies for Regional Integration: South and East Asian Case Studies.* London: Anthem Press.

Lall, S. (1987). *Learning to Industrialize: The Acquisition of Technological Capability by India.* Basingstoke, England: Macmillan Press.

Lall, S. (2001). *Competitiveness, Technology and Skills.* Cheltenham, England: Edward Elgar.

Lardy, N. R. (2002). *Integrating China into the Global Economy.* Washington, D.C.: Brooking Institution Press.

Lardy, N. R. (2003). "Trade Liberalization and Its Role in Chinese Economic Growth." Paper prepared for IMF and NCAER Conference "A Tale of Two Giants: India's and China's Experience with Reform and Growth," New Delhi, November 14–16.

Maddison, A. (2007). *Chinese Economic Performance in the Long Run, 960–2030.* Paris: OECD.

Ministry of Commerce, PRC (2011). "Invest in China Website." www.fdi.gov.cn. Beijing: Ministry of Commerce of the Peoples Republic of China.

OECD, WTO, and UNCTAD (2010). *Report on G-20 Trade and Investment Measures September 2009 to February 2010.* Paris and Geneva: OECD, WTO, and UNCTAD.

Panagariya, A. (2004). "India's Trade Reform." In S. Berry, B. Bosworth, and A. Panagariya, eds., *India Policy Forum 2004,* vol. 1. New Delhi: National Council of Applied Economic Research, and Washington, D.C.: Brookings Institute.

Panagariya, A. (2006). "India and China: Trade and Foreign Investment." Unpublished paper. Columbia University, New York.

Panagariya, A. (2007). "Why India Lags behind China and How It Can Bridge the Gap." *World Economy* 30(2), pp. 229–248.

Plummer, M. (2007). "Best Practices in Regional Trade Agreements: An Application to Asia." *World Economy* 30(12), pp. 1771–1796.

Rodrick, D. (2006). *What's So Special about China's Exports?* NBER Working Paper 11947. Cambridge, Mass.: National Bureau of Economic Research.

Suominen, K. (2009). "The Changing Anatomy of Regional Trade Agreements in East Asia." *Journal of East Asian Studies* 9(1), pp. 29–56.

Whalley, J., and T. Shekhar (2010). "The Rapidly Deepening India-China Economic Relationship. CESifo Working Paper Series no. 3183. Available at www.cesifo.de.

Wignaraja, G. (2008). "Ownership, Technology and Buyers: Explaining Exporting in China and Sri Lanka." *Transnational Corporations* 17:2, pp. 1–15.

Wignaraja, G. (2010). "Are ASEAN FTAs Used for Exporting?" In P. Gugler and J. Chaisee, eds., *Competitiveness of the ASEAN Countries: Corporate and Regulatory Drivers.* Cheltenham, England: Edward Elgar.

Wignaraja, G. (2011). "Innovation, Learning and Exporting in China: Does R & D or a Technology Index Matter?" *Journal of Asian Economics,* in press. Available online 3 March 2011.

Wignaraja, G., and D. Lazaro (2010). *North-South vs. South-South Asian FTAs: Trends, Compatibilities, and Ways Forward.* UNU-CRIS Working Papers no. W-2010-3. Bruges, Belgium: United Nations University Comparative Regional Integration Studies.

Winters, A., and S. Yusuf (2007). Introduction to A. Winters and S. Yusuf, ed., *Dancing with the Giants: China, India and the Global Economy*. Washington, D.C.: World Bank.

World Economic Forum (2010). *The Global Competitiveness Report 2010–11*. Geneva: World Economic Forum.

WTO (2007). *Trade Policy Review: India*. Geneva: World Trade Organization.

WTO (2010). *Trade Policy Review: China*. Geneva: World Trade Organization.

WTO (2011). "World Trade 2010: Prospects for 2011—Trade Growth to East in 2011 but Despite 2010 Record Surge, Crisis Hangover Persists." Press release. Geneva: World Trade Organization.

Yusuf, S., K. Nabeshima, and D. H. Perkins (2007). "China and India Reshape Global Industrial Geography." In A. Winters and S. Yusuf, eds., *Dancing with the Giants: China, India and the Global Economy*. Washington, D.C.: World Bank.

Zhang, Y. (2009). "Peoples Republic of China." In J. Francois, P. Rana, and G. Wignaraja, eds. *National Strategies for Regional Integration: South and East Asian Case Studies*. London: Anthem Press.

Zhang, Y., W. Zhongxin, and S. Zhang (1998). *Measuring the Costs of Protection in China*. Washington, D.C.: Peterson Institute for International Economics.

CHAPTER 12

....

AUSTRALIAN COMMERCIAL POLICIES

....

PETER LLOYD

"COMMERCIAL policies" will be taken to mean those government border and non-border policies that affect the competitiveness of Australian industries. These policies have been contentious in Australia since the time of Federation over 100 years ago. They have occupied as much time in parliamentary debate as any other economic topic. The issue underlying this debate is that an increase in a tariff or a subsidy or another measure that raises producer prices will raise the real incomes of some Australian households (e.g., owners of capital and workers employed in the industry) and lower the real incomes of other households (notably consumers and business buyers of the products). There is still a lively debate about commercial policies.

Border protection of particular industries has been reduced steadily and substantially since the mid-1980s, though it is still significant for a few industries. However, assistance through nonborder policies is substantial and increasing. The debate has broadened in the last two decades or so to cover new areas of policies, notably innovation and technology development, and more emphasis, too, is put now on "globalization" issues such as the role of multinational corporations and global production strategies.

This chapter reviews commercial policies in Australia, examining both long-term trends and recent developments. Australia is fortunate in having time series that are long and of excellent quality. Indeed, they are probably as good as those available in any other country. These enable us to track changes in commercial policies in detail and to describe the distribution of the rates of assistance across industries. This review will cover trade in services as well as trade in goods and the international movement of capital and labor, and it will consider the style of policy-making.

1. HOW OPEN IS THE AUSTRALIAN ECONOMY?
THE MACRO EVIDENCE

A measure of openness commonly used in Australia, as in other countries, is the trade ratio; that is, the sum of the value of annual exports and imports of goods relative to the value of the national product in the year. It is preferable to include services trade along with goods trade, and to use a constant price measure in place of a measure where the value of trade and of national product are in current prices. Fortunately, the Penn World Tables has constant-price time series of the trade ratio for goods and services (as recorded in the balance of payments statement) covering 188 countries. Figure 12.1 plots the series from 1950 to 2004 for Australia.

These series show two features. First, Australia is toward the lower end of the distribution of these trade ratios. In the latest year available, 2004, the figure was 39.7% (cf. neighboring New Zealand at 77.3% and the UK at 59.9%). At first sight, this low ratio is surprising, and it has been interpreted by some as evidence that the economy is not very open. Australia is a middle-sized country in terms of GNP, and it has an endowment of natural resources (both agricultural land and mineral resources) per capita that is far above the world average. Both of these predict a high trade ratio. On the other hand, however, Australia is distant from major markets in Europe and North America. Australian economic historians have emphasized the "tyranny of distance" (Blainey, 1966). This is confirmed by recent empirical studies of observed trade flows using gravity models that show distance from major markets is a strong trade disincentive for Australia (e.g., Adams et al., 2003).

The second feature is that the trade ratio has increased rapidly since the mid-1980s, whereas it had been almost stationary from 1950 to 1980. Indeed, it is now double the level that held around 1980, when it was around 24 per cent. This no doubt reflects several influences, including the opening of the Australian economy, the opening of potential export markets, and the discovery of large mineral resources in the 1980s and later.

The problem here is that as a measure of openness, trade ratios depend on two quite distinct sets of factors. One set is the factors that determine comparative advantage; endowments, country size, technology, tastes, and distance. The second

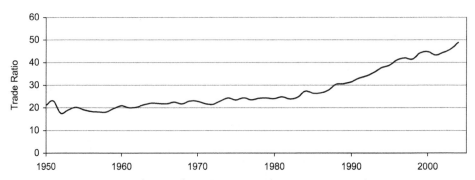

Figure 12.1. Australian trade to GDP ratios (in constant prices): 1950–2004.

set is the level of trade restrictions, both in Australia and in export markets. To separate these two sets of factors, one needs to develop direct measures of the policy stance. I shall focus on policies in Australia.

2. THE POLICY STANCE IS GENERALLY OPEN

Trade in Goods

Tariffs have been the main instrument of industry assistance in Australia for most of its history. Lloyd (2008) constructed 100-year series of the average tariff rate on goods imported into Australia. There are two main series, one for all imports and one for dutiable imports only.[1] Australian economists have generally considered that the latter series for dutiable imports only is preferable. For most of its history, a majority of imports by value have entered duty free because of various concessions applying to imports of materials, components, and other intermediate inputs that are used in the production of goods in Australia and are not competitive with goods produced in Australia. Thus the average tariff on dutiable imports only is an average of rates that are protective of goods produced in the country. Figure 12.2 reproduces both series for the period 1903–04 to 2004–2005.

From the longer-term perspective, the single most important feature of these two series is the high peak of average tariff rates in the years of the Great Depression. The last 70 years have been largely an unwinding of these Great Depression rates.

Two particular events mark this unwinding. One is the 1973 Tariff Cut. In July 1973, the government introduced an unprecedented across-the-board cut in tariff

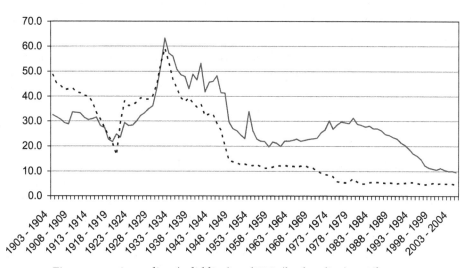

Figure 12.2. Australian (solid line) and U.S. (broken line) tariff rates.

rates by a uniform 25%.[2] However, the automobile industry and several other protected industries succeeded in having the tariffs on their products restored to the pre–Tariff Cut levels within one or two years. These factors and other piecemeal increases in tariff rates meant that the Tariff Cut had no enduring effect on average tariff levels. The second is the strategy of phased annual reductions in tariff rates introduced in the 1988 Economic Statement. This strategy has continued without interruption to the present time. It has had and continues to have a much greater effect than all other piecemeal reforms, including the 1973 Tariff Cut. Both policy changes were introduced by Labour governments. A typical example is the tariff on assembled motor vehicles. This product group is one of the most important groups of products protected in Australia, both because it is one of the largest groups in terms of the value of production and because it is the largest single protected product group in Australian household budget expenditures. Before the Tariff Cut the MFN tariff rate on this product group was 45%, one of the peak rates in the Australian Tariff. With the Tariff Cut, it fell to 33.75 (= 45 x 3/4) but it rose again to an all-time peak of 57.5% for the period 1978–1979 to 1987–1988. It fell in every year after the Economic Statement until it reached the current level of 10% in 2004–5.

Beginning with the year 1968/69, the statutory authority advising the Australian government on border policies (the Tariff Board and its successor statutory authorities up to the present authority, the Productivity Commission) have produced annual series of nominal and effective assistance for the manufacturing sector. Since this sector has accounted for 90–95% of imports since World War II, these series are good proxies for the average nominal and effective rates of assistance for imports of all goods. These estimates are made at the four-digit level of the Australian Standard Industry Classification code and aggregated to the two-digit manufacturing subdivisions and then to the total manufacturing level. Unlike the series of average tariff rates, they include the effects of all major nontariff measures affecting imports: quantitative import restrictions, local content schemes, and certain export incentives and subsidies.[3] Subsidies is a group of beyond-the-border policies used for protective purposes. Standard trade theory interprets the nominal rate as the distortion of the price to consumers and therefore the rate that is relevant to the measurement of the consumer welfare loss, and the effective rate as the distortion of the value added per unit of output or the effective price of producers and therefore the rate that is relevant to the measurement of producer costs.

Figure 12.3 plots these two series. (Breaks in the series occur because of minor changes in classification and data sources.) For the manufacturing sector as a whole, the effective rates have been generally 150–175% of the nominal rates for the same years; for example, in 2003–4 the average nominal rate was 2.8%, whereas the average effective rate was 4.5%. This is because of the widespread exemption from duty of imported intermediate inputs in Australia. Both series have fallen without a significant reversal since the series began.

Recent advances in tariff theory have shown that for the purpose of measuring the deadweight costs imposed on the national economy, the appropriate average

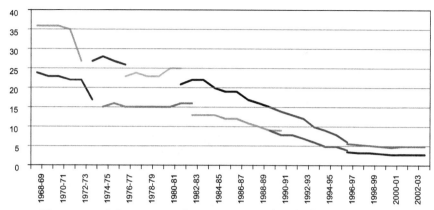

Figure 12.3. PC estimates of average nominal and effectives rates (%).

measure is the Trade Restrictiveness Index (TRI). This is the average *nominal* ad valorem rate that yields the same utility loss as the differentiated structure of tariffs and nontariff measures (NTMs). Feenstra (1995) produced a partial equilibrium version of the TRI. It can be shown that this version is a function of the arithmetic mean and the variance (or standard deviation) of the nominal rates. The variance is a measure of dispersion that picks up the much higher welfare costs of the spike and peak rates.

Fortunately, the Productivity Commission and its statutory predecessors have calculated the standard deviation of the nominal rates for most years as well as the mean rate. Using these two series, Lloyd and MacLaren (2008) have produced a new series of the TRI for the manufacturing sector in Australia over the 31-year period 1973–74 to 2003–4. This is the best series of the average level of assistance available to the sector. It includes the effects of almost all NTMs as well as tariffs, and it reflects properly the higher welfare costs of spike and peak rates of distortions. It is the theoretically correct measure of the average rate.[4]

Figure 12.4 plots this series for the TRI. This series of the TRI has two interesting features. First, by derivation, this measure is greater than the average nominal rate.[5] Hence the standard use of the average nominal rate of assistance understates the average level of trade restrictions. A fortiori, the use of the average tariff rate, as in figure 12.2, understates the average level of restrictions and to a greater degree because this measure does not include NTMs. Second, the measure peaked in the year 1982–83, when it reached 25%. This peak contrasts with the series for the average nominal and average effective rates of assistance in figure 12.3, which has no clear peak. The explanation of this difference is that the series for the average nominal and average effective rates of assistance do not take account of the variance among rates. The mean rates do not reflect properly the increase in assistance given to the textile, clothing, and footwear and motor vehicle industries in the early 1980s that caused the variance to increase when the mean fell. Third, the TRI has declined every year since then.

The outcome of these continual reforms in the last 25 years or so is that Australia has, in terms of its policy stance, opened its importable goods sector very substantially.

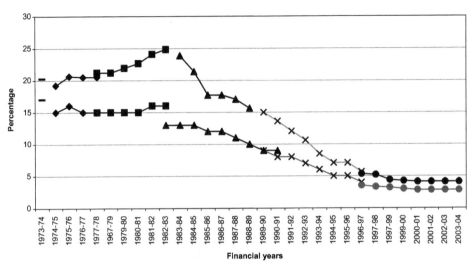

Figure 12.4. Average nominal rate of assistance to Australian manufacturing, 1973–74 to 2003–4: Arithmetic Mean and TRI.

It went from being one of the OECD countries that protected its import-competing industries most highly to one that is now among the most open.[6]

Trade in Services

From the time of the signing of the Uruguay Round General Agreement on Trade in Services, services have been regarded as internationally tradable.

Service industries are affected by three sets of instruments of government policy:

- Tariff on their inputs
- Subsidies and other budgetary outlays and tax concessions on inputs and outputs
- Industry regulations

In Australia, the first two have in recent years been tracked in detail by the Productivity Commission. The first of these instrument sets impose substantial costs on services industries, whereas they benefit the goods-producing industries. The second is positive. In the latest year for which statistics are available, 2007–8, the service industries received total budgetary assistance of $2,273.7 million. For the first time, this assistance was greater than the amounts granted to manufacturing industries ($1817.1 million) and to agriculture industries ($2,220.1 million), both of which are much smaller than the services industries in terms of the aggregate value of gross output or value added. The combined assistance from the two sets of measures together was negative and large for service industries. This has been the pattern for many years.

The effects of the third set of instruments of industry assistance are, unfortunately, difficult to measure. Internationally tradeable services are delivered by a variety of modes, some regulation is applied at the border and some is beyond the border, and regulation to services is industry-specific. For example, the passenger air transport industry is regulated through bilateral air services agreements, whereas the regulation of the financial services sector is mainly through restrictions on the entry of foreign providers.

Thus, the measures of assistance are not comparable to those for traded goods. Moreover, in some service industries most of the assistance from government comes from the state governments, and this assistance is not included in the estimates of assistance to manufacturing, mining, and agriculture industries.

In the absence of time series of levels of all assistance to service providers, it is not possible to be precise about trends in assistance to service industries. Undoubtedly, however, the general trend has been toward opening the tradeable services to international competition. From about the same time that the federal government significantly opened the goods sector to international competition, that is, from the mid-1980s, a number of measures were taken to open up some service industries. For example, the financial services industries were opened up by the floating of the Australian dollar in 1983 and other deregulation of financial services. Similarly, air passenger transport services have been partially deregulated by a general liberalization of bilateral air services agreements and the Open Skies Agreement with New Zealand. Foreign investment regulations have been relaxed, thereby opening up some service industries where the mode of supply is wholly or predominantly by commercial presence; for example, hotels, electricity generation, and distribution and transport.

There have been no comprehensive studies of assistance to service industries, and some, such as education and health care, have not been studied at all.[7] Yet we know some industries remain heavily protected from foreign competition, mainly by regulatory regimes; for example, retail banking[8] and gambling. Many of the restrictions on foreign competition are prohibitions. Almost certainly, there is greater variance in the levels of assistance provided to service industries than to goods industries.

3. Focusing on the Big and Small Pictures

The discussion above and most of the debate in Australia has concerned *interindustry* variation in levels of assistance. This section adopts what might be called a zoom lens approach, looking at the big picture of *intersectoral* relations and, at the other end of the magnification scale, looking at the *intraindustry* variation in levels.

The Big Picture

To assess the effects of the protection of import-competing activities, we need to consider assistance to exporting activities. Standard general equilibrium theory (the Lerner symmetry theorem) tells us that import taxes act as export taxes, penalizing efficient export producers. But this only holds if exporters do not receive an equal or greater level of assistance through export subsidies and other forms of budgetary assistance. In the past, the Australian governments had a policy of "tariff compensation," offering compensatory assistance to some exporters for the antiexport effect of protection of import-competing manufacturing producers.

In Australia, the Productivity Commission measures assistance from all forms, including export assistance, and calculates nominal and effective rates of assistance for three goods sectors: manufacturing, primary production (agriculture and forestry and fishing) and mining. For the latest year available, 2007–8, the average effective rate of assistance to manufacturing was 4.5%, whereas that to primary production was higher, at 7.5%. Mining received a zero level of net effective assistance (0.0%; Productivity Commission, 2009, table 2.7). Mining is an export-oriented sector, and primary production is a mixture of exporting and import-competing industries. The export tax effect of import protection is now small, much smaller than it was in previous decades when assistance to import-competing producers in both the manufacturing and primary production sectors was much higher on average.

This conclusion is confirmed by a study by Anderson, Lloyd, and MacLaren (2007). Using improved time series of assistance to agricultural producers prepared for the new World Bank megadatabase of distortions in the agriculture sector, they reexamine the extent to which industry assistance policies in Australia have been biased against exporters in the agriculture sector and against the sector in general. Figure 12.5 reproduces their graph of the nominal rates of assistance to producers in this sector. Agricultural exporters received some assistance. Assistance to agriculture producers has fallen dramatically—the average nominal rate of assistance fell from 16% in the early 1970s to less than 2% in 2004—but assistance to manufacturers fell even more rapidly. Thus, the anti-agriculture bias, which had been in place for seven decades, has all but disappeared. This database shows that assistance to agricultural producers in Australia is the lowest of the 78 countries in the database, with the solitary exception of New Zealand. Subsidies and regulatory interventions to assist farmers have been close to eliminated. Within the agriculture sector, there is now no significant bias against exporters.

The service sector is penalized by tariffs, as noted, but does receive budgetary assistance, and some service sector industries receive positive assistance from the third source of industry regulation. No estimates of the combined assistance from all sources are made for the services sector. It is likely that the large service sector is penalized vis-à-vis the goods-producing sectors.

The effect of these intersectoral differences depends on the mobility of resources between sectors. Both primary production and mining depend on essential land-based resources, and this reduces the intersectoral mobility of resources considerably. Given the large intrasectoral variance in effective rates within all sectors, it is likely that the main consequences of the economy-wide pattern of assistance at the present time are from intrasectoral reallocation of resources.

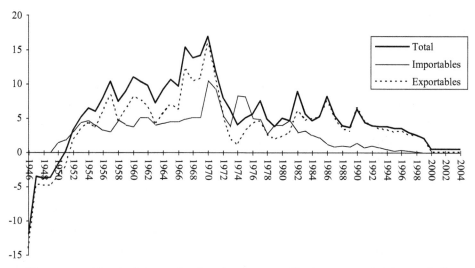

Figure 12.5. Nominal rates of assistance to exportable, import-competing, and all agricultural industries, Australia, 1946–47 to 2004–5.
Source: Anderson, Lloyd, and MacLaren (2007, fig. 4).

The Small Picture: Intraindustry Competition

At the other end of the focus, we can look within each industry in each sector. The recent development in trade theory of the model by Melitz (2003) emphasizes the effects of government interventions on firms within industries. This is the first model of intraindustry trade that is based on firms that are heterogeneous in terms of their productivity and exporting performance. This model has gained great popularity in a very short time. It indicates that exiting of low-productivity firms and other firm-level margins of adjustment following the lowering of barriers to trade are a source of improved factor productivity and increases in real income. These factors are in addition to those captured by traditional trade models in which the industry, not the firm, is the unit of production. Unfortunately, there are no empirical Australian studies using firm-level data of outputs, exports, and imports because disclosure rules prohibit the release of firm-level data collected by the Australian Bureau of Statistics.

4. International Factor Flows and Growth Effects

Australia is one of the few economies in the world that has received net inflows of both capital and labor in almost every year since World War II. Indeed, this record extends back to the creation of the Australian Federation in 1901, apart from the years of the two world wars and the Great Depression.

Total net borrowing in all forms as represented by the deficit on current account of the balance of payments statements has been large in the last three decades. In the decades of the 1980s and 1990s, it averaged 4.8 and 4.3% of GDP. In first eight years of the decade of the 2000s, it has averaged 3.5%. These rates are toward the upper end of the world distribution of these rates. As with trade ratios, the observed upward trend is partly the result of liberalization of borrowing regulations, especially in relation to FDI, and partly the result of Australia becoming an increasingly attractive destination for foreign outward direct and portfolio investment because of the stability of its political system and currency.

There is no simple relationship between overseas borrowing and aggregate capital formation, as foreign borrowing may crowd out domestic borrowing; however, such large-scale borrowing must have increased the rate of capital formation. In a centenary review of the 100 years of national economic history since Federation, Treasury (2001, p. 61) concluded that "the ability to 'tap into' the world economy has allowed Australia much greater investment capacity and correspondingly higher economic growth, in turn producing higher per capita income and increased wealth."

Trade economists emphasize foreign direct investment (FDI) inflows, as a vehicle of acquiring foreign technologies, management skills, and know-how, and spillovers to domestic-owned firms. Approval of foreign investment proposals is carried out by the Foreign Investment Review Board (FIRB). Unlike the system applying to goods and service industries, this Board is not an independent statutory authority; it is a branch of the Commonwealth Treasury Department. In recent years the government, through the operations of FIRB, has relaxed restrictions on foreign investment inflows. One unfortunate development was the granting in the 2005 Australia–United States Free Trade Agreement of preferences to U.S. foreign investors in the form of lower threshold levels for review of foreign investment proposals, though in practice this has probably had little effect because almost all proposals are allowed.

Partly as a result of this relaxation of border controls, Australia's stock of FDI has been growing at a much faster rate than its trade in goods and services. The FDI inflows as a percentage of Gross Domestic Capital Formation increased from 23.2% in 1990 to 28.6% in 2000 and to 34.4% in 2007. Foreign direct investment, by either mergers and acquisitions or greenfield operations, have reshaped many industries, including notably infrastructure service industries. Australian FDI outflows increased even more rapidly; from 9.6% of gross domestic capital formation in 1990 to 22.0% in 2000 to 30.6% in 2007 (UNCTAD, 2008, app. table B.3). Consequently, Australian firms have become much more integrated into the global operations of multinational corporations.

Since the time of Federation, Australia has had a proimmigration policy. Like the series for net foreign borrowing, net overseas migration[9] has been positive since Federation in all but a few years immediately after Federation and during the Great Depression and the two world wars (Department of Immigration and Multicultural Affairs (2001, table 3). In absolute numbers and as a share of population increase, it has been rising in the decade 2000–2010. In the latest year, 2008, net overseas migration was 213,500 persons. These represented 59.5% of the population growth (+1.7%), despite a recent rise in the domestic birth rate. Almost one in four of the total population was born overseas.

The rate of net overseas migration understates the contribution of migration to the population growth. Unlike net foreign borrowing, there is no reason to expect crowding out of natural births; instead, past immigrants have their own children. The contribution to the growth of the labor force is similar to that of the total population.

The effect of immigration on average skill levels is uncertain. Compared to other net immigration countries, Australia puts a strong emphasis on economic criteria in selecting immigrants, particularly on skill and education levels. However, immigrants are heterogeneous in terms of their skill levels, human capital, language skills, and other labor force characteristics.

We also need to consider the relationship between the openness of the economy with respect to factor flows and the openness with respect to produced goods and services. There is no strong reason to expect a direct relationship between these two. However, international trade theory raises the possibility that openness of the goods sector may affect the rate growth of real expenditure that results from factor accumulation. Immiserizing growth theory raises the possibility that high levels of protection of goods industries from foreign competition may even result in increased factor supplies having a negative effect on real national expenditures through an adverse movement of the terms of trade. This is unrealistic, but more generally, this model demonstrates that border protection may lower the benefits from factor accumulation. Furthermore, New Growth theory has added more reasons why border protection may lower permanently the rate of growth; it may raise the cost and reduce the variety of capital and intermediate inputs and reduce the productivity of R & D.

The literature since the 1990s has made an important distinction between the effect of trade liberalization on the *level* of average real income and the effect on the *rate of growth* over time of real income per capita per year. Standard gains from trade refer to the former effect only. A number of empirical studies claimed to have found a rate-of-growth effect. While this is still controversial, Estevadeordal and Taylor (2008) have confirmed a positive rate-of-growth effect from trade liberalization, using a difference-in-difference times series approach.

In Australia, economists have posited that the high levels of protection of manufacturing industries in the first four decades following World War II depressed the rate of growth of real output and output per capita. Casual evidence supports this. The rate of growth of real per capita income in those decades was slow relative to that in other high-income OECD countries, whereas in the past 20 years or so when the economy has been opened up, the rate of growth of per capita income has substantially exceeded the OECD average (see Anderson, Lloyd, and MacLaren, 2008, and fig. 12.1 here).

Athukorala and Chand (2007) have formally tested this relationship with a small-scale growth model of the Australian economy, using data covering the period

1871–2002. Their study reveals a persistent statistically significant negative relationship between the average tariff rate and growth of GDP. The elasticity of the growth rate with respect to the tariff rate is -0.28%.

This link between higher protection and lower growth has another implication. It indicates that comparative static analyses of the costs of protection understate these costs. Note, too, that the neglect of intraindustry trade effects discussed in the previous section has a similar effect. In the last two decades, computable general equilibrium models have been used in Australia to analyze unilateral and regional changes in border protection, probably more than in any other country. They have played a significant role in increasing our knowledge of the effects of protection and in persuading governments to reform protectionist policies, but they still omit several substantial negative effects of government policies.

5. AUSTRALIA JOINS THE REGIONALISM RUSH

Like many other countries, Australia has signed multiple regional trade agreements (RTAs). It has signed six RTAs: with New Zealand (called the Closer Economic Relations agreement [CER], which came into effect in 1983), Singapore (2003), the Australia–United States Free Trade Agreement (AUSFTA, 2005), Thailand (2005), Chile (March 2009), and ASEAN (the ASEAN-Australia-New Zealand Free Trade Area [AANZFTA]). Six is about the average for all countries. All are bilateral agreements except that with ASEAN, which was signed jointly with New Zealand.

Until the recent conclusion of the RTAs with the USA and ASEAN, preferential goods trade had been unimportant for Australia, after the end of the Imperial Preference system, when the UK acceded to the EU in 1973.[10] This has changed substantially now. If agreements with China and Japan are signed, Australia will have preferential trading agreements with all major trading partners except the EU. However, the coverage of commodities subject to preferences and the margins of preferences vary considerably. In the case of the CER Agreement with New Zealand and the agreement with Singapore, all tariffs are eliminated on all goods. In the case of the agreement with Chile, all tariffs were eliminated on 97% of the goods currently traded when the agreement came into effect, and the remaining tariffs will be eliminated by 2015. On the other hand, the agreements with the United States, Thailand, and ASEAN all have important exclusions from free trade provisions, and in the Agreement with ASEAN each of the 10 members has made separate access commitments. These exclusions mostly relate to agricultural goods, which are an important part of our total merchandise exports, or to the heavily protected motor vehicles and clothing, textiles, and footwear industries. They are, therefore, much more important than indicated by the number of tariff lines. Moreover, preferences that vary among commodity groups in this way will increase the variance of the average levels of assistance among industry groups.

All of the six agreements already signed go well beyond liberalizing trade in goods. All six have provisions liberalizing trade in services. The provisions in the agreements with New Zealand, Singapore, the United States, and Chile are on a more liberal negative list basis. All six have provisions relating to other areas of trade in goods and services such as trade remedies, sanitary and phytosanitary measures, and technical standards, but the coverage in relation to these and other measures varies considerably from agreement to agreement. All are WTO Plus in several respects.

All six also have provisions relating to the movement of capital and/or labor, but the coverage varies greatly in this area. The CER is most unusual, in that it provides for complete freedom of movement of residents, for work and temporary or permanent residence,[11] but it has no provision at all relating to the movement of capital. However, there are few restrictions on the movement of capital between the two countries. In the other five agreements, the provisions relating to labor movement cover the temporary movement of labor only, mostly for area business and investment.[12] All five have provisions relating to investment, but they mostly concern investor protection and do little to liberalize market access.

The CER is by far the most opening of all these agreements. Indeed, it is the most regionally open of all RTAs in the world, except for the EU, and in a few respects is more liberal than the EU (see Lloyd, 2002).

In January 2004 the Australian and New Zealand prime ministers announced the intention of creating "a single economic market" (SEM) modeled loosely on the EU single market. Essentially, this seeks to completely integrate the economies of the two countries. Under the Trans-Tasman Travel Arrangements, trans-Tasman migration has been an important part of the net migration into Australia (and an even more important part of the outmigration from New Zealand). For Australia, New Zealand has been the second most important source of permanent settlers after the UK. In the latest year, 2008–2009, 34,000 New Zealand citizens came to Australia as net permanent and long-term arrivals, that is, 14% of the total from all sources. In the current SEM work program, the governments of the two countries are looking at filling in the holes to complete the single market, including the possibility of adding an investment component to CER to reduce remaining barriers to trans-Tasman capital flows.

The trend to regionalism is likely to continue for Australia. It is currently negotiating five more bilateral agreements—with China, the Gulf Cooperation Council countries, Japan, Korea, and Malaysia. It is negotiating, along with the United States, Peru, Vietnam, and possibly other countries, to join the Trans-Pacific Partnership Agreement (TPA), an agreement between Brunei Darussalam, Chile, New Zealand, and Singapore that came into force in 2006. Australia is also negotiating a trilateral Pacific Agreement on Closer Economic Relations Plus. This is a proposal for a regional free trade area involving Australia and New Zealand and the Pacific Forum Island countries. In this proposal, a program allowing for the seasonal movement of workers has been mooted. This goes beyond business-related labor movement and is regarded as important by the Pacific Forum Island governments. Australia is considering, by way of joint feasibility studies, bilateral RTAs with India and Indonesia.

One curious feature of the emerging pattern of regionalism involving Australia is that trade between Australia and some of the other countries is covered by more than one agreement. Singapore and Thailand are signatories to both the bilateral agreements with Australia and the AANZFTA. Malaysia and Indonesia will join this list if bilaterals are signed with these two countries. If the TPA negotiations are successful, Singapore will become a party to three RTAs involving Australia. This form of multiple agreements is a result of perceived inadequacies in prior agreements, but it adds considerably to the complexity of trade rules.

In this context, the TPA is considered particularly important, as it had been envisaged by the members that this agreement would expand by admitting more members, and one of the objectives of the TPA is to create an agreement that could be seen as a model within the Asia-Pacific region. It is one of the most liberal RTAs, and the four countries have signed other bilaterals that are among the most liberal; as noted, the provisions in the Australian agreements with New Zealand, Singapore and Chile are in general more liberal than those with the other three bilateral partners. Some hope the TPA will become the vehicle for the establishment of an Asia-Pacific area-wide agreement and that it will replace the complex network of existing agreements (e.g., Mortimer and Edwards, 2008).

6. A New Pattern of Policies and Policy-Making in Australia

Traditionally, in Australia the debate about commercial policies affecting the goods industries has focused on tariffs, but there has been a major shift in the pattern of assistance over the last three decades. In the threefold classification of forms of assistance to specific activities used by the Productivity Commission (tariffs, budgetary assistance, and industry regulation), the share coming from budgetary assistance has steadily increased. When average nominal and effective rates of assistance were at their peaks in the early 1980s, budgetary assistances provided less than 5% of total assistance to the manufacturing sector, though it was about one-half of total assistance to primary production. The Productivity Commission began a new series, starting for 2001–2002, of assistance from budgetary outlays and tax concessions combined to the four sectors (primary production, mining, manufacturing, and services) combined. In that year, budgetary outlays and tax concessions accounted for 37.3% of the total gross assistance. (Recall that this assistance does not include assistance by regulation to service sector industries.) When one subtracts the negative assistance to all industries from tariffs levied on input, the assistance from budgetary outlays and tax concessions combined was 76.7% of total net assistance to all sectors. In the latest year available, 2007–2008, the corresponding percentages of total gross and net assistance were 47.1% and 87.7%, respectively (Productivity Commission, 2009, table 2.5). Subsidies have been the main form of assistance to specific activities since some time in the 1990s. This has been due to a combination of steadily reducing tariff rates and steadily increasing budgetary assistance. It is a major change in the traditional pattern of border assistance in Australia.

Within the total budgetary assistance, the share going to traditional output-based subsidies for specific industries has declined, and the share of assistance going to R & D has soared. In 2006–2007, these shares were 25% and 29%, respectively.

A general feature of this trend is a much stronger emphasis now on technology development. (See the Productivity Commission's annual Trade and Assistance Review.) The general shift in government policy is illustrated by the change in the name of the department responsible for advising the government on industry policy. Previously it was the Department of Industry, Tourism and Resources; now it is the Department of Innovation, Industry, Science and Research.

Many new kinds of subsidies have been introduced. There are several programs designed to develop so-called green technologies, for example "clean coal." Before the national election in 2010, the Labor government had sought to introduce an emission trading scheme for greenhouse gases, which has important implications for the so-called "trade-exposed" sectors. This was abandoned after the failure of the climate change negotiations in December 2009, and the present Labor government has set up a parliamentary committee to determine whether it will introduce an emissions trading scheme, a carbon tax, or some other policies to mitigate climate change. However, these policies are best regarded as environmental rather than commercial policies. In 2008 and 2009, the government introduced a number of measures to assist particular industries as part of its strategy to combat the global financial crisis. The government is intervening to affect the profitability of particular industries in more ways than ever before.

Running alongside the shift in forms of assistance has been a major shift in the method of policy-making. For more than 80 years, the conflicts resulting from commercial policies between groups of households and the political groups that represent them have been moderated in Australia by a process of public enquiry through an independent statutory authority. These enquiries have sought to find whether proposed changes in commercial policies are in the national interest, though this concept has been elusive. This process of public enquiry has been developed further in Australia than any other country. Its advocacy of promoting efficient industries and its policy recommendations made a major contribution to the lowering of protection in the 1970s and 1980s in Australia. (For a historical account of the major enquiries and subsequent government actions, see Productivity Commission, 2003. For a frank insider account by the former chairman of the statutory authority of the time, see Rattigan, 1986.) Indeed, Australian trade economists and former officials have recommended on more than one occasion that the Australian system of enquiry by an independent statutory authority be adopted by other countries.

This system of public enquiry has, however, changed drastically in the last 10 years. In the days when the statutory authority was the Tariff Board (1921–1973), the

Australian government was required to send a reference to the authority whenever it was considering a change a tariff rate or bounty measure. In the days when the statutory authority was the Industries Assistance Commission (1974–1990) and the Industry Commission (1990–1998), the government was required to send a reference to the authority whenever it was considering a change in any form of "long-term" assistance. When the present Productivity Commission replaced the Industry Commission, this 80-year-old practice of a mandatory enquiry by the authority was abandoned. In 2008, when it wanted to review assistance to the motor vehicle and to the textile, clothing, and footwear industries, the government appointed two ad hoc reviews. In the past, such reviews had always been conducted by the Productivity Commission or its predecessor authorities. These two reviews were public enquiries, and their reports were published, but they were not conducted by an independent statutory authority. With ad hoc reviews, there is a suspicion that the government may select an enquiry group that is sympathetic to the government's views. These reviews resulted in large increases in nontariff assistance to the two industries. They have been and still are the most heavily assisted manufacturing industries, and the Productivity Commission (2009, p. 53) expects that if the review recommendations are fully implemented, they will reverse the steady decline in assistance to these industries over the last 20 years.[13]

The situation has changed in another respect. As budgetary assistance has become more important as a form of industry assistance than the tariffs and other border measures traditionally used in Australia, fewer of the measures giving assistance are subject to public enquiries. Some measures of budgetary assistance are introduced following a recommendation of a public enquiry, but many are just announced in the annual budget or at other times. The Australian government, like other governments, wants the freedom to introduce budgetary measures unencumbered by a process of public enquiry. Offsetting these trends to some extent, references to the Productivity Commission and other public enquiries are used more frequently now to enquire into changes in regulatory arrangements than used to be the case.

None of the regional trading agreements that the government has signed or is now negotiating or contemplating have been subject to open public enquiries, though the government has consulted some stakeholders and invited submissions. The growing importance of RTAs makes this a major gap. In November 2009, the government sent a reference to the Productivity Commission dealing with the general issues of bilateral and regional trade agreements. The Draft Report released in June 2010 contains some recommendations relating to the way the government investigates and legislates for bilateral and regional agreements (Productivity Commission, 2010).

Currently, the Australian system is very strong on transparency. The annual reviews of assistance and of industry regulation by the Productivity Commission are a model of public information about current government policies. The WTO puts great emphasis now on transparency in member countries as a means of countering protectionism. But transparency is not enough. All changes in commercial policies should be subject to public enquiries, preferably by an independent authority, if the great progress that has been made in reforming commercial policies in Australia is to continue.

NOTES

1. The U.S. International Trade Commission has long-term series of the same two averages. The U.S. and Australian series follow a remarkably similar time path through the twentieth century (see Lloyd, 2008).

2. One important category of goods was exempted from this cut: tariff items that were matched by an excise duty on like goods produced in Australia. These were revenue duties on the "sin goods" (alcoholic beverages, tobacco and tobacco products, and petroleum products.)

3. Some forms of assistance provided by Commonwealth, state, and local authorities through budgetary outlays and tax expenditures are excluded. Perhaps the most notable exclusion is the phytosanitary, or quarantine as they are called in Australia, regulations that ban imports and give substantial protection to many agricultural and fishery products produced in Australia. The intention of these laws is to protect species from viruses and other diseases present in foreign biological stocks, but they are regarded by foreign producers as protective. Australian agricultural economists have argued that the bans ignore the economic benefits of lower import prices and are unduly trade-restrictive (see Anderson, McRae, and Wilson, 2001). Two of Australia's trading partners—New Zealand (in relation to apples) and the Philippines (bananas) have brought complaints to the WTO alleging that Australian procedures breach the Sanitary and Phytosanitary Agreement.

4. There are small errors in the weights and the calculation of ad valorem equivalents of the NTMs.

5. The measure is $T=\{E^2[t]+Var[t]\}^{1/2}$, where $E[t]$ is the arithmetic mean and $Var[t]$ is the variance. In fact, the TRI is the mean of order 2 (see Lloyd and MacLaren, 2008, p. 253).

6. For comparative tariff data, see WTO (2009. Unfortunately, there is no reliable comparative data for NTMs. Kee, Nicita, and Olarreaga (2009) provide estimates of the TRI for 78 countries. Their estimates of NTMs are indirect econometric estimates of the ad valorem equivalents of NTMs derived from UNCTAD statistics of the incidence of core NTMs. For Australia, where we have direct estimates of the ad valorem equivalents, their estimates are far too high and quite implausible.

7. The Productivity Commission, working with researchers from the Australian National University and Adelaide University, had a research project from 1998 to 2000 that did studies of different methods of quantifying levels of assistance (including regulatory assistance) to service industries. They made estimates of the assistance to selected service industries (see Findlay and Warren, 2000). These studies were pioneering, but they have not been continued.

8. The main restriction on foreign suppliers is the Four Pillars Policy, intended to preserve the four major banks, which includes conditions on foreign banks acquiring any of them.

9. Net overseas migration is net permanent plus long-term migration, including net movement of Australian residents.

10. From 1907 until the UK joined the EEC in 1973 the former Imperial Preference scheme gave preferences to certain goods sourced from the UK and some other Empire (later Commonwealth) countries. These preferences were important.

11. Technically, these provisions are outside the CER agreement itself, under a separate and older agreement, the Trans-Tasman Travel Arrangements.

12. While AUSFTA has no provisions relating to the movement of people, the United States introduced, subsequent to the agreement, a special category of visas for Australians wishing to obtain temporary work in the United States.

13. In another decision in 2009 relating to imports of books, the government rejected advice from the Productivity Commission. The Commission had recommended a relaxation of the parallel importing restrictions on imports under copyright laws, but the government saw fit to maintain the present restrictions.

REFERENCES

Adams, R., P. Dee, J. Gali, and G. McGuire. (2003, May). *The Trade and Investment Effects of Preferential Trading Arrangements: Old and New Evidence*. Productivity Commission Staff Working Paper. Melbourne: Productivity Commission.

Anderson, K., P. J. Lloyd, and D. MacLaren. (2007). "Distortions to Agricultural Incentives in Australia since World War II," *Economic Record*, 83, 461–482.

Anderson, K., C. McRae, and D. Wilson, eds. (2001). *The Economics of Quarantine and the SPS Agreement*. Adelaide and Canberra: Centre for International Economic Studies and AFFA Biosecurity Australia.

Athukorala, P., and S. Chand. (2007). "Tariff-Growth Nexus in the Australian Economy, 1870–2002: Is There a Paradox?," Australian National University, Research School of Pacific and Asian Studies, Working Papers in Trade and Development No. 2007/08.

Blainey, G. (1966). *The Tyranny of Distance*. Melbourne: Sun Books.

Department of Immigration and Multicultural Affairs. (2001). *Immigration; Federation to Century's End 1901–2000*. Canberra, Department of Immigration and Multicultural Affairs.

Estevadeordal, A., and A. M. Taylor. (2008). "Is the Washington Consensus Dead? Growth, Openness, and the Great Liberalization, 1970s–2000s," NBER Working Papers 14264.

Feenstra, R. C. (1995). "Estimating the Effects of Trade Policy," in G. N. Grossman and K. Rogoff (eds.), *Handbook of International Economics*, vol. 3. Amsterdam: Elsevier.

Findlay, C., and T. Warren, eds. (2000). *Impediments to Trade in Services: Measurement and Policy Implications*. London: Routledge.

Kee, H. L., A. Nicita, and M. Olarreaga. (2009). "Estimating Trade Restrictiveness Indices," *Economic Journal*, 119, 172–199.

Lewer, J. J., and H. Van Berg. (2003). "How Large Is International Trade's Effect on Economic Growth?," *Journal of Economic Surveys*, 17, 363–396.

Lloyd, P. J. (2002). "Completing CER," in A. Grimes, L. Wevers, and Ginny Sullivan (eds.), *States of Mind: Australia and New Zealand 1901–2001*. Wellington: Institute of policy Studies.

Lloyd, P. J. (2008). "100 Years of Tariff Protection in Australia," *Australian Economic History Review*, 48, July, 99–145.

Lloyd, P. J., and D. MacLaren. (2008). "An Estimated Trade Restrictiveness Index of the Level of Protection in Australian Manufacturing," *Australian Economic Review*, 41, 250–259.

Melitz, M. J. (2003). "The Impact of Trade on Intra-industry Reallocations and Aggregate Industry Productivity," *Econometrica*, 71, 1695–1725.

Mortimer, D., and J. Edwards. (2008). *Winning in World Markets: Review of Export Policies and Programs*. Canberra: Commonwealth of Australia.

Productivity Commission (2003). *From Industry Assistance to Productivity: 30 Years of "the Commission."* Melbourne: Productivity Commission.

Productivity Commission (2009). *Trade and Assistance Review 2007–8*. Melbourne: Productivity Commission.

Productivity Commission (2010). *Bilateral and Regional Trade Agreements, Draft Research Report*. Melbourne: Productivity Commission.

Rattigan, A. (1986). *Industry Assistance: The Inside Story*. Melbourne: Melbourne University Press.

Treasury (2001). *Economic Roundup, Centenary Edition*. Canberra: Commonwealth Treasury.

United Nations Conference on Trade and Development (UNCTAD). (2008). *World Investment Report 2008*. Geneva: UNCTAD.

World Trade Organisation (WTO). (2009). *World Tariff Profiles 2008*. www.wto.org.

CHAPTER 13

··

THE EUROPEAN
TRANSITION ECONOMIES

··

TORBJÖRN BECKER AND ANDERS
FREDRIKSSON

THIS chapter discusses trade policy in the European Transition Economies. The countries covered are the Eastern European countries that became independent in 1989, the new nations formed by the breakup of former Yugoslavia, the countries west of the Ural that formerly were part of the Soviet Union, and Russia. It adds up to 21 countries covered over a time period that involves a fundamental transition from planned to market economies. Trade policies have certainly been one of the key reform areas in the transition process. But for many of the countries discussed, it has to be viewed in a broader light of integration with the EU.

The chapter consists of an introduction, a section on the historical developments in the region over the past two decades, a section on tariffs, and a section on trade in the region.

In the account of developments over the past two decades in section 1, the countries of the region are classified into four groups: Central Eastern Europe and Eastern Balkans, the Baltics, South Eastern Europe (SEE) and finally, the Commonwealth of Independent States (CIS) countries. This is largely based on geography, independence status in 1989, and progress in economic integration efforts over the last 20 years. While this classification makes sense along some dimensions, each group still includes countries with different economic policies. But since the scope of this chapter is to provide an overview of each group of countries as a whole, it will necessarily make certain oversimplifications. A separate subsection deals with each group.

The first group, Central Eastern Europe and Eastern Balkans, consists of Poland, the Czech Republic, the Slovak Republic, Hungary, Slovenia, Romania, and Bulgaria. The Czech Republic and the Slovak Republic were not independent nations but part of one country, Czechoslovakia, until January 1, 1993.[1] Slovenia, independent since 1991, was part of Yugoslavia at the time of the breakup of the Eastern Bloc but has followed an economic integration path similar to that of the first group of countries.

The second group is the Baltics: Estonia, Latvia, and Lithuania. The process of economic integration with Western Europe has come since independence from the Soviet Union in 1991, setting these countries apart from the first group. But there are many similarities between the two groups: countries in both the Baltics and in Central Eastern Europe and the Eastern Balkans are members of the EU, and prior to EU accession, they all joined the WTO.

Until the end of the 1980s, Poland, Czechoslovakia, Hungary, Romania, and Bulgaria were state-controlled and centrally planned economies belonging to the Council for Mutual Economic Assistance (CMEA), the organization through which economic activities were organized in the Eastern Bloc. Discussing the development of trade policy for Poland, the Czech Republic, the Slovak Republic, Hungary, Romania, and Bulgaria therefore consists largely of the account of their transformation to become members of the EU.[2] Slovenia has followed a similar path after independence.[3] Discussion of trade policy in terms of approaching the EU also holds for Estonia, Latvia, and Lithuania, countries that followed a European integration and trade policy path similar to that of the Central Eastern European countries. Becoming members of the EU has meant adoption of the EU "acquis communautaire"—in particular the rules of the internal market; moving to free trade with all EU 27 members and adopting the EU trade policy in relations with non-EU members.[4]

The third group, SEE, is made up of the countries—except Slovenia—that formerly belonged to Yugoslavia: Croatia, Bosnia and Herzegovina, Serbia, Montenegro, UNMIK[5]-Kosovo, and the Former Yugoslav Republic (FYR) of Macedonia. Albania has been placed in this group as well. For these countries, further integration with the EU is a likely outcome, although the progress in this process differs markedly between countries.[6]

Moldova, Belarus, Ukraine, and Russia constitute the fourth group of countries. They were all part of the Soviet Union and are now part of the CIS. This is probably the most diverse group of countries, despite their close historical and economic ties. For example, Moldova is a small low-income nation with European integration as a possible goal, whereas Russia is a high-powered economic force due to its energy exports. It also carries significant weight as a military force beyond its borders and has no intention to join the EU. This diversity is also reflected in the speed and direction of trade policy reforms.

Table 13.1 provides basic information about the different countries, including dates of independence, EU accession, and regional and multilateral trade agreements.

Table 13.1. Country facts on independence and key trade arrangements

Region	Country	Independent	European integration: Trade-related preaccession agreements relevant for Central Eastern Europe, Eastern Balkans, Baltics					Preaccession agreements relevant for SEE		Agreements relevant with CIS countries	EU member	Euro	OECD	Regional integration CEFTA/BFTA	CIS	CEZ	EAEC	WTO
			Trade and cooperation agreement	Interim trade agreement	Free trade agreement in force	Europe agreement in force	Agreement w. EFTA	Interim agreement signed	SAA in force	PCA								WTO
Central Eastern Europe	Poland		1989	1992		1994	1992				2004		1996	CEFTA 92–04				1995
Central Eastern Europe	Czech Republic	1993	1990[1]	1992[1]		1995	1992[1]				2004		1995	CEFTA 92–04				1995
Central Eastern Europe	Slovak Republic	1993	1990[1]	1992[1]		1995	1992[1]				2004	2009	2000	CEFTA 92–04				1995
Central Eastern Europe	Hungary		1988	1992		1994	1993				2004		1996	CEFTA 92–04				1995
Central Eastern Europe	Slovenia	1991	1993	1997		1999	1995				2004	2007		CEFTA 96–04				1995
Eastern Balkans	Romania		1991	1993		1995	1992				2007			CEFTA 97–07				1995
Eastern Balkans	Bulgaria		1990	1993		1995	1993				2007			CEFTA 99–07				1996
Baltics	Estonia	1991	1992	1994	1998	1995					2004			BFTA 94–04				1999
Baltics	Latvia	1991	1992	1994	1998	1995					2004			BFTA 94–04				1999

		1991	1992	1994	1998	1995	2002	2001	2004		
Baltics	Lithuania	1991	1992							BFTA 94-04	2001
South Eastern Europe (SEE)	Croatia	1991				2001	2002	2001	Cand.	CEFTA 03-	2000
South Eastern Europe (SEE)	Bosnia and Herzegovina	1992					2008	2008		CEFTA 07-	OG
South Eastern Europe (SEE)	Serbia						2010	2008		CEFTA 07-	OG
South Eastern Europe (SEE)	Montenegro	2006					2008	2007		CEFTA 07-	OG
South Eastern Europe (SEE)	UNMIK/Kosovo	2008								CEFTA 07-	
South Eastern Europe (SEE)	FYR Macedonia	1991				2000	2001	2001	Cand.	CEFTA 06-	2003
South Eastern Europe (SEE)	Albania		1992				2006	2006		CEFTA 07-	2000

(continued)

Table 13.1. (continued)

Region	Country	Independent	European integration: Trade-related preaccession agreements relevant for Central Eastern Europe, Eastern Balkans, Baltics						Preaccession agreements relevant for SEE	Agreements with CIS countries	EU member	Euro	OECD	Regional integration CEFTA/BFTA	CIS	CEZ	EAEC	WTO
			Trade and cooperation agreement in force	Interim trade agreement	Free trade agreement w. EFTA	Europe Agreement in force	Agreement Interim agreement in force	SAA signed		PCA								
CIS member	Moldova	1991								1998				CEFTA 07-	CIS			2001
CIS member	Ukraine²	1991								1998					CIS	CEZ		2008
CIS member	Belarus	1991													CIS	CEZ	EAEC	OG
CIS member	Russia	1991								1997					CIS	CEZ	EAEC	OG

Sources: European Commission documents from the Enlargement webpage, EFTA webpage, CEFTA webpage, WTO Regional Trade Agreements gateway, OECD webpage.

OG—Observer Government at WTO.

Cand—Candidate for EU membership.

EA—Europe Agreement.

SAA—Stabilization and Association agreement with EU.

PCA—Partnership and Cooperation Agreement with EU.

CIS—Commonwealth of Independent States (Armenia, Azerbaijan, Belarus, Georgia, Kazakhstan, Kyrgyz Republic, Moldova, Russia, Tajikistan, Ukraine, Uzbekistan) (note that Georgia left the CIS after the armed conflict with Russia in 2008).

EFTA—European Free Trade Association.

CEFTA—Central European Free Trade Agreement (currently Albania, Bosnia and Herzegovina, Croatia, Macedonia, Moldova, Montenegro, Serbia and Kosovo).

BFTA—Baltic Free Trade Area.

CEZ—Common Economic Zone (Belarus, Ukraine, Russia, Kazakhstan).

EAEC (or EVRAZES)—Eurasian Economic Community (Belarus, Kazakhstan, Kyrgyz Republic, Russian Federation, Tajikistan), a customs union.

¹ Signed by Czechoslovakia.

² De facto member but not signatory.

1. DEVELOPMENT SINCE 1989

....

The move from plan to market in the European Transition Economies that started in earnest in most countries at the end of the 1980s has been the driving force of the vast majority of economic reforms over the last two decades. This section describes trade policies, together with key elements of this broader transition process. Two central themes in this transition are, first, the breakup of the Soviet Union and its extended economic and political sphere, and second, the EU accession process.

Poland, the Czech Republic, the Slovak Republic, Hungary, Slovenia, Romania, and Bulgaria: The Path toward EU Membership

At the time of the breakdown of communism and the Eastern Bloc in 1989, a reorientation toward Western Europe started or was already under way in Czechoslovakia, Poland, and Hungary. Hungary and Poland had implemented some market reforms prior to 1989. One example of such a reform was allowing for small private businesses in Hungary during the 1980s. In Czechoslovakia, on the other hand, the economy was largely centrally planned and state controlled. Czechoslovakia split into the Czech Republic and the Slovak Republic in 1993, but the period of reorientation toward the west began when Czechoslovakia still existed.

One of the first steps toward closer economic cooperation with Western Europe had started in 1988 with Hungary signing a Trade and Cooperation agreement with the European Community.[7] Poland and Czechoslovakia followed suit and signed such agreements in 1989 and 1990, respectively. These trade agreements aimed at normalizing trade relations, applying the most-favored-nation (MFN) principle and eliminating quantitative import restrictions (except in "sensitive sectors" such as coal, steel, textiles, and agriculture).

When the leaders of Poland, Czechoslovakia, and Hungary met in the Hungarian city of Visegrad in 1991, one of the aims was to increase integration among themselves and to work together toward EU membership. The Visegrad countries made a joint effort to get a clear roadmap from the European Community, including criteria that would need to be fulfilled and a timetable that would lead to full membership. During the first years of transition, the European Community did not commit to such a schedule, and the discussion within the EU was one of "deepening" cooperation between present members versus "widening" (to allow the EU to expand to include the former Eastern Bloc countries). At the Copenhagen summit in 1993, the EU did commit to admitting its eastern neighbors at some future date, if a number of criteria were met.[8]

Prior to Copenhagen, however, in December 1991, the Visegrad countries all signed a "Europe Agreement" (EA) with the European Community. Although these agreements did not come into full force until 1994–1995, the parts relating to trade, the Interim Trade Agreements (ITAs), applied from early 1992.

The Europe Agreements formed the legal ground between the EU and the countries aiming at membership. The implementation of the ITAs, and the move toward closer integration with the EU in general, meant both establishing free trade with the EU countries and adopting the EU trade policy in relations with non-EU members.

In the area of trade with the EU, the ITA stated that free trade in industrial goods between the country and the EU should be established within 10 years. Economic legislation within the country should be harmonized with EU legislation. The ITAs recognized that the restructuring of the Eastern Bloc economies would take time and therefore allowed some protection on the part of the Visegrad countries, while the EU was required to reduce import tariffs at a faster pace ("asymmetry"). At the Copenhagen summit in 1993, a more accelerated schedule for the reduction of tariffs was established (Berend, 2009; Kaminski, 1994).[9]

In addition to the integration process with the EU, the Visegrad countries established in 1992 the Central European Free Trade Agreement (CEFTA), which was encouraged by the EU. Apart from goals of increased integration, increased regional trade would also protect the Visegrad countries, with trade flows ever more linked toward Western Europe, from shocks originated within the EU. In addition, if trade were liberalized with the EU but not with regional partners, it could lead to trade diversion.[10] The CEFTA agreement consisted of bilateral agreements between the countries involved and was similar to the EAs, in that it aimed at establishing free trade in industrial goods between Poland, the Czech Republic, the Slovak Republic, and Hungary within 10 years.[11] A series of adjustments of the initial agreement in practice made trade in most industrial goods tariff-free within five years (Richter, 1998).

In 1992/93, the Visegrad countries had first gone through a phase of rapid trade liberalization, which was then followed by some measures of increased protection. These early developments are discussed in Koteva (1993), Rodrik (1992), and Winiecki (2002) and are briefly summarized here.

At the onset of transition, all three countries largely abandoned trade licenses and quotas, although their removal was more gradual in Hungary than in Poland and Czechoslovakia. In particular, Hungary used a "global quota" to protect agricultural products and foodstuffs. Being the most gradual reformer of the three, Hungary had average tariff levels of 13–16% in the early 1990s (Koteva, 1993). In the face of a balance-of-payments crisis in the mid-1990s, a temporary import surcharge of 8% was imposed (Winiecki, 2002; WTO, 1998). This measure was then removed in 1997.

Poland adopted a very liberal import tariff schedule, with rates averaging 5% at the end of 1990. However, calls for protection of industry and agriculture and for raising government revenue resulted in increasing import tariff rates. With these increases, particularly prevalent for agricultural goods, import tariffs stood at 11.5–18% in 1992/93 (Koteva, 1993)[12]. An import surcharge of 6% was also introduced in 1992 but then gradually phased out until 1997 (European Commission, 1997g).

Czechoslovakia adopted a liberal tariff schedule at the onset of transition, with rates averaging 5%. Although tariff levels were only marginally increased to an average level of 6% in 1992, a temporary import surcharge on foodstuffs and consumer goods of 20% was introduced at the end of 1990 and hence increased protection. By 1993, the import surcharge had been reduced to 12%. From its formation, the Slovak Republic used an import surcharge of 10% that was dismantled in 1996/97 (European Commission, 1997i).

After the initial period of liberalization, some of the protectionist measures, for example, increased levels of agricultural protection, made the Visegrad countries look more like their western neighbors.

The ITAs required that quantitative import restrictions in the EU should be eliminated immediately, except for the "sensitive sectors" of steel, coal, textiles, and clothing. The ITAs, furthermore, classified industrial goods into six categories for which tariffs should be reduced: products of immediate trade liberalization; liberalization within one, four, and five years; plus the two groups containing steel/coal and textiles/clothing. Kaminski (1994) reports that, depending on the country, the group of products to be liberalized immediately accounted for 30–50% of the preagreement export value to the EU, that is, a substantial fraction. The sectors for which the EU imposed more restrictions, that is, steel/coal and textiles/clothing, accounted for 4–14% and 14–28% of the preagreement export value to the EU, respectively.

Romania and Bulgaria also signed EAs. The ITA for these two countries came into force in 1993.[13] For Slovenia, the only country from the former Yugoslavia that was included in the same enlargement process as Central Eastern Europe, the ITA of the EA came into force in 1997. Slovenia (1996), Romania (1997), and Bulgaria (1999) also joined CEFTA.

Vachudova (2005) discusses the political developments in Romania and Bulgaria during the 1990s and the lack of reform actually taking place in order to meet the criteria for EU accession. When the EU evaluated progress in the Eastern European candidates in 1997, the lack of progress in adoption of the *acquis communautaire* in both countries led to the conclusion that they were not ready to cope with competitive pressures and market forces within the EU (European Commission 1997a, 1997h). These and other considerations delayed the process of EU accession and economic integration in the Eastern Balkans.

Slovenia experienced a gradual transformation of its economy during the early 1990s and, building on links established when it was still part of Yugoslavia, had Western Europe as its main trading partner throughout the transition period.[14] Similar to the other ITAs, trade between Slovenia and the EU was to be liberalized gradually. However, since Slovenia had signed its agreement later than the other countries, it had to liberalize trade at a faster pace. Signing the ITA with the EU, joining CEFTA, and signing a free trade agreement with Croatia, all in 1996–1998, contributed to speeding up trade liberalization. After entering into these agreements, approximately 80% of Slovenian imports were subject to preferential treatment, and the effective level of import protection was low (World Bank, 1999). As in other countries, agriculture was an exception.[15]

The Baltic Countries

Estonia, Latvia, and Lithuania gained independence when the Soviet Union broke up in 1991.[16] The path of reorientation toward, and integration with, Western Europe and the EU looks similar to that of the previous group of countries. However, at the time of independence from the Soviet Union in 1991, it was not at all obvious that a close integration with Western Europe would follow. The EU's relationship with Russia and the CIS, the issue of citizenship for ethnic Russians in Estonia and Latvia, and desire by the EU to have the Baltic states focus primarily on increased economic integration among themselves were some of the factors affecting the extent of EU-Baltic integration in the first half of the 1990s.[17] Western integration was desired by the Baltic states, but it was not a priority of most EU members at the time. However, the political breakthrough regarding enlargement in Copenhagen in 1993 and the accession of Sweden and Finland—"Baltic neighbors"—into the EU in 1995 acted to strengthen the EU-Baltic integration process.

Similar to the countries discussed earlier, the Soviet Union had signed a Trade and Cooperation agreement with the EU in 1990. In principle, this covered also the Baltics. After independence, however, the EU negotiated separate agreements with each of the Baltic states in 1992. In 1994/95, the next level of formal trade integration followed—after a discussion of the citizenship issue—with the signing and ratification of free trade agreements between the EU and each of the Baltic countries. Several factors contributed to the EU taking the step toward deeper economic integration: the breakthrough in Copenhagen; the signing of free trade agreements by Finland, Sweden, and Norway—at the time potential EU members—with the Baltic states; and the establishment of the Baltic Free Trade Agreement (BFTA). In contrast with the Central European case, the free trade agreements were not part of EAs, perhaps reflecting a lack of full commitment from the EU at the time to open the road toward membership. However, EAs with the Baltic countries were signed in 1995.

The Baltic countries were keen to adapt to EU institutions and trade policies from the outset, and the free trade agreements with the Baltic countries were more "liberal" than the corresponding trade agreements discussed for the first group of countries. From the date of the agreement in 1995, trade with Lithuania was to be liberalized within a period of six years, with Latvia within four years, and for Estonia trade was liberalized immediately. The EU was to abolish all quantitative restrictions and tariffs over this period of trade liberalization. Some products such as textiles, fishing, and agriculture were treated separately. In line with the ITAs with Central Eastern Europe, the Baltic countries were allowed to temporarily impose protectionist measures.[18] Lithuania and Latvia protected agriculture and textiles, although signaling that they intended to comply with the criteria of EU accession (Čičinskas, Cornelius, and Treigiene, 1996). Estonia on the other hand was reluctant to impose any restrictions on trade and was largely at free trade with the EU after 1995.

SEE: Croatia, Bosnia and Herzegovina, Serbia, Montenegro, UNMIK-Kosovo, FYR of Macedonia, Albania

Yugoslavia followed a different socialist development path from the other Eastern European countries. With respect to trade, it was not a CMEA member, it maintained closer links with Western Europe, and it signed trade agreements with the EU in the 1970s and in 1980. Compared to that of other Eastern European countries, Yugoslav trade was more oriented toward Western Europe, although it also contained a substantial CMEA component. Yugoslavia also traded with the United States and, as did some other Eastern European countries, with developing countries.[19] Albania on the other hand followed an "autarchic" development policy and was largely isolated from world trade up until the late 1980s. But by 1992, it signed a Trade and Cooperation Agreement with the EU.

At the onset of the Yugoslav wars, the EU suspended its trade agreements with Yugoslavia. As Slovenia (1991), Croatia (1991), FYR Macedonia (1991), and Bosnia and Herzegovina (1992) became independent nations, new national borders were drawn between them and the remaining parts of the federation (consisting of Serbia and Montenegro). From 1992 until the end of the Yugoslav wars in 1995, Serbia and Montenegro was subject to sanctions by the UN.[20]

In the late 1990s, the newly formed nations of the SEE region had their own trade policies, tariff structures, and nontariff barriers. Serbia and Montenegro, in addition, conducted somewhat independent trade policies even prior to the independence of Montenegro in 2006.

Trade Policy Developments in SEE since the Late 1990s: Approaching Europe

The international community launched the Stability Pact for SEE in 1999, after the NATO intervention against the Federal Republic of Yugoslavia over Kosovo. One of the goals of this process was economic reconstruction, cooperation, and development. The EU, in turn, launched the Stabilization and Association Process, which is the framework for integration between the SEE countries and the EU. For the SEE countries, this process plays a role similar to that of the EAs, which the EU signed with the countries discussed previously.

Following the Stability Pact and after initial discussions and preparations in 2001, 28 bilateral free trade agreements were signed during 2002–2003. These agreements established free trade in all the bilateral relations between Croatia, FYR Macedonia, Bosnia and Herzegovina, Serbia and Montenegro, Albania and, in addition, Romania, Bulgaria, and Moldova. This was generally considered a great success, given the recent history of the region and the amount of negotiation that had taken place (Sida, 2004; World Bank, 2005a). The treaties covered industrial products. Trade in agricultural goods on the other hand continued to be characterized by protection (Sida, 2004). Another major step toward regional integration was taken in 2006, when an expanded CEFTA further liberalized trade in the region and replaced the web of bilateral agreements.[21]

Similar to the position that the EU had taken on regional integration in Central Eastern Europe and in the Baltics, increased SEE regional integration was highly desired by the EU. Given the Yugoslav wars, political reasons for the EU to encourage regional integration may have been even stronger for the SEE. The EU also explicitly emphasized that benefits from the EU would depend on deepened regional economic integration taking place (World Bank, 2005a). The free trade agreements signed were thus much welcomed by the EU.[22]

For its part, the EU took several steps to increase trade with the SEE countries. Although some previous agreements existed, the granting of Autonomous Trade Measures (ATMs) to the SEE countries in 2000 virtually eliminated tariffs and quotas on most products imported from them. Some agricultural products were exceptions. This asymmetric trade liberalization measure was followed by the start of negotiations of a Stabilization and Association Agreement (SAA) between the EU and each SEE country. Similar to the trade part of the EAs, the SAA contains measures that will gradually liberalize trade, asymmetrically, over a 10-year period.

The ATMs and the SAAs together imply a faster liberalization of restrictions to EU imports from the SEE region than was the case for the EAs signed with previous accession candidates. However, the region faced some obstacles that limited reforms and EU integration in the early years of the decade 2000–2010. First, the region started the process at a lower level of economic development than previous accession countries and lacked administrative capacity to undertake reforms; this lack was especially the case in FYR Macedonia, Bosnia and Herzegovina, and Albania (SIGMA, 2002; Vachudova, 2005). Second, public sector corruption—as measured for example by Transparency International—was and remains a greater problem in the region than was the case in the Visegrad countries.[23] Finally, complying with the International Criminal Tribunal for Former Yugoslavia (ICTY) was an additional criterion affecting the integration prospects for Serbia and Montenegro, and initially also for Croatia (European Commission, 2005a; Vachudova, 2005).

Croatia and FYR Macedonia signed SAA agreements in 2001 and are currently candidates for accession to the EU.[24] Both countries, together with Albania, are members of the WTO. Albania made significant progress toward trade liberalization in the 1990s, with reduction in tariff rates and the removal of nontariff barriers, but the institutional capacity lagged behind (SIGMA, 2002). Albania, as well as Montenegro, Bosnia and Herzegovina, and Serbia signed SAAs in 2006–2008, but as of March 2010 the latter three agreements still await EU ratification.[25] Furthermore, these three countries have yet to become members of the WTO, although some progress has been made in the membership negotiations.

In terms of progress of European integration as of October 2009, the European Commission (2009) reports that accession negotiations with Croatia "are nearing the final phase" (p. 2); FYR Macedonia "has made significant progress in meeting key challenges" (p. 2); Montenegro and Albania in general show progress in implementing agreements but need to show concrete results on rule of law and corruption (p. 14);

reforms are lacking in Bosnia and Herzegovina (p. 14); the Interim Agreement (prior to the SAA) should now be implemented in Serbia, but there is still progress to be made in terms of cooperating with the ICTY (p. 15); and the Commission is concerned (p. 7) about CEFTA being paralyzed due to disagreements over the Kosovo status issue.[26]

The CIS States: Moldova, Ukraine, Belarus, Russia

The CIS was formed in 1991 by 12 out of the 15 former republics of the Soviet Union. The three Baltic countries were the only former republics that did not join the CIS in 1991, although Georgia left the CIS after the armed conflict with Russia in 2008. A free trade area was, in principle, established between the 12 CIS countries in 1994, but progress toward the realization of free trade was slow, and the agreement was never ratified by the Russian parliament.[27] Instead, starting in 1994/95, Belarus and Russia, later joined by Kazakhstan, the Kyrgyz Republic, and Tajikistan, formed a customs union, the Eurasian Economic Community (EAEC). In addition, a free trade agreement, the Common Economic Zone (CEZ), was also established by Belarus, Russia, Kazakhstan, and Ukraine in 2004.

Yet the degree of implementation of the agreements has been questioned. For example, exceptions to common external tariffs were common in the EAEC; the extent to which Ukraine has desired further eastern integration has varied over the years; and the agreements have been incompatible with both a closer relationship with the EU and with WTO membership for the CIS countries (Fantini, 2007; Olcott et al., 1999; World Bank, 2005a). In addition to the multilateral agreements, a large number of bilateral free trade agreements have been signed between the CIS members. As an example, Ukraine has a total of 12 bilateral free trade agreements, covering all original CIS members as well as FYR Macedonia.[28]

Parallel to the efforts for CIS integration, Moldova, Ukraine, and Russia signed Partnership and Cooperation Agreements (PCAs) with the EU. These agreements, now part of the EU's broader "European Neighborhood Policy" (ENP), have been in effect since 1997–1998 and cover different aspects of the relations with the EU. Trade between the three countries and the EU should adhere to WTO principles such as MFN treatment. Compared to the original EAs and the SAAs, however, the PCA regulates, rather than liberalizes, trade with the EU. In the cases of Moldova and Ukraine, the EU granted them Generalized System of Preferences (GSP), meaning lower tariffs on some imports, although coverage is limited. Trade between Belarus and the EU is covered by the Trade and Cooperation agreement that was originally signed with the Soviet Union in 1990. Relations between the CIS countries and the EU have also been characterized by the EU classification of the countries as nonmarket or transition economies, which has opened up a large number of antidumping actions (World Bank, 2005a).

The following subsections discuss briefly some specific aspects of trade and trade policy developments in the four countries.

Moldova

Moldova suffered a large decline in GDP and in exports in the 1990s as a result of the collapse of the Soviet Union and the Russian financial crisis in 1998 and is today very poor by European standards.[29] With respect to proximity to the EU and access to EU markets, the country falls somewhere between the SEE region and the other CIS countries. From an EU perspective, the country is included in the ENP.

Moldova is part of CEFTA and thus has free trade with the SEE region. When Romania joined the EU, however, it had to abandon its 1994 free trade agreement with Moldova, and it also left CEFTA. Thus, Moldova no longer borders the region with which it has a free trade agreement. In 2005, in the "EU/Moldova Action Plan," the possible extension of Autonomous Trade Preferences to Moldova was considered (European Commission, 2005b) and then granted in 2008. This meant a removal of tariffs on industrial goods and improved access for agricultural products. However, trade in some important products, including wine, is still restricted. More generally, EU barriers to import of agricultural products—Moldova's main exportable output— are likely to have slowed down a reorientation of Moldovan exports toward the EU (Ronnås and Orlova, 2000).

One of the issues that restrict Moldova's market access to the EU is the problem of controlling the origin of goods in Moldova (European Commission, 2008). This is a nontrivial issue, since Moldova does not control its eastern province Transnistria, and the semiindependent Transnistria customs authority complicates the fulfillment of "control of origin." Illegitimate trade in this region is an issue that goes far beyond trade policies and will require a broader resolution of the underlying conflicts.

With respect to tariffs, Moldova has kept a low level of protection since the mid-1990s, with average MFN import tariffs of approximately 5%. The country also became a member of the WTO in 2001.

Belarus, Ukraine, and Russia

A discussion of trade policy developments for Belarus and Ukraine is by necessity characterized by the geographical location of the two countries between the EU and Russia and the legacy of Soviet economic structures. Both countries are heavily dependent on imports of Russian energy and are transit countries for Russian gas exports to the EU. Although the Ukrainian share of imports coming from Russia decreased from around 60% in 1990 to around 40% in 2003 (World Bank, 2005b) and has continued to decline, the country continues to depend heavily on gas and oil imports from Russia. With respect to Belarus, 60% of its imports came from Russia in 2008.[30]

During the Soviet period, the different republics received heavily subsidized gas from Russia, in exchange for manufactured goods, agricultural products, and other goods. Although Russian exports are not as heavily subsidized as previously, Ukraine and Belarus still benefit from gas imports below the prices that other countries in Europe pay. Subsidized prices, lock-in effects, and transit routes have made gas a contentious issue for these two countries. On several occasions since transition, arguments over gas supplies have become international disputes that have spilled over to the rest of Europe. The issues have included accusations that Ukraine was reselling gas bought at subsidized prices to its Western neighbors; Belarus and Ukraine not paying gas bills and therefore having supplies shut off; quadrupling of the gas price for Ukraine (and Moldova); and accusations that Russia was using its monopoly pricing power to affect internal politics in the recipient countries and trying to gain control of the distribution network inside Belarus and Ukraine themselves (Fantini, 2007; Nygren, 2009; Olcott et al., 1999).

For Russia, the EU 27 is by far the most important trade partner (see section III for further details). Mineral fuels and related products constitute the largest share of Russia's exports to the EU. These raw materials are not subject to any tariff barriers in the EU. However, it has been argued that Russia's exports suffer from EU protection of "sensitive areas" such as coal, steel, textiles, and agriculture, areas in which the CIS countries often have a comparative advantage (Machold, 1998).

Ukraine's reorientation of trade toward the EU has been slow compared to Russia and the former CMEA members that are now EU members. Most Ukrainian exports are in sensitive areas and therefore heavily protected by the EU. The GSP status Ukraine enjoys most likely produced moderate results in terms of improved access to the European market. Half of the 30% of Ukrainian eligible exports actually received GSP benefits, according to a World Bank 2005 study, while the European Commission places this ratio at 72% in 2010.[31] The GSP status means reduction in, not elimination of, tariffs in the subset of areas where it applies.

Another reason for Ukraine's relatively slow trade growth with the EU is that it did not become a member of the WTO until 2008. This made the country more susceptible to antidumping actions by developed countries (World Bank, 2005a). Furthermore, before joining the WTO Ukraine did not have access to the dispute settlement mechanisms the WTO offers. After joining the WTO, Ukraine has started negotiations over a free trade agreement with the EU and EFTA.

The relationship between the EU and Russia is perhaps less developed than in 2002–2003. Initiatives to create a Common European Economic Space have yet to materialize and negotiations over an agreement to replace the PCA are ongoing. Russia also pushed an eventual WTO entry further into the future by stating that it would join only as part of a customs union with Belarus and Kazakhstan. As of 2007, Russia and Belarus have similar average MFN applied import tariffs of 11%, double the protection level of Ukraine. In addition to tariffs, domestic regulations have typically been substantial barriers to trade in CIS countries.

2. TARIFF PROTECTION

Table 13.2 reports average MFN applied tariff rates in the SEE and CIS countries that are part of this study. It also reports the trade-weighted average of applied tariff rates. The most recent tariff data from the WTO, averaged for all, industrial, and

Table 13.2. Tariffs

Region	Country	Average MFN applied tariff rates Simple average						Average applied tariff rates Weighted average					
		Year	All goods	Year	All goods	Agricultural goods	Industrial goods	Year	All goods	Year	All goods	Agricultural goods	Industrial goods
SEE	Croatia	2002	6.0	2008	4,8	10,3	4	2002	4.7	2006	4,5	14,2	3,8
SEE	Bosnia and Herzegovina	2001	5.4	2008	6,8	12,4	6	2001	5.1	2007	8,5	19,2	6,4
SEE	Serbia	2001	9.0[1]	2008	7,4	14,2	6,3	2001	5.8[1]	2006	6,1	15,9	5,3
SEE	Montenegro	n/a	n/a	2008	4,9	11,1	4	n/a	n/a	n/a	n/a	n/a	n/a
SEE	FYR Macedonia	2001	14.3	2008	7,7	13,7	6,8	2001	11.1	2007	6	18,4	4,4
SEE	Albania	2001	8.5	2008	5,2	7,8	4,8	2001	8.5	2007	5,2	7	4,9
	Average SEE		8.6		6,1	11,6	5,3		7,0		6,1	14,9	5,0
CIS	Moldova	2001	5.1	2008	4,7	11,2	3,7	2001	2.8	2007	2,7	8,5	2,1
CIS	Ukraine	2002	7.9	2008	5,5	13	4,4	2002	3.9	2007	5,1	19,1	4,2
CIS	Belarus	2001	10.6	2008	10,8	13,3	10,5	2001	8.1	2007	7,7	16	7
CIS	Russia	2001	10.8	2008	10,8	14,2	10,2	2001	8.9	2006	11,4	22,8	9,3
	EU	2003	4.4[2]	2008	5,6[3]	16,0[3]	4,0[3]	2003	3.1[2]	2007	2,7[3]	4,6[3]	2,7[3]
Column		1	2	3	4	5	6	7	8	9	10	11	12

[1] Number refers to Serbia and Montenegro.
[2] Number refers to EU15.
[3] Number refers to EU27.

Sources: Columns 1, 2, 7, 8: World Bank (2005A), Annex table 3.1. Columns 3–6, 9–12: WTO, Tariff Profiles.

agricultural goods, respectively, is presented (columns 3–6, 9–12). The table also presents 2001–2003 average tariff levels from a 2005 World Bank study (columns 1–2, 7–8). No breakdown in industrial and agricultural goods is made for this earlier point in time.[32] The 10 countries that have become EU members had to adopt the EU common external tariffs and are not included separately in the table.

The 2008 tariff rates in column 4 are not very high. The average SEE tariff rate of 6.1% is close to the EU level and compares favorably with other regions such as Latin America (10%) and Africa (13.8%)[33]. As discussed, Moldova has had a liberal tariff regime since the mid-1990s, whereas Russia and Belarus have a higher level of protection. All countries except Bosnia and Herzegovina, Belarus, and Russia have reduced average applied MFN tariff levels (comparing columns 2 and 4), with the FYR Macedonia showing the largest tariff reduction. The pattern of tariff reduction also shows up when comparing trade-weighted tariffs over time (columns 8 and 10). However, while Serbia and Ukraine have reduced MFN applied tariffs, the trade-weighted tariffs have actually increased. It is also noteworthy that the EU has substantial agricultural tariff protection (column 5) but the trade-weighted tariff protection is low (column 11). That might be the result of a downward bias imparted when using trade weights to estimate average tariffs.

The speed of implementation varied between the countries. For Romania, a 2007 EU member, tariffs remained high throughout the first part of the decade 2000–2010. Average applied MFN tariffs stood at 15% for industrial and 30% for agricultural products at least until 2004, well above EU levels of 3.6% and 16.2%, respectively (information from the European Commission's yearly evaluation reports of Romania as a candidate country). Tariffs have since dropped down to EU levels. In the case of Estonia, trade was completely liberalized, including in agricultural goods. On accession to the EU, Estonia would have to apply the Community's Common Customs Tariff, and from 2000 it has been raising rates to align its tariffs with those of the EU.

3. Trade in the European Transition Economies

This section provides a brief analysis of the extent of trade and of trade flows in the European Transition countries since 1993. The breakdown of the Communist Bloc and the following period of transition to market economies implied abrupt changes in economic conditions throughout the bloc. Former centrally planned and state-organized trade relations between CMEA members broke down. Quotas, licenses, trade in inconvertible currencies, or even barter trade relations were largely abandoned. Instead, countries were exposed to world market prices on imports and exports. Not only trade with Western Europe but also trade between former CMEA members underwent price liberalization. The CMEA countries were exposed to competition from Western products and Western quality, meaning that low-quality Eastern European products could not compete. These factors all contributed to a sharp decline of trade in most countries.[34]

Table 13.3 below shows total exports of goods and services, total trade in goods and services, the trade balance, and the openness data for the region for the years 1993, 2000, and 2007. Openness is defined as the sum of exports and imports divided by GDP. Table 13.3 also shows basic GDP data and the trade balance to GDP ratio for 2007. Table 13.3 presents the countries in three subgroups: the 10 current EU members, the SEE countries, and the CIS countries included in the study. Below each group of countries are shown its share in world exports, share in total trade, and average degree of openness.

The Level of Trade

Trade in the region has increased substantially over the period covered. Columns 4–6 of table 13.3 reveal that the share of the 10 countries that have joined the EU in world exports has more than doubled over the time period, and stood at 3.7% in 2007. For the SEE and CIS countries in the study, there is a substantial increase in shares of world exports as well.

The increase in trade over the last two decades is also reflected in the openness measures, reported in columns 14–16. Whereas the trade-to-GDP ratio has increased in the world as a whole, the increase in openness ratios is larger for both the present EU members and for the SEE countries over the periods for which data exist.

The most open economies in the study are the Slovak Republic, Hungary, Estonia, the Czech Republic, and Slovenia, whereas the larger countries—especially Russia, Romania, and Poland, trade less as a fraction of GDP.[35] This is most likely due to a combination of factors, including country size and attractiveness to foreign investments into the trade-oriented manufacturing sector. From the group of most open economies, Hungary stands out as the country for which trade as a fraction of GDP shows the most dramatic increase; it was during the years 1994–2000 that trade increased at the fastest pace. The early openness measures of the Czech and Slovak republics may be exaggerated, due to the fact that to a large extent, early trade was bilateral between the two countries.[36] This effect would exacerbate the "opening up" toward other countries in the data.

Trade Balances in the Region

Since the start of the transition process, the countries in the region have tended to run significant trade deficits, leading in most cases also to large current account deficits. In the years prior to the 2008–2009 crisis, many countries in the region were running double-digit deficits as a percentage of GDP. Russia is an exception due to its substantial exports of oil, gas, and minerals. Indeed, its trade balance varies closely with international prices for energy and minerals.

Table 13.3. Trade data

Country	GDP 2007 BUSD	Population 2007 Millions	GDP/cap. 2007 kUSD	Total exports EX			Trade balance (EX-IM)			Trade balance (EX-IM)/GDP	Total trade (EX+IM)			Degree of openness (EX+IM)/GDP		
				1993 BUSD	2000 BUSD	2007 BUSD	1993 BUSD	2000 BUSD	2007 BUSD	2007	1993 BUSD	2000 BUSD	2007 BUSD	1993	2000	2007
Poland	425	38,1	11,1	19,7	46,5	173,3	0,8	-11,0	-12,2	-2,9%	38,6	103,9	358,8	0,45	0,61	0,84
Czech Republic	174	10,3	17,0	19,2	35,9	139,5	0,3	-1,7	8,7	5,0%	38,1	73,6	270,3	1,09	1,30	1,55
Slovak Republic	75	5,4	13,9	7,6	14,4	64,9	-0,6	-0,5	-0,8	-1,0%	15,7	29,3	130,5	1,18	1,43	1,74
Hungary	138	10,0	13,8	10,2	34,6	111,3	-3,2	-1,7	2,2	1,6%	23,6	70,8	220,5	0,61	1,50	1,59
Slovenia	47	2,0	23,5	7,4	10,7	32,9	0,1	-0,7	-0,8	-1,7%	14,8	22,2	66,6	1,16	1,11	1,41
Romania	166	21,5	7,7	6,1	12,2	50,5	-1,3	-2,1	-23,7	-14,3%	13,4	26,4	124,8	0,51	0,71	0,75
Bulgaria	40	7,6	5,2	4,1	7,0	25,1	-0,8	-0,7	-8,7	-22,1%	9,1	14,7	58,9	0,84	1,17	1,49
Estonia	21	1,3	15,9	1,1	4,8	15,6	-0,1	-0,2	-2,4	-11,3%	2,4	9,8	33,5	1,37	1,73	1,57
Latvia	29	2,3	12,7	1,6	3,3	12,1	0,4	-0,6	-5,8	-20,2%	2,8	7,1	30,1	1,18	0,90	1,05
Lithuania	39	3,4	11,6	n/a	5,1	21,1	n/a	-0,7	-5,2	-13,3%	n/a	11,0	47,5	n/a	0,96	1,22
Region average														0,93	1,14	1,32
Share in world trade				1,63%	2,20%	3,72%					1,66%	2,29%	3,86%			
Croatia	59	4,4	13,2	n/a	9,0	25,1	n/a	-0,7	-4,4	-7,6%	n/a	18,6	54,6	n/a	0,87	0,93
Bosnia and Herzegovina	15	3,8	3,9	n/a	1,6	5,7	n/a	-2,6	-4,9	-33,1%	n/a	5,7	16,3	n/a	1,14	1,11

(continued)

Table 13.3. *(continued)*

	GDP	Population	GDP/cap.	Total exports EX			Trade balance (EX-IM)			Trade balance (EX-IM)/GDP	Total trade (EX+IM)			Degree of openness (EX+IM)/GDP		
	2007	2007	2007	1993	2000	2007	1993	2000	2007	2007	1993	2000	2007	1993	2000	2007
	BUSD	Millions	kUSD	BUSD	BUSD	BUSD	BUSD	BUSD	BUSD		BUSD	BUSD	BUSD			
Serbia	40	7,4	5,5	n/a	0,7	12,4	n/a	-0,4	-9,6	-23,9%	n/a	1,7	34,4	n/a	0,28	0,85
Montenegro	3,8	0,6	6,2	n/a	n/a	1,7	n/a	n/a	-1,0	-27,2%	n/a	n/a	4,3	n/a	n/a	1,12
FYR Macedonia	7,9	2,0	3,9	n/a	1,7	4,2	n/a	-0,5	-1,5	-18,8%	n/a	4,0	10,0	n/a	1,12	1,26
Albania	11	3,1	3,4	n/a	0,7	3,0	n/a	-0,7	-2,9	-26,6%	n/a	2,0	8,9	n/a	0,56	0,83
Region average														n/a	0,79	1,02
Share in world trade				n/a	0,17%	0,30%					n/a	0,20%	0,37%			
Moldova	4,4	3,7	1,2	n/a	0,6	2,0	n/a	-0,3	-2,3	-52,5%	n/a	1,6	6,3	n/a	1,25	1,43
Ukraine	143	46,3	3,1	8,5	19,5	64,0	-0,1	1,6	-8,2	-5,7%	17,0	37,5	136,2	0,52	1,20	0,95
Belarus	45	9,7	4,7	n/a	6,7	27,6	n/a	-0,4	-2,8	-6,3%	n/a	13,8	58,0	n/a	1,33	1,28
Russia	1277	141,9	9,0	66,1	114,4	392,2	13,3	52,0	111,3	8,7%	118,8	176,9	673,1	0,71	0,68	0,53
Region average														n/a	1,12	1,05
Share in world trade				n/a	1,78%	2,80%					n/a	1,43%	2,51%			
World				4724	7937	17359					9558	16119	34746	0,38	0,50	0,63
Column	1	2	3	4	5	6	7	8	9	10	11	12	13	14	15	16

Sources: IMF International Financial Statistics (IFS), National accounts-section. For Montenegro, Moldova, Bosnia and Herzegovina: IFS, Balance of Payments-section. GDP figures for Montenegro and population figure for Serbia from WTO. World trade figures from IMF World Economic Outlook. World trade figures from WTO. World GDP figures (not shown) from IMF WEO database (sum of the 182 countries covered).

Trade balances depend on many factors, including trade policies. In this region, the transition and EU integration process has been an extremely important factor affecting trade flows. The promise of economic growth and eventual access to the EU has made many of the countries in the region very attractive to foreign capital inflows, enabling them to run very large current account and trade deficits. The fact that Russia has not been running deficits can also be viewed as its failure to attract substantial foreign investments, despite its significant needs to invest and modernize.

Behind the raw numbers of trade deficits lie very different economic processes, which in turn affect future trade flows. For example, a trade deficit financed by foreign direct investment (FDI) flows tends to lead to investments that create or facilitate future output and exports. On the other hand, trade and current account deficits that are financed by households borrowing abroad to invest in real estate or buy foreign cars are less likely to have a positive impact on future exports.

The trade balances in this region are certainly a mix of these types of behaviors and other factors. For example, it seems that the Visegrad countries fit the picture of FDI-financed trade deficits, whereas the Baltic states have relied more heavily on foreign bank loans to finance their deficits. The important lesson is that trade data can both highlight and hide important economic processes and vulnerabilities.

The Direction of Trade

Table 13.4 presents merchandise exports for the countries in the region, grouped by destination, for 1993, 2000, and 2007. Table 13.4 shows that the EU 15 is the most important export partner for most of the countries in the region. Although "EU 15" is no longer a political or economic entity in itself, it largely represents "Western Europe" at the onset of the transition process.[37] The transition countries are, to a large extent, integrated into traditionally Western European trade flows and, for most countries, the reorientation toward Western Europe happened early in the transition period.

Yet trade with other regions has grown even faster, resulting in a declining EU 15 export share between 2000 and 2007. Seven out the ten present EU members show an export share to EU 15 that increased between 1993 and 2000, and then declined. Accounting for this decline is increased trade among the 10 countries themselves. All current EU members, except the Czech and Slovak republics, show increasing export shares to countries within this subregion.[38] In the SEE region, Croatia and Bosnia and Herzegovina show increasing shares of exports destined to the region itself, whereas the opposite holds for Albania and FYR Macedonia. It is also noteworthy that Slovenia maintains its export share to the SEE countries, all being part of the former Yugoslavia (except Albania).

It appears that regional integration has taken place, at least in the case of the Visegrad countries and the Baltics. Russia has reemerged as an export partner for the Baltic countries and remains the most important export country for Ukraine and Belarus. Neither the United States nor China has emerged as important export partners for the countries in the region.

Table 13.4. Direction of Trade: share of total merchandise exports from a country (row) to a region or country (column)

Merchandise export share to

	EU15			"EU10"			SEE			Russia			CIS (excl. Russia)			US			China		
	1993	2000	2007	1993	2000	2007	1993	2000	2007	1993	2000	2007	1993	2000	2007	1993	2000	2007	1993	2000	2007
Poland	0.69	0.70	0.63	0.05	0.11	0.16	0.00	0.00	0.01	0.05	0.03	0.05	0.03	0.04	0.05	0.03	0.04	0.02	0.01	0.00	0.01
Czech Republic	0.54	0.69	0.64	0.28	0.17	0.21	0.00	0.01	0.01	0.04	0.01	0.02	0.01	0.01	0.01	0.02	0.03	0.02	0.02	0.00	0.01
Slovak Republic	0.30	0.59	0.57	0.51	0.31	0.30	0.01	0.01	0.01	0.05	0.01	0.02	0.03	0.02	0.02	0.01	0.01	0.02	0.01	0.00	0.01
Hungary	0.58	0.75	0.60	0.04	0.08	0.19	0.00	0.02	0.03	0.00	0.02	0.03	0.00	0.01	0.03	0.04	0.05	0.03	0.01	0.00	0.01
Slovenia	0.62	0.64	0.54	0.05	0.08	0.15	0.15	0.15	0.16	0.04	0.02	0.04	0.01	0.01	0.02	0.03	0.03	0.02	0.00	0.00	0.00
Romania	0.41	0.64	0.58	0.06	0.08	0.14	0.01	0.02	0.02	0.05	0.01	0.01	0.05	0.03	0.04	0.01	0.04	0.04	0.09	0.01	0.01
Bulgaria	0.47	0.46	0.49	0.06	0.04	0.11	0.01	0.11	0.08	0.10	0.02	0.02	0.01	0.03	0.03	0.07	0.04	0.03	0.05	0.00	0.01
Estonia	0.48	0.68	0.50	0.15	0.12	0.20	0.00	0.00	0.00	0.23	0.07	0.09	0.08	0.03	0.03	0.02	0.02	0.03	0.00	0.00	0.01
Latvia	0.32	0.65	0.38	0.10	0.16	0.34	0.00	0.00	0.00	0.29	0.04	0.13	0.17	0.04	0.05	0.01	0.04	0.03	0.01	0.00	0.00
Lithuania	0.67	0.48	0.38	0.18	0.24	0.27	0.00	0.00	0.00	0.04	0.07	0.15	0.03	0.09	0.09	0.01	0.05	0.03	0.01	0.00	0.00
Croatia	0.57	0.52	0.43	0.21	0.13	0.14	0.06	0.15	0.22	0.00	0.01	0.01	0.00	0.01	0.01	0.02	0.02	0.01	0.00	0.00	0.00
Bosnia and Herzegovina	0.40	0.66	0.45	0.17	0.11	0.27	0.15	0.12	0.22	0.12	0.03	0.00	0.00	0.00	0.00	0.09	0.03	0.00	0.00	0.00	0.01

	1	2	3	4	5	6	7	8	9	10	11	12	13	14	15	16	17	18	19	20	21
Serbia			0.39			0.21			0.21			0.05			0.02			0.01			0.00
Montenegro			0.65			0.33			0.01			0.00			0.00			0.01			0.00
FYR Macedonia	0.35	0.43	0.55	0.19	0.05	0.14	0.07	0.32	0.11	0.11	0.01	0.01	0.00	0.00	0.00	0.06	0.13	0.02	0.01	0.00	0.00
Albania	0.73	0.94	0.86	0.03	0.00	0.01	0.12	0.04	0.03	0.00	0.00	0.00	0.00	0.00	0.00	0.04	0.01	0.01	0.00	0.00	0.03
Moldova[1]	0.06	0.22	0.30	0.27	0.13	0.18	0.00	0.00	0.01	0.36	0.45	0.24	0.27	0.14	0.18	0.00	0.03	0.03	0.00	0.00	0.00
Ukraine	0.27	0.16	0.16	0.25	0.14	0.12	0.00	0.00	0.01		0.24	0.26	0.08	0.07	0.12	0.05	0.05	0.02	0.11	0.04	0.01
Belarus	0.13	0.09	0.29	0.10	0.19	0.14	0.01	0.00	0.00	0.41	0.51	0.37	0.20	0.09	0.10	0.02	0.01	0.01	0.01	0.02	0.02
Russia	0.45	0.36	0.41	0.18	0.17	0.13	0.00	0.00	0.01				0.00	0.13	0.15	0.05	0.08	0.02	0.07	0.05	0.05
Column	1	2	3	4	5	6	7	8	9	10	11	12	13	14	15	16	17	18	19	20	21

EU10—the 10 new member countries in EU from Eastern Europe.

SEE—the SEE countries of this study.

CIS—Armenia, Azerbaijan, Belarus, Georgia, Kazakhstan, Kyrgyz Republic, Moldova, Tajikistan, Turkmenistan, Ukraine, Uzbekistan.

[1] The latter data point for Moldova comes from 2006 data, not 2007.

Source: IMF Direction of Trade Statistics.

4. CONCLUSION

The European transition countries discussed in this chapter were divided into four groups based on geography and time of independence. The EU has been a driving force for many of the economic policies and reforms these countries have undertaken, not least with regard to trade. An alternative grouping of countries that largely coincides with the classification used here could be based on the attractiveness and speed of EU integration: (1) the countries that were eager and ready to join the EU right after transition started; (2) those that became independent along the way and, while eager, were not ready to join the EU; and (3) those with less clear ambitions with regard to the EU. The first group would comprise the 10 new member states; the third group would include Russia and Belarus, and perhaps also Ukraine and Serbia; the bulk of the remaining countries would belong in the second group. This classification would also represent groups of countries that have followed similar trade policies, which signifies the importance of EU integration for trade policies and economic reforms more generally.

NOTES

1. The official name until 1990 was the Czechoslovak Socialist Republic and, from April 1990, the Czech and Slovak Federal Republic.

2. For discussion of the pre-1989 trade policies and trade patterns of the CMEA region, see e.g. Ellman (1989). A substantial fraction of the trade of Czechoslovakia, Poland, Hungary, Romania, and Bulgaria consisted of the bilateral trade with the Soviet Union. The Soviet Union provided energy and raw materials, and the other CMEA members provided goods such as industrial (Czechoslovakia) and agricultural products (Hungary). For the five countries as a whole, 63% of trade was conducted with other CMEA members in both 1970 and 1983, although the share differed between countries and over time (Ellman 1989).

3. Yugoslavia was not a member of CMEA. Its trade policy history therefore looks somewhat different than that of the other countries in Central Eastern Europe.

4. The EU trade policy is described in a separate chapter.

5. United Nations Interim Administration in Kosovo.

6. As of March 2010, Croatia and FYR Macedonia were candidates for EU membership.

7. Throughout most of this chapter, we will use the term "EU" when we refer to the European Union and also when referring to the European Community (the relevant term until 1993).

8. These criteria became known as the "Copenhagen criteria." Vachudova (2005) discusses early relations between EU and the Visegrad countries.

9. The countries also signed agreements with the European Free Trade Association, which at the beginning of the 1990s included the future EU members Austria, Finland, and Sweden.

10. See Adam et al. (2003) for a discussion of the EU´s attempts to increase regional trade within Central Eastern Europe, the Baltics, and SEE, respectively.

11. The Czech and Slovak Republics had signed a customs union at the breakup of Czechoslovakia. The CEFTA agreements consisted of one bilateral agreement between the Czech and Slovak republics and Hungary, one agreement between the Czech and Slovak republics and Poland, and one agreement between Poland and Hungary.

12. For Poland, Koteva cites several sources on the level of protection, with tariffs ranging from 11.5% to 18% in Poland in 1991–1993. The Rodrik (1992) figure for August 1991, 13.6%, and the figure of 12.2% for 1992 from World Bank (2007) fall within this range.

13. Under Ceaucescu, Romania had signed a Generalized System of Preferences Agreement with the EU in 1974 and an "Industrial Products" agreement in 1980.

14. Differently from most other countries in the Eastern Bloc, Yugoslavia had several trade agreements with the European Community, the first of which was signed in 1970.

15. Agriculture was largely outside the scope of the ITAs. The agricultural share of GDP was higher in Eastern Europe than in EU 15 and a larger share of the population was employed by the sector. A low agricultural productivity, the reduction of state subsidies, the opening up of trade in agricultural goods, and the extent of EU support of its agriculture all contributed to a fall in agricultural output and a large trade deficit in agricultural products in the Eastern European countries. Moving toward EU membership meant opening up to free trade in agricultural products with EU 15 countries. In a first wave of liberalization, the "least sensitive products" phased a total and reciprocal liberalization of trade. In consecutive waves in 2001–2003, the "double zero" measure implied reciprocally increased quotas and reduced export subsidies for certain processed products. It was followed by the removal of duties and the creation of tariff-free quotas (European Commission, 2000a; OECD, 2002). The new member countries have also had to adapt to the various requirements of the EU Common Agricultural Policy.

16. Much of this discussion of the Baltic countries draws on van Elsuwege (2008).

17. The three Baltic countries had similar production structures in the Soviet planned economy and exchanged products with other parts of the Soviet Union, but there was very little regional trade. In the case of Lithuania, 80–90% of trade was with the Soviet Union, where Russia accounted for around 50%, and with Ukraine and Belarus also having large shares. Half of the 10–20% of trade that was not oriented toward the Soviet Union was with other CMEA countries (Čičinskas et al. 1996).

18. See Kaminski 1994.

19. See e.g. Carter and Singleton (1982) and Bartlett (1991) for the economy of Yugoslavia.

20. The conflict over Kosovo continued after 1995. In the region, there has also been civil conflict in FYR Macedonia in 2001 and in Albania in 1997.

21. On joining the EU, previous members of CEFTA have left the agreement. Croatia was the first SEE country to join CEFTA in 2003. For current CEFTA members see table 13.1 or www.cefta2006.com (available October 31, 2011).

22. Other free trade agreements exist in the region. One set of agreements are the bilateral agreements between Turkey on the one hand and Croatia, Bosnia and Herzegovina, FYR Macedonia, and Albania, respectively, on the other.

23. The Transparency International (www.transparency.org) Corruption Perception Index runs from 1 to 10 and is a subjective measure of public sector corruption. The lower the number, the more corrupt the country is perceived to be. For 2009, the average for the Baltic countries was 5.5, for the Visegrad countries and Slovenia 5.2, and for Romania and Bulgaria 3.8, whereas it was 3.6 for SEE. As a comparison, the average EU 15 score was 7.3.

24. Croatia and FYR Macedonia also have free trade agreements with EFTA.

25. In addition, in anticipation of the SAA, Interim Agreements on trade and trade-related matters have been signed by all SEE countries.

26. Kosovo is also part of the SAA process, but at an early stage.

27. Olcott et al. (1999) discuss the (lack of) CIS integration in the 1990s. They also discuss how a system of state trade, characterized by Soviet-style planning, currencies that were not fully convertible and, to some extent, barter trade, existed into the mid-1990s. To the extent that barter trade still exists, it is most common in Belarus, which may also imply that Belarusian trade data are the least reliable.

28. Information based on WTO's "Regional Trade Agreement portal" (www.wto.org).

29. See Ronnås and Orlova (2000) for an account of Moldova's experience during the 1990s.

30. See the country sheets, at http://ec.europa.eu/trade/creating-opportunities/ bilateral-relations/, for trade data for individual countries from 2008. In section 3, trade data and trade flows in the region, using IMF Direction of Trade Statistics, are presented.

31. World Bank (2005a) and European Commission (2010), respectively.

32. Sources: "Tariff Profiles," at http://stat.wto.org/TariffProfile/WSDBTariffPFHome. aspx?Language=E (available October 31, 2011) and World Bank (2005a), annex table 3.1.

33. Authors' own calculations based on average MFN applied rates from the "tariff profiles" of all African and Latin American countries included in the WTO database.

34. See for instance World Bank (2005a) for discussions of the large drop in trade during early transition and of the quality of the region's trade data.

35. Bulgaria and Moldova also show high openness measures, which is explained by a large import/GDP fraction. These countries run substantial current account deficits. See the discussion below.

36. The share of total Slovak merchandise exports that goes to the Czech Republic has decreased from 42% to 13% between 1993 and 2007, and the share of total Czech merchandise exports that goes to the Slovak Republic has decreased from 22% to 9% over the same time period.

37. The EFTA countries Sweden, Finland, and Austria became EU members in 1995.

38. See the first subsection of section 3 for a discussion of the effects of the breakup of Czechoslovakia.

REFERENCES

Adam, A., Kosma, T., and McHugh, J., 2003. Trade Liberalization Strategies: What Could Southeastern Europe Learn from the CEFTA and BFTA? IMF Working Paper 03/239. Washington, D.C.: IMF.

Åslund, A., 2003. A Foreign Trade Policy Strategy for Ukraine. Washington, D.C.: Carnegie Endowment for International Peace.

Baldwin, R., 1994. Towards an Integrated Europe. London: Centre for Economic Policy Research.

Bartlett, W., 1991. Economic Change in Yugoslavia: From Crisis to Reform. In Ö. Sjöberg and M. Wyzan, eds., Economic Change in the Balkan States: Albania, Bulgaria, Romania and Yugoslavia. London: Pinter, pp. 32–46.

Berend, I., 2009. From the Soviet Bloc to the European Union: The Economic and Social Transformation of Central and Eastern Europe since 1973. Cambridge: Cambridge University Press.

Carter, B., and Singleton, F., 1982. The Economy of Yugoslavia. London: Croom Helm.

Čičinskas, J., Cornelius, P., and Treigiene, D., 1996. Trade Policies and Lithuania's Reintegration into the Global Economy. Stockholm Institute of East European Economies Working Paper 111. Stockholm: Institute of East European Economies.

Ellman, Michael, 1989. *Socialist Planning*. Cambridge: Cambridge University Press.

European Commission, 1997a. Commission Opinion on Bulgaria's Application for Membership of the European Union. Brussels: European Commission.

European Commission, 1997b. Commission Opinion on the Czech Republic's Application for Membership of the European Union. Brussels: European Commission.

European Commission, 1997c. Commission Opinion on Estonia's Application for Membership of the European Union. Brussels: European Commission.

European Commission, 1997d. Commission Opinion on Hungary's Application for Membership of the European Union. Brussels: European Commission.

European Commission, 1997e. Commission Opinion on Latvia's Application for Membership of the European Union. Brussels: European Commission.

European Commission, 1997f. Commission Opinion on Lithuania's Application for Membership of the European Union. Brussels: European Commission.

European Commission, 1997g. Commission Opinion on Poland's Application for Membership of the European Union. Brussels: European Commission.

European Commission, 1997h. Commission Opinion on Romania's Application for Membership of the European Union. Brussels: European Commission.

European Commission, 1997i. Commission Opinion on Slovak Republic's Application for Membership of the European Union. Brussels: European Commission.

European Commission, 1997j. Commission Opinion on Slovenia's Application for Membership of the European Union. Brussels: European Commission.

European Commission, 2000a. Farm Trade with the CEECs: Preparing for accession. *European Commission Directorate-General of Agriculture Newsletter*, June 23.

European Commission, 2005a. Croatia: 2005 Progress Report.

European Commission, 2005b. EU/Moldova Action Plan.

European Commission, 2008. Council Regulation (EC) No. 55/2008 of January 21, 2008, Introducing Autonomous Trade Preferences for the Republic of Moldova and Amending Regulation (EC) No. 980/2005 and Commission Decision 2005/924/EC.

European Commission, 2009. Communication from the Commission to the European Parliament and the Council: Enlargement Strategy and Main Challenges 2009–2010. Brussels.

European Commission, 2010. Countries, Ukraine. Available at http://ec.europa.eu/trade/creating-opportunities/bilateral-relations/countries/ukraine/, October 31, 2011.

Fantini, M., 2007. The Economic Relationship between Russia and the EU: History and Prospects. In J. Gower and G. Timmins, eds., *Russia and Europe in the Twenty-First Century—An Uneasy Partnership*. London: Anthem Press, pp. 247–266.

Kaminski, B., 1994. The Significance of the "Europe Agreements" for Central European Industrial Exports. World Bank Policy Research Paper 1314. Washington, D.C.: World Bank.

Kaminski, B., and de la Rocha, M., 2003. Stabilization and Association Process in the Balkans: Integration Options and Their Assessment. World Bank Policy Research Working Paper 3108. Washington D.C.: World Bank.

Koteva, M., 1993. Trade Policy Reform: Lessons from the Experience of Developing Countries and Central and East European Economies in Transition (With Special Reference to Bulgaria). Oslo: Norwegian Institute of International Affairs.

Machold, S., 1998. Europe and Russia's External Economic Relations, an Assessment. *Economic and Political Weekly* 33: 113–120.

Nygren, B., 2009. Rysslands relationer med OSS-länderna. In A. Jonsson and C. Vendil Pallin, eds., *Ryssland, Politik, Samhälle och Ekonomi*. Stockholm: SNS Förlag.

OECD, 2000a. Regulatory Reform in Hungary: Enhancing Market Openness through Regulatory Reform. Paris: OECD.

OECD, 2000b. Regulatory Reform in Poland: Enhancing Market Openness through Regulatory Reform. Paris: OECD.

OECD, 2002. Agricultural Policies in Transition Economies: Trends in Policies and Support. Paris: OECD.

Olcott, M., Åslund, A., and Garnett, S., 1999. Getting It Wrong—Regional Cooperation and the Commonwealth of Independent States. Washington, D.C.: Carnegie Endowment for International Peace.

Richter, S., 1998. The CEFTA and the Europe Agreements. *MOCT-MOST* 8: 91–119.

Rodrik, D., 1992. Foreign Trade in Eastern Europe's Transition: Early Results. NBER Working Paper 4064. Cambridge, Massachusetts: NBER.

Ronnås, P., and Orlova, N., 2000. *Moldova's Transition to Destitution*. Sida Studies no. 1. Stockholm: Sida Studies.

Sida, 2004. *An Overview of Trade and Trade Policy Developments in South Eastern Europe 2001–2003*. Econ Analys AB. Stockholm: Sida.

SIGMA, 2002. SIGMA Balkans Report 2002: Republic of Albania Trade Policy. Support for Improvement in Governance and Management in Central and Eastern European Countries.

Vachudova, M. A., 2005. *Europe Undivided: Democracy, Leverage, and Integration after Communism*. Oxford: Oxford University Press.

van Elsuwege, P., 2008. *From Soviet Republics to EU Member States. A Legal and Political Assessment of the Baltic States' Accession to the EU*. Vol. 1. Leiden: Martinus Nijhoff.

Winiecki, J., 2002. *Transition Economies and Foreign Trade. Routledge Studies of Societies in Transition*. London: Routledge.

World Bank, 1999. Slovenia: Economic Transformation and EU accession. Vol. 2. Main Report., Washington, D.C.: World Bank.

World Bank, 2005a. From Disintegration to Reintegration. Eastern Europe and the Former Soviet Union in International Trade. Washington, D.C.: World Bank.

World Bank, 2005b. Ukraine's Trade Policy: A Strategy for Integration into Global Trade. Washington, D.C.: World Bank.

World Bank, 2007. Trends in Average Applied Tariff Rates in Developing and Industrial Countries, 1981–2007 (Unweighted in %), Excel spreadsheet downloaded from www.siteresources.worldbank.org/INTRES/Resources/469232-1107449512766/tar2007.xls, available October 31, 2011.

....

CHAPTER 14

TRADE LIBERALIZATION IN A SMALL OPEN ECONOMY: THE CASE OF ISRAEL

....

MICHAEL MICHAELY

1. THE BEGINNING: BACKGROUND

....

Israel started its existence with an extremely restrictive commercial policy. But to put this in context, a general background should be provided.[1]

The State of Israel was formally founded on May 14, 1948, on a part of Palestine, which had been ruled by Britain under a mandate given in 1921 by the League of Nations (prior to World War I, it was a part of the Ottoman Empire). When the State was declared, Israel was in a midst of an intensive and crucial war. The war gradually subsided during the first half of 1949. By mid-1949, the hostilities were almost over. By that time, too, the organs of the State were mostly put in place. It would be thus meaningful, in discussing Israel's economic policy, to start at about this point—mid-1949 (it is, of course, no accident that also data concerning some major instruments and attributes start from around this time).

In fashioning economic policy in general and trade policies in particular, several major historic developments and general social-economic attributes must have played a predominant role. These were, primarily:

(1) Under the pre–World War II mandatory regime, economic policy could have been characterized as liberal (in its free-market sense) and conservative (in its macro-economic aspects). Palestine belonged then to the Sterling Block. Following a "currency board" monetary policy pattern and an absence of a borrowing facility for the government (i.e., dictating government expenditures to be roughly equal to

its revenue), no autonomous monetary or fiscal policy could be practiced. Trade policy, like that of Britain itself, manifested in general a low level of tariffs. Tariff protection was practiced once in a while. But it was constrained, besides the government's general free-trade approach, by the fact that Palestine's economy was largely bi-sectoral. Manufacturing (which was not indeed highly developed, or largely diversified) was mostly the domain of the Jewish sector, whereas agricultural production was dominated by the Arab sector. Protection of one good or another was thus necessarily perceived as benefiting one ethnic sector and hurting the other—adding a political constraint to the feasibility of imposing protective tariffs.

The regime changed completely, for obvious reasons, during World War II (the period from the fall of 1939 to mid-1945—and, in fact, a year or two beyond it). The Middle East as a whole became almost completely isolated from the outside world (so far, of course, as civilian exchanges were concerned). A system of foreign-exchange control and rationing of imported goods was introduced. On the other hand, trade *within* the Middle East, as well as with the sizable Allied military forces stationed in the region, expanded many-fold. The Jewish sector in Palestine was better equipped than most of the region's other members to establish and expand many varieties of industrial production, demand for which was ample. Thus, the war led to a radical expansion in size, and in the varieties of production, in the manufacturing sector (again, mostly Jewish). Much of this dwindled fast, with the gradual opening of trade during 1945–1947 and the major contraction of the size of the Allied forces in the region (and, in particular, in their needs for construction of all sorts). Added to it was a boycott imposed by the neighboring Arab countries during the postwar years, on imports from the Jewish sector in Palestine. But the experience of the war left an important legacy: protection of manufacturing activities (imposed, as the actual case was, not by design but by circumstances) would lead to a large expansion of local activities. This legacy was part of what policymakers in Israel inherited in the early years.

(2) A crucial element was what may be termed the "frame of mind" of policymakers—reflecting prevailing perceptions and norms in the society at large. To start with, the upbringing of most society members did not incorporate, by and large, a free-market ideology. The Palestinian Jewry at this juncture originated mostly in eastern Europe, with ideologies and perceptions shaped largely there. These were benevolent, including a strong requirement for self-sacrifice—indeed, perceptions without which the establishment of the new Jewish identity in Palestine would not have taken place; but reliance on free-market mechanisms was definitely not part of this ideology or tradition. To the contrary, socialism (but not communism!), in one version or another, was the professed belief of most ideologists and policy-makers, as well as of a major share of the public. Some contributions to modes of thinking were also due to descendants from Germany; but these, too—in different ways—did not reflect a free-market tradition.

Moreover, a major share of Jewish economic activity during the prestate years— the predominant element of agriculture, as well as much of manufacturing and services—had been planned, guided, and largely financed by quasi-government

Jewish public organizations. It was hence taken as a matter of faith—and was probably true—that reliance on the free market would have made the whole new settlement effort futile. Hence, many concluded that further economic activity in the new State of Israel should not rely on the operation of free-market mechanisms.

(3) Still another factor were the recent experience of the two wars—World War II and, even more, the just-concluded War of Independence. As in various other war economies, economic activities were closely regulated; and wide-scale rationing was practiced. An experience that was judged highly successful (and rightly so) was that of Jerusalem during most of 1948, which was under siege and in which fundamental elements for survival (including water) were minimal. A pervasive mechanism of control and rationing made the situation manageable. This led, again, to the perception that a similar mechanism might work well under the circumstances of the new state—which were quite unfavorable. Indeed, the person in charge of the 1948 rationing mechanism in Jerusalem was made, under various ministerial guises, the "tsar" of the controls and rationing schemes in Israel for the first three years of its existence. The system was largely identified with his name; and its demise, which we shall review later, included his disappearance from economic policy-making.

(4) Somewhat compensating for these tendencies and perceptions was the strong reliance of the new State on economic support of the United States, and in particular, of its Jewish community, whose economic environment and ideology were obviously inclined to the free operation of markets. While these did not dictate Israel's economic policies, nor were even involved in the State's running of its affairs, this reliance on, and close association with the U.S. Jewry served as an important constraint. Even if for this factor alone, it was obvious that making Israel a full-fledged, Soviet-style planned economy would be inconceivable, even if the atmosphere in Israel had led some to wish to introduce such an economy.

(5) A still other major attribute of Israel's economy and society at the State's inception—or, rather, at its first few years—was the dramatic size of the wave of immigration to the country. Within the first year of its existence—from mid-1948 to mid-1949—its Jewish population increased by about 30%; and by the time this wave subsided—in early 1952, that is, within less than three years—population about doubled. Evidently, even partial absorption of such large migration would require the use of a major share of the economy's resources. An important (indeed, crucial) part of these resources was provided by inflow of capital from abroad—whether unilateral donations or borrowing from abroad. But these were mostly channeled to and through the government, or semigovernment organs such as the Jewish Agency, thus inevitably enhancing the government's role and share in the economy. Beyond this, it was felt that the marshalling of domestic resources could not be performed just through the use of "conventional" public-finance instruments (primarily, taxation), leaving then the allocation mechanism to the free market: this would not be adequate for the task.

(6) Finally, the general international climate should be noted. The late 1940s were a period in which many countries—certainly almost the whole of Europe—were still rallying from the impact of World War II. In the majority of countries

controls, rationing and heavy government interventions were still prevailing; and overvalued currencies (mostly against the U.S. dollar) were the rule. With Israel emerging then from its own war, the lesson it drew from the postwar era was definitely not one that would assign a dominant role to the free market.

Thus, the stage was set, at the State's inception, for a framework in which the government's share and involvement in economic activity and in its guidance were paramount. Given a high share of imports in the economy's aggregate resources—and a very low share of exports—policies addressed to the country's international transactions, and in particular to its imports, thus became a crucial element.

2. 1949–1951: An Overwhelmingly Controlled Economy

The guiding principles of economic policy during these early years were widespread use of price controls and, consequently, of a rationing scheme, and a complete control of international transactions, in which the rate of exchange was fixed (and constant) and free transactions in either foreign exchange or in imports were almost completely absent. Indeed, the fixed foreign exchange rate was deemed crucial to the system, through its determination of the (domestic) price of imports. Similarly, a government-determined allocation of foreign exchange, and through it of imports, was a cornerstone of the government's involvement in resource allocation.

Imports were allocated by licenses. First, overall quotas were assigned to "competent" ministries, and, through them, to importers (often, final users). Thus, for instance, inputs for agricultural production were licensed through the Ministry of Agriculture, and so on. During the period under consideration, the system worked in a haphazard way, through ad hoc decisions. In later years, from 1953 onward, the system became better organized and rationalized. An annual foreign-exchange budget was then determined (run, like the conventional budget, by the Ministry of Finance). In it, aggregate expenditures were set to be equal to (expected) foreign exchange revenues (excluding short-term borrowing from abroad). The budget specified allocations to the "competent" ministries. The latter, in turn, issued import licenses for which foreign exchange allocation was assured as long as they fell within the authorized budget.

An overwhelming element of economic policy and economic activity during these years were strongly expansionary fiscal and monetary policies. The government sustained a massive budgetary deficit (beyond the part financed by unilateral transfers and long-term borrowing from abroad), and this was financed predominantly by borrowing from the banking system (a central bank was not yet established). The accumulated short-term debt (which included also the outcome of the war finance) created (as the system worked) an accompanying expansion of bank reserves and, consequently, a further expansion of money supply.

The foundation of massive inflation was thus there. But, for a while, the system of controls worked tolerably well. Price controls (and rationing) kept the inflation repressed, creating in the process some forced saving. But within a year or so—from the middle of 1950 onward—as the "repression" became inevitably more intensive, discontent and cracks in the system became gradually more prevalent. Black markets became widespread; and, with them a general perception that the system did not provide for equality as it was supposed to do. Most important was the development of a black market for foreign exchange (pretty well organized, with a uniform and publicly known rate of exchange). The demand for foreign exchange in this market was partly of the "conventional" source—to shift liquid assets from domestic holdings (of a currency whose future value was deemed bleak) to holdings abroad. But more important was the motivation of acquiring foreign exchange to finance imports that were allowed, under a variety of schemes, to be brought "without allocation of foreign exchange" (these goods came from lists of both "luxury" consumer goods and, on the other hand, some "essential" imports not provided for in the budget). The deviation of the "black-market" exchange rate from the official, formal one, during the period under consideration, is presented in table 14.1.

The trend seen from these data is obvious: a rapidly increasing divergence of the two rates (temporary fluctuations were due predominantly to frequent changes in the facilities provided for "imports without exchange allocation"). By the end of 1951—toward the close of the period under review—the "black" rate reached almost eight times the level of the official rate.

By and large, this reflects the divergence between prices of imported goods, which may be regarded as having been sold in a "free" market (in a limited sense), and those imported within the controlled system. This divergence reflects also the one that existed in general, in the economy, between black market prices and

Table 14.1. "Black" and Formal Exchange Rates, 1949–1951 (Quarterly averages of end-month quotations; Israeli pounds per $)

Quarter		"Black" rate (1)	Formal rate (2)	Ratio (1)/(2) (3)
1949:	3	.421	.341	1.23
	4	.498	.357	1.40
1950:	1	.573	.357	1.61
	2	.635	.357	1.78
	3	.748	.357	2.10
	4	.862	.357	2.41
1951:	1	1.349	.357	3.78
	2	1.221	.357	3.42
	3	N.A.	.357	N.A.
	4	2.402	.357	6.73

Sources: "Black-market" rates: data from Michaely (1963), p. 102, table 42. Formal rate: data from Michaely (1971), p. 102, table 2-1.

controlled prices (the former applying, as it were, mostly to imported goods). Data on *quantities* transacted in the "black" market were, for obvious reasons, absent; but all anecdotal evidences indicated that they, too, increased rapidly and intensively. The system thus came to be regarded as nonfunctioning and, to a large extent, corrupt, and a sense of disillusion with the whole tenor of economic policy became pervasive. This was manifested, inter alia, by a strong shift of votes in elections toward parties that stood for a more "liberal" economic policy.

Toward the end of 1951, it became evident that a radical reform was due, and should be expected. Moreover, the severity of regulation and the sense of disillusion were so strong that such reform could not be conceived as a temporary, "stop-go" move but as a permanent feature. As we shall see, this unhappy period yielded a foundation for a future consistent and persistent trend of economic liberalization.

Throughout this period, there was little room for "commercial policy" in the conventional sense, that is, imposition of barriers on imports (or equivalent measures for exports) as means of protecting domestic activities. Introduction of tariffs for protection would be redundant, given the control of imports through the foreign exchange regulations. And the latter only rarely were intended to provide protection for local activity. We shall return to this issue in discussing the next period.

3. 1952–1955: RADICAL TRANSFORMATION

In February 1952, a "New Economic Policy" was introduced.[2] Essentially, it consisted of bringing prices closer to their equilibrium levels, thus eliminating, or heavily diminishing, controls and the need for rationing. An essential accompanying policy change was the abandonment of expansionary macro-economic policies (a reversal of which actually started several months earlier, in the fall of 1951). The repressed inflation would thus turn into an open inflation (so far as official prices were concerned). And in due course this inflation, too, should subside, with increased prices, given no expansion of money, leading to contraction of real money supply, thus lowering demand for goods and services. Indeed, this process materialized very rapidly, with inflation becoming quite minor within about a year.

A major policy element—again, due to the crucial role of imports in the economy—was the introduction of devaluation. This was done in stages. A system of multiple exchange rates was introduced, with a shift of transactions to higher exchange rates (and the addition in 1953 of a still higher rate) being effected gradually. By the end of 1954—some three years after the process began—almost all transactions were subject to the highest rate, of IL 1.80 per U.S. dollar. Starting, on the eve of devaluations with a rate of IL 0.357 per U.S. dollar, the exchange rate thus increased fivefold in the process. As measured by *official* prices, the *real* exchange rate increased during this period by a factor of about 2 to 2 1/2 (use of some combination of official and black market prices would obviously lead to an estimate of a larger increase of the real exchange rate, since domestic prices would then appear to have risen less).

The outcome of this process was, thus, a gradual reduction of the intensity of controls and the severity of rationing. Once more, this was most important in the sphere of foreign exchange and of imports. Again, a representation (though by no means an estimate, or measurement) may be found in comparing the black market exchange rate with the official rate. It appears that the ratio between the former and the latter—which was, we recall, close to 8 at the end of 1951—fell to 1.28 at the end of 1955[3]. Thus, by the end of 1955, the official exchange rate may be assumed to have been close to its equilibrium level (or to what it would have been in the absence of controls.[4]

During this period as well, imports were restricted by the control mechanism—though much less severely than before (that is, excess demands for imported goods were relatively smaller).[5] Hence, in this period as well as in its predecessor, there was not much need or requirement for, or use of, tariffs for protection of local activities. Similarly, as before, allocation of imports was rarely determined on the grounds of such protection. Thus, use of conventional instruments of commercial policy applied to provide protection was still an exception during these years. Tariffs were mostly devised to yield revenue, often by absorbing (at least partly) the quota profits enjoyed by recipients of import licenses.[6]

4. 1956–1961: "Classical" Protection

This period started with an important act of liberalization. Imports of the majority of essential raw materials—and, within a short time, also of machinery and equipment—became free in the sense of import licenses being granted freely. Secondary regulations were still applied to issues such as the exporting country or the mode of payment.[7] This liberalization was accompanied by the imposition of tariffs, designed in principle so that they should lead each good to be imported by a size equal to what it was under the controls system.[8] The impulse to this change—beyond, of course, the realization of its benefit—was some sense of relief in the conduct of the country's international transaction. An accumulation of some minimum level of foreign exchange reserves, and the assurance of a substantial size of foreign resources, for the following five to six years, from the payments of reparations by Germany, made policy makers more inclined to let the market work—at least to some extent—rather than making imports strictly and immediately controlled.

This change was highly beneficial for general economic activity in the country. Yet it also led, in a well-known fashion, to a higher effective protection of import-competing activities. Such protection became, indeed, a major determinant of commercial policies in this period.

In import policy, granting of protection to domestic activities became during this period (1956–1961) the dominant factor. This was done in the general framework of a pervasive scheme of what in a later era would be termed "industrial policies"—a framework of mostly ad hoc decisions concerning the availability of government finance (long and short term), granting of monopoly rights, allocation of land, and similar measures. Within this framework, the control of imports was probably of utmost importance. This was done, again, not through access to an even partly free market (i.e., through the use of tariffs or other import levies) but through quantitative restrictions applied by the import licensing system. By and large, imports were totally prohibited when an import-competing domestic activity existed. Moreover, not even the actual existence but the *promise* of a future existence was sufficient: most often, when the undertaking of an investment (local or foreign) was discussed ("negotiated" would probably be a better term) by the potential investor and the government (whose principal agent was mostly the Ministry of Commerce and Industry), prohibition of imports was normally offered to the potential investor. No proof of damage, or promise of future alleviation of the need for protection, was normally required: the very claim that imports would compete with a local activity was sufficient for import prohibition. The only occasion of hesitation would occur when domestic production of primary goods (quite few) was concerned, where the protection of such activity would mean negative protection of the domestic activity using the intermediate input on hand. By and large, the liberalization of imports of inputs and machinery, enacted during 1956, was not reversed.

In figure 14.1, the commodity nature of the system of protection is portrayed through its representation by levels of the *effective* exchange rate applying to the imports of each good. This rate includes, beside the formal rate (uniform during this period, at the level of IL 1.80 per U.S. dollar), components such as tariffs, other impositions on imports, and—when estimates could be generated—quota profits from imports. The estimates were made, for 138 goods, for each of the years from 1956 to 1960, and the *averages* for the period were ranked. The good with the lowest effective rate would appear as 1, and the good with the highest rate as 138. Goods were classified into three categories: processed raw materials (69 goods), machinery and equipment (14); and consumer goods (55). Figure 14.1presents the *frequency distribution*, by the goods' rankings, in each of these three categories.

Figure 14.1 reveals the essential properties of the commodity structure of import policy. On the one hand are goods classified as "machinery and equipment," the effective exchange rates (i.e., the levels of protection) for which are consistently the lowest. On the other hand are "consumer goods," with consistently the highest effective rates. In between are "processed raw materials," the rates for which are highly diversified, though they tend to be on the low side. This pattern agrees with the one suggested by the general description of the attributes of protection during this period.

Another property that should be noted is the treatment of *exports*, which were quantitatively much less important than imports or import-competing activities. Policy-makers at that period were fully conscious of the adverse effects of the promotion of import-competing activities on the exporting activities. Hence, almost from the inception of deliberate policies of protection from imports, export-promoting policies were also introduced. First, these took a variety of forms, mostly of a smaller scale and on an ad hoc basis.

Later, beginning around 1953–1954, a more uniform mechanism of subsidizing exports in the form of a retention quota—granting import licenses to reward exporters—was introduced. But the main form of export subsidization was put in place in early 1956. It applied to most exports in a uniform—though uniquely so— method. The concept of effective protection was rather well known and familiar in Israel after 1953 or 1954 (it was known by the term "the rate of exchange for value added" or "for value saved"). The export subsidization scheme was thus meant to provide a uniform subsidy *for value added*. This required, of course, knowledge of what the "value added" actually was. Indeed, the government introduced and maintained a machinery for estimation of the proportions of value added (of total value) for individual goods. Needless to say, this was far from perfect, yet it reached a reasonable level of uniformity in subsidizing the value added in export activities. This level was certainly lower than the *average* level of promotion of import-competing

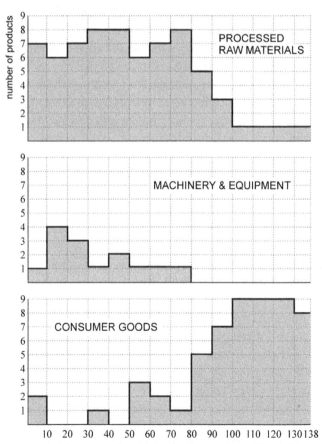

Figure 14.1. Ranking of importer's effective exchange rates, by principal commodity group.

Source: Michaely (1971, fig. 5).

activities through the quantitative barriers on imports. But it served at least to partly offset the antiexport bias involved in the system.

5. 1962–1969: Shifting from Non-tariff Barriers to Use of the Price Mechanism

A new phase in the history of commercial policy started in February 1962. The second "New Economic Policy" introduced then—precisely 10 years after its predecessor—consisted, first, of a substantial *formal* devaluation, of 67% (from IL 1.80 to IL 3.00 per U.S. dollar)—the first since late 1954. The change of the *effective* rates, though, was smaller, particularly on the export side, since the devaluation was accompanied by an elimination of the (uniform) export subsidy: in exports, thus, the effective exchange rate was raised by only just over 10%. The devaluation of the effective exchange rate in imports, though still lower than that of the formal rate, was nevertheless substantial—about 37% (compared with the 67% increase of the formal rate).

The devaluation was not accompanied by appropriate macro-economic policies. Mainly due to this—but partly also due to the modest scale of devaluation, which was almost absent in exports—it failed to achieve its designated targets. The *real* (effective) exchange rate fell back, to its predevaluation level, within a short time (in exports—just over a year); thus, the devaluation failed by and large to affect the conduct of international transactions. In this sense, hence, the "New Economic Policy" was a passing episode, not leaving much of a trace in the history of the country's economic policies.

Another component of the "new" policy, however, which at the time was considered secondary, proved to be of crucial importance. This was the principle that control of imports should change, over the whole field, from the use of quantitative restrictions (through licensing and prohibitions) to the use of the price mechanism; that is, quantitative restrictions (QRs) should be eliminated and be replaced by tariffs (and similar levies on imports). The policy principle also stated that the newly imposed tariffs should be *equivalent* to the QRs—namely, leading to the same size of imports (though at some unspecified future time protection was expected to be lowered). In most instances of protection, this would mean imposition of prohibitive tariffs (since imports had been excluded altogether).

At the time of its introduction, it was assumed that the process of substitution would last some one or two years. It proved to be much longer. Its implementation was assigned to the Ministry of Commerce and Industry—which strongly opposed the introduction of the "New Economic Policy," with all its components. The Ministry designed a specific mechanism of conversion. A committee was established. Representatives of the local producers (or of trade associations) and of labor were members of the committee. The committee discussed separately each good as it was introduced into the process by the Ministry. The role of the committee was, first, to decide whether conversion should be applied at all for the activity on hand. Second, granting the removal of QRs, the committee would determine the appropriate level of the equivalent tariff.

The guidelines for the work of the committee in deciding which activities should be liberalized meant anything but the removal of protection. The main principle was termed "not elimination, but more efficiency." If local producers proved (mostly, claimed) that in the foreseeable future they would lower costs, the branch of activity would be exempted from liberalization. Several other guidelines pointed in the same direction; that is, of restricting the extent of conversion and minimizing its impact on local activity.

The process of deliberations was slow and tedious—as it was certainly meant to be. The committee started work in May 1962. Within a year—by May 1963—it rendered decisions to apply the conversion to 98 goods. These employed about 10% of total labor force in manufacturing; and contributed in roughly the same proportion to total value added produced in this sector. In the next couple of years, the process proceeded at roughly the same pace. Thus, by mid-1965, the transformation from protection through QRs to that provided by tariffs apparently applied still to only a fraction—probably a large minority—of manufacturing activity (agricultural production, it should be noted, was completely and universally excluded from the process—and remained so for a long time).

The newly imposed tariffs were, of course—by the nature of the process—not uniform. Their average level was around 50%, with a median somewhat above it, and a large variance. But with the import component being in Israel at that time (and even much later) rather high, *effective* protection rendered by these tariffs was much higher. It was estimated that these ranged from 20% to 250%, with a median of around 100%.[9]

The process of transformation was brought to a halt during the years 1965–1967, when the economy suffered from a severe recession. It was renewed in 1968 and by the end of the 1960s came to its conclusion. Despite the limitations imposed on the machinery handling it, and the relatively high level of tariffs, it was of great significance. For well-known reasons, protection by the price mechanism is superior to that granted by quotas. It is less certain (as seen by the entrepreneurs); it is provided at a given level; and—probably of major significance—no absolute protection is provided to *new* activities. In the general atmosphere of the conduct of economic activity and of the nature of commercial policy, the decade of the 1960s could certainly be regarded as forming a major step toward liberalization[10].

6. 1970–1989: GRADUAL SHIFT TO FREE TRADE

In the early 1970s, a new stage of liberalization policy was started. It was implemented in numerous steps; these were, however, mostly not ad hoc moves but components of a general process with some overall guidelines. These were primarily as follows.[11] (1) *Variance* in the system was contracted. The tariff schedules were collapsed, at least part of the time, by something approximating the "concertina method"—leaving the lowest tariff rates untouched and cutting the rates by larger proportions the higher the tariff levels. (2) *Effective*, as well as nominal, protection was addressed; that is, cutting tariffs in forms that will lower effective protection, and avoid increasing it. Again, the principle followed was the reduction of variance in the system. In fact, a *uniform* effective rate of protection (not low, though) was set as a target for the process (3). As before, agricultural products were left out of the reform altogether.

Although it seems that substantial liberalization would have proceeded in any case, it was greatly helped by two commercial treaties which Israel concluded—with the EEC (becoming later the EC and then the EU); and with the United States. These helped significantly in "selling" the liberalization—making it more widely accepted than it would have otherwise been.

A preferential agreement with the EEC was already concluded in 1970 but took a concrete shape only in 1975, when a free-trade agreement was signed. The agreement provided Israel with immediate (or, almost so) elimination of barriers on the EEC's imports from it, whereas Israel's concessions were to be implemented over a longer period—with final elimination of tariffs only by 1989. The Israel-U.S. Free Trade Agreement came into effect in September 1985.[12] It specified a phased tariff reduction process, aiming at complete tariff elimination within a decade (by January 1, 1995). The agreement was indeed fully implemented, and U.S.–Israeli trade became by that date free of all tariff or nontariff barriers except in the area of agricultural products. A series of supplementary agreements with the United States were later concluded (in 1996, 2001, and 2004), aiming at achieving free trade—or, mostly, *more* free, with mutual preferential concessions—in the area of agricultural trade as well.

Several figures may serve to indicate the intensity of the process of tariff reductions[13]. In 1968, the average nominal protection rate for manufactures was 45%, with a large variance—the highest rate (close to 100%) applying to clothing. The average *effective* protection rate was as high as 96%—again, with large variance, and the highest rate (in this case for "basic chemicals") at the level of 273% (and in fact many rates exceeding 200%). In 1977, the average nominal rate fell to 16% (with a highest rate, for "wood products," of just 39%). Even more impressive was the fall of the average protection rate—from 96% in 1962 to a mere 25% in 1977.Thus, it appears that during the 1970's a dramatic tariff liberalization took place.[14]

The process was interrupted by an unfavorable macro-economic environment—a rapidly accelerating inflation that started in the late 1970s and was stopped only by a very successful stabilization policy introduced in mid-1985. By that time, though, Israel's trade with the majority of its partners—the United States and the EC—was mostly free. High protection still prevailed in trade with the rest of the world—primarily with Asian countries. Removing, or lowering, barriers on this trade would later become the next (and final) phase in the general process of Israel's trade liberalization.

Throughout most of the process, export policy was meant, as before, to offset partly the anti-export bias emanating from import protection. The devaluation of

February 1962 was accompanied, it may be recalled, by the elimination of the uniform (per value added) export subsidy. But within a few years export subsidies (on a smaller scale) were re-introduced, in one form or another. By the time import protection was mostly removed, export subsidies as well mostly disappeared.

7. 1990–2000: CULMINATION OF LIBERALIZATION

The stage was now set for the next and final act of Israel's trade liberalization; namely, the removal, or contraction of, barriers on imports from "the rest of the world."[15] These trade flows not only did not participate in the preceding liberalization process but, to the contrary, often manifested increased protection—primarily through nontariff barriers. Thus, toward the end of the 1980s these trade flows were as restricted, overall, as Israel's total trade was in the early 1960s. Liberalization of this component of Israel's trade, which took part over just a few years, was hence more intensive, less gradual, than Israel's general commercial policy changes manifested earlier.[16]

It became gradually obvious to Israel's policy-makers that the discrimination against imports from "third" countries led to serious trade diversion, making Israel pay for a fraction of its imports substantially more than it would in the absence of discrimination. Eventually, the realization of this policy failure prevailed, and helped to overcome the strong resistance of the manufacturers involved in the relevant activities to the relaxation of barriers on competing imports.

A guideline for this transformation was clearly included in the principles of the major stabilization policy introduced in mid-1985. But implementation started only in the late 1980s. The unique feature of this phase of the liberalization policy was its *unilateral* form. Unlike the majority of earlier tariff reductions or eliminations, steps were taken by Israel on its own discretion, without expecting (or negotiating) qui pro quo measures by Israel's trade partners.

Mechanisms for this phase of liberalization were established in the fall of 1990; and implementation started by the fall of 1991. Its major components were two: (1) the elimination of nontariff barriers (NTBs) of all forms; (2) a gradual contraction of all tariffs to take place over a period of five to seven years, to an almost completely uniform—and low level of tariffs, within the range of 8–12%. This would naturally imply also a rather uniform and low level of effective protection. The policy also included the elimination of the remnants of export subsidies that were still practiced at the end of the 1980s.

The policy did indeed follow its preannounced schedule; and was completed in time. Thus, toward the year 2000, almost full import liberalization was achieved, and Israel reached a position of nearly free trade. Once more—with one important exception, agricultural goods. Though some liberalization was implemented there, too, particularly within the framework of Israel's free-trade agreements with the United States and EU, this sector has remained protected to this day (2011). As in many other industrial countries, the agricultural sector is politically strong though its size is small. The share of the protected activities in agriculture in Israel's aggregate production of tradables does not amount to more than a few percent. Thus, the existing protection in agriculture, though clearly visible, does not amount to a significant deviation from a generally free-trade policy.

8. ISRAEL'S EXTERNAL TRANSACTIONS: IMPORTS, EXPORTS, AND THE IMPORT SURPLUS

The analysis of this chapter has been concerned with Israel's commercial *policies*— the central subject matter of the chapter and of this book as a whole. But to put it in context, a brief presentation of the essence of the transactions to which these policies apply would be of benefit—though this addition does not presume to investigate causal relationships between policies and economic performance.

Israel's major trade flows during the period surveyed here are presented in table 14.2 in the context of the whole economy; that is, as proportions of the country's product (GDP). The table is divided into two. First, part A records the (annual) data for the 1950s (1950–1959). It is presented separately because this is the subperiod in which a radical transformation took place, whereas the process of transformation became more gradual in later years. During this subperiod, a very large increase of the *real* (as well as nominal) exchange rate took place (by about a factor of 2.5). This relative change of the price of tradables to nontradables (thus also to the price of the national product) requires the use, in a comparison over time, of *constant* prices in the evaluation of performance—or else apparent movements would reflect (partly at least) price rather than real changes. Beyond the 1950s, fluctuations of the real exchange rate still occurred, but these movements were not sustained for long, nor was any long-term trend of much significance revealed. Thus, an alternative estimate for the later years using *current* prices would not have led to much distortion.

Some clear features appear in the process of change in the 1950s (part A). First, the *import surplus* declined heavily—from over 30% to over 10% of GDP.[17] Second, a large contraction of *imports* took place—from over 50% to over 30% of GDP. Third, the increase of the export ratio as a proportion of *itself* was as remarkable as the contraction of imports—it about doubled. But, since exports amounted at the beginning (and also towards the end of this period) to such a small fraction of product, the contribution of export expansion to the contraction of the import surplus was far smaller than that of the reduction of imports. Hence, the combined proportion of imports and exports in GDP—the trade share—declined materially—though this happened only at the very beginning, following which the share remained about

Table 14.2. Shares of major trade flows, 1950–2008 (percentages of GDP, in 1995 prices)

	Ratio of imports of goods and services	Ratio of exports of goods and services	Ratio of trade = (1) + (2)	Ratio of import surplus = (1)–(2)
A. Annual	(1)	(2)	(3)	(4)
1950	37.3	4.5	41.8	32.8
1951	29.3	4.8	34.1	24.5
1952	25.8	6.0	31.8	19.0
1953	26.8	7.5	34.3	19.3
1954	24.7	8.9	33.6	15.8
1955	23.4	8.1	31.5	15.3
1956	25.0	8.4	33.4	16.6
1957	22.8	9.2	32.0	13.6
1958	23.8	9.6	33.4	14.2
1959	22.6	11.2	33.8	11.4
B. Five-year averages				
1960–64	26.4	15.5	41.9	10.9
1965–69	26.2	15.5	41.7	10.7
1970–74	35.8	20.0	55.8	15.8
1975–79	36.6	22.6	59.2	14.0
1980–84	35.5	25.3	60.5	9.9
1985–89	36.5	29.0	65.5	7.5
1990–94	41.2	28.2	69.4	13.0
1995–99	47.7	33.9	81.6	13.8
2000–04	50.9	40.4	91.3	10.5
2005–08	52.5	46.0	98.5	6.5

Source: Manipulated from data in Statistical Abstract of Israel, volumes of 2004 and 2009, table 14.1.

stable. By this yardstick, the Israeli economy became, over this period, *less* open to the outside world; but this is just the reflection of the fact that Israel had, of necessity, to reduce its dependence on the provision of resources from the outside world.[18] It should be noted that this diminished dependence, and in particular the contraction of imports, *did not* come at the expense of domestic activity (except for a brief period, mainly in 1953): nearly full employment prevailed most of the time, and the national product increased by no less than 250% from 1950 to 1959 (or even by over 90% from 1952—after the wave of migration subsided—to 1959).

Developments over the long period starting at the end of the 1950s—presented in part B—are mostly quite different. Imports, rather than declining, expanded very impressively—about doubling, from around 25% to over 50% of GDP in recent years. Even more remarkable was the expansion of *exports*—not only as a proportion of itself (increasing about fourfold from the late 1950s to the present) but also constituting a large share of GDP (that is, expanding by no less than 30% or 35% of GDP).[19] Hence, the combined proportions of imports and exports—the trade share—increased dramatically, about threefold (from about 33% at the beginning to close to 100% at its end—in 2008). The *absolute* increase of exports exceeded the size of import expansion; thus, the import surplus declined materially, almost to its disappearance.[20] But this time, the contraction of the import surplus did not involve a decline of trade but, to the contrary, came along with a dramatic increase of trade.

Thus, throughout most of the 60 years of Israel's existence surveyed here, its economy turned from a largely closed one to a truly open one by both yardsticks—those of *policies* and of *performance*. The title of this chapter, presenting Israel as an *open* economy, gradually became fully justified.[21] It may be noted that this remarkable increase in Israel's economic openness to the outside world was accompanied by an equally remarkable expansion of the country's general economic activity. Thus, aggregate GDP increased from 1950 to 2008 by a factor of 34—an annual growth rate of about 7%; and per capita GDP increased during this period by a factor of about 6. This is an impressive performance in an international context, especially when such a long period is observed (the growth rate was much more substantial during the first two decades—through the early 1970s). By this yardstick, Israel became by the beginning of the twenty-first century a fully developed economy—on par with the average European country (per capita GDP in 2008 was close to $25,000). It would take a thorough research effort to explore a potential causal effect of one phenomenon, the increased openness, on the other—the rapid economic growth; but a guess that a positive relationship does exist would probably not be too wild.

9. POLICIES REGULATING TRANSACTIONS WITH THE PALESTINIAN TERRITORIES

Before concluding this analysis, mention should be made of an aspect of Israel's policies that concerns a specific component of its international transactions, with unique features, namely: transactions with the Palestinian Territories.

The territories of the West Bank and the Gaza Strip were occupied by Israel in June 1967 from, respectively, Jordan and Egypt. From that moment on, these territories' international economic transactions—either with Israel or with the outside world—have been determined completely by Israel (at some later stage, we shall see, through an agreement). It should be noted that overwhelming differences in size make the Israeli transactions with the territories far from being of symmetrical significance. To illustrate: although the population of the two territories equaled in 1968 about one-third of Israel's population, a radical difference in per capita GDP—that of the territories being, in 1968, just roughly 10% of Israel's—made the GDP of the two territories reach only slightly over 3% of that of Israel. Hence, any trade flow between the two partners is of much greater significance to the territories than to Israel. The present discussion concerns, thus, transactions of only minor importance for Israel.

The events of 1967 turned the two territories from being completely closed to Israel to being completely open. Israel's imports from the two territories have been, however, subject to quotas, primarily on several agricultural products. In addition, they have been hampered by discretionary, often ad loc, physical restrictions. These took often the form of border checks (virtual "borders," of course) of varying severity. These checks have originated, to a large extent, from security considerations, and have naturally been more severe—turning often to become prohibitive—during tense periods, such as those of the "intifadas." *Price* restrictions, though—such as tariffs—have always been completely absent with regard to Israel's trade with the territories.

The trade of the West Bank with Jordan (the pre-1967 "East Bank") became subject, from the beginning, to the policy of "open bridges." Trade relations between the two "Banks" had been naturally extensive when they formed parts of the same political entity. The motivations of the "open bridges" policy were two. One was the desire not to disrupt completely and abruptly the West Bank's pattern of trade and specialization, to avoid great economic loss. The other was a desire to remove the threat of serious competition with Israel's agricultural that which would emerge from free imports from the West Bank. Jordan has cooperated with this policy, allowing imports from the West Bank—subject to a "rule of origin": the goods exported to Jordan should originate in the production of the West Bank (or of Gaza), and not of Israel.

Of much more significance than the movement of goods between Israel and the two territories is the movement of *labor*—from the latter to the former. For many years, this movement was virtually free (with much of the "migrant" Arab labor taking the form of daily commuting between Israel and the West Bank and Gaza). The flow of migrant labor to Israel dwindled during the last two decades, with the deterioration of security, particularly following the second "intifada," which started in 2000 and mostly subsided about five years later. The labor from the territories employed in Israel has largely been replaced by other foreign workers—mainly from the Far East. This substitution is judged, today, as being mostly nonreversible. But while the migration of labor from the territories to Israel was free it assumed a very substantial size. At its peak, almost a third of the territories' labor force was employed in Israel, and the proportion of the territories' gross national product (not *domestic* product!) originating from the income of this labor was similar. This labor movement was, for the reasons indicated earlier, of much less significance for the Israeli economy in the aggregate. It was important, though, in several sectors of the economy—particularly in agriculture, construction, and services.

The impact of this labor migration was certainly a major contributor to the *small* size of trade in goods between the two partners. This was a classic demonstration of the movements of factors (i.e., labor—capital movements have been almost absent) and of goods substituting for each other. In particular, this labor movement led (beside other, less important factors) to the fact that the relative abundance of low-level, nonskilled labor in the territories did *not* lead to the establishment, or expansion, of manufacturing activities, which are intensive in this factor.[22]

For many years, imports of the territories from the outside world—which naturally could be conducted only through Israel; and custom duties on such imports—obviously ruled by the Israeli tariff schedule—were collected by Israel's custom authorities. This has remained essentially true to this day; but important changes and qualifications have been introduced in the so-called Paris Protocol, signed by Israel and the PLO as part of the "Oslo Agreement," which led to the establishment of the Palestinian Authority in early 1994.[23] This agreement formalized the effective customs union that had existed due to the absence of borders. It specified that the movement of goods between the two sides should be (with a few exceptions) "free of any restrictions including customs and import taxes." The main exception is (presumably temporary, due to expire over four years) quota restrictions applied mostly to imports of various agricultural products by Israel. Free movement of labor, on the other hand, is *not* guaranteed: Israel might regulate it according to what it regards as relevant economic and security circumstances. The essential feature of the agreement is its specification that the Israeli tariff duty should be (as it has been throughout) the common tariff of the two partners. Important exceptions are provided—most important of which is probably the right of the Palestinian Authority to apply its own, separate tariff schedule and import rules to its imports of motor vehicles. Some exceptions are intended to enable the Palestinian Authority to import goods from countries (predominantly Arab) with which Israel does not maintain trade relations. Since the predominant part of the territories' imports comes through Israeli ports, the overwhelming part of custom revenues would be collected by Israel. The agreement provides that custom revenues should be allocated on the principle that the identity of the import's final destination determines the right to the customs revenue. Thus, Israel acts in fact as a collecting agency of the duties belonging to the Palestinian Authority, and a procedure for tax clearance is established. For several years, the agreement functioned mostly as it was intended. But, once more, deterioration of security has limited its significance in recent years.[24]

10. SUMMARY: AN EVOLVING PROCESS OF LIBERALIZATION

For the first few years after its establishment—formally, in May 1948—the State of Israel was highly controlled and regulated. A combination of circumstances—history, the ideology of its founders, emergence from an intensive war, and an overwhelming wave of immigration—led to the government playing a dominant role in direct activity and control policies. Nowhere was that expressed more than in the country's international transactions, particularly imports, the control of which was pivotal in a overall policy of price controls and rationing.

Within a few years, though, by the end of 1951 or early 1952, transformation and liberalization started. It was a long, gradual process, which took practically half a century. It was more persistent at times and slow or nonexistent at other times. But it was rarely reversed, and at the end, toward the turn of the millennium, it made Israel an almost completely open economy.

Several major stages of this process may be distinguished. First, during 1952–1954, the (formally nominally fixed) exchange rate was radically increased, bringing it close to an equilibrium level. This obviated the need for restriction of imports as a means of allocation and led to commercial policies more closely following their traditional, conventional targets. The following stage, taking place in the second half of the 1950s, was ambiguous. Imports of inputs and of machinery were largely liberalized. Other imports—of final consumer goods—became less strictly controlled, but the barriers imposed on them became a crucial instrument of affording protection to competing domestic activities. The following stage, starting in the early 1960s, was crucial. It presumably constituted only of a change in the *form* of protection—from the use of quotas to the use of prices, namely, tariffs and similar levies—granting in principle the same level of protection of each activity as the nontariff barriers. In fact, though—as both theory and other experiences would tell us—this became a significant lowering of protection. In the next stage, taking place in the 1970s and early 1980s, tariffs were lowered, and mostly eliminated, on the major part of Israel's imports—those originating in the United States and the EU. Finally, during the 1990s, tariffs were similarly eliminated or radically lowered on imports from Israel's other partners—the "rest of the world" (mostly meaning Asian countries).

Thus, by the end of this process of transformation—toward the end of the twentieth century—Israel's international transactions became virtually free, though with one proviso: the process of liberalization was only partly applied to the agricultural sector, where imports have still remained highly controlled (often prohibited) even to the present day. But it should be noted that the domestic activities protected in this manner amount to only a low percentage of Israel's aggregate economic activity.

Several features may be observed in this process of opening. First, as has been noted, it was slow, and at times halting; but it was never reversed to any significant extent. Second, policy-makers were always aware of the antiexport bias involved in the protection of imports. Export subsidy schemes were often applied—particularly when it became clear that the foreign exchange rate was getting far below its equilibrium level. Unlike import protection policies, export promotion schemes were applied most of the time in a rather uniform manner; and they did not constitute long-term features—having been removed and reapplied (not necessarily in the same fashion) pretty often. Another feature was the attention given (in both import protection and export promotion policies) to the concept and levels of *effective* protection. These were often embodied explicitly in the formation and changes of commercial policies.[25]

In its international trade, Israel has persistently and radically become a more open economy during the period surveyed. To cite only a few salient indicators: the share of imports in GDP (in real terms) increased between 1950–1954 and 2005–2008 from 26% to 53%—about doubling; the share of exports increased from 16% to 46%; and the combined trade share increased from 42% to 99%. In absolute size (again, in real terms), imports (of goods and services) increased during this period by a factor of about 50 and exports increased by no less than 350. Even on a per capita basis, exports multiplied by the remarkable magnitude of about 60. Thus, from its establishment to the early years of the twenty-first century, Israel's economy turned from one involving a rather moderate size of trade to a truly open economy.

ACKNOWLEDGMENT

I am indebted to my colleagues Nadav Halevi and Ephraim Kleiman for helpful comments.

NOTES

1. An extensive analysis of this background may be found in Kleiman (1997).

2. To give this introduction an extra weight, it was formally declared by the all-powerful prime minister, David Ben-Gurion, rather than by the minister of finance. The term "New Economic Policy" was, certainly not accidentally, similar to that coined by Lenin when he announced, in 1921, the introduction of a large dose of free-market activities into the Soviet system.

3. This fall was as evident even immediately and proceeded during 1952–54. But it is difficult to make estimates for this period, during which there was no single official rate but a multiple-rate system. It may be noted that not just the ratio but even the absolute level of the black market rate declined during the period: it was IL 2.800 per U.S. dollar at the end of 1951 and fell to IL 2.303 at the end of 1955. The estimates are taken from Michaely (1971, p. 99, table 4-5).

4. As long as some restrictions exist in the foreign exchange market, the black market rate must exceed, at least to some extent, the official (controlled) rate. This would indeed appear (once more, to a rather limited extent) in all estimates of the black market rate in Israel prior to the full liberalization of the markets in 2000.

5. Throughout 1952–54, the control mechanism became less restrictive, in this sense, by moving imported goods from one exchange rate to a higher one in the multiple-rate system.

6. In a study by Gafni, Halevi, and Hanoch (1958), the authors devised a scheme for classifying tariffs into three categories: (1) revenue tariffs, (2) import-constraining tariffs, and (3) protective tariffs. The method of classification most probably overestimated the size of the latter group, since it included all tariffs on goods of which some domestic production existed. Yet in the estimates for 1955 (formally, the fiscal year 1955/56), less than 10% of the tariff items were judged to belong to the "protective" category.

7. A large share of Israel's trade during this period was conducted through payments and clearing agreements; and the import licensing mechanism was often used to direct imports toward partners to such agreements.

8. The liberalization started in April 1956 and applied to wood or timber, hides, and inputs for textiles. In the summer of 1956, it was extended to inputs for metal production and of some foods. In October 1956, inputs for the production of plastics, rubber and paints, tools, and office equipment were added. Toward the end of 1958, the imports of passenger cars were also liberalized (with extremely high tariffs and other levies). This information is drawn from Morag (1967, p. 217).

9. These estimates are drawn from Barkai and Michaely (1963).

10. This evaluation would also be gained from the "index of liberalization" provided in Halevi and Baruch (1991, p. 42, fig. 2-1).

11. This analysis draws on the presentation in Halevi and Baruch (1991, ch. 7).

12. It was the first trade preferential agreement of the United States, signifying its turning away from the U.S. traditional universal most-favored-nation policy.

13. The data are taken from Halevi and Baruch (1991, p. 111, table 7-1).

14. In agricultural goods, the process was less impressive. Between 1968 and 1977, the average nominal protection rate fell from 27% to 22%, and the effective rate from 61% to 25%.

15. These barriers were then on place not only because, unlike Israel's trade with its major partners (the U.S. and EC) this trade was *not* addressed by preferential agreements but also because for a long time many thought that allowing these imports would make Israel's manufactures face "unfair" competition. This perception found its expression in much of the political pressures borne by policy-makers.

16. The discussion of this phase of liberalization draws heavily on Gabai and Rob (2002).

17. Use of constant prices of *that* period—say, 1956 rather than the 1995 prices used in table 14.2—would have shown a fall from around 45% to around 16%; that is, again, a fall by almost two-thirds.

18. It would take us too far afield to explore here the reasons for the need to reduce this element of Israel's dependence on the outside world.

19. In addition, a remarkable change in the *structure* and diversification of exports should be noted. In the early 1950s, exports were highly concentrated: about half consisted of citrus fruits and the rest in just a few individual goods. By the turn of the century, citrus fruits amounted to just a fraction of 1% of aggregate exports. Israel's export structure became one of the world's most diversified, consisting mostly of a large variety of manufactured goods and of services, with a large component of high-tech products.

20. At *current* prices, exports and imports (of goods and services) were practically equal during the recent years 2005–8; that is, no import surplus exists at present.

21. The analysis presented in this chapter is restricted to *commercial* policies; that is, to policies related to international transactions in goods and services. It does *not* address at all policies applied to the *capital* market. The interested reader may find an analysis of the latter in Michaely (2007).

22. For an exploration of this relationship, in general and in the West Bank and Gaza in particular, see Michaely (2003).

23. The following description of the "Paris Protocol" draws heavily on Kleiman (1994).

24. The Agreement addresses also a variety of other issues concerning economic relations of the two partners—such as the imposition and collection of VAT, or the monetary and banking mechanism; but these fall beyond the scope of this discussion.

25. Still another feature, falling beyond the scope of this analysis, should be noted. In the *order* of liberalizations of the goods market versus the capital market, Israel followed the conventional-wisdom prescription: freeing first the goods market. The capital market has also become virtually free, but here, the process of opening took place mostly since the second half of the 1980s and primarily during the 1990s. Consult Michaely (2007).

REFERENCES

Barkai, Haim, and Michael Michaely (1963). "More on the New Economic Policy." *Economic Quarterly (Rivon Le'kalkala)* 39, pp. 210–232. (in Hebrew).

Gabai, Yoram, and Rafael Rob (2002). "The Import Liberalization and Abolition of Devaluation Substitutes Policy: Implications for the Israeli Economy." In Avi Ben Bassat, ed., *The Israeli Economy, 1985–1998*. Cambridge, Mass.: MIT Press. Chap. 9, pp. 281–307.

Gafni, Arnon, Nadav Halevi, and Giora Hanoch (1958). *Israel's Tariff Structure and Functions*. Research Paper 3. Jerusalem: Falk Project for Economic Research in Israel. (in Hebrew)

Halevi, Nadav, and Joseph Baruch (1991). *Israel*. Vol. 3. In D. Papageorgiou, M. Michaely, and A. M. Choksi, eds., *Liberalizing Foreign Trade*. Oxford: Blackwell.

Israel. Central Bureau of Statistics. *Statistical Abstract of Israel* (various years). Jerusalem.

Kleiman, Ephraim (1994). "The Economic Provisions of the Agreement between Israel and the PLO." *Israel Law Review* (Hebrew University of Jerusalem) 18(3–4), pp. 347–373.

Kleiman, Ephraim (1997). "The Waning of Israeli Etatism." *Israel Studies* 2(2), pp. 146–171.

Michaely, Michael (1963). *Foreign Trade and Capital Imports in Israel*. Tel-Aviv: Am Oved. (in Hebrew)

Michaely, Michael (1971). *Israel's Foreign Exchange Rate System*. Jerusalem: Maurice Falk Institute for Economic Research in Israel.

Michaely, Michael (1975). *Israel*. Vol. 3 of *Foreign Trade Regimes and Economic Development*. New York: Columbia University Press for the National Bureau of Economic Research.

Michaely, Michael (2003). "Goods versus Factors: When Borders Open, Who Moves?" *World Economy* 26(4), pp. 533–553.

Michaely, Michael (2007). "The Liberalization of Israel's Foreign Exchange Market." In N. Liviaten and H. Barkai, eds., *The Monetary History of Israel: The Bank of Israel*. Oxford: Oxford University Press. Vol. 2, chap. 3, pp. 67–97.

Morag, Amotz (1967). *Public Finance in Israel: Problems and Development*. Jerusalem: Magnes. (in Hebrew)

CHAPTER 15

ASEAN ECONOMIC INTEGRATION: DRIVEN BY MARKETS, BUREAUCRATS, OR BOTH?

HAL HILL AND JAYANT MENON

1. INTRODUCTION

The 10-member Association of Southeast Asian Nations (ASEAN) was established in August 1967. It is arguably the most durable and successful regional association in the developing world. In a region that had been plagued by conflict during the preceding quarter of a century, and divided by a diverse colonial past, ASEAN has first and foremost forged diplomatic cohesion among its population of almost 600 million people. Formed initially by leaders of five of the member countries,[1] the Bangkok Declaration was broad and general in its seven objectives. These included:

> To accelerate the economic growth, social progress and cultural development in the region.... To promote regional peace and stability.... To promote active collaboration and mutual assistance ... in the economic, social, cultural, technical, and administrative spheres.

Subsequently, ASEAN has developed into a close-knit grouping with around 700 meetings each year on economic, political, cultural, educational and security matters. The Association has also been able to effectively project itself regionally and internationally through a wide range of initiatives.

Four broad characteristics define ASEAN. First, it is a region of great diversity, probably more so than any other grouping in the world. Indeed, its economic, political, cultural, and linguistic diversity is greater than that of the European Union, for example. This diversity was accentuated by colonial-era experiences, with Brunei, Malaysia, Myanmar, and Singapore part of the British Empire, Cambodia, Laos, and Vietnam annexed by the French, Indonesia ruled by the Dutch, and the Philippines under first Spanish and then American rule, while Thailand was never formally colonized.[2] Political structures are equally diverse, including freewheeling democracies (Cambodia, Indonesia, the Philippines), communist states (Laos and Vietnam), a constitutional democracy with a highly influential monarchy (Thailand), heavily managed democracies with one party in continuous rule since independence (Malaysia and Singapore), a military-dominated authoritarian state (Myanmar), and an all-powerful sultanate (Brunei).

The Association includes one very wealthy nation (Singapore) alongside some of the world's poorest, on mainland Southeast Asia. The per capita income of the richest is about 80 times that of the (imperfectly measured) poorest member. The world's two largest archipelagic states (Indonesia and the Philippines), together with the city-state of Singapore and the tiny oil sultanate of Brunei, are included. The world's fourth most populous nation (Indonesia) and three states with populations of between 60 and 90 million people (the Philippines, Thailand, and Vietnam) are included, while Singapore and Laos have less than 5 million people and Brunei less than half a million.

Second, most of the countries have achieved rapid economic development for most of the past quarter century, and longer in some cases. Four of them—Indonesia, Malaysia, Singapore, and Thailand—were classified by the World Bank (1993) as "miracle" economies. Since the late 1980s, the three former command economies of Indochina have successfully engineered a transition from plan to market with significantly increased growth rates and sharp reductions in poverty. The region's economic dynamism and steadily expanding cooperation have constituted a virtuous circle, with the increased regional harmony created by the formation of ASEAN providing an enabling and more conducive business environment. Nevertheless, membership of ASEAN has been no guarantee of economic success. Two of its members, Myanmar and the Philippines, in the early development economics literature both expected to be success stories, have underperformed, the former disastrously so.

Third, ASEAN diplomacy and cooperation have been characterized by caution, pragmatism, and consensus-based decision-making. The so-called "ASEAN Way" has entailed noninterference in the internal affairs of member states and lowest-common-denominator decision-making. The Association's leaders have deliberately avoided creating a strong supranational regional institution, and the ASEAN Secretariat has been deliberately underpowered, serving more as a diplomatic facilitator and conference organizer rather than a strong EU-type agency. These characteristics constitute both strengths and weaknesses: they explain the Association's durability, but they limit its effectiveness and capacity for strong and decisive action.

Fourth, and related to the third observation, ASEAN has never been, and probably never will be, an EU-type organization, or even a NAFTA-type economic bloc. That is, it is unlikely to adopt a common external trade regime, with completely free commerce among the member states, in the foreseeable future. In fact, although it appears in a formal sense to be a quasi-preferential trading bloc, in practice, most of its trade liberalization measures have been multilateralized as part of unilateral domestic reforms in each country. Moreover, the Association is even less likely to develop formal mechanisms for macroeconomic policy coordination, leading for example to a common currency and central bank. A key challenge for ASEAN is therefore to define a role for itself, especially since Asia's two giants, China and India, are now growing faster than the ASEAN economies in aggregate. Will it, as some commentators contend, be forever at the crossroads, institutionally unable to establish a stronger variant of economic cooperation, and therefore confined to being a looser association, a forum for leaders to discuss issues of regional interest?

This chapter aims to provide a stand-alone introduction to the ASEAN economies, and traces ASEAN's evolution with a focus on its programs of economic integration. We also critically evaluate its past performance and, based on this, examine prospects for its future.

Our organization is as follows. Section 2 provides an overview of the 10 economies and the development of ASEAN as an institution. Section 3 examines ASEAN economic cooperation and integration with reference to merchandise trade, which was the principal focus of initiatives for the first quarter century. Section 4 then investigates a range of "trade plus" measures, including efforts to develop a broader range of closer economic relations both within and beyond the region, against the backdrop of expanded membership, the Asian financial crisis, the rise of China, and rapidly evolving regional commercial architecture. Concluding observations are presented in section 5.

2. ASEAN AND ITS ECONOMIC DEVELOPMENT

2.1. The Evolution of ASEAN

There are four more or less distinct phases in the evolution of ASEAN (see table 15.1). The *first phase* commenced with its establishment in 1967, in a highly uncertain regional and global environment overshadowed by conflict. This was at the height of the Cold War, the Indochina conflict was at its peak, and China was in the throes of its Cultural Revolution. Indonesia had only recently renounced its intention to "crush" Malaysia, Malaysia and Singapore had separated after a brief union, Malaysia and the Philippines were in dispute over Sabah, and there were (or had been recently) significant leftist insurgencies in all but Singapore. Thailand was widely regarded in the West as a likely next "domino" to fall to the communist advance.

Table 15.1. ASEAN—Major dates

Date	Event
8 August 1967	Bangkok Declaration establishes ASEAN.
23–24 February 1976	Major Bali Summit.
8 January 1984	Brunei Darussalam joins.
28 January 1992	AFTA/CEPT launched.
28 July 1995	Viet Nam joins.
23 July 1997	Lao PDR and Myanmar join.
15 December 1997	Vision 2020 to accelerate economic integration.
30 April 1999	Cambodia joins.
6–8 May 2000	ASEAN+3 announce Chiang Mai Initiative.
7 October 2003	ASEAN Economic Community launched.
22 February 2009	Expanded CMI launched.

Source: ASEAN Website, www.aseansec.org.

Earlier attempts at establishing a regional association, such as the Association of Southeast Asia (ASA), and a possible three-nation "Malay" grouping, Maphilindo, had not progressed. A major facilitating factor in the 1967 meeting and declaration was regime change in Indonesia in early 1966, with the Soeharto administration signaling its intention to rejoin the international community, to focus on economic development, and to seek better relations with its neighbors. Then, as now, ASEAN has been able to progress only as fast as its dominant power.

The vision of the leaders therefore focused primarily on establishing regional harmony. While all were strongly anticommunist in outlook, they explicitly emphasized socioeconomic cooperation and development rather than defense and security. In 1969 the ASEAN foreign ministers commissioned a study on ASEAN economic cooperation to be conducted by the United Nations. The resulting report, known as the Kansu Report (after its leader, Professor G. Kansu), was completed in 1972. But it was not widely circulated, and was not formally published until 1974 (as United Nations, 1974). Its recommendations on economic cooperation reflected both popular thinking at the time and the inclination of ASEAN member countries. Specifically, it proposed trade liberalization through selective, or product-by-product, tariff negotiations, package deal arrangements for large industrial projects, and financial cooperation.

Meanwhile, various cooperation activities had commenced, including reports by various committees covering commerce and industry, agriculture, tourism, transport, and telecommunications. As early as 1971, for example, the commerce and industry committee was exploring the possibility of trade fairs and cooperation, trade liberalization, harmonization of trade statistics, and industrial complementation projects. The spirit of the Kansu Report was broadly accepted, including in principle the notions of joint industrial projects and of reciprocity among the parties involved.

The *second phase* commenced with the Bali Summit of the five leaders in February 1976. This marked the beginning of a formal set of regional cooperation measures. These comprised the ASEAN Preferential Trading Agreement (APTA), the ASEAN Industrial Projects (AIPs), the ASEAN Industrial Complementation (AIC), and the ASEAN Industrial Joint Ventures (AIJVs). The APTA, the most significant of the four, represented the first attempt to promote intra-ASEAN trade through institutional integration and regional trade preferences. The AIPs, on the other hand, were designed to establish in each member country a large-scale, intergovernmental project. The AIC and the AIJVs were aimed at promoting specialization in complementary products and facilitating the pooling of resources.

These initiatives were broadly consistent with the Kansu and other reports. They reflected the desire on the part of leaders to "put some flesh on the bones" of regional cooperation, at least in a minimal, nonthreatening sense. They were generally similar to other regional initiatives being promoted in the developing world, notably in Latin America, the Caribbean, and East Africa. A major trigger was the reunification of Vietnam in April 1975 and communist takeovers in Cambodia and Laos. Meanwhile, ASEAN became a more active organization in international affairs. It began to caucus as a group, for example in the United Nations and on issues of common concern, such as market access for its labor-intensive manufactures and tropical cash crops. Dialogue-partner relationships with a wide array of countries and regions were established, and some of these formed the basis for subsequent regional architecture initiatives. In addition, ASEAN began to be active diplomatically, especially with its attempt to isolate Vietnam for its role in the removal of the murderous Khmer Rouge regime in Cambodia.

However, none of the four economic cooperation programs had any significant impact on regional economic relations (Imada and Naya, 1992). Indeed, they were explicitly designed to have minimal effect. In spite of the early enthusiasm, the APTA had little impact on intraregional trade. The tariff cuts were not implemented on an across-the-board but rather on a product-by-product basis. Hence the commodity coverage was narrow, the tariff cuts were too small to have any discernible effect on trade,[3] and in addition implementation was halfhearted.[4] Moreover, APTA failed to deal with nontariff barriers (NTBs), which were generally a more serious impediment to trade than tariffs. The AIP, AIC, and AIJVs also had limited success. In the case of the AIJVs, for example, the Philippines and Thailand were in dispute over wanting to produce the same automotive parts (Ajanant, 1997). More generally, the failure of these initiatives was symptomatic of the members' unwillingness and unpreparedness to pursue either trade liberalization or regional integration at the time. Notions of infant industry were still popular.

There was little further progress during the 1980s. Brunei's accession in 1984 occurred as that country became independent. During 1984–1987, the Philippines was engulfed in economic and political crisis and effectively disengaged from ASEAN. The collapse in commodity prices in the mid-1980s pushed both Indonesia and Malaysia—and by extension Singapore—into recession, in turn prompting swift and effective reforms, but lessening interest in the broader regional agenda.

A *third phase* commenced in 1992 with another leaders' summit at which the ASEAN Free Trade Area (AFTA) was announced. This marked a clear break with the past. The emphasis was on stronger economic cooperation: for the first time, "free trade" was the regional objective, there was a clear timetable for implementation, and a "negative list" approach was adopted, in that all goods trade was to be included within AFTA unless explicitly excluded. The six leaders agreed to reduce the common effective preferential tariff (CEPT) rates to 0–5% by 2008, with an interim target of 20% by 1998–2000. This deadline was subsequently advanced to 2005 at the Fifth ASEAN Summit in 1995, and later to 2003. The leaders also agreed that each country would have at least 85% of its tariff lines in the "Inclusion List" by 2000, and 90% by 2001.

Here, too, a range of regional and external drivers was at work. First, there was general recognition that the 1976 measures were cosmetic and ineffective. Second, there was increased self-confidence in the region. Indonesia in particular had weathered the mid-1980s debt crisis effectively, and introduced sweeping policy reforms. Third, substantive regional associations were coming into vogue elsewhere, especially with the signing in 1991 of the EU Maastricht Accord and the imminent extension of NAFTA to Mexico, a middle-income competitor in the crucial U.S. export market. Fourth, China was now growing very fast, and attracting large foreign direct investment (FDI) inflows. The ASEAN leaders felt they had to present the region as a competitive single-market alternative to China. Fifth, other changes in the regional and global commercial architecture were gathering momentum and threatened to overshadow the slow-moving ASEAN. Notable here were the establishment of the Asia Pacific Economic Cooperation process in 1989 and the promulgation of the Uruguay trade round in 1995.

The ASEAN leaders built on this renewed vigor by seeking to extend ASEAN's geographic spread and commercial depth. By the early 1990s, Vietnam had clearly signaled its intention to adopt market-oriented reforms and to look outward. The earlier antipathy toward this communist regime gave way to pragmatism, fueled in both cases by a common apprehension toward China. Thus Vietnam joined in 1995, followed by Laos and (with a delay owing to its domestic political instability) Cambodia. Despite some reservations, ASEAN also invited Myanmar to join, partly for geopolitical reasons and partly in an effort to economically and politically engage one of the world's most isolationist states.

In its commercial engagement with the three reforming states of mainland Southeast Asia, ASEAN has played a constructive role. Membership in ASEAN has reinforced their outward orientation, built confidence in their reform momentum, and enabled these latecomers to learn from their more advanced neighbors. The four mainland states negotiated phased-in arrangements for accession to AFTA and other agreements. Thus, Vietnam was given until 2006 to bring down tariffs on products in its Inclusion List to no more than 5%. For Laos and Myanmar, it was 2008, while Cambodia, owing to its delayed accession, had until 2010. As of 2009, almost 80% of the products of the new member countries had been moved into their respective Inclusion Lists, and of these, about two-thirds have tariffs within the 0–5% range. Thus, the implementation of the AFTA accords for this grouping is on track.

By the mid-1990s, and consistent with the global trend in preferential free trade agreements (PTAs), ASEAN began to cautiously develop arrangements for trade in services, investment, harmonization of customs and other fields. The ASEAN Framework Agreement on Services (AFAS) was signed on December 15, 1995, at the Fifth ASEAN Summit Meeting in Bangkok. This was an ambitious agreement with two main objectives: to substantially eliminate all restrictions (both discriminatory and market access measures) to trade in services among member countries, and to liberalize trade in services by expanding the depth and scope of liberalization beyond those undertaken by member states under the General Agreement on Trade in Services.

Given the importance of FDI in the region, ASEAN was one of the first regional groupings in the "South" to adopt formal instruments to try to promote and protect crossborder investment among its members. A number of agreements were signed, the most significant of which was the Framework Agreement on the ASEAN Investment Area (AIA) in October 1998, which was subsequently expanded and consolidated into the ASEAN Comprehensive Investment Agreement (ACIA) in February 2009.

However, just as the original leaders' dream of "one Southeast Asia" was being realized, in mid-1997 the Asian financial crisis (AFC) suddenly erupted. What transpired in its aftermath is now well known. Notwithstanding its ferocity, the impact of the AFC was surprisingly short-lived. Most of the crisis economies experienced a V-shaped recovery, although they have generally returned to somewhat lower growth trajectories. For ASEAN as an institution, the crisis had two principal effects. First, the region as a whole lost some of its commercial attractiveness, especially as China and India were largely unaffected by the crisis. Moreover, ASEAN was seen by many as an ineffective and feeble institution, unable to respond decisively at a time of crisis. In addition to the AFC, it was unable to play any role in the two other major regional flashpoints of that period, the Timor crisis of 1998–1999 and the forest fires of 1997–1998.[5]

Second, the crisis led to a general rethink about the future of economic cooperation, and the need for some sort of coordinated macroeconomic response capacity to avert such future events. This led to the current *fourth phase* in the evolution of ASEAN, dominated by two key features. These are the return to growth (at least until 2008 and the onset of the global financial crisis), and the struggle to define its rationale and identity, against the backdrop of a fast-changing regional and global environment, including a plethora of initiatives affecting commercial policy architecture.

Four features have dominated the commercial policy architecture in the first decade of the 21st century, and all have posed new and difficult challenges for ASEAN. These developments, and their implications for ASEAN, are discussed in more detail in section 4 below.

The first is the spread of PTAs. Singapore in particular, frustrated with the slow pace of ASEAN, began to break ranks and embark on a bold strategy of PTAs.

Although causing strain within the grouping, this had momentum or domino effects, with other ASEAN countries, especially Thailand, feeling compelled to follow.

Second, there has been a recognition that ASEAN is too small to address some of the broader, post-crisis macroeconomic coordination issues. For example, ASEAN is too small to seriously contemplate coordinated macroeconomic policy, such as for example a common exchange rate. In the case of emergency and crisis prevention measures, including currency swaps and fiscal standby agreements, the huge international reserves accumulated in North Asia dictate that these economies will be the major players in any regional and international agreements on such issues.

Third, ASEAN has now largely completed the "easy phase" of intra-regional trade liberalization. As of 2009, zero tariffs applied to 64% of the products in the Inclusion List of the ASEAN-6. The average tariff for ASEAN-6 under the CEPT scheme is down to 1.5%, from 12.8% when the tariff cutting exercise commenced in 1993.

What remains are the politically more sensitive areas, heavy industry and food crops in particular. An unstated tenet of ASEAN trade liberalization is that the concessions would be "multilateralized" as long as it was politically acceptable domestically for the signatories to do so. But for more contentious liberalizations, progress has been slower and exemptions have proliferated. For example, Indonesia has imposed rice import bans periodically. As food prices rose sharply in 2008, there was a free-for-all in the regional rice markets, with talk of a "Mekong rice cartel" among exporters, and the then president of the Philippines (now the world's largest rice importer) announcing that her country would buy rice "at any price." Each country has sought to protect its steel industry. Malaysia has been reluctant to liberalize its auto trade barriers for fear of competition from Thailand, the regional leader in this industry. In addition to these barriers at the border, a further obstacle to the notion of "ASEAN as a single market" has been the proliferation of sub-national barriers, particularly in Indonesia, where many provincial and kabupaten governments have introduced illegal levies on cross-border transport (McCulloch, 2009).[6]

Fourth, the rise of fragmentation trade called into question the viability of all forms of PTA's that do not multilateralize their concessions. East Asia has been the dominant player in this fast-growing segment of international trade, which involves the physical relocation of stages of the production process that can be transferred to lower-cost sites.[7] Parts and components in the electronics and automotive industries have been the major segment of this trade, although it is now spreading rapidly to (poorly measured) services trade through BTO facilities. Within East Asia, the ASEAN countries stand out for their heavy dependence on production fragmentation trade. In 2005–2006, for example, parts and components accounted for 44% of ASEAN manufactured exports, up from 29% in 1992–1993. The shares are higher still for some countries: 64% for the Philippines in 2005–2006 (up from 24% in 1992–1993), 53% in Singapore (from 32%) and 51% in Malaysia (from 37%). Over this period, ASEAN's share of world trade in parts and components also rose significantly, from 7.8% to 10.9% (Athukorala and Menon, 2009).

Clearly, the management of global production facilities, sourcing inputs to the final product from many countries, is fundamentally incompatible with PTAs: some countries may be signatories to various PTAs, and these agreements are unlikely to be mutually compatible. The response of governments and multinational enterprises (MNEs) in these industries has been to locate such activities in free trade zones, thus placing their operations on a free trade footing. More recently, governments have come to recognize the impracticality of any form of trade barriers—unilateral or preferential—in this segment, through the establishment of the International Technology Agreement (Bhagwati, 2008), to which the major Southeast Asian electronics exporters are signatories.

2.2. The ASEAN Economies: An Overview

Table 15.2 summarizes the key socioeconomic features of the 10 countries, with are diverse in practically every respect. The richest country, Singapore, has a per capita income of about 50 times that of the poorest, Cambodia.[8] In Purchasing Power Parity (PPP) terms, the range is narrowed, but is still more than 25:1, larger than for any other regional association in the world. Of course, the range is exaggerated by Singapore, whose per capita income is 5 and 3.5 times that of third-ranked Malaysia. But even excluding Singapore (and Brunei), the range is very large, about elevenfold. In terms of economic size, however, Indonesia is the dominant economy, with over 35% of ASEAN GDP, almost double that of second-ranked Thailand. Three intermediate-ranked economies, Malaysia, Singapore, and the Philippines (with relative sizes depending on which GDP series is employed) follow, and then the four small mainland states, of which Vietnam is by far the largest. Cambodia and Laos are still officially regarded as "least developed states," reflecting their poverty and (along with Vietnam) the historical legacy of deep conflict.

The demographics of the 10 countries also vary considerably. Here, also, Indonesia is by far the largest, with 39% of ASEAN's population, followed by three mid-sized populations, in order the Philippines, Vietnam, and Thailand. Myanmar's 50 million is a very approximate estimate. Malaysia is approaching 30 million, while the remaining four states are considerably smaller. Population densities provide a clue to comparative advantage in land-intensive activities. Apart from the special case of Singapore, the Philippines and Vietnam have the highest population densities, with the three poor mainland states much less heavily settled. Indonesia's average density, of course, obscures its huge demographic imbalance, with the main island of Java containing regions with among the highest population densities in the world.

There are also large differences in economic structure, reflecting both levels of development and relative resource endowments. The two poorest Indochina states (and almost certainly Myanmar) are still heavily agrarian economies, with one-third or more of their GDP from agriculture, while the richer economies have largely shifted out of agriculture. Several of the economies have experienced rapid industrialization over the recent decades, with this sector accounting for at least one-quarter of GDP in Indonesia, Malaysia, Singapore, and Thailand. Services, as expected, dominate the Singapore economy. For a complex set of reasons, they also account for more than half of the still low-income Philippine economy.

Table 15.2. ASEAN—Key Socioeconomic indicators

Country	GDP, 2008 Current PPP int'l $bil	GDP, 2008 Current US$bil	GDP per capita, 2008 Current US$	GDP per capita, 2008 PPP Current Int'l	Population, 2008 Total (mil)	Population, 2008 Density (per sqm)	Percent of GDP (value added), 2007 Agri	Ind	Man	Ser	Human Development Index, 2008 Value	Rank	Poverty headcount ratio at $2/day, PPP (% population)
Brunei Darussalam[1]	19.7	14.6	37,053	50,199	0.4	75	1	71	10	28	0.9	30	
Cambodia	28.0	9.6	651	1,905	14.7	83	32	27	19	41	0.6	131	68[2]
Indonesia	907.3	514.4	2,254	3,975	228.3	126	14	47	27	39	0.7	107	54[3]
Lao PDR	13.2	5.2	837	2,134	6.2	27	40	31	20	29	0.6	130	77[4]
Malaysia	383.7	194.9	7,221	14,215	27.0	82	10	48	28	42	0.8	63	8[2]
Myanmar[1]	68.0	26.2	446	1,156	58.8	75					0.6	132	
Philippines	317.1	166.9	1,847	3,510	90.3	303	14	32	22	54	0.8	90	45[5]
Singapore	238.5	181.9	37,597	49,284	4.8	7,024	0	31	25	69	0.9	25	
Thailand	519.1	260.7	3,869	7,703	67.4	132	12	46	36	43	0.8	78	12[2]
Viet Nam	240.1	90.7	1,052	2,785	86.2	278	20	42	21	38	0.7	105	48[5]

Notes:

[1] GDP, GDP per capita and total population data are from the IMF World Economic Outlook Database, October 2009.

[2] 2004.

[3] 2005.

[4] 2002.

[5] 2006.

Sources: World Bank, 2009 World Development Indicators; IMF, World Economic Outlook Database, October 2009; UN, 2009 Human Development Indicators.

Welfare indicators correlate closely with per capita income. Thus the indices for Singapore and Brunei are well above that of the others (although internationally their rankings are well below their per capita income rankings), with Malaysia and Thailand a good deal higher than the other six economies. Those for the three poorest mainland states are among the lowest in the world. Poverty incidence, as measured by the percentage of the population living on less than $2/day, is still very high in these three (again with accurate estimates for Myanmar unavailable), and still over 40% in Indonesia, the Philippines, and Vietnam. Poverty incidence has fallen rapidly, however, in all cases of sustained rapid growth in the region.

These socioeconomic indicators highlight several distinctive features of the ASEAN grouping, and they have important implications for how it operates. It is unlike any other regional grouping with respect to its balance of economic power. Singapore, by far the richest economy, has less than 1% of the population and is ethnically distinct. By contrast, the largest economy, Indonesia, is barely in the middle-income developing group, and its per capita GDP is below the ASEAN average. This contrasts with NAFTA, dominated by one rich economy, and with the European Union, with its four major economies together with a diverse group of member countries on average considerably richer than that of ASEAN. It also differs from the South Asian Association for Regional Cooperation (SAARC), South African Development Community (SADAC), and the Southern Common Market (MERCOSUR) in this respect, with India, South Africa, and Brazil, respectively, the dominant economies (though not the richest in the first and third case).

Moreover, owing to its unique historical, political, economic, and cultural characteristics, Singapore is unable to provide the leadership that might otherwise have been expected of the country that is the richest and has historically been the most economically dynamic—except by example: in the high quality of its economic policy, legal, and other institutions and its superb infrastructure. Indeed, leading security analysts sometimes characterize its principal challenge as "dealing with vulnerability." Although referring primarily to its defense and foreign policies, the sentiment also has broader implications for the country's policies, ranging from large defense expenditures to an extraordinarily high savings rate and huge foreign exchange reserves.[9]

There is also greater diversity in economic structure—and hence scope for intraregional specialization and commerce—than is commonly recognized. There are net food exporters (most of the mainland states) and importers (most of archipelagic Southeast Asia); resource-poor and resource-rich nations (the latter Brunei and Malaysia especially, on a per capita basis); net labor importers (the four higher income states) and net labor exporters; while Singapore and to a lesser extent Malaysia have advanced R & D capacity and higher education resources, alongside their neighbors with much weaker human capital bases.

The ASEAN economies are diverse with respect to not only their levels of development but also their institutional and commercial policy environments. Three of the economies, Singapore, Malaysia, and Thailand, were classified by Sachs-Warner as "always open." Singapore has never deviated from this open borders approach, apart from a very mild and brief period of import substitution as part of its short-lived union with Malaysia. By contrast, the four poorer economies of mainland Southeast Asia have been largely closed to the international economy, in the case of the three Indochina states until they commenced a historic and increasingly decisive reorientation from plan to market. Indonesia and the Philippines have for extended periods erected high barriers to international trade and investment, but since the mid-1980s have become increasingly open.

The various estimates of openness and the summary indicators of commercial policy regimes in the 10 countries presented in table 15.3 confirm these generalizations. With respect to trade/GDP ratios, Singapore is one of the most open economies in the world, with Malaysia, Vietnam, Thailand, and Cambodia also having figures above 100%. The tariff data show a broadly similar picture, with weighted averages below 10% for most of the economies and only marginally higher for Cambodia and Vietnam. The higher figures for these two economies in part illustrate their success in converting opaque trade barriers into transparent tariffs. Smuggling remains extensive in the economies with remaining trade barriers, long porous borders, and weak administrative capacity. Myanmar, Laos, and Indonesia stand out in this respect. The dispersions in tariffs across sectors is generally declining, with a switch from above- to below-average protection for manufactures observable in several countries. Like tariffs, NTBs are generally declining, but they remain significant in some cases for the usual political economy reasons. Highly protected sectors are often those dominated by state-owned enterprises in the former command economies and Indonesia.[10]

Employing the stock of FDI relative to GDP as a crude measure of openness, Singapore has one of the highest ratios in the world, with very high figures (over 40%) for Brunei, Cambodia, Malaysia, and Vietnam. Of course, these indicators of openness do not necessarily imply the existence of secure, transparent, and low-corruption business environments. Subjective, perceptions-based indicators, for all their limitations, portray a somewhat different story. For illustration, we also include in table 15.3 three widely used comparative indicators: the index of economic freedom, regulatory quality as measured by the World Bank's Governance Indicators, and the World Bank's *Doing Business* series. On these indicators, the rankings generally correlate quite closely with per capita income. Singapore stands far apart from its neighbors, with rankings at or very close to the top in all three series. Brunei follows, with Malaysia and then Thailand some way further behind. Although reforming quickly, the former command economies are still regarded as having uncertain business climates, weak property rights, or high levels of corruption, and in some cases all three. However, in aggregate they do not rank far behind Indonesia and the Philippines, illustrating in turn the slower pace of reform in the latter two. Whereas 15 years ago the original ASEAN-5 group was well in advance of the transition economies, the distinction is now increasingly blurred.

Table 15.3. ASEAN trade and commercial policy regimes

Country	Trade/GDP, 2007 (%)	FDI Stock/ GDP, 2007 (%)[1]	Average tariff, 2006 (wtd,%)	Index of Economic Freedom[2] rank	Regulatory Quality[3] rank	Ease of Doing Business[4] rank
Brunei Darussalam	95	82	na (v low)		75.8	14
Cambodia	138	49	10.8	106	34.3	22
Indonesia	55	14	4.3	131	45.4	19
Lao PDR	87	28	9.3	150	9.7	24
Malaysia	200	43	3.4	58	60.4	4
Myanmar		29	3.9	176	1	
Philippines	85	13	3.2	104	51.7	21
Singapore	429	160	0	2	99.5	1
Thailand	144	35	4.7	67	59.9	3
Vietnam	167	60	13.3	145	32.4	13

Notes:

na = not available.

[1] FDI data are estimates for 2007.

[2] Measures 10 components of economic freedom, assigning a grade in each using a scale from 0 to 100, where 100 represents the maximum freedom. The 10 component scores are then averaged to give an overall economic freedom score for each country.

[3] One of the six dimensions of governance captured by the World Bank's Worldwide Governance Indicators. Reflects the ability of the government to provide sound policies and regulations that enable and promote private sector development.

[4] This index averages the country's percentile rankings on 10 topics, made up of a variety of indicators, giving equal weight to each topic. A high ranking on the index means the regulatory environment is conducive to the operation of business.

Sources: World Bank, 2009 World Development Indicators; UNCTAD, 2009 Foreign Direct Investment Database; Heritage Foundation and Wall Street Journal, 2009 Index of Economic Freedom; World Bank, 2009 Worldwide Governance Indicators; World Bank, 2009 Doing Business.

3. "Old Issues": Merchandise Trade

Two features dominate ASEAN trade. First, the ASEAN economies trade predominantly with the rest of the world. That is, extraregional trade is much larger than intraregional trade. Since 1970, intraregional trade has generally constituted between 15% and 30% of total ASEAN trade (see figure 15.1). These seemingly low shares of intra-ASEAN trade have attracted a lot of critical comment, and some have used it to question ASEAN's viability as a regional grouping. An important point to bear in mind in interpreting these shares is the fact that the ASEAN economies are also only a small share of global trade flows. When this scale factor is adjusted for, through the computation of trade intensity measures for instance, the picture that emerges is quite different. For 2006 for example, all intra-ASEAN flows record an index of greater than unity, and many are in the double-digits and range to a maximum of 53.

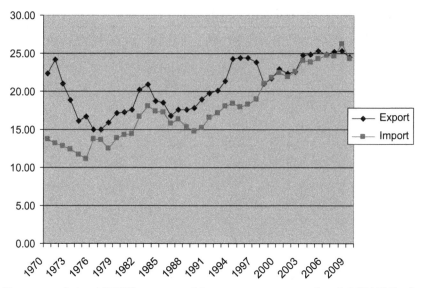

Figure 15.1. Intra-ASEAN exports and imports as a percent of total ASEAN Trade.
Source: Data for 2009 from the ASEAN Secretariat in *Handbook of Statistics Online*. Geneva: UNCTAD, 2010.

There is also a general upward trend in the intra-ASEAN trade shares, reflecting the rising importance of the group in world trade. In the earlier period, commodities dominated this trade, with Singapore the entrepot for resource-rich Indonesia and Malaysia. This in turn explained the volatility in shares. While still important, intra-regional trade is now considerably more broad-based, with manufactures playing a larger role, increasingly as Singapore-centered global production networks. Note that these statistics refer only to merchandise trade and do not include the fast-growing but poorly measured services trade. It is also important to contrast the much lower intra-ASEAN share with that of the EU figure of around 70%. Since, as will be argued below, most AFTA trade concessions are multilateralized, the observed increase in intra-regional trade shares must be explained by complementarity and market-driven factors rather than deliberate policy measures.

Second, Singapore dominates intra-ASEAN trade flows, as revealed in table 15.4.[11] The largest single trade flow is between Singapore and Malaysia, as it always has been historically. Singapore's trade with Indonesia and Thailand is also very large. The largest non-Singapore trade flows involve the region's second most open economy, Malaysia, with the two neighbors with which it shares a land boundary, Indonesia and Thailand. The matrix also shows the small scale of official trade of the poorer mainland states, although Vietnam is rising fast. The countries also differ with respect to the importance of ASEAN within their total trade. For both Singapore and Malaysia, ASEAN markets constitute more than one-quarter of total exports. The share is much lower for Indonesia, where natural resource exports to extraregional markets are important, and for the Philippines, whose commercial patterns have always been the least ASEAN-centered of the five original member countries.

Table 15.4. Major intra-ASEAN trade flows in 2008,% of total intra-ASEAN trade

ASEAN Country	Partner					
	Indonesia	Malaysia	Philippines	Singapore	Thailand	Viet Nam
Indonesia	0	2.6	0.8	5.1	1.5	0.7
Malaysia	2.5	0	1.2	11.7	3.8	1.0
Philippines	0.2	0.8	0	1.0	0.6	neg
Singapore	14.2	16.3	2.9	0	5.2	3.5
Thailand	2.4	3.9	1.3	3.9	0	2.0
Vietnam	neg	0.8	0.7	1.1	0.5	0

Notes: neg = very small, <0.5%.
Source: IMF, 2010. Direction of Trade Statistics.

Two important implications for the governance of regional economic architecture flow from this analysis. First, it does not make sense for ASEAN to contemplate the formation of a customs union, since the major trade is outside the region. That is, the costs of trade diversion would almost certainly exceed the benefits of trade creation. Second, Singapore's dominance of intra-ASEAN trade flows, and the country's nonnegotiable commitment to open borders, mean that any attempt to set a common external trade regime at anything other than that defined by Singapore is not feasible, since Singapore would be a veto player. In other words, a common external ASEAN trade regime would have to be at Singapore levels. This does not necessarily preclude the adoption of free trade within ASEAN alongside differing trade policies for each state. Such an arrangement would imply a two-tier trade policy for all but Singapore, which is technically feasible but would obviously be administratively cumbersome and subject to widespread corruption. In any case, the fact that less than 10% of intra-ASEAN trade avails of AFTA concessions suggests that this approach is virtually irrelevant. The margins of preference between the AFTA and MFN rates are already very low, and the administrative procedures render the AFTA option unattractive. We return to this issue later.

4. "New Issues": Services, FDI, and Regional Economic Architecture

Since the early 1990s, ASEAN—AFTA and related initiatives in particular—has had a deeper regional economic integration objective. What light does its experience shed on the broader question of whether PTAs can accelerate economic integration? The regional trade liberalization experience was discussed earlier. In this section, we address this question with reference to a range of issues beyond the first-round efforts that focused on merchandise trade.

4.1. Deepening Integration: Services Trade, FDI, Labor

Following AFTA, ASEAN has also signed agreements relating to trade in services, intraregional investment, and labor movements. The ASEAN economies are increasingly integrated in all these respects, but they are all market-driven, with little if any formal implementation of the regional initiatives.

Under the 1995 AFAS, negotiations over the liberalization of services have focused on five sectors: financial services, transport, telecommunications, tourism, and professional business services. Progress has been limited, however, owing to the lack of political commitment to open up the services market, weaknesses in negotiation frameworks, legal restrictions, and institutional limitations (Rajan and Sen, 2002). These problems have been compounded by the global tendency to liberalize the services sector last, whether in the form of a general market liberalization or specifically privatization and FDI liberalization.

Of course, although it is notoriously difficult to measure, intra-ASEAN service trade is intense, driven by proximity (which generally matters more for services than merchandise trade) and complementarity. In the majority of ASEAN countries, tourists from the region are the major visitors. In financial services and telecommunications, Singapore and Malaysia are major investors throughout the region. The flows of intraregional education and health services are growing rapidly. These are essentially market-driven transactions, which can be facilitated by simplified visa arrangements (such as the current ASEAN-wide visa-free facility) and other harmonization measures that lower transaction costs. However, it would hardly make sense for ASEAN governments to give preferential access to neighboring service providers over the best-practice global alternative.

In the case of FDI, there are a number of sequentially related agreements, starting in 1987 with the ASEAN Agreement for the Promotion and Protection of Investment, commonly known as the ASEAN Investment Guarantee Agreement. More than a decade later, the Framework Agreement on the ASEAN Investment Area was signed in October 1998 at the Thirtieth Meeting of the ASEAN Economics Ministers (AEM). The most significant initiative of the AIA was the preferential, or discriminatory, treatment afforded to ASEAN investors in member countries for a fixed period of time. This preferential treatment was to take the form of access to particular industrial sectors available only to ASEAN member countries on a reciprocal basis.[12] However, in 2007, the Thirty-Ninth Meeting of the AEM effectively nullified this preferential treatment when the provisions were extended to foreign-owned ASEAN-based investors. In February 2009, the ACIA was signed; it was intended to be more comprehensive, in that it deals with liberalization, promotion, facilitation, and protection and adopts also a single negative list approach.

Regional investment flows have risen rapidly over this period. But these are predominantly market-driven, and there is no evidence that they have been induced by the special provisions offered under the AIA and ACIA initiatives. That is, although some of ASEAN's investment provisions may represent a medium for regional protectionism or sectoral sheltering rather than liberalization, in practice they appear to have little impact (Jarvis et al., 2009).

Singapore, with its extraordinarily high savings rate and international reserves and its large government-linked corporate sector, has emerged as a major foreign investor, globally and regionally. Its scale is such that in several ASEAN countries it is among the top three foreign investors. Its investments are in a broad range of sectors, including banking, telecoms, hotels, and real estate. As the major regional headquarters for MNEs, it is also a base for the companies investing elsewhere in the region. Malaysia, too, has become a major investor abroad, with a similar set of drivers at work—high savings rates, loss of comparative advantage in labor-intensive activities, and an activist sector. For example, both countries have emerged as major investors in Indonesia over the past decade in a diverse range of sectors, including banking, palm oil, hotels, and telecommunications. Thailand is now a major investor in the small neighboring Indochina economies in a wide range of service, manufacturing, and resource-based activities, and despite the Thai-Cambodian hostilities.

Table 15.5 provides estimates of realized FDI by for each ASEAN economy by source—ASEAN and extra-ASEAN—for the period 2006–2008, which are indicative of longer-term shares. Extra-ASEAN economies dominate these flows, and are typically five to seven times larger than those originating from within ASEAN. This applies to all economies, including the mainland transition economies, which, in the early reform phase, received much of their FDI from neighboring ASEAN countries. It also needs to be noted that the intra-ASEAN share in total FDI flows to the region is less than the corresponding share for trade. This is to be expected, given that among the ASEAN-10, only Singapore is an outward investor of any significant

Table 15.5. ASEAN shares of FDI and trade

Country	ASEAN share of inward FDI, 2006–2008[1] (%)	ASEAN share of exports, 2009 (%)	ASEAN share of imports, 2009 (%)
Brunei	7.8	17.1	51.8
Cambodia	30.8	12.9	37.3
Indonesia	27.4	21.1	28.7
Lao PDR	21.5	80.6	85.8
Malaysia	27.2	25.7	25.4
Myanmar	14.6	50.4	53.7
Philippines	0.1	15.2	25.4
Singapore	3.4	30.3	24.0
Thailand	31.6	21.3	20.0
Vietnam	17.5	15.1	19.6

Notes:
na = not available.
[1] . . . Data for 2008 are preliminary.
Sources: ASEAN Secretariat website, www.aseansec.org.

scale. The implication is that preferential investment schemes within ASEAN are unlikely to make economic sense for the foreseeable future.

Regional labor markets are becoming increasingly integrated. Here, too, ASEAN has signed several formal accords since 2000, including the January 2007 ASEAN Declaration on the Protection and Promotion of the Rights of Migrant Workers. Discussions on implementation of this agreement are continuing. However, intra-ASEAN labor flows occur independently of these arrangements, and are largely market-driven, dictated by large intercountry wage differentials and open labor markets. Labor flows to, from, and within the ASEAN countries are significant. Several lower-income countries are major labor exporters, particularly the Philippines, where remittances are the fourth largest in the developing world. The two richer countries, Singapore and Malaysia, together with tiny Brunei, have always had very open labor markets, with 20% or more of their workforces temporary foreign workers. In neither case is there a deliberate preference for workers from other ASEAN countries, but in practice, proximity and ethnic/cultural similarities result in the majority of these foreign workers coming from neighboring countries. This is particularly the case with Malaysia, where about 75% of the workers are estimated to be from Indonesia. Given Malaysia's delicate ethnic mix, it is widely believed that the dominant Malay community tacitly supports these large inflows. The Philippines is the second largest source of migrant workers, with particularly large inflows to the East Malaysian states.

Table 15.6 provides one set of estimates of the stock of temporary intra-ASEAN migrants in 2006. Recognizing that they are almost certainly a considerable underestimate, one can say that they highlight the major flows. The three richer economies, Singapore, Malaysia, and Thailand, all with broadly open international labor markets, are the major recipients, while Indonesia, Malaysia, and Myanmar are the major senders. Among the 5.5 million recorded workers, three large concentrations stand out, accounting for about two-thirds of the total: migrants from Myanmar working in Thailand, Indonesians in Malaysia, and Malaysians in Singapore. Malaysia is unusual in that it is both a significant recipient and sender, receiving predominantly low-skilled workers and sending higher skilled ones. Some of the other flows, while small in aggregate, are significant for the countries concerned. For example, about 10% of the Lao workforce is estimated to work in Thailand, on a permanent or casual basis.

4.2. The Rise of PTAs

As noted, with the exception of ASEAN itself, the countries of Southeast Asia generally eschewed preferential trading arrangements until the late 1990s, preferring a combination of multilateral and unilateral measures. The former had resulted in a global trading environment that generally supported export expansion with few serious trade barriers, apart from some agricultural and labor-intensive manufactured products. There were meanwhile a series of significant domestic liberalizations in the 1980s and 1990s, most particularly in the three communist states, but also in Indonesia and the Philippines.

Table 15.6. Bilateral estimates of migrant stocks in ASEAN, 2006 (in thousands)

Source country	Destination										
	Brunei	Cambodia	Indonesia	Lao PDR	Malaysia	Myanmar	Philippines	Singapore	Thailand	Vietnam	ASEAN
Brunei Darussalam	Neg	Neg	Neg	Neg	Neg	Neg	1	Neg	Neg	Neg	1
Cambodia	Neg	Neg	Neg	2	7	Neg	Neg	Neg	232	Neg	240
Indonesia	6	Neg	Neg	Neg	1,215	Neg	5	96	1	Neg	1,323
Lao PDR	Neg	1	Neg	Neg	Neg	Neg	Neg	Neg	257	Neg	258
Malaysia	68	1	Neg	Neg	Neg	Neg	Neg	994	3	Neg	1,066
Myanmar	Neg	Neg	Neg	Neg	92	Neg	Neg	Neg	1,382	Neg	1,475
Philippines	23	1	Neg	Neg	353	Neg	Neg	136	3	Neg	516
Singapore	3	1	Neg	Neg	87	Neg	Neg	Neg	2	Neg	92
Thailand	11	129	Neg	3	86	Neg	Neg	Neg	Neg	Neg	229
Vietnam	Neg	157	Neg	15	86	Neg	1	Neg	20	Neg	279
ASEAN	111	290	Neg	20	1,925	Neg	8	1,226	1900	Neg	5,480

Source: International Labour Organization, *Labour and Social Trends in ASEAN 2007: Integration, Challenges and Opportunities* (Bangkok: International Labour Office, 2007).
Note: Details may not add up to totals due to rounding-off errors; Neg indicates less than 1,000, or no estimates available.

Table 15.7. FTA status by country, as of January 2010

Country		Under negotiation		Concluded		Total
	Proposed	Framework Agreement signed/under negotiation	Under negotiation	Signed	Under implementation	
Brunei Darussalam	4	0	1	0	8	13
Cambodia	2	0	1	0	6	9
Indonesia	6	1	1	1	7	16
Lao PDR	2	0	1	0	8	11
Malaysia	3	1	5	2	8	19
Myanmar	2	1	1	0	6	10
Philippines	4	0	1	0	7	12
Singapore	5	0	9	2	18	34
Thailand	6	4	3	0	11	24
Viet Nam	2	0	2	0	7	11
Total	36	7	25	5	86	159

Notes:

1. Proposed—parties are considering a free trade agreement, establishing joint study groups or joint task force, and conducting feasibility studies to determine the desirability of entering into an FTA.

2a. Framework Agreement signed/under negotiation—parties initially negotiate the contents of a framework agreement (FA), which serves as a framework for future negotiations.

2b. Under negotiation—parties begin negotiations without a framework agreement (FA).

3a. Signed—parties sign the agreement after negotiations have been completed. Some FTAs would require legislative or executive ratification.

3b. Under implementation—when the provisions of an FTA becomes effective, e.g., when tariff cuts begin. As of January 2010.

Source: ADB Asian Regional Integration Center 2010, Free Trade Agreement Database for Asia.

Since 2000, there has been little progress with multilateral liberalization, and domestic reform has slowed significantly. Not unrelated to these developments has been the proliferation of various forms of PTAs. Table 15.7 lists each ASEAN country's participation in PTAs as at January 2010: 91 PTAs have been signed or are under implementation, 32 are under negotiation, and 36 are proposed. These numbers include a variety of agreements, ranging from the comprehensive to the so-called trade-lite, and thus they are not strictly comparable.

Singapore has been the major ASEAN adopter of PTAs, with 20 concluded and 14 under negotiation or proposed. It accounts for over one-quarter of the regional PTAs under implementation. Its government decided to be proactive in this commercial diplomacy, frustrated with the slow pace of ASEAN and alert to commercial opportunities elsewhere. It might appear puzzling that free-trade Singapore would embark on this route, since it has little to offer by way of reciprocal market access. However, it has made some concessions in its more protected services sector, and it has used the PTAs to extract useful concessions from partner countries (for example, extensive access to Indian landing rights for Singapore Airlines.) It has also suited other countries to engage with Singapore as a "training exercise" in preparation for negotiations with larger, more complex economies. Singapore is seen as small, nonthreatening, and with a nonexistent agricultural sector, tradition- ally the area of greatest sensitivity in trade negotiations. Singapore's participation in these PTAs has attracted subdued criticism from its ASEAN partners, but it has not seriously threatened the viability of ASEAN.

Thailand has also been active with PTAs, particularly under the prime minister- ship of Thaksin. This is somewhat ironical since Thailand, although traditionally a relatively open economy, has achieved little progress with its own trade reform since the 1980s. The governments of Indonesia, the Philippines, and the other four main- land Southeast Asian states have thus far engaged very little in PTAs—reflecting mainly their concerns with domestic reform and a generally reactive approach to international commercial diplomacy. The smaller transition economies, in particular, have struggled to cope with the demands of formalizing their trade regimes, convert- ing their many implicit and obscure NTBs into tariffs. This is also in the context of securing membership in the WTO (except for Laos, which is still an applicant) and then implementing the formal requirements, all in an institutional environment of very limited analytical expertise in their bureaucracies and many competing demands from the international donor community.

Three general observations need to be made about these agreements. First, they vary considerably in their scope, depth, and coverage. The larger economic powers, notably Japan and the United States, are able to extract specific requirements, for ex- ample, the exclusion of sensitive agricultural products in the case of Japan, and intellec- tual property rights in the United States. Where ASEAN rules apply, the agreements are more likely to be multilateralized and have less restrictive (ROOs). Some of the agreements are very minor and have little functional significance.[13] Second, there is considerable variation in the capacity of the ASEAN governments to implement these agreements. Singapore, for example, has a high-quality analytical and negotiating ca- pacity, while Laos has practically none of these resources at its disposal and is struggling to satisfy the requirements for WTO membership. Thus, PTAs involving the transition countries are a clear distraction from the more important task of general trade reform.

Third is the issue of whether these and the broader regional initiatives discussed in the following section will collapse into a plurilateral, pan-Asian agreement. This approach has gained further impetus from the October 2009 East Asian Summit in Hua Hin, Thailand, where the Japanese and Australian prime ministers put forward proposals for an ASEAN+6 and a free trade agreement (FTA) including all of the Asia-Pacific Economic Cooperation (APEC), respectively, and with the former receiving ASEAN support. Both proposals are substantially driven by political and strategic objectives. What if any contribution do they make to clearing up the current, distorted trade policy landscape?

According to one school of thought, these multiple and overlapping PTAs could be consolidated into a single East Asian PTA. However, details of how these PTAs can somehow be folded into a much broader multilateral agreement remain sparse.

It is also perplexing that advocates of this approach often argue that bilateral agreements are able to achieve much deeper integration because only two parties are involved, but then inexplicably expect the same results from a consolidated agreement involving many more parties.

Even if the "consolidation approach" may be able to address the proliferation of often overlapping PTAs, and make the best of the current mess, other options could achieve the same outcome without creating yet another FTA. Two such alternatives include the multilateralization of preferential accords, and the dilution of ROOs. The original members of ASEAN have employed the multilateralization approach with success, and today close to 90% of the preferences of their PTA are available to non-members on an MFN basis. This is a model of how so-called open regionalism can work. As a result, overall tariffs have fallen sharply on trade with all countries, because the PTA liberalization program has been more ambitious and rapid than the WTO alone could have delivered. Consequently, utilization rates of remaining preferences have also fallen to negligible levels. Joining a new East Asian PTA would be a step backward, as it would bring this process of multilateralizing preferences to a halt.[14]

If members of the PTA are not yet ready to give up reciprocal preferences, then liberalizing ROOs could be an interim step in preparing the groundwork for that process. This could be done by harmonization, and expanding the so-called rules of cumulation (i.e., the number of countries whose value added qualifies). If rules of cumulation are sufficiently expanded and then harmonized across different agreements, the outcome could no longer require formal multilateralization of tariff accords. Here again, a new and larger PTA is not required, and it would in fact be a less desirable option.

Both these alternatives could be applied to intra- and extraregional PTAs. The consolidation approach, on the other hand, is only designed for intraregional PTAs. But most PTAs are extraregional. An ASEAN+3 PTA (i.e., ASEAN plus Japan, China, Korea) would address only 6% of all PTAs of the countries concerned, while an ASEAN+6 PTA (i.e., ASEAN+3 plus Australia, New Zealand, India) could potentially neutralize a quarter of them. But these figures in turn prompt the question why most PTAs are extraregional to begin with. A common explanation is that they are designed to restore market access in traditional trading partners that may have joined a regional PTA (see Menon, 2007b). If this is true, then a new, consolidated East Asian FTA might itself spark a new wave of extraregional PTAs. With more countries outside the region than inside, an East Asian PTA could actually be counterproductive, leading perversely to an increase in the total number of PTAs. "Consolidation," therefore, does not appear to provide a solution, and may actually contribute to the problem by adding another strand to the spaghetti bowl or, worse still, inducing a new wave of extraregional PTAs.

4.3. From ASEAN to the East Asian Summit, and Beyond?

ASEAN has developed an elaborate set of extraregional agreements, ranging from general statements about the desirability of closer economic relations to what on paper appear to be firm commitments to economic integration (see for example

Plummer and Chia, 2009). Until around 2000, the former prevailed, and involved little more than official dialogues and sporadic business cooperation programs. However, in recent years, ASEAN has made significant commercial policy commitments, initially in the form of ASEAN+3, or APT (China, Japan, and [South] Korea), and more recently ASEAN+6 (adding Australia, New Zealand, and India). In turn, ASEAN+6 has morphed into the ASEAN Economic Community and the East Asian Summit. In addition, there are various formal agreements with other economic communities, such as the AFTA-CER, involving ASEAN and Australia–New Zealand, and ASEAN Plus One, where ASEAN may negotiate with a particular country (or bloc) on a specific issue.

With these regional economic integration efforts ASEAN is geared toward creating an ASEAN Economic Community (AEC). The ASEAN leaders had originally intended to create the AEC by 2020, but in early 2007 they advanced the deadline to 2015. The AEC envisions ASEAN as a competitive economic region with a single market and production base. At the Thirteenth ASEAN Summit, held in Singapore on November 20, 2007, the ASEAN leaders adopted the ASEAN Economic Blueprint to serve as a guide for establishing the AEC. The blueprint contains 17 "core elements" and 176 priority actions to be implemented within a Strategic Schedule of four periods (2008–2009, 2010–2011, 2012–2013, and 2014–2015). Given the diversity within ASEAN, and sensitivities regarding different issues/sectors, it was agreed that liberalization of goods, capital, and (skilled) labor flows were to proceed at different speeds according to member countries' readiness, national policy objectives, and levels of economic and financial development. Thus, despite the blueprint and the various priority actions and schedules, it remains to be seen to what extent concrete liberalization initiatives will be implemented, or whether the blueprint will remain essentially a vision statement.

In addition, ASEAN participates in a range of broader regional and multilateral initiatives. These include APEC and WTO-based negotiations (e.g., the current Doha Round). Its official position is that it regards these processes as consistent with its objectives and therefore supports them. However, in practice, it does not appear to have played an effective catalytic role in recent years. One ASEAN country, Indonesia, is a member of the G20, which appears to be morphing into the principal global forum for addressing key development issues, such as the measures to prevent a recurrence of financial crises, and climate change. It is too early to judge whether Indonesia attempts to represent ASEAN interests at these meetings. Institutionally, ASEAN also has observer status at the G20. In sum, ASEAN is moving cautiously and uncertainly toward being at the center of a potentially large, yet still undefined, economic grouping.

Meanwhile, ASEAN has been an active participant in the ongoing, though still largely inconclusive, discussions concerning broader macroeconomic coordination. Following the 1997–1998 Asian financial crisis, East Asia launched several interrelated regional cooperation initiatives, particularly for early detection and management of financial and macroeconomic vulnerabilities, as well as broader macroeconomic coordination. Some of these have developed faster than others, and all have occurred within the framework of APT, with the involvement of China, Korea, and Japan.

The three major initiatives undertaken by the finance ministers of APT are the introduction of a regional economic review and policy dialogue process (ASEAN+3 ERPD); the establishment of a regional reserve pooling arrangement, the Chiang Mai Initiative (CMI); and the development of local-currency bond markets, the Asian Bond Markets Initiative. The first two were launched in May 2000, and the third, which has progressed at the slowest pace, three years later.

The ASEAN+3 ERPD mechanism is intended to improve information sharing, promote dialogue among policy-makers, and foster collaboration on financial, monetary, and fiscal issues of common interest. Initially, the CMI involved an expanded ASEAN Swap Arrangement involving all ASEAN members, and a network of bilateral swap agreements and repurchase facilities among ASEAN+3. The size of the CMI fund has grown from $36.5 billion in 2001–5 to $84 billion in 2008, and to $120 billion in May 2009. Since its inception, however, it was clear that the CMI was much more than this, in that it was actually an institutional mechanism to pursue further negotiations, rather than a final agreement on swap arrangements.

The biggest step forward took place in May 2009, when the ASEAN+3 Finance Ministers agreed on the governing mechanisms and implementation plan for the CMI multilateralization (CMIM). Japan and China would contribute identical shares of the total reserve pool (32%), together with Korea (16%) and ASEAN countries (20%). The Finance Ministers also agreed to establish an ancillary institution in the form of an independent regional surveillance unit to monitor and analyze regional economies and support CMIM decision-making—the Asian Macroeconomic Research Office (AMRO), to commence in May 2011 in Singapore. Looking forward, the success and relevance of this fund will depend on boosting its size from its current $120 billion, an amount that is unlikely to be sufficient in the event of a major regional crisis. Moreover, as long as countries continue their attempts to "self-insure" in the form of accumulating very large (and low-return) foreign exchange reserves, it is unlikely to play much of a role. Much will also depend on how the Office performs, and how crucial issues of surveillance and conditionality are operationalized.

5. RETROSPECT AND PROSPECTS

Now in its fifth decade of existence, how should one evaluate ASEAN? To what extent has it contributed to the region's economic dynamism? Is it a building block or a stumbling block toward greater Southeast Asian and Asia-Pacific economic integration?

ASEAN has significant achievements to its credit. First, it still exists as an effective functioning entity, which is more than can be said for several other past and present regional organizations in the developing world. Second, for a region characterized by great diversity and considerable past tension, Southeast Asia has by and large been free of major conflict since the mid 1980s, as the three Indochina states progressively reentered the regional and international mainstream. Of course, border skirmishes persist, the creation of East Timor as an independent nation-state was a challenging experience, and Burma remains an international pariah state beyond the reach of ASEAN diplomacy. Third, and most important, ASEAN in aggregate has been a region of rapid economic development and rising living standards. One can debate the direction of causality between this outcome and the establishment of the Association, but undeniably the determination of the region's leaders to forge more harmonious relations has facilitated economic development. The engagement with and the nurturing of the three Indochina states in their early stage of economic liberalization, after decades of acrimony and one of the most destructive wars in recent memory, has been a signal achievement.

Fourth, ASEAN has been diplomatically skillful in effectively playing "balance of power" politics (Acharya, 2009). There is no clear economic and political leadership in East Asia, with the economic giants of the past and the future—Japan and China respectively—engaged in a battle of constant diplomatic rivalry. Courted by both powers, ASEAN has thus been able to advance its own interests considerably, and become either the arbiter or driver of almost every major initiative on regional commercial and security architecture. ASEAN's pivotal position has been maintained as Asian regionalism has extended to embrace South Asia, and in particular the inclusion of the third major Asian power, India.

Yet, on the other side of the ledger, ASEAN has not progressed very far in terms of becoming a formal economic entity. This proposition can be illustrated with reference to the standard theory of customs unions (table 15.8). In over four

Table 15.8. Indicators of economic integration

Indicator	ASEAN	EU	NAFTA	CER	MERCOSUR
Free trade in goods	Part	Yes	Yes	Yes	Part
Free trade in services	Part	Yes	Part	Yes	Part
Capital mobility (FDI)	Part	Yes	Part	Yes	Part
Labour mobility	No	Yes	No	Yes	No
Competition law converging	No	Yes	No	Yes	No
Monetary union	No	Yes	No	No	No
Unified fiscal policy	No	Part	No	No	No

Source: Author's interpretation.

decades, it has not progressed beyond the first phase, of loosely exchanging trade preferences, while still maintaining their separate, and still quite variable, trade regimes. As noted, it is very unlikely to progress to the next stage, of a customs union with common external tariffs. Deeper integration, affecting factor markets and a common macroeconomic policy regime à la the EU, is even further off the horizon.

Moreover, ASEAN runs the risk of being consigned to the status of a diplomatic talk-shop. In the words of one its former Secretary Generals, in a frank report to leaders: "Regional economic integration seems to have become stuck in framework agreements, work programmes and master plans" (Severino, 2006, p. 247). The Association has a long history of issuing declarations, action plans and charters, yet with limited capacity—and in some cases arguably intention—for implementation. It has generally prevaricated on whether to become a formal customs union. It has developed a plan for labor market integration, while some of the largest labor movements in the world (relative to the size of the recipient economy) have occurred outside this framework. Even after one of the deepest economic crises in the region's history, the Association was unable to develop a set of emergency support mechanisms. At its root, the "ASEAN Way" is an institutionalized mechanism that renders very unlikely the prospect of a fundamental change in direction. The most likely outcome is that the country's policy regimes will converge over time, to the point where preferential arrangements become redundant. As the region's commercial hub, Singapore sets the standard in this respect, and one to which the lower-income members of ASEAN might aspire.

And so it is not surprising that ASEAN's greatest achievement in the economic sphere has been more to do with what AFTA has indirectly induced, rather than mandated. Recognizing that most of the region's trade is extraregional, the original ASEAN members, in order to minimize the potential costs of trade diversion, have been reducing their external tariffs in conjunction with reduced barriers to intra-ASEAN trade. The ASEAN6 countries have also undertaken several waves of multilateralizing preferences, voluntarily offering their AFTA concessions to nonmembers on a nondiscriminatory basis. When the preferences are fully multilateralized, the margins of preference are zero, as is the potential for trade diversion. This was the case for more than two-thirds of the tariff lines for the ASEAN6 countries through to 2002 (Feridhanusetyawan, 2002), and the proportion has increased since then (Menon, 2007a).

Furthermore, because preferential tariff reduction schedules have been ambitious and rapid, AFTA has accelerated the pace of multilateral trade liberalization in the ASEAN+6 countries. Instead of jeopardizing multilateralism, it has hastened these countries' movement toward their goal of free and open trade. In this way, AFTA's greatest achievement may have less to do with what it prescribes or mandates, and more to do with what it promotes indirectly through its members' long-standing commitment to openness.

NOTES

For helpful comments on earlier drafts, we are grateful to seminar participants at the Australian National University, the Cambodia Development Research Institute, the Centre for Strategic and International Studies (Jakarta), and the Institute for Strategic and International Studies (Kuala Lumpur). Anna Cassandra Melendez provided excellent research assistance. Any remaining errors are our own.

1. Indonesia, Malaysia, Philippines, Singapore, and Thailand.

2. A word on country names is relevant here: Myanmar is also referred to as Burma, especially by those who do not recognize the legitimacy of the current regime, while Laos is officially known as the Lao PDR (Peoples' Democratic Republic), and Brunei is short for Brunei Darussalam.

3. Until 1981, most of the items on the list had tariff reductions of just 10%. In that year, the size of the tariff cuts for products already listed was increased to 20–25%. But this was still regarded as too low by the business community, which argued that cuts of 30–50% would be needed to have a perceptible effect (Saw, 1982). More generally, as Ariff (1991) points out, a major problem with the APTA was the failure to consult and involve the business community.

4. The first list, presented to the Fifth ASEAN Economic Ministers meeting in Singapore in July 1977, contained only 71 products (15 from Indonesia, 14 from each of the other four) for the 10% reduction in tariffs. These products constituted just 2.5% of intra-ASEAN trade in 1975 (Saw, 1982). Although the number of items grew quickly, the scheme still only covered 5% of intra-ASEAN trade in 1986 (Edwards and Wong, 1996). The right of members to exclude "sensitive" items from the list was so widely exploited that only minimally traded goods were included. Moreover, some of the "concessions" were memorable, including snow plows and specially created but fictitious trade categories.

5. Writing at this time, the late Hadi Soesastro (1999, pp. 158–59), one of the leading thinkers in ASEAN on regional cooperation, observed: "The public has been largely disappointed with ASEAN. Its perception is that of a helpless ASEAN, an ASEAN that cannot move decisively, an ASEAN that is trapped under its organizational and bureaucratic weight, and an ASEAN that fails to respond to real, current problems and challenges."

6. In addition to these formal and informal trade barriers, studies of the region's logistics have drawn attention to the high trade costs in some of the lower-income ASEAN economies, resulting from poor infrastructure, limited competition, and regulatory impediments in the customs agencies. See Brooks and Hummels (2009) and Shepherd and Wilson (2009).

7. See Athukorala (2006a), Athukorala and Menon (2009), and Kimura (2006) for detailed examinations of this trade.

8. Data are not always available for Brunei and Myanmar, Brunei because it is so small as to not always be included in comparative international statistics, and Myanmar because its statistical system is considered unreliable. In the rankings, Brunei's per capita income may safely be assumed to be similar to Singapore's, and Myanmar's probably a little below that of Cambodia. So assertions about the range of incomes are unaffected by their exclusion.

9. These features also have implications for Singapore's role within ASEAN. As a senior official once caustically noted in private, the other ASEAN members not infrequently tell Singapore to "provide the funds and then shut up."

10. Various trade policy country studies illuminate these NTBs in more detail and examine the trade reform agenda in the respective countries. As illustrations, see for example Athukorala (2006b) on Vietnam, Bird et al. (2008) on Indonesia, and Fane (2006) on Laos. See also the ASEAN Secretariat website for detailed listings of NTBs by country, at www.aseansec.org/16355.htm.

11. A word of caution is necessary in interpreting these trade shares. While aggregate trade flows are reasonably accurate, as they can be verified from major OECD trading partner statistics, some intra-ASEAN trade flows are at best approximate, owing to widespread physical and technical smuggling. For many years, Singapore has not released its trade statistics with Indonesia, for fear that any discrepancy with the Indonesian statistics might trigger accusations that the island state is complicit in smuggling. Smuggling from Burma is known to be extensive, as it was in the communist states of Indochina until their major trade liberalizations.

12. Access was to be provided through national treatment provisions within six months of the AIA signing. These exclusions were to be progressively phased out by 2003, extended to 2010 in the case of new members.

13. For example, out-of-season fruits and vegetables could motivate a PTA, such as in the U.S.-Chile agreement (that also included copper), or the proposed Indonesia-Pakistan agreement related to citrus fruits.

14. For further discussion, see for example the exchange of views in the *Far Eastern Economic Review* between Kawai and Wignaraja (2008) and Hill and Menon (2008).

REFERENCES

Acharya, A. (2009). *Whose Ideas Matter? Agency and Power in Asian Regionalism*. Ithaca: Cornell University Press.

Ajanant, J. (1997). "AFTA: An Introduction." In K. K. Hourn and S. Hunter, eds., *ASEAN Free Trade Agreement: Implications and Future Directions*. London: ASEAN Academic Press, pp. 13–24.

Ariff, M. (1991). *The Malaysian Economy: Pacific Connections*. Kuala Lumpur: Oxford University Press.

Athukorala, P. C. (2006a). "Product Fragmentation and Trade Patterns in East Asia." *Asian Economic Papers* 4(3), pp. 1–27.

Athukorala, P. C. (2006b). "Trade Policy Reforms and the Structure of Protection in Vietnam." *World Economy* 29(2), pp. 161–187.

Athukorala, P. C., and J. Menon (2009). "Global Production Sharing, Trade Patterns and Determinants of Trade Flows in East Asia." *ADB Working Papers on Regional Economic Integration*. Manila: Asian Development Bank.

Bhagwati, J. (2008). *Termites in the System: How Preferential Agreements Undermine Free Trade*. Oxford: Oxford University Press.

Bird, K., H. Hill, and S. Cuthbertson (2008). "Making Trade Policy in a New Democracy after a Deep Crisis: Indonesia." *World Economy* 31(7), pp. 947–968.

Brooks, D., and D. Hummels, eds. (2009). *Infrastructure's Role in Lowering Asia's Trade Costs: Building for Trade*. Cheltenham: Edward Elgar.

Chia, S. Y., and M. Pangestu (2005). "Regionalism and Bilateralism in ASEAN." In S. Jayasuriya, ed., *Trade Policy Reforms and Development: Essays in Honour of Peter Lloyd*. Cheltenham: Edward Elgar, vol. 2, p. 121–152.

Edwards, R., and K. Wong (1996). "Regional Cooperation: ASEAN, AFTA and APEC." In R. Edwards and M. Skully, eds., *ASEAN Business, Trade and Development: An Australian Perspective*. London: Butterworth-Heinemann, pp. 1–16.

Fane, G. (2006). "Trade Liberalization, Economic Reform and Poverty Reduction in Lao PDR." *Journal of the Asia Pacific Economy* 11(2), pp. 213–226.

Feridhanusetyawan, T. (2002). "Preferential Trading Arrangements in the Asia-Pacific Region." *IMF Working Paper 149*. Washington, D.C.: International Monetary Fund.

Hew, D., ed. (2005). *Roadmap to an ASEAN Economic Community*. Singapore: Institute of Southeast Asian Studies.

Hew, D., ed. (2007). *Brick by Brick: The Building of an ASEAN Economic Community*. Singapore: Institute of Southeast Asian Studies.

Hill, H., and J. Menon (2008). "Back to Basics on Trade." *Far Eastern Economic Review* (June), pp. 44–47.

Imada, P., and S. Naya, eds. (1992). *AFTA: The Way Ahead*. Singapore: Institute of Southeast Asian Studies.

Jarvis, D., S. F. Chen, and T. B. Tan. (2009). "Investment Liberalization in ASEAN: Progress, Regress or Stumbling Block?" In J. Chaisse and P. Gugler, eds., *Expansion of Trade and FDI in Asia: Strategic and Policy Challenges*. London: Routledge, pp. 138–185.

Kawai, M., and G. Wignaraja. (2008). "A Broad Asian FTA Will Bring Big Gains." *Far Eastern Economic Review* (April), pp. 46–48.

Kimura, F. (2006). "International Production and Distribution Networks in East Asia: Eighteen Facts, Mechanics and Policy Implications. *Asian Economic Policy Review* 1(2), pp. 326–344.

Lloyd, P. (2005). "What Is a Single Market? An Application to the Case of ASEAN." *ASEAN Economic Bulletin* 22(3), pp. 251–265.

Menon, J. (2007a). "Building Blocks or Stumbling Blocks? The GMS and AFTA in Asia." *ASEAN Economic Bulletin* 24(2), pp. 254–266.

Menon, J. (2007b). "Bilateral Trade Agreements." *Asian-Pacific Economic Literature* 21(2), pp. 29–47.

Menon, J. (2009). "The Proliferation of Bilateral Trading Agreements." *World Economy* 32(10), pp. 1381–1407.

McCulloch, N., ed. (2009). *The Rural Investment Climate in Indonesia*. Singapore: Institute of Southeast Asian Studies.

Plummer, M. (2006). *ASEAN Economic Development and Integration*, Singapore: World Scientific Publishing.

Plummer, M., and S. Y. Chia, eds. (2009). *Realizing the ASEAN Economic Community: A Comprehensive assessment*. Singapore: Institute of Southeast Asian Studies.

Rajan, R., and R. Sen. (2002). "Liberalization of Financial Services in Southeast Asia under the ASEAN Framework Agreement on Services." CIES Discussion Paper. Adelaide: CIES, University of Adelaide.

Sally, R., and R. Sen, eds. (2005). "Revisiting Trade Policies in Southeast Asia." Special issue, *ASEAN Economic Bulletin* 22(1).

Saw, S.-W. (1982). "ASEAN Preferential Trading Arrangements." In S.-W. Saw and H. Hong, eds., *Growth and Direction of ASEAN Trade*. Singapore: Singapore University Press, pp. 136–147.

Severino, R. (2006). *Southeast Asia in Search of an ASEAN Community*. Singapore: Singapore University Press,

Shepherd, B., and J. Wilson. (2009). "Trade Facilitation in ASEAN Member Countries: Measuring Progress and Assessing Priorities." *Journal of Asian Economics* 20(4), pp. 367–383.

Soesastro, H. (1999). "ASEAN during the Crisis." In H. W. Arndt and H. Hill, eds., *Southeast Asia's Economic Crisis: Origins, Lessons and the Way Forward*. Singapore: Singapore University Press, pp. 158–169.

Soesastro, H. (2006). "Regional Integration in East Asia: Achievements and Future Prospects." *Asian Economic Policy Review* 1(2), pp. 215–234.

United Nations, 1974. Economic Cooperation for ASEAN. Report of the United Nations Task Force Study Team, Headed by G. Kansu, monograph.

World Bank (1993). *The East Asian Miracle*. Washington, D.C.: World Bank.

World Bank (2009). *World Development Report 2009: Changing Economic Geography*. Washington, D.C.: World Bank.

INDEX

....